FOURTH EDITION

THE PROFESSIONAL JOURNALIST

A Guide to the Practices and Principles
of the News Media

JOHN HOHENBERG

Columbia University, Emeritus

University of Kansas

New York · Chicago · San Francisco · Atlanta
Dallas · Montreal · Toronto · London · Sydney

To Theodore M. Bernstein
W. Phillips Davison
Fred W. Friendly

OTHER BOOKS BY JOHN HOHENBERG

THE PULITZER PRIZE STORY: *An Anthology*
FOREIGN CORRESPONDENCE: *The Great Reporters and Their Times*
THE NEW FRONT PAGE: *An Anthology*
BETWEEN TWO WORLDS: *Policy, Press and Public Opinion
   in Asian-American Relations*
THE NEWS MEDIA: *A Journalist Looks at His Profession*
FREE PRESS/FREE PEOPLE: *The Best Cause*
NEW ERA IN THE PACIFIC: *An Adventure in Public Diplomacy*
THE PULITZER PRIZES: *A History*

John Hohenberg is Professor Emeritus of Journalism at the Columbia University Graduate School of Journalism, was the Meeman Distinguished Professor of Journalism at the University of Tennessee in 1976–1977, Gannett Visiting Professor of Journalism at the University of Kansas, 1977–1978 and administered the Pulitzer Prizes for 22 years. He won the 1974 award of the Society of Professional Journalists/Sigma Delta Chi for distinguished teaching in journalism and received two of the Society's prizes for his books. In 1976, he won a Pulitzer Prize Special Award for his services to American journalism. He was a working newspaperman for more than 20 years in New York, Washington and abroad.

Library of Congress Cataloging in Publication Data

Hohenberg, John.
   The Professional Journalist.
   Includes index.
   1. Journalism.   I. Title.
PN4775.H44   1978   070.4   77-8573
ISBN 0–03–018226–3

PREFACE

This fourth edition of *The Professional Journalist* reflects major changes of substance, practice and technology in American journalism. It also takes account of a considerable shift in professional attitudes in the wake of an electronic revolution in both print and broadcast journalism. New methods, new themes and new approaches to the news have made necessary the inclusion of much additional information and extensive revisions in every chapter of this standard work.

Some of the new practices are clearly caused by the speed with which the computer and the terminal have come to dominate the most important part of the daily American press. It is a movement that was just beginning when the third edition of this book was published only a few years ago. Now it is an accomplished fact, and journalists are deeply affected by it. The same is true of the liberation of television news coverage from film through the invention of the miniature videotape camera, which makes electronic news coverage immediately available to newsrooms and television studios.

But useful as these technological changes are, there is also a significant rearrangement of journalistic values. For at long last, the upheaval in American society during the latter part of this century has had a measurable impact on both American journalism and its practitioners. There is a greater awareness today of the public responsibility of the news media, sharpened by the Watergate scandals and the conflicts of the media with the courts. In many news organizations, too, there is more concern over the rights of women and ethnic minorities. Subjects that few editors would have bothered to cover less than a generation ago now are seen sometimes on Page 1 and on television's evening news programs — environmental issues, equality of education, civil rights, consumerism, secrecy in government and the like.

If there is a common theme that runs through these pages, it is the dedication of the American journalist to the public interest. For the fourth edition, there is a stronger emphasis on public service journalism and on the work of the investigative reporter in all news media. The contributions of social science to journalism are enlarged upon in an expanded chapter on the reporting of public opinion, polling and elections. Moreover, in all types of reporting, stress is placed on the techniques and substance of interpretive writing and analysis.

The latest decisions of the U.S. Supreme Court on free press issues, the wave of judicial gag orders and contempt citations and issues involving equal time are described and discussed in chapters on the news media and the law, crime reporting and the coverage of the courts. There is extended coverage of specialized reporting such as science, environmental issues, consumerism, civil rights and the position of minorities. Other discussions include the latest moves of The National News Council, ombudsmen and the issue of the public's right of access to the media; education, and the new developments in school busing and other difficult issues; the ethics and the moral position of the journalist on such issues as the handling of secret or classified information, the protection of sources and contempt of court.

Necessarily, a very large part of the new material in this volume has been devoted to a description of the new computer and terminal systems for newspapers and wire services and their effect on the journalist's work, plus a glossary of computer and other electronic terms. Indisputably, the coming of electronic newsgathering to television through videotape, the minicam and the microwave transmission system has also made a considerable difference to broadcast journalists. These new developments, too, are described in detail. From the coverage of politics and government to sports, from finance to the family pages, the portable terminal is going to make a big difference to newspaper people and so will the minicam to their colleagues in broadcasting.

Among the hundreds of changes that have been made in this edition, new examples of excellence are used to illustrate the work of newspapers, wire services, radio and television. For the print media, reliance has continued on the materials of the Pulitzer Prizes, particularly those that have elevated the standards of journalism. For the wire services, Presidential election reporting and international news coverage of major stories are added as illustrative material. In the expanded sections on broadcast journalism, Presidential campaigning and advanced forms of news organization for television also are included.

Like the three preceding editions, the preparation of this volume has been a pleasant task because of the acceptance of the original work by so many schools, colleges and universities as well as professional news organizations with training programs.

The volume is organized in four sections. The first presents a broad view of the work of journalists and their principal tools — language, methods and fundamental procedures. In the second, these tools are put to a variety of practical uses in the print and broadcast media with enlarged chapters on the wholesalers of news, the wire services and broadcast journalism. The third section deals with reporters' work in all its aspects, from problems of attribution to such issues as free press and fair trial. The final section is given over entirely to interpretive journalism — politics and government, public opinion and polling, national and international coverage, the specialties and public service and investigative reporting.

Throughout, there is instruction in writing — given in detail and with illustrations from the best available work done by American journalists. In particular, the work of writers under the new electronic dispensation is analyzed and discussed.

My thanks go to the following for material assistance in the form of advice and the use of texts, partial texts, background information and much-appreciated cooperation in general:

William Attwood, publisher, and David Laventhol, editor, *Newsday*, Garden City, N.Y.; Barry Bingham Jr., publisher, and Carol Sutton, assistant to the publisher, with Geoffrey Vincent and John C. Long of the *Louisville Courier-Journal and Times*; Paul Banker, managing editor, the *Baltimore Sun*; Robert C. Bergenheim, publisher, *Boston Herald-American*; Louis D. Boccardi, executive editor, the Associated Press, with Wes Gallagher, ex-president, and Ronald E. Thompson, general executive; Malcolm A. Borg, executive vice president, *The Record*, Hackensack, N.J.; Benjamin C. Bradlee, executive editor, and Howard Simons, managing editor, the *Washington Post*; Wallace Carroll, former editor, *Winston-Salem* (N. C.) *Journal & Sentinel*; Otis Chandler, publisher, and William F. Thomas, editor, the *Los Angeles Times*; Norman A. Cherniss, editor, Riverside (Calif.) *Press-Enterprise*; Edward R. Cony, executive editor, the *Wall Street Journal*; J. Montgomery Curtis, vice president, Knight-Ridder Newspapers; Robert P. Early, managing editor, the *Indianapolis Star*; Katherine Fanning, editor and publisher, *Anchorage* (Alaska) *Daily News*; William H. Fields, executive editor, *Atlanta Constitution*; Reuven Frank, former president, NBC News; Louis G. Gerdes, executive editor, *Omaha World-Herald*; Evarts A. Graham Jr., managing editor, *St. Louis Post-Dispatch*; Martin S. Hayden, editor, the *Detroit News*; James F. Hoge Jr., editor-in-chief, the *Chicago Sun-Times* and *Daily News*; John Hughes, editor, *The Christian Science Monitor*; Larry Jinks, executive editor, San Jose (Calif.) *Mercury-News*; Clayton Kirkpatrick, editor, the *Chicago Tribune*; Dick Leonard, executive editor, the *Milwaukee Journal*; Reg Murphy, publisher, *San Francisco Examiner*; Arthur E. Mayhew, executive editor, *Delaware County Times*, Chester, Pa.; Bruce H. McIntyre, editor, *Pontiac* (Mich.) *Press*; George Merlis of the American Broadcasting Company; Michael J. O'Neill, editor, and Floyd Barger, former executive editor, *New York Daily News*; Cruise Palmer, executive editor, *Kansas City Star and Times*; Gordon Pates, managing editor, *San Francisco Chronicle*; Gene Roberts, executive editor, and John E. McMullan, former executive editor, *Philadelphia Inquirer*; A. M. Rosenthal, executive editor, *The New York Times*; Richard S. Salant, president; William J. Small, senior vice president, and Donald W. Richardson, deputy director of news, all of CBS News; H. L. Stevenson, editor-in-chief, and Kenneth Smith, promotion manager, United Press International; Joseph M. Ungaro, managing editor, Westchester-Rockland (N. Y.) Newspapers, and Thomas Winship, editor, the *Boston Globe.*

For their careful reading of the manuscript of this fourth edition, their criticisms and their suggestions for improvements, I am grateful to Professor John B. Bremner of the William Allen White School of Journalism at the University of Kansas, Dean Henry F. Schulte of the Newhouse School of Public Communications at Syracuse University, and Professor John Breen of the Department of Journalism at the University of Connecticut. I am greatly indebted, as well, to Roth Wilkofsky, my editor, and to Ruth Chapman, who has supervised the preparation of all four editions of this book for publication, at Holt, Rinehart and Winston.

All are hereby absolved of responsibility for what is written here. I also acknowledge, with thanks, the copyright ownership of the material herein reproduced with the permission of the news organizations involved.

JOHN HOHENBERG

August 16, 1977

CONTENTS

PART TWO: THE WRITER AS JOURNALIST

Part One

BASIC PRACTICE IN JOURNALISM

Chapter 1
The Journalist

American journalism is undergoing enormous changes in these concluding years of the twentieth century. All forms of news media are breaking out of established patterns through the advances of science. In dealing with substance, the journalist has been and will continue to be profoundly affected by the social forces that are reshaping American society.

Nothing quite as dramatic has happened to the profession in more than a hundred years.

THE JOURNALIST AND SOCIETY

For all its imperfections, journalism is expanding its influence in the United States. Its impact on public thinking sometimes is of so critical a nature that it has become a factor in the formulation of public policy. It is, as well, a barometer of public attitudes, a consideration of importance in assessing social change.

These extended functions of the journalist have in turn stimulated a wide range of new activities, new attitudes, new methods and new ideas in a profession that had demonstrable need of them. And as our jour-

nalistic horizons have brightened, a new technology has developed. Today, therefore, American newspapers are being produced in large part
by vastly different processes through the uses of the computer and various forms of electronic terminals. In effect, production has become an
editorial function and the old-time composing room is in the course of
extinction.

For the great world-wide wire services, with Americans as leaders,
the high speed transmission of news and pictures is no longer a dream
but a reality. As for television, with its matchless potential for bringing
all peoples directly to the scene of events, new miniature cameras plus
videotape and microwave transmission have released the tube from its
dependence on film. Electronic newsgathering [ENG] is now the order
of the day. And now that we have seen men walking on the moon and
pictures coming from Mars, no one can predict all that the twenty-first
century will bring. But one thing is certain: television will expand as
our principal newsgiver.

The New Journalist It follows that journalism offers unique opportunities to those with the youth, vigor, requisite skills and courage to do
the work. Like any other profession, journalism has its own disciplines
and its share of necessary routine. It also has standards of practice and
conduct even though these cannot—under the First Amendment—be
enforced. In addition, the hours of work are generally difficult to miser-
able and it is not easy to maintain much of a family life.

Despite these drawbacks, it appears that more young people than
ever before are being attracted to newspapers, the wire services, the
news magazines and the broadcast media. Schools of journalism and
their progeny, the colleges and institutes of communications, often
have more applicants than they can decently handle. Although all is
not as well ordered between the profession and the schools as it should
be, journalism education after less than a hundred years is well established in the United States. And the advanced degree, once so rare in
journalism, is now commonplace.

The Greatest Problem Inevitably, the growth of journalism has aroused
greater criticism of its performance and closer scrutiny of its functions
than at any time since the "Brass Check" era of Upton Sinclair. This is
to be expected; moreover, the journalist, despite his well-known sensitivity to outside criticism, will have to meet it.

What is not so settled a prospect is the time of testing that American
journalism has been undergoing in the courts, in the Congress and in
some state legislatures. While the highest court in the land has stood
firm for the time being against the imposition of prior restraints on
publication, it has not intervened to halt the judicial practices of jail

threats and sentences for contempt in an effort to force journalists to reveal their sources. This is a part of the price of success for American journalism—a price that would be too great if it finally impinged on the principle of a free press.

The Surge of News The expansion of news communication has given the journalist a greater measure of responsibility than ever before. It has also immeasurably enlarged the audience for news.

Never before has so much information been available to so many people through so many different sources in so short a time. And as yet, the news revolution is only in its initial stages.

Science and Journalism More new channels are in prospect for television through the liberating devices of science. With newspaper production in process of change, it is certain that archaic distribution methods will be the next to go. And none can predict what profound consequences will follow the inevitable expansion of cable television.

Many new developments also are in prospect by reason of the computer and the communications satellite, the terminal and the laser beam with its glass fiber light technology, multichannel cables and intercontinental facsimile. Nor can the "black boxes" of information retrieval systems be overlooked.

Videotape, the minicam (a hand-held videotape camera) and the electronic newsgathering systems that have evolved from them are by no means the last word for television news. And the terminals, combined with photocomposition and offset printing, are not the be-all and end-all of change for newspapers.

With the coming of cheaper power transmission, made possible by light-wave technology, many other things are likely to happen. The British Broadcasting Corporation's Ceefax and Reuters' News-View open up instant wire service communication to cable television subscribers who are willing to experiment. The same systems eventually will also be used to call up the latest pictures and data bank material from libraries.

In Japan, an even more radical experiment has been conducted in the "wired city" of Tama New Town, 30 miles northwest of Tokyo. Here, a government supported project, in which Japan's largest newspapers participated, made available home-delivered newspapers either on facsimile machines or TV screens. The first was actually a small printed paper. The latter provided up-to-the-minute information that was flashed on TV. Through other devices, children were taught at home by a centrally located TV teacher and women (or men) were enabled to do their marketing by scanning the latest supermarket bargains on TV.

Curiously, the newspapers viewed the project more as a promotion for

Scene in the Milwaukee Journal's city room. Here are staffers at work on their video display terminals—an animated scene close to an edition deadline. (Copyright, Milwaukee Journal. Used by permission.)

the press than as competition because all the Tama New Town information was produced at high cost and its papers could not be as complete as the current product.

While the United States is not going in for such stunts to date, the Associated Press is taking the lead in a new 10,000-word-per-minute transmission through which the entire New York Stock Exchange's daily transactions are transmitted to member papers in three and a half minutes. Both AP and United Press International also have special news services at 1,200 words per minute. It is a foregone conclusion that, once these high speed reports are adapted to computers for a majority of American dailies, the current 66 words per minute teletype transmission will be abandoned.

Beyond all doubt, those who dominate so powerful a communications system have enormous power to influence the public's initial perception of events. What they do with it, and what government is likely to do to try to control them, are other questions that time must answer.

THE ROLE OF THE JOURNALIST

Early in the twentieth century, it was the reporter's role to try to be an objective recorder of fact. This was the era of the pad-and-pencil reporter who ran for the wire first, asked questions later. In most newspaper city rooms throughout the land, staffs tended to be—with a few exceptions—male, white, native American, mostly Christian and educated at the high school level. The news, in the perception of the average editor, usually turned out to be what a comfortable, middle class America wanted to read.

Even so, there were bold and provocative journalists then who refused to be confined to the stenographic role that had been ordained for them. Many of these were reporters, mainly for magazines, who proudly called themselves "muckrakers," an epithet that had been coined by Theodore Roosevelt. And there were editors and publishers like Joseph Pulitzer who espoused the crusade as a social weapon.

Between them, they exposed the shame of the cities, the plundering reign of corrupt machines, the ruthless profit-seeking of great industrial monopolies and the human tragedies of the sweatshop and child labor. Pulitzer went so far as to challenge President Theodore Roosevelt over the acquisition of the Panama Canal Zone, bore up under the threat of a Federal prosecution and prison sentence, and escaped punishment.

Changing Times Such pioneering examples of public service journalism and investigative reporting have left a deep imprint on the kind of journalism that is practiced today. For in modern American newsrooms, both print and electronic, there are reflected the tremendous changes that came to American society in the wake of two World Wars, a Great

Depression, two smaller but no less ruthless wars, and the turmoil of the inner cities that exploded into burnings and riots.

This amounts to something more than a change in the social composition of the nation's news staffs. For even though modern American journalists tend to be university-trained and include in their ranks respectable numbers of women, blacks and other minorities, both ethnic and religious, that transformation still has a way to go.

What counts a good deal more is the change in the outlook and motivation of many of the newer journalists. Instead of merely skimming over the glossy surface of events and going on to something new each day, the best of this new breed exhibit an almost passionate devotion to the necessity for probing beneath the surface and reporting in depth. This is the kind of dedication that is giving to journalism a larger and more meaningful dimension.

It is risky, to be sure. Not every enthusiastic, crusading young journalist is going to expose almost unbelievable chicanery at the very peak of government, as was the case in the Watergate inquiry; more likely than not, such investigators will often make embarrassing mistakes. Yet, if they can be kept within the bounds of journalism's normal disciplines, they should be—and usually are—encouraged.

Too often in the past, the deadening effects of routine journalism have turned off the brightest recruits to the profession. Of course, there is always a certain amount of routine work that must be done, and done with professional skill. Of course, the younger journalists as a rule are bound to be assigned to such jobs as a matter of training, if for no better reason. But this should not, and in better news organizations, does not foreclose opportunities for the kind of challenging assignments to which most journalists respond.

The Professional Role There is nothing particularly new about this concept. Long ago, Joseph Pulitzer gave this definition of professional responsibility: "What is a journalist? Not any business manager or publisher, or even proprietor. A journalist is the lookout on the bridge of the ship of state. He notes the passing sail, the little things of interest that dot the horizon in fine weather. He reports the drifting castaway whom the ship can save. He peers through fog and storm to give warning of dangers ahead. He is not thinking of his wages or the profits of his owners. He is there to watch over the safety and welfare of the people who trust him." [1]

The novel aspect of Pulitzer's observation is that it appears to be far more credible today than it was when he wrote it. For in the early years of the 20th century, most newspapermen were severely restricted in what they could do and what they could write; indeed, very few

[1] Joseph Pulitzer in *The North American Review* (May 1904).

Here is the way electronic camera coverage works. The cameraman is preparing to take his microcam from the truck. The microwave dish antenna already is in place to send pictures directly to the studio for transmission. Although most others term the process electronic news gathering (ENG), CBS prefers electronic camera coverage (ECC). Whereas minicam is the general term for such miniature cameras, CBS calls them microcams. (Copyright, Columbia Broadcasting System. Used by permission.)

Right. A CBS camera crew covering the arrival of the Italian liner Michelangelo. (Copyright, Columbia Broadcasting System. Used by permission.)

even had bylines. The prevalence of objective journalism, with its emphasis on basically factual coverage, deprived all but a handful of elite journalists of the tools "to give warning of dangers ahead."

Now, in the closing years of the century, it is commonly accepted that the role of the journalist is something more than the gathering and communication of the news and opinions of the day; for, in all that he does, says and writes, he must also seek the truth. Unhappily, since news and truth are not always synonymous, this is seldom easy to do. Moreover, it can scarcely be assumed that what is true today will necessarily remain true tomorrow.

Time has an uncomfortable way of changing the perspective from which events are viewed. Unlike the historian, who is preoccupied with the past, the journalist deals with the present and, very often, the future as well.

The Testing of the Journalist It follows that the first rule of journalism is to take *nothing* for granted. There is no doubt that the journalist of ability tends to question established values and conventional wisdom to a greater extent that the members of any other profession. And this is as it should be.

Skepticism has always been the hallmark of journalism. No news organization can exist for very long if it continually registers contentment with things as they are, if it does not delve beneath the surface of events, if it fails to sound the alarm over the shortcomings of society.

Journalism in its broadest sense, incites change.

The element of credibility, too, enters into everything the journalist says, does and writes. In its simplest form, this calls for the accurate reporting of factual material, from the exact time of an earthquake to the closing words of a Presidential address, from the precise shade of the bride's gown to the correct spelling of the name of a murder suspect.

But of what use is it to report the middle initial of a speaker and his title with unfailing accuracy, yet fail to record the inconsistency of his remarks; to make certain that the city budget's total expenditure is correct to the penny, yet fail to point out that it is inadequate to take care of the requirements of the city's schools, its needy and its aged?

It is in these larger areas of journalism that the journalist is tested far more than in the achievement of factual accuracy, necessary though it is. For in all things, he must be worthy of public belief and public trust. Thus, far from conforming to some vague standard of objectivity, the journalist often finds that almost all expert assessments of the news are subjective.

Given the imperfections of the human condition, it could scarcely be otherwise.

A Matter of Values The reason for this intermingling of the precepts of journalism with the public interest is not hard to find. For the strength of the journalist inevitably depends on the extent to which he merits public support, and not from the advertiser, the counting house or a censorious government. It is a hard but demonstrable truth that whenever a news organization has gone over to sheer commercialism, it soon allows itself to be used by special interests, betrays its trust and shows itself to be both weak and unworthy of belief.

But wherever the journalist practices his profession with skill, courage, honesty and resolute independence, he is a primal force in any open society. The greater his freedom, the broader are his responsibilities. For by his very nature, he becomes deeply involved in social change, in the fundamentals of public service and the struggle for progress toward a better life.

Every journalist of consequence considers himself to be a public servant and believes that he and his organization are ultimately accountable to the public. On this base he rests his values. In a very real sense, therefore, he makes representative government possible, for he is the essential link between the governors and the governed.

The Integrity of the Journalist The professional aspect of journalism has prevailed over those who regarded it in the past as a money-making device or a bald technique that could be practiced by semi-literate tradesmen under rigid editorial direction. Still, journalism *is* a business in somewhat the same sense that law and medicine are—a most necessary and important business that sustains the independence of the news media by keeping them solvent.

But it is also true that where there is no profession of journalism as we know it, there cannot be any business of journalism. Neither one exists in a closed society. There, the entire enterprise of informing the public is smothered in the embrace of an all-powerful government and bound with propaganda controls, censorship and condign punishment of offenders.

It would be a mistake, however, to assume that the journalist is always free to practice his profession as he wishes under the relatively tolerant conditions of Western civilization. Here, he is subject to different but no less real pressures.

He knows that he must keep the money men of journalism out of the editorial department if he is to maintain his fidelity to the public interest. But he also must be aware of the even greater danger of lapsing into an insensitive partnership with government for the sake of some temporary benefit. No journalist, whether for high-mindedness or baser motives, can serve his profession and also such organizations as the Central Intelligence Agency, the Federal Bureau of Investigation, or the local Chamber of Commerce. Nor will any reputable news organization permit its integrity to be compromised by sanctioning such dual loyalties.

In consequence, it follows that there is almost constant tension between government and press in an open society, for the watchdog function of the journalist is one of his most potent professional activities. Now and then, when he pushes his inquiries into the deeds and misdeeds of government with striking results, he sometimes antagonizes conservative public opinion.

The cry is then raised that the journalist has endangered national security or, even worse, given away precious government secrets. These charges, however, are far more likely to be based on anguished political rhetoric than truth, as was the case when both Richard Milhous Nixon and Spiro Agnew made such accusations in their vain efforts to retain, respectively, the presidency and the vice presidency.

Sometimes, elements of the news media do overreach themselves. However meritorious the majority of news organizations and individuals may be, a few journalists in every era are guilty of abuses ranging from mistakes in judgment to faulty reporting, from inexcusable sensationalism to vicious partisanship, libel and worse. Yet, where the tradition of self-government is strong, as it is in the United States, the sins of the journalist are tolerated for the sake of the undoubted benefit that a free press brings to free people.

It is precisely because most journalists have a passionate regard for their integrity that their impact on public opinion remains one of the most vital factors in shaping our society.

TRAINING FOR JOURNALISM

What makes a journalist? Some say moral values; others, a superior education. Some believe it is a flaming competitive spirit, a persistence that will not be denied; others, a sense of style, a flair for the dramatic, a crusading interest in digging out the truth and serving as a guardian of the public weal.

Although no response can be complete in itself, there is an essential element implicit in both the superior journalist and his assessment of his profession. It is a love of his work and a fierce and uncompromising belief in its importance. And this is as true of the men and women who have made television and radio the dominant dispensers of much of our breaking news as it is of those who have brought newspapers, news agencies and news magazines to a high level of performance in the United States.

The Qualities of the Journalist Any survey of leading American journalists is bound to conclude that they are highly motivated, diverse in both character and talent, and extremely independent. But it is difficult, perhaps impossible, to single out any one quality that is common to all.

Bob Woodward and Carl Bernstein, the young reporters who did more than anybody else to break the Watergate scandal, showed persistence, vitality and implacable courage in their long campaign for the *Washington Post*. To their managing editor, Howard Simons, those were the qualities that distinguished them. He wrote: "(They) worked against enormous odds, heightened by the final stages of a Presidential campaign. There was explicit and implicit intimidation of sources. There were explicit attacks on the reporters' credibility and motives, and on those of the newspaper, its owner and editors. But despite these odds, the *Washington Post* and its two reporters continued their investigation." [2]

Even in their wildest dreams, Messrs. Woodward and Bernstein could never have forecast the outcome in subsequent years—a formal Senate inquiry, the resignation of President Nixon, a Pulitzer Prize for the newspaper and instant fame for the two reporters.

Another young reporter, Neil Sheehan, demonstrated the strongest moral purpose as well as persistence in obtaining the Pentagon Papers—the record of how the United States was thrust into the Vietnam War—for publication by his newspaper, the *New York Times*. In summing up his experiences, he commented: "In writing the First Amendment, the Founding Fathers imposed upon us a duty, a responsibility, to assert the right of the American people to know the truth and to hold those who govern them to account. In the pursuit of this responsibility, some of our colleagues, a number of them my friends, have given their lives in Vietnam. No one intimidated them and no one is coming to intimidate us." [3]

[2] Letter of 29 January 1973 in *Washington Post* Pulitzer Prize exhibit.
[3] From the *New York Times*'s 1972 Pulitzer Prize exhibit.

Mary McGrory of the Washington Star, *winner of a Pulitzer Prize in Commentary.* *(Copyright, the* Washington Star. *Used with permission.)*

When Barbara Walters left the National Broadcasting Company's "Today" show to go to the American Broadcasting Company's Evening News at $1,000,000 a year, there was considerable critical examination of her. After an initial adverse reaction, Walter Cronkite of the Columbia Broadcasting System said of her: "She has shown exceptional talent in interviewing. She is aggressive and studies her subject." [4]

One of the most admired of the nation's professional journalists, Mary McGrory of the *Washington Star*, won distinction through entirely different qualities. A Pulitzer Prize jury report, in recommending her for an award for Distinguished Commentary, said of her: "Her work (is) rich in insights and forceful analysis. Her writing is perceptive, her reporting vigorous. Her wit and cogency lead the reader to fresh perspectives and a sharpened understanding of national events." [5]

The courage and daring of Peter Arnett during the eight years in which he covered the Vietnam War earned for him a reputation as one of the greatest of war correspondents and also won him a Pulitzer

[4] Time (3 May 1976), p. 55
[5] From the *Washington Star*'s Pulitzer Prize exhibit, 1975.

Prize. His organization, the Associated Press, said of him at the time: "He is a reporter who probes behind the official version of what is taking place. Whenever possible, he likes to rely on what he sees, rather than on what is said at press briefings and in communiques. Consequently, he spends much of his time—probably more than any other correspondent—slogging through the mud with troops in the heat and dangers of Vietnam."[6]

It was such reporting that finally brought the truth about Vietnam to the American people, creating such a violent reaction that President Lyndon Baines Johnson declined to run for re-election in 1968 and the Democrats were unable to elect another President until Jimmy Carter's successful race in 1976.

Finally, Clark Mollenhoff, for many years an investigative reporter for the *Des Moines Register*, has stressed technical excellence as a necessary journalistic quality. He says: "The point is to make your case. Getting evidence that's admissible in court is what it's all about. You can't always do it, but every time you neglect that you cut into your own credibility."[7]

Courage, persistence, vitality, moral purpose, aggressiveness, outstanding talent as a writer, technical excellence—all these are characteristics of the professional journalist to some degree. The beginner, examining the record of his seniors with a sinking heart, no doubt will ask himself how he can qualify for a career in journalism against such competition.

The answer is to start knocking on doors and refuse to be discouraged.

The Requirements For those who wish to make a beginning in journalism, regardless of the media involved, the minimum requirements may be summed up as follows:

- A thorough education, sound training and a willingness to accept discipline.
- Familiarity with the basic skills of the journalist.
- The will to work at tasks that are sometimes frustrating and seem unrewarding at the outset.
- A deep respect for one's personal and professional integrity.

For reporters, whether they serve the print or broadcast media, the coverage of the news is still the most important aspect of their work. But they have learned, as well, through the disclosures of Watergate and the Vietnam war, to examine the meaning of the news and look behind every official announcement.

No matter how skilled they may be in these pursuits, however, they

[6] From the Associated Press Pulitzer Prize exhibit, 1966.
[7] *Newsweek* (10 May 1976), p. 82.

can be only as good as their sources and they must learn to protect such sources. In addition, they are always dependent on the full and unwavering support of their own news organizations. And while it is vital for them to respect confidences and safeguard informants when necessary, it is of even greater consequence for them to know when to hammer on closed doors.

For writers, it is basic to learn to present the news clearly, fairly, honestly, accurately, concisely and interestingly, and to know how to interpret it when the meaning is obscure. True, the familiar word, the short sentence and the single idea to each sentence whenever possible are essential to the writer. But they are of little moment without style — the priceless ingredient that separates the professional from the amateur.

For editors, news directors and producers, even more than for their fellow journalists, there must be curiosity, vision and drive. It is scarcely enough for a newspaper editor to see that hard news is written in the past tense or for a news director to preserve the immediacy of radio and television by putting much of his report in the present tense.

Mere techniques are not as important as good judgment.

The Deadline Rule No journalist can afford the luxury of waiting until he believes his work is perfect. There comes a time when he must adhere to the old deadline rule, "Go with what you've got."

At that moment, the writing of the story must begin. The newscast must be taped or put on live. And if, when that moment of truth arrives, there is some material that is not sufficiently developed for use, another old newsroom saying still applies, "When in doubt, leave out." And the doubtful material should stay out until it is checked.

It seems so simple to set these things down in a few paragraphs. Yet, it requires a lifetime of experience to put them into practice as a professional.

The journalist, in sum, requires a special faith in his work and a formidable inner discipline if he is to stay the course. Herbert Bayard Swope, the executive editor of the New York World, used to tell his staff in a hoarse and awesome roar: "I don't know of any sure way to success but there is a recipe for certain failure. Just try to please everybody and you'll surely fail."

James Thurber wrote his own advice to young journalists in verse:
Get it right
   Or let it alone
The conclusion you jump to
   May be your own.*

*From *What Happened to Charles* in *Further Fables for Our Time.* Copr. © 1956 James Thurber. Published by Simon & Schuster. Originally printed in *The New Yorker.*

The School of the Streets In the early part of the century when the press was king, members of editorial staffs referred to themselves as "newspapermen" with a special note of pride. And the highest compliment that could be paid to a few women in the nation's city rooms was that "they work like a man."

Newspaper people were usually trained on the job then, and the established ethics, practices and procedures were passed from one generation to another in the city rooms. The expression, "the newspaper business," like "show business," came more naturally to those who worked at it than "our profession." For veterans of the city room, that is still true; even among the younger generation, there remains a very special feeling about being identified as a newspaperman or woman.

The gathering, preparation and publication of the news in the lively and less demanding era of the 1920s in the United States were handled competently, and often brilliantly, by skilled newspapermen who often had no particular training except in the hard school of the streets. They were professionals in every sense but, on the whole, they did not consider themselves to be members of a profession.

The very term *journalist*, applied so generally now to the entire field of news communication, then conjured up the image of a dilettante who wore spats, carried a cane and liked to have a red rose in his buttonhole. Such men were thought of as trained seals—special writers akin to columnists—rather than reporters. And they were thoroughly disliked.

A Matter of Status Journalism had glamor in those days, but little or no prestige. What Ben Hecht and Charles MacArthur put on the stage in *The Front Page* reflected the raffish and fun-loving character of Chicago's journalism and a lot of what went on in New York, too. Of course, not everybody could play the role of Hildy Johnson, the hero of *The Front Page*, although New York had its own fabulous police reporters and others, from Kansas City to San Francisco, solved crimes, exposed gangsters and attacked grafting police.

Far above them were the true "gentlemen of the press," the ones with status. Among the leaders were Walter Lippmann (a Harvard man) who ran the *New York World's* editorial page and Heywood Broun (a Harvard dropout) who turned from sports writing and criticism to become the founder of the Newspaper Guild; H. L. Mencken and George Jean Nathan, the friendly iconoclasts of *Smart Set* magazine; Ring Lardner, a superior Chicago sports writer and later a master of the short story; Grantland Rice and Frank Ward O'Malley of the *New York Sun*; Elmer Davis of the *New York Times*, who became a pioneer in radio broadcasting, and Richard Harding Davis, Irvin S. Cobb, Stephen Crane and Will Irwin of points east, south and west.

Between these members of the elite and the less favored figures in newspaper city rooms, a great gap existed. And as for radio, outside such pioneering stars as Graham McNamee, Gabriel Heatter and Lowell Thomas, it was a time when almost any out-of-work actor could read a newspaper over the air or "rip and read" wire service news.

First of all, the difference between the few on top and the working press in general was apparent in personal prestige and public recognition. But more important, salaries for the rank and file were lamentably low — so low that a well qualified reporter as late as the 1930s received only $25 or $35 a week and $50 was considered a good wage.

In fact, before the era of New Deal reforms, newspaper people worked six and seven days a week and put in long hours every day without daring to suggest overtime pay. The image of the journalist, understandably, became fixed as a poorly paid scrivener of little account and almost no future unless he turned to press agentry or show business. It took journalism many years to eradicate this out-at-the-seat, down-at-the-heels image.

The Big Change In the profession as a whole today, there is no doubt that university-trained men and women for the most part staff all but the relatively small newspapers and broadcast operations. Graduates of journalism schools in particular have won a respected place for themselves. Yet, it is considerably less than a century ago that Joseph Pulitzer was riddled with abuse by his fellow editors for daring to suggest that journalists were educated, not born.

That battle has been fought and won. The newest journalists, as a result, tend to be well-educated, well-trained, thoroughly grounded in the humanities and knowledgeable in the social sciences. True, they differ widely in both their way of life and their philosophical approach from their elders; but then, the concerned attitudes of youth near the close of this century are quite a change from the careless and carefree 1920s. And that is all to the good.

There have been other beneficial changes, too. The nearly all-male newsroom went out with the entry of the United States in World War II. But despite the manner in which women helped keep newspapers, wire services, news magazines and radio going while so many men were in the armed forces, they had great difficulty in maintaining their foothold once peace came. It was the militant women's rights movement of the 1970s that helped increase the number of women in newsrooms, both in the print and electronic media. And at length, with Carol Sutton of the *Louisville Courier-Journal* as the first woman news executive of a major newspaper, they began moving slowly into the top rank of journalism.

As for minority journalists — the blacks, Puerto Ricans, Mexican Americans and Americans of Oriental descent — it has taken them much longer to break into the profession. There was a time, and it is not so long ago, when a newspaper editor believed himself to be liberal-minded if he had one or two black reporters on his staff. That time has long since passed for much of the metropolitan press, as well as the broadcast media where the lack of minority representation is far more visible.

The argument that minority journalists are scarce has been met in part by training programs that were undertaken by leaders of the news media and major journalism schools. Generous fellowships also have been initiated at leading institutions to encourage young people from minority groups to strive for professional recognition.

There has been even more stimulus for minorities in journalism through the progress of such outstanding black journalists as Albert E. Fitzpatrick, who became managing editor of the Knight-Ridder group's *Akron Beacon-Journal,* and Carl Rowan of the *Chicago Daily News,* whose column has been widely syndicated and who became a familiar television commentator.

However, despite all these heartening developments, the movement for more women and minority journalists in the United States still has quite a way to go.

The View from Academe Where the news media were once looked down upon or ignored by the elect of academe, they are considered now to be worthy of extended study as the harbingers of change. Philosophers worry about their morals. Political scientists are concerned about their effect on the process of government. Legal scholars gravely weigh the merits of free press versus fair trial. And social scientists have taken to an almost endless examination of the motivation of newspapers, news magazines, wire services and the electronic media. Even practicing historians have not scorned the task of delving into the meaning of today's events not later than tomorrow, perhaps in the very next edition or news program.

As for the journalists, those incapable rogues of yesteryear, they have been weaned away from their poor-men's clubs and plumped down in the classroom and on the lecture platform as people of consequence. Yet, it is only a little more than two generations ago that the first school of journalism was founded at the University of Missouri in 1909 and the first student journalists left Columbia University with their assignments in 1912, followed by jeering New York newspaper reporters.

Today, about 65,000 students classified as "journalism majors" are enrolled in 190 of the nation's four-year colleges and universities.[8]

[8] This takes in all forms of communications including advertising, public relations and journalism education. *The Journalism Educator* (January 1977, pp. 3–9) reported about 19,000 undergraduates were in news-editorial sequences and about 9,000 in broadcasting, with 4,180 of the former and 1,900 of the latter qualifying for baccalaureate degrees. Currently, there are 64 accredited schools of journalism or communications and 266 colleges and universities that offer majors in journalism or communications.

About 14,000 journalism degrees are granted each year, nearly 1,500 of them at the master's and doctoral levels. This is a five-fold increase in enrollments in little more than a decade.

Does this mean that every young person who sits at a video display terminal for the first time wants to be another Woodward or Bernstein, every young woman a Mary McGrory or a Barbara Walters? Probably not. Since the number of new journalists who can be absorbed in the field each year is strictly limited, it is entirely likely that the nation's colleges and universities are now educating news audiences, news makers and news technicians as well as professional journalists.

This happened in the arts when courses in drama, music and painting attracted university students in far larger numbers than could be absorbed in such specialized fields. It turned out, as we now know, that audiences as well as performers were being instructed.

In his annual survey of journalism enrollments, Professor Paul V. Peterson of Ohio State University says he doesn't believe glamor has much to do with journalism's popularity among students. He thinks it more likely, as he says, that many young people choose it as a field of study because they believe in its potential for "changing the world." He adds: "There is no indication at this time that any real relief from the crunch of students can be expected in the near future." [9]

Despite the elevation in the status of the journalist on campus, journalism still has not realized Joseph Pulitzer's concept of it as one of the great and learned professions. Most journalism schools and faculties concede that they must make a better adjustment to the workaday aspects of the profession. And the professional journalists themselves, as is the case with lawyers and law schools, will have to find ways of closing the gap between them and academe.

What Is a Professional? You may well ask, therefore, what distinguishes the professional of today from the craftsman of yesterday.

On the surface, it could be concluded that the journalist's image has improved in the United States through higher pay, better working conditions, improved attitudes, more thorough education and a less raffish way of life. But these are mainly the results of the swing toward professionalism, not its basis.

Actually, one of the strongest motivations for professional conduct has been the threat to the journalist's constitutional rights and privileges. This began with the publication of the Warren Report, based on an investigation of the murder of President John F. Kennedy, and has grown apace ever since. It has caused journalists, in larger measure than ever before, to turn to a defense of their freedoms wherever they are challenged.

[9] *Journalism Educator* (January 1976), pp. 3–8; (January 1977), p. 9.

This circumstance has helped create a community of interest among print and electronic journalists (the term is Eric Sevareid's) that has never existed before. For it has dawned upon all concerned that an infringement on the freedom of one journalist may very well establish a pattern that could affect the freedom of all journalists in the United States.

There has been, in consequence, a heartening rise in the kind of internal criticism that is so necessary to a strengthening of the professional spirit within journalism. This is most evident at meetings of professional journalistic organizations, which flourish in large numbers, and in the willingness of a minority of news organizations to experiment with such novelties as public-supported news councils and ombudsmen who represent the public interest.

Journalism also has assumed the outward trappings of other professions in its interest in research, its promotion of community projects, its acceptance of national prize contests and other honors. Beyond the graduate level, one of the most significant developments in journalism education has been the midcareer studies program. This includes the pioneering Nieman Fellowships at Harvard, which are for an academic year; the Bagehot Fellowships, principally for journalists specializing in economics, at Columbia; shorter and more general fellowships at Stanford and elsewhere; the Alicia Patterson Fellowships, which are granted for research and book projects, and the always popular two-week refresher seminars of the American Press Institute at Reston, Virginia.

These are notable advances for a group that celebrated the corner saloon as a major center for professional courtesies and discourtesies barely 50 years ago.

STATE OF THE PROFESSION

Journalism, as it is practiced in the United States today, is a crowded, highly competitive profession. However, not everybody who claims to be a practicing journalist actually is one. Respectable and useful though their operations may be, government information officers, public relations and advertising people, and the growing army of journalistic technicians scarcely qualify as members of, to use an old and vividly descriptive term, the working press.

The Hard Core Leaving aside the additional thousands of part-time and occasional employees who drift in and out of newsrooms, there is a hard core of approximately 70,000 full-time, bona fide journalists who are primarily responsible for informing the American people.[10] These

---

[10] John W. C. Johnstone, Edward J. Slawski, and William W. Bowman, *The News People* (Urbana, Ill., 1976), pp. 8–9. There has never been a census of working journalists,

are the staff members of the nation's daily and weekly newspapers, news agencies, news magazines and radio and television stations.

In good times, about 4,000 new journalists a year may be required to fill existing and recurring vacancies. About half of these generally come from journalism schools, the rest being recruited mainly from four-year colleges and universities. Daily newspapers at both journalism schools and colleges serve as informal training centers.

It is, therefore, an empty exercise to debate whether journalism graduates have more or less acceptance than those with degrees in the liberal arts or sciences. The not unpleasant truth is that both are in demand; however, in most newsrooms, journalism graduates often have an early advantage because of their professional training.

Where Do Graduates Go? Granted that there are many more journalism school graduates and other candidates than there are job openings in the field, what happens to them once they seek to become professionals?

The Newspaper Fund, which has conducted annual surveys of journalism school graduates for many years, has found that the largest placements are among daily and weekly newspapers while the smallest are among television stations, magazines and news agencies. Moreover, based on the most recent samplings, it would appear that about 40 per cent of the journalism school graduates go into nonmedia jobs — teaching, the military, graduate schools, management, sales work and the like.

Of those who actively pursued media careers in the year after graduation, a study of recent reports indicates that 23 per cent were on daily or weekly newspapers, 6 per cent in radio news, 5 per cent in television news, 3 per cent in magazines, 1 per cent in news agencies and the rest in public relations, advertising and similar media work. In fact, the proportion in public relations and advertising appears to exceed 15 per cent.[11]

There is no question, however, that the daily newspaper remains the largest single employer of journalism graduates, varying between 15 and 18 per cent of the new journalists in various surveys. The competing media are more hospitable to holders of journalism degrees and others with three to five years' experience.

---

so these figures are based on a national probability sample of such journalists, and on a poll of 1,061 news organizations, which gave an estimate of 69,500 full-time working journalists. This broke down into 38,800 on dailies, 11,500 on weeklies, 1,900 on news magazines, 3,300 on wire services and 14,000 in the broadcast media. My own "informed guesstimate" is closer to 60,000; the broadcast figure, admittedly based on the claims of such organizations, seems high. In the nation's communications industry as a whole, about 500,000 persons are employed.

[11] This represents an average for Newspaper Fund reports covering much of the 1970s. The samples used in the surveys ranged from 900 to 2,000 persons. In a typical year, the survey found about 2,500 journalism graduates were hired by daily newspapers.

The Press The requirements of the press are greater than those of the other news media because newspapers are by far the largest single compilers and distributors of news in the United States.

As an overview, there are more than 1,750 daily newspapers in the United States. They sell in excess of 60 million copies every 24 hours. Their gross receipts are about $12 billion annually, almost $9 billion in advertising and the rest in circulation. About two-thirds of the nation's dailies sell for 15 cents, nearly 150 charge 20 cents and a handful go for a quarter.

While there has been a contraction of the press in key metropolitan areas of the nation, the suburban and small city dailies have shown surprising growth. But it is the chains that have, with few exceptions, expanded the most. The nine largest — Knight-Ridder, Chicago Tribune Group, Newhouse, Gannett, Scripps-Howard, Dow Jones, Los Angeles Times Group, Hearst Newspapers and New York Times Group — control 37 per cent of daily newspaper circulation. And chain profits, even in recession years, are reported to range between 15 and 33 cents on the dollar.

Employment in the newspaper field has declined from a peak of 385,000, including editorial, reached in 1973.[12] Computerized production in the main has resulted in a cut of 7,000 to 10,000 in the work force which is bound to continue. Conversely, since some mechanical duties are going into editorial, the outlook is for a moderate editorial work force expansion; nothing, however, like the expected mechanical decline.

There is another important factor in current newspaper economics. Most of the leading corporations in the field have diversified their interests. They have acquired more broadcast properties, gone into periodical and book publishing, and are also merchandising various kinds of information and retrieval systems. Some have become conglomerates with properties that have no relation whatever to journalism.

All this has made newspaper publishing the tenth largest industry in the country. It has been done at the price of eliminating newspaper competition in all but a few cities in the United States and, to a certain extent, consolidating other sources of information. Nor is the trend likely to be reversed.

True, sales of daily newspapers have not kept up with population growth for more than a quarter of a century and total circulation, particularly in recession years, has shown small but significant losses. However, those who expected newspapers to curl up and die because of television have retreated with those others who predicted the demise

---

[12] Statistics from American Newspaper Publishers Association and *Editor & Publisher International Year Book*. Profit estimate from *The Bulletin of the American Society of Newspaper Editors* (April 1976), pp. 4–5.

of movies. With the exception of a few chronic losers in metropolitan areas, most newspapers are thriving.

Broadcast Media Although the broadcast media do less recruiting than newspapers, they generally outbid the press for experienced talent.

That is because broadcast journalism, as Walter Cronkite puts it, is a "postgraduate business" for which newspaper and wire service experience is very often a prerequisite. While it is true that a few first-rate broadcast journalists have turned to newspaper work, the general trend is the other way. And the broadcast media are now beginning to develop their own talent.

The difficulty is, however, that opportunities for young journalists are fewer in the electronic media than in print. For while television and radio revenues run to about $7 billion annually, with profits in the range of 15 to 20 cents on the dollar in good times and more than that for the leaders, total full-time employment for the broadcast industry is only a little more than 100,000, more than half of it in radio. Of these, perhaps a little more than one-sixth are full-time employees in the electronic newsrooms and devote all their time to journalism.

The largest pool of broadcast journalists, those employed by the three networks, numbers between 2,500 and 3,000 full-time employees working with a combined budget of around $200 million in an average year. As for radio, despite the development of all-day news and some laudable radio enterprise journalism, there has not been much change to date in personnel practices.

Cable TV The imponderable is cable television, which since its development in 1949 has spread to 10.8 million homes in the United States, which are serviced by 3,450 systems using 190,000 miles of cable. Some estimates place the probable total in the 1980s at 25 million subscribers, which would cover between 50 and 60 per cent of American homes. If a cable system is developed for home transmission of newspapers, that total could increase sharply.

However, restrictive Federal Communications Commission regulations have been hobbling the growth of the system. In particular, between the FCC and the pressures of commercial broadcasting, the efforts of cable operators to introduce pay TV have made slow headway with only about 500,000 subscribers to show for three years of work.

The hard-pressed cable industry got a lift, however, when Teleprompter Manhattan Cable Television began using hair-thin optical fiber, made of glass, to carry electrical impulses transformed into light—a cheap method of power transmission based on light-wave communications technology. Fiber power lines, if sufficiently developed to replace coaxial cables, could turn cable TV into a major source of news dissemination and make at least 60 channels available.[13]

News Magazines While news magazines have been an important factor since the 1920s in maintaining the flow of information and opinion to the American public, their news staffs are more compact than those of the rival media. In actual size, they have never been more than a small part of the total and their numbers have always been few.

Caught between an expanding broadcast journalism for national and international news and the monopoly position enjoyed by the bulk of the daily press for local news, the magazines in general have been hurt far more than any other element in American journalism. The great picture magazines have all gone to the wall—*Look*, *Life* and their sometime smaller competitors. Such powerful general circulation magazines as the *Saturday Evening Post* and *Collier's* also have died.

With the steep rise in postal rates throughout the 1970s and other inflationary costs, the news magazines are facing a serious challenge to the continuation of their services in their present form. *Time*, with four million circulation, remains the leader, closely followed by *Newsweek*, which has crossed the three million mark, and *U. S. News & World Report*, with about two million. But all have had to go through a certain amount of belt-tightening in secondary areas of coverage.

The circulation gains of the checkout counter tabloids, such as the *National Enquirer*, have increased competition among the news magazines. And, unfortunately, there always will be people who buy the "skins," the exhibitionist sheets. But the success of *People*, a junior partner of *Time*, would seem to indicate that a bright venture in magazine journalism can still succeed without pornography or fake horror headlines. However, except for clerical help and researchers, there is little hope for beginners in this highly specialized field.[14]

The Challenge For the beginner, the most difficult part of journalism is to find a place in this highly competitive field. Personnel people advise

[13] Ronald R. Kriss, "Cable TV: The Bottled-up Medium" *Columbia Journalism Review* (July/August 1976), pp. 26–28. Les Brown, "TV's Use of Fiber Transmission Begins," *New York Times*, 9 July 1976, p. 1.

[14] The Newspaper Fund said in the latter 1970s that 18 per cent of journalism graduates who responded to its annual survey reported they had found jobs in the news media at $200 a week, 34 per cent between $150 and $200, and the remainder at less than $150. For experienced journalists, top minimums under Newspaper Guild contracts have topped $500 a week. These include *Washington Post*, $504.25 for reporters after 4 years, $529.50 flat for rewrite and copy desk; *New York Times*, $461 after 2 years; *New York News*, $432 after 6 years; *Buffalo News*, $390.17 after 6 years; *St. Louis Post-Dispatch*, $390.05 after 5 years.

Starting minimum salaries for reporters include *New York Times*, $432; *New York News*, $366.09; *Chicago Sun-Times & News*, $250.64; *Washington Post*, $238.25; *Sacra-*

scattering resumes in a particular geographic area, followed by visits to responding organizations. Editors, besieged by applicants, usually counsel newcomers to start on small dailies or weeklies. Yet, while the smaller papers are often receptive to younger people and are usually deluged with applicants, they can seldom afford to hire more than one at a time. And the wire services, as a general rule, do not assign beginners to larger bureaus.

The new journalist, however, cannot afford to be discouraged or dismayed. In surveying his prospects, he ought to concentrate on the cities or areas of the country he knows best and cultivate a useful specialty (law, medicine, science, education, religion, economics, architecture). It also helps to apply to the largest employers of news people, as well as to search out the smaller newspapers or radio stations that may welcome a beginner. And for the inveterate gamblers, it's still worth taking a chance on going directly to the scene of a major news event that continues over a considerable period in order to try to land part-time or temporary assignments.

It takes more determination and better preparation than ever before to become a journalist today. For those who are willing to stick it out, the work is rewarding.

Motivation Fifty years ago, many a young man and woman took to journalism as a menial necessity while nourishing secret hopes of making it as a novelist, dramatist or even a poet. They were following the examples of Ernest Hemingway of the *Kansas City Star*, Carl Sandburg of the *Chicago Daily News*, and Eugene O'Neill of the *New London* (Connecticut) *Telegraph*. But it was given to few to achieve such eminence.

In the years between the two world wars of this century, there was also a lot of dreaming about the romance of working in far-off places among strange peoples. Much of this stemmed from the popularity of *Personal History*, the autobiography of an adventurous foreign correspondent, Vincent Sheean, and others who rushed into print with similar sagas. *The Desert Song*, a Sigmund Romberg operetta based on one of Sheean's experiences, helped spread the legend.

But all too unhappily, publishers didn't pay many young men or

---

mento Bee, $225.19. For the Associated Press, the top minimum is $368.25, United Press International, $349.07. At magazines, top minimums include $510.10 flat for general editors at *Newsweek*, $425 after 2 years for writer-reporters at *Time*, Inc.; $495.86 after 5 years for senior editors at *Consumer Reports*; $395.50 for editors at *Scientific American*.

The calculation for TV correspondents is more difficult, since it consists of a weekly figure for base pay plus special fees dependent on advertising content. But in major news centers like Washington, D. C., $30,000 a year is a fair approximation of earnings for experienced TV correspondents. And many earn more.

All this is a far cry from the $25 to $35 a week that was the lot of the professional journalist in the early 1930s.

women to go wandering around the world as they wished and few who did won large audiences. As for those who sought fame as war correspondents, it did not come to the Richard Harding Davis types in World War II but, instead, to a wizened little man with a dreadful thirst and a sloppy uniform, the immortal Ernie Pyle. And in Vietnam, television's first war, the photographic record showed that the correspondents were as dirty, tired and bedraggled—and as brave—as the troops with whom they moved.

Then, too, there have always been hopeful impresarios who plunged into journalism with aspirations for empire in the manner of Henry Luce, the founder of Time, Inc.; William S. Paley, who put together the Columbia Broadcasting System, and a one-time door-to-door radio salesman in the Canadian Arctic who became Lord Thomson of Fleet, the greatest of British press barons. But not many can achieve such power and riches.

Great wealth, artistic fame, glamor and romance—these are not, as a rule, the dividends that journalism pays in spite of the talented and fortunate handful who seem to prove the contrary in every generation.

These are the realities:

Journalism today is practiced for its own sake—and its own rewards—by thousands of dedicated, skilled and highly professional men and women. Its social and moral values are high for those who work at it. Its fascination is compounded each day of novelty, surprise, satisfaction, fulfillment, sometimes disappointment, and occasionally even shock over the ceaseless variety in the story of mankind.

There is no limit to journalistic ventures in the public interest in these hard and difficult times; nor are they, by any means, confined to the eminent and the powerful in the profession.

It was no gilded legal expert from Washington but a tenacious local reporter, Gene Miller of the *Miami Herald,* who twice won Pulitzer Prizes for producing the evidence that freed four persons in three different cases after they had been wrongfully convicted of murder. And it was no famous syndicated columnist or news commentator with a fancy hairdo, but a young and well-nigh penniless free lance reporter, Seymour M. Hersh, who uncovered the horror of the My Lai massacre in the Vietnam War.

Nor did the mighty news and television organizations of the land take the lead in attacking predatory interests that were polluting air, earth and water. In such successful crusades, the annual Pulitzer Prize gold medal for public service was awarded first to regional newspapers—the *Louisville Courier-Journal,* the *Milwaukee Journal,* the *St. Louis Post-Dispatch* and the *Winston-Salem* (North Carolina) *Journal & Sentinel.*

It was well-merited recognition for the hard-work, dedication and responsibility that are characteristic of the profession at its best. And basically, the urge to achieve such results is among the strongest motivating factors in journalism today.

THE MEDIA — PRINT AND ELECTRONIC

When nearly two-score reporters scrambled from a press bus at the Trade Mart in Dallas on November 22, 1963, prepared to cover a speech by President John Fitzgerald Kennedy, they saw a young newspaper-woman hang up a telephone and run toward them. She was Marianne Means of Hearst Headline Service, who said, "The President's been shot. He's at Parkland Hospital."

Tom Wicker of the *New York Times,* who heard her, wrote afterward: "One thing I learned that day; I suppose I already knew it but that day made it plain, A reporter must trust his instinct. When Miss Means said those eight words—I never learned who told her—I knew absolutely that they were true." [15]

This instinctive feeling for news has been remarked on by many reporters under the most difficult circumstances. While the Diem regime in South Vietnam was still proclaiming it could stop the Communist advance in 1975, Peter Arnett coolly informed the Associated Press in New York that he expected the fall of Saigon but would remain at his post there. His message was:

"I was here at the beginning and I think it's worth the risk to be here at the end."

His instinct as a war correspondent had told him that total collapse was only a matter of days and he was right. When the North Vietnamese and the Vietcong marched into Saigon, he was there to report the event.[16]

Norman Cousins, a distinguished magazine editor, once demanded in an outburst against the mounting dangers of the atomic age, "Who speaks for man?" More precisely than anyone else, it is the journalist. For if the nineteenth century was the era of the novelist, then surely the twentieth century belongs to the journalist.

Different News Patterns There is an insatiable demand for news in the United States. It is available in the home or at the office with a twist of the radio or television dial, in the newspaper that is delivered at the door or the news magazine taken from the mail. It comes across in traffic through automobile radios. Citizens' band radios have popped up by the millions with all kinds of gossipy consequences. And, of course,

---

[15] Tom Wicker in The Kennedy Years (New York, 1963).
[16] AP Log (5–12 May 1975), p. 1.

the corner newsstand remains a primary dispensing station. The public never seems to tire of hearing the latest, even if it is only about a change in the weather.

Despite such eagerness and such conditioning of a vast public, the American news media as a whole are painfully aware that they could be far more efficient in dispensing their product.

For newspapers, this means a break with a century-old tradition of immobility. The hard fact is that ten other countries, including the United Kingdom, Japan and Sweden, buy more newspapers than the American daily rate of 326 per 1,000 population.[17] Optimists project a potential sale of 80 million newspapers a day in the United States by 1985, based on the expectation that there will be 20 million more households then. However, within less than a decade, sales have already dropped from 1.2 dailies per household to fewer than one. And, with the increasing trend toward smaller families and "singles" living, the end is not yet in sight.

Thus, the old practice of forcing the consumer to buy the same product in an entire community or region has given way to newer concepts. The most popular is called "segmented marketing," issuing different editions for various parts of the circulation area with both news and advertising tailored to fit each area's needs. The chains have been doing this for some time, as have the news magazines and radio, but it took awhile to bring around such great dailies as the St. Louis *Post-Dispatch* and the *New York Times*.[18]

In meeting the public demand for community editions, the metropolitan press is following the population shift from the inner cities that gave rise more than two decades ago to the prosperous suburban press. Satellite printing plants, and even newspaper production by electronic means, are far more than experimental future developments if this trend continues, as is likely.

Toward a National Press Another major result of the changes in American society is the appearance of the specialized national newspaper.

At the top level, this is typified by the *Wall Street Journal*, which in a decade has jumped from 800,000 to 1.5 million in daily circulation, a tribute to the gospel of affluent living. For sheer efficiency, this compact and lively publication is far ahead of its rivals. It is produced around the nation in a dozen printing plants, some serviced by facsimile transmission, through which identical editions can be reproduced over great distances.

The jet age has also made it possible to distribute newspapers like the *New York Times* and *Washington Post* in numerous cities, but this is still a very expensive matter for both the producer and consumer.

[17] UNESCO, *World Communications*, 4th ed.
[18] *The Bulletin of the American Society of Newspaper Editors* (April 1976), pp. 4–5.

At a less exalted level, the checkout counter tabloids appear to have solved the distribution problem by featuring timeless gossip about celebrities and merchandising their product in the food chains. Like it or not, the *National Enquirer* and its three main rivals have zoomed to eight million circulation—a throwback to the tabloid journalism of the 1920s which operated under the philosophy that anything goes.

By contrast, a serious and respected national weekly, the *National Observer*, the *Wall Street Journal's* junior partner, suspended publication in 1977 because it was unable to attract that kind of mass readership. But the public will go for news of specials in lamb chops and toilet paper in the "shoppers," freely distributed advertising sheets that have increased in number from 6,000 in 1960 to more than 15,000.

Thurman R. Pierce, Jr., vice president for print media at the J. Walter Thompson advertising agency, writes in Advertising Age:

"A look at major trends—economic, social, demographic, life-style, whatever—all point to a nice future for newspaper readers, advertisers and stockholders."

The question remains, however: "What kind of newspapers will we have?" Circumstances, social change, scientific improvements and the demands of readers are bound to have a dramatic effect on the fortunes of the press in the foreseeable future.

The Impact of the Electronic Media Television has its limitations, too. Despite its power and influence as a universal means of communication, its prime time news programs continue in the main to be a bulletin service that cannot fill one page of a full-size newspaper. No matter how talented television's people may be—and some are very gifted—it is difficult for them usually to do more than touch on such complicated matters as a government budget, Medicare, national health insurance, urban renewal, road building and the fight against pollution.

David Brinkley once said, "I think the question of our replacing newspapers is perfectly silly. We can't do it; we wouldn't if we could." And more recently he argued that television couldn't devote much time to news that could interest only 10 per cent of the viewing audience.[19]

Yet, television can on occasion contribute magnificently to the public interest in the coverage of important set events. The pity of it is that the full-scale documentary is out of favor with TV executives because it is so expensive, and so seldom appealing to a mass audience. About two dozen specials based on American history were shown during the Bicentennial celebration but only one, Part II of the Roosevelt story, "Eleanor and Franklin," placed in the top 50 of the Nielsen ratings.

On commercial television, a program such as the Hallmark Hall of

---

[19] Brinkley's quoted statement in proceedings of the American Society of Newspaper Editors, 1965, pp. 41–44; his paraphrased statement in *The New York Times*, January 23, 1977, Sec. 3 p. 27.

Fame's "Valley Forge" wound up near the bottom of the ratings, but Part II of the dramatization of the Charles Manson murder case, "Helter Skelter," was among the top programs. Public television showed that such an outcome wasn't inevitable, however; its historic series, "The Adams Chronicles," was the highest-rated series ever put on by PBS.

As one critic commented, "On commercial television, with its mass audience criteria, the country's past would seem not to have much of a future." [20]

For sheer impact on the public mind, there has never been anything as powerful and pervasive as American radio and television. It has the largest audience in the world.

More than 200 million radio receivers and 7,000 transmitters are in use in this country. They cover 99 per cent of all American households, 60 million automobiles and 11 million public places. As the figures indicate, many homes have more than one set. And all this has come about in a little more than 50 years.

Television's growth has been even more spectacular since its beginnings in 1946. Today, almost 1,000 stations in all categories transmit to nearly 100 million sets, covering almost 98 per cent of American homes. Of the total, nearly 70 per cent are color television, a relatively recent innovation.

As tens of millions of viewers will testify, television is superb in the coverage of national conventions and elections, space shots, sports events and other spectacles—some call them "media events"—that can be brought to the public at first hand. What television cannot do is to give all the news with suitable interpretation and background, except when special arrangements are made for a take-out program around midnight.

The economic wastefulness of excessive rivalry has obliged the print and broadcast media to enter into cooperative coverage where possible. Thus, the two great American news agencies and the three networks have formed the News Election Service to function during Presidential elections. And the *New York Times* and the Columbia Broadcasting System have jointly financed a Presidental campaign polling operation. The media often can and do complement each other in general news coverage. [21]

The Money Factor Televison's advertising earnings of around $6 billion annually are based more on its effectiveness as an entertainment medium than on its key role as news giver to the nation. While some station owners have discovered that advertisers also will support strong local news programs, as well as the nightly network news, old habits and old beliefs are hard to break. The swing of thoughtless local news-

[20] Les Brown in the *New York Times*, Section 2, 23 May 1976, p. 1.
[21] NES began in 1972, the Times-CBS Survey in 1976.

casters toward treating news as entertainment, plus the hiring of consultants to "beef up" news programs, has been of serious concern to many a first-rate journalist.

One of them, Ron Mires, a California news director has written:

"I'm concerned . . . about the future of television news based on today's rush to discard journalistic value in favor of entertainment values. . . . The answer would seem to be a compromise: To produce a news program which retains solid content, but includes enough of entertainment values to attract top ratings." [22]

Julian Goodman, while president of the National Broadcasting Company, even appealed to advertisers to support public service programs. When he tried to line up advertisers for a three-hour, prime-time program on the energy crisis, he said: "I would hope that many businesses that now find themselves caught in the social and governmental pressures of this decade, with a need to explain themselves to a concerned and influential cross-section of America, might take advantage of the sort of audience news documentaries attract." [23]

Very little happened.

The Magazines' Dilemma Timeliness will always be a function of journalism, but newspapers seldom can be first with news and pictures that they themselves do not originate. As for magazines, their deadlines make it imperative for them to lean heavily on enterprise journalism, exclusive features and entertainment. Television has preempted the presentation of most breaking news and radio has the rest.

Thus, for the future, it is likely that American periodicals, which once numbered almost 10,000 and boasted of astronomical circulations, will be reduced to magazines that perform specialized services for limited audiences, preempt a particular field or emphasize general news and opinion. With a few exceptions, the all-purpose magazine of general circulation has lost much of its base.

There is no doubt of the essential prosperity of the leading magazines, which share in an annual advertising income of $1.5 billion plus their rising sales prices. Even though daily newspapers publish TV schedules, the enterprising *TV Guide* is the leading magazine with 20 million circulation, followed by the unchanging *Reader's Digest*, with 18 million; *National Geographic*, 9 million; *Family Circle* and *Woman's Day*, 8 million each, and *Better Homes & Gardens*, 7.8 million. In a different category, the Sunday magazines also continue to do well: *Parade*, with 19 million circulation and *Family Weekly* with 11 million.[24]

[22] Fifth Columbia-duPont Survey of Broadcast Journalism, p. 102.
[23] Ibid. pp. 107-108
[24] Statistics from Magazine Advertising Bureau of the Magazine Publishers Association.

But all will have to wrestle with continuing problems of rising mail rates and newsprint costs for years to come.

The Boom in Books Unlike magazines, the book publishing industry in the United States has increased both sales and readership during the period coinciding with television's greatest growth. Mainly, this has been caused by the popularity of the paperback book, for book publishers, like others, have had their troubles and consolidation has been the rule in the industry.

Yet, with an annual gross income of nearly $4 billion, about 500 book publishers in the United States are printing more than a billion books a year and bringing out some 40,000 new titles and new editions annually. Population growth and broadened educational opportunities for millions of young people account for some of the heightened activity in the world of print, as do book clubs and 12,000 book stores, but not all of it.[25]

Book publishers, for example, know from experience the surge of sales that accompanies television's exploitation of books. The circumstance that Woodward and Bernstein's *The Final Days* came out at a time when they were in great demand on television because of their movie, *All the President's Men*, created a bonanza for them and their publisher. That kind of exploitation also helped sell *Jaws*, another paperback blockbuster.

Such circumstances, plus the extraordinary frankness of language and sexual reportage made possible by a permissive age, have created new markets for books all over the United States. In any event, it all proves that reading hasn't exactly gone out of style.

THE PUBLIC MIND

Despite the undoubted accomplishments of the American information system and the repeated assurances that it is the best the world has to offer, it is obvious that a considerable segment of the American public is not as well informed as it should be. Even among well-educated audiences, repeated polls have shown that few know their Congressman or woman and they seem to retain little knowledge of what they see and hear if it has no special interest for them.

Surveys have also disclosed deplorable areas of public ignorance. During the Bicentennial celebration, a Gallup Poll showed that less than half the American people knew that the First Amendment is the basis for our freedom of the press.[26] A poll on the Vietnam war demonstrated that 20 to 25 per cent of the respondents did not know that the

---

[25] Statistics from *Publishers Weekly* and the *New York Times*, 24 Oct. 1976, Sec. 4, p. 8.

[26] The *Bulletin of the American Society of Newspaper Editors* (May–June), 1975, p. 21.

Vietcong was the military arm of the Communist National Liberation Front. Almost the same number, in fact, didn't know that the Communists controlled China before the first Presidential visit there in 1972.

Social scientists can document such findings at all levels of public intelligence. And poll takers know from experience that up to a quarter of the respondents in nation-wide surveys are likely to be in the lower IQ range.

Louis Harris and Associates, in a study conducted for the National Reading Council, estimated that 21 million Americans of age 16 and over are such poor readers that they cannot understand a classified advertisement.[27] Making additional allowances for the trick phrasing of questions, the obtuseness of interviewers who conduct the polling, and a certain amount of misunderstanding between those who ask the questions and those who answer them, the result must still be taken as a danger signal. The American mass communications system and American education are far from perfect.

In these distracting times, getting people to read or to listen and watch, and then remember, is a universal problem. Very often, a mass audience is conditioned to accept first what it wants to hear, to see, or to read. The unexpected, the unpleasant and the unfamiliar usually have to be accompanied by a considerable shock—or endless repetition—to make an impression on the mass mind.

For despite all the glib talk about manipulating either the mass media, the public or both, it is easier said than done. To sell soap or hamburgers or brassieres over television is one thing; to sell a Presidential candidate or change a long-held public commitment to social progress is quite another. For there is always a time of reckoning when an audience, however large or small, discovers it has been deceived through underhanded trickery. The machinations used by President Nixon and his associates to win the 1972 election in the end were his ultimate ruin.

The Editors' Problem There are severe limits on what a mass audience can absorb. People are far too busy with their own immediate concerns and interests to have itemized knowledge of such complicated matters as the background of major Supreme Court decisions at home or the political upheavals abroad that have created so many new nations in Asia and Africa.

In mass communication terms, the feeble public response to certain kinds of stimuli is appallingly familiar. It is known as "weak feedback." The message—the news—goes out with a lot of strength behind it but the echo—the response—is often very faint. Between the sender and receiver of the message, there is invariably a lot of interference.

[27] Reported in *Education* magazine (October 1971).

The result is often imperfect and even garbled reception, particularly in the era of brief radio and television bulletins.

If this situation were taken at face value, our news media would prepare their output for an audience with an IQ capable of coping only with Mother Goose. Such an approach has been attempted both in print and on the air, as witness the brief revival of gossip news in the press and "happy talk" news shows, but the public has scarcely been enlightened.

In a nation with more than 60 million people in school, more than 12 per cent of them in institutions of higher learning, it would be a grievous mistake to underrate either the public will or the public intelligence. The evidence of functional illiteracy at the lower levels of our society should not be considered out of context, as H. L. Mencken was prone to do with his scornful essays about the "booboisie."

The responsible journalistic principle is never to overrate the background knowledge at the public's command and never to underrate the intelligence of the minority.

Surveys have shown repeatedly that the average citizen spends about 30 minutes a day with his newspaper, even though the television set in the same household may be on for hours at a time. If he reads around 250 words a minute, and stays with it for the full half hour despite the distractions that often accompany newspaper reading, the most he can cover is 7,500 words. Chances are that it may be less.

Small wonder, then, at the journalistic insistence on using every device of style, organization, language and presentation to capture the reader's attention and keep it. Similarly, the television anchor man or woman with a 30-minute program knows that viewer interest is a fragile quality and may be broken at any moment by interruptions; the mere fact that the set is on doesn't mean that people are either watching or listening.

There has been a long and fruitless argument over whether the public's dependence on the electronic media for its breaking news has decreased its support for newspapers. The fact is that both are present in the literate American home. Certainly, it is worrisome to editors that polls show newspaper readership is declining and that young people are not great newspaper readers on the whole. But then, they never have been. And with the coming of the 15 to 25-cent daily, there is a legitimate question about how many papers our youth can afford to buy. Among adults, nearly all surveys show that since 1957 there has been little change in the accepted proportion of 70 per cent who buy and read a newspaper every day.

Radio and television can't be beaten on bulletin news. And with the coming of the minicam and videotape, plus the new electronic miracles through which pictures are transmitted directly from the locale of the news, television is bound to be first with news pictures. But for complete news, reported in depth and interpreted with honesty and good judgment, there is still no substitute for a newspaper of the first rank.

INTERPRETATION

Whether a reporter works for a newspaper or a wire service, radio or television, it is not sufficient for him to report that a new nuclear power plant is planned in his area, that the state budget will be substantially increased, or that the federal government has announced a one per cent rise in the cost of living for the previous month.

These stories must also cover the degree of public concern over atomic radiation from the proposed plant, the probability of a rise in state taxes evolved by the budget increase, and the obvious return of double digit inflation with the federal announcement of what amounts to a 12 per cent annual inflation rate. This process is known as interpretation, for it supplies meaning to the news.

Once, editors obliged reporters to run around or telephone until they found somebody in public office who could be quoted on the probable effect of such developments. Some reporters are still alive who remember offering their own views to lazy or ignorant public officials and getting them to agree to be so quoted on these matters. A little of that still goes on today; but, for the most part, the reporter no longer must pretend that he can't think.

This is not to say that interpretation is required of everything that happens, from yesterday's storm to tomorrow's fashions, or that interpretive material must not be documented. Indeed, both restraint and proof are requisites in the use of what always has been, and still is, a sensitive process. It is not for amateurs.

News—and Opinion Once it was widely taught and sincerely believed that the news columns of the American newspaper were composed of facts, while the editorial page was reserved for opinion, and that the two never mixed.

This was the supreme concept of journalistic objectivity. Yet, even where this dubious proposition was enforced, it was never really possible to make it work. Such rigid objectivity exists only in the minds of those who believe there is such a thing as "pure news" that flows in its pristine state from some mysterious source, uncontaminated by the addition of color and flavoring.

The mere process of deciding whether to print an article or omit it is an exercise of opinion by the editor. Whether an article carries a large headline or a small one, whether it is put on Page 1 or back with the want ads, similarly, is not the result of any objective process but one of editorial choice.

The reporter who covers a speech and the rewrite man or woman who puts the story on paper both exercise their legitimate judgment on what facts to feature, what quotes to use, what material to leave out. So does the editor who puts together a radio or TV news program. The concept of objectivity, as it was defined at the turn of the century, is therefore an amiable myth.

What was and is valid is the fundamental premise of honesty, fairness and impartiality in the presentation of news. The American newspaper was founded on that basis. The best ones have always endeavored, within the limits of human frailty, to present the news fairly and honestly in the news columns, leaving persuasion to editorial writers and featured columnists.

This is a realistic assessment of the function of the journalist who covers the news. It presupposes that the gathering and writing of the news also involves the necessity of telling what it means, whenever necessary. It does not follow, however, that the newspaper has the right, covertly exercised, to try to persuade the reader to adopt its view by allowing editorialization in the news columns. This is equally true for the electronic media, which is why many more station managements are permitting the use of editorial segments in their news programs.

Reporting, explaining, backgrounding, analyzing and interpreting the news are all proper parts of journalism today. They belong in the news columns and the broadcast reports. It has always been valid to use expert opinion on a particular subject, usually in the form of an interview, to make a complicated news development more intelligible to the public. It follows that where the reporter is also a specialist, his analysis—properly identified as such—is well worth using.

The line must be drawn at persuasion, recommendation and exhortation, techniques that clearly are outside the framework of the news and belong in the editorial columns or the editorial segment of a news broadcast. Where interpretation goes over this line, it becomes editorial comment and should be so labeled.

The Meaning of the News A majority of American editors and broadcasters believe in interpreting the news today and insist that it is necessary to public understanding. The wire services and newspaper syndicates send interpretive dispatches to their clients almost as quickly as they send the news. The responsible press prides itself on its specialists and the validity of their interpretive reports in many fields. Interpretation is accepted by such newspapers as a necessity. And when the electronic journalist is able to do a documentary in which there is reasonable time for interpretation and explanation, he thinks of it as a high point in his career. Lamentably, he usually has to settle for a "quickie" overview—a mini-documentary of brief duration that is woven into the news report.

All this is a far cry from the era when Walter Lippmann was the editor of the *New York World* in the early years of the century and had to do things differently. As he once explained:

> When I first went to work on a newspaper, which was after World War I, the generally accepted theory was that it was the duty of the news columns to report the "facts" uncolored by "opinion" and it was the privilege of the editorial page to express opinions about what was reported in the news columns.
>
> To this simple rule of the division of labor between reporters and editorial writers, we all subscribed. In practice we all, reporters and editorial writers, broke the rule and this led to many disputes, good-natured and some not so good-natured. The news columns would have opinions with which the editorial writers disagreed. The editorial pages would contain statements of fact that the news editor had not certified.
>
> In the course of time most of us have come to see that the old distinction between fact and opinion does not fit the reality of things . . . the modern world being so very complicated and hard to understand, it has become necessary not only to report the news but to explain and interpret it.[28]

Thus, when the Senate passes by a narrow majority a bill to which the President is opposed, the objective method would be to report the result and let it go at that. But the interpreter would show at once that the measure is probably doomed by Presidential veto because a two-thirds Senate vote is needed to override and it obviously will not be forthcoming. He doesn't have to "hang" this on anybody, as the newsroom saying goes. It is the truth.

It is equally true, at the local level, that the objective reporting of facts frequently obscures important developments instead of clarifying them. It means exactly nothing if a reporter writes two days before election that the mayor, who is seeking re-election, has announced that he will not raise taxes in the coming year. In all honesty, the interpretation must be included that the pledge is in apparent conflict with another of the mayor's campaign promises to raise the pay of police and firemen, for City Council members already have warned there will be no money in the treasury for such increases unless new taxes are imposed.

Or take the example of a seemingly humdrum Moscow announcement that the Soviet Union fears another bad harvest and wants to buy more American grain. The objective reporter would write the story briefly in just that manner and the objective editor would probably bury it on the business page. But actually, this would amount to a case of unintentional dishonesty. It is essential, in any such report, to add the vital background that such purchases early in the 1970s caused rises in the cost of feed grains to American farmers. The interpretation

[28] *The Bulletin of the American Society of Newspaper Editors* (1 January 1956), p. 7

would have to be added, however, that it would be difficult if not impossible to predict immediately whether the proposed Soviet deal would have a further inflationary effect.

Who Writes What? These questions immediately arise:

"Who is to decide which news requires interpretation and which does not?

"How will the reporter know when to interpret, and to what degree?

"When does the reporter need a source to document his interpretation and when can he do it on his own?

"And who decides on the validity of the interpretation?"

For experienced journalists who have earned the trust of their employers and the public, these questions seldom offer problems that are insuperable. To be valid, any interpretation should be so written that an editor —and the general public —can readily understand the basis for the journalist's judgment. Sometimes, a mere citation of essential background will be sufficient to sustain the interpretation. At other times, a source may be required to support the interpretation.

Frequently, the editor is in no position to decide what to do and the reporter on the spot, particularly on an out-of-town assignment, must tell the meaning of the news to the best of his ability and must make the basic decisions. If the editor disagrees with what is done, it is his right to change the copy—but few editors nowadays would throw down the work of a trusted reporter without a lot of hard thinking.

There is no clear-cut formula for making such decisions. But this scarcely means that a qualified journalist, who knows the news at first hand, should not make an effort to tell the public what it means. The fear of making a mistake in judgment should not be permitted to paralyze the intellect of the journalist, nor the freedom of the editor to publish such work. The news organization that fears controversy is not likely to last very long.

Do all interpretations of the news turn out to be the same? Of course not. Once, when a distinguished Red Army general suddenly retired, an American correspondent in Moscow interpreted the move as a disgrace while his chief rival indicated the general might be in line for a major Politburo appointment. The former turned out to be correct. Were the correspondents guessing? Probably. But they shouldn't have. Unless a reporter is reasonably sure that he is right in his interpretation, he shouldn't use it. Guessing doesn't pay.

When old-line editors learn of such shenanigans, they renew their long-held objections to interpretation. They continue to insist that intepretation is opinion and therefore has no place in the presentation of the news. True, one's opinion plays a role in making any interpretation of the news; it would be nonsense to pretend otherwise. But when a writer decides to pluck a sentence out of the middle of a speech and feature it, that also is a matter of opinion; at the very least, he should be required to explain to the public why that particular sentence is so important and defend wrenching it out of context.

Interpretation and the Newcomer The newcomer to a news organization, even if he has a lot of experience, is seldom called upon immediately to do stories that are sensitive and require careful interpretation.

Each paper or station has different methods, different routines, different requirements. What is acceptable to one may be anathema to another. It takes time to learn what the policies of any news organization are. And during the process of learning, the best rule is to proceed with caution and act responsibly in dealing with the meaning of the news.

In an age when publicists in and out of government make so many exaggerated claims and announcements, it would be an abdication of editorial responsibility merely to use what was said and fail to assess credibility in one way or another. The interpretive method, in such cases, is indispensable in the handling of the news.

WHY NEWSPAPER TRAINING?

It is neither a tradition nor an accident that, despite the diversity of mass communications, the newspaper retains its place as the principal spokesman for the news media.

Unlike radio and television, the newspaper is not licensed and need not have any particular regard for the Federal Communications Commission and the wishes of the White House for prime time for Presidential announcements. Nor is the newspaper beholden to any other branch of government.

Unlike the news magazines with their weekly deadlines, the newspaper appears several times daily and can communicate quickly with the public even on ponderous matters of public record. Moreover, with the exception of a small percentage of gutless publishers, the newspaper has an editorial page through which good editors can exercise leadership. Not many electronic editorialists, by contrast, have made much of an impression. To a greater extent than media with a larger stake in national advertising, the newspaper—with its highly diversified local advertising interests—is less subject to advertising pressure where such pressure exists.

In brief, the newspaper still leads all its competitors in the news media because it is the most independent among them, the strongest and therefore the best able to resist pressure. In consequence, the press is still the principal rallying point for public opinion after the government itself and it remains the foremost vehicle for public service.

When the electronic media do look to the press for support on some matter affecting the public interest, they usually get it. Thus, the sustained coverage of the House Judiciary Committee's hearings on the move to impeach President Nixon won wide acclaim from the press. As R. W. Apple Jr. wrote in the *New York Times:*

> The presence of the cameras held the members to a reasonable standard of decorum and guaranteed that all would be in their seats. It also gave those who feared that they were voting against the grain of their constituents a better chance to explain themselves than could a whole year of speeches, newsletters and news conferences.
>
> If television is permitted to cover future Congressional debates on momentous questions it could work a profound change in Congressional politics — in some ways as profound as its impact on Presidential politics since 1960. Through a means the Founding Fathers never dreamed of, the Representative could truly become the Federal office-holder closest to the people.[29]

Apple was perfectly right. In the six days of its hearings from July 24–30, 1974, climaxed by its vote to recommend three articles of impeachment against President Nixon, the House Judiciary Committee attracted 70 million viewers. At the same time it destroyed the arguments of the White House that the Watergate inquiry was just a "media conspiracy." The 46 hours of TV coverage by the networks cost them $5 million in advertising billings, no small mark of the electronic media's devotion to the public interest.[30]

There is still another major reason for the continued leadership of the newspaper on matters of principle and other common interests of the news media. By their very nature, the nation's best newspapers, their syndicates and the wire services continue to be primary sources of the news for the electronic media. This does not mean that the networks and some of the outstanding local stations do not have competent staffs or that they do not originate news of their own. Indeed, they do. The wire services in particular continue to be the source of most national and international news, not only for radio and television but also for a very large percentage of newspapers. And it is obvious that a limited electronic news staff can scarcely expect to compete with the better newspapers in local coverage, except on a big breaking story with dramatic visual impact, when the minicams take over.

The Newspapers' Dilemma It follows that familiarity with newspapers and wire services in the United States becomes almost mandatory for most of those working in other journalistic fields. Of course, television has begun training newsmen and women without previous journalistic experience, particularly the representatives of minorities, and some magazine writers have never worked for any other medium. But for

---

[29] *The New York Times*, 31 July 1974.
[30] *The Fifth duPont-Columbia Survey of Broadcast Journalism* (New York, 1975), p. 61.

most journalists, the hard discipline of newspaper or wire service training is still basic to the profession and nearly all news organizations, even at this late date, still prefer their staff people to have it.

This poses many problems. The journalist who wishes to specialize in the electronic media or magazine writing finds difficulty in accepting the rather exacting routine of newspaper and wire service work. Often, resentment is aroused on both sides.

Then, too, the competing media unsystematically raid the smaller newspapers (and occasionally some of the larger ones) as well as the wire services for young talent. Finally, the newspapers understandably resent being used as a training ground for the other media and do everything they can to prevent their best young staff members from leaving.

The flourishing public relations field represents still another factor in the competition for the best of the young journalists. Almost without exception, the 5,000 companies and specialized departments of advertising firms operating in public relations advise their young prospects to get newspaper or wire service experience first. If they engage radio or television specialists, they are often professionals who are recognized as outstanding in their own field. In recruiting for the United States Information Agency and medium to top level public relations posts, the federal government has similar practices.

All this makes newspapers and wire services wary of engaging young journalists who do not appear to have much of a commitment to the press as a way of life. The embryo novelists, dramatists and poets of yesteryear are little in evidence in the city room now, having found a safer and more agreeable refuge in school and college English departments. In their places have come young adventurers who hope that television one day will discover their fascinating appeal for mass audiences and place a fortune at their feet.

Mostly, it doesn't happen that way at all. Regardless of the kind of organization that engages young journalists, they seldom make much progress without first proving themselves. And despite the currently unfashionable position of the work ethic among advanced thinkers, there is no possible way for responsible journalists to avoid a difficult and arduous regimen in either the print or electronic media.

Newspapers can scarcely be blamed for refusing to spend three to five years in the painstaking and often expensive training of young journalists if they know they are eventually going to lose the newcomers to television, radio, public relations or the news magazines.

The Four Ideals Yesterday, many an editor thought that he had done a good job if he told the news. Today, the public requires much more and the definitions of news, as well as its content, are changing rapidly.

Regardless of the advances of science and technology, however, the practice of journalism in the open societies of the Western world will be based in the future, as it has been in the past, on four ideals that often seem utterly unattainable.

The first is the never-ending search for the truth.

The second is to push ahead to meet changing times instead of waiting to be overtaken by them.

The third is to perform services of some consequence and significance to the public interest.

The fourth and by all odds the most important is to maintain a steadfast independence.

If these goals seem to be beyond the reach of journalists in an imperfect world, it is nevertheless in character for them to struggle toward them. For all their faults, and they are many, they are fated to attempt the impossible—to find, gather, organize, explain, interpret and disseminate the news, ideas and opinions of the day to an ever-increasing audience.

The degree of their accomplishments may be measured in the extent to which the public is informed on matters that vitally affect its interests. Journalists may seldom hope for unqualified success. But if they fail, then assuredly the whole basis of self-government—an informed electorate—fails as well. In this sense, the journalist remains an indispensable "watchdog" in any system of representative government.

Chapter 2
The
News
Operation

Science has wrought massive changes in American news operations. Hundreds of American newspaper city rooms are now so automated as to be unrecognizable to journalists of another era. And through the perfection of electronic newsgathering, the nation's television newsrooms have broken out of the straitjacket of film.

What follows is a summation of the principal features of the most basic of all news operations, that of the daily newspaper. The routines for TV, radio and the wire services are considered in relevant chapters.

THE COMPUTER AGE

Most American daily newspapers are now using computers. It is estimated that during the 1980s, at the current rate of changeover, not a single Linotype machine will remain in their composing rooms; instead, production will be done by a combination of terminals, computers, photocomposition machines (cold type as opposed to hot type) and offset printing presses. As a sign of what is ahead, not a single typewriter is used for news writing today in the New York headquarters of the Associated Press; everything, from writing and editing to distribution, is done on terminals.

The Computer For the uninitiated, the introduction of electronics into journalism may seem confusing. Actually, the new processes have made life in the nation's news rooms much more pleasant. They are now easier to work in, quieter, and incredibly more efficient than they were in an earlier era that glorified the romantic side of the press. As a result, newspapers are now produced with smaller work forces and through less expensive and vastly improved methods. And electronic newsgathering has given television news a new and important dimension.

The electronic machines and processes, therefore, are not to be feared but welcomed. And since many thousands of journalists are now familiar with them, and use them daily as integral parts of their work, the beginner should take heart. It is not particularly difficult to adjust to the new methods of journalism.

Basic to the major changes is the computer, an electronic machine for sorting, storing and processing the news that works at very high speeds. It has a fabulous memory, is far more accurate than any other tool that has been used to process the news, and can perform tasks in a brief time that would take a team of persons years to accomplish. The Mark I computer, the first of these formidable instruments, went into operation at Harvard in 1944 to calculate ballistic trajectories for the U. S. Navy but it has since been enormously improved. The newer generations of computers are an intrinsic part of every modern newsroom today.

Within a single day, a typical computer can make several billion calculations without mistakes as it stores information, changes it, organizes it and puts it out as tape, cards, microfilm, impulses to operate a photocomposition machine, or a laser beam. The machine can be programmed to perform quickly and efficiently a great many functions that formerly tied up a composing room for hours. It also can "talk" with other computers—those, for example, that transmit news from wire services at high speeds directly to the computers of members of client news organizations.

John H. McMillan, executive editor of the Huntington (West Virginia) *Advertiser and Herald—Dispatch* writes: "With a computer able to store all the words in a typical newspaper and able to tell a typesetting machine how to organize those words on newspaper pages, the possibilities for automatic production of newspapers are obvious. Also obvious is the fact that editors will control production as they write and edit into computers. The potential for improvement in the quality of our products is enormous—if we are up to the challenge."

Philip Meyer, a Washington correspondent for the Knight-Ridder Newspapers who was among the first journalists to make use of the computer in public opinion surveys and other reportorial operations, has this word of caution: "The computer can be dangerous because it makes things too easy. It cannot substitute for human intuition and judgment and it cannot make decisions for you. The temptation can be great to let it do so, particularly for those of us who, owing to the nature of our occupation, are chronically in a hurry." [1]

Other Machines and Processes Here are brief definitions of other electronic machines that have come into general use in journalism and one process, pagination, that is in development:

Video display terminal (VDT) This is a marvelously adaptable machine that has replaced the typewriter in most daily newspapers and is also used for editing copy. It has a typewriterlike keyboard attached to a small TV screen, on which the news appears as it is written or edited.

The copy comes up silently on the screen as the writer types. With the use of a *cursor*, a small block of light one character in size that the writer can control, copy can be changed, corrected and rearranged at the touch of a key. When a take (page) is completed, it can be stored at the touch of another key or it can be sent either to an editor's desk or to the composing room to be set. This is done through a bank of computers. Editors, too, can call up any story they wish or inspect schedules to select the material in hand.

Optical character reader (OCR), or scanner, is another type of terminal. It was the early star of the electronic movement in the city room and is still used in conjunction with a special kind of typewriter, usually the IBM Selectric. The OCR converts this typewritten material into electrical impulses that are then recorded either on punched tape or stored in a computer for later editing, usually on a VDT.

Cathode ray tube (CRT) is a VDT used by the Associated Press and some newspapers for writing and editing copy, which is stored and dispatched by computer. When the copy is sent by AP at 1,200 words per minute, it is generally received and stored directly in the newspaper computers until editors call it up. Because not all newspapers can handle high speed transmission, the 66 wpm teletypes are still used. United Press International uses its VDTs in the same way.

Photocomposition This is a photographic printing process on paper. It replaces the old typesetting system that used hot metal type and the Linotype machine. Instead, the photocomposition machine receives electronic signals making up the letters of a news account or other material and transfers them to paper by photographic means. The paper,

---

[1] John H. McMillan in "A Primer for the Newsroom on New Technology," prepared by the New Technology Committee of the Associated Press Managing Editors, pp. 5–7. Meyer in *Precision Journalism* (Bloomington, Ind.: Indiana University Press, 1973) p. 112.

in column lengths, is pasted up by experts on page-size sheets. With headlines, illustrations and advertisements, each sheet then becomes the basis for the offset printing process (see below).

The first photocomposition machines in the 1960s set about 20 lines a minute, an advance over the 14-line-a-minute Linotypes. Within five years, phototypesetters were made that could turn out 150 lines a minute—about a full-size newspaper column every 60 seconds. Now, the third generation of phototypesetters produces a column in three seconds and can also print a number of different type sizes simultaneously.

Material for use in photocomposition machines may be transmitted by an operator at the keyboard, from a tape, or directly from a computer. As for headlines, they can be attached to the stories for which they are written in whatever type sizes an editor may designate. Many are set at the same time as the story.

When phototypesetters are used in conjunction with computers, and VDTs, they are very accurate. More errors occur when they are manually operated. When there is an error in a line, a new tape must be produced and a paste-up man must impose the single corrected line over the original film printout, which can be a messy business. To avoid such complications, many newspapers now do proofreading on VDTs, so that corrections are made on the screen and error-free tapes usually result.

Pagination This is a process that seeks to shorten the time for the pasteup process of type from the photocomposer. It is in use now on some publications for making up and placing advertisements on a page and is in process of development for editorial matter. What happens is that editorial text, produced on a phototypesetter, is arranged in page form by electronic means with designated headlines, pictures and stories at desired length. The editing is generally done by VDT, the makeup on a pagination device. The arrangement of editorial matter on a page is more complicated than advertising primarily because of the use of graphics and headlines.

Offset is an indirect printing process. The positive image of a page is obtained by pasting up type proofs, pictures and ads. This is then sent to the camera room where a full-page negative of the page is produced. The negative, in turn, is transferred to a thin metal plate by an automatic plate-making machine. An oil-based ink adheres to the parts of the plate retaining the image of the page, the rest is washed clean by water. Next, the inked image is imposed on a rubber roller as a negative which, when transferred to paper, again becomes positive and presents a sharper, cleaner appearance than hot metal letterpress printing. Most American daily newspapers now use it. Illustrations, in particular, are much clearer as a result.

Effects of the Change The most important consequence of the swing to electronics is the decimation of employees in newspaper composing rooms and the virtual elimination of the "punchers," the teletype operators, from the wire services. What has happened, in effect, is that production of newspapers has become centered in the editorial department.

With the savings that have accrued from the cut in mechanical staffing, some publishers have chosen to boost stock dividends. The more farsighted ones, however, have decided to invest more of their resources in the editorial product. In place of the cluttered city rooms and black holes that served as composing rooms in some of the old-time newspapers, many of today's newspaper offices are as well lighted and furnished as any other modern office. Nor is the change limited to the metropolitan giants. On numerous papers of more modest size, there is complete automation with all editing being done on terminals and almost every reporter having one for writing.[2]

It follows that the well-equipped reporter can't get along any more with just pad and pencil. Leading newspapers are equipping bureaus and sports reporters with two-way portable terminals that can be plugged into a power source on assignment and brought into direct communication with the office.

Putting It Together The total effect of the new system is to reduce the number of times a story has to be keyboarded and simplify the process of getting it into type.

A reporter at City Hall, for example, uses his portable VDT to send a story to the paper on deadline. It comes up on an editor's screen at once, is swiftly edited, dispatched with a touch of a single key to the phototypesetter, and is quickly available in proof. Since a space has been held for it on Page 1, it is quickly pasted in and the completed page goes to press. Within minutes, the edition is ready to roll with a story that could not have made that edition under the old hot metal system of production.

Speed and economy are two of the obvious benefits, but that is not all. The swing toward automation has also given the middle group in print journalism—the desk people and copy editors—a unique and sometimes a decisive, influence on the way a newspaper presents the news and opinions of the day. For they are the ones who really put out the paper and what they do on deadline can scarcely be masterminded from above at all times. In no other profession is top management so

---

[2] Sources for the material on new machines include "A Primer for the Newsroom on New Technology," op. cit.; *Editor & Publisher*, (27 September 1975), p. 15; Meyer's *Precision Journalism*, op cit., and demonstrations arranged for me through the kindness of the Associated Press and a number of newspapers in Tennessee.

dependent on the intermediate managers and processors for presentation and production. If this were not so, a newspaper could not be put out efficiently.

Delegation of Authority The publisher is a newspaper's top executive. The five departments — editorial, advertising, mechanical, circulation and business — are responsible to him or her. It is the publisher who must make the final decisions.

Because of the way time, space and people shape the news, many newspaper publishers delegate authority over editorial policy to their editor-in-chief. However, the editor-in-chief, customarily, finds he has all he can do to run the editorial page and the columnists, represent the paper as both its voice and its conscience, and keep in touch with the working news operation. The delegation of power, therefore, usually continues down the line with sole responsibility for the news going to the managing editor.

This individual, whether known by the loftier title of executive editor or the more usual one of managing editor, thereby becomes solely responsible for getting out the paper and guiding the news staff. Whether the managing editor's superiors like it or not, the paper is bound in a sense to reflect something of that person's character and interests. This is inevitable. News does not occur in a vacuum and it cannot be handled by robots.

THE ORGANIZATION

It is apparent that, except on the smallest newspapers, no one person can give detailed direction over all aspects of gathering, writing, processing, editing and publishing news. The news organization in practice has tended to divide roughly into three parts that are generally known as the news side, the city side and the various departments such as life-style pages, sports, financial and amusements. The managing editor is responsible for all of them, but in practice they operate more or less under the general directives he gives to the individual editors.

The News Side Changing news patterns and procedures have shaken up a lot of old ideas about the standard table of organization for newspapers as well as the electronic media. Once the standard press operation was delegated to a managing editor, a city editor, a few departmental editors and their assistants and that was it. Today, from the leading metropolitan and suburban papers to the dailies in cities of medium size, the organization of the staff is dependent on circumstances. A suburban paper in the 150,000 circulation range has come up with a directorate that consists of a managing editor, three assistant managing editors who take charge of various aspects of the news, and a separate editor who handles nothing but investigations. Other papers vary the pattern, including everything from separate investigative teams to editors in charge of self-criticism (the *Washington Post*) and ombudsmen to represent the public (*Louisville Courier-Journal* and *Times*).

It is difficult, therefore, to generalize about news organizations. But despite the many functional changes that have been made, the so-called news side still is the key to the entire news operation. It usually consists of the managing editor, his various assistants, the news editor, the telegraph and cable editors, the head of the copy desk (slot man or woman) and copy editors, the makeup editor and the clerks who assist in their work. On medium to smaller-size papers, some of these functions are of course combined.

With the exception of departmental copy—financial, sports and the like—all news copy flows to the various components of the news side for processing. This includes copy from the city desk, the suburban desk, and the telegraph and cable desks. Generally, the entire copy flow is directed at one top-level executive who is either an assistant managing editor or the news editor (the title matters less than the actual functions). This editor, with perhaps one assistant, has the fantastic responsibility of handling and evaluating all news copy for the paper. It must be scanned for length and given an appropriate headline to indicate its importance in the day's news. The news editor marks directions on the copy for others to carry out.

From this desk the copy flows to the copy editors (a title not only more dignified than copyreader but easier to distinguish from proofreader, who performs a mechanical function primarily designed to catch typographical errors in the composing room). After being read on the copy desk for errors of fact, style, grammar and spelling and trimmed to appropriate length, the copy is given its designated headline. It then goes to the composing room to be set in type.

The makeup editor takes over at this point with a dummy of Page 1 made by the managing editor or news editor after a brief editorial conference before the edition. There also may be dummies for a split page (first page, second section) or for pages 2 and 3. But the rest of the paper must be dummied by the makeup editor with whatever news remains. It is this editor's job to direct the assembling of the paper in the composing room—a procedure that electronic processes are bound to simplify in a few years.

The telegraph and cable editors on the news side are frequently the same person; in fact, the job of makeup editor may be added as a third responsibility. Where there is no special Washington or foreign staff— and usually only the largest papers have their own—the telegraph-cable editor's job consists of keeping up with the wire service file.

To sum up the news side process: It is an entity that is closely tied to the rest of the newspaper—the mechanical side, which produces the paper, the circulation department, which distributes it; the advertising department, which generally places its ads on a page first and therefore sets the size of the news hole, and, of course, the business department, which must meet all expenses.

The City Side On the nation's largest newspapers, the old city desk is no longer recognizable. With the movement of many city dwellers to the suburbs, the coverage of new areas has outgrown the make-shift device of creating suburban editors. In addition, the superior suburban newspapers have demonstrated that they can hold their own in competition with the giants. Thus, some large newspapers have found it necessary to create what they call a metropolitan editor, with jurisdiction over the coverage of both city and suburban areas.

Yet, whether this person is known as a metropolitan editor or city editor, the executive in charge of local news by no means exerts the unlimited authority and prestige that once went with the job even though the field of local coverage has been vastly enlarged. In fact, on papers that are putting out different suburban editions, the city-turned-metropolitan editor has greater responsibility than ever before. It is curious, therefore, that the old awe-inspiring image of the city editor is now preserved only in ancient stage comedies about the newspaper business and droll reminiscences by exjournalists.

On the larger metropolitan and suburban newspapers, the top local news executive still controls the work of most of the news staff. On the city or metropolitan desk, there are also at least one assistant and sometimes several others including an assignment editor for the reporters, a production editor who works with the rewrite bank, a liaison editor with the photo desk, and a swing shift editor who relieves the others on their days off. Necessarily, on a smaller paper, one person may do all these jobs, write the headlines and often handle makeup as well.

Departmental Desks The lines of authority between the city desk and the departmental editors are as rigidly observed as those between the city desk and the news desk. Everything proceeds in channels, almost as if it were a military organization; in view of the time factor, some such discipline is not only desirable but necessary. The sports side, for instance, has its own space assignment and fills its pages, going to the managing editor for general directives. The same is true of business-financial, amusements, and the rest of the departments.

The Individual What this organization amounts to is a mechanism whose operation is governed by the managing editor, but whose separate parts have such a high degree of individual movement that they revolve at approximately the same pace and in the same direction by a seeming miracle. Without very much individual attention, except possibly during the single brief editorial conference that is usually held daily in most newspaper offices, the deskmen and deskwomen carry on efficiently. The activities of individuals, however, are limited very largely to their own group or department.

A local reporter, for instance, takes an assignment from an assistant city editor. The understanding is that he or she will call back that same assistant, who knows what the story is. If the assistant who has given the assignment goes off duty, the callback is handled by a replacement, who has been filled in. Except in an emergency, the reporter stays within this chain of command. The rule is that no reporter offers opinions on the writing of headlines or captions or the play of the story in the edition unless that reporter works on a very small paper or is asked to do so. Even if the reporter has been working with somebody on rewrite, any callback still must be routed through the city desk.

The same restrictions that affect reporters apply to the other individuals on the newspaper's staff. A copyeditor does not have the right to consult directly with a reporter on the meaning of a sentence, unless instructed to do so. The copy has to come back through the news desk and city desk to the writer, who then passes it back through the same channel. In no case, without specific permission, is it possible for a writer or reporter to go to the composing room to make changes in a story. A young reporter once did it to slip his byline on one of his stories and was fired for his pains.

This channeling of the individual, in a profession that is seemingly so casual, is always something of a surprise to those who are first being introduced to journalism. There is good reason for it. If a story could be changed without the knowledge of the copy desk, the headline might not be fixed to conform to the new version. If a reporter could fix copy after handing it in without telling the city editor, many a city editor would be out of touch with the handling of the news. A news organization is run without the boxes or lines of authority that designate the military chain of command, which is all to the good; but, even if the lines of authority are few and not clearly visible, they are kept tight and must be strictly observed.

THE NEWS STAFF

Most newspaper city rooms are functional, workaday places. The pattern of operations varies according to the size and location of the plant and its commitment to the demands of the electronic age.

Large operations like those of the *New York Times* and *Washington Post* are centrally directed and highly organized. Others like the *Wall Street Journal* are decentralized, working through electronic means with composing rooms that are many miles away and press rooms that are scattered all over the country. The *Journal* and the *Los Angeles Times* are two pioneers in the use of facsimile transmission of news pages to distant press rooms. While most papers are not prepared to go that far yet, even smaller ones are swinging over to automation because of the large savings in the cost of labor in the mechanical department.

The Package This situation will not remain static. In viewing the future of the newspaper, Otto A. Silha, president of the *Minneapolis Star-Tribune*, forecasts dramatic changes: "We're told it would cost $250 billion to wire the whole nation for electronic communications," he says. "If that happens, which I believe possible, it will be done in support of a complete home communications system, in which frame-grabbing on the video display tube will bridge the gap between electronics and print." [3]

Right now, leading full-size dailies are shifting away rapidly from the standard eight-column format and the tabloids are dropping the five-column page. Some of the largest and most important full-size dailies in the country have gone to a format of six columns for news, nine for advertising, among them the *New York Times* and *Washington Post*. In the case of the *Times*, the management has calculated a 5% saving annually on newsprint that would amount to more than $3 million a year. Interestingly, when the *Times* was first published on September 18, 1851, its editorial format was six columns. [4]

How Many to a Staff? News staffs vary widely in size and organization. A survey of small city dailies showed that a daily of 5,000 circulation had four full-time and one part-time staffer while another of 8,400 circulation had just six full-time staffers. Most larger dailies have staffs running into the hundreds, with the giants employing more than 1,000 persons on the news side alone.

Size, however, is no particular measure of accomplishment. The six-member staff of the tiny *Panama City News-Herald* has won a Pulitzer Prize gold medal for public service for campaigning against corruption in Bay County, Florida. The same honor has gone to two small North Carolina weeklies, the *Whiteville News Reporter* and the *Tabor City Tribune,* for attacking the Ku Klux Klan, and to the *Watsonville (California) Register-Pajaronian* for a political exposé.

Does automation make a difference in the size of news staffs? Not so far. A more recent survey of small city dailies has shown that one editor is needed for each 2.5 reporters, [5] which shows little change from preautomation years. On larger papers, more editors are required; on a number of them, stenographers are hired to do the typing on some of

[3] *The Bulletin of the American Society of Newspaper Editors,* (September 1976), p. 5
[4] *Editor & Publisher,* (19 June 1976), p. 12.
[5] *Editor & Publisher,* (27 September 1975), p. 14

the terminals to save the time of higher-priced editorial help. There is a growing tendency to dictate instead of write in a few places.

Wherever staff services are too skimpy to give a paper adequate coverage, it is obvious that wire service and syndicate copy are being used to plug up the news hole. In a fully automated shop, this amounts to a considerable saving although, under current circumstances, editors on fairly large papers estimate that as much as one-quarter to one-third of their total copy—a lot of it syndicate material—comes in the same way as always and has to be reprocessed.

But a filler-stuffed paper is a poor product, whether it is crammed with old-fashioned boiler-plate or current time copy extracted from a computer. Such products can have little appeal, since even the least sophisticated reader can tell almost at a glance that they provide only token coverage of the news of a community. A standard filling, no matter how professionally and competently done by the news side, will not really satisfy readers unless there is some evidence of local and departmental work as well. The image that a paper reflects of the world immediately around it will be distorted. It takes an individual staff, working against time and circumstance and sometimes even against itself, to bring a newspaper to life.

PMs and AMs There are about 1435 afternoon newspapers and about 335 morning papers in the United States plus about 20 "all day" papers. As far as the news staffs are concerned, the main characteristic of an afternoon newspaper is change. Except for news from overseas, where there is a large time differential, an afternoon newspaper's first edition can have little more fresh news than the final edition of a morning newspaper as a rule.

Thus, P.M. first editions are often stuffed with features, interpretive pieces on politics and news analyses to provide something different. Then, as the day progresses and more news develops, subsequent P.M. editions are heavier on news and the early stuff goes out. But for economic reasons, the time span over which P.M.s operate is being reduced and so are the number of editions (some are merely Page 1 makeovers).

A normal morning paper operation, by contrast, is fairly stable. Unless the deadline is moved up to the middle of the afternoon (and some large circulation A.M.s are doing just that), a morning paper can go in with a fairly complete and newsworthy first edition. Therefore, except during political campaigns and the coverage of major sports events, not as many changes need be made for the few later editions.

Sunday newspapers—and there are about 600 of them in the nation—are entirely different operations. Separate sections devoted to life style, entertainment, business and finance, housing, books and the like often are produced during the week, with news, sports and editorial/interpretive sections being saved for early Saturday night deadlines. The fat, many-featured Sunday paper has proved to be so durable that some typical Sunday sections also are being put out during the week to bolster the daily paper.

With the coming of automation, the line between P.M. and A.M. operations is becoming blurred. One of the largest P.M.s, *Newsday,* with a circulation that spreads over all of New York's Long Island, has a first edition deadline earlier than most morning paper final editions. And some larger morning papers are going in with their first editions early in the afternoon. Long ago, the old afternoon paper with seven or eight editions and a 5:30 P.M. final edition vanished from the streets; today, more often than not, an afternoon "final" is likely to go to press anywhere between noon and 1:30 P.M. Automation may add a few minutes to that spread, but not much.

Scope of News The scope of the day's news also makes a difference to a staff in the conduct of its operations. During a baseball World Series or a football Super Bowl, for instance, there is a tacit understanding that only the most essential news will be processed while the games are in progress. Teleprinters and composing rooms are tied up when sports interest is at its height. Other events that keep newspaper staffs busy, such as the death of a President of the United States or a spectacular new outer-space development, also almost automatically curtail the handling of secondary material.

Another consideration is the amount of advertising for a particular day, since on most newspapers advertising determines to a very large extent the size of the paper and the amount of available news space on a given day. Finally, a news operation may be affected by unusual weather conditions—a hurricane that knocks out power and snarls communications, a heat wave that sends the potential readers scurrying from the city, or a blizzard or cold wave that makes newspaper delivery a problem.

The reporters, processors, and managers know all these things and govern themselves accordingly. The date book, a daily list of coming events, and the wire service schedules are their guides. It is seldom that a "downhold" order has to be explained when big news is breaking, and this is as true for the broadcast media as it is for print.

CHANGING NEWS PATTERNS

Because of its proximity to developing events and ideas, the middle group in journalism often is the first to identify what is and what is not news. There is a considerable time lag, as a rule, before the most influential group in journalism, the editors and publishers, can assay the flow of events. And it is even longer before public reaction, the final and ultimate news force, makes itself felt.

Who Says It Is News? Thus, a young editor handling a night desk for a wire service in Washington, D. C., can take over the entire national and world facilities of his organization to put out a major news bulletin if he believes it worthwhile. Another young editor on the dogwatch for a morning newspaper and in sole charge of its editorial staff during the last hours of publication can send in Page 1 with a late break. An even more youthful executive in charge of news for a television station in the late evening can interrupt a program with big news.

These editors have no time to weigh the consequences of a mistake and, indeed, seldom worry about it. Actually, the probability of error in such instances is small. By background, experience, and training people in the middle group are well aware of what is generally considered to be news. They also know the gradations of interest.

There is no formula for this. Nor is there a book of news tables that one can consult, as an engineer whips out his book of logarithms. The things that are and are not news vary from one day to the next, from one country to another, from one city to another, and without doubt from one paper to another.

Identical News On events of all conceivable varieties it happens over and over again that leads are practically identical on competing publications and the electronic media. Those who are unfamiliar with journalistic procedures may conclude quite wrongly that this is the result of some secret method of comparing notes and deciding on a standard presentation. Actually, this rarely happens, unless everybody uses the same wire service account, and that certainly is not a matter for consultation.

The fact is that the middle group in journalism is so cohesive by reason of its training, and even its general education and cultural background, that its news approach tends to vary only through circumstances.

The test of a newspaper's individuality is whether its editors try for a fresh approach, rather than a standardized one, to show the public that one newspaper is not just like every other—and does not want to be.

The Making of a Journalist A journalist who works for a particular newspaper or station in Chicago, Kansas City or St. Louis does not take on the thinking, customs and various other peculiarities of that news organization forever after. Nor does a member of the working press necessarily subscribe to the editorial beliefs of such a news organization unless he or she works with policy matters entirely, writes editorials or is a top management official.

The body of knowledge and experience common to good journalists makes professionals out of news people and gives them their capabilities. In radio and television, as in newspapers, Joseph Pulitzer was right. Journalists are made, not born.

It is seldom that a working professional finds any difficulty in fairly and honestly reporting the news, even in a hot political campaign. The journalist is trained to do an honest job, regardless of any personal convictions as a citizen. For those who are in a position to mold or execute policy, however, the only decent thing to do if they differ substantially from their management is to resign, or at the very least, to abstain from writing political editorials for the duration of the campaign.

Journalists who permit their personal integrity to be breached are no journalists at all.

A Sense of Morals It is judgment, finally, that determines how, why, and in what manner the news of the day must be handled; either the judgment of the editor, or in the absence of editorial instructions, the members of the middle group of journalism.

It is, therefore, a tribute to their sense of responsibility that so much good stuff does appear in the columns of the American press in spite of the daily temptations to grab for circulation in every sex case and cheesecake picture. Drivel is written, it is true; and some newspaper accounts are still told in the florid and unrestrained spirit of the Gay Nineties. Newspapers are by no means the sole offenders here; the custodians of television, literature, and the stage have much to account for, too.

While many good newspapers have died because they could not keep up with the times and survive in the face of today's rigorous inter-media competition, it is worth noting that, in the main, the better newspapers are the ones that have gained in prestige since the beginning of the television era. Among them are the *Wall Street Journal, Washington Post, New York Times, Los Angeles Times, Newsday, Boston Globe* and *Miami Herald,* to mention only a few. And sex does not happen to be outstandingly popular in their columns unless it happens to be defined as sociology.

This is not to argue that racy, or even gamy, news should not be published and that certain types of pictures should be virtuously suppressed. This kind of material should be measured by the same kind of editorial standard as any other kind of news; if it is in the public interest, it should be published. Nobody pretends that such judgments come easily.

There are still newspapers that are so afraid of giving offense to someone that they distort or even falsify the news out of the very loftiest of motives. It is, unfortunately, not a legend that a timid suburban weekly reported a distinguished citizen had died suddenly, but neglected to report that he did so by diving out a sixth-story window. And there are still radio and television programs that neglect to mention hard facts that are displeasing to the federal government or major advertisers, or if they are used, tone them down.

But these things are not typical of the best in American journalism. Its leaders today believe as much in vigorous use of freedom of the press as did their more violent predecessors. But they have a livelier sense of responsibility as well.

Chapter 3
The
"Why"
of News Style

Social change in the latter part of the twentieth century has had a moderating effect on the strict rules that once governed the use of written and spoken English by most American news organizations. Grammatical distinctions are no longer as precise as they once were. Nor is the meaning of a word considered to be fixed for all eternity. Some expressions that once were thought of as vulgar or slangy now are in daily use. And a few mild obscenities also appear regularly in the best of publications and are even used, somewhat hesitantly, in newscasts.

The rise of feminism has upset a lot of notions about the treatment of women in the news, among the casualties being such terms as "housewife" and others that appear to put women in a second class status. Even greater changes have come about in the drive of blacks and other minorities for equal treatment, including the increased emphasis on abandonment of descriptions of figures in the news by race or color except where these are pertinent.

The upshot has been a thorough re-examination of that ancient instrument of torture in the newsroom, known to editors as the style-book and to many a disgruntled reporter as the 'copy editors' revenge." Actually, despite all the grumbling that any stylebook evokes among writers, it is a necessary and basically useful compendium of style and usage. If it did not exist, it would have to be invented; without it, reporters and writers would be at constant war with editors.

In effect, stylebooks are standards set by responsible news organizations for the guidance of their staffs and by news agencies for their members or clients. Newspapers take such things far more seriously than the broadcast media because what appears in print is more carefully examined than what is said before a microphone. Good stylebooks can do much to improve the presentation of the news. They should, of course, be administered sensibly and (it is not completely unheard of) with good humor.

THE EDITORIAL MIND

While Lewis Jordan was the news editor of the *New York Times*, he wrote of its new "Manual of Style and Usage," which he revised and edited:

"The intent is to give preference to that which safeguards the language from debasement: to maintain, for instance, distinctions like that between *imply* and *infer*; to avoid faddish neologisms like the verbs *host* and *author*, while avoiding the timeworn and the trite; to shun slang and colloquialisms in inappropriate contexts, but to use them without self-consciousness when the context is appropriate." [1]

As an example of the changes in *Times* style in the 14 years since the last edition of its stylebook, the newspaper formerly identified a married woman on first reference as Mrs. John Doe but now calls her Jane Doe on first reference and Mrs. Doe thereafter. The stylebook continues to use honorifics for men and women except for Ms., but warns:

> In referring to women, we should avoid words or phrases that imply that *The Times* speaks with a purely masculine voice, viewing men as the norm and women as the exception." [2]

Among the terms that are banned are such disparaging references as *doll, weaker sex* and *little woman*. But writers are also cautioned against undesirable subtleties of meaning that can be conveyed by otherwise innocuous terms like *housewife, comely brunette, grandmother, sculptress, divorcee* and others. The rule is that writers should ask themselves whether similar terms would be appropriate if applied to men in the same context. It also is applied generally when descriptions are given of someone of another race or religion.

[1] *The New York Times Manual of Style and Usage* (New York, 1976).
[2] Ibid, pp. 124–225.

The *Times's* rule against obscenity, vulgarity and profanity, formulated in 1896 when Adolph S. Ochs bought the paper, was shattered — with those of many other papers — by the publication of the White House Watergate transcripts. Now, the *Times's* stylebook concedes that "profanity in its milder forms can on some occasions be justified." [3] And while the *Associated Press–United Press International Stylebook* permits the use of obscenity, profanity or vulgarity if there is a "compelling reason" for it, such usage must be accompanied by a precautionary warning to editors at the top of the story. [4] Journalistic morality continues to rest in the eye of the beholder.

The Electronic Stylebook From the standpoint of acceptance among editors, the most influential manual of usage in the United States is the *AP–UPI Stylebook,* which was revised for the first time in 20 years in 1977. Because these two major American news agencies blanket the nation and have a profound influence abroad, their manual is closely read.

In its newest manifestation, there are few breaks in traditional style except in the matter of courtesy titles. Here, AP and UPI decided to eliminate *Miss, Mrs.* and *Mr.* from all sports wires, retained *Miss* and *Mrs.* for the news wires but gave any woman the option to be called Ms. More important changes in style were dictated by the dominance of the computer in wire service work. As William R. Barrett, an assistant UPI managing editor, put it in a detailed notice to clients of changes in usage: "The old ways we have been doing things have to be discarded in these days of modern technology and computers talking to computers. Computers need certain information always in the same place so they will know what to do. In other words, they are programmed to look for certain things in certain places and they react certain ways as a result. The reasoning behind having a standard which all wire services will follow is so receivers of the information can develop programs to uniformly accept the information." [5]

A digest of wire service stylebook usage and procedures appears in Chapter 15.

Hemingway's Lesson Years after he left the Kansas City *Star*, Ernest Hemingway recalled the first principles of news writing as laid down in the *Star's* stylebook that he used. The first paragraph follows:

> Use short sentences. Use short paragraphs. Use vigorous English, not forgetting to strive for smoothness. Be positive, not negative.

As quoted by Charles A. Fenton in *The Apprenticeship of Ernest*

[3] Ibid, p. 147–148
[4] *UPI Reporter* (14 October 1976).
[5] UPI Message to Editors, sent March 22, 1976.

Hemingway, the writer who won both the Nobel and the Pulitzer Prizes had this to say about the influence of the stylebook:

> Those were the best rules I ever learned for the business of writing. I've never forgotten them. No man with any talent, who feels and writes truly about the thing he is trying to say, can fail to write well if he abides by them.

A Lack of Standards Despite all the pressures toward uniformity of usage and procedures in journalism, however, it is a mistake to assume that everybody is going to follow either what the *New York Times* does or what the wire services do. Each news organization, finally, is the arbiter of what it intends to say or print and how and when it will be done. Not many, for instance, prescribe a manner of writing as does the *Kansas City Star.*

One illustration of the bewildering variety of uses to which the language can be put is the classical newspaper insistence, for much of this century, that individuals should be defined as "persons" and large, indefinite groups as "people." With few exceptions, nearly all broadcast journalists use "people" instead of "persons," as sanctioned by *Webster's Third New International Dictionary.*

Thus, a typical newspaper story of an automobile accident amost always began, "Two persons were killed today in an auto accident . . ." Or, in reporting politics, most reporters would write, "More than 1,000 persons heard the governor's speech." But in referring to groups, all journalists would, of course, agree on "the American people," or "Catholic people." Broadcast journalists generally were alone, until recently, in using "people" instead of "persons."

Today, with the exception of newspapers where traditional editors still hold the line, the distinction has all but vanished. Instead, there is such confusion over usage that the *New York Times* reported, in an eight-column inside headline, that "244 *people* with incomes of $200,000 or more" paid no income tax. But in the Washington datelined story by one of the paper's economic specialists, the text reported that "there were 244 *persons*" who had paid no income tax.[6] [Italics added]

This is the *Times's* stylebook ruling on the subject:

> In general, use *people* for round numbers and groups (the larger the group, the better *people* sounds), and *persons* for precise or quite small numbers. *One million people were notified. He notified 1,316 persons. He said 30 people had been asked to volunteer. Only two persons showed up. Seventeen persons were injured.* The important thing is to avoid the ridiculous. *As we all know, persons are funny.*" [7]

[6] The *New York Times,* 6 May 1976, p. 19.
[7] The *New York Times Manual of Style and Usage,* p. 157.

In this book, those writing for newspapers will be advised to use "persons" for individuals, "people" for groups unless their particular news organization has a contrary rule. Those writing only for the broadcast media, however, should use "people" in general because that is the way people talk.

The Need for Discipline The most radical changes in journalistic style nearly always accompany the success of a new medium of mass communication. Thus, Briton Hadden's carefully devised "Timelanguage" kicked up a public fuss when Henry Luce began publishing *Time* magazine. Its stress on inverted sentences caused Wolcott Gibbs to complain in *The New Yorker:*

> Backward ran sentences until reeled the mind.
> Where it all will end, knows God.

With success, *Time's* language moderated. It is not now—for all its color and peppery editorial comment—the Timelanguage that Hadden so carefully planned. Conservatism often comes with success and age, even in the handling of structure and style.

There are some who believe the informality of electronic media is, in effect, a license to write a newscast in a sloppy manner. Not so. The *AP Radio News Stylebook* begins with this admonition:

> The first essential to being a good radio news writer is being a good news writer. You must know news and you must know how to handle it. It is a mistake to assume (and it has been assumed by some) that writing news for radio is a much easier task than writing it for other mediums. Radio news writing demands greater compression, which calls for greater skill.[8]

USES OF THE STYLEBOOK

The stylebook, thus, becomes a primary tool of the journalist as a catalogue of procedures. If a newspaper does not have one of its own, then it must abide by the standards of the wire service it uses in these days of high speed electronic transmission.

Differing Styles It would be almost hopeless to seek agreement even among leading papers on the finer points of newspaper style. Appended to this text is a stylebook based on practices that seem to have majority acceptance.

Editors write stylebooks. They are often genuinely enthusiastic about them and never seem to tire of discussing obscure points in them. Reporters and rewrite men, whose copy is polished against the unyielding whetstone of the stylebook, are less demonstrative for un-

[8] Andrew C. Lang, *The AP Radio News Style Book*, p. 5.

derstandable reasons. They are seldom consulted on what goes into the stylebook, on most papers, and obviously have less interest in it. Thus, stylebook rules can and do become points of contention between writers and copy editors. But the copy editor, having the last look at the copy, is usually the ultimate winner.

What a Stylebook Can Do Most stylebooks, at the very beginning, dutifully enter a disclaimer that they cramp a writer's style of composition. The AP has a more positive view of the function of a stylebook:

> Presentation of the printed word should be accurate, consistent, pleasing to the eye and should conform to grammatical rules. The English language is fluid and changes incessantly. . . . Because of the constantly changing usage, no compilation can be called permanent. Nor can any one volume be infallible or contain all the wisdom and information of the ages. When there is a doubt, consult an authoritative source and stay with it.

What a Stylebook Cannot Do No stylebook can substitute for the hard work, acquired skills, and natural artistry that are the mark of the professional writer of news.

It cannot be used to decide what points are most important in a story, nor can it develop hints on how news should be presented or organized. No rules have yet been devised to substitute for thinking.

These are the limitations of stylebooks. But to a certain extent, many of them do not attempt to fulfill some of the functions for which they are designed. Their authors seldom bother to explain basic newspaper procedures that are too often taken for granted, beginning with the mechanics of copy preparation and including the complications of slugging, markups and other technical operations. The stylebooks that deal with such things usually brush them off with a few primer-like sentences. Consequently they remain mysteries to some reporters to the end of their days.

PREPARATION OF COPY

Copy preparation is the beginning of the newsmaking process. If it is done sloppily, or inaccurately, it can lead to endless confusion. In an automated shop, an improperly marked story can disappear into a computer, never to be seen again. What follows applies to newspapers that use typewriters or a combination of typewriters and OCRs. The same page format applies to preparation on VDTs, except that the slugging process (described in a "header sheet" for most news organizations) is a bit more complicated. That is also true for OCR copy that is edited on VDTs. As for wire service copy preparation, that is described in Chapter 15; broadcast copy preparation in Chapter 16.

Nonautomated newspapers prepare copy on typewritten sheets of

8½ x 11 copy paper plus carbons. For OCRs, the typing is done on IBM Selectrics and any editing changes or corrections are made in a special ink. Regardless of method, the principal mistake news writers make is to try to crowd too much copy on a take—or page.

Copy for the first take of a story should begin one-third of the way from the top with margins an inch or more at either side and a bit more at the bottom. Most terminals take the guesswork out of this, automatically indicating the beginning point and determining the margins. Regardless of method, all sentences and paragraphs should end on a take and it is best to try not to split words at the end of a line.

Standard Procedure The first thing that goes on a story is the name of the writer, top left, with a few words to indicate the source of the story (name of the reporter, AP, UPI, *Journal* clip, etc.). Reporters doing their own stories write "assigned" after their name. Those using the phone use "by phone"; others, rewriting publicity, say "handout." Essentially the same information goes in a terminal "header" block, but spaces are provided for the material along with the slug, the name of the story, which is generally one word. On nonterminal copy, the slug goes an inch or so under the writer's name.

When a story ends on one page, it should be given an end mark such as xxx, #, or even the word "end," with the time off. If it runs to more than one take or page, the word *(more)* is written in the lower right hand corner. After the first take, all succeeding ones begin with copy about an inch and a half from the top.

Working with Terminals Some old-line reporters and writers complain that the electronic era is interfering with their creativity, that the terminal is reducing literary quality. No doubt, the journalists who had to give up the quill pen for the typewriter also felt aggrieved. In reality, working with the terminals isn't all that difficult. A bright beginner should be able to work with a terminal after 48 hours or so and the finer points will come with practice. Most of the newcomers who have learned to operate terminals agree with this view. Some say they would prefer not to go back to typewriters. All of which would seem to indicate that the electronic hazard is mainly in the mind.

How to Prepare Copy

Opposite is the first take of an unedited news story, written by the reporter whose name appears in the upper left-hand corner. The word "assigned" shows that the reporter also was the writer. The word "police" is the slug. Note the generous margins and the wide indentation of paragraphs. The word (more), lower right, shows the story is not finished. Copy on terminals generally resembles this, except that more information is required at the top in "header" boxes provided for the name, date, etc.

Harrington - assigned

POLICE

Police Chief Warren G. Westervelt asked Mayor Caruthers
yesterday to add 500 men to the city's police force before Jan. 1.

"I can't prevent crime in the streets unless I have the
men to do it," Chief Westervelt said. "We simply don't have enough
police to make this city safe."

Asked at a news conference how much the enlarged police
force would cost and where he would get the money to pay the
additional men, he replied:

"I don't know. That's the mayor's problem. Go ask him.
All I can tell him is what's needed."

At City Hall, it was learned that the mayor was angered
by Chief Westervelt's outburst. "I want to talk to him before I say
anything about his proposal," the mayor said.

The two officials will meet at City Hall in the
mayor's office at 10 a.m. today.

MORE

IDENTIFYING A STORY

Slugging used to be a haphazard process. With terminals, it has to be precise, particularly with those that allow only a limited amount of characters for a slug. Thus, for all newspaper writers, the slug should be descriptive. For example, a story about the mayor would be slugged "mayor," about the United Nations, "UN," Other descriptive and familiar slugs are "fire," "plane," "train," "slay." If there are a lot of stories about one event, such as an election or the Olympic Games, each would carry an added designation such as "election," or "games," which would be shortened to two letters for terminal use.

Purpose Slugs have many purposes in addition to story identification. On nonautomated papers, the process through which the story is edited and set may be traced by the recording of the slug in various departments. On terminals, the slug is needed to call up a story on the screen for editing or transmission to the composing room. The slug also is used to identify the headline designated for the story and its place in the paper. When changes are made in the story, such as new leads, inserts, adds or corrections, the slug quickly identifies the piece that is affected. (New Lead Mayor, Insert A Yanks, Add Moscow, etc.) The word "kill," which means a story is to be eliminated, cannot be used as a slug. Neither can "must," an editor's designation for a piece that must be published.

Differences in Page Numbering Some newspapers number their takes consecutively, as in the foregoing. Others follow wire service procedure (see Chapter 15) and use "1st Add Storm" instead of "Storm Page 2," "2nd Add Storm," instead of "Storm Page 3," and "3rd and Final Add Storm" instead of "Storm Page 4" with an end mark. Sometimes, an add will run several pages but the principle is the same; then, the add numbers run consecutively: "1st Add Storm, Page 2," etc. It doesn't really matter which system is followed as long as the slugging is consistent, the page numbers are checked and the ends of adds and of stories alike are carefully marked.

How to Edit Copy

Opposite is the first take of an edited new lead. The slug shows that the writer has topped a story previously handled. Instructions, lower right, show where the old story will pick up. The names after that of the writer are those of reporters and the wire service that was the source of the story. For an OCR, the editing would be done with a special ink and pen. For a VDT, instead of topping a previous story, the whole thing can be reconstituted and reset faster than doing it the old-fashioned way, provided the piece isn't too long.

Harrington rew Sessons, Mainwaring and AP

NL POLICE

Mayor Caruthers ~~has demanded~~ asked Police Chief Warren G.

Westervelt's resignation, ~~it was learned~~ to last night.

Furious over the Chief ~~Westervelt's demand that~~ request for 500 more

~~men be added to the city's~~ police ~~force~~ before Jan. 1, the Mayor

bluntly told him by telephone that he was through.

~~It was learned~~ At Police Headquarters, ~~that~~ the 65-year-

old chief ~~intended to~~ indicated that he would apply this week for retirement after 41 years

of service on the force. Neither he nor the mayor would comment

publicly.

The break between the two officials came ~~with dramatic~~ Soon

~~and unexpected suddenness~~ after Chief Westervelt had demanded an increase

in the size of the city's 8,000-man police force. ~~He had been~~

~~under increasing pressure in recent weeks to check the rising crime~~

~~rate, the worst in the city's history.~~

end NL POLICE

~~pikup 2nd graf "I can't prevent"~~

STYLE AS A MANNER OF WRITING

Style is a two-faced word in journalism. In the sense of the foregoing discussion, it refers to uniform rules of spelling, syntax, abbreviations and similar matters. In its most important sense, however, style refers to an individualistic manner of writing. Editors or news directors who fail to separate the two are likely to have trouble getting the best out of their writers.

The ambivalence of the editorial mind with regard to style is at once the delight of the critics of journalism and the despair of the well-educated newcomer. While writers are always encouraged to try to develop a more readable style, they are also limited by the dictates of the stylebook.

Little can be done about this. Both are vital in journalism, particularly in newspaper work. The best advice that can be given to a newcomer is to memorize the stylebook, work to develop a highly personal style of writing and then hope for the best.

HANDLING A STORY ON A VDT

Barbara Abel is ready to write a story about a parade for the city desk of the Milwaukee Journal. She signs on at her Hendrix 3400 VDT, presses the SLUG key, and this form pops up at the top of the screen:

SLUG:		⊢ABEL⊣SLUGIT⊣01Z	STATUS:	R1	TIME:	09:23 MON	REF:		⊢
EDN:		DAY:	PAGE:		SET:	012			OK:

CY is entered for City Desk, PARADE is the slug, 01 is the page number (the z is dropped because that signifies the last take), R1 means the piece is routine (urgent, or U, means faster handling) and 1 means it is the first version. One L is the name of the edition and 012 is the code for body type. Barbara writes a take and the city desk gets it:

SLUG:	CY⊣ABEL⊣PARADE⊣01	STATUS:	R2	TIME:	09:23 MON	REF:	ABEL⊣PARADE
EDN:	ONE L	DAY:	MON	PAGE:	SET:	012	OK:

Automatically, when the story comes up for editing on a city desk VDT, it becomes version R2. There happens to be another PARADE slug, so the desk changes Barbara's story to FROLIC and decides to set it in wide measure and put it on a page designated as H. The codes appear in these spaces and the take goes to the copy desk:

SLUG:	LD⊣ABEL⊣FROLIC⊣01	STATUS:	R2	TIME:	09:23 MON	REF:	ABEL⊣PARADE
EDN:	ONE L	DAY:	MON	PAGE:	HHH	SET:	042	OK:

When the copy editor finishes with the take on another VDT, Barbara's second and last takes are ready and these, too, are handled and sent to the composing room. This is the second take slug when it reaches the composing room at 10:10 a.m.:

SLUG:	NA‐ABEL‐FROLIC‐02Z	STATUS:	R3	TIME:	10:10 MON	REF:	ABEL‐PARADE
EDN: ONE L	DAY: MON	PAGE: HHH	SET: 042			OK:	SR

Chapter 4
The Uses
of Language

When Walter Cronkite used the pronunciation "Feb-yoo-ary" for the second month of the year on the CBS Evening News, he gravely informed his 28 million viewers that he had looked it up in a good dictionary. Not many younger broadcast journalists would have thought it necessary.

Such public displays of concern for the purity of the English language also occur now and then in newspaper work. When Red Smith won a Pulitzer Prize for his sports writing, the jurors praised his care and respect for the uses of language.[1] That hasn't happened very often on sports pages, where almost anything goes nowadays.

Cronkite and Red Smith are typical of the older generation of journalists, who are deeply concerned over the deficiencies in basic writing skills that are so painfully apparent among many newcomers to journalism, including graduates of our finest universities. A learned article by three journalism professors has called it "a spelling and grammar crisis." [2]

[1] Smith won the 1976 Pulitzer Prize for Distinguished Commentary.
[2] Thomas A. Bowers, Richard A. Cole and L. E. Mullins in *Editor & Publisher* (30 August 1975), p. 42.

Numerous hurry-up remedies have been proposed to bring the new journalists up to the mark, none of them very practical. For if recruits don't know the basic rules of grammar and spelling, for whatever reason, they will have to learn them. Such deficiencies are bound to disqualify a newcomer quicker than anything else.

The news media cannot be casual about the uses of language. They must transmit news, opinions and ideas to mass audiences as efficiently as possible. Their standards in the uses of language must be at least as high as those of the best-educated elements among their readers, listeners or viewers if they are to retain the public's respect.

Slovenly language may not prevent 50,000 people from buying a book or seeing a play, but it would be well-nigh fatal, if continued for very long, to the reputation of a news organization.

A GRAMMATICAL CHECK LIST

There are no exceptions to the rule that correct grammatical usage is essential to good journalism. The preciseness of language sharpens the meaning of fact. That is why the two go hand in hand.

Here, in condensed form, is a grammatical check list. It includes some of the principal shortcomings of professional journalists and suggests procedures that are generally acceptable in American newsrooms:

Adjectives It is customary in every professional work on writing to caution against the use of adjectives, certainly sound advice. Most writers, even inexperienced ones, quickly learn that adjectives are treacherous and select the few they use with care. When Georges Clemenceau was editor of the newspaper, *La Justice,* he told a new reporter, "Young man, when you write a sentence you are to use a noun, a verb, and a complement. If you use an adjective, you must ask my permission."

Adverbs The flat adverb sometimes is mistaken for an adjective. "Go *slow,*" is correct usage, *slow* being a flat adverb. (An adverb without the usual "ly" adverbial ending.) But, "He drove *careful,*" is obviously wrong, *careful* being an adjective that modifies a verb. The rule is that adverbs, flat or not, modify verbs whereas adjectives modify nouns.

Therefore, if the modifier specifically refers to the subject, it must be an adjective; if it refers to the verb, it must be an adverb. Thus, "He drove carefully," would be a correct use of the adverb.

In the use of copulative (linking) verbs (appear, feel, look, seem, smell) the writer must choose carefully between the use of a predicate adjective and an adverb modifier. "He feels bad," connotes illness. To write, "He feels badly," would mean that something was wrong with his sense of touch.

Antecedent A noun or noun equivalent, whether word, phrase or clause, is referred to by a personal or relative pronoun. The pronoun and antecedent must agree in number. The pronoun, *it,* is nearly always a danger signal in copy because it may be the source of a grammatical error. Always check the antecedent.

Articles There is a notion among some editors that an article can be dispensed with in many sentences. The result has been to encourage the growth of a kind of telegraphic writing in which "the," "a" and "an" are bowled over like ninepins. Some samples:

> Sense of the meeting was against zoning.
> Rash of activity broke out in City Council last night.
> Dedication of bridge is set for Tuesday.

There is inconsistency, as well, in the dropping of articles. The indiscriminate omission of articles saves little space, leads to confusion, and annoys readers.

Collective Nouns Congress, the cabinet, and the government are among the collective nouns that are singular in American usage and plural in Britain. Plural nouns such as police and fish should not be mistaken for collective nouns.

Ellipsis The omission of words necessary to complete a sentence involves the use of ellipsis. There is a rule, modified by exceptions, that a word may be omitted if its meaning can be supplied or understood from a corresponding part of a compound sentence. The word to be supplied must be in the same grammatical form as the one to which it corresponds. This is correct: "One person was killed and another injured." This is incorrect: "One person was killed and 12 injured." To be correct, the word "were" would go after 12.

Not Only In using the term *not only* the writer must watch parallel construction or the meaning of his sentence may be twisted. The rule for correlative conjunctions is that one must parallel the other; that is, it must follow the same part of speech. Thus, the expression, *not only,* is usually paired with the expression, *but also.* It would be incorrect to write, "The defendant was not only found guilty of grand larceny, but also of assault." To make sense, the "not only" must be moved to after the word "guilty." Then, each of the phrases directly precedes the preposition "of" and is parallel in construction. Other correlative conjunctions that are used in pairs and that follow the same rule include such expressions as *either—or, neither—nor,* and *both—and.*

Number Disagreement in number between subject and verb is an unwelcome feature of much news copy. Singular verbs crop up with dismaying frequency after plural subjects, particularly when a qualifying clause intervenes that confuses the writer. It is incorrect to write, "Part of their silver and linen were stolen." The subject is the noun *part* and it takes a singular verb. The same error may be detected in this sentence: "A box of rifles and hand grenades, discovered on the ship, were seized by the federal agents." The singular form of the verb should have been used. However, in the following sentence, a plural verb should have been used: "Much flame and smoke, while obscuring the building, was seen for miles around." In a compound subject joined by *or, nor, either—or,* or *neither—nor* the verb agrees with the subject nearest to it. This sentence, therefore, would be correct: "Neither the captain nor his men were seen." But when a simple subject is modified by an expression such as *in addition to* or *together with,* the verb still must agree with the subject and therefore it remains singular: "The sergeant, together with his companions, was injured."

Preposition at End of Sentence At one time ending a sentence with a preposition was a grammatical crime in the first degree. The only recourse for a culprit, when detected, was to throw himself on the mercy of the court. The rule against prepositional endings has been relaxed here and there—but when one is used in news copy a good excuse had better be given.

Sequence of Tenses The rule of good sense should be applied to a determination of the proper sequence of tenses. It has become so complicated that the average writer is bewildered by rules. The first thing to remember is that the alignment of tenses in a sentence should follow the rules of parallelism and normal time sequence. Thus, it is normal to write: "The President says he feels fine." Also, transposing to the past tense, it is correct to write: "The President said he felt fine." But, in an exceptional case, the parallel construction must be broken to take account of circumstances. For instance, it would be silly to write: "Columbus said the world was round." It still is. (Well, anyway, it's pear-shaped.) Therefore, the correct method of writing current truths expressed in the past is: "Columbus said the world is round." There is further variation when reference is made to an event preceding the simple past. Then, the past-perfect tense must be used as follows: "The President said that he had been ill." However, when the sentence itself indicates the priority in time of various events, it is not necessary to do so by juggling tenses. Thus, it would be correct to say: "The President recalled that this was the anniversary of his illness a year ago." But it is not correct to report: "The President said he will go to Chicago." What actually happened was that he "said he would go to Chicago." When in doubt, the writer should examine his sequence of tenses and ask himself whether they make sense. Then, he ought to think of the suffering reader or listener.

Split Infinitive Infinitives are split at will in some universities, but copy desks still worry about slipping an adverb between "to be," or "to have," or "to split." The general rule is that a writer must have good reason for splitting an infinitive.

Subjunctive The subjunctive mood is honored primarily by newspapers and wire services. In certain simple conditional clauses some editors with more self-assurance than others will permit the indicative mood to be used. Such a clause is given in the following sentence: "If the mayor was involved, he did not say so." In the case of a purely hypothetical clause, the subjunctive is used as follows: "It's as if the moon were made of green cheese." When a conditional clause is contrary to fact, then the use of the subjunctive is mandatory, as in the following: "If Justice Smith were no longer a member of the Supreme Court, he would probably take up mountain climbing."

That and Which The easiest way to separate this old puzzler is to use "Bernstein's Law," as follows: "If the clause could be omitted without leaving the noun it modifies incomplete, or without materially altering the sense of what is being said—or if it could be reasonably enclosed in parentheses—it should be introduced by 'which'; otherwise, by 'that.' For example: "The Holston River, which flows east of Knoxville, Tennessee, is muddy." (A nondefining clause; it could be omitted or parenthesized.) But: "The river that flows east of Knoxville, Tennessee, is the Holston."[3] To repeat the rule: "That" introduces a limiting or defining clause; "which," a nondefining clause.

Verbs The historical journalistic insistence on the use of verbs in the active voice, where possible, is perfectly sound, but the device may become banal with overuse.

The intransitive verb is not to be despised. Some of the world's most moving and dramatic events can be told best with the use of an intransitive verb. For instance:

ROME—The Pope is dying.

There are times, too, when a verb in the passive voice is most effective, as in the following:

HOUSTON—A space shuttle was fired into orbit today.

Not all the smashing, lashing, dashing, crashing pile-up of verbals can create the effect of a simple, unaffected statement of big news. Where verbs in the active voice contribute to the clarity and mood of a story, of course, they are to be preferred, but some of the excesses of indiscriminate use can only be deplored.

[3] Theodore M. Bernstein, *Watch Your Language* (New York, 1958), pp. 169–170.

Writers are well advised not to switch from active to passive voice, and vice versa, in the same sentence.

Verbals This is the grammatical chamber of horrors.

Exhibit A is the dangling participle. A participle is a verb used as an adjective. When it dangles, it is an erratic modifier. For example: "Walking from the dark room, his eyes blinked." He did the walking, not his eyes. Dangling participles may be avoided by putting the participle in direct contact with the noun or pronoun it modifies. For example: "Walking from the dark room, he blinked."

Exhibit B is the misused gerund. A gerund is a verb used as a noun. It may take a modifier, but if so, the noun or pronoun must be in the possessive case. It is incorrect to write: "He did not approve the candidate speaking first." What was not approved was *the candidate's speaking*, and that is the way it should have been written. The intent of the sentence is the basis for determining whether the gerund takes a possessive. Try the words, *act of*, in the above sentence as a test. In the sentence, insert these words before the gerund *speaking*: "He did not approve of the candidate (act of) speaking first." It is awkward. Therefore, the use of the possessive, the *candidate's speaking*, is indicated.

Will and Shall The grammatical rule governing *will* and *shall* is too generally disregarded in most newsrooms. The language, "I shall go," or "I should like," seems too precious for journalistic use. Actually, the distinction is a good one and should be maintained. Shall is used with the first person and *will* with the second and third persons when simple future or mere expectation is to be expressed. In expressing determination, command, promise, or obligation, the order is reversed. The first condition is met by this sentence, "I shall try if you will help me." The second condition is illustrated as follows: "I will be heard," or, "You shall obey me."

Who and Whom There is no nonsense about the correct use of *who* and *whom*. The simple rules are still in effect on every copy desk in the land, and writers are held strictly to account. The error in usage here is one of the most common in journalism, and one of the easiest to detect.

A sentence properly using *who* as the subject of a clause follows: "The Mayor was the only candidate who, in the committee's opinion, would be acceptable to the voters." Another sentence in which *whom* is properly used as the object of a verb is: "The Mayor was the candidate whom the committee preferred." A simple test may be made by recasting the sentence and substituting the pronouns he or him for who or whom. The first sentence would then read: "In the committee's opinion, he would be acceptable." Thus, *who* is the correct pronoun.

USAGE

Some words and expressions are frequently misused by news writers. Below are some that have achieved notoriety:

all-America Often misused as All-American, referring to members of All-America football teams.

all right Often incorrectly spelled alright. The expression is two words, like under way.

all-round Misused as all-around. The correct expression is all-round athlete.

as a result of Usually misused as "the result of. . . ." Often, something happens as a result of. . . . In other words, more than one result is usually possible.

author This is a noun. Do not use as a verb.

banquet Usually it is a dinner. There has not been a dinner in New York worth calling a banquet in years.

boat A small craft, propelled by oars. It is often misused for a ship, which is larger and is a seagoing craft.

bride A woman about to be married, as well as a newly married woman. Her husband is not a groom, but a bridegroom.

broadcast Present and past tenses of the verb are identical.

burglary Usually misused. There must be breaking and entering before a larceny can be called a burglary. The act of stealing is more often a theft or a robbery.

by A preposition expressing relations of place or direction and commonly referring to persons. "Through" may refer to either persons or things.

capital Washington, D. C., is the capital. The building is called the capitol.

casualties In war these refer to both dead and injured. The term means losses from any cause.

chair Misused as a verb. To say that someone chaired a meeting is incorrect. He or she presided.

claim Often incorrectly used. It is not right to say that a district attorney claims a defendent is guilty. This is a charge, an accusation.

compare Two like objects are compared to each other. Two unlike objects are compared with each other.

comprise Do not confuse with compose. Comprise means to consist of.

counsel Used as a noun, this refers to a person who gives advice. He may be part of a council, which is a deliberative body.

data This is plural. The singular, datum, is seldom used.

different than Use different from.

don't   It means do not and must never be used for doesn't, meaning does not.

due to   Must refer to a noun, if used. It is wrong to write, "She agreed to go, due to her husband's insistence." This is correct: "Her agreement to go was due to her husband's insistence." Often "because of" will serve the purpose better.

false titles   Expressions such as movie queen Elizabeth Taylor, television comic Flip Wilson, and concert pianist Van Cliburn, are false titles. They should not be used as such. Instead, use them after the names of persons, as modifiers.

farther   Refers to physical distance. Further is used for time and all else.

figuratively   Do not confuse with literally.

finalize   Do not use.

forecast   Present and past tenses of the verb are identical.

from   A man does not die from heart failure. He dies of heart disease.

hanged   A man is hanged. A picture is hung.

infer   Conclusions reached by a reader or viewer; not to be confused with imply, which is what a writer or speaker does when he makes allusions or suggestions.

it's   Means it is. *Its* is a pronoun in the possessive case.

kind of   Do not follow with the article *a*.

lawyer   A member of the bar is a lawyer, not an attorney. However, a lawyer may be an attorney (adviser) to an accused person.

less   A reference to quantity: "Less than one-third remains." Fewer refers to numbers: "Fewer than ten attended."

lie, lay   Lay is the past tense of lie. "He lay down." Lie is present tense. "It lies there."

like   A preposition that expresses comparison. "He pitched like Tom Seaver." It cannot be substituted for the conjunction *as*. "The prisoner did as he was told." Not "like he was told."

majority, plurality   If only two candidates are running for office, the winning margin is a majority. If more than two are in the contest, the margin of the votes of the first candidate over the second is a plurality but the first candidate also may have a majority of all votes.

media   A plural noun.

narcotics   Do not use the expressions, dope and drugs, when narcotics or habit-forming drugs are meant.

none   Singular, except when the usage is awkward.

numbers   Do not start a sentence with numbers. Spell them out instead.

over   Not to be used for the expression, more than. Over means above. The expression, more than, means in excess of.

per cent   May be one word or two, depending on your editor.

plenty   A noun. Not to be used as an adjective or adverb.

practically   Means the opposite of theoretically. "The crop was practically worthless." Virtually means in essence, or in effect, but not in fact. "He rules virtually as a dictator."

principal   An adjective meaning chief or main. Principle, a noun, means a general truth.

proven   The correct word is proved.

providing   Provided is better. "The plane was due at Orly at 8 A.M., provided its schedule was maintained."

raise   Children are reared. Pay is raised.

reason is because   Do not use. Because means "for the reason that."

render   Fat is rendered, but not music.

St. James's   The United States has an ambassador at the Court of St. James's, not St. James.

Scots   The people of Scotland are Scots. They drink Scotch and soda sometimes.

sustain   Injuries are received or suffered, not sustained.

toward   The final "s" has been dropped in toward, afterward, forward.

transpire   Means to become known gradually, and should not be used in the sense of to happen or to occur.

try   The old college try has made this verb into a noun.

whether   Do not use as whether or not, unless an alternative must be given the same weight.

SPELLING

Editors are not alone in complaining that newcomers are poor spellers. Young lawyers, doctors, and engineers also have been criticized for the same failing.

The following list includes words that have been chronically misspelled for many years by both older and younger generations of journalists:

accessible	atoll	commitment
accommodate	ballistic	consensus
affect	battalion	contemptible
aggression	bettor	council
all right	buses	counsel
analogous	canoeist	curlicue
anyone	capital	defense
appall	capitol	deity
appendicitis	carrot	demurrer
arraignment	changeable	dependent
assault	claque	dietitian

diphtheria	indomitable	passenger
discernible	inevitable	peaceable
dissension	ingenious	permissible
drunkenness	ingenuous	Philippine
ecstasy	innocuous	phony
effect	inoculate	plaque
embarrass	inseparable	Portuguese
endorse	insistence	propeller
eying	judgment	queue
frivolous	kidnaped	recommend
fulfill	kimono	regrettable
furor	liaison	renege
gaiety	likable	sacrilegious
gauge	mangy	sanitarium
glamor	Manhattan	saxophone
guerrilla	marshal	seized
hemorrhage	naphtha	supersede
hygiene	nickel	vacillate
hyperbole	niece	vilify
immolate	ninety	weird
impeccable	observer	whisky
incalculable	occult	xylophone
incompatible	occurred	zephyr
incorruptible	oculist	
indispensable	offense	

The pitfalls in this list are not entirely of a writer's own making. Some of these words have several accepted spellings, but only one is used generally in American journalism. (Observer is accepted by most newspapers, but observor is equally correct.) Others are correct by American standards, incorrect by those of Britain and other Commonwealth countries. (We spell glamor, offense; the British, glamour, offence.) There are also homonyms—words that sound alike but are spelled differently and have different meanings (council, counsel). Of course, there are also many words that are exceptions to the normal rules of spelling.

Good spelling requires a good memory. It means, too, that dictionaries must be consulted frequently. Except for pathological cases, those who spell poorly either were never trained correctly in school or are too careless now to change their ways.

CONCISENESS

Sometimes news phrases are wordy. They may be tautological. Or, worst of all, they may be incorrect.

Every editor has a list that violates the journalistic virtue of conciseness in one way or another. Below in bold type are some of the most frequent offenders, with suggestions for improvement and comments in regular type face:

at the present time   At present, now.
big in size   Big *is* size.
biography of his life   That is what a biography is.
checked out   As used by TV detectives, who check out clues, this is a redundant expression. Drop the "out."
combined together   Drop the "together."
consensus of opinion   A consensus means opinion.
dead body   A body is presumed to be dead.
early pioneer   How late is a pioneer?
entire monopoly   Either it is a monopoly or it is not. Drop "entire."
hallowe'en evening   E'en is a contraction of evening.
head up   As coined by the Togetherness Boys, the expression means to head a committee. The "up" is superfluous.
high-powered rifle   Rifles are. If it is only a pop-gun, say so.
knots per hour   Knots measure speed per hour.
most unique   It cannot be. Drop "most." It is like saying somebody is very dead.
present incumbent   Drop the "present."
repeat again   That is what repeating is — again.
ten P.M. tonight   It is no better when it is written, "Five A.M. this morning."
true facts   Facts are presumed to be true.
two alternatives   An alternative refers to a choice between two things.
unknown person   Correct expression is unidentified person.
well-known   Do not use. If a person is well known, people will realize it without being told. The same is true of the use of "prominent citizen."
win it   This is a fad expression used by sportscasters: "The Yankees win it, 6–5." The "it" is superfluous.

There are other pet hates among journalists, such as Sahara Desert and Sierra Nevada Mountains. (Sahara means desert, and Sierra means mountains.) The list could grow to unreasonable length. It is intended primarily as a compilation of the most common offenses.

PUNCTUATION

The unskilled writer frequently uses too much punctuation.

There are too many quotation marks around single words and partial quotations. There are too many dashes and hyphens, too many commas, semicolons and colons, and not enough periods. This is a broad complaint, to which there are, of course, numerous exceptions. But in an effective writing style punctuation should be distinguished by its sparseness and utility. Here is some good advice from the AP–UPI *Stylebook*:

> Punctuation is the visual inflection. The marks should clarify meaning and, like shouting, should be employed sparingly. Skillful phrasing avoids ambiguity, insures correct interpretation and lessens need for punctuation. When punctuation is used, it should be employed solely to bring out what is intended. If punctuation does not clarify, it should be omitted.

Some of the principal errors in the use of punctuation are discussed below.

Periods The period is the most useful of all forms of punctuation. The main error made by news writers, in general, is that they do not use enough periods. Nor do they use them at sufficiently frequent intervals. A period should be used more often than it is.

Quotations The failure to place commas and periods inside quotes is frequently noted in news copy. Another error is the placement of quotation marks in several paragraphs of quoted material that follow one another. All that is required is to place a quotation mark at the beginning of each paragraph in the series and to omit it from the end of all paragraphs except the last quoted one. Often quotes are placed around single words or phrases when they are not needed. In general, writers should avoid quoting a word or phrase unless there is a specific justification for it. To quote a word or phrase because it is unusual or slangy or cute is an error, unless it can be directly attributed to someone in the story and has a special meaning that requires quotation marks. As for double attribution, it should be used sparingly and with great care.

Hyphens and Dashes Hyphens pull language together. Dashes perform the opposite function. Both are used far more than is necessary. The rules for hyphenating compound words are given at length under *compound* in *Webster's New International Dictionary*, a standard guide. A dash should be used only when there is an abrupt change of thought.

Commas In newspaper style, there is no comma following the last element in a series. For books, in a series of three or more elements, all the elements are separated by commas. In this book, newspaper usage is followed.

CAPITALIZATION

Many newspapers in the United States are embracing lower-case style. The so-called down style is more convenient, easier to handle, and probably faster to work with than the more formal and more correct full capitalization that is characteristic of the most carefully edited publications.

When a newspaper uses lower case or down style, it often goes farther in this direction than it may wish. The reason is that copy editors are generally so rushed, and so few in number, that they do not indicate carefully what is to be capitalized. And no terminal will help them out, as printers used to do.

The result is that, in many a newspaper of excellent reputation, there will be uncapitalized words on Page 1 (and elsewhere) such as Congress, the United States Supreme Court, the Federal Bureau of Investigation, the United States Air Force and sometimes the United States itself. In all except the most fanatically down-style papers, these excesses are accidents.

In checking the stylebooks of newspapers the inexperienced journalist will find quickly that a certain basic minimum of proper nouns must be capitalized. A newspaper is not intended to be a copy book, but it also should not be a typographical nightmare.

Such are the basic uses of language that must be known to every journalist. They must be practiced faithfully. Without them journalism would be chaotic and undisciplined. Wisely used, these techniques emphasize the expressiveness and versatility of the English language. They frame the manner in which journalists express themselves and give their work depth and meaning.

Chapter 5
News Writing
Is
Clear Writing

Experienced journalists know that they must do more than merely make themselves understood. They must also be certain that they are never misunderstood. For news, in these complicated and critical times, can be very confusing to people, and sometimes to specialists as well, if it is not clearly written and told.

There is no mystery about clear writing. The principles have been known for thousands of years and put into practice by the masters of literature since the time of Homer. Winston Churchill explained his own experience in these vivid terms:

"By being so long in the lowest form (at Harrow), I gained an immense advantage over the cleverer boys. I got into my bones the essential structure of the ordinary British sentence—which is a noble thing."

That "noble thing," British or American, is the basis of clear writing.

WRITERS AND EDITORS

Until television began making inroads into newspaper readership, most editors were far too complacent about the manner in which their staffs handled the language. The long, straggling sentence and the imprecise word, the inaccurate modifier and the unintended slip in grammar were often shrugged off when they got into print. Not in recent years, however. At almost every meeting of editors, and even those of publishers now and then, the improvement of staff writing skills is a matter of urgency.

There are some who are inclined to blame the public decline in reading efficiency, as tabulated in countless reports of low-scoring reading tests in schools, for at least a part of the problems of print journalism. Others argue that the terminal and the computer are making word technicians out of writers of taste and sensitivity.

The answer to this comes from computer experts who point out that a machine by itself can scarcely eliminate deficiencies in the use of language. As they brutally put it: "Garbage in, garbage out."

The View from Washington While Charles Seib was the Washington Post's ombudsman and resident press critic, he wrote a column that celebrated the joys of clear writing. This was his theme: "Newspapers continue to dish up a daily diet of turgid prose, cliche-ridden and indigestible. It is a chore to read and hard to understand. . . . This isn't a plea for the restoration of arbitrary rules by newspapers. It is a plea for more consideration for the reader. Survival may be in the balance." [1]

The AP Log picked up the complaint and sent it to all editors, which was a commentary in itself.

The View from Cambridge Taking a broader view, Ralph F. Lewis, editor and publisher of the Harvard Business Review, was even more disconsolate. Far from limiting his criticism to newspapers, he wrote: "When one reads as many manuscripts as each of us editors does, it is very easy to feel that the English language is falling apart." [2]

Edwin Newman, an NBC commentator who has written a best-selling book on the subject, agrees with this view. "Language," he says, "is in decline."

A Hopeful Note In a survey of newspapers that have resisted television's inroads, some of which have achieved the highest circulation records in their history, J. Montgomery Curtis reports that such papers as the *Wall Street Journal, Detroit Free Press, Buffalo Evening News* and *Charlotte*

[1] *The Washington Post*, February 27, 1976.
[2] *New York Times*, 4 June 1976.

Observer emphasize their improved writing in broadening their appeal to readers.

The *Wall Street Journal,* he points out, has "an unusually high story count accomplished by brevity and balanced by thorough treatment of at least two and sometimes three stories a day, many of which can be read for the sheer pleasure of reading." He adds that the *Detroit Free Press* has placed "a premium on good writing." [3]

Nevertheless, newspapers in general have some distance to go before they can satisfy their critics. Nor can television be exempted by any means from censure for the use of muddy language.

ON UNDERSTANDING NEWS

If there were a simple definition of news upon which all could agree, the failings of journalists as writers would be easier to diagnose and correct. But none exists. In consequence, it is obvious that those who try to write about the news are in deep trouble if they are in doubt at the outset over the essential character of the news.

Actually, the concept of news varies among the media. To morning newspapers, it is what happened yesterday. To afternoon newspapers, it is what happened today. To news magazines, it is what happened last week. To wire services, radio and television, it is what happened a moment ago.

There is nothing static or stylized about the news; nor, for that matter, should there be any rigid rules and decrees for writing about it. News is a living, growing, expanding entity, constantly changing direction, constantly producing the dramatic and the unexpected. In the early years of this century, the notion of producing an atomic bomb or landing men on the moon was not news; indeed, both were considered impossible. A generation ago, few thought there was news in the ecology, the consumer movement or the struggle for equal opportunity for women.

What is News? Every definition of news, therefore, raises questions of its own. How can you tell an event, which is news, from a pseudo event, which may be inspired by a tiny group of demonstrators to draw attention to themselves? Can you pretend that there is news in a media event, something actually created by the presence of the media or even bought and paid for by one news organization or another? Do reporters become news, or are they participants in the news, when they permit themselves to be drawn into the events that they are supposed to

---

[3] J. Montgomery Curtis, former director, American Press Institute, and vice president, Knight-Ridder Newspapers Inc., Report to American Newspaper Publishers Association, 5 May 1976.

cover? All these are intensely practical questions that no definition will cover.

Most journalists have their own pet definitions. Keith Fuller, president of the Associated Press, suggests that when somebody says, "Gee whiz, I didn't know that," it's news. Turner Catledge used to tell the staff of the *New York Times* when he was its executive editor, "News is anything you didn't know yesterday." A cynic's definition is: "News is what editors say it is." And finally, here is a statement of fact: "News is what is broadcast or printed in newspapers."

All these are flawed, particularly the last. There is no guarantee that all news media provide news.

Characteristics of News The basic qualities of the news are accuracy, interest and timeliness. To these must be added a fourth, explanation. Of what use is an accurate, interesting and timely report of a news event if people cannot understand it?

Even on the basis of these four requirements, no journalist could devise an infallible formula for recognizing news although all except dullards know quickly enough when they have missed a story. It is not something that can be done by slide rule, examined under a microscope or calculated on a computer.

There are too many variables. The news of President Nixon's denial that he led the Watergate coverup was accurately reported, but the denial turned out to be untrue. Henry Kissinger was always making news when he was secretary of state by commenting to reporters on foreign developments, but he usually detracted from his own credibility by permitting quotation only as a senior American official. And any number of pretty women of high and low degree made news from time to time by publicly announcing that they had had a love affair with a President, usually deceased.

Then, too, a major news event may go unrecognized. When the uranium atom was split at Columbia University in 1939, most newspapers gave it only cursory attention; in fact, President Franklin Delano Roosevelt himself didn't understand it until Albert Einstein explained it to him.

Is News Always Bad? Critics invariably point out that crisis, disaster and catastrophe are the common stock of journalism. They argue that the news media are primarily a catalogue of horrors involving individuals and society.

There is some truth in this, but it is not the entire truth. Pulitzer Prizes have been awarded for campaigns to improve urban life, to preserve our national resources from predatory interests, to attack pollution, to uphold the administration of justice, to free those unjustly accused and wrongfully convicted. It is nonsense to imply that the media must have bad news to stay in business or that they necessarily put on circulation when there is a catastrophe. Storm coverage seldom sells an extra paper or attracts an extra viewer to the TV screen, but it must be done. And trials of prominent persons are no longer the sensation they were in less sophisticated times. The trial of Patty Hearst on a charge of armed bank robbery did not turn into a circus, as some had feared.

Public-spirited newspapers for years have conducted civic campaigns for urban renewal and fought for the passage of bond issues to rebuild decayed sections of American cities. They have led in the exposure of frauds against the public interest and have reached into high places to help bring malefactors to justice. Television documentaries, few though they are in number, have awakened public interest in such varied subjects as expositions of American foreign policy, the history of the Chinese revolution and the exploration of polar wastes. At the height of the urban rioting that so distressed the nation, the Gannett newspapers patiently sought to publish examples of progress in American race relations. And after the tragedy at Kent State University, when National Guard bullets killed four students during an antiwar protest, the Knight Newspapers diligently sought to place the responsibility where it belonged. These, surely, are not the mark of a ghoulish profession, intent only on capitalizing on shock and sensation.

True, any editor or news director who wants to feature pornography, knife-wielding delinquents, phony Hollywood romances, mindless violence and similar fare can do so with little effort. But it takes work to find news in happy children, contented families and peaceful nations. These, too, are a part of journalism although they are often not as prominent in the news as the events that scare the public.

Any sensible newspaper, news magazine, wire service or news program tries to give the public a balanced view of the community, state and nation, and the world beyond our borders. To do it requires an enormous amount of skill, money, patience and understanding. The less-exploited categories of news cannot be handled with the simplicity and dash of old-fashioned cops-and-robbers journalism. When the bad, the good, the not-so-bad and the not-so-good can be brought into balance and written about with clarity, grace, and understanding, the journalist may be satisfied that he has done a day's work.

TOWARD A BETTER UNDERSTANDING

Once police blotters, courts, and government offices provided most of the news. Today, no self-respecting editor can ignore science, health and education; the environment, consumerism and civil rights; housing, highways and urban redevelopment; aerospace, automotive and boating news, and developments in a score of other areas that were scarcely touched upon in years gone by. Surveys of public opinion are mandatory for all news media today. Business news has crowded its way off the financial pages and landed on Page 1, along with news of inflation and various attempted controls. With unemployment a national problem of great concern during bad times, labor news now is devoted to a great deal more than strikes and picket lines and anti-union fulminations. And energy has become a major national problem.

It is no longer a novelty to see thoughtful, critical work on serious music, books, the drama, ballet and art on the entertainment pages along with the usual movie reviews or to hear competent critics on television. Family pages have become more interesting, generally, instead of being repositories for old publicity handouts from the grocery chains and flour companies and accounts of publicity-inspired junkets. As for society pages, once the domain of the local elite, they now feature blacks, Orientals, Chicanos and others along with the wife of the leading banker or the daughter of the major department store owner.

Even sports pages have felt the change. Women sports writers are no longer a novelty. And sports such as golf, tennis, boating, auto racing, bowling, fishing and hunting are demanding some of the attention that was once reserved to football, basketball, baseball, horse racing and boxing. The more sophisticated sports writers are becoming more critical, too, of the dollar chasing in the sports arena and the notion that athletes are little more than gladiators.

Is Conflict Always News? Most American journalists think of conflict as an essential element in much of the news—from the town hall to the White House and from the playing fields to the divorce courts. But there is more to the news than conflict. Just before his retirement as the president of the Associated Press, Wes Gallagher suggested that there should be more "accountability reporting," which he called explanatory rather than accusatory. He went on: "Many times there are no fancy villains, just imcompetents and publicity seekers. We must clearly explain the problems of a complex civilization. Accountability reporting is an extremely difficult type of reporting and editing, requiring expertise in many areas. It requires hard, grinding work. Some reporters do not have the patience for it." [4]

Even when editors decide to explore such problems in depth and find reporters capable of doing it, writing the story becomes a major problem. It is generally easier to produce a readable story about an exposé or a murder than it is to write about the financial troubles of New York City or the consequences of an oil shortage. However, there can be no question about the public requirement for both kinds of news. And no editorial formula can be devised to simplify the problem of presentation.

[4] AP Log, 27 October–3 November 1975.

More People, More Subjects What has happened, in brief, is that good editors have come to identify their assessment of the news with the public interest more often than not. And this is a significant change for the better.

Not so long ago, an appalling amount of news space and air time was lavished on the foibles of the notorious, the wealthy, the fashionable, the beautiful, the mighty and the wicked; about sex goddesses, gangland crime and associated themes. At the lowest level of journalism, there are commercial publications and local broadcasters who still mine these muddied fields. But responsible news organizations have concluded that the public demands something better.

After all, many Americans today have a larger income than ever before, considerably more leisure time and a widening sphere of activities. They have a better life and a higher living standard than ever before despite inflation and erratic swings of joblessness. Necessarily, they are vitally interested in social security, better health, the education of their children. They are understandably concerned by anything that touches their pocketbooks, beginning with taxes. And while they do not understand science, they have found out with a shock that a far-off land can suddenly deny them oil and force them to wait in line for hours for a few gallons of gasoline for their automobiles.

Nor is that all. Americans may not, as a people, be as self-centered as a European public but they worry just as much about the consequences of social issues that touch their lives, from juvenile crime to racial integration, from school busing to national health insurance. They realize the need for a strong defense, for they spend upward of $100 billion a year for it, but they have their doubts about trusting their safety completely to atomic energy.

They still want their sports, pictures and other familiar features. And they have boundless curiosity about people like themselves, far more than the exotic types of yore. While they can take their heroes or leave them alone, this being the age of the anti-hero, the Dream Girl heroine still seems to have a more or less faithful audience. But comics, the old standby of newspaper circulation, are rapidly shrinking in size and one of the greatest, "Pogo," has dropped out. If there is any permanent and universal interest in the news that remains constant, it is the weather. And that, too, is unpredictable sometimes.

A New Kind of News Editors who probe for fresh approaches to the news usually follow this dominant theme of reader and viewer self-interest. Many of them now talk about "use-papers" as well as "newspapers." For example, the *New York Times*, *Los Angeles Times* and *Washington Post* are publishing special entertainment, leisure time and calendar-of-events sections during the week. The *Des Moines Register* and other papers have been putting out information about what people could get for free. The old travel and garden sections, once stuffed with handouts, are being dressed up. All this isn't news in the usual sense, but it's what some people want to know.

Lee Hills of the Knight-Ridder Newspapers says newspapers ought to be more relevant to their readers. And Robert Marbut of the Harte-Hanks Newspapers has suggested working harder on what readers want to know. Among the few that have solved the problem, the *Wall Street Journal* has a comparatively simple definition of what satisfies its readers. As its president, Warren Phillips, puts it: "We expect to do a superior job of covering the story that's the No. 1 preoccupation of Americans today, and that is news of our evolving economy and how it affects peoples' lives and jobs."

READING AND WRITING

News comes from many sources. Television, radio, wire services, newspapers, magazines and word-of-mouth share in the dissemination process, depending on the event, time of day, and location and occupation of the individual.

Under the circumstances, it is remarkable that so much news does get through and that a lot of it is reasonably well understood. To anybody who has lived with the news disseminating process for any length of time, the public's patience and doggedness in seeking out the news despite all difficulties represent a heartening faith in the democratic process. True, as all surveys agree, there is a healthy public skepticism toward the news media, particularly in the reporting of controversial events. But that is something the journalist has learned to live with. It is the reason for his constant effort to turn up more facts, to check his sources, to document events as completely as possible and to develop meaningful interpretation.

While it is possible for a newspaper to be entertaining, and some are, television is the prime entertainment medium. But television, too, has realized that entertainment is not enough; the network news periods are more selective and the news content on responsible local stations has increased. The all-news radio stations—dull and repetitious though most of their programs are—serve a useful function, as does radio news in general. And the alert news magazines are a constant prod to the faster media to do a better job. Because, as every journalist knows, the public demand for news is insatiable.

How People Read Since television is the major source of breaking news to the nation, it follows that the newspaper must develop into a more efficient medium of communication if it is to maintain its standing and prestige. This means that a greater account will have to be taken of the public's reading habits.

How do we read? Certainly not a word at a time. Only children who are beginning to read do that as a rule. Average adults recognize words in groups—sometimes two or three words at a time. They take about a third of a second for each group; then they pause for about a quarter of a second between one group of words and another in order to assign provisional meanings to what they have read. As they go on, their provisional understanding may change. They then will go back to look at a key word group. Once satisfied that they have the proper understanding of the sentence, they go on. This stop-go-backward-forward movement is characteristic of the average reader.

Improved Reading Eye cameras at the Armed Forces Information School have developed a pattern in repeated examinations of military personnel. A beam of light focuses on the eyes of a reader, thus permitting pictures to be taken of reading habits. The restless, jumping movements of the eyes show the pattern: one word group, a pause; another word group, a pause; then a shift back to a previous word group, a pause; then, on to the next unfamiliar word group. At 250 words a minute, an average of a little more than four words a second, this process explains why a ponderous writer has trouble in communicating with the average reader. He simply cannot always make himself understood.

However, it has been shown that the average slow reader can be trained to speed up and also increase comprehension because, fundamentally, slow reading is not necessarily an indication of a sluggish mentality.

We have not yet reached the era, however, in which those who seek the news are willing at all times to train themselves in comprehension, as do those who go in for an appreciation of fiction, drama, classical music and art. Newspapers, of course, can and do try to educate their readers as well as inform them, but mass training for improved reading and comprehension is a slow and uncertain process. The American Press Institute has held a seminar on the subject. Thoughtful editors have decided to expand their traditional "newspaper in the classroom" programs. But the desire to read will have to be stimulated first of all by inculcating a love for reading—and that cannot be done without improved writing.

Clarity in Writing It is self-evident that writers whose work is clear, simply organized and easy to understand are more likely to find an audience in today's complicated world than a ponderous genius. Writers who are opaque in their presentation, whether they deal in science, semantics, news or love letters, are only storing up trouble for themselves. It takes more effort to be clear, simple and direct. Sometimes it also takes more courage. Journalists must use the language that people understand if they intend to communicate the kinds of news that people want.

The 5Ws and H The traditionalists of journalism have clung for more than a century to the 5Ws and H—*who, when, where, what, why* and *how*. There is nothing wrong with this, except that they spawned the belief that everything had to be told in the first paragraph of a story. Nothing is more calculated to drive people away from newspapers.

Charles Seib cited the following example from his own paper, the *Washington Post:*

> A revolutionary $3 billion foreign military aid bill carrying $1.5 billion in weapons credits for Israel and unprecedented Congressional powers to monitor the $12 billion annual U. S. overseas arms trade won Senate approval yesterday, 60–30.[5]

It was, he commented, "too much too soon for the average reader." Other editors gave this example of a mouthful of lead from the AP:

> WASHINGTON—Total crude oil runs averaged 11,238,000 barrels daily during the week ending Friday, the American Petroleum Institute reported today. This compared with 10,960,000 barrels daily in the previous week and 12,223,000 barrels daily a year ago.

To which this editorial comment was appended: "What does it all mean?"[6]

It means, in a few words, less complicated writing. Such leads have given the 5Ws and H a bad name. As a result, the old 60 to 100 word lead is seldom seen any more—and a good thing, too. But mere word-counting is not going to create clarity in writing; after all, a short sentence can mix up a reader faster than a long one. The disposition of modern editors is to insist, wherever possible, on a single idea in the lead sentence with the rest of the news woven into the body of the story. Sometimes the important factor may be the *who*, or the *why*, but modern writers beware of cramming everything into the top of the story. The inverted pyramid type of news organization, which uses facts in diminishing order of importance, is scarcely the perfect way to tell a story.

As for word-counting in sentences, few editors worry about it any longer. They do believe, on the whole, that a reasonable sentence length for a newspaper is in the shorter rather than the longer range, somewhere around 15 to 25 words. And yet, on a Sunday not long ago, an industrious editor found these average sentence lengths on these front pages: the *Washington Post*, 38 words; the *New York Times*, 33

---

[5] *AP Log*, 12 April 1976.
[6] *APME News* (June 1974), p. 14.

words. By contrast, such writers as Saul Bellow, Woody Allen and Jimmy Breslin averaged 11 to 12 words a sentence in recent books.

Charles Seib commented: "News stories can't be judged on the same basis as fiction or even Breslin's free-style journalism. But an average of over 30 words per sentence is too much for comfortable reading. Particularly when the tube is waiting just across the room."

PROBLEMS OF MASS COMMUNICATION

Language is as old as man. "Nothing," says the *Columbia Encyclopedia*, "is known of its origin but its existence reaches back so far into the dawn of human life that the estimated 6,500 years that writing has been in use are trifling by comparison. Next to North Chinese, English is the most widely used language of the 1,000 or more speech communities that exist in the world."

Yet, the first of the recognized line of English dictionaries was Nathan Bailey's in 1721.

Much of the pioneering work in language study to advance the efficiency of communication was done by Professor Edward Lee Thorndike, the educational psychologist, at Teachers College, Columbia University. From Thorndike and his associates, who counted nearly 20 million words in a wide range of English literature, have come accurate determinations of the frequency of use of thousands of words. This demonstration gave a firm basis to the notion that effective written language should contain a high proportion of words that are familiar to the average reader.

The English Language Consider the size of the English language, which most authorities now estimate at more than 700,000 words and it is growing rapidly. Out of these, as has been demonstrated by Professor Edgar Dale and Mrs. Jeanne S. Chall, at Ohio State University, some 3,000 words are familiar to fourth-graders and presumably to the average reader as well. In fact, a quarter of written English is generally believed to be composed of ten words—*the, a, and, to, of, in, I, it, is,* and *that*.

There are about 850 words that form what we know as basic English—basic because they are four out of every five words we use. Thorndike's research showed that 10,000 words make up some 98 per cent of written English. Teachers often require a vocabulary of 30,000 words.

Between the 10,000–30,000-word range, therefore, lies the bulk of any writer's vocabulary. At the lower range is the average man's understanding of English words. It is obvious that above this point reader recognition tends to shrink rapidly.

Dr. Rudolph Flesch, in *The AP Writing Handbook,* gave this advice to the wire-service's writers:

> Don't use words that are not generally used in everyday conversation, if you can help it. Remember, the AP isn't in the business of increasing people's vocabulary. If you *have* to use a word that *may be* unfamiliar to an ordinary reader, explain it. Follow the example of the reporter who explained that tularemia is rabbit fever. In particular, be sure to explain geographical terms for readers who live at a distance.

What Do They Understand? It is easy to conclude that a writer can avoid trouble with an audience by using short words and shunning the polysyllabic words. It is not quite that simple, however.

The word *peace* is on the Dale-Chall list of words intelligible to fourth-graders. But what is peace? Try to define it. The author once belonged to a seminar of professors of various graduate schools at Columbia University. For four years, on and off, the seminar members tried to arrive at a definition of peace that would please all. Finally, with a great deal of reluctance, the following was agreed on: "Peace is the absence of war."

Many simple words have widely varying meanings. By *democracy,* most Americans think of a state in which government protects individual freedoms; but Russians, who also lay claim to democracy, consider it to be a system that places the state's interest above all individual rights.

The word, *table,* has many meanings. To cite only one source of conflict, it conveys a diametrically opposite meaning when used as a verb in the United States and at the United Nations. In the United States, to table a resolution means to drop it, shelve it, pigeonhole it, prevent action on it. But at the United Nations, when a diplomat introduces a resolution, he speaks of tabling it—presenting it, asking for a vote on it, putting it on the table.

Nor do words have meanings that are fixed for all time. Yesterday, "creep" was a description of movement, "square" was a geometrical form and a banana was a fruit. Today "creep" denotes an objectionable person, "square" is a name for the hopelessly conventional, "going bananas" means to be driven out of one's mind, and "top banana" is a comic.

It is not sufficient, therefore, to use words that are on somebody's list for reading comprehension. Whether they are short or long, they must be easily understood within the context of the experience of both readers and listeners.

Tired Words It has been fashionable, for as long as there has been instruction in writing, to warn against the use of tired words. The cliché, the word or expression that has been used so often that it is hackneyed, has been made as obnoxious as a snake at a picnic.

These are some of the trite expressions that have been rightly condemned:

Along these lines	A goodly number
Meets the eye	Budding genius
A long-felt want	At one fell swoop
Sadder but wiser	Method in his madness
Launched into eternity	Busy as a bee
Last but not least	Cool as a cucumber
Green with envy	Blushing bride
With bated breath	Wild and woolly
Fair maidens	Dull thud
The great beyond	White as a sheet

Dr. Bergen Evans once presented the following as an example of cliché-stuffed writing. It was a description of an audience reacting to a political orator.

> They know they are in the presence of a man who gets down to brass tacks, hits the nail on the head, and doesn't beat around the bush; a man who means business, who is fully aware that although we have entered the atomic age, we have not relinquished the faith of our fathers, and who believes that although we cannot rest upon our laurels we must not rush in where angels fear to tread. Such a speaker is a man after our own hearts. He has his feet on the ground. He knows the score.

To encourage the timid writer, who freezes at the typewriter for fear of writing something trite or awkward, Dr. Evans also added this clarification:

> If the phrase is sincerely meant, spoken deliberately with a full awareness of its exact meaning and its shopworn state, or gaily borrowed in ridicule, it is not a cliché, no matter how often it has been spoken. It is a cliché only when it comes without meaning, though often with a most pompous pretense of meaning, from an unmeaning mind.

The point is worth stressing. Nobody advocates piling one tired word on another or stringing out dreary, shopworn phrases in a news story. But where a word or phrase transmits the exact meaning that a writer wants to convey, it is no longer a hackneyed expression but a useful symbol of understanding.

Debasing the English Language At every level of our society, there are temporarily fashionable words and phrases that are misused and overworked. Many of those who know better have made a fad out of using the word "terribly" as an adverbial synonym for "very." Just how this started, no one knows, but it leads to aberrations like this: "She wasn't a terribly bright child," or, "He wasn't terribly impressed." The word "real" is even more generally used as another adverbial substitute for "very," with even more appalling grammatical results, to wit: "He had a real fine time" or "Wojciechowicz played a real fine game at guard."

These are a small part of the penalty for permissiveness in the oral and written use of the English language. There are other phrases that are just as debasing. Even well-educated Americans are falling victim to the tendency to drop the words "You know" and "I mean" into ordinary speech so that they become a monotonous refrain, which sounds something like this: "I read a terribly good book last night, yunno, a book that holds your attention and, yunno, tells it like it is, eyemean, it's a real fine book." Ow.

Teachers are not exempt from this linguistic plague. Some have their own baffling language, which includes such expressions as a "learner-centered merged curriculum," an "empirically validated learning package," and a "life-oriented curriculum." This weakness for the windy phrase and pompous word has led to such sentences as this: "Underachievers and students who have suffered environmental deprivation can be helped learning-wise by differentiated staffing and elaborated modes of visualization."

Gobbledygook The worst offenses of all are committed in the name of government. Gobbledygook perverts the meaning of much that is done in Washington, the governments of the 50 states and the thousands of city and town halls in the land. The Watergate transcripts were littered with such expressions as "at this point in time," instead of simply saying "now," plus such doubletalk as "stonewalling," for "resisting." And everybody has a "bottom line."

Such expressions in official Washington deserve the coined name of *gobbledygook.* American policy, for example, no longer favors certain countries; it "tilts toward" them. Civilians in a war zone are not killed; they are "wasted." A problem is not examined; it is "scoped." And if costs are embarrassingly high, they are disguised as "social diseconomies." If a project is well conceived, it is called "maximally valuable"; if it is abandoned, however, it is "defunded." A wild guess is dignified as a "ballpark estimate" and even the most vagrant procedure is cloaked under the grandiloquent term, *game plan.* Nor are officials powerful today; in the modern idiom, they have "clout."

These additional illustrations come from Wallace Carroll, a Southern editor and former Washington correspondent:

"The President doesn't make a choice or decision: he exercises options. He doesn't send a message to the Russians: he initiates a dialogue—hopefully (and what did we ever do before the haphazard 'hopefully' came along?) a *meaningful* dialogue. He doesn't try to provide a defense against a knockout blow; he seeks to deny the enemy a first-strike capability. He doesn't simply try something new: he introduces innovative techniques."

Such expressions defile the clarity of newswriting. Nor does it help any to drop the word *clearly* into a sentence to show that an effort is being made to avoid obscuring an issue. Clearly is one of the most overused words in the English language.

The Jargon of Journalism For the millions of Americans who are interested in the news, the writer is bound to make a special effort to guard against the jargon of journalism. It can wither the freshest news. It can make certain types of stories sound alike regardless of how or when they occur.

Thus, during the Christmas holidays, crowds in growing America invariably set new records as they flock from the city to their family hearths. Heat waves almost automatically begin July 1 and cold waves December 1 in the more temperate parts of the country. On summer week ends, along both coasts, thousands rush to the seashore.

When opposing politicians meet, it is often a showdown. In the United Nations, of course, this is either a crisis or a deadlock. When representatives of the United States and the Soviet Union meet at a conference table, they usually clash. On election day the voters invariably troop to the polls under (check one: cloudy, rainy, snowy, fair) skies. Investigations are either quizzes or probes. When someone is criticized, he is flayed. If he is merely questioned, he is grilled. If he says nothing, he is likely to be termed defiant. If the police seek a suspect in connection with a crime, they throw out a dragnet. When they arrest him, he is seized — or jailed. If they do not have a clue or are too lazy to find one, mystery surrounds the case.

A ship that has a mishap too often limps into port, which would be quite a performance if it ever happened. When there is a collision of automobiles, trains, planes or ships, it is a crash. And, of course, if more deaths occur, the death toll mounts as the probe begins. When royalty visit an American community, they never fail to reign over the city today.

Perhaps the worst offender in this department is the sports page.

Red Smith, the Pulitzer Prize winning sports columnist, once presented the following mythical interview between a sports editor and an applicant for a baseball writer's job:

> Q. What is baseball? A. The national pastime.
> Q. Good, very good. Now what is the game played with? A. The horsehide and ash.
> Q. Excellent. And what else? A. The sphere, hassocks . . .
> Q. Yes, yes. I see you have the idea. And what is the game played on?

A. It is played on the velvety sward.

    Q. What does the rookie run like? A. A deer.

    Q. What has he for an arm? A. A rifle.

    Q. Describe the man who has played baseball for five years. A. An old pro with know-how.

Few writers can be original as often as they would like. Nobody, however, is justified in trying to convey meaning by using clusters of tired words and phrases plus journalistic jargon. It is often just as easy to give the reader or listener a clear, simple story of what happened. It is also refreshing.

READABILITY

There is no easy way to learn to write, as readability experts will agree. A writer must keep everlastingly at it. Mistakes will be made. They must be corrected. Whenever there is time, poor or indifferent stories should be rewritten. Other writers should be studied to see how they obtain their effects.

The Writing Habit Writing never gets done unless it is made an essential part of the day's work. No matter how much Eugene O'Neill drank in his younger years, he was always setting words on paper regularly. The same is true of every writer who develops professional competence. There is no hope for the potential genius who waits for inspiration to strike, particularly in a newspaper office where writers use terminals.

Writing habits are important. Talent is important. Knowledge of the audience is important. Knowledge of language is important. But nothing is quite as important as sticking at it. This is the only writing formula that really works.

A Message The principal criticism of readability studies has been that there is no conceivable way of measuring the thought content of a word, sentence, article, book or newspaper. And this is the crucial problem in writing—to create understanding through the communication of thought.

The difference between *The Reader's Digest* and Thoreau, for example, is not in the length of their sentences or the number of syllables in their words, but in what they have to say and how well they say it.

Walt Whitman wrote:

> I celebrate myself, and sing myself,
> And what I assume you shall assume,
> For every atom belonging to me as good belongs to you. . . .

Highly personal, nothing to worry about in the "Reading Ease" department, but "Song of Myself" requires something more than a casual glancing through.

Or consider the "Reading Ease" of Lewis Carroll:

'Twas brillig and the slithy toves
   Did gyre and gimble in the wabe
All mimsy were the borogroves,
   And the mome raths outgrabe. . . .

All things considered, the King of Hearts in *Alice in Wonderland* was something of a readability expert, too. He said this was the way to tell a story:

"Begin at the beginning, and go on until you come to the end, then stop."

Try to improve on that.

Chapter 6
Watch
These
Things!

The urge to tell a good story is a familiar human trait. All writers like to make their work inviting for readers, listeners or viewers.

Sometimes, unhappily, a story is *too* good. The pressure for a sharp lead, a bright phrase or a good quote is too great. The writer cracks, strains for effect, falls into distortions and worse.

The following discussion lists some of the ways in which writers can safeguard their work from such perils and at the same time produce an interesting story.

ATTITUDES

Writers in all forms of journalism are well advised to maintain a cool, detached, even skeptical attitude as they approach their material. Their task calls for a high degree of skill in the use of language, organization and dexterity on both the typewriter and the terminal. The newsroom is no place for histrionics, displays of temperament, excitement or loud talk. Everything depends on the ability of the writer to concentrate and to work efficiently.

It takes a certain amount of enthusiasm, of course, even to attempt to do a job like this. If enthusiasm is not carefully controlled, even repressed, disaster can result, for enthusiasm is a heady brew that often overwhelms native caution and even ordinary good sense. During Jimmy Carter's campaign for the Democratic Presidential nomination in 1976, televised projections indicated he had lost the Wisconsin primary and at least one newspaper, the *Milwaukee Sentinel,* put out the story under a banner headline. Carter even conceded defeat but later returns brought him victory, which he celebrated by posing for pictures holding the erroneous headline. It was a parallel to President Harry S Truman's famous 1948 victory, in which he waved a copy of the *Chicago Tribune* proclaiming that he had been beaten by Thomas E. Dewey.

This can happen to anybody who writes for the news media. There is nothing devious or sinister about it. Even at the highest levels of journalism miscalculations occur because of overconfidence or misplaced enthusiasm, sometimes both. It is obvious that there are many more such chances for that kind of thing at lower levels — which is one reason why enthusiasm for anything is a quality that is likely to be suspect in the average newsroom. If uncontrolled, it has a tendency to warp the soundest judgment. A calm, questioning attitude is safer.

ATTRIBUTION

The leaking of military information and other post-Watergate disclosures at the top level of government in Washington have led to a national debate over what is known as "sourcing." In its simplest form, this is the practice of attributing news to the proper source; what has produced the debate is the important practice of protecting sources.

Those who criticize the lack of attribution in pieces about wrongdoing in the executive branch or sex scandals in the legislative branch say that it gives the reporter a chance to make up "facts" or quote the janitor. The trouble with this approach is that no reporter of consequence has been found guilty of such a crime. True, Bob Woodward and Carl Bernstein cited no authority for their celebrated report that President Nixon, in his final days in office, got down on his knees and prayed and had Secretary of State Henry Kissinger do it, too. But, in his TV interview with David Frost, Nixon confirmed it.

The justification for not using a source, something that must involve the top people in any news organization, is that there is no other way to make the information known and that the public interest requires it. Thus, when the *New York Times* published the Pentagon Papers, with much classified information on how the United States was drawn into the Vietnam War, the decision was made by the publisher, Arthur Ochs Sulzberger, and the source has never been given by the newspaper itself despite admissions from Daniel Ellsberg that he provided the material. Similarly, Katharine Graham, the publisher of the *Washington Post,* took the responsibility for her newspaper's Watergate disclosures and the validity of the mysterious "Deep Throat" as a source.

Obviously, such high level journalistic decision-making is not for the beginner. The rule is that every news story, whether large or small, should have a source. Preferably the source should be identified fully. But whether the source is identified or not, some indication of the origin of the information should be given so that the public can evaluate the relative worth of the source.

The best attribution is to name the source. The next best is the name of the organization, office, or group represented by the source as spokesman. The least satisfactory is some variation of the phrase "informed source" if the origin of the news must be held in confidence. Only columnists, commentators, and similarly privileged characters are entitled to use themselves as the authority for the correctness of their news, and withhold all mention of sources. Such a privilege does not extend to the ordinary news writer.

The insistence on sources causes inexperienced writers to clutter up their leads for newspaper and wire services. Titles or names of news sources, locations of news conferences, and other necessary but not consequential details need not always go into leads. Such subsidiary information may be tucked into succeeding paragraphs.

The caution against the use of excessively long titles, names of persons who cannot easily be identified in a community, and other details should be observed in beginning most news stories. When the President, a governor, mayor, or some other widely known personality makes news, however, it is essential to begin with name and title.

For radio and TV, the source is usually indicated at the beginning of the sentence but the anticluttering rule still holds despite that.

CHECKING COPY

Several safeguards are generally used in copy whether it is produced on terminal or typewriter. They are eliminated before the story is set, taped or put in a script for a news program.

Names When there is a new and strange name in the news, several methods are used to call attention to it in handling stories. The name may be repeated and placed in brackets. The bracketed letters (CQ) or (OK) may be inserted after the name to show that it has been checked for accuracy. These and other attention-calling devices must be eliminated before the story is used.

Figures The use of figures in the news always entails risks and much checking, but that is no excuse for not using them. For reasons of style, figures are never used to begin a sentence but are spelled out instead. This is one way of being certain that a figure is correctly used.

Another is to repeat a key figure in brackets. Still another familiar safeguard is to use the letter (M) after a figure in the millions and the letter (B) after a figure in the billions. The surest way of all to be certain that figures are correct is to go over the story with great care before it is handed in.

CLAIMING CREDIT

With reduced competition among newspapers, the somewhat repulsive practice of claiming credit for every small news development has abated in the press but it is growing in broadcast journalism.

The phrase, "It was learned today," when connected to a newspaper lead, was a modest way of claiming credit for an exclusive break in the news. As long as the breaks were big enough to justify the use of the claim, nobody really objected. Many competing newspapers, however, used the refrain so often, and on so many nonessential angles of the news, that it became discredited to a large extent within the profession. TV, however, will even credit a correspondent with asking a question at a news conference.

In addition, the sources of the news can make things difficult by controlling the breaks. Therefore, when a story is really big and really exclusive, it advertises itself and there is no actual need for the extensive claiming of credit. Now and then one still sees a lead advertising that "The *Evening Gazette* learned exclusively today" of some news development, but many editors think the practice is too flamboyant. TV has yet to learn the lesson.

The writing of news suffers also from overstatement through the use of such credit-claiming verbs as "disclosed" or "revealed." If there is a real disclosure or a real revelation, the use of such verbs is, of course, justified. But it arouses merriment even among less sophisticated readers for a reporter to write, with ponderous solemnity, that the United States Weather Bureau "revealed" tomorrow's weather would be fair and warm.

The lead that points out "revelations" and "disclosures" which are the product of routine reporting belongs with the rest of the trappings of gas-light journalism. It should remain in the files of newspaper morgues.

CURRENT TIMING

The timing of important meetings creates special problems for newspaper writers. Unlike broadcast news, the news written for a newspaper may not be read for hours later by the public.

News as It Happens   No newspaper wants to announce that a parade will begin during the afternoon when its first edition will be sold along the line of march. But no editor can authorize a story saying that the parade is under way until it happens.

Editors and writers face similar dilemmas in handling political rallies, session of Congress, legislatures, or city councils, political speeches, court hearings, and other events that may be in progress during the paper's hours of publication. For those who insist on merely past-tensing the story and running it without waiting for confirmation, a reminder should be given of the many events that have been canceled at the last minute and of instances in which leading characters in the news failed to perform as scheduled. It is no answer at all to "date the paper" by using the future tense to describe an event that already has happened by the time the edition arrives on the scene.

In order to be accurate and still not make the paper seem too old, writers generally get around the problem by omitting the actual time of a current event (except on wire services) and using such leads as follows:

> The Legislature was summoned today to act on Governor Moore's budget proposals.
> The Republican State Convention was set to open today with Marvin McAllister as the leading contender for the gubernatorial nomination.
> United Nations delegates assembled today for a vote in the Political Committee on new United States plans for limiting atomic armaments.
> A 21-year-old clerk was held for arraignment today as a suspect in the murder of his 23-year-old girlfriend.
> The sidewalks of New York blossomed with green today as 50,000 marchers lined up for their St. Patrick's Day parade along Fifth Ave.

Starting the Action   This technique is known as getting the action under way. It is used so that, even if the paper is picked up hours after the event is over, readers will not be so painfully aware that they are perusing very old news. What the writer has done is to use something that actually did happen, but preceded the action on which the story is based. Thus, the legislature was summoned before it actually met, the delegates were ready for their convention, the UN diplomats assembled preceding the opening of their meeting, the suspect was held preceding his arraignment, and the marchers lined up before the parade began.

In no case, it may be observed, does the lead say that the event in question actually began. The technique is to anticipate what is about to happen by writing a "squinting" lead. To accompany such anticipatory leads the body of the story should make it clear that the main event is just developing. In the case of the United Nations story, or any other having to do with a deliberative body, this could be written as follows:

> Before the delegates went into session, the U. S. Mission appeared hopeful that its resolution would be approved. The Americans counted on the assistance of the British to help lead the fight against Soviet opposition.

A less skilled writer can always say in a lead, in such cases, that something is "scheduled" or "expected" to happen, but only an amateur writes that something "was to" happen. The "was to" lead has few defenders in professional journalism.

The Present Tense Most broadcast news is written in the present tense. Newspapers also resort to the present and future tenses to try to bridge the gap between events at the hour of publication and the necessary time lapse in getting out the edition. These are samples of a useful if awkward device for the harried writer:

> A Congressional committee convenes today to investigate the nation's defense program.
> The United Nations meets today on the crisis in the Middle East, with the United States demanding a cease fire.
> The New York Yankees and the Boston Red Sox open the baseball season today.

When Did It Happen? For a quite different reason, newspapers generally dislike stories that specify something happened "this morning" or "this afternoon" for publication in undated leads. The terms are too imprecise. Editors prefer the simple use of "today" or "yesterday" with the exact time specified in the body of the story if it is needed.

Afternoon papers usually describe anything that happened in the early hours of the morning, from 12:01 A.M. on, as "early today" or "before dawn today." They refer to the late afternoon or early evening in leads as "late today." There are no such niceties in morning-paper practice because AM writers are not pressed to bridge the gap very often.

DATELINES

Newspapers generally do not dateline news of the community in which they are published. They also drop datelines from a given area surrounding the community, the radius being anywhere from 25 to 50 miles, depending on the city and the paper. In addition, datelines are omitted from such general stories as storms, holidays, elections, and similar material. When datelines are used, they should be written as a part of the lead, beginning exactly where news accounts normally would start on the page or terminal, with the text of the lead following them without a break. The wire services and many newspapers use only the place name and not the date in the dateline, since the paper itself carries the date. The use of a dateline in a newspaper should be a guarantee that its reporter was there, or that whatever wire service or syndicate copy it uses conveys the same guarantee of good faith. That also holds true for radio. On television, of course, there can be no faking of datelines. The public can see for itself whether the correspondent is on the scene or in the studio at home.

DISTORTION

In an effort to attain a striking effect, inexperienced writers sometimes resort to allusions of a literary nature, epigrams, parodies of popular songs or sayings, and similar bits of chicanery to brighten up a story. This kind of thing is not for amateurs. It is difficult enough for a professional to do well.

Now and then, a piece of this kind will come off, but it is seldom worth the trouble it causes a writer to dream up such a synthetic approach to the news. If the story is good enough, it does not need this type of tinsel; if not, perhaps it should not be used.

An Artificial Effect In any case, the risk of distorting a story by such devices is the best argument against wasting time and news space to seek an artificial effect. Even feature material and other types of soft news generally are not improved by freaks and tricks unless they are witty and original. These are qualities that are hard to come by in journalism.

The twisting of substance is not the only source of possible distortion. Sometimes writers begin stories with top-heavy clauses because they are tired of writing simple declarative sentences. Even editors fall prey to the lure of change for change's sake. There was once a city editor in New York who refused to let his writers begin any story with an article or a noun, common or proper. Naturally, the unhappy writers began spraying the journalistic landscape with participial phrases and clauses that inevitably tended to overdramatize the news. The epidemic did not last long, but while it raged, it damaged the self-esteem of several score reporters and writers and probably caused a certain amount of head-shaking among several hundred thousand readers.

Unnatural Prose The warning to avoid unnatural prose may be illustrated by the following type of nuisance lead:

Quit.

That's what Housing Commissioner Ringwood did today.

It is a ridiculous way of writing news or anything else. A simple statement that Commissioner Ringwood resigned is shorter and more pointed. It takes more than a trick approach in a lead to startle today's reader of news.

James Thurber is credited with having written the ultimate in ridiculous leads when he turned out the following as a young reporter in somewhat mild protest against unnatural news writing:

Dead.

That's what Joe Schmaltz was today after he fell down a manhole.

EDITORIALIZING

Despite the new-found freedom to background and interpret certain types of news, writers should not inject their own point of view in a story unless they are authorized to do so. The principle of separating the news from editorial opinion is fully supported in every responsible area of American journalism, even though there is no general agreement on where one ends and the other begins. The intent, at least, is clear. Putting it into practice becomes a matter for empirical treatment.

Personal Pronouns In an era when TV creates news personalities, there is a tendency to revive personal journalism. Although the pronouns "I" and "we" are beginning to creep back into the copy of reporters who write eyewitness accounts of big news, they still are forbidden to most writers for newspapers. For that matter, the editorial "we" is still taboo except on the least sophisticated small-town papers.

Inadvertent Comment Sometimes editorial comment is inadvertent, particularly in stories by inexperienced writers. Few journalists of experience would attempt to thrust their own point of view into a story. For one thing, they know it will be taken out. For another, it is the worst sin that can be committed in the writing of straight news next to inaccuracy.

Inadvertent editorial comment takes different forms. A New York city editor likes to tell how he picked up a piece of copy by a beginner who was writing about an "elderly" man. He called the neophyte to his desk.

> "Young man, how old is elderly? Let's get it in the story."
> "Why, the man in the story is fifty years old."
> "I am fifty years old," the city editor said sternly, "and I do not consider that I am elderly. Merely give the man's age and do not characterize him as old. Let's have no more editorialization in copy."

Loaded Words The news writer who uses superlatives is likely to be caught in the vice of editorializing by picking up a loaded word.

Most of these phrases are developed by public relations specialists who like to try to influence people subtly through the news columns. Thus, such concepts as socialized medicine should be quoted and attributed to a source if they are used to describe government-sponsored health insurance. The same is true of a campaign slogan such as the "right-to-work" proposals, which generally oppose both labor's closed and union shops. Editors may even be disturbed by a seemingly innocent phrase such as "honoring a picket line." It would be less partial to report that a picket line either was crossed or not crossed.

There are many loaded words, the use of which tends to prejudice the public in one way or another. It is the responsibility of the writer to avoid using them.

ELEGANT VARIATION

H. W. Fowler's stricture against the literary crime known as elegant variation has been used, in some instances, to justify monotonous writing.

For instance, in wire-service copy it is often observable that the expression, "He said," is used in almost every sentence in some stories. The justification is that "said" is the perfect word and, given the stricture against elegant variation, there is no reason why "said" should not be used over and over again. The practice has now spread. Few reporters will bother to strain for the exact shade of meaning to describe how a man spoke as long as he knows in advance that the desk will eliminate it.

The result has been unfortunate, on the whole. It takes a Hemingway to handle the beauty and rhythm of English in such a way that the use of such expressions as "he said" or "she said" in every sentence makes good reading. Nobody would call a banana an "elongated yellow fruit" or describe a brunette as a "maiden with raven tresses." That constitutes prima facie evidence of elegant variation. The protest here is against lazy reporting.

Stories of speeches and press conferences are often lifeless. Some of them are mere stenographic records of what happened. If reporters were encouraged to try to define exactly the manner and circumstances of an oral statement, a little of the dullness of speech reporting might be dissipated. In place of a too rigid observance of the elegant variation precaution, there is perhaps some need for a common sense variation to try to find the exact word. "He said," after all, is only one form of statement and is bound to be used more than others. A man also may have insisted, recalled, protested, admitted, conceded, declared, murmured, rasped, shouted, or even thundered. Those who write "said-

said-said" are safe from ridicule. They do not, however, contribute to the fine art of making the news interesting.

Louis D. Boccardi, as executive editor of the Associated Press, once said, "We are a basic news service but if the complex stories we all must cope with these days tell us anything, they say that the basic 'he said' approach is almost never enough any more."

GOOD TASTE

No decent journalist intentionally harms individuals in the news. Nor do responsible news organizations attempt to profit through morbid public interest in disgusting news involving sexual matters.

Not all copy intended for the columns of the *American Medical Journal* and similar publications finds its place in the news media. The media also are not, and by their very nature cannot be, prudish where the public health or the public interest is at stake. It is one thing to publicize necessary information on venereal disease, for instance, and quite another to use material on abnormal sexual practices to boost circulation. Between the guidelines of the public interest and good taste the news media try to maintain a decent and helpful course of conduct toward the community.

The rule of good taste also must be followed in making reports based on strong language in public affairs. Usually it is unnecessary to use profanity or blasphemy merely as a matter of straight reporting. The fact that someone said it is not sufficient excuse to repeat it. But when the President of the United States used strong and gamy language in the Watergate tapes, the news media had no choice but to make his conduct known to the public. In such cases, profanity becomes news, and there is a sound excuse for violating the canons of good taste.

There are, of course, laws in many states that protect juvenile offenders and relief clients from undue publicity, but the news media have their own unwritten rules of conduct as well. They vary widely. Underlying them all is the assumption that a news organization which is to win and hold the respect of the community must observe the ordinary courtesies and practices that show good taste.

For many years dialect stories have not been used in responsible newspapers, and dialect itself has been edited out of reports of conversations where there was no real need for it. The dialect story no longer is particularly funny.

Persons who figure in the news, in most parts of the country, are no longer identified by race, color, or nationality unless there is some point to it. Stories that poke fun at crippled persons or embarrass women, stories that make difficult reading or listening in the home in front of children and sexy pictures of an extreme nature are used only by the most frivolous of the news media.

However, it should not be assumed that efforts to maintain a high standard of journalism in the matter of taste constitute a kind of blue-nosed self-censorship. That is very far from being the case. A good news program or newspaper can be just as lively as a bad one.

HARD WORDS

Every writer knows that some words automatically characterize a news story.

First One of the most overused is the word *first*. If something is done for the first time, supposedly that is news. Sometimes, routine events are overly dramatized by the use of such a headline word, often with threadbare justification. The first man on the moon was news, but the first in line at the opening of a new grocery store can scarcely be in the same category.

The same is true of the headline word *last*. It is used too often and with too little reason.

Largest The largest crowd in some place's history, the lowest temperature on record in another place, the smallest person in a third, the largest in a fourth, the oldest settler, the closest football game, the prettiest girl, the cutest baby—all these superlatives are supposed to be the automatic signal for a story. And by and large, they are for some news organizations although the public is satiated with such mummery by now.

The trouble is that the theory of unique occurrence has been used so often and for so many years that the public is likely to be bored with it unless the claims made are amply justified.

In the reporting of speeches, the public has been cudgeled with appeals, demands, assurances and proposals until it seems as if no fresh approach is possible on stories of this kind. The old, frayed headline words ought to be examined with care before being worn again to dress up a very tired old story. They are just about worn out.

"MISTER"

Many newspapers refuse to "mister" anybody except the President of the United States. That goes for the wire services and broadcast media as well. In this manner they escape the problem of whom to address as Mister and whom to call just plain Jones or Smith. Some newspapers use Mr. with the names of all men in the news columns (but not sports) except for criminals.

The style for the use of Mr. always creates problems. Generally stated, most American newspapers do not use Mr. with the full name of a man except on the society page. But after introducing him in the news column by his full name (Thomas J. Hamilton), he is referred to as Mr. (Mr. Hamilton) whenever further mention is made of him.

MS.

Many American daily newspapers and both American wire services are willing to use Ms. if a woman requests it, but it has not yet achieved general usage. Nor do many papers follow the news magazines in using last names only in referring to women a second time, except in the sports pages. A United Press International survey concludes: "Many newspapers apparently have adopted the style voluntarily, others say they do it because the news services started doing it and some candidly admit they use *Ms.* when they cannot determine a woman's marital status."

The practice on larger newspapers varies widely. The *Los Angeles Times* uses *Ms.*, The *Denver Post* prefers not to but will yield if a woman insists, The *Chicago Tribune* permits its use in articles on feminism, but the *New York Times* bars it because "it has not been universally accepted." [1]

Practice also varies for the use of such terms as chairwoman and spokeswoman, but not many favor chairperson. And nobody so far has compromised on the use of terms such as manpower, manning tables or the Rights of Man. Militant feminism, too, has limits, as the struggle over the Equal Rights Amendment has demonstrated.

NEGATIVE NEWS

Editors, as a rule, dislike stories that denote lack of action in a developing situation. This is the source of the frequent admonition to news writers to be "positive, not negative." There is a lot more to this than merely refraining from using the word "not" in a lead. That is often an entirely academic matter in all the news media.

What Is Negative News? The substance of the prejudice against so-called negative news is not in the wording, but in the assertion in a lead that nothing is happening. When a bride halts outside the church and says she is not going to be married, that is the most positive kind of news—particularly for the bridegroom. When the President of the United States announces he will not run for re-election, the only thing negative about such news is his intention. But when a writer notes that strike talks "marked time today," or diplomatic reactions "were awaited today," or a political convention "continued today," he is merely saying that nothing has happened.

[1] *New York Times*, 2 February 1976.

For better or worse, the editorial feeling against negative substance in leads has been translated into certain basic procedures as well. Some of these are merely a play on words and mean very little, except that they gratify an editorial whim. Others convey a positive meaning by dropping negative terms.

Changing Negative Leads   Here is an example of a news story that has been given greater force by changing from a negative to a positive approach:

> **Negative**   Police Commissioner Hamilton said today that he would not adopt Mayor Riddle's plan of shaking up the police force.
> **Positive**   Police Commissioner Hamilton today rejected Mayor Riddle's demand for a police shakeup.

The negative approach in the following example deadens the essential conflict in the story. The positive translation makes the news vital by placing it in proper perspective. The positive lead also is shorter.

> **Negative**   There was no chance left today that the Warrington Woolen Mills would remain in this city instead of moving to the South.
> **Positive**   The Warrington Woolen Mills, a major source of local income, moved South today.

Emphasizing Negatives   There is another reason why editors worry over negative leads. In criminal cases, where the news is that someone has been found not guilty, journalists sometimes contract severe cases of nerves over using the story in precisely that form.

Many news organizations have adopted the practice of describing a verdict of "not guilty" as a verdict of "innocent." In some cases they have gone beyond this defensible practice to say that someone pleaded "innocent" instead of "not guilty," although there is, of course, no such plea as "innocent" in law.

No one who has ever been the victim of a dropped-out "not" can fail to be sympathetic to the effort to replace "not guilty" with "innocent" where it applies. When it does become necessary to use the words "not guilty," then an additional safeguard in transmission (but not in actual publication) is to adopt the old cable practice of repeating the negative as follows:

NOT RPT[2] NOT GUILTY

Other ways of emphasizing a negative in copy include spacing between letters (n o t), underlining them (not), or capitalizing the word (NOT guilty). In any case, the risk is evident because no such device can be used in the paper or on the air. As long as everybody concerned is aware of the risk, there is less chance of a dropped negative. Few

---

[2] *Rpt* is the abbreviation for the word repeat.

editors, though, are happy about taking such risks if they can legitimately avoid them.

NOW

The use of a verb in the present tense indicates immediacy. It is not necessary to use "now," "at present," and "presently," when the time is so definitely set by the verb tense. Only the amateur journalist sprinkles his copy with "nows" and "presentlies" when they are obviously redundant.

OMISSION OF NECESSARY DETAIL

One of the sources of murky writing is the constant effort to shorten sentences at the expense of clarity. The dropping of articles is one symptom. An even more annoying trend is the use of inference to identify leading actors in a news story.

This situation frequently occurs in the writing of news that involves persons who are not generally known to the public and who therefore must be introduced in some way other than by using their names in the lead. For instance:

> A messenger boy saved 30 fellow-employees from a fire that razed McMichael's Supermarket today.
> Sammy James, 17, gave the alarm. . . .

It is only inference that leads the public to identify Sammy James as the messenger boy referred to in the lead as the hero of the fire. If the words, "The messenger," were placed before Sammy's name, there would be no doubt. There is no reason for such omissions.

ONE IDEA TO A SENTENCE

The principle of one idea to a sentence is not new, but it has gained wide acceptance as a means of clarifying news writing. An example of limiting a sentence to a single idea, taken from the file of early Pulitzer prizes, follows:

> The biggest shadow in the world—235,000 miles high, 105 miles wide and 75 miles thick in its densest part—fell across San Diego today, the shadow of the moon as it crossed the face of the sun.

Such was the beginning of Magner White's classic description of the eclipse of the sun, published in the *San Diego Sun* on September 10, 1923. It is possible to do the same with any story in the news. Catchall sentences, either in the lead or the body of a news account, are seldom necessary.

It is the misuse of the 5 Ws and H that contributes to catchall sentences. Ideally, news stories should attempt to answer these questions whenever they are pertinent, but never in one sentence. Certainly there is no rule that obliges a news writer to lump everything in a lead. The most effective leads, in fact, are the ones that direct the public's interest into the body of the story.

A Better Method Careful news writers make every effort to limit themselves to one idea to a sentence. This is particularly necessary in handling complicated, swiftly developing news stories where clarity is mandatory.

The rule does not cover every sentence in a news story, of course; nor is it desirable that it should. Graceful writers who know how to use the English language can be trusted to construct both stories and sentences as they believe best. There is no doubt whatever that the process of one idea to a sentence, where it applies, increases comprehension. It is particularly applicable to broadcast journalism.

Nobody advocates going back to kindergarten style and writing, "Oh, see the cat. It is a gray cat. Its eyes are green." Readers are usually able to absorb a complicated idea, but it is too much to ask them to grapple with a complicated sentence at the same time.

PARAGRAPHING

The brevity of the news paragraph on many newspapers is often a puzzle to the inexperienced news writer. He is used to the traditional paragraph of the English theme, which may run a full page or so but never just one sentence. The petty tyranny of the schoolmarm and the assistant professor of English has paralyzed his senses, so that he understands only with difficulty that the paragraph in journalism is often a mere typographical device for maintaining attention.

Beginning Paragraphs Differently Once the newcomer to journalism grasps that thought, he is suddenly assailed with a lot of well-meant advice to begin each paragraph differently.

Where variety can be achieved without strain or unnatural language it is, desirable. But frequently, inexperienced journalists who try to vary the beginnings of their paragraphs find that they have made a literary hash out of their stories.

Sentences should flow naturally from one to another. If several begin the same way with good reason, nobody is going to worry about it as long as the story is interesting.

Longer Paragraphs Some newspaper editors dislike the old three- or four-line journalistic paragraph. These editors encourage the use of normal paragraphing and gain, to some extent, in coherence. It is difficult to say just how far the trend toward longer paragraphs in newspapers will go; it is, after all, a matter of editorial taste and not of public demand. There is no evidence of substance to show that the public really cares very much about this technical matter.

Block Paragraphs When a story is written in block paragraph style, each paragraph except the first one theoretically can be separated from the rest, shaken up in a hat, and then reassembled without making much difference to the story. It is a beautiful, but impractical, theory. Few stories can be written in such a way, even for wire services. One paragraph in a news story usually does depend in some way on the preceding paragraph as a matter of coherence, if nothing else.

Just about the only time that the block paragraph device really works is when a big story breaks and the object is to get as much type on Page 1 as possible in a hurry. Then, the impact of the news itself acts as a kind of unifying force for the story even though the paragraphs do not mesh.

Block paragraphing supposedly is a device that permits a story to be cut easily from the bottom. If the makeup editor is not watchful, it can create a minor crisis. For when block paragraphs are used, indiscriminate trims can result in this kind of a paragraph at the end of a story:

> Mrs. Peterson wiped the tears from her eyes, embraced her new daughter-in-law, and said:

End of story.

PAST TENSE

It is traditional that straight news is written in the past tense for newspapers and the headlines that top it are cast in the present tense for the most part. Experienced journalists are seldom bothered by this familiar dichotomy but newcomers to the profession usually have their troubles. They also are bothered by the present and present-perfect tenses in broadcast journalism and use them for newspaper stories.

A Difference in Tenses Why, they ask, should there be one tense for text and another for headlines in newspapers? Why can't it all be done simply, as in radio? The answer is that the two standard practices developed separately but for many years have been joined to create the effect of immediacy on newspaper pages.

When an atomic submarine stays under water for months, when jet air travel creates new records for transoceanic travel, when a President is elected, or when a Pope dies, the newspaper story is written in the past tense. The event is thus recorded. It is part of the history of the day. Thereby the newspaper derives an air of permanence and authority that cannot be captured by any other medium of quick information for a mass audience. But the headline, being written in the present tense, tops this substantial and permanent account with an urgency that supposedly communicates the immediacy of the event to the reader.

The Future, Past-Tensed The uses of the past tense are sometimes strained. In order not to "date" an afternoon paper, which must print while the news is happening, future events often are introduced through the use of the past tense. For instance:

> WASHINGTON—The White House announced today that the President would meet Congressional leaders at 5 p.m.

Past-Tensing an Advance Here is an example of the use of the past tense in an advance story of a parade or similar event:

> WASHINGTON—In warming weather, thousands of marchers, musicians and multicolored floats assembled today for the Presidential inaugural parade.
>
> The President himself was with his family, preparing for the one-mile walk along Pennsylvania Ave., past stands built to seat honored guests. Almost a million people gathered along the line of march . . .

A close reading of the account shows that the parade had not begun. Even from the lead, it is apparent that the piece purports to do nothing more than to give the arrangements for the inaugural parade which is to begin later in the day.

When Not to Past Tense The trouble with past-tense news writing begins when an effort is made to stretch it to cover categories other than hard news. In such matters it is far better to adopt the standard present-tense characteristics of radio and TV news handling. Often a mild little news event, which may seem unnecessarily pompous when written in the booming hard news style, becomes quite acceptable if it is present-tensed. Here is an example:

> Residents of one apartment in the Washington Houses project of the New York City Housing Authority have found a solution to one of their major problems. An exposed pipe in the bathroom of their apartment leaks water every time the tenants in the apartment above use the facilities. So the tenants below take an umbrella to the bathroom with them.

PSEUDO EVENTS — AND REAL ONES

Newspapers, including some of the greatest in the land, showed that they were vulnerable to terrorist demands in 1976 when they published full texts of Croatian separatist propaganda to save the lives of passengers on a hijacked air liner. Thus, a real event, the seizure of the air liner by the Croatian terrorists, was used to foist pseudo news on the public. No one can doubt the good faith of the editors involved. They could not have known, at the time the publication demand was made, that the Croatians did not take real bombs aboard the plane even though a "planted" bomb on the ground already had killed one policeman. The real situation was discovered only after the terrorists were seized and their hostages released.

The story, however, illustrates the lengths to which zealots will go to foist their views on the public. For journalists in general and editors in particular, there is no rule in such crises except the rule of good sense.

QUALIFYING A STORY

The urge to oversimplify is powerful. It assumes everything in the news to be black and white, which is seldom the case. That is why the careful news writer will always qualify whatever he writes in the interest of accuracy. Few stories can be written without qualification of some kind.

Two-faced Qualifiers Because of the complexity of much of the news today, ingenious writers have invented words and expressions that can only be described as two-faced qualifiers. For instance:

> Mayor Joseph Westfall indicated today he might run for re-election. . . .

Obviously the Mayor said nothing bearing directly on the subject; otherwise, the word "indicated" would not have been used in the lead. Hence, "indicated" may be a trick word. The reader is entitled to ask how the Mayor did his indicating. Was it by a wink, a shrug, a broad grin, a brisk rubbing of his hands when he was asked the question? Surely, it would be more accurate to report exactly what happened instead of using "indicated," a two-faced qualifier.

What Is "Possible"? Another two-faced qualifier—"possible"—is used with painful frequency in news writing:

> District Attorney Frank Garbutt showed a possible inclination to recommend acceptance of the defendant's plea of guilty to second-degree murder.

What makes the prosecutor's attitude possible? Or impossible? Either he will or will not recommend acceptance of the plea. To use his exact words would be the fairest way of reporting the facts. Interpreting their meaning by using the word *possible* can only confuse the public.

Nor is "possible" used only in this context. It has been general practice for police reporters to say that accident victims have a "possible skull fracture." There is no such medical term, of course. It should not be used until the diagnosis shows whether there is a skull fracture.

Qualifying "Qualified" Perhaps the worst of all the two-faced qualifiers is the word *qualified* itself. It is used in this context when writers do not want to do an "iffy" lead:

> UNITED NATIONS, N. Y.—Russia gave qualified acceptance today to U.S. plans for a new round of arms limitation agreements.

In other words, what Russia did was to say that the United States plan was acceptable provided certain conditions desired by the Kremlin were met. Often, such conditions in themselves are completely unacceptable to the United States. It would be just as fair to write that Russia "in effect" rejected, or gave a qualified rejection, to the United States plans. The words *in effect* are frequently used to try to show the real meaning of a set of proposals.

Reporters in the News It is seldom a good idea for reporters to let themselves be drawn into the news as participants. But when it does happen, the reporter should withdraw from coverage of the event with the assent of his editors. This is what happened when Tom Wicker of the *New York Times* was asked by rioting convicts at Attica Prison to be one of their negotiators with the prison authorities. What Wicker did was to stop being a reporter and become a mediator; thereafter, he assumed his normal function as a journalist.

RUMORS AND REPORTS

The use of rumors in news stories causes endless trouble, even when the rumors turn out to have some substance. A wise writer, supported by an experienced editor, rarely resorts to the practice of dropping a rumor high up in a story on the theory that it is "just for luck" and nobody will notice if it is not substantiated. Such practices discredit journalism as a profession and undermine its structure of responsibility to a discerning public.

What Is a Report? There is an enormous difference between the use of unverified material, such as rumors, and news that is unquestionably correct but cannot be given immediate official confirmation. Such "soft" news is called a report—a journalistic use of the word that has a special meaning when it is applied to pending events. The journalistic type of report differs from the conventional report, which usually describes a document of some kind.

To illustrate, there were many authentic reports from Peking of the turmoil that broke over the succession to Mao Tse-tung but it was a long time before they could be confirmed.

Another familiar use of the term is in the circulation of perfectly valid reports of who will win Nobel Prizes, usually put out by semi-official sources 24 hours in advance. Such reports invariably have preceded the official announcement of the prize awards.

Rumors Journalistic semantics, however, have no arbiter and are loosely and sometimes irresponsibly used. A rumor will be given a respectable disguise as a report, at times, in order to make a story look a little more solid than it actually is.

A careful reading of the documentation for the so-called report will disclose its fundamental weakness, in many cases, so that nothing is really gained by dressing up a rumor and using it.

No responsible news organization will use a story reporting that a murder jury stands 7–5 for acquittal, when it is obvious that the only basis can be corridor rumors or betting odds. Nor are wild guesses as to the outcome of a nominating convention or election to be dignified as reports. A journalistic report should be limited to material that the journalist has good reason to believe is true, but currently unverifiable. Used in that sense, the technique is extremely useful.

SPECIFIC NEWS WRITING

News writing must be specific. It is often a waste of time to string generalities together.

Give Meaning to the News Generalities too often blur the news picture. Instead of writing that a man is tall, it is better to describe him as six feet four. Instead of reporting that a speaker was nervous and upset, it would be more effective to write that he shouted and banged on the table.

If statistics are to be used, they must be given some meaning. To say that New York City's subways have only one candle-power illumination confuses the public. It is more informative to write that the average New York subway rider sometimes reads his paper by less light than Abe Lincoln had when he studied by firelight.

Certain other types of news must be related to specific audiences if they are to have meaning. Five dead in a San Francisco fire is of little interest in New York, except if it is stressed that the persons involved were from New York.

Color, Quotes, and Names Colorful details often can create news where none could previously be found. When a builder announced that he was putting up a 40-story building in mid-Manhattan, he received no special notice because there are taller structures in the area. When he said he intended to paint his skyscraper bright red, he made Page 1.

Direct quotation frequently can increase interest in the news. Most readers like conversation and novelists dote on it because it makes for a lively, colloquial style. There is no law against it. Editors want all the good quotes they can get.

It should never be forgotten that names make news. Also, that people like to know about other people. Even buildings and bridges have names, and they should be used. Some of the most fascinating places in America have wonderful names—Death Valley, California; Ten Sleep, Wyoming; Paradise Valley, Washington.

To tell the news effectively, all these devices of journalism should be used where they are applicable. It is a formidable armory of weapons for any writer—action, color, topical material, unusual facts, special appeal, personal references, brief descriptions, and meaningful quotes.

TIME ELEMENT

There is so much confusion over the use of the words *today* and *yesterday* in leads that many newspapers now substitute the day of the week for them. Commonly, the use of "today" in leads is stressed in afternoon papers and datelined stories for morning papers. The word *yesterday* is generally used for undated (nondateline) leads in morning newspapers. For radio and television, there is no problem. "Today," "tonight," and "yesterday"—and all other elements of time—are used when they apply.

Placing the Time Element For all news media, the time element ought to be included in the story where it naturally belongs. Usually, it is placed close to the verb in the opening sentence. For example:

> A new military jet plane flew today from London to Dulles Airport near Washington, D.C., in record time.

When Tomorrow Is Today The problem of the time element is not limited to its placement in the lead sentence. In a morning newspaper bearing the date of July 1, for example, all dispatches using a date except those filed after midnight will necessarily bear June 30. Therefore, a datelined story about events on July 1 is written as follows:

> CENTRAL CITY, June 30—Governor Amberwell said today that he would announce tomorrow whether he will be a candidate for re-election.

The reader will have to do a double take to realize that the "tomorrow" in the story actually means "today" and that "today" means "yesterday." It would be less confusing to drop the date from the dateline and use the day of the week as a time element. Thus, if July 1 happened to be a Wednesday, the story would read:

> CENTRAL CITY—Governor Amberwell will announce Wednesday whether he will be a candidate for re-election.

The reader thereupon is asked to remember that July 1 is Wednesday, or today. There seems to be little to choose between the respective formulas. Both are widely used.

Where Yesterday Is Taboo Just as there are two schools of thought regarding the use of the day of the week and the date of the month to show when a news event occurred, so do editors differ in the stress that they place on the use of any kind of time element.

There are some, mostly on the laissez-faire morning newspapers, who do not really care if today or yesterday is in the lead, as long as the story somewhere specifies when the event occurred.

On afternoon papers in particular, however, a breed of editor still exists who will not tolerate the use of the word *yesterday* in any lead when it can be avoided. Such editors want the reader to know his news is fresh, that it happened today, and they want the word *today* in the lead. Apparently they do not recognize the existence of radio or television, where the newscast of an hour ago is old stuff.

TITLES

There is an unfortunate tendency among journalists to turn identifying phrases about people in the news into titles. Thus, a piece about John Jones, who led several expeditions of mountain climbers to the Himalayas, becomes "Himalayan mountain climber John Jones." And an obit about James Smith, who once served as an assistant commissioner of internal revenue, begins "Former Assistant Commissioner of Internal Revenue James Smith." In the case of Jones, the error is the use of a false title. In the Smith obit, it is poor judgment to use such a long title before the man's name; instead, a qualifying phrase or clause after the name would be more acceptable. The urge to bestow titles on news figures or to make up titles for them is a journalistic weakness that should be shunned.

"WRITE LIKE YOU TALK"

Writing for wire services, newspapers, and news magazines has become less formal in this generation and is likely to be even more relaxed in the next. Yet, except for an occasional feature story, journalists try to preserve the precision of the written word. For example, Theodore M. Bernstein remarks in *Watch Your Language* that he is suspicious of the

"Write Like You Talk" school of editor and observes: "Whatever the people say is okay by me; the people speak real good."

As Bernstein explains, "Writing is and must be a more precise form of expression than extemporaneous speaking."

For radio and television, however, it is necessary to give the illusion of informality even though the news is often more tightly written. The Associated Press, in its rules for broadcast journalism, observes: "Generally speaking, it is best to employ a conversational, informal style in writing for the air." But that does not mean the electronic news writer can afford to sink into tortured, unnatural, or excitable prose any more than his colleagues of the press.

Nobody can justify a "Write Like You Talk" news report regardless of the medium for which it is written. But the skillful, informal news account that bridges the gap between the public and the news media can often be extremely effective, particularly when it gives the illusion of conversation. It is a wise journalist, however, who knows when to try it and when to revert to safer and more traditional methods.

Part Two

THE
WRITER
AS
JOURNALIST

Chapter 7
Basic
News
Structure

The electronic revolution has removed much of the constraint that marred the telling and writing of the news in the earlier years of this century. Most writers, regardless of the medium involved, try to present today's news in a natural and unaffected style.

Nearly all the artificial rules for writing have been discarded. The inverted pyramid style of news organization is no longer considered ideal. Writers with an original turn of mind are sought out and encouraged by thoughtful editors instead of being put on night rewrite to "straighten them out," which was what used to happen so often to bright, innovative people.

The new order is not an unmixed blessing, however. While the competition of television has forced the print media to abandon the rigid postures of former years, the coming of the terminal and the computer has produced a different kind of pressure in the nation's city rooms. A lot of good writing is done on terminals, it is true. But in less finicky shops, the urge is to manufacture copy by the yard—to "get it out" at all costs. What can happen under such circumstances is that the quality of the newspaper may plunge despite the introduction of the most modern production methods. It is a trend that wise editors are resisting, and with considerable success. But writers are well advised to take account of both the advantages and disadvantages of the electronic era.

There is no guarantee that there will be better writing just because newsrooms are automated. It still takes talented men and women to shape the news in such a way that the public will want to read—and to try to understand it. In expert hands, the news story should be as flexible and graceful as any other art form based on fact, thought, feeling and language. News is life. The patterns of news should reflect it.

ORGANIZING THE NEWS

Except for bulletin-type material, much of the day's news falls into a two-stage organizational pattern when it is told at normal length. The opening sentence, paragraph or section of several paragraphs is called the lead (misspelled lede by some who should know better). The remainder, to which the lead is joined, is called the body of the story and consists of documentation for the lead and whatever elaboration is necessary.

Some news, particularly when it is written for the broadcast media or the news magazines, lends itself to chronological treatment. Now and then the forms of fiction (but not the practice of it) are recommended as a novelty, particularly the short story. Even the old-time essay, the *feuilleton* so beloved of European journalists, can be used with distinction in news analyses and other interpretive articles. And for longer pieces and series, some of the forms of the nonfiction book may be applied with generally gratifying results.

The point is that there is nothing automatic about the telling of the news. A complicated development in economics, such as the effect of the raising of the prime interest rate and its impact on the economy, necessarily must be told far differently from a human interest story about a blind woman student who has just received her M.D. Nor can the public's interest in a potentially important new source of energy be dealt with in the same way as a jam session for the pet charity of the First Lady, performed at the White House.

A Varied Approach With both journalistic style and format in the process of change, experimentation is a distinctive element of the writer's work for all the media. There is also great pressure on the broadcast media to continue to increase the amount of prime time allotted to news and documentaries. Faced with such a challenge, which might at last permit broadcast journalism to break out of its dominant news bulletin format, both newspapers and news magazines will have to develop more news of their own as well as more effective ways of writing and presenting the news in general.

Certainly, it is no longer necessary to begin every story with what is known as the "Bang-Bang-You're-Dead" type of lead. The news magazines and the writers for broadcast journalism have proved that with ease. Often, the devices of the news feature are imposed on the telling of the news—the brief anecdote, the chronological approach, the recollection of some previous or similar event, the impact of a forceful personality, an interesting remark, a snatch of dialogue and similar material.

Many newspapers have experimented with some of the broadcast techniques of presenting the news. For that reason, the personal, present-tense style of broadcasters and commentators has had an impact on both newspaper and news magazine pieces to which it can be adapted. Some newspapers have even attempted to become daily news magazines, but with somewhat appalling results. News is—and must remain—the dominant feature of newspapers.

In the discussion of basic news structure that follows, the emphasis is on writing for newspapers. Writing for television is discussed in Chapter 16, and for wire services in Chapter 15.

BUILDING BLOCKS OF NEWS

Regardless of how a .news story begins, the function of the lead is to focus the attention of the reader. This is true whether the article is long or short, so-called straight news or feature, background or in depth reporting, analysis or interpretation. Necessarily, the lead and its phrasing are bound to determine in large part the organization of the story. Here are examples of various types of opening statements:

Straight News

> IDAHO FALLS, Idaho—The Teton Dam, which had been the target of law suits by ecologists, burst today, flooding the upper Snake River Valley and forcing the evacuation of some 30,000 persons.
>
> —*United Press International*

A Feature

> It was raining when Sylvester Young Sr. got there yesterday morning, the kind of good, soaking rain the city needed a month ago.
>
> Young, a member of the Kansas City Police Department for nearly 23 years, paused for a minute at the intersection of 44th and Highland. Just down the street police had surrounded a house that contained, they thought, some bank robbers and some hostages.

A patrolman came up to Young and asked him gently, "That your boy in there?"

"Yeah," Young said. "I've talked to him."

So there it was. Dozens of police cars, barricaded streets, guns galore. And one of the men wanted on suspicion of robbing the Central Bank of Kansas City yesterday morning was Sylvester Young Jr., the son of the long-time Kansas City police detective . . .

—Kansas City Times

An Investigative Story

Several times each decade, natural disasters—hurricanes, floods, tornadoes—devastate entire areas of the United States. And the nation watches and reads in dismay.

Then, the President declares a national emergency and rushes in massive aid and the nation turns its attention elsewhere, assured that all will be set right.

The *Philadelphia Inquirer* went back to Wilkes-Barre, Pa., two years after the worst natural disaster, in terms of property damage, in the nation's history. There it found that very little had been set right . . .

—Philadelphia Inquirer

(*One result of the Inquirer series was that full-scale action came to Wilkes-Barre which two years later was back to normal.*)

An In-Depth Reporting Story

In hearing room No. 1 there is a rape trial. In hearing room No. 6 an arson and burglary trial. In room No. 8 a murder trial. In room No. 3 a sexual-assault trial.

There are at least 40 other cases waiting outside in the hall to be tried.

This is a typical day at the Eastlake Juvenile Court Building, a structure tucked neatly in the shadow of the County-USC Medical Center. Along with the memories of crimes and the sadness of broken lives pervading these rooms, there is pressure—the pressure of a public demanding action, the pressure of too little time, too many cases and too few people to handle them . . .

—Los Angeles Times

The Follow-Up Story

WASHINGTON—The TV public service ad shows cartoon character Fat Albert, with the voice of comedian Bill Cosby, arriving with friends to play baseball in a junk-strewn sandlot. After some chatter, Fat Albert proclaims: "Let's clean it up and play ball with Johnny Horizon."

On the outfield fence in the background is a poster with the face of Johnny Horizon, an outdoor type with a square jaw and a cowboy hat, looking on in approval. No one, it might seem, would object to this do-gooder. Yet Johnny Horizon, the Interior Department's anti-litter and environmental protection symbol, has become a figure of controversy. Johnny, who has helped sponsor thousands of beautification and conservation projects since 1968, is under attack from the very agency that created him . . .

—*Wall Street Journal*

National Affairs Reporting

WASHINGTON—For 1968, with U.S. involvement in Vietnam at full blast, President Johnson asked for a $76.5 billion defense budget—to "combat aggression."

For 1973, with the Vietnam War winding down, President Nixon asked for a $78.3 billion defense budget—because "we can only negotiate and maintain peace if our military power continues to be second to none."

For 1975, with U.S. forces free from war at last, the President asked for a record $85.8 billion defense budget—to "build an enduring structure of peace in the world."

Each year, the official rationale is different but the pattern remains the same. Defense costs are spiraling, in times of war and peace. By 1980, according to a study by experts at the Brookings Institution, the U.S. defense request will soar to $112.8 billion—and if five per cent inflation is figured in, the total jumps to $144 billion . . .

—*Newsday*

International Affairs Reporting

It is the same sun that rises each day over Singimarie Pachuniper, a tiny village in eastern India, and Kao, a tiny village in central Niger in the middle of Africa.

Dawn comes first to a refugee camp for farmers in Singimarie where 6-year-old Saku Barman rises unsteadily to his feet and totters out of an open lean-to into a listless day of numbing hunger.

Six hours later, dawn comes to the Sahara nomad camp in Kao where a spindly 4-year-old girl named Hameda weakly gets to her feet to face the same sort of day.

Once in the sun, Saku and Hameda, though 5,500 miles apart, cast the same shadow. They are the shadows of ghastly apparitions, of walking child skeletons, doomed by the same natural and man-made forces to a short, unhappy existence on Earth . . .

—William Mullen in the *Chicago Tribune*

A MATTER OF STYLE AND TASTE

These leads, so varied and so colorful in their approach to the news, illustrate the differences in style and taste that are characteristic of much of the writing for modern American news organizations. To be sure, there are still many writers and editors who prefer the direct approach—the single sentence that tells exactly what happened. But when time and space permit, and when the story justifies more of an effort in the telling, there is no doubt that the indirect approach is more effective.

In all save the straight news wire service lead, the writers of leads for the major newspapers quoted above have tried to add a dimension to the news. Once, old-fashioned editors would have termed this "backing into the news." Some, in fact, would have turned back much of the copy on the ground that reporters have put themselves, their views and their emotions into their stories. It is a measure of progress for American journalism as a whole that writers have won more freedom in the way they present the news.

The lead, of course, can give only the flavor of the story when the indirect approach is used. What the writer is saying to the reader is, "Come, let me tell you a story. It begins on a rain-swept city street corner, a juvenile court, an African hut baking in the sun . . . It is about something that will interest you."

The technique is much the same as that of the TV camera tilting up the wall of a skyscraper at the beginning of a story about an energy crisis or swinging over a restless sea of angry faces at the outset of a report on a strike. The writer and the camera both are trying to arouse the anticipation of the public rather than slam the news in their faces with scant ceremony and no regard whatever for public sensitivity.

Documenting Leads Whether the lead is one sentence, several sentences, one paragraph or several paragraphs, it can scarcely stand up unless the body of the story provides sufficient documentation to make the whole a credible performance. Any statement in the lead must be supported by factual material or the story simply cannot be used. And this is true whether the lead represents a "teaser" approach, a side issue that leads into the body of the story, or an attempt to present a summary of conclusions.

To illustrate the principle of documentation with a few simple examples:

If the lead of a story about an automobile accident says that two persons were killed, the body of the piece must contain their names, ages and addresses or, at the very least, an explanation of why these cannot be provided in detail. In the case of a speech, interview or news conference, a lead based on what was said must be supported by pertinent quotations to show the source of the paraphrase. When someone dies of other than natural causes, any suspicion of suicide or murder must be backed up either with an authoritative statement from a responsible public official or a recital of the factual evidence that justifies the conclusion.

The Boundary of Interest Writers with marginal experience in journalism often complain that it is impossible to be interesting about all subjects. Very true, for the public can scarcely be expected to rush to read about something in which the writer is profoundly uninterested. It takes a specialist, very often, to carry the public through a story about such arcane subjects as price fixing, the gross national product or the mathematics behind a poll of public attitudes.

The old-time editor had a mystical belief in the ignorant reporter. The theory was that if a reporter without special background covered a scientific meeting on the risks of atomic power, he could somehow make the problem clearer to an uninformed audience. This was a case of ignorance feeding on ignorance in the hope that knowledge would be the end result. It was never very rewarding, but the belief dies hard.

E. B. White once said, "Anything can be made interesting." Perhaps. It depends on who is doing the writing and the degree of interest the writer brings to the job at hand.

The Break from Routine If an inspired writer can be counted on to arouse an audience, a bored writer almost certainly will destroy interest in a promising subject. Let us assume, for example, that an electrical engineer who died at the age of 95 leaves his alma mater $20,000,000 in his will. The routine newspaper writer, far from inquiring into the facts with telephone call to the engineer's family, will grind out a familiar Form A story beginning:

> Robert P. Wilkinson, who died two months ago at the age of 95, left $20,000,000 to Eastern University, according to his will which was filed for probate today.

However, a writer with just a spark of interest in Mr. Wilkinson's motivation would make the telephone call to the engineer's family and come up with a quite different story, beginning:

> When Robert P. Wilkinson was approaching his senior year at Eastern University 75 years ago, a kindly dean at the School of Engineering obtained a $500 scholarship for him because he couldn't pay for his tuition.
> Today, when Mr. Wilkinson's will was filed for probate two months after his death at the age of 95, Eastern University received a gift of $20,000,000 from a grateful alumnus.

Any editor has a right to assume that a writer will carry out minimal basic research on most items that are destined for publication. Unhappily, such an assumption is not always well based. The journalist is always pressed for time; all too often, that becomes the excuse for giving routine treatment to something that looks like a routine item.

Let us suppose, for example, that a relative of Mrs. Marjorie Robinson, 73, of 226 Volunteer Road, telephones the city desk to report that she will be married tomorrow to Cyrus Hadley, 76, a retired lawyer, who lives in New York City. It will be her third marriage, Mr. Hadley's second, and the details of time, place and officiating clergyman are all given. The writer grinds it out as a routine item:

> Mrs. Marjorie Robinson, 73, will be married tomorrow to Cyrus Hadley, 76, a retired New York City lawyer, at the First Congregational Church of Central City . . .

But in the newspaper's library, there is a clipping file on Mrs. Robinson that shows she was born in New York City, was married at 18 and obtained a divorce from her first husband two years later, then was married for a second time to Herbert Finchley Robinson, a local architect, who died three years ago. Who was the first husband? A telephone call to Mrs. Robinson causes her to say that he was Cyrus Hadley, then an impecunious law student. Now the story is anything but routine. It could begin:

> Fifty-three years after their divorce, Marjorie Robinson, 73, and Cyrus Hadley, 76, will be remarried tomorrow. Mrs. Robinson doesn't remember why she gave up on Mr. Hadley the first time.
> "It was so long ago," she said, "and it doesn't matter very much now . . ."

Do It Differently   The principle is clear enough. If it is fundamental for reporters never to take anything for granted in journalism, it is equally basic for writers never to succumb to deadly routine if they can avoid it. The rule is: "Do it differently if you can." And it works for any kind of story, from the simple human interest feature to the removal of the President of the United States.

Saul Pett, in a copyrighted article for the Associated Press, broke all the familiar rules in beginning his remarkable "An American Ordeal: The Deception and Descent of Richard M. Nixon." This was the way Pett handled his lead:

> WASHINGTON—Thomas Jefferson, the third President of the United States, made this observation on Aug. 19, 1785:
> "He who permits himself to tell a lie once finds it much easier to do it a second and third time, till at length it becomes habitual; he tells lies without attending to it, and truths without the world's believing him. This falsehood of the tongue leads to that of the heart, and in time depraves all its good dispositions."
> One hundred and eighty-seven years later, the 37th President of the United States met with his most trusted assistant at four minutes after ten in the morning of June 23, 1972. Routinely, Richard M. Nixon and H. R. Haldeman discussed a variety of subjects, none of them of great moment.
> "Now," Haldeman said, with the tone of a man with a list, "on the investigation, you know the Democratic break-in thing, we're back in the problem area because the FBI is out of control . . ."
> The President told Haldeman to tell the FBI, "Don't go any further into

this case, period!" The reasons, he made clear, were political but the pretext would be national security. Then the two men casually moved on to other subjects while in a basement across the street from the White House a reel of tape quietly turned.

Thus was begun a process by which a "third-rate burglary" five days before was turned into a third-rate conspiracy and, 26 months later, a world leader was toppled . . .

THE INVERTED PYRAMID

Editors on the whole aren't quite as willing to discard the inverted pyramid form of news organization as are brand new Ph.D.'s in mass communications. When a major story is breaking near a deadline the format is still both convenient and useful. And for a running story (of a trial, political convention, hurricane or other natural disaster), there is still no better form of assembling the news quickly so it can be topped frequently and easily with new leads. For short items in the news, the familiar mold is often the most compact as well.

The truth is that those who most dislike the inverted pyramid often are also the ones who either don't know how to use it or won't bother to take the trouble to learn. Since it is the pattern in which much breaking news is presented, it is obvious that a certain amount of experience and writing skill is needed to handle the organization of the work. True, the inverted pyramid can be an invitation to dullness and routine but the better writers in daily journalism know how to avoid such traps.

In addition, there is a basic misconception about the inverted pyramid. Inexperienced writers assume that it always separates facts in the diminishing order of importance, with the main fact on top. Not so. Often there are several developments that must be woven together for a fairly detailed lead, with each being documented in turn in the body of the story. Putting such a story together with the proper transitional sentences or paragraphs and making the whole thing read coherently is quite a performance even for an experienced journalist.

Structure and Style Here is the beginning of Thomas O'Toole's story for the *Washington Post* of a landing on the moon, which illustrates the complexity of the inverted pyramid structure and the uses of an agreeable journalistic style:

> HOUSTON—Apollo 16 astronauts John W. Young and Charles M. Duke landed among the moon's volcanic highlands last night, but a six-hour delay in landing forced cancellation of one of their three planned traverses of the lunar surface.
>
> Young and Duke landed on the moon's Cayley Plains at 9:23 P.M. after being delayed for six agonizing hours in lunar orbit by a faulty electrical

circuit in the command craft Casper, piloted by Apollo 16 astronaut Thomas K. (Ken) Mattingly.

"Wow, down," exulted Duke when the landing craft Orion touched down at the landing site called Descartes. "Old Orion is finally here, Houston. Fantastic."

Young and Duke landed northwest of the spot they were aiming for, but no more than 500 feet from their target.

"Perry Precision has landed on the Plains of Descartes," Duke said. "All we have to do is jump out the hatch and we've got plenty of rocks."

Duke and Young described the landing site as rolling country surrounded by mountains and covered with big boulders.

"It's really nice to have the shadows out there," Duke said. "We've got some good altitude out there."

The landing came almost six hours behind schedule, which meant that Young and Duke would be delayed more than 15 hours in taking their first lunar traverse. It also meant that the last of their three seven-hour traverses would be lost or cut drastically short because of the loss of time . . .

Is the inverted pyramid pattern the only one that could be used to tell this story under pressure of an edition deadline, with the facts changing all the while? Obviously, while the story is developing, it is the most convenient. And once two or three columns of such an account appear in print, not many editors will order a complete write-through to provide a fancier job for the final edition. This, in brief, is why the inverted pyramid has survived.

Criticism of the Inverted Pyramid The most forceful criticism of the inverted pyramid was made by Herbert Bayard Swope while he was executive editor of the *New York World*. He pointed out that it forces a newspaper to tell a story three times — in the headline, the lead and the body of the story. Swope used to proclaim it a "space waster," which it is.

On more esthetic grounds, journalists with an interest in creative writing argue that the inverted pyramid is a grotesque art form because it places the climax of a story at the beginning instead of near the end. Necessarily, it destroys any feeling of suspense, or so its critics say.

Perhaps the most telling criticism is that the inverted pyramid is an outdated form, an illogical holdover from the days when newspapers were first with the news and had no rivals except the town crier. Why, critics ask, must a newspaper of the first rank present its news on Page 1 in the same form as broadcast hours earlier, even if it is given at greater length?

The *New York Times*'s response is that it is a paper of record. The *Wall Street Journal*, taking a diametrically opposite course, prints the day's news in capsule form and expands on its own exclusive material. Most of the nation's dailies fall somewhere between these two leaders for lack of any clear policy. However, writers of discernment and talent break out of the pattern whenever they can.

A WELL-ORGANIZED STORY

Despite the usefulness of the inverted pyramid in deadline situations, there is no sense whatever in making a stencil out of it. The form has become so familiar to the reading public that it is, in a broad sense, predictable. Therefore, when the principal facts of a story are known and a writer has the time to try something different, the result can turn out to be a welcome deviation from routine. Here, for example, is the beginning of a straight news story that cries out for a touch of originality and a feeling of human sympathy:

> A clergyman who was falsely accused of kidnaping two children at gun point died today of a heart attack at a police station while he was protesting his innocence.

When Tom Fitzpatrick of the *Chicago Sun-Times* covered the same story, this is the way he wrote it:

Setting the scene

The well-worn Bible was on the living room table, still open to the passage that the Rev. James Jackson had been reading when the knock came at the door.

His glasses were still on the table, too, right where Mr. Jackson had placed them as he got up to greet the policemen and the 7-year-old boys who would cause his death.

Developing the main character

Mr. Jackson was 62 years old and the pastor of St. Luke's Community Church, which holds its services in the Washington Park YMCA at 50th and Indiana.

He had done so much work with the young people in his neighborhood that it wasn't surprising that the boys would know that Mr. Jackson lived on the third floor of the old building at 4550 S. Cottage Grove and that he drove a black car.

"He was such a wonderful man, my grandfather was," the young girl was saying now.

Mrs. Olivia Williams, 27, was sitting in the same chair her grandfather always used when reading. It is near the window and it offered him the opportunity to look at the passing cars on Cottage Grove when his eyes grew tired from reading.

"I keep thinking that this is some awful dream," Mrs. Williams said now. "I keep thinking maybe I'll wake up and it won't be true."

But it is true that Mr. Jackson is dead, and on Wednesday afternoon his widow got on a bus and went downtown to buy some new clothes to wear to his funeral, which will be held Saturday.

The tragedy, normally the lead

Mr. Jackson died Monday after suffering a heart attack while being questioned in the brand-new police building at 51st and Wentworth.

He had been taken into custody after the two young-sters told police that he had kidnaped them at gun point and forced them into his home.

"But I haven't been out of the house all day," Mr. Jackson pleaded when the boys made the charge. "Ask my wife and sister. They've been with me all the time."

The two women pleaded with the police but it was to no avail.

Documentation of the lead

The mothers of the two boys were with the police at the time and they kept shouting terrible things at Mr. Jackson and demanding that the police "get to the bottom of this thing."

"But I've never even seen these two boys before," Mr. Jackson said over and over again. "I don't even know them. I've never held a gun in my hand in my whole life and I certainly don't even have one."

Details of the arrest

"Sorry," said one of the police officers. "You'll have to come down to the station. Get your hat and coat."

Mr. Jackson was distraught. There was nothing he could do but follow orders. He was under arrest.

At the station, the mothers signed complaints charging Mr. Jackson with illegal restraint and he was taken into a small room for more questioning.

"I don't even like to think about it," Sgt. Sam Babich said Wednesday. "It was just an awful thing. Those kids fingered him and there was nothing else we could do.

"They picked out his car and they knew where he lived and they told a pretty convincing story."

It was while Mr. Jackson was attempting to refute this "pretty convincing story" that he suffered the heart attack. The police rushed him to Provident Hospital but there was nothing anyone could do.

The climax

Oh, yes, there was one thing. When the boy who had been making most of the charges heard that Mr. Jackson was dead, he did what he could.

"I think we'd better tell you we weren't really telling the truth," the youngster said. "Rev. Jackson never did anything to us. We just made up the story because we ditched school and we had to have a good excuse."

Mr. Jackson's wife was in the police station when the 7-year-olds and their parents emerged from an inter-rogation room and headed for the door. There were tears in her eyes but Mrs. Jackson spoke with great control.

Conclusion

"Son," she said to the boy who had done most of the talking, "whatever you do, as long as God gives you life, don't ever tell another lie. You told a lie today and it cost a good man his life."

The effectiveness of the piece depends almost entirely on the manner in which it is organized, once the anecdotal approach catches the reader's attention. But even tight and logical organization would not suffice, were it not for the neat manner in which each part of the story is joined to the next without artifice or strain. The writer's reportorial eye for color, detail, and nuances of speech thus turned what might have been a routine story into an interesting and dramatic narrative.

This is the kind of thing experienced writers put together without thinking too much about detailed organization or fussing about artistry. Having had to learn how through years of practice, they do what comes naturally.

Chapter 8
Biography for the Millions

Coming out of the national trauma of the Vietnam War and Watergate, the public mood in the United States swung sharply away from frustration, rage and protest to some of the diversions of the earlier years of this century. It came as no surprise to journalists that this calmer but still far from secure and satisfied society showed a renewed interest in news of people. They had always known that names make news.

Like the jazz-age journalism of the 1920s, this swing toward the personal element in the news started at the lowest level. Taking advantage of the relaxed atmosphere of the 1970s, when so many social taboos were dropping, the weekly "checkout counter" tabloids mercilessly exploited the lives of the rich, the famous and the notorious. While they did not go quite as far as the "skin" magazines, which merchandised sex and nudity, they left very little to the imagination.

Here and there, gossip columnists cropped up in newspapers and began to attract both attention and a considerable following. With the death of Walter Winchell, the practice had died out for a time in print journalism although it survived on late-at-night radio and some of the TV talk shows. But with the numerous disclosures of the love affairs of some of the late occupants of the White House and a round of Congressional sex scandals, the public appetite for gossip revived with a vengeance.

THE "PEOPLE" SYNDROME

While news of people has always been a staple of journalism, it is handled in varying ways by different news organizations. In the latter part of the twentieth century, the more responsible newspapers are carrying "people" columns in which local and wire service items about personalities are strung together. There are also many more features about unusual individuals, men and women in the news, personality pieces pegged to anniversaries or new activities of familiar people and, of course, the much-overworked personal interview.

This kind of material is present to an even greater extent in the news magazines, reflecting the success of *People* magazine and its minor league imitators. The wire services and feature syndicates, as might be expected, also provide such copy in volume. And television, by its very nature, creates the greatest interest of all in the "people" syndrome.

Necessarily, much of this is pretty thin stuff and scarcely passes muster as news. A considerable part of it is generated by professional press agents and less skilled publicity seekers. And some of it, particularly when it deals with a famous personality in which there is great public interest, comes under the heading of a "media event," or anti-news.

What Can Be Done about It Often, when it is deluged with unnecessary details of the doings of glittering personalities, a bemused public may well wonder who is exploiting whom. For after every publicity binge, questions do arise and there are not always ready and satisfactory answers. Did the media needlessly exploit a powerful Congressman, an elderly alcoholic who took to pursuing a fan dancer? Was it necessary to brand a former First Lady as a heavy drinker? Was it a part of the "watchdog" function of the press to delve into the sexual habits of members of Congress, as depicted by their self-admitted former mistresses?

These are hard questions that most professional journalists will answer in the affirmative, although a good many will have their own private doubts. But the public as a whole seldom goes along completely with the journalists in such matters. It is one thing to glorify such stars of the amusement world as Robert Redford and Elizabeth Taylor, or such public favorites as Jacqueline Kennedy Onassis. This is just fan magazine fare. But when it comes to scandal involving public figures with a political following, there is always going to be a kickback whether the journalist is right or not. And editors and broadcasters must be prepared for it.

True, it is easy to avoid trouble by not using controversial material. That, however, insures the quiet of the graveyard, not a notably flourishing atmosphere for the news media. The fact is that "people news" is often problem news and it must be handled, and handled responsibly. There is no way around it.

The filing of the will of J. Paul Getty, the American oil billionaire, is just one illustration of the complexities of "people news." This was the way the *Wall Street Journal* handled the beginning of the story:

> LOS ANGELES—Billionaire J. Paul Getty left the bulk of his estate to the art museum he endowed in Malibu, Calif., according to a will filed for probate in Superior Court here.
>
> The oil magnate, who died Sunday at his home in England, also left bequests of annuities and common shares of Getty Oil Co., of which he was president, to one of his ex-wives and 11 other women . . .

This was the lead of a more extensive story, which went all over the world on the wires of the Associated Press:

> LONDON—(AP) J. Paul Getty, who died June 6 at the age of 83, named 12 women in his will. A number of them can recall romances or near romances with the American billionaire.
>
> Eight of the women live in Europe, four in California. He had known some for half a century, others for little more than a decade.
>
> Mr. Getty was married and divorced five times, but only one of his former wives, Louise Lynch Getty of Santa Monica, Calif., is listed in the will. She was awarded $55,000 a year for life.
>
> Penelope Ann Kitson, 53, an Englishwoman who refused to marry Mr. Getty, received the largest lump sum, 5,000 Getty oil shares valued at $826,500, plus $1,167 a month for life . . .

WHEN PEOPLE MAKE NEWS

There is a quieter and equally essential aspect to news of people. The history of many cities and towns can be traced in the reporting of its births and engagements, its birthdays and anniversaries, its marriages, its celebrations, its illnesses, its deaths and memorials. Whether such news is of ordinary people or the leaders of a community, it is bound to be welcomed by their families, friends and even casual acquaintances. It is, moreover, one of the principal assets of a local daily or weekly newspaper because the broadcast media cannot use it in any volume.

The British historian, Sir Denis Brogan, used to read scores of local papers on every one of his many tours of the United States, particularly for items about people. "I found out a lot more about America and the American spirit through its local press than I ever did in Washington," he often said.

The Brief Biography Because so many beginners are given the chore of handling such brief and basic news, it is often regarded as the lowest common denominator of journalism. It need not be if the reporter is alert and has the energy to make inquiries. The trouble is that aspiring newcomers, so eager to prove themselves and make something out of what is apparently nothing, can stumble over a mere name while reaching out for the journalistic horizon.

Throughout the three centuries in which newspapers have existed, editors have preached the importance of getting such personal details as names, ages and addresses and getting them right. There is nothing novel about such advice, but it deserves to be repeated because it is so often disregarded. Newcomers to journalism too often smile with a superior air when they receive such a mini-lecture and a few minutes later some of them are bound to misspell a name or get an address wrong. Nor are they alone.

The story is still told in New York city rooms of the political writer, who had been out of the country for three years and came back to cover a mayoral campaign. Without bothering to look up the clips, he referred to a former mayor as "the late John Patrick O'Brien." No sooner had the edition hit the street than he received a telephone call in which a man with a solemn, deep voice identified himself as follows: "Good afternoon, my friend. This is the late John Patrick O'Brien."

The Impersonal "Personal" It is possible to do a brilliant two paragraph "personal," but it doesn't happen very often. Generally, it is a good rule to let the item go as a brief, accurate statement of fact. It is very difficult to use words that sing about a meeting of the Rotary Club or the 95th birthday of Grandmother Mary Ann Jones. An accurate piece, done in clear but unadorned language, generally shows better judgment.

Procedure Newspaper practice in handling names is based on completeness, including middle initial if any and title or designation. Honorifics for men are usually dropped. Naturally, if there is any doubt, you use the name in the same way as its owner does. The fighter may have been born Cassius Clay, but his name is Muhammad Ali. And there is only one Catfish Hunter.

The broadcast media, thriving on the informality of oral journalism, have fewer rules than printed journalism. If a title (such as senator or mayor) precedes a name, then the first name is usually dropped.

Middle initials are generally omitted as well. The only time middle names are used is where confusion would result by dropping them, as in changing a name like John Paul Jones. Titles invariably precede names to make it easier for listeners and viewers. As for nicknames, they go into the script in parentheses to give the announcer the option of using or dropping them. Mostly, they are used.

Gossip The heads of responsible news organizations are always wary of using gossip. This is something more than a matter of good taste and avoidance of the banal. For a lot of libel suits start with an unverified item of gossip that can, and sometimes does, creep into an otherwise impeccable news report. This is why most gossip columns are referred to staff-employed libel lawyers before they are used.

For reporters and writers, therefore, gossip is something to be approached as circumspectly as a rumor. Both take a lot of verification before they can be used. It is much better procedure to write personals in such a way that they reflect dignity, fairness and good taste. The average person, reading about his marriage or anniversary in his newspaper, or hearing about it in a news broadcast, should not have to blush, cringe or feel apologetic in front of friends.

Fact and Fancy This clear separation of gossip and fact also applies to the language that is used in the writing of personal items. No reporter should try to do a simple personal item in the cliché-ridden style of an unsophisticated country weekly. People do not have blessed events, unions in holy wedlock, or tragic departures. They are born. They are married. They die. The simple verbs and the basic expressions should be used, not disguised under threadbare phrases that were not original in the journalism of a century ago. Familiarities in the news columns are not permitted, and feeble good humor is best eliminated, something the local broadcast media might take to heart.

SOCIAL ITEMS — AND NEWS

There was a time when news of society was based on an avid public interest in the activities of socially prominent persons in New York, Newport, Bar Harbor, Southampton and a few other Eastern centers. Pages devoted to society and women's news either were very exclusive, or crammed with gossip about the so-called 400 of society.

Those days have gone. Even in metropolitan centers, editors are given wide latitude in the processing of the social item. Of the thousands of personal items submitted for publication, newspapers are accustomed to use as many as they can after suitable checking — one of the indices that determines whether or not an item is to be used.

Although similar in subject matter, a social item about a birth or an engagement cannot be given the same treatment as a news story. The social item, having no general news appeal, usually makes no particular point of identifying the persons involved in the opening sentences. It is also written in a restrained, rather formal style.

Births Social items about births are usually one-paragraph accounts giving the names of the parents, date of birth, name and sex of the child and sometimes its weight and the number of other children in the family. The following is standard:

> Mr. and Mrs. R. Bruce Louchheim, of Redding Road, Fairfield, Conn., announce the birth of their second son and fourth child, Arthur David Louchheim, on Jan. 4. Mrs. Louchheim is the former Miss Sara Jean Mainwaring of Greenwich, Conn.

The restrained, fact-studded style of this social item contrasts oddly with news stories about births. For instance, there is little resemblance between this announcement and the following, done in news agency style:

> BROOKLYN—The wife of a $150-a-week department store clerk gave birth here today to quadruplets—two boys and two girls. The four babies and their mother, who already had six daughters, were reported "doing fine" at Kings County Hospital.
>
> The four babies, ranging in weight from three pounds one ounce to four pounds, were born within a 30-minute period to Jeanne May Sammons, 36, who had twins four years ago. The children were placed in separate incubators, the boys in one and the girls in another.
>
> The father, Crawford Sammons, 38, sells men's hats in a downtown department store. He said he planned to look for a larger apartment soon.

Engagements and Marriages The processing of social items dealing with engagements and marriages also follows a formal and well-established pattern. There are differences only in degree, based on the prominence of the persons or families involved. These are emphasized, not particularly in the manner in which the item is written, but in the additional facts that are presented and the play which the announcement is given on the page.

In engagements the items feature the names, educational and professional backgrounds of the principals, their home addresses, the identities of their parents and their marriage plans. It is rare to give the ages of engaged persons on the society page, or delve into their previous marriages, if any. This is an example:

> Mr. and Mrs. William Mellon Dudley, of East Moriches, L.I., announce the engagement of their daughter, Helen Gray, to Mr. Samuel James Delafield, son of Mr. and Mrs. Pendleton Delafield, of 1140 Fifth Avenue, New York, and Westhampton Beach, L. I.

Engagement news stories are handled without such formality. Due regard is given for the ages and previous marriages of the subjects, and any other details that may seem pertinent. The following is an example of a story about an engagement:

LAS VEGAS, Nev.—What happens when a brother act meets a sister act? You guessed it.

Lonnie and Bill Ringwood, 25-year-old twin singers at a local hotel, announced their engagements today to the Pettison Sisters, whose act immediately preceded theirs. Lonnie said he had made arrangements to be married to June Pettison, 23, at the same time that his brother and June's sister, Annette, 21, took their vows. The double ceremony will be some time next week.

"It just shows what can happen when you keep watching the same girls every night in the week," Lonnie said.

When marriages are processed as social items, they are reported with just as much reserve as engagements but, where appropriate, colorful details are added. The bare announcement of a marriage includes the names, parents and backgrounds of the principals, but not their ages, and the church and clergyman. When there is room, and interest in the bride and bridegroom warrants it, the bride's dress, flowers, and attendants are described and the names of the groom's best man and the ushers are also given.

The following is a typical society-page account of a marriage:

Miss Gail Demarest, daughter of former Senator and Mrs. Arthur J. Demarest, was married yesterday to John David Sandeson of Spokane at the First Presbyterian Church.

A cousin of the bride, the Rev. Dr. Henry Hallam Knight of the Community Church, officiated. Mr. Sandeson is the son of Professor William Finch Sandeson, of the State University, and Mrs. Sandeson.

The bride wore a gown of white silk taffeta and Chantilly lace and carried white orchids and stephanotis. Her attendants wore yellow silk, with bouquets of yellow and white flowers.

Mrs. Winfred G. Paynter, sister of the bride, was matron of honor, Mr. Sandeson's brother, Kenneth Sandeson of Pullman, was best man.

After the ceremony, there was a reception at the Metropolitan Hotel attended by Mayor George W. Worthy, Comptroller J. Cornell Simpson, and other officials in both the city and state administrations.

Miss Demarest, an alumna of the State University, is now an instructor in English there. Mr. Sandeson is completing work at the University on his Ph.D. in history.

When the couple return from a wedding trip to Canada, they intend to make their home in the University district.

When a marriage attracts sufficient attention to merit more general treatment in the news columns and on television, the social form is, of course, discarded.

Announcements All newspapers and local broadcast media receive many requests for the use of announcements of meetings, dances, benefits, luncheons and dinners by social, civic, fraternal and charitable organizations. Because of the volume of such news, all items must be written briefly and simply. Nothing makes a newspaper or a newscaster more ridiculous than to try to inject a personal slant or heavy humor in what is essentially a news note.

Birthdays The birthdays of the famous, the honored and respected, the eccentric, and the patriarchs always provide material for writers of news. Some are amusing, some sad; many are philosophical, looking back over life and picking out its lessons. The feature is a hardy perennial but it always has been popular, when it is written without affectation. This is an example of how such stories are done:

> HUNTINGTON—Mrs. Carrie D. Spear is celebrating her 100th birthday today in hale and hearty condition—and to what does she attribute all this? Year after year of beer.
>
> The cheerful, alert lady, whose doctors describe her as "nothing short of amazing," doesn't smoke but she likes her beer. At every lunch and dinner, when the 15 other elderly guests of the Hilaire Farm Nursing Home have their tea or milk, Mrs. Spear has a glass of beer. Asked last night to what she attributed her long, healthy life, she giggled and said, "I reckon I'm a museum piece today because I drink so much beer. That keeps me going."
>
> —*Newsday*

OBITS

The difference between a seasoned journalist and a beginner can be quite marked when they handle an obituary. The beginner, with an insulted air, is likely to hasten through the job as a bit of distasteful routine. The veteran will do careful and even painstaking work because he knows how tricky obits can be.

Principal Points in Obits Each life is different. Each obit, therefore, should be different, but getting at the facts is not always a simple matter. Bereaved families, eager relatives, helpful friends and undertakers are not always the most reliable sources, and old clips are seldom complete. Nor can physicians always be reached and persuaded to give the cause of death if the certificate is not available. For that reason the cause of death sometimes has to be omitted.

If obits were written only for the scrutiny of families, they would be wooden and mealy-mouthed affairs. They are not. They depend on detail, and more detail, for effectiveness. In a few hundred words they should convey exactly why a particular death was news.

All the devices of journalism—the colorful incident, the well-remembered saying or quip, the personal traits, anecdotes and observations of friends and associates — should be used whenever possible to show what manner of person it was who died.

For obits that have no additional news angle, and therefore go either on the obit page or on Page 1 for big news names, the first few paragraphs sum up the circumstances of death. These are the name, age, identification by position, business, trade, or profession, and time and place of death. The age, being of special importance, sometimes is given a short sentence by itself after the opening sentence.

Then follow, in whatever order is pertinent, the cause of death, home address if it is different from the place where death occurred, those who were at the deathbed, other survivors, and funeral arrangements. As a point of style, most obits say that a man is survived by his wife, not his widow, and a woman is survived by her husband, not her widower.

When a death is announced in the morning papers or the AM cycle of a wire service, the afternoon papers and the PM wire service cycles switch to a second day angle — the funeral services. Where there is no competition, of course, the same obit can run all day.

When death occurs in unusual circumstances, the story is handled in an appropriate manner. Sometimes there is a brief feature angle to the story, as was the case in this short piece:

> HOUSTON, Tex. (AP) — Mrs. Eva Deschner, who rallied from serious illnesses many times in the last two years and told her family she would not die before her 97th birthday, died Wednesday on her 97th birthday.
>
> "Mother always was a strong-minded woman," said a daughter, Mrs. Julia Gabler.

The Advance Obit Except for the deaths of a Churchill or a Kennedy, obits are generally summarized in a few crisp sentences for the broadcast media. During newspaper strikes, both local radio and television stations have made efforts to supply the kind of detailed obituary notices that are common in good newspapers. The results have not been impressive to date.

There are, of course, many newspapers on which the obit is so stylized that the details could be filled in on a blank form without making a great deal of difference. The stories read like it, too. But the better newspapers really care about making obits mean more than just a lot of printed matter to run beside the paid ads. The *Nashville Tennessean* has pioneered on a regional level in interviewing prominent persons for obituary material, to be held for use when they die, and the *New York Times* has done the same thing on a national and international level, as well. C. P. Snow, the British novelist who was interviewed for this purpose by the *Times's* chief obit writer, Alden Whitman, later referred to him good-humoredly as a "ghoul." To which Whitman replied, "The eye of the beholder in this, as in other matters, is where ghoulishness is perceived—and resides."

For the famous, it is the general practice on both newspapers and wire services to run the news of the death in relatively brief form, then carry an obit, usually prepared in advance, under a dash. Here is a piece about the death of Marianne Moore, the poet:

> NEW YORK—Marianne Moore, the Pulitzer Prize-winning poet, died today at her home, 35 W. Ninth St., after a long illness. She was 84 years old.
>
> Miss Moore had been a semi-invalid for nearly two years, following a series of strokes, but she remained cheerful under constant nursing care, received visitors and often chatted with friends by telephone. She was universally recognized as one of the most original poets of this century.
>
> Funeral services are being arranged.
>
> ———————
>
> With her dark cape and tricorn hat perched jauntily atop her braided gray hair, Marianne Craig Moore seemed much more like an amiable member of a small-town ladies' club than one of the most admired, honored and influential of American poets. She habitually depreciated herself, saying, "I'm a happy hack as a writer."
>
> She wasn't. T. S. Eliot often said that her poems formed a part of the small yield of durable poetry written in this era. Malcolm Cowley, the critic, called her "What Are Years" one of the "noblest lyrics of our time." In 1952, she was awarded the Pulitzer Prize, the National Book Award and the Bollingen Poetry Prize.
>
> Heaped with these and many other honors, she might have been excused if she had put on a more solemn air about herself but she never did. "The only reason I know for calling my work poetry," she said, "is that there is no other category in which to put it."
>
> Unlike most poets, Miss Moore loved crowds and public events. With her Mary Poppins-like face, her bright smile and her elfin style (she was only five feet three), she was an all-American presence, attending everything from Broadway first nights and fashionable balls to public receptions and sports events. She was an inveterate baseball fan and, in 1968, opened Yankee Stadium by throwing out the first ball.
>
> There was nothing about Miss Moore's background to indicate that she would become a world-renowned poet or, indeed, that she had any particular bent for literary endeavor. She was born in Kirkwood, Mo., a suburb of St. Louis, on Nov. 15, 1887, the daughter of John Milton and Mary Warner Moore. Her father, a construction engineer, was put in an institution before she was born and her mother took her and an elder brother, John, to Carlisle, Pa., where Mrs. Moore taught at Metzger Institute.
>
> Miss Moore was graduated from Bryn Mawr, taught for a short time, then moved to New York with her mother and became a librarian. She began publishing bits of poetry, but did not come to public attention in a big way until 1925, when her "Observations" won the Dial Award. From then on, her progress was meteoric. In all, she wrote only 120 poems, which occupy 242 pages in "The Complete Works of Marianne Moore," published on her 80th birthday.

Characteristically, she celebrated the weak and cautioned the strong, as she did in the opening lines of her "What Are Years":

> What is our innocence,
> what our guilt? All are
> naked, none is safe. And whence
> is courage: the unanswered question,
> the resolute doubt—
> dumbly calling, deafly listening—that
> is misfortune, even death,
> encourages others
> and in its defeat, stirs
> the soul to be strong? . . .

It was a theme to which she returned, as was evident in a fragment from "Nevertheless":

> The weak overcomes its
> menace, the strong over-
> comes itself. What is there
> like fortitude!

Toward the end of her days, her bent for self-depreciation grew on her and caused her to say once to a visitor:

"I'm all bone, just solid, pure bone. I'm good-natured, but hideous as an old hop-toad. I look like a scarecrow, like Lazarus awakening. I look permanently alarmed."

The wire services and most large newspapers maintain current hold-for-release obituaries on file of as many big news names as possible. Often newspapers put some of these in type and, in the case of national and international leaders, make up a whole page or more of news and pictures in advance to be used when the subject dies. The broadcast media are able to call on their film libraries, as well as the wire-service advance obits, for quick reports when someone of stature dies. Similar material is kept available for years on Presidents, former Presidents and many other famous persons here and abroad.

FUNERALS

It is the current fashion to avoid a show of emotion in covering a funeral, except when there is extraordinary justification for such a display. Editors prefer to have the event convey its own impact, as was the case in the funeral of the assassinated black leader, Martin Luther King Jr. Although the reporting of most funerals is brief and restrained, giving only the basic facts of time, place and procedure, the last rites for a famous person often attract more attention. The rules, however, do not change. Whether journalists work with a typewriter, a terminal, a microphone or a camera, they must depend on their artistry to communicate the meaning and spirit of the event without bathos.

This was the way one newspaper began its account of funeral services for James A. Farley, who presided over Franklin D. Roosevelt's first successful campaign for the Presidency:

> James A. Farley was buried yesterday after a final salute from the great clan of politicians whose ambitions and stratagems were the consuming joy of his long life.
>
> A crowd of 1,500 at St. Patrick's Cathedral attended the funeral of the master politician in a friendly gathering that was as much a glowing political event as a religious ceremony of final passage.
>
> "Life for so many of us can become such an anticlimax," the Rev. Robert J. Gannon said in the funeral homily about his longtime friend. "It's nice to go when everyone is still saying, 'Stay.' "
>
> This struck the theme of the crowd, which mourned the passing of the 88-year-old man, but even more reminisced about his life with smiles and laughter. There also was the display of some of the man's personal letters—signed "Jim" in green ink—that marked Mr. Farley's course through one of the most successful individual careers in the history of American politics . . .
>
> © *The New York Times* Co. Reprinted by permission.

Chapter 9
How News
Fits
Time and Space

One of the oldest problems in journalism deals with the necessity of fitting the presentation of the news into a given time and space. For the broadcast media, this has always been a critical matter. Until the coming of new methods of production, the print media had more leeway and many a newspaper could put together its editorial content without much detailed planning and scheduling well in advance. Now, however, the dominance of the computer in the city room plus the swing to wider news columns and narrower advertising columns has made precise measurements of the news mandatory for all well-managed newspapers.

There is no longer any justification for overwritten material for any news organization. Precision is the order of the day. Whatever editors order for use, with the possible exception of a big story that breaks almost on deadline, generally must be written to an exact space limit. And it can't be held back for more details; on terminals, there is room for only one take at a time and it must be sent on its way with a touch of the proper button almost as soon as it is finished.

The manner in which newspapers are handling the problem in the light of modern methods and procedures is discussed in this chapter. The adaptation of it to broadcast journalism follows in Chapter 16.

THE WRITER'S CHANGING JOB

Few writers have ever felt completely secure about their work. Staring momentarily at a blank page in a typewriter on deadline was bad enough, but the twinge of panic quickly passed once the keys began to rattle under flying fingers. It is different sitting in front of a blank, dark, terminal with its roving eye, the cursor. Even when the letters begin popping up on the screen, there is no reassuring sound; sometimes, to the beginner, it almost seems as if the machine is doing the writing.

It is no longer sufficient, in consequence, for writers to know their editors and their audience, to know what is to be communicated and to know their own capabilities. They must also master the machines and learn to work within limitations but without sacrificing their skill with words and their style. All this sounds terrifying; actually, like anything else writers must do, it is a matter of becoming accustomed to new ways of working, new requirements, new standards.

Editorial Instructions In the era when pencil and paper and paste pot and shears were the be-all and end-all of an editor's working equipment, a writer and editor communicated almost by osmosis. The editor might say to someone on the rewrite bank, "Take so and so on the telephone and let's have a piece on what he's got." Or, the same editor might drop a bundle of clips and some wire copy on a writer's desk and suggest, "Let's have a few paragraphs when you get around to it."

Life in the city room was often casual, easy. There wasn't much talk about space limitations or precise word counts. Here and there, a few of the more careful editors had writers set the stops on their typewriters to approximate the number of characters in a line of type, thus making it possible to have a general idea of exactly how long a story would run. But mostly, editors worked by guess and by instinct and writers had to be mind readers.

It sometimes happened that a writer would hand in the first take of a story to the city desk and start on the second take, only to have first take come back to him with a smudged pencil mark beside the third paragraph. Or maybe the fourth. To the initiated, that meant the editor wanted the indicated material used as a lead and the change was promptly made.

Other than that, every man (there were very few women) was his own city editor. In retrospect, it is remarkable that such good work was done by both editors and writers with so little confusion. For there was one rule that never seemed to fail when there was doubt about the length of a story. It was: "Keep it short!" And the wise writer always did.

Writing to Space The writer who works with terminals and computers in a shop that uses photocomposition and offset printing must be much more precise, for editors now are obliged to be more systematic. Even in the remaining noncomputerized city rooms, the notion has taken hold that it isn't a bad thing to "write to space." With the constant rise in newsprint costs, a continued laissez faire policy would be the worst kind of editorial folly.

The difference between editors of yesteryear, those disorganized wretches, and their modern counterparts is that the editors of today virtually control news production as well as news gathering and presentation. They have had to learn to be systematic, and for many it has been an effort. As Robert C. Maynard wrote when the *Washington Post* installed electronic equipment:

"We are discovering that we have a long way to go and much to learn before a smooth relationship between news and the computer becomes possible."

There are so many different systems and combinations of systems that it is difficult to lay down a set of rules that will apply to all who use them to write the news. Obviously, with the focus of production turning from the composing room to the city room, the emphasis first of all is on clean, compact, usable copy. To judge space, most writers are asked to set their terminals or electric typewriters to produce a fixed set of characters per line (terminals run usually up to about 80 spaces for each line).

In nearly all automated city rooms, the usual editorial instructions are used on copy in place of computer jargon but with a difference. It didn't matter much in the old days if a writer missed slugging a page—the copy desk or the printer might catch it very quickly. Now, if an unslugged page goes into a computer for storage in some undetermined manner, the editor who wants to call it up on his machine may never find it. Thus, precise instructions on each page of copy are mandatory and each news organization has its own rules—usually the name of the writer, story slug in one word, sometimes the date and the specified section of the paper in which it is to appear.

In any event, if an editor asks a writer for 30 words for a given item, that is what should be written. Or, the order may be for 100 words as a substitute for a story of twice that length; possibly, in another case, for a 60-word new lead that will pick up a reconstituted story. Such precise instructions aren't common, but they can be followed.

Other editors link the length of news accounts to the varieties of headlines that are suggested for them, except for major stories. For example, a single-line, one-column head in small type can carry an automatic space limit of 60 words. A slightly larger one-column headline will specify that the story must be held to 150 words. A short spread head may be pegged to no more than 400 words. Beyond that point, a limit in wordage may be specified for each story that is assigned.

Whatever the understanding between editors and writers, the successful operation of the system depends on teamwork and mutual support. With the cost of newsprint at more than $300 a ton in the United States, and with larger newspapers using anywhere from 100,000 to 275,000 tons each a year, space is a very precious commodity and it must be allotted wisely.

Checking Results Except for tighter space requirements and greater care with minimal technical instructions, the writer's work, by and large, is not greatly affected by the electronic revolution in the city room. But when the editor comes to check the results by calling up a writer's story on a terminal, there are procedural differences that retard the flow of copy. Once, a few strokes of a big black pencil and a scribbled word here or there were sufficient — and the copy desk and the printers could be trusted to unscramble the editorial hieroglyphics. Not so with a terminal. Chicken-scratch editing won't work.

In one system, when a reporter writes on a special typewriter, the IBM Selectric, both he and the editor must use special pens with a particular type of ink for editing or correcting. Next, the corrections have to be typed between the lines before the story goes into an OCR or scanner that converts the whole into electronic signals for computer storage and use in photocomposition.

In another system, the OCR material plus corrections goes into a video display terminal for editing and eventual routing to computer and photocomposition. Still another combination calls for both writer and editor to use the VDTs. The point is that the complications begin with the editor, for each system has its own electronic devices for correcting, changing or substituting copy and none of them is as simple as a pencil stroke.

The equipment is marvelously flexible, it is true, and the system goes far toward eliminating errors but it does take time to operate. And unless there is a printout of what has been edited, in different type from that used by the writer, the writer will never know what changes were made in his copy unless he has a photographic memory.

The battered old mill, Underwood or Remington, plus the pencil work on the scratched-up, cigarette-scarred city desk, never produced fancy-looking copy but the system worked well for as long as newspapers put up with the expensive and inefficient hot metal composing rooms. With the arrival of cold type and the computer, the chill of an unaccustomed efficiency has settled over the city room. The old ways were less responsible and more fun. But the new ones make it more likely that the press will remain solvent, and therefore capable of survival.

FIRST TEST FOR THE WRITER

Many a beginner sits around the city room for hours on end, sometimes for days, with little more to do than imbibe atmosphere. Then, without warning, comes the first test. Sometimes it is an obit or a bit of wire copy to be rewritten; occasionally, a long-winded reporter gives in a less than monumental piece about a fire, a theft or an auto accident. Whatever the material, once the writer asks the city desk for space, the instructions come back to do a "short"—perhaps four lines on the typewriter or terminal, maybe as much as eight or ten. And do it right away.

All of a sudden, the writer is caught up in the struggle against the limits of time and space in a highly personal manner. Many a man and woman has asked inwardly under such circumstances, "How can I tell a *story* in such a short time and with so little space?" Often, it can't be a *story* because the material isn't there; it's just an item to be set down crisply and clearly without fuss.

Now and then, however, there will be material for a story in a short account and that's the way it should be written. It follows that not many good "shorts" are done in inverted pyramid style. Sometimes, chronological order is effective. Frequently, the punch of a short-short story can be compressed into a few lines. A delayed beginning, a clever tag line, a quote, a keen observation—all these devices may be used to make "shorts" come alive.

There is no name for this kind of story organization, except possibly a box because that is how some good "shorts" are published. In structure they resemble a square because there is usually an equal division of space between the lead and the body of the story. These are "shorts" that relieve the monotony of straight news:

> LONDON—The debut of Ruggiero Raimondi, a 6 foot 2 inch baritone, was out of sight at Covent Garden last night. He sank through a faulty trap door on stage while singing the lead role in Mozart's "Don Giovanni."
>
> When he finally pulled himself out of the hole, the audience gave him an ovation and the critics praised his bravery.

> YORK, Neb.—When Caril Ann Fugate was 14, she accompanied Charles Starkweather on a murder spree in which 11 persons were killed. He died in the electric chair and she went to prison for first degree murder.

Today, at 32, she won parole from the Nebraska Center for Women and set out for a new life under a different name in Michigan, saying: "I just want to settle down, get married, have a couple of kids, dust the house and clean the toilets. I just want to be an ordinary dumpy housewife."

SINGLE-INCIDENT LEADS

The simplest form of organization for a story is one that is based on a single-incident lead. The account may have more than one news idea in it, but these are not of such importance that they must be clustered right after the first paragraph, as is true for an inverted pyramid. Therefore, the organization takes the form of a ladder:

Lead incident
  Documentation
  ―――――――――

    Second incident
     Documentation
     ―――――――――

        Third incident
         Documentation

The length of such a story may be calculated easily by limiting the number of news ideas that are selected for development and using only the most essential documentation for each. It can be written precisely to space.

There isn't anything very rigid about this format. It won't be found in a handy set of tables, like chi square values, and nobody is going to stand beside the typewriter or terminal and proclaim, "For this story, you use a single incident lead." The writer makes such a determination in a few seconds before beginning the story without consulting anybody.

Writing about Speeches The average speech, which is not necessarily Page 1 material but still is worth publishing, usually can be handled in the ladder form of organization.

It should be noted, in the following account, that the rule of one-idea-to-a-sentence is reasonably well observed. Only the central news idea is in the lead. The speaker's name, the time and place of the meeting, the reason for the speaker's remarks and similar details are scattered through the story where they logically belong. Formerly, all such material was rounded up into a block-buster of a lead. The device of scattering speech detail through the story is almost a regulation pattern for news writers today. It is also used, more or less, for the handling of political meetings, legislative proceedings, hearings of various kinds and similar events that must be written in a given space, and without superfluous detail.

Here is the way a story about a speech could be handled, using the simplest form of organization:

Lead incident

The new director of the city's Museum of Modern Art promised today that he would broaden its benefits to the community.

Documentation for lead

Dr. Frederick V. R. Langsam, the director, who succeeded the late Albert Arnold Bunker, made public his plans in a "White Paper on Art."

The "White Paper" was summarized in a speech by Dr. Langsam before his Board of Trustees at the Museum's auditorium.

"We are going to send some of our best pictures, including some Picassos, into the deprived parts of this community," he said.

At the Museum itself, he added, such modern devices as indoctrination films and pocket-size tape-recorded guides would be used to explain the collection to the public.

Second incident

Dr. Langsam also said he might find some surprises in the Museum's treasure-trove of art, now stored in various warehouses.

Documentation for 2d incident

"As a good museum man," he explained, "I know that fashions in art change and some works of modern artists that have been stored now will find an appreciative public. This city is likely to have some surprises."

Third incident

The Museum's director conceded frankly that the Museum's public image needed improvement.

Documenation for 3d incident

"People have thought of us as a stuffy old barn run by a lot of fuddy-duddies," he said, "and maybe they have been right. We're going to open up from now on, I can tell you."

Added detail

Among the measures Dr. Langsam proposed in his "White Paper" were improved relations between the Museum and the city's public schools. "Let's bring art to the children instead of leading the children into the Museum by the hand," he urged. He also wants to close the gap between the Museum and the State University to strengthen the Museum's reputation among art scholars.

Dr. Langsam was a professor of art history at the State University before he assumed his present post. During his academic career, he won a reputation for springing surprises, known as "Langsam's Happenings," to attract the public to academic surroundings. He said there would be no "Happenings" at the Museum.

One of the difficulties about writing reports of speeches is the need for attributing all statements, in quotes or paraphrase, to the speaker. On some city desks it is the fashion to use a monotonous "he said—he said—he said" on the theory that this is exactly what he did and it is the best word to use. At the other extreme is the writer who uses such nonsensical variations as "he opined" or "he averred."

Surely there is room between these two extremes for an exact determination of what actually happened. If reporters did not take the care to make such observations, they would overlook good headline verbs in their leads. A speaker may have demanded, charged, challenged, accused, warned, shouted, insisted, explained, asserted, pointed out, or any number of other variations thereof. However, except when a speaker has taken a formal position, it should never be reported that he has stated or declared his views. These are formal words—statements and declarations. They should be reserved for such situations.

The single-incident lead, as applied to speeches, lends itself readily to other news accounts in which all main points need not be jammed into the first two or three paragraphs. This is an example:

> Doctors at City Hospital have used an artificial tube and valve fashioned from the patient's skin to replace a shattered larynx and restore the voice of a State University freshman.
>
> The student, Campbell B. Stinchfield, 18, of Chicago, greeted reporters with, "Hello, everybody. Come right in." They were his first spoken words since he was injured in an automobile accident on Route 162 near the city's southern limit.
>
> In two operations, the new larynx, made from skin taken from Stinchfield's thigh, was installed.
>
> The operation was performed by Drs. Wilford J. W. Carstairs and Helge O. Halvorsen.
>
> Dr. Halvorsen said the procedure was the first of its kind and "rather simple, although it will take a year or two to get the kinks out."

MULTIPLE-INCIDENT LEADS

The story with several angles that must be featured high in the lead, and documented in turn, becomes a fairly complicated matter to organize. Once again, the selection of the news ideas that are to be featured is the key to the amount of space that will be required. This type of organization is somewhat more akin to the inverted pyramid, but it cannot be bitten from the bottom as recklessly as that old sponge for printer's ink.

This is generally the organization scheme for a multiple-incident lead, when writers have the time to figure out exactly how they want to construct it. Assuming three major news ideas must be included near the top of the story, the ladder would assume a somewhat different shape:

Lead Incident
_____

Second Lead Incident
_____

Third Lead Incident
_____

Connecting Paragraph
_____

Documentation for Lead Incident
_____

Documentation for Second Lead Incident
_____

Documentation for Third Lead Incident
_____

Other details

If each major news idea is easy to express, the three top incidents may be summarized in one paragraph each. Often this is not possible, and two or more paragraphs may be required to give the highlights of each news idea. It is likely that a key quotation, a textual paragraph of importance, or some other part of the documentation, may have to be thrust high in the story to call it immediately to the readers' attention. This is why no estimate can ever be made on the length of leads for all news stories. In some cases they may be a sentence, in others 400 or 500 words.

A multiple-incident lead, of course, can be butchered by a writer who ignores connectives. The separate parts of a story, where possible, should be made to hang together. When they do not, the result is scarcely a story but a series of bulletins strung together in what is known as block-paragraph style. Cut them up, toss them in a hat, draw them out, and rearrange them, and they will still read as block paragraphs. The temptation of an amateur writer, trying to glue his paragraphs together, is to write involved sentences. It is disastrous to yield to it. Following are some of the simplest connective words and phrases that help make a story coherent:

also	with
but	without
soon	later
before	however
after	nevertheless
meanwhile	as to
in spite of	about

next   for instance
finally   nearby
better   farther off
worse   whatever

Redoing a Story The easiest way to illustrate the difference between the handling of a single- and multiple-incident lead is to redo the Museum of Modern Art story by crowding the main points into the lead. It follows:

Lead incident	Some of the city's prized Picassos are going to be sent from the Museum of Modern Art into slum areas.
Documented lead incident	The Museum's new director, Dr. Frederick V. R. Langsam, promised its trustees today in a "White Paper on Art" that he would send the Picassos and other art treasures into parts of the city that had had little previous exposure to culture.
Summary of other points	In a speech at the Museum's auditorium, he also pledged he would change the institution's "stuffy old barn" image by exhibiting art in the schools, resorting to explanatory movies and recorded guides for visitors and
Transition graph, to be followed by detail	taking some of its art works out of storage. Dr. Langsam, who succeeded the late Albert Arnold Bunker, said, "We're going to open up from now on, I can tell you."

The remainder of the documentation would be picked up, each section in turn, with the paraphrase in each case illustrated with quotes. Naturally, the virtue of such organization is to jam the principal news at the top. The main fault is that the reader is likely to lose the thread of the story and forget all about the documentation. However, in major speeches during political campaigns or those outlining local, national, or state policy, a writer has no alternative but to get the news at the top.

Tabular Leads The multiple lead may be better fixed in the public mind by using a tabular system of organization. In the new beginning for the Museum of Modern Art story, for example, the first paragraph may stand and then be followed with this.:

> The Museum's new director, in a "White Paper on Art," also pledged:
> 1. To exhibit art in the schools.
> 2. To use explanatory movies and recorded guides for Museum visitors.
> 3. To change the Museum's "stuffy old barn" image.

The documentation of the lead and the two following points then would proceed as has already been indicated. Sometimes the figures for the succeeding points are omitted and bullets or paragraph marks are used instead. It adds up to the same thing. Another device for summary purposes is to use key words or phrases, followed by the gist of remarks about them, such as:

> Dr. Frederick V. R. Langsam, the director, laid down these other main points in his "White Paper on Art":
> Schools — Art exhibits would also be sent there.
> Communications — Explanatory movies and tape-recorded guides will be used in the Museum itself to aid visitors.
> Image — The Museum's "stuffy old barn" image is going to be changed.
> "We're going to open up from now on, I can tell you," Dr. Langsam told the Museum's trustees in a speech in its auditorium.

Generally it is awkward to use the key word or phrase system for summary purposes high in a story, but it fits in very well at the end of stories that must be written tightly in order to touch on a few additional points made in a speech.

This is another form of tabular lead on a story more difficult to do than the relatively easy speech form:

> The River City Police Department is riddled by lax discipline, old-fashioned administration and inefficient procedures.
> While the city's police force is as large and well-paid as those in municipalities of comparable size, standards for performance, promotions and job applications are sagging.
> These were the salient conclusions made public at City Hall today of a year-long survey by a panel of experts into the work of the Police Department. Mayor Harold V. Dawkins, who pledged that such a study would be made during his successful campaign for election, stressed these major points in the report:
> 1. The Police Department's record-keeping is inaccurate and open to serious question on other counts.
> 2. Less than 20 per cent of the force is assigned to patrol work on weekends, when crime usually reaches a peak.
> 3. Patrol post boundaries are outmoded and patrolmen are assigned arbitrarily to three shifts in equal numbers, although high crime hours are at night.
> 4. Many patrolmen frequent bars while on duty, despite efforts of supervisory officers to halt the practice.
> "This survey," Mayor Dawkins said, "indicates that a thorough going reform is needed in the organization of our Police Department and I'm going to see that a beginning is made, regardless of who is hurt. River City is entitled to better police protection . . ."

Necessarily each of the tabular points must be documented in both these leads in order to provide the reader with a decent explanation of them. As may also be seen, there is always the possibility that the copy desk may let the lead stand, if it is so ably summarized, and carve off the documentation, thus leaving the reader in dazed ignorance of why these striking statements are so.

THE STORY ASSEMBLED

In the multiple incident lead that follows, the general form of story organization is clearly outlined by the manner in which the main points are assembled. The various angles are blended into the opening paragraphs without numbers, dots or other tabular devices:

> CENTRAL CITY—An estimated 600 of the 1,263 inmates at State Prison ended a 24-hour takeover of two wings of the prison last night by releasing five hostages after an agreement with state officials.
>
> Governor Harold Anderson announced that Warden Nicholas Golubovic and three guards had been freed by rebel inmates after a meeting with newsmen and state officials to air grievances at the maximum security institution.
>
> A fourth guard was released at the start of the meeting as a sign of good faith.
>
> In an effort to assure that prisoners would not be harmed, officials agreed to a unique arrangement—Central City citizens, not otherwise identified, would escort prisoners back to their cells to make sure no physical abuse occurred . . .

The easiest way to go into the body of the story would be to use a transitional sentence saying that order was restored at a particular time and the governor's announcement followed. Then, the governor's quotes, documenting the lead, would read in easily with the remaining detail following in summary form.

An Original Pattern Despite the demands of space and time, not all such organization schemes can be carefully contrived. There is a type of narrative that falls into a natural story pattern and in effect tells itself if the writer has the wit to see it. For such pieces, old hands at telling the news say, "Get out of the way of the story." It makes its own pattern, as the following illustrates:

> ATLANTIC BEACH—The former Miss Judy John became the bride of Mr. Pete John at Lou's Restaurant yesterday and all hell broke loose.
>
> A whirling, stomping, jumping, shouting gypsy party exploded in the big dining room after a go-between led dark-haired, 21-year-old Judy from her mother to the groom's mother. That was the ceremony. Miss John was now Mrs. John, the bride of her second cousin.
>
> There were no wild Romany violins to get the blood racing. Instead there was the bump-thump of a non-gypsy rock group who called themselves the Initial Phase. They played mechanically, their eyes darting from side to side.
>
> Lou's is a short walk from the beach, but it was a dismal day and the only cars parked outside were dozens of pickup trucks with out-of-state license plates. The gypsies had been in town for three weeks. Somebody said they'd elected a king but nobody seemed to know his name or where he was.

There was only one answer to a non-gypsy's question about gypsies: "Give me $5 and I'll read your palm. You don't have five? ... Make it two." The gypsy women sparkled in gold and vivid reds, greens, and blues. They wore sashes and scarves and headbands and pounds of gaudy jewelry.

Judy John came out to the bar and sat down at an empty table. Out on the dance floor, her 22-year-old groom was hopping around with one of the rainbow girls. "I'm tired. I've danced with everybody here, I think," Judy said. She was wearing a white wedding dress but around her neck was a huge necklace of gold coins. "It doesn't mean anything. It's just pretty," she said. The marriage had been arranged by her mother and the groom's, but she was happy, she said.

The restaurant's proprietor, Lou Calabrio, wore a strained smile. The gypsies had come at noon, carrying their own hams and chickens, he said. They had cooked and served their own food, and the restaurant had provided the booze. There were supposed to be 75 guests, but 250 showed up.

—Newsday

THE "OFF-BEAT" STORY

The off-beat story often may be useful, lively and economical of space. The trick is to begin in such a manner that the reader's curiosity will be piqued so that he follows the story. There are many effective devices through which this can be done.

The Unexpected Event Sometimes, there is a happening that can be turned to good advantage in the news columns—an event so unexpected that it makes news. This is one way of handling such an occurrence:

When Thomas Dunn raised his baton at Town Hall yesterday to rehearse the Festival Orchestra of New York, 22 beagles came loping on stage.

Mr. Dunn seemed not to be as surprised as the beagles. They sniffed the stage, the musicians, and appraised the bass violin as a possible substitute for a hydrant. The sound of recorded barking off-stage didn't upset them; like well-behaved visitors, not a beagle barked back.

Mr. Dunn gestured and the French horns piped hunting calls, but the beagles paid no attention whatever. They were well aware that there were no rabbits at Town Hall. So the orchestra played on and the beagles were left pretty much to their own devices.

It was all according to plan, except for the beagles' unnatural silence. For the work being rehearsed was the Hunting Symphony by Leopold Mozart, father of Wolfgang Amadeus, who wrote instructions in the score for dogs to bark in response to the opening notes of hunting horns.

Mr. Dunn brought in the Buckram Beagles, a Long Island hunting pack, from Brookville, complete with the Master of Beagles and three uniformed whippers-in. But there wasn't a bark in the pack during the afternoon, which would have pained the composer no end.

EYEWITNESSES TO HISTORY

Frequently, reporters are the eyewitnesses to history and their accounts of their own experiences become a part of the national experience. Such was the position of George Esper, the courageous AP bureau chief who stuck to his post in Saigon (now Ho Chi Minh City) after the American evacuation on April 29, 1975. It was his duty to flash this message next day:

> SAIGON (AP)—South Vietnam has declared unconditional surrender to the Viet Cong, ending 30 years of warfare.

After a month behind enemy lines, Esper wrote this story for the AP report of May 31, 1975, beginning as follows:

> SAIGON (AP)—The gaudy lights of Tu Do Street, the Times Square of Saigon, have been dimmed.
>
> The only neon that flashes boldly and brilliantly is the one which emblazons the life-like picture of the late North Vietnamese Leader, Ho Chi Minh, which hangs from the Independence Palace where President Nguyen Van Thieu once held sway. Thieu now lives in exile on Taiwan.
>
> The French restaurants with the fine wines are virtually empty.
>
> There is scarcely an American in sight. And middle class Vietnamese no longer want to be seen in public with the few Americans who remained behind after the American evacuation April 29.
>
> While there has been no evidence of a bloodbath or mass reprisals so freely predicted abroad, the spirit of many of the 3½ million Saigonese appears to have been killed. But for the first time in 30 years, the guns have fallen silent, refugees are returning to their ancestral villages, fields are being plowed instead of bombed and shelled and homes are being rebuilt.
>
> Movie houses that once featured American and French films now show only the life of Ho Chi Minh. The bars and the night clubs are closed, some of them turned into barracks for the Provisional Revolutionary Government soldiers.
>
> The orphans that some Americans predicted would be killed by the PRG or made Communists appear to be well taken care of. Children still play in the parks as they always did, but I have seen youngsters with arms folded or manacled, marched up the street by PRG soldiers in shame and disgrace for thievery.
>
> Some of the same children who made a business of begging under the former regime are doing the same thing under the new government . . .

It takes masterful reporting to do such work. Not many are capable of it in journalism, regardless of age and experience, and only a handful in this century have dared report from behind enemy lines, with or without the permission of their news organizations.

That Day in Dallas Contrast Esper's story with the even more dramatic chronological narrative of the assassination of President Kennedy, as told by Merriman Smith of United Press International. Only a few hours after the first bulletins from Dallas shocked the nation on November 22, 1963, Smith hurried to a typewriter and wrote his famous story that won the Pulitzer Prize. The piece began quietly and simply, without pretense or fuss:

> DALLAS, Nov. 23 (UPI)—It was a balmy, sunny noon as we motored through downtown Dallas behind President Kennedy. The procession cleared the center of the business district and turned into a handsome highway that wound through what appeared to be a park.
>
> I was riding in the so-called White House press "pool" car, a telephone company vehicle equipped with a mobile radio-telephone. I was in the front seat between a driver from the telephone company and Malcolm Kilduff, acting White House Press Secretary for the President's Texas tour. Three other pool reporters were wedged in the back seat.
>
> Suddenly we heard three loud, almost painfully loud, cracks. The first sounded as if it might have been a large firecracker. But the second and third were unmistakable. Gunfire.
>
> The President's car, possibly as much as 150 or 200 yards ahead, seemed to falter briefly. We saw a flurry of activity in the Secret Service follow-up car behind the Chief Executive's bubble-top limousine. Next in line was the car bearing Vice President Lyndon B. Johnson. Behind that, another follow-up car bearing agents assigned to the Vice-President's protection. We were behind that car.
>
> Our car stood still for probably only a few seconds, but it seemed like a lifetime. One sees history explode before one's eyes and for even the most trained observer there is a limit to what one can comprehend.
>
> Everybody in our car began shouting at the driver to pull up closer to the President's car. But at this moment we saw the big bubble-top and a motorcycle escort roar away at high speed.
>
> We screamed at our driver, "Get going! Get going!"
>
> We careened around the Johnson car and its escort and set out down the highway . . .

In this manner, Smith's account continued. There was a historic quality about his work. It has stood the test of time; even today, it still brings the reader to the scene. It arouses compassion for the fallen President, sympathy for the shocked newsmen and women who struggled to find out what had happened and how it had happened. This is journalism at its best.

Chapter 10
News Nobody Likes

Science has given a shocking immediacy to the reporting of disaster news in this difficult era. Through the marvel of magnetic tape and the minicam, all the horrors that befall mankind are brought pell-mell into the nation's living rooms while helpless victims are still dying and the moans of the injured can still be heard.

Nor are newspaper people very far behind the television cameras in their more detailed coverage of fire and flood, earthquake and storm, wreck and explosion and every other kind of deadly mishap. Reporters with their portable terminals can flash their stories directly from the scene, or close by, to their waiting editors.

It all makes for high drama. But it also places an enormous burden on the news media to give an accurate dimension to the disaster before it is even over. As any reporter knows who has ever been at the scene of a developing story of this kind, few people can be located at once who have the faintest idea of what is going on. Rumors are usually spread by imaginative types and sometimes by panicky survivors. And it is sometimes sheer luck that inflated figures of probable casualties are not circulated to the discredit of all concerned.

A No Win Situation Nobody profits from a disaster, least of all a newspaper cut off from its advertisers and sometimes from its own plant, or a television or radio station that gives its time to public service in an emergency. Nor can it fairly be said that the more common stories of fire losses, auto, train and airplane accidents, ship collisions and the like are of particular benefit to the news media. They don't "sell newspapers" because the regular circulation procedures of the press are disrupted in a stricken community. And on television, a dim-witted part of the public that lusts for entertainment at all costs often resents looking at disaster material.

Why, then, do the news media go to such effort to cover this type of news regardless of risk and cost? Quite simply, it is a part of the tradition of journalism. Radio and television, the most immediate sources of the news, serve as the good watchmen. The news agencies and newspapers follow up, in the most intricate detail, with casualty lists, the extent of damage and the myriad additional facts that cannot be made available to the public by the electronic media in comparable volume.

Covering disaster news isn't exciting or glamorous, as anybody knows who has ever walked wearily through mud, rain and darkness to the scene of a fatal wreck. Like the news of a defeat in war, such material cannot benefit anybody as a general rule. It is the news nobody likes. But it is also the news the public must have.

STORMS

What is a storm? The news media must be precise in announcing that a tornado, hurricane, or blizzard has struck the area. The United States Weather Bureau designations are offered as standard here, but it should be noted that they differ slightly from the standard of the familiar Beaufort's Scale. These are the Weather Bureau's definitions:

DESIGNATION	MILES PER HOUR
calm	less than 1
light air	1–3
light breeze	4–7
gentle breeze	8–12
moderate breeze	13–18
fresh breeze	19–24
strong breeze	25–31
near gale	32–38
gale	39–46
strong gale	47–54

DESIGNATION	MILES PER HOUR
storm	55–63
violent storm	64–73
hurricane	above 74

Beaufort's Scale, devised by Sir Francis Beaufort, R. N., in 1805, describes a whole gale as one that uproots trees and defines a hurricane as a wind of more than 75 miles an hour velocity. Actually, hurricanes, tornadoes, cyclones, and typhoons are all members of the cyclonic family. A cyclone is a system of winds that may be several hundred miles wide and circulates about a center of low barometric pressure. It travels at 20 miles an hour or more, and usually from west to east in the United States.

Commonly, a tornado — the most destructive and violent of all local storms — consists of winds rotating at 200 miles an hour or more. It may last from a few minutes to hours, cut a path of destruction from a few feet to a mile wide, and move forward anywhere up to about 300 miles at a speed of up to 68 miles an hour. The hurricane, a severe cyclone that originates in tropical waters, is a huge wind system as much as 500 miles in diameter. It is slower than a local twister, moving at 10 to 15 miles an hour. In the western Pacific, it is called a typhoon.

There is also a meteorological rarity, called a neutercane, that is a cross between a hurricane and tropical storm, but exists mainly in subtropical latitudes.

The severity of rain and snowstorms is measured by the number of inches of precipitation over a given period. By custom, the public has come to accept any snowstorm of prolonged intensity as a blizzard; actually, the Weather Bureau defines a blizzard as fine, dry snow driven by a wind of 35 miles an hour or more, reducing visibility to less than 50 feet, during a period of low temperature.

Casualty Lists In these days of instant reportage, with the public watching and listening as news people go about their work, it is folly to guess at a total of dead and injured. It never was sound practice, but in the earlier years of the century reporters at least had time to do their work and weren't often tempted to gamble. Under current circumstances, the safest thing for any reporter to do on reaching the scene of a disaster is to say quite frankly what people can see for themselves — that no one has any accurate casualty figures and that it may take some time to arrive at an accurate count.

True, there is always pressure when a wire service or rival reporter for radio or television jumps out in front with a figure derived, usually, from a wandering official who is even more confused than the press corps. But the reporter has to assume, sometimes against the body of evidence, that editors are reasonable people and will wait a reasonable time for a more soundly based figure.

No reporter should accept a casualty estimate from a hysterical or unqualified person. Nor should those who claim to have been eyewitnesses to an accident be permitted to give their stories without a precautionary warning that the statement will require verification. Often, eyewitnesses turn out to be very inaccurate and biased reporters.

Figures even from authoritative sources should be checked carefully, and the sources identified as far as possible so that first reports from a disaster scene are not ridiculously out of line. If there are conflicting estimates, which may seem to be worth examining, a casualty figure within a certain range—from the lowest to the highest—may serve as a temporary expedient.

As soon as possible, reporters should begin working on their own to gather their figures, documented by the names of the dead and injured. If a count shows that twenty bodies have been recovered (and it is one of the most distasteful parts of a reporter's job to make such a tally), then the reporter eventually must have twenty names in his list of dead. Until the list is complete, partial identifications are acceptable if they are so specified. The list of the injured, and their identities, is compiled from the various hospitals and emergency shelters at which persons are treated.

The efficiency and judgment of reporters invariably are tested by the manner in which casualty figures see-saw from the time a disaster occurs. When the first estimate is 50 or 60 dead and it eventually narrows down to 14, that is simply bad reporting and bad judgment. No such wide swing in casualty figures is ever justified. There may be a variation of five or ten, in a major disaster, or the figures may mount hour by hour as more bodies are discovered and the missing are accounted as dead, but in no case should wild guesses be made at a final total.

The same precautions should be taken in characterizing the extent of the tragedy, the estimates of property loss, and the explanation for the size of the death toll. While eyewitness stories frequently are dramatic, and bear on the reasons for the extent of casualty lists, no account that seems to a reporter to be fanciful should be turned in until it has been checked.

The main story, whether in print or broadcast media, should be handled conservatively with the emphasis on understatement if there is doubt about the extent of the disaster. Nothing is gained by flinging adjectives about, when a whole town has been shaken to its foundations. People do not want to be thrilled by magnificent prose. They just want to know what happened.

A DISASTER STORY

When tornadoes swept through Omaha on May 6, 1975, more than 100 staffers of the *Omaha World-Herald* worked all night to cover the disaster and, despite difficulties, a complete paper hit the streets with all the news next day. This is how the Page 1 lead began:

> Armed troops patroled broken businesses and shattered houses in west Omaha and southwestern suburbs early today after at least two tornadoes created bomblike destruction in thousands of buildings.
>
> "The only time I have seen something this devastating was in the South Pacific during the war," Gov. J. J. Exon said after flying over the 2,000-block area that was dealt the heaviest blows.
>
> "I've lived in tornado country all my life and I've never seen anything comparable to this for property destruction. This is certainly the biggest loss in property damage that has ever hit Nebraska."
>
> In the wake of the storm there were these statistics:
>
> —Three and possibly five dead; at least 141 injured.
>
> —At least 500 living units destroyed.
>
> —Damage to "thousands of units."
>
> —About 35,000 homes without power for varying periods of time.
>
> —Damage estimates ranging into the hundreds of millions of dollars with one business alone reporting a $5 million loss.
>
> "Unbelievable, unbelievable," said Public Safety Director Richard Roth, who was with Mayor Zorinsky from the time the sirens sounded . . .

Radio news usually follows the same basic themes, except that it is often present-tensed and tries to update every hour. As for TV, the bulk of on-the-spot disaster reporting has to be ad libbed to fit the transmission of videotape directly to the office. This is the most difficult and demanding kind of reporting, for if the story is big and the pictures are good enough the whole thing goes right on the air. The only rule to follow in such circumstances is to qualify every fact that is likely to change as the story develops.

Newspapers, too, have their problems under these circumstances because of the massive detail they must print—casualty lists, eyewitness accounts, tales of individual heroism or tragedy, the inevitable investigations and the coverage of hospitals and morgues. Unlike the electronic media, the newspapers may have only one chance at a rounded disaster report—a single edition may be all that is left. And it must be made as complete as possible.

GENERAL WEATHER NEWS

There are many ways of telling weather news and the journalist uses all of them, whether the weather is good or bad. Even if there is no story in the newspaper, the United States Weather Bureau forecast is always published in one of the ears on Page 1—the boxes on either side of the nameplate. Either the government forecast or the paper's own prediction, obtained from private forecasters, is printed in a prominent position inside the paper. As for the electronic media, weather is one of their most prominent features and many stations have their own specialists.

Forecasts Most daily newspapers also run the government weather table from various major cities, the regional weather forecast, the long-range weather forecast and the weather map with appropriate explanations. Radio and television run radar maps and give appropriate explanations. At airports and Coast Guard stations, meteorologists also are called upon frequently for interviews by all the news media.

The enormous amount of statistical weather data given to the public means that reporters should make it their business to be reasonably familiar with the principles of weather forecasting. No journalist can for very long escape writing or talking about the weather. When a weekend or a holiday is near, when there is a big sports event or an outdoor convention of consequence, the weather is an important part of the story. It cannot be ignored.

The basic facts that must be used in any weather summation include the latest forecast, mean and hourly temperatures when pertinent, humidity, barometric pressure, wind strength and direction and a comparison with the record highs and lows for that particular date and season. In hot weather, Americans torture themselves with a measurement called the temperature-humidity index (THI), which tries to estimate human discomfort (as if that were possible). To determine THI, wet and dry bulb temperature readings are added, then multiplied by 0.4 and 15 is added to the product. In theory, when the THI passes 75, half the people will be uncomfortable; when it reaches 80 or more, everybody feels awful.

Highs and Lows It is an amiable and harmless journalistic custom to salute a "record" high or low for a particular date, which is slightly synthetic, since most government and other weather records are less than 100 years old. When all highs and lows for a single date such as May 12 or December 13 are compared in the record, it is obviously possible to have a "record" day occasionally. The ancient journalistic weakness for "firsts" can also be satisfied by checking on the weather for the first day of the season, the first storm of the winter, the first heat wave of the summer, and the hottest and coldest days of the month, season or year. To those who play the game of highs and lows, a reminder should be given that the "record" is not always established on the hour but may come between hourly readings. Like everything else, the reporter must ask the Weather Bureau for the record because the information is not always volunteered; nor is it a good policy to depend on such supplementary services as the weather information supplied in some cities by telephone companies.

There is one other precaution that is recommended to everyone who writes about the weather, whether the story deals with disaster or is just a routine short. A glance out the window, just before writing, will sometimes save everybody trouble. Weather forecasting is far from perfect, and even the most efficient meteorologists have been known to change their predictions within an hour or less.

In resort cities and localities weather news sometimes is used for its promotional value. Thus, Florida media are likely to play the news of cold weather in northern states, from which so many tourists come, or rain in a rival tourist paradise such as California. Local weather, too, is more likely to be newsworthy in such areas.

Heat Waves, Cold Waves, and Storms When the hot spells of summer and the cold spells of winter set in, they are news. The classic patterns of weather reporting then are spread over several days, with hourly temperatures featured and enlarged upon by appropriate comparisons with previous days or years. It is comparatively simple to document a heat wave or a cold wave with statistics from the usual sources. They are plentiful and available for the asking. The accompanying events also are familiar and generally easy to cover. Crowds take to the parks, lakes, mountains and seashore in the summer heat, with a certain amount of official and business activity being curtailed at extreme periods. During the winter a sub-zero cold spell can seriously disrupt both business and transportation but much of this material can be obtained from official sources, chambers of commerce and transportation information. Gathering such data takes time, but usually it is plentiful.

The troublesome part of handling extremes in the weather for use in the news media is to determine which deaths, injuries and losses are directly attributable to them. Such casualties seldom are officially proclaimed. Reporters have to exercise their best judgment—and a considerable amount of restraint—and editors are presumed to check on them. Nevertheless, broadcasts and banner headlines announcing that ten persons have died of the cold summon up images of frozen bodies found in remote places. In reality, most of them are likely to be victims of heart attacks that may or may not have been induced by overexertion. The same is often true of deaths attributed to the heat. It would be a nice exercise in general reporting to determine, in any given heat or cold wave, how many persons actually died because of extreme weather conditions. There is, as a rule, too much poetic license in such reportage; it taxes the public's credibility in its news media.

Writing the Story The most difficult thing for a newcomer to journalism to understand is that a heat wave, cold wave or storm, which is known to have occurred in the area, must be announced in the media and explained from beginning to end. There is nothing unusual about this. A hundred thousand people may have seen the Super-Bowl football game and millions of others may have watched it on television, but the newspapers and subsequent regular broadcasts still record the fact that there was a game, which side won, what the score was and the pertinent details. The evidence is impressive that the public is often particularly interested in getting more detail, background information and color on news of which it has some advance knowledge.

Since the weather is a universal topic of discussion, the first rule in any weather report is to begin at the beginning by telling what is right or wrong with the day, what the results are and why, and whether improvement can be expected. The following are typical leads used by wire services, newspapers and the major television news roundups. Some may be edited for other forms of broadcast news merely by changing the past tense of the verbs into present perfect and eliminating the time element if desired:

> A cold wave from northern Canada rolled over the northeastern part of the nation today, forcing the temperature in the city to two degrees above zero. No relief was in sight. . . .

> The mercury shot into the 90s today on the fifth day of the August hot spell, but thundershowers forecast for tonight promised temporary relief. . . .

> Whipped by a 30-mile-an-hour wind, a snowstorm pelted the city today and reached a depth of four inches in the first five hours. The Weather Bureau forecast an all-night fall, with a probable depth of 12 inches before morning.

One of the characteristics of weather stories is the use of vigorous verbs and sweeping general statements of conditions, which conceivably can lead to an impression that things are worse than they really are. It is one of the risks of writing colorfully about facts that are more or less generally known. Between the dry-as-dust official phrases of the weather report and the hopped-up writing of an overenthusiastic wire-service writer doing an undated lead, there is a sound middle ground that reporters should seek. It is to tell the story colorfully and accurately, with emphasis on the information that interests the public.

Here is the way two major news organizations handled leads on important weather stories:

> One man was missing and another critically injured after 90-mile-an-hour winds slammed the Dundalk Marine Terminal yesterday, causing an estimated $15 million damage and closing the giant terminal.
>
> Gusts recorded at up to 94 m.p.h. in Dundalk apparently were the worst of a violent March windstorm that steam-rollered a broad swath across the state between noon and 4 P.M.
>
> The winds tore ocean-going freighters from their moorings, flattened trees and walls, flicked roofing from entire blocks of houses and snapped the main mast of the ship Constellation in the harbor.

Nearly 40,000 customers of the Baltimore Gas & Electric Company were without power at one point yesterday afternoon . . .

— Baltimore Sun

BUFFALO, N.Y. (AP) — Snow-stricken Buffalo's cleanup from the worst storm in the city's history moved forward today with the arrival of more men and snow-removing equipment.

More than 13 feet of snow have fallen thus far on the paralyzed city for the winter of 1976–77.

Air Force planes ferried in 200 Army engineering troops and a work crew from New York City, along with snow blowers, snow scrapers and trucks. And the federal government said Buffalo would get about $200,000 to hire the unemployed for snow removal.

More than a dozen persons died in the storm, most of them stranded in autos. An estimated 250,000 Buffalo area workers were off the job and losing $12–$15 million daily. The Salvation Army served 20,000 meals to the stranded and homeless . . .

EARTHQUAKES

Four out of five earthquakes occur around the borders of the Pacific Ocean. They also may be experienced with some degree of frequency from the West Indies across the Atlantic and Mediterranean and on to the Himalayas and East Indies. All in all, 1,200 seismograph stations detect about a half million temblors a year. But of these only about 1,000 cause specific damage although up to 100,000 or more may be felt in some slight degree.

The measurement of earthquakes is done on the Richter Scale, designed by the geologist, C. F. Richter. Under it, the magnitude of the quake is made proportional under certain conditions to the logarithm of maximum recorded amplitude. These are typical Richter Scale figures of earthquake magnitude:

2   — smallest shocks to be reported.
4.5 — smallest shocks causing slight damage.
6   — shocks that cause moderate destruction.
8.5 — largest known earth shocks.

While there is a considerable body of material about earthquake forecasting, such predictions should be handled with great caution. Headlines announcing a future quake, or broadcasts suggesting it is time to take to the hills, are not notably popular either in Japan or along the San Andreas Fault on the American Pacific coast. Such forecasts do not have irrefutable scientific acceptance to date.

The locality in which a small earth shock occurs also has something to do with the amount of interest it creates. A mild tremor means very little in most parts of Japan, where there are thousands of earth movements every year. But anything that even sends pictures to swinging on the walls in the New York City area, where earth shocks are rare, stirs up the public and stimulates a kind of controlled alarm in the news media. The major China quake of 1976 (8.5 on the Richter scale) was a brief sensation in the United States, then was treated almost routinely.

FIRES

Like the news of storms and other natural disasters, news of fires must be handled with the greatest care in accounting for casualties. The same procedures recommended for the compiling of lists of storm dead and injured are advisable. The top police and fire officials at the scene and hospital authorities all can be helpful in insuring the accuracy of fire casualty lists, but often final identifications must wait on the appearance of relatives at a morgue or funeral home. These are heart-rending scenes, which are difficult for even an experienced reporter to witness.

There are other hazards in the reporting and writing of fire stories. In a report on the cause of a fire, it should be borne in mind that anything said by a fire chief or fire marshal is not privileged. Therefore, if the authorities suggest the blaze was set, it is not the job of the reporter to accuse anyone of arson unless a suspect is arrested and booked on such a charge. It is also dangerous, in reporting the cause of a fire, to attribute negligence to the owners of a house or other building although such risks frequently must be taken if fire authorities choose to make a public statement to that effect. The only course a reporter can take, in such an event, is to seek a reply promptly from the person or persons accused.

Basic Data Certain information is mandatory in any fire story, in addition to the casualties and the probable cause. The exact address of the structure involved is not enough. It must be described as a residence, office, loft, or factory building. The number of stories should be given and the type of construction, whether it is frame, brick, concrete or fabricated steel. If it is a building of a particular type, such as a tenement or a substandard dwelling, that should be reported. The time the blaze was discovered, how many fire alarms were turned in, the number of firemen and vehicles that responded, the time when the flames were brought under control or put out, and the effect on nearby buildings and traffic are generally included in the average fire story.

If it is possible to give a fair and accurate estimate of damage, that is obviously one of the features of such a story. The size of damage estimates, however, frequently depends on who gives them—whether it is the owner of a building or a fire official or an insurance adjuster. When there is doubt, the news media should give the legitimate damage estimates that are made and such explanations as are available.

Stories of heroism or narrow escapes from death, eyewitness accounts and other material generally associated with disaster coverage are often the principal part of a fire report, if there have been no casualties. Otherwise they are mentioned fairly high in the lead, and then documented in the body of the story at an appropriate point.

Multiple Coverage It makes no difference to newspapers that at least a part of their audience has seen fire pictures on television and that broadcast journalists have already covered the story. Perhaps that will change in time. But for the present, the print media continue to cover fires of consequence with news and pictures as completely as ever. Newspaper reporters, well aware that the minicam can do many things they cannot do, try for exclusive angles, particularly in suspicious fires, but so do broadcast journalists.

In any case, fires get a lot of attention and newspaper fire pictures still win Pulitzer Prizes, as witness Stanley Forman's remarkable photograph of a baby sitter and a small child plunging from a collapsed fire escape in Boston. After it was published in the *Boston Herald American,* it won the 1976 Pulitzer award for spot news photography and it also brought about new safety regulations for fire escapes.

A Fire Lead Here is the *Herald-American*'s lead on that fire story, illustrating how the various angles can be woven into a newsworthy pattern:

> A young woman fell to her death, a small girl was injured and a firefighter was saved by a chance hand-hold yesterday when a fire escape collapsed at the height of a suspicious blaze in the Back Bay.
>
> Diana Bryant, 19, a resident of the five-story brick building at 129 Marlborough St., fell into a rear alley when the topmost fire escape gave way.
>
> She was taken to Massachusetts General Hospital in critical condition and died hours later of multiple head and body injuries.
>
> The child, identified as Tiare Jones, who will be 3 in September, also plunged into the alley. She suffered breathing difficulties in the ambulance to the New England Medical Center but was revived by ambulance attendants.
>
> Tiare was later reported to be suffering a mild concussion and possible internal injuries. She was kept in the hospital for observation.
>
> Her mother, Mrs. Patricia Jones of St. Alphonsus St., Roxbury, said she was the godchild of Miss Bryant, a family friend who was caring for her.
>
> The victims were seconds away from being rescued by Firefighter Robert O'Neil who was saved from the fall only because he had one hand on a rescue ladder while holding his other out to guide them to it.
>
> At that point, in O'Neil's words, "It just let go." He was left dangling on the swaying ladder.
>
> "There was no warning," he said. "I didn't think there was any reason to worry. It appeared to be a routine rescue."

O'Neil swung himself onto the ladder and climbed swiftly to the ground where the injured were being given emergency treatment . . .

TRANSPORTATION ACCIDENTS

All forms of transportation accidents—automobiles, buses, trains, ships, aircraft and now space ships—are reported as they occur. It is unhappily true that the individual automobile crash, because it is the most common, receives comparatively less attention than the others although it is responsible for more than 50,000 deaths a year—approaching the American death toll in both the Korean and Vietnam Wars. There is a striking difference in the treatment given by the news media to two deaths in an air crash as compared with two deaths in an auto crash. Two deaths of astronauts in a space ship are, of course, far more spectacular than anything else and receive the full treatment on television and in headlines.

It is, without doubt, patently unfair to air travel to feature air crashes and play down automobile wrecks, particularly in view of the excellent safety records of the commercial airlines. It is also scarcely responsible journalism to underplay the role of the automobile as the great killer of our society. But, good or bad, these are the news values that exist today and only public pressure can change them. When rocket travel comes of age, presumably the treatment of aircraft accidents will be somewhat more fair.

Automobile Accidents Many attempts have been made by the news media to dramatize the slaughter on the nation's highways. For a time, it was considered a public service to give a blood-curdling tinge to accounts of auto crashes, but the technique had less effect than publicity that has been given to cancer research in connection with cigarette smoking. With the exception of accident reports in crusading newspapers, news stories generally have returned to a straight news treatment of automobile accidents.

Over holidays and summer weekends, it has been the custom to feature the auto death forecast of the National Safety Council and moodily comment on whether or not it was exceeded—an editorial chore that seems to have had little more effect than a shock treatment. The fact is that the day-by-day totals of automobile accidents are shocking enough, to those who are impressed by such things, and the holiday death forecasts serve only to pile horror on horror.

There seems to be no point in tinkering with automobile accident news. In place of the awesome national roundup of hundreds of deaths during a holiday period, the names, ages, and addresses of the victims and the time and circumstances of their deaths are more meaningful news in their own communities. Contrast the following two stories for human interest:

> The nation's highway death toll soared to 575 last night for the four-day Christmas holiday. Of the traffic fatalities, 36 were in New York State.
>
> The death total was below the 620 predicated by the National Safety Council for the four-day period. It also was unlikely to exceed the record of 706 for a four-day holiday in the United States.
>
> A 14-year-old girl plunged into the flaming wreckage of a truck yesterday near Bridgeport and dragged its unconscious driver to safety. Then she put out the fire on his clothes with her new, red Christmas jacket.
>
> The heroine, Mathilda Johnstone, of New Haven, was riding in the family car with her mother, Mrs. David Wills Johnstone, when the truck sped past them on U.S. Highway 1. A few minutes later, it went out of control, plummeted from the road into a ditch and overturned.
>
> As soon as Mrs. Johnstone stopped the car, Mathilda rushed to the truck and rescued the driver, Sam Don Persson, 28, of Silver Lake. He was reported in fair condition last night at Bridgeport Hospital.

The difference between these two accounts is that a writer tried to make an individual incident come alive in the second instance, while the first was just a tabular summary of a weekend of accidents. It illustrates one of the axioms of journalism — there is more human interest in one person than in a crowd of 10,000.

Ship Accidents The news of tanker oil spills, ship collisions, fires at sea, and other nautical disasters usually breaks first by radio. Very often, it is followed by intensive radio coverage either through communication with rescue vessels or aircraft, messages from such agencies as the Coast Guard or RCA Communications, assistance from amateur radio operators, or announcements from owners of ships involved. Until the rescue vessels reach port, if mishaps occur at sea, reporters must be communications experts and the one with the best resources usually gets the most complete story.

In the case of a ship accident offshore that is worth the trouble, newsmen may be authorized to hire planes or tugs to go to the scene. This is always done by television cameramen and the picture syndicates when there is a major disaster at sea, unless the scene is too far from shore. When survivors are being brought to shore in lifeboats, newsmen have to spend many long hours on the beaches, sometimes in storms, waiting to get the first-person accounts of the disaster.

With the coming of the supertanker that transports oil half way around the earth, any considerable oil spillage from such vessels has become big news. Public concern for oil conservation, the safety of wildlife and beach pollution have made it so and the news media have reacted accordingly.

The first time radio was used in a sea rescue, on January 23, 1909, Operator Jack Binns on the "Republic" sent the first distress call (it was then CQD, not SOS). He told of a collision involving his ship and the "Florida" off Nantucket Light and appealed for help. As a result, all but six of the "Republic's" passengers were saved.

Many years later, in the following account based on an Associated Press report, it may be seen that radio still gives the news of disasters at sea:

> A German freighter burst into flames on the Atlantic Ocean today, but all save one of the 23 men aboard were rescued.
>
> The body of the dead crewman, who could not be identified immediately, was left aboard the 259-foot freighter, Caldas, 40 miles off the fishing village of Chincoteague, Va.
>
> The Coast Guard reported the ship's last distress call at 12:53 P.M., which read: "Fire on board. Smoke coming into wireless room."
>
> The Coast Guard reported that 17 crewmen had abandoned ship and had been picked up by the American freighter, Somerset Trader. The captain and four others who stayed aboard the Caldas in an attempt to save her had to take to lifeboats themselves soon afterward. They were picked up by the Coast Guard cutter Kiwana.
>
> All were later transferred to the freighter Atlantic Heritage, bound for Philadelphia.
>
> A Coast Guard C-130 rescue plane and the Coast Guard cutter Cherokee from Norfolk also aided in the effort to save the stricken freighter. The Coast Guard said the 14-year-old vessel had a gaping hole in its starboard side and a 10-degree starboard list, but was still afloat tonight.

Often, in ship disasters, it is necessary to "write around" or "talk around" the number of casualties when it is difficult to determine exactly what happened. Sometimes, it is specified in the lead that 130 persons were on board, but the body of the story says there is no immediate word on what happened to them; or, as the radio messages pile up, some indication is given that part of the passengers were rescued and the fate of the rest is not known. In any event, whenever there is a disaster on land or at sea, it is a familiar precaution to hold out hope for the missing until a body count indicates that they are dead.

Train Accidents In many ways, the coverage of an accident on a crowded train is the most difficult of all except the natural disaster. Here, no one has a passenger list such as is generally available after ship and aircraft disasters. The problem of identifying survivors is one that tries the patience of even the most painstaking of veteran reporters. Radio and television give the first news but the newspapers must follow up.

The first news of a train accident usually comes from someone living near the scene. Often, the railroad people themselves do not know what happened until they conduct an inquiry. A good reporter, who is on the job quickly and moves around, often finds out more than anybody else at the scene of such a disaster.

If the train has not gone off a bridge or been destroyed by fire, an accurate count of the dead and injured can be made fairly quickly. Where there is uncertainty over which passengers survived, a reporter faces a long and difficult job of checking. At that point, the news is likely to develop everywhere at once—hospitals, police stations, funeral establishments, railroad waiting rooms, even over the switchboards of the news media that receive appeals from anxious relatives or friends for information about possible survivors.

Here is the first break on a railroad accident that illustrates the problems of initial coverage:

> A five-car Jersey Central commuter train, carrying about 100 passengers, plunged through an open drawbridge into Newark Bay today.
>
> At least forty persons died and 21 others were injured, a railroad spokesman estimated. The accident occurred shortly after 10 A.M. near Elizabeth, N.J.
>
> By early afternoon, skin divers had recovered 13 bodies.
>
> The train had started from Bay Head, a North Jersey shore resort, and was bound for its Jersey City terminal. Passengers at the terminal take the Hudson Tubes for New York City.
>
> Two Diesel locomotives and the first two passenger cars crashed through the open span and were quickly submerged in 40 feet of water. The bridge is 50 feet above Newark Bay.
>
> A third car remained dizzily suspended, half in the water and half out, for almost three hours. Then it, too, plunged to the bottom of the bay.
>
> No reason was given immediately for the failure of the engineer to stop the train before roaring across the drawbridge. . . .

Except where the final death toll has been determined, it is standard practice to base the lead on the accident itself. The extent of the casualties, with suitable qualifications, can be given in the second paragraph and easily changed. This procedure holds good for the electronic media as well as print. The reason for not engaging in necessarily unfounded speculation is evident in the above story. With the exact number of passengers uncertain, and only 13 bodies recovered, it is evident that the estimate of 40 dead and 21 injured can be little more than an educated guess by the railroad spokesman on whom it was pinned.

Aircraft Accidents There are two general types of coverage for aircraft accidents.

When commercial planes alone are involved, a combination of methods used in ship and train accidents is usually advisable. The federal, state and local authorities responsible for regulating air traffic may have part of the story. The local airport may prove to be a valuable source for obtaining the last messages from the aircraft involved and their locations.

It is true that the companies have passenger lists of a sort, but they can never be taken at face value. That is because of the substantial percentage of "no shows" (persons with reservations who do not use them) and the standbys who go aboard at the last minute to fill vacancies. Stewardesses are supposed to take the names of all passengers aboard, and their seat locations, but these lists seldom are available after an accident; on occasion, they aren't even compiled because the stewardesses are too busy serving drinks and food.

In any case, it takes time to check through the ticket stubs and find out who actually did go aboard a plane that is later involved in an accident. If the disaster scene can be reached, it tells much of the story and survivors fill in many of the details. But often the wreckage is inaccessible and organizations such as the State Police must be relied upon for first reports. If the United States Air Force has a base in the vicinity, the commander or his information officer may prove helpful, too. But much of the work must be done by the news media without much guidance—and often a lot of interference as well.

When an Air Force, Navy, Army, or Coast Guard aircraft is involved in an accident, the rules change sharply. The Defense Department's procedures for issuing information on aircraft accidents often curb independent reporting. The news media, in such cases, must depend on the military for initial reports of casualties. The restrictions become even tighter when a military aircraft carrying a nuclear weapon is involved. The laws concerning disclosure of atomic information provide stiff penalties for the unauthorized issuance of information in such cases. When H-bombs were lost off Palomares, Spain, following an Air Force accident there, the Spanish authorities leaked the news long before the Pentagon confirmed it.

Here is the essential part of a report of an accident involving a commercial aircraft, which illustrates many of the general problems of coverage:

> CHARLOTTE AMALIE, Virgin Islands (AP)—An American Airlines jet with 88 persons aboard crashed into an embankment at the end of the airport runway yesterday, ripped across a busy highway and exploded in flames.
>
> Hospital authorities said 52 passengers and crew members were treated for injuries, leaving 36 persons killed or unaccounted for.
>
> Civil Defense officials reported earlier that 47 bodies were removed from the wreckage, but it was determined later that some of the body bags used at the site contained only portions of badly charred victims.
>
> The survivors were taken to Knud Hansen Hospital, the only hospital on St. Thomas Island. A hospital announcement said 19 persons were admitted and two were flown by helicopter to Puerto Rico. The others were treated and released.

Three persons on the ground who were hit by debris also were treated at the hospital.

The plane struck at least seven automobiles and smashed into a Shell Oil Co. service station and a tavern, a fire official said. Two cars were crushed under the smoldering fuselage.

American Airlines in San Juan, P.R., announced that the Boeing 727 was Flight 625 from Providence, R.I., with a stop at New York's Kennedy Airport. They said the craft carried 81 passengers and a crew of seven.

SOARING INTO SPACE

The space story is one for specialists. After American astronauts had landed on the moon six times between 1969 and 1972 and a Soviet-American expedition into space had carried out a successful docking experiment in 1975, the public in the United States appeared to take these wonders for granted. And yet, both American astronauts and Soviet cosmonauts died in the earlier stages of space experiments and there is no guarantee that more such tragedies will not occur.

Television is at its best in the reporting of such spectacles as space flights. American television, in particular, has shown the world what its skill and advanced technology can accomplish; the Soviet Union's controlled television has grudgingly followed some American practices in letting the world in on its secrets. The print media have had to be content with factual reporting from American space centers and occasional first-person narratives, descriptive material that is better shown on television and massive coverage of home towns, families and backgrounds of news-making astronauts.

Chapter 11
Handling the Story on Rewrite

Everybody in journalism recognizes the difficulties of writing under pressure. The "bleeders"—those who write with great effort—consider it a triumph of mind over matter when they are able to turn out a decent story under such circumstances. But for specialists, it is an art that is practiced with both care and devotion.

It has always been true, from the time of the quill pen, that writers with a particular talent for fast, accurate and interesting work on deadline are rarities in journalism. The media may expand dramatically in marvelous ways. The tools of the trade may change with striking effect. But whether the chosen instruments are pad and pencil, typewriter and copy paper, terminals and computers or magnetic tape, somebody of professional competence has to use them to produce on deadline.

For television newscasts, writers develop carefully timed and tailored scripts to accompany the pictorial material that inundates broadcast newsrooms. For news magazines, they weave together compact and coherent pieces from thousands of words filed by their correspondents and other sources. Equally difficult tasks are handled by the writing specialists for newspapers and wire services — the men and women who work at the rewrite desks and write on demand. For them, every minute is precious.

THE FINE ART OF REWRITE

To those outside the profession, who have no reason to give any thought to newspaper or wire service techniques, the words *rewrite man* or *rewrite woman* sound as if they should be applied to a tired hack.

Consider only one circumstance that is familiar to anyone who has ever worked in a city room for even a short time:

Several reporters are out on a story, covering various angles at widely separated points. Two or three editors are giving them directions as they phone in. Somebody else is checking wire service copy and watching for bulletins as they come along. The managing editor is holding Page 1, and the circulation director is in the city room to see what the fuss is all about.

At such a time, the whole burden of the operation rests on the person at the rewrite desk. The writer is geared to such moments, with notes and wire copy piled around the desk in seeming disarray. Everybody watches that desk. But the writer, with a glance at the clock, begins work nervelessly — a paragraph or two at a time — so the editors can begin reading and producing headlines and layout. Then, take after take flows from the machine into production until the deadline is reached and the story is done. Without argument. Without fuss.

No hacks could be trusted to do this kind of writing day after day, week after week. Even if some have tried it, they haven't lasted very long. They don't have the know-how.

What Is Rewrite? The term *rewrite* is a misnomer. Originally, the rewrite man was called that because he actually did redo the work of semiliterate reporters. Today there are far different requirements.

When a President is elected or a war begins, when a Pope dies or a hurricane strikes a great city, the story must be written quickly. The lead must be available within a matter of seconds if the account is for a wire service, a newspaper deadline or immediate broadcast.

Nor do great events alone receive such spectacular treatment. In the ordinary run of local news it may be necessary to give quick handling to a fire, a robbery, a baseball or football game, the death of a prominent citizen or even an interview with a million-dollar sweepstakes winner.

In such situations, skilled writing specialists are called on. It is no time to spin theories or philosophize over the news. And it is no place for amateurs. This is the spot that was made for the rewrite man or woman.

The Necessary Ingredients The first quality of those who work at rewrite is the ability to turn out clear, accurate and interesting copy without hesitation under all conceivable circumstances. If it is done on a typewriter, it should be as clean as an expert stenographer's. If it is produced on a terminal, typographical errors are bound to delay and interfere with the quick completion of the job. Whatever the method, the copy itself should be more readable than that of less practiced writers.

Facility and adaptability are other qualities that are mandatory on rewrite. Such writers may handle in the same working day a dramatic straight news story, a light feature, a thoughtful interpretive piece, or even a street tragedy tinged with human interest. Their least desirable quality is temperament.

Anybody who wants to stay on the rewrite bank for very long must demonstrate sharp and accurate news judgment. Editors cannot forever be telling their writers what the lead should be. They must know, based on their background, their current reading and specialized knowledge. However, if it happens that an editor wants a lead other than the one that has been written, the slant should be changed without fuss.

It is the unhappy fate of deadline writers, who are always in the middle between reporters and editors on newspapers, to be blamed by all sides for any failure and to receive little credit for success. The records of the Pulitzer Prizes contain the names of lamentably few journalists whose specialty was rewrite; and yet, newspapers could not be produced without them.

The Rewrite Habit When Alexander Graham Bell invented the telephone, he also created the journalistic situation that made rewrite necessary. Charles E. Chapin, who terrorized the staff of the *New York Evening World* while he was its city editor, is generally believed to have been the first in New York journalism to have reporters telephone their facts to a writing specialist in the office instead of returning to do their own stories.

As afternoon newspapers in metropolitan centers began issuing more editions per day — at one time some of the biggest papers put out as many as eight editions regularly — it became necessary to use reporters principally to gather the news. The term *legman* came into being, and many a metropolitan reporter simply became a fact-gatherer for the rewrite man.

From the afternoon papers the practice of rewrite spread to the morning field whenever reporters were too far from the office to come in, too close to a deadline or too inept to do their own pieces. There was a time immediately before World War II when rewrite was even more general than it is now, and editors began to realize that something valuable was slipping away from journalism—the firsthand account of a news event.

At just about the time that efforts were being made to restore the balance between rewrite and reporting, the United States entered the war and women took over in many a city room. With many younger men in service, it was the first time that most editors realized rewrite didn't necessarily have to be done by a man. But despite the demonstrable competence of rewrite women, men resumed control of nearly all these specialized writing jobs after World War II.

However, with the drastic decline in the number of daily newspaper editions, morning papers in particular began giving reporters more chance to get their own copy before the public. The added time between editions meant that rewrite wasn't quite as important as it had been and a few women were rather grudgingly admitted to the one-time male preserve. The pressure for more staff-originated copy—investigations, in depth reports, features and other specialized pieces—had a similar effect in the afternoon field.

But not for long. Once cold type and pasteups replaced hot metal and the makeup of a page of type in a metal form, more time had to be allowed to get editions to press. Once again, the emphasis was on speed and accuracy on deadline and rewrite men and women returned to favor. With the terminals and computers dominating so much newspaper production today, rewrite is still important.

From an experiment, rewrite became a habit. It is now a necessity.

WHAT WRITERS CAN DO

Competent writers can illuminate the bare details of reporters' work with considerable newsworthy material. Being detached from the event itself and under no compulsion to leap to the telephone with every new detail or file on a portable terminal, writers can afford to take a broader view and try to make their stories amount to more than a surface account. Frequently, they succeed.

For one thing, writers who are handling a continuing story will usually have a good idea of the background, the principal characters and the scene. For another, reporters who are out on such a story cannot consult the newspaper library, or morgue, for the fill-in information that is often so necessary to make a piece authentic as well as interesting. The two are not necessarily synonymous.

Nor can reporters divine what is happening at other points that may have an important bearing on the development of the story. In a sense, therefore, writers in the office actually are in a better position to tell what is going on than are the reporters in the field.

Finally, writers have direct and immediate contact with editors and can discuss operations with them. Where reporters would be hopelessly snarled up by space estimates or the lack of important background, writers handle such things in stride. Yet, for all their advantages, not even the cleverest member of the rewrite bank can make a story seem as real as that of a reporter who knows how to describe the sights, sounds and smells associated with the news. The best writers, in fact, are those who are too wise to try to counterfeit reality by imagining a news scene in too great detail. That way lies error and a resultant failure of credibility. Reporters will always be the legs, eyes and ears of a newspaper; no terminal, computer or camera can substitute for them.

A Writer's Duties What writers do varies from paper to paper and from bureau to bureau of a wire service. The scope of the job depends largely on how much work an individual writer can handle well without making mistakes or falling into a panic. Some on rewrite do nothing but obits and shorts. Others handle the main stories of the paper day after day. Still others, with a gifted telephone manner, are used to backstop reporters by making calls on breaking news or on various other types of stories.

In general, any first-rate member of a rewrite battery should be able to turn out between 1,500 and 3,500 words a day on the average without feeling strain. Not all of this will be in the paper at day's end, of course. News changes. As it does, earlier developments are dropped for the latest material.

There is always something for writers to do, even if others on the staff are sitting around. They may be rewriting and checking clips from other sources or pulling together wire copy from various points. They may be assigned to handle a campaign or an investigation, weaving the work of a dozen reporters into a coherent whole (and without much credit in the bargain).

Sometimes, returning to the dim beginnings of rewrite, those with time on their hands may be asked to redo a reporter's bungled feature. When news pressures slacken on the late shift, they may be given some publicity or other material to work up into a story for the next day. Or they may be asked to bring up to date obits that have been put into type against the time that famous persons die, do advance stories on parades, speeches, conventions, trials and similar set events, or develop comment by telephone on some news break.

These, of course, are all side issues to the main job of the rewrite battery, which is to write a considerable proportion of the hard news. Throughout the nation there are papers with competent staffs of reporters on which rewrite people are not such dominant figures. But there are many more, particularly in metropolitan areas, where editors depend on their rewrite staff to handle the principal local stories and sometimes others in the state and nation as well.

Feats on Rewrite Writers have performed seemingly incredible feats ever since the practice of writing from someone else's notes began. One of the first, Will Irwin, wrote the magnificent story of the San Francisco earthquake of 1906, "The City That Was," from wire service and other fragmentary reports that came to him in the city room of the *New York Sun*. Trials, conventions, elections, murders, international conferences — every aspect of the news in fact — all have been handled through similar techniques.

Some writers have had the stamina to organize the most complicated kind of news and write a story of 3,000 or 4,000 words in a relatively short time, using no more than a few hours. In extraordinary cases the fastest and most competent of them have been known to do stories of 800 to 1,000 words in about 10 or 12 minutes after taking suitable notes from a reporter. Nor are such electronic virtuosos merely stenographers, spinning words out of a notebook. Even under trying conditions they are expected to do a thoroughly readable job, and usually they are able to deliver.

REWRITE PROCEDURES

There are no blueprints for working on a rewrite desk. No accepted body of procedure has ever been drawn up for this difficult and demanding job. Yet, there are certain things that good writers do to reduce the hazards of processing the news. These are some of them:

Listening to Reporters The old movies on the late-late show have made a burlesque out of the relationship between reporters and writers. Not even so serious and accurate a film as "All the President's Men" and others of that genre have been able to restore the balance. The writer, invariably male, is usually depicted as a character, sometimes with a hat on, who keeps snapping "Yah — yah — yah" into the telephone out of the corner of his mouth, presumably to let the reporter know somebody is on the line. Or he may make nasty remarks about the reporter's professional and personal life.

If this were done on a major story, it would hopelessly jam the delicate machinery of news gathering and news transmission. The rewrite and reporting processes must be handled smoothly, and with a minimum of friction, or they break down. It is not unheard of for a reporter to hang up on an inconsiderate writer, which always requires a lot of explaining and causes unnecessary anguish.

Reporters are trained to tell their stories by beginning with a brief summary, then giving the pertinent details and incidentally spelling out difficult or unusual names and repeating figures. When they finish, they generally ask, "Any questions?" Considerate writers then conclude the communication process by filling in the blanks without coarseness, wisecracks or "yah—yah—yahs."

The wiser and more experienced members of the rewrite bank always remember to ask reporters, if there is time, whether they have suggestions for a lead. But no writer with a professional newspaper background will ever try to tell reporters their business or suggest improved methods for covering a story. These are mainly the business of the editors.

Writing Methods Writers develop their own habits, and no two are alike. All good ones know, as soon as they finish taking notes or reading clips and wire copy, how they would like to start the story. Often, the lead "feels" right the first time it is tried, and the writer then knows the story will pretty well tell itself. If the lead seems awkward, or not quite apposite, most writers today will take another try at it if they have the time. However, no one can do what Lauren (Deak) Lyman did when he wrote the Pulitzer Prize story of the secret departure of the Lindbergh family for England in 1935—13 leads before he hit the "right" one for the *New York Times*.

The first principle of writing on a rewrite desk is to keep copy moving. Under no circumstances can writers delay starting a story, merely because the edition deadline is an hour off, unless directed to do so.

They must be careful of slugs, page numbers, editing directions, and, above all, end marks on stories.

It is easy, of course, to tell an inexperienced young journalist to begin writing. However, few can do it without practice because they do not really have the power of decision that comes with assurance, practice and knowledge. What happens to most beginners is a severe attack of "buck fever" on their first days on rewrite. This is a journalistic ailment that renders its victims helpless and pitiful. The symptoms are a patchwork of false starts, a frantic burst of typing followed by a glazed stare and a depressed feeling of utter frustration.

The only cure is to keep eternally at it until the day comes when the lead magically begins forming on paper or terminal. Nobody can say what alchemy of the mind brings this about, but it does happen to those who are destined to write the nation's newspapers and its wire-service reports. It is given to some to be expert deadline writers after only a few years of all-round experience. Others never learn, although they have deservedly good reputations as journalists, because they are not comfortable when they must write under pressure. It takes a writer with a clear mind, few inhibitions, good technical ability and much self-confidence to do the rewrite job.

Rewriting Clips Most editors maintain that they always have clips from other papers checked before they are rewritten, and some actually manage to do so. The rewriting of clips to get short spreads, routine departmental items, fillers and similar material has been done for a long time and is quite likely to continue. There is at least one major news organization that runs a clip desk, illustrating its reliance on the material developed by others.

There is no question here of news piracy. The line between picking up news that is public property and news that belongs exclusively to one news organization is easily recognized. If the morning paper has a story of a speech by the mayor at the opening of a fair, it is much easier for an evening paper to rewrite the story rather than detach a reporter (at time and one-half cash) to cover a routine event that will be old by the time its first edition goes to press. But if the morning paper or TV has a story that the mayor did not appear at the fair because he is about to undergo an operation for cancer, nobody will dare pick up the story until it has been checked and confirmed. If the story is unconfirmable, the only way it can be used is to credit it to the source that first used it—something a competing newspaper hates to do.

Newspapers generally copyright the contents of each edition and therefore contend that all material in the edition, not otherwise accounted for, belongs to them. Of course it does, in the form in which it appears. No one, though, can copyright the body of human knowledge. Nor can facts be copyrighted that are issued as common property. Some use such facts sooner than others, either through differences of edition time, superior reporting or sheer accident. But all are entitled to use facts that are generally known.

UPDATING

When it becomes necessary to rewrite a clip from another paper or combine such old news with fresh material developed by a reporter or wire service, that is the job of the rewrite battery.

The first effort should be to try to get something fresh on the story by making a telephone call. There is nothing deader than rewriting an old clip that was originally based on an older handout. If writers can get nothing new, they should at least update the news by featuring a different slant and using a lot less of the whole story. The writer who merely repeats a previously published story, or picks up words and phrases at random, does not last very long.

The practice of updating old news is called using a "second-day angle." In the case of the first edition of an afternoon newspaper, which is in the position of using facts already in a morning paper with no new development in sight, the technique is usually to base a lead on the next anticipated turn in the story.

How to Do It If a person's death is announced in a morning paper, for instance, the afternoon paper rewrite could feature the arrangements for the funeral. In the event of a fire or accident the next succeeding angle would be the inevitable investigation. The story of a speech would be followed by the reaction to it, if any, and the announcement of an arrest would be continued with the expected arraignment of the prisoner. The verbs that are dear to the hearts of writers searching for second-day angles in old stories include such workhorses as emerged, confronted, faced, awaited, expected, held, seemed, appeared and others in the general area denoting continuing action. For instance:

> George J. Dockweiler emerged today as a narrow victor in the election for City Council president. Final results from yesterday's election showed he had defeated Ernest Quentin, his Democratic rival, by 22,652 votes. . . .

> Maxim Carpescu, owner of the Hotel Mabuhay, was confronted today with a $50,000 damage suit from a guest who charged she slipped and broke her leg in one of his bathtubs. The complainant, Mrs. Ernestine Garrabrandt, filed suit yesterday. . . .

> Three teen-age robbery suspects faced arraignment today in the theft of $15.22 from a South Side grocery store. They were captured last night. . . .

> The toll in the Southeast Railway wreck stood at ten dead today and appeared likely to go higher. Rescuers searched in the debris all night. . . .

Writers for both print and broadcast media often have to use such methods to update material on which there is nothing new. On many an afternoon paper or wire service overnight cycle the rewritten "today" leads are so smoothly past-tensed that they have to be looked at twice to determine if they are based on breaking news or second-day angles.

Morning papers having the whole day's news for their field are not so dependent on updating the previous story while waiting for a fresh break. The *Associated Press,* too, in recent years, has leaned toward the practice of doing away with second-day angles unless they are necessary. Instead, the AP simply uses the present perfect tense for its second-day leads on overnight files, if there are no new or anticipated developments, and drops the time element (yesterday or last night) into the body of the story.

For instance, if the mayor of a city spoke last night at the opening of the Salvation Army's drive for funds and the speech was reported in the morning newspaper, the afternoon lead could begin:

> Mayor Jones has appealed for funds to help the Salvation Army. Opening the organization's drive for funds last night at the Hotel Astor, the Mayor said, etc. . . .

Or, if the mayor made an appointment several days ago but delayed its announcement until today, the present perfect tense could be used to get around the cumbersome time element as follows:

> Mayor Jones has appointed Walter D. Smith, 52-year-old lawyer, as deputy housing commissioner. The appointment was made Monday and announced today at City Hall. . . .

An improper use of the present perfect tense, however, can confuse and even mislead the reader. If a story is new, it should be indicated by using the word *today* or *yesterday* (or Monday or Tuesday) in the lead instead of resorting to the "something-has-happened" approach, news that could have occurred any time.

It should also be noted that while the present perfect construction is eminently sensible, and is used by the broadcast media, wire services and major newspapers, many editors stubbornly insist that the time element must go in the lead of any straight news story.

To illustrate, the two "something-has-happened" leads about Mayor Jones could also be written as follows for an afternoon newspaper to satisfy a captious editor:

> The annual Salvation Army drive for funds was under way today following an appeal from Mayor Jones. Under the Mayor's leadership, the drive began last night at the Hotel Astor with a dinner. . . .

> Mayor Jones made public today the appointment of Walter D. Smith as deputy housing commissioner. The 52-year-old lawyer was appointed Monday, but the announcement was held up until today at City Hall. . . .

To young journalists who have lived all their lives with radio and television news, the lengths to which some editors go to try to avoid "dating the paper" seem excessive. Nobody really thinks that the public's belief in the credibility of the press will be shored up by shuffling words in updated copy. But old routines die hard.

Mistakes in Second-Day Leads The best rule to follow in "freshening up" an old story is to dig up a few new facts of some significance, or drop the whole business. Old news does not sell either newspapers or news magazines; as for the electronic media, there simply is no time for a news rehash. The continual process of probing and reporting is the best guarantee that a few old-line rewrite tricks will not be used in an effort to disguise the bankruptcy of editorial direction.

True, second-day leads are always useful in anticipating the next development in a breaking story; but if that next development does not come very soon, then an artificial story should not continue to take up space or time in the day's report. Probably the grand-daddy of all second-day leads is the following, which is still sometimes seen in an afternoon paper's obit page that carries death notices published in the morning paper or heard over radio or TV:

> J. Samuel Methfessel, a philanthropist who gave away $20 million, is dead today.

It may be observed, in all truth, that Julius Caesar also is dead today. The stretched second-day lead is, in this case, both an eyesore and an embarrassment to a decent newspaper. It would be much better—if it is absolutely necessary to repeat the obit—to report that Mr. Methfessel died yesterday, to lead with the funeral plans as is usually the case, or to begin with a colorful incident from the philanthropist's life. Almost anything is better than a nonlead, also known in pure New Yorkese as a "nothing lead."

In recent years, a number of editors have tried to do away altogether with the artificial second-day lead and some have made great progress. One of the innovators, Roger Tatarian, while he was editor of the UPI, offered the heretical notion that—in instances where it applied—a reporter's personal story of an event would be well worth publishing. Other devices to do away with the rehash included the use of chronological stories to reconstruct some major news event, the engagement of experts to criticize a cultural event or explain a new development in economics, the increasing trend toward lavishly illustrated stories, and even the publication of reporters' diaries when they are on a long and significant story.

REWRITING WIRE COPY

Since 1918 when the Associated Press obtained an injunction against International News Service to prevent the lifting of AP news, the wire services have been understandably nervous about picking up news from each other. There is nothing in any law, moral code, or sensible procedure that obliges any of the news media to submit tamely to being beaten on a story. If that happens, a recovery must be made by every legitimate means and rewrite is often the vehicle for the job. There is, however, little reason for extensive rewriting of wire copy for newspaper use. The wire services have competent writers of their own. The services usually do a first-class job because it is their business to give their members or clients what they want.

However, some city editors are nervous about permitting AP or UPI copy of local origin to get into their papers, with credit. The same is true of wire copy that originates in any other area that should have been covered by a staff reporter. The question could be asked of the city editor, "Why wire copy? Where was your reporter?"

It is standard practice, of course, to backstop any local story with wire copy even if it is covered by a staff reporter. The writer combines facts, where necessary. Some papers rewrite wire copy on the doubtful premise that "our people do it better." What editors probably want to do is to make certain that their papers differ from the opposition, where it exists. The criticism is widespread that American papers are too standardized because of the overly generous use of wire copy.

In any event, it is the job of the rewrite bank to redo wire copy. These are fairly standard practices on newspapers:

1. *Wire Copy of Local Origin.* In general, such wire copy may be rewritten without credit to the agency unless some special arrangements apply. Except in Washington, it is rare to see a local story credited completely to a wire service.

2. *Regional Wire Rewrite.* In most metropolitan areas it is standard practice for papers to use a dateline on news coming from outside a 50-mile limit from the city of publication. The result is that stories within that area are usually rewritten by the papers.

When wire copy goes into the paper under a dateline, and is not substantially changed, credit must be given to the agency. If the paper adds material of its own and gives the story a different slant, then the wire-service logotype is dropped.

The rule is that when the form and meaning of a wire story are substantially changed so that it is no longer truly the story of the originating agency, the wire-service credit must be removed. This does not apply to the normal processes of editing, or even transposing paragraphs to use a different lead.

3. *National Wire-Copy Rewrite.* Wire-service copy from Washington and abroad is cut so sharply by many small papers (and some big ones) that the result sometimes is practically meaningless. For this reason the European practice of combining wire-service accounts is becoming popular. It is to be regretted. The line, "From Combined Services," is usually a tip-off that a paper has decided to give only bulletin service on events that do not directly help circulation.

4. *Undated Leads.* There is, however, a real need often for combining agency accounts with whatever news a paper's own staff is able to get. This applies to stories that break over a wide area, such as a storm, a major accident or other disaster and similar news that comes in from many points.

Writers perform a unique service by doing what is known as an undated lead (that is, without a dateline). In effect, this is a story of a national event written locally. The following is an example:

> Tornadoes ripped savagely across the Carolinas and Virginia today, killing at least six persons and injuring more than 150 others.
> The deadly black funnels blasted factories, offices and homes along a

150-mile strip. Trees were uprooted. Billboards were ripped up. Rivers flooded their banks. Power and telephone lines sagged in tangles that paralyzed communications.

The undated lead would run for no more than 200 or 300 words, in this type of account, and then break into news stories from various spots that were severely affected. Necessarily, papers in the area might well have more material than wire services so the device of an undated lead would give a broad view of the damage.

Wire services and the broadcast media use such undated leads with even greater frequency than newspapers in handling national or international events that cover a number of major news centers.

5. *Weaving Wire Copy Together.* When AP, UPI, and local copy must be combined without substantial rewrite, it becomes a job for the telegraph, cable or copy desks rather than rewrite.

In such a situation the news desk itself must make the decision on which story to use as the basic account. If AP is to be the main account, then material from UPI and local sources may be bracketed into AP if it is done clearly. For instance, in a general AP story about the Middle East, UPI might have an essential fact which a paper taking both services would want to use. It could be done like this:

(According to UPI, Arab diplomats were meeting secretly at Cairo to try to determine a course of joint action.)

The same kind of treatment might be accorded a fact developed locally that would fit into a basic wire-service account. The principle, in any case, is to set off and clearly identify one wire service from another. AP and UPI cannot be woven together unless they are rewritten with the logotypes of both being removed.

When there are two wire-service stories on the same subject and under the same datelines, naturally they may be worked in together if they are from the same agency. If they are from different agencies, one may be bracketed into the other or one may follow the other, separated by a dash. When a brief elaboration follows a basic story and originates from a different source, as would be the case with a short AP piece from Washington being tacked on a major UPI story from the same city, the additional material is called a "shirttail."

THE OBLIGATION OF TEAMWORK

Writers are only as good as the reporters who turn in the facts. They see through the reporters' eyes, hear through the reporters' ears, go to the scene on reporters' legs. They are the reporters' closest collaborators. Their obligation is to support the reporter.

When there is doubt about an angle of the story, and there is conflicting information, the best rule to follow is the old faithful of journalism: "When in doubt, leave out." But if the broadcast media and the wire services say one thing, and one of the paper's most reputable reporters says another, it is customary for the paper to go with the reporter until he is proved unreliable. The rule is "You don't let your own reporter down." When the reporter has no time to develop background or check on a detail, it is the duty of the writer to send for clips from the library to see if he can save everybody time and effort.

These are some of the things that any writer can do to make the relationship with the reporter smooth, sensible and valuable to the organization. In a word, the obligation is for teamwork.

Chapter 12
Sharpening the Lead

Among the very few things that journalists agree on in a time of social unrest and massive change is the requirement for better writing of the news. And that starts with the lead.

Anybody who has ever worked for the news media dreams of doing the perfect lead which, of course, has never been written. Nor is it likely to be, given the imperfect nature of journalism and the time pressures that hobble the writer. In any generation of journalists, there are not many who can produce sharp, and sometimes original, leads. And this is as true of the broadcast media as it is of print. With the exception of Edward R. Murrow and a handful of others, few have spoken memorable words in television's newscasts.

Artists or Technicians? Too often, news writers become mere word technicians, their art impaled on an editorial spike. They bury ideas under a mound of stale and stilted language. They become bemused by the notion that things must sound official rather than interesting—a professional weakness that is not necessarily limited to journalism.

Writers of little talent and scant judgment load their leads with official sources, official titles, official phrases, even official quotes, and wonder why their work is condemned as long-winded, cumbersome and dull.

The doleful truth is that all the devices of "officialese," which are supposed to impress the public with the importance of the news, seldom do so. The measured cadences of the government report, the sonorous public relations man, and the advertising specialist actually dam the flow of the news when they clutter up a lead.

The superior journalist has always known this and acted accordingly. The ones who know how have never been afraid to use the writers' art to communicate, clarify and even illuminate the news. That art, and the professional ability to use it, are among the greatest needs of journalism today.

A writer, with a few words, can illuminate a scene and convey a mood through sheer artistry. Mary McGrory of the *Washington Star* did it during the Watergate trial of H. R. Haldeman, once President Nixon's chief of staff at the White House, when she set aside the official transcript toward the end of the hearing and began a story:

> On the 30th day of the trial, H. R. Haldeman's eyes are like two burnt holes in a blanket . . .

Nor did Miss McGrory save her best writing for leads. Of another of the Watergate trials, she wrote: "The defendants came on like Chinese wrestlers, bellowing and making hideous faces as if to frighten the prosecutors to death." And when Gerald R. Ford was lifted out of the House of Representatives and plumped down in the White House by appointment, she called him "a blind date who has been proposed to." And this was her description of the House Judiciary Committee's vote to impeach the President:

> The question was really on Richard Nixon's fitness to continue in office. It was answered in an atmosphere of deepest melancholy.

The point is beyond argument. Those who are able to capture the essence of the news in a fine lead also have the talent and the will to demonstrate superior ability in whatever else they write. For all the magic of machines, nothing can match the power of the written word.

GOOD LEADS—AND BAD

In writing a lead, the first instinct of the news technician is to "play it safe," to "hang it on somebody," as the journalistic saying goes. The first instinct of the artist is to tell the story.

Patterns for Leads Suppose a crowd has collected about a wrecked automobile at a street corner outside a park. A passerby stops and taps a truck driver on the arm.

"Hey, Mac. What happened?"

"Two kids got killed. Car jumped the curb."

In effect, the truck driver has performed the same function as a writer summarizing a news event. He has answered the essential question posed for anyone dealing with hard news:

"What happened?"

The news writer could tell it just as plainly and simply. But no! In the ancient news formula so dear to the news technician, the lead must contain both the facts and the source of the facts, whether or not it is necessary to give the source the same prominence as the facts. Under this procedure, assuming the facts in the street incident just referred to came from the police, the traditional news writer would produce something like this:

> Police Chief J. W. Carmichael announced today that two children were killed outside Prospect Park, at Jackson Ave. and 16th St., N.W., when a "recklessly driven" automobile jumped the curb near where they were playing at 2 P.M. and ran them down.

This forty-word horror contains all the bad habits of the traditional news writer. A tragedy such as this need not have its lead embellished with the name of a police chief or a partial quotation from his words of wisdom to make the story sound formal, official and important. The principal reason why these things are put in is that the reporter, writer, or editor—as the case may be—feels the news must be "hung on" some official to make it safe, particularly when there is an allegation of reckless driving.

The routine radio and television broadcasters, sticking to the same procedure, compound the error by "over sourcing" the story. That is, they feel they have to stick to the usual broadcast procedure of giving the title of the source and the official holding the title before proceeding to the news. This is what makes much daytime radio news so deadly. The writing needn't be that bad.

The Crime of Monotony There are two arguments against this kind of writing, whether it is done for newspapers or for the broadcast media. First, it is dull. It makes a monotonous official sing-song out of an event that should arouse a community. Even more important, a question of accuracy in involved. Either the facts are accurately reported, or they are not. If they are accurate, the reporter does not need the police chief to guarantee them in the lead but can refer to him elsewhere. If the story is inaccurate, whatever the police chief says will not excuse the publication of such an account.

The name of the police chief, therefore, should be used only in the context in which it has some meaning. The event, not the source, should be stressed. The source is a secondary consideration. Yet, without some thought and effort, a lead that is shorter but even more prosaic may emerge:

> Two children were killed and 12 others injured today when an automobile hit them outside Prospect Park.

This is the good old news-story blueprint lead for accidents of all types. It has been used for fifty years by lazy or inexpert news writers and could be kept standing, with blanks for the figures of dead and injured, the place and the type of vehicle.

Answering the Question The story does not really attempt to answer the question: "What happened?" It grinds out statistics and records in prosaic language. Yet, in an event of this kind, the news writer should try to take readers to the scene—to let them see it, hear it, smell it. That is possible only by describing the action as is done below:

> Two children at play were killed today when a speeding yellow sports car jumped the curb outside Prospect Park and ran them down. Twelve others in the group were injured.
> Police Chief J. W. Carmichael attributed the tragedy to reckless driving. The driver, slightly injured, was. . . .

Thus, in three sentences totaling 40 words, the facts are packed into the beginning of the story in such a way that the public has a vivid image of what happened and how it happened. Facts—action—color—these are the ingredients of a fast-moving lead on a spot news story.

In place of the humdrum "two killed, twelve hurt" approach, readers are shown how this automobile accident differs from all other automobile accidents. It is a specific, rather than a general, lead. It uses vigorous verbs in the active voice rather than the less appropriate passive voice. It eliminates needless attribution and locations, since it may be assumed that they will be written into the story as it develops. The awkward phrases and needless quotes of the official type of writing in the first lead are also dropped.

In essence this is the difference between sharp leads and dull leads. The dull leads are the product of habit, lazy writing and carelessness. They become weighted down with needless attribution, needless quotes, hackneyed phrases. To make a lead sharp requires a good news sense and a decent command of the English language. Above all, it must make an honest attempt to answer the primary question: "What happened?"

WHAT A LEAD REQUIRES

The happy inspiration that produces a quotable lead seldom strikes the news writer as he struggles with his story, particularly on a deadline.

He has to make do. But every lead, quotable or not, can be accurate, clear and precise.

The Deadly Way There is no more deadly way to begin a story than to use the "so-and-so said" lead when it does not really apply. For instance:

> WASHINGTON (AP)—The White House announced today the submarine Nautilus has completed . . .

It was the announcement that the Nautilus, an atom-powered submarine, had cruised under the ice across the North Pole. The APME Blue Book commented wrathfully:

> Would the man who wrote that lead call up his wife and tell her, "The White House announced today . . ."? Darn right he wouldn't. But here was rugged old habit. Senator Claghorn said . . . Deputy Sheriff Glubb said. . . .
> Why, in Gutenberg's name, deaden the announcement of a thrilling achievement with those wooden words . . . somebody said? What was so important about the source that it had to get in front of the news?

Two more wire services leads, of which the AP itself heartily disapproves, are:

> JERUSALEM (AP)—A dispute between Israel and Syria brought another round of claims and counter-claims today.

> RIO DE JANEIRO (AP)—Diplomatic sources today said African and Asian coffee producing nations will have equal say with Latin American countries in formulating policies of the proposed international coffee organization.

The first lead is so determined to be impartial that it squeezes all the action out of what could have been a significant Middle East story. If a specific case had been described the curse of dullness might have been lifted.

In the second lead the most frayed of all attributive devices is needlessly thrust into a story of interest to all Americans because it concerns their cup of coffee. Sometimes, diplomatic sources must be used to explain that individuals and organizations cannot be named, but it seems ludicrous to use the device in a lead about a cup of coffee.

The wire service leads that follow provide a welcome contrast. Lightness, humor, imagination and originality make these openings sparkle—and if wire services can do it, newspapers most certainly have no excuse not to try:

> WASHINGTON (AP)—The Supreme Court yesterday knocked out the International Boxing Club. By a 5–3 vote the court upheld the decree of a U.S. District Judge ordering the IBC in New York and Chicago to break up its giant prize-fighting empire.

BRIGHTON, England (UPI) — Mrs. Pamela Bransden slowly counted five, snapped into a hypnotic trance, and gave birth to an eight-pound baby. It was as easy as that.

Today she relaxed at her home here, delighted that she had become Britain's first self-hypnosis mother.

LONDON (AP) — Buckingham Palace bounced to the beat until 2 A.M. today and Queen Elizabeth II joined the hired help. It was the annual party for the palace household staff. . . .

LEADS FOR ALL OCCASIONS

The sharp news lead crops up in every conceivable situation. It may be produced by a great name of journalism or by a relative unknown. It may set the stage for the telling of a momentous news story. Or it may describe the weather.

These are some of the classics that are recalled whenever American journalists discuss the fine art of sharpening a lead:

(*By Walter R. Mears, AP special correspondent, on Jimmy Carter's election as President of the United States*)

WASHINGTON — Democrat Jimmy Carter defeated President Ford and won the White House early Wednesday, ending eight years of Republican rule and crowning his long campaign out of the political wilderness.

(*By Lindesay Parrott in the* New York Evening Post *on a St. Patrick's Day parade*)

Fifty thousand Irishmen — by birth, by adoption and by profession — marched up Fifth Avenue today.

(*By H. Allen Smith in the* New York World-Telegram *on a one-sentence routine weather forecast*)

Snow, followed by small boys on sleds.

(*By Harry Ferguson, UPI executive editor, on the execution of Bruno Richard Hauptmann*)

The State of New Jersey, which spent $1,200,000 to capture and convict Bruno Richard Hauptmann, executed him tonight with a penny's worth of electricity.

(*By Hugh Mulligan, AP special correspondent, on a dull day during the Vietnam war*)

SAIGON — Rama Dama Rau, Premier Ky's personal astrologer who predicted five years ago that the war would be over in six months, was drafted today.

(*By Shirley Povich in the* Washington Post *on Don Larsen's perfect World Series game*)

The million-to-one shot came in. Hell froze over. A month of Sundays hit the calendar. Don Larsen today pitched a no-hit, no-run, no-man-reach-first game in a World Series.

(By Robert J. Casey in the Chicago Daily News *describing what happened after a Texas explosion wiped out a public school)*

They're burying a generation today.

(By Charley Williamson in the Yonkers (N.Y.) Herald Statesman *on events in Elmsford, N.Y.)*

Tranquility ran rampant in Elmsford last night. No accidents, no fires, no traffic violations, no wife-beatings and no dog bites.

SOME PRECAUTIONS

In the urge to be bright, clever, or profound an inexperienced writer frequently overlooks the basic reason for a lead—to tell the news. No matter how fine the lead may be, it is not worth using if it fails in this test.

It may not be necessary to use the attribution of the news in the opening sentence, or even in the first two or three paragraphs, but it must be in the story somewhere. The public always has the right to know the source of his news, if it can be divulged. It also should be told why a news source cannot be identified, if that happens to be the case.

Sourcing True, the newspapers directly involved still have refused to give their prime sources in the Watergate inquiry (the *Washington Post*) and the publication of the Pentagon Papers (the *New York Times*). But such cases do not come along very often; in fact, the average journalist can go through a very active and useful career without coming up against such a decision involving government at the highest level.

To reporters who have to deal each day with officials who have a penchant for secrecy, the identification of sources becomes a problem. Unnecessary secrecy should not be tolerated. More indentification of such sources would help reduce journalism's perennial credibility problem.

When the news source is of major importance, it must be featured. No one would consider beginning a Presidential news conference by eliminating the name of the President of the United States. The story would have no meaning. For example, when Japanese bombs began dropping on Pearl Harbor, it was imperative to inform the nation that the announcement came from the White House, that it was genuine, and that it meant we were at war.

QUOTES IN LEADS

Similarly, the effort to sharpen leads by dropping unessential quotes or partial quotes should not be made a pretext for eliminating quotes from the whole story. Quotes frequently are the essential documentation for a lead and should be used immediately after a paraphrase that summarizes them.

The reason why full quotes are seldom used as a lead sentence is that they often do not tell the story as well as a writer's paraphrase. When they do, however, they should be used. The brief statement by President Johnson in 1968 that he would not be a candidate for reelection was widely used as a lead.

Here, however, is a quote lead that takes a lot of explaining:

> "I was furious when that disreputable young man had the audacity to sit in my antique rosewood chair."
>
> That's how tiny, 82-year-old Louise Freeland today described her brush with a gun-toting escaped convict whom she talked into surrendering to Sheriff's officers.

It might have been better to tell what happened, even if the story is a sidebar to a main account, rather than let the quotes stand as the lead.

As for partial quotes in a lead, the tendency has been to dispense with them unless they are the key to the story. It is usually more helpful to use such material as a complete quote to document a paraphrased lead. Too many writers have quoted words and phrases that did not have to be quoted, thus casting doubt on the sense in which they were used. In a story about a Nebraska mass killer who was caught, one AP account said, "Her stepfather had urged Starkweather to 'stay away' from the Bartlett home." The "stay away" quote was meaningless.

These are details—the string around the news package. They must be watched, but they should not be made more important than what is inside the package.

EFFECTIVE NEWS LEADS

Here are some effective leads with a brief discussion of how and why they are used by American newspapers and wire services, which serve both the print and electronic media.

Straight News Leads These leads, frequently called straight news or hard news leads, topped major stories that were widely played in the American news media at the time they occurred. Each effectively summarizes what happened.

> SAIGON (AP)—North Vietnamese and Viet Cong forces marched into Saigon Wednesday and put an abrupt end to a century of Western influence over the often-bloodied Indochina peninsula.

> Desegregation, symbolized by the school bus, came yesterday to the Boston public school system, the oldest in the nation, after nine years of controversy.
>
> —*Boston Globe*

The bloodiest prison revolt in U.S. history was crushed at Attica (N.Y.) Prison yesterday in a hail of gunfire and clouds of tear gas.

But the toll of the five-day rebellion by 1,281 convicts was enormous — 10 prison employees and 28 inmates dead, more than 100 persons injured and much of the prison a shambles.

— *Rochester (N.Y.) Democrat & Chronicle*

All these leads stress action, emphasizing the differing news situations. It would have been easier and briefer, perhaps, to have begun the quake and prison stories with a "deadpan" total of casualties and pinned the news on a source. But the writers in each case were conscious of the unique character of the story and tried to set the stage in the opening sentences.

Such leads may be a phrase, a sentence, several sentences, a paragraph, or several paragraphs but they must delineate the action, the locale, and the meaning of the story or they fail in their effect. The following four-sentence lead meets all these conditions and gives a moving account of a tragedy:

HYDEN, Ky. — It would have been a glorious day for children to make snowmen. The white drifts swept over high boots and the big black tree limbs took on cottony linings.

But there were no sleds and no happy shouts here yesterday. The town of Hyden was trying to cope with a coal mine disaster that ended the lives of 38 men on nearby Hurricane Creek, only two days before the New Year.

— *Louisville Courier-Journal*

The Personal Lead The use of the first person singular used to be discouraged as a reportorial device, except for columnists and other privileged characters in journalism. All that has changed radically. There is now a fetish for reporters' notebook stories, personal views of a developing news situation, even breezy commentaries sometimes disguised as news. This is partly the effect of television, with its stress on the personalities of anchormen and women, and partly a belated tribute to Tom Wolfe, Jimmy Breslin and others who used to call themselves "New Journalists." Sometimes it works, sometimes it doesn't. But it is invariably interesting, as witness the following:

(By Reg Murphy, while editor of the Atlanta Constitution, after being released by a kidnaper)

When the tall, heavy, garishly dressed stranger appeared at the door, it was clear this was trouble.

He said, "I'm Lamont Woods," in a Southern accent quickened by exposure to speech patterns elsewhere.

I let him into my living room for a moment but hustled him out quickly because of the anxiety within him. My wife, Virginia, stayed out of sight but went to the window as we left and noted that he was driving a dark green Ford Torino. She tried for the license plate but couldn't see it.

And so I went driving into the Wednesday dusk with a man we both knew was trouble. Neither of us guessed then that it would amount to 49 hours of terror at the hands of a kidnaper telling a bizarre political tale and demanding $700,000 ransom. . . .

(By John Roderick of the AP upon reaching Peking, the first American journalist to return to his former base since the Communist takeover in 1949)
PEKING — This is my first dispatch from China in 22 years. The news I have to report would have been incredible only a few weeks ago — Americans are welcome in the People's Republic.

The "You" Lead Then there is the "you" lead, which is intended to make a personal appeal to the reader, listener or viewer to get involved in a complicated situation. Here is an example, fairly typical of a trend toward consumerism in the news:

WASHINGTON (UPI) — If you are one of 30 million Americans working for a company with a private pension plan, Congress has given you a new bill of rights. It is the Employee Retirement Income Security Act and it promises that if you have worked long enough to earn a pension, you will receive one at retirement age. Nothing — including bankruptcy, plant closings, dismissal or resignation — can stand in the way.

And here is a personal way of handling what could have been a dull routine paragraph:

Give Ohio back to the Indians? Absolutely, the Indians say.
Testimony before a House appropriations subcommittee showed today that Indian tribes have filed Ohio land claims that total 117 million acres. That is roughly four times the area of the state.

The lead that asks a question and the lead that begins with a quote were far from favorites among old-line editors but both are cropping up with greater frequency today. The urge to vary the beginnings of news stories is great and these are ways of doing it. To be effective, they have to be bright. And a writer cannot always be bright in handling routine news items of the kind cited.

The Contrast Lead One of the stand-bys of feature-type news leads is the contrast lead. In its most familiar form it reports the election of a company president who began as a $4-a-week office boy. Sometimes, to vary the monotony, this saga may be split into two sentences, the first of which refers to the humble beginning and the second to the hero's latest triumph.

This stencil has grown faded with use. Infrequently, a writer with an original turn of mind can adapt the same theme to a new subject with wit and effectiveness. When Van Cliburn, the pianist, returned from a musical triumph in Moscow, one reporter wrote:

Harvey Lavan (Van) Cliburn Jr. of Kilgore, Tex., came home from the Soviet Union yesterday with seventeen pieces of luggage. They bespoke his triumph as a pianist in Moscow. He had three when he went over.

The Delayed Lead Sometimes a situation can be exploited in an interesting way so that an ordinary item stands out. This technique usually results in a delayed lead, inducing the reader to delve several paragraphs into the text to find out what has happened. In the profession, it is called "backing into a story." While it has its advantages, it can also be a headache if it is improperly handled. This effective delayed lead is from *Chicago Today,* before it was merged into the all-day *Chicago Tribune:*

Dwight David Eisenhower once said he would rather win the Medal of Honor than be president. Dwight Harold Johnson — who was named for Dwight Eisenhower — said once to a friend that "winning the medal has changed my life so much I don't know if I'll ever get my head straight again. But I know this. Nobody's a hero forever."

Friday, April 30, in the drizzle of a Detroit dawn, Dwight Johnson died but not as a hero. He died in the emergency room of a Detroit hospital with three bullet wounds in his side and one in his head. He was shot, according to police, by a store owner he had tried to rob.

The Anecdotal Lead Magazines used to begin many articles with anecdotal leads, provided the anecdotes were bright and applicable and not too wasteful of space. The practice seems to have dwindled in recent years in favor of a more direct news approach. However, newspapers have been so eager to pick up pointers from magazines to interest mass audiences that the anecdotal lead has had a rebirth in the news columns. Here is one that began a series on divorce in the *Louisville Sunday Courier-Journal* and *Times:*

David and Kay Craig's two-year-old marriage is a second one for both and their story is one that is being repeated with increasing frequency across the country.

Each was married for the first time at 18. David's marriage lasted through five years and two children. Kay's first marriage ended in divorce after a year and eight months.

The Craigs (not their real name) are among the 13 million Americans who, according to the Census Bureau, at one time or another have been through a divorce. More than four million Americans currently list their marital status as divorced. The rate of divorces in this country has been and still is steadily increasing.

When the anecdote is short and pointed, as this one is, it can be used to bring the reader quickly into a news situation that might not attract his attention if it were routinely written. The trouble with anecdotal leads, as some magazine editors concede, is that they do not really attract as many readers as unusual statements—the basis of good straight news leads.

Besides, few anecdotes are good enough to occupy the amount of Page 1 space that could otherwise be used for a news lead.

Gag Leads There is no sadder face in a newsroom than that of the writer who has just been ordered to write a funny story. When a situation is funny, the practiced news writer lets it tell itself and modestly disclaims credit for a humorous effect. Journalistic humor requires the skilled and practiced hand of an Art Buchwald.

Knowing the limitations, the experienced journalist seldom trifles with humor. As E. B. White of *The New Yorker* once wrote, "Humor can be dissected as a frog can. But the thing dies in the process and the innards are discouraging to any but the pure scientific mind." Nevertheless, the inventive mind of the journalist sometimes is able to produce a delightful change of pace in the dull routine of an average day's news.

Here was what Hal Cooper wrote for the Associated Press when a woman broke her leg trying to climb out of a locked London public toilet:

LONDON—What's a lady do when trapped in a loo?

And Peter Kann of the *Wall Street Journal,* trying to jog the public memory to recall the offshore Chinese islands of Quemoy and Matsu, then held by the Nationalists and shelled every other day by the Communists, wrote:

QUEMOY—Some years back, during an election campaign, former Mississippi Gov. Ross Barnett was asked what he would do about Quemoy and Matsu.

"Appoint them to the fish and game commission," he replied.

But more often than not, the journalist who is asked to be funny on deadline feels like emulating Dorothy Parker; when asked to define humor, she once said, "Every time I tried, I had to go and lie down with a cold wet cloth on my head."

Chapter 13
"Go with What You've Got!"

When I was a young reporter, struggling for just one more fact by making a telephone call a few minutes before the edition deadline, a long-forgotten deskman pointed at the clock and snapped inelegantly, "Go with what you've got!" Without doubt, the additional fact might have helped my story; equally without doubt, it would not have made the paper because my lead would have been too late. I have never forgotten the rough and ungrammatical advice; nor, for that matter, have I let others around me forget it. For whether they write for a newspaper or wire service, radio or television, a news magazine or perhaps even a book publisher, there comes a time when the story must be told as it stands. Otherwise, it may not be told at all.

WRITING BY THE CLOCK

Those who write for deadlines can gauge their efforts by the clock. If they have an hour to do a developing news story, they are in luck. Usually they have about 20 or 30 minutes, enough for an adequate story. Sometimes there are only five or ten minutes to do the job.

And for wire service writers, whatever breaking news they have goes at once if they intend to make the A wire.

The terminals and the computers in the nation's newsrooms have not eliminated the need for this kind of work. Nor have they simplified the process; in one sense, they have added complications because the instructions for the computer, coded in "header" lines at the beginning of the story and at the tops of its various parts, are a bit more intricate than the simple one-word slug. The only point at which the terminal helps at all is in putting the story together, and that applies only to the video display terminals. In any system in which typewriters still play a part, the whole thing still has to be pieced together.

Don't Crowd the Deadline One of the principal rules for newspaper deadline writing always has been not to crowd the deadline except possibly with the lead story. Since copy can be set for printing at a much faster rate with cold type systems, some editors contend that they can include more late-breaking news in their papers under the new dispensation. At times, this is true. But when a story has to be put together in bits and pieces, as will be seen, it still takes time to assemble them for a pasted-up page. And the pagination machine can't help too much. In short, the rule against crowding the deadline is still very much worth observing.

This is the rationale behind the editorial admonition to keep copy moving along in a well-regulated flow:

The separate pages of a well-regulated newspaper move into production on an orderly schedule for placement on the presses. Pages with large advertising layouts are plugged up and sent in early with copy that isn't likely to change, usually feature material. The same is true of most departmental pages, copy for which is prepared well in advance whenever possible. That leaves a cluster of fairly "open" pages plus Page 1 for developing news, but these also must be moved along on schedule if the edition is to go out on time.

That places the burden for deadline production on the writers. Now, few writers have the kind of temperament that will allow them to wait until five or ten minutes before a deadline to begin a lead. Nor can every story be held right to the last second before a deadline. That way lies madness, for when copy piles up on the news desk and pages are jammed in clusters in production, everything goes wrong. Thus, editors must insist on a smooth flow of copy right up to deadline.

Organize! From these observations, it follows that the literary manner of a deadline story is by no means as important as its organization. If a developing story is not done in such a way as to permit easy expansion and contraction, quick handling on a deadline becomes impossible. This is not as difficult to do as it seems. With just a little thought, a reasonable scheme for building almost any developing story can be worked out and maintained under pressure.

This is the writer's business. Sometimes, editors are helpful in making suggestions; generally, however, they leave writers to their own devices for fear that they will freeze on deadline and produce nothing. There is good reason for such editorial concern, for many a story on a rapidly changing event is made up of a succession of new leads, inserts and adds, a constant challenge to the talent and ingenuity of writers.

The wonder is not that such assembly-line writing jobs read as well as they do, but that they are even put together. The process is intricate, and made more so by the terminals. It requires experience, patience, coolness, great skill at organizing detail, and a maximum of staff cooperation.

Of all these, the most important word is, "Organize!"

PARTS OF THE STORY

Developing stories can be no better than their parts because each part is often written separately and out of sequence. To add to the confusion, there is no standard nomenclature for the separate parts although the widespread use of computers eventually will bring that about. For the present, only the wire services have agreed on standard nomenclature to tie their material in with the computers of members or clients. In the following summary, the terms and symbols that are more widely used will be described in order to make sense out of the deadline writing operation. Where terminology differs, the operation itself will be recognizable.

New Lead The term *new lead* is used by many newspapers to denote a new start on a story that is in type. It is often referred to as a *new top,* particularly by the broadcast media. Symbols vary widely and include NL, *Nulead, 1st lead* and 1st LD, the last being the most prevalent for computer use.

Wire services for many years have been accustomed to top their stories with a *1st LD,* then a *2nd LD,* and so forth, which has caused some newspapers to follow the practice. However, the term *new lead* still lingers on and will be used here for illustrative purposes. The difference in terminology arose because newspapers, having specified editions, did not need as many fresh tops as the wire services and broadcast media.

Expanding the New Lead There are two basic numbering systems in wide use in print journalism. (Broadcast scripts, being differently organized, will be discussed in Chapter 16.) Many newspapers number the separate pages of a news story consecutively, while others follow the first take with *1st ADD* and the slug; 2nd ADD, and the slug, up to *4th and Final Add, and the slug,* or however long the story is. The same thing happens when a story is topped.

In topping an existing newspaper story slugged *storm,* for example, a writer would begin with the slug *New Lead Storm* on the first page of copy. This would be followed, under one system, by *New Lead Storm – 2, New Lead Storm – 3,* etc., until the final page, which would be marked at the end: *End New Lead Storm, Pick Up Type,* or *Pick up Earlier.* Under the more cumbersome system of writing adds, which is used by wire services and many large newspapers, *New Lead Storm* would be followed by *1st Add, New Lead Storm, 2nd Add, New Lead Storm,* etc., until the final page when the same kind of concluding instructions would be written.

Fixing the Old Story If the old story is still in the computer memory system and not in the paper, it can be joined to the new lead very simply on a video display terminal with appropriate editing or corrections. What then results, in effect, is a fresh story.

But if the old story is in the paper and the fresh top is for a new edition, then the procedure (and it is the same for cold and hot type) is to make a *markup* to show where the new and old stories fit. The paragraphs to be killed would be indicated. At the paragraph where the new lead is to be joined to the old story, the instruction would be written: *Pick Up after New Lead Storm,* usually shortened to *PU NL Storm.* Computer language varies, so there are varying symbols for the latter.

What Happens under Automation In the automated city room, much of this cumbersome system can be dispensed with. As the case was put recently by Dick Leonard, editor of the *Milwaukee Journal,* a leader in the field of automation, "We can produce type almost instantly and it is easier to reset the story." [1] Thus, for all except stories of greater than normal length, a new lead that is longer than a paragraph or two means that the whole story will be subbed, as the expression goes. For non-automated or partly automated newspapers, wire services and the broadcast media, however, the old system still is almost intact.

How the System Works Here is an example of how a new lead is written down into an existing story so that the two join smoothly at a designated paragraph. The technique is known as "making a clean pick up."

[1] Letter to author 9 August 1976.

THE OLD STORY
Slug: Storm

The first snow storm of the winter swirled over Centerville today, but the Weather Bureau said it would not last long.

With the first flurry of white flakes at 10 A.M., Forecaster F. L. Maynes announced that the snow was expected to melt rapidly. The 10 A.M. temperature was 31 degrees and Maynes said, "It's likely to go up above the freezing point."

But, he went on, "There is just a chance that the temperature will stay just where it is, and if that happens we'll be in for a real storm."

The Street Superintendent, A. R. Ward, took no chances. He put his entire force on a standby basis, tested his snow plows and arranged to hire snow removal trucks if they were needed.

xxx

THE NEW LEAD
Slug: New Lead Storm

An all-day snow storm tied up Centerville today and threatened to reach a depth of 15 inches before tomorrow.

At least five persons died in auto accidents that were attributed to the storm. In the first four hours, up to 2 P.M., the snow reached a depth of four inches.

It snarled traffic, played havoc with bus schedules and made walking dangerous.

The snow crossed up the Weather Bureau. It predicted at first that the snow would change to rain. A later forecast warned of an all-night snow fall that would pile at least 15 inches on the city.

End New Lead Storm
Pick Up Type

In the markup that indicates where the new lead would join the old story, it is clear that the pick-up point in the storm piece is the second paragraph of the old story. The new lead has been written with this in mind. The details of the storm would be added to the part of the story that remains in the paper.

Lead All A *lead all,* as its name implies, tops a new lead. It is seldom used, for it is seldom needed. On newspapers, when a lead all is ordered, it is kept very short and generally is written so that it reads into the old story at the second paragraph. In wire service terminology, a *lead all* is simply a *2nd LD.*

How to Mark up a Story

On the opposite page is a markup. On the left is a story of a subway delay, pasted on a sheet of copy paper. The crossed-out portions show what is to be eliminated. The directions indicate what material is to come for the next edition and where it is to join the old story. The T.R. means "turn rule," an old printing directive that results in a black line, a reminder that the directions must be eliminated when the story is assembled. In any system that uses typewriters, the markup procedure is still useful. On a video display terminal, the whole process can be done on the screen by an editor in short order and the reconstituted story can be reset in a brief time.

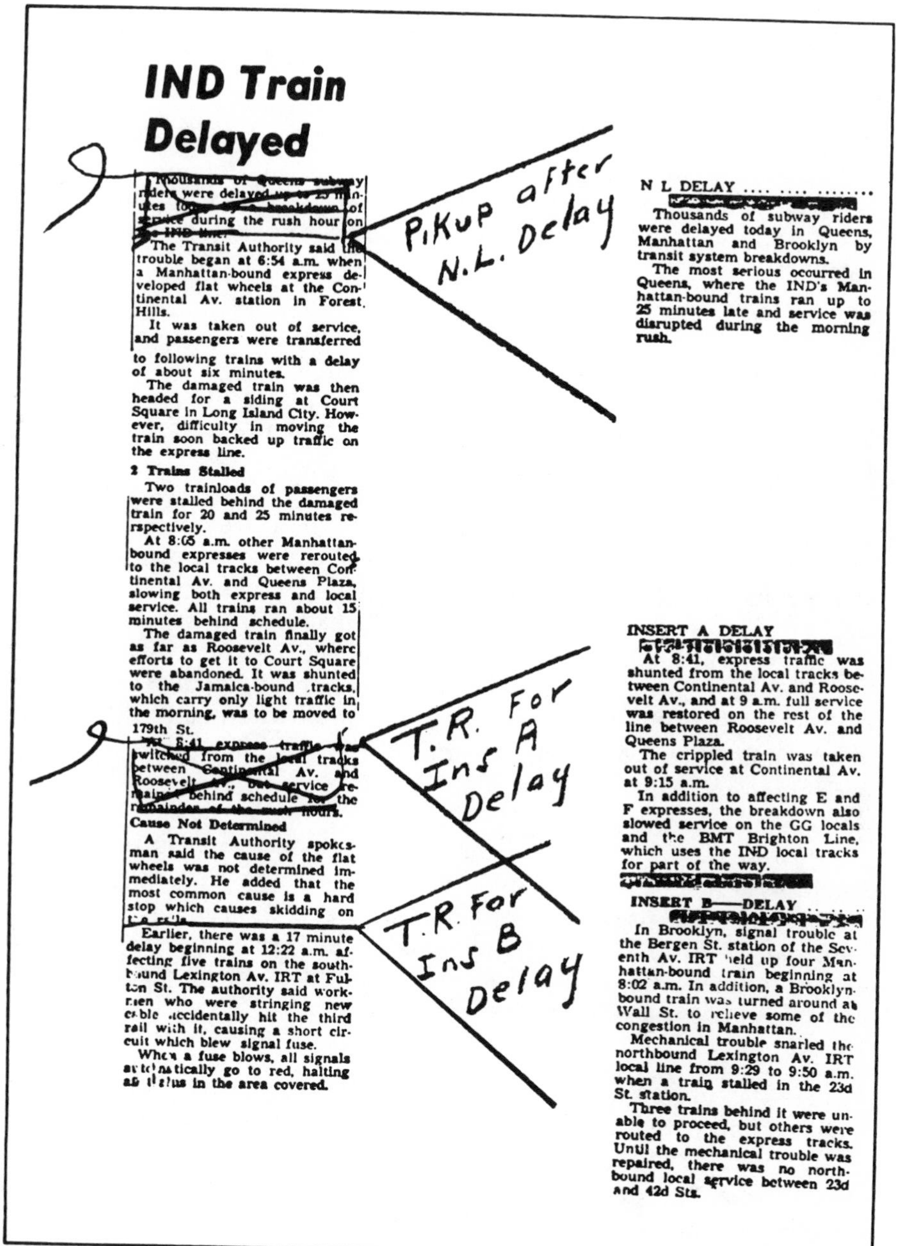

IND Train Delayed

[handwritten: PiKup after N.L. Delay]

Thousands of Queens subway riders were delayed up to 25 minutes to during the rush hour on IND line.

The Transit Authority said the trouble began at 6:54 a.m. when a Manhattan-bound express developed flat wheels at the Continental Av. station in Forest Hills.

It was taken out of service, and passengers were transferred to following trains with a delay of about six minutes.

The damaged train was then headed for a siding at Court Square in Long Island City. However, difficulty in moving the train soon backed up traffic on the express line.

2 Trains Stalled

Two trainloads of passengers were stalled behind the damaged train for 20 and 25 minutes respectively.

At 8:05 a.m. other Manhattan-bound expresses were rerouted to the local tracks between Continental Av. and Queens Plaza, slowing both express and local service. All trains ran about 15 minutes behind schedule.

The damaged train finally got as far as Roosevelt Av., where efforts to get it to Court Square were abandoned. It was shunted to the Jamaica-bound tracks, which carry only light traffic in the morning, was to be moved to 179th St.

[handwritten: T.R. For Ins A Delay]

At 8:41 express traffic was switched from the local tracks between Continental Av. and Roosevelt Av., but service remained behind schedule for the remainder of the rush hours.

Cause Not Determined

A Transit Authority spokesman said the cause of the flat wheels was not determined immediately. He added that the most common cause is a hard stop which causes skidding on the rails.

[handwritten: T.R. For Ins B Delay]

Earlier, there was a 17 minute delay beginning at 12:22 a.m. affecting five trains on the southbound Lexington Av. IRT at Fulton St. The authority said workmen who were stringing new cable accidentally hit the third rail with it, causing a short circuit which blew signal fuse.

When a fuse blows, all signals automatically go to red, halting all trains in the area covered.

N L DELAY ....

Thousands of subway riders were delayed today in Queens, Manhattan and Brooklyn by transit system breakdowns.

The most serious occurred in Queens, where the IND's Manhattan-bound trains ran up to 25 minutes late and service was disrupted during the morning rush.

INSERT A DELAY

At 8:41, express traffic was shunted from the local tracks between Continental Av. and Roosevelt Av., and at 9 a.m. full service was restored on the rest of the line between Roosevelt Av. and Queens Plaza.

The crippled train was taken out of service at Continental Av. at 9:15 a.m.

In addition to affecting E and F expresses, the breakdown also slowed service on the GG locals and the BMT Brighton Line, which uses the IND local tracks for part of the way.

INSERT B——DELAY ....

In Brooklyn, signal trouble at the Bergen St. station of the Seventh Av. IRT held up four Manhattan-bound train beginning at 8:02 a.m. In addition, a Brooklyn-bound train was turned around at Wall St. to relieve some of the congestion in Manhattan.

Mechanical trouble snarled the northbound Lexington Av. IRT local line from 9:29 to 9:50 a.m. when a train stalled in the 23d St. station.

Three trains behind it were unable to proceed, but others were routed to the express tracks. Until the mechanical trouble was repaired, there was no northbound local service between 23d and 42d Sts.

Just about the only time that the *lead all* has any meaning is after a *new lead* has cleared production and a fresh break in the story occurs before the edition deadline. In such cases, the editor has the choice of using a *bulletin,* which sits atop the old story separated by a dash, or a brief new top that is joined to the old story. Generally, it is just as easy to do a *lead all* with the fresh break in a terse paragraph that turns the new material smoothly into the previous story. This is an example:

Lead All Storm
Mayor Wallis closed nearly all city offices today as an all-day snow storm tied up traffic and threatened to reach a 15-inch depth before tomorrow.

End Lead All Storm
Pick Up Type

The markup would indicate the second paragraph of the previous new lead as the pick-up point. If there were time, the Mayor's statement would also be inserted into the story at an appropriate point in order to document the lead all.

Insert An *insert* should be written in such a way that it will fit smoothly into an old story or a new lead. A lazy way of doing this is to begin an insert with the words, "meanwhile," "earlier," or "at the same time." These threadbare devices do not make for a smoothly joined story and should not be used, except on a deadline.

If an insert corrects material previously sent, it merely replaces the old paragraphs. If it adds to or elaborates on detail already in the story, it may be necessary to condense some of the type that is in the paper to make room for the new material. If that is done, it should all be a part of the same insert.

As is the case with a *new lead* or *lead all,* an insert must be accompanied by a markup except on production systems that use video display terminals. This applies to wire service and special copy sent by wire, too. To illustrate what happens to an insert, the mayor's statement, if put into the storm lead above, could easily be substituted for the third paragraph in this manner:

Insert A Storm
The Mayor took his emergency step as the snow snarled traffic, played havoc with bus schedules and made walking dangerous.
"I am asking all city department heads to close their offices by 2:30 P.M., he said, "with the exception of those that are directly concerned with clearing the streets. This is an emergency."

End Insert A Storm

It is a good practice to name succeeding inserts with letters of the alphabet. In this way the sequence of inserts can be maintained, and there is also an automatic check on how many have been written. This is standard newspaper procedure but is not usually followed by wire services.

Add Here is a case of confusion twice compounded. On newspapers that use the *add* system of numbering pages, the addition to a story presents no problem and is merely numbered in sequence to show where it should go. On papers that number the pages of a story consecutively, an *add* also goes at the end. It doesn't help much that some editors drop off the additional "d." But as long as everybody understands the system of the particular paper, it doesn't matter.

In the storm story, for example, the five persons whose deaths were attributed to the storm could be listed by name, age, address and occupation in an *Add Storm.* If greater prominence was desired, the names could be inserted higher in the story.

Bulletin In the days when newsboys hawked newspaper extras and there were devices for inserting news on Page 1 without stopping the presses, the *bulletin* was a big deal in the city room. It is less useful now except when it is part of a wire service report or gives an important sports result. For the ordinary run of news on a newspaper, of what utility are a few words in boldface, topped by headlines in boxcar type, against the continuing narrative that any reader can hear by flipping on his radio or television set? And with pictures, too?

The newspaper bulletin, when used, consists of about 40 or 50 words and is placed on top of the story to which it refers, separated by a dash, if a *new lead* or *lead all* cannot be written. This would be a bulletin for the storm story:

Bulletin Precede Storm
   Two autos collided on snowswept Route 82 north of Centerville at 2:40 P.M. today, killing at least six persons.

3 em dash

End Bulletin Precede Storm

For a fresh news break of overwhelming importance that refers to nothing already in the paper, no editor in his right mind would go with just a few words. For example, if word was received of the death of a President of the United States while an edition was on the press, sufficient detail would be incorporated in a fresh Page 1, technically known as a replate, to make publication something more than a gesture.

Flash A *flash* is reserved for the biggest kind of news, outside the sports pages. It is an attention-calling device to give warning of a major news development. Typically, it consists of a dateline, three or four words, the name of the sender, and the time. It cannot be used in print because it is so curtailed; it always must be followed by either a bulletin or some type of lead. This is a flash:

WASHINGTON – PRESIDENT IS DEAD

It saves time, in the long run, to send a lead rather than a flash because it eliminates one step in the information process. The flash, being shorter, however, is likely to be faster by a few seconds. It also gives control of the wire to the source that has sent the flash and produces silence until a bulletin has been sent.

Kill Another journalistic word that must be used with great care is *kill*. It means that material to which it refers should be destroyed.

On routine corrections it is advisable to use a different term, *eliminate*. For example, in doing a note on the previous storm insert, the correction would be: *"Eliminate Third Pgh New Lead Storm."*

The word kill should be saved for extraordinary situations. The mandatory instructions, *Must Kill,* can never be used on a newspaper without the permission of the editor in charge unless the reporter is filing from a distant point and is on his own.

Sub As its name indicates, a *sub* substitutes for a previous news account. *Sub Weather,* when it is written, would automatically dispose of the weather story that is in the paper. It is a newspaper term and is seldom used in wire-service practice.

Of course, a sub is usually impractical except when it is short and eliminates a short previous account. In the weather story that has been built up over several hours, it would be foolish to do the news a second time for some purely esthetic reason.

The Effect of Terminals All these technicalities used to be of great importance, but terminals and fast printing by photographic means have made it less necessary to transmit the news in dramatic bits and pieces. An entire new story can be sent and put into type now in the time it used to take to handle a short lead.

PIECING THE STORY TOGETHER

When the lead to a long news story is expected shortly before the deadline, much of the story must be written in anticipation of the lead. It must also be done in such a way that, regardless of what happens to shape the lead, the earlier part of the story will fit it.

This technique of writing a story backward is known in newspaper work as doing *B copy* or *B matter.* Some newspapers call it *A copy* or *A matter.* Still others slug it *running* or *lead to come.* For purposes of discussion, *B copy* will be used here as the term for the earlier part of the story that is written in anticipation of a lead to be done a few minutes before the deadline.

Running stories of this type often have to be written in several pieces, one stacked atop the other. The way they are assembled, in the order in which they appear in the paper, is *lead* (not *new lead*), *A copy*, and *B copy*. Often the *A copy* is eliminated as a needless and complicating step so that the two pieces that remain are merely lead and *B copy*.

B Copy This is a process that wastes space. It should be used only on major stories, or on sports events calling for detail that is written before the lead is begun.

It is wasteful because, by its very nature, *B copy* includes material that could easily be chopped from the end of a story. Except when it is done in chronological order, *B copy* contributes little to the art of good news writing.

Its sole justification is that no paper can go with just a paragraph or two on the outcome of an election, convention, trial, contest, sports event, or similar account. Thus, when a writer anticipates the passage of a new law, or a verdict, or an election of a mayor or governor, or the end of a football game, *B copy* is used.

The trick is to write it in such a way that it will easily join to any lead that is written, regardless of how the lead may begin or end. In effect, the documentation for the lead is bound to be in the *B copy* somewhere.

Therefore, the way the *B copy* begins is important. In doing an election story, the *B copy* could start:

B Copy Vote
The polls closed at 7 P.M.
During the day there was a heavy turnout of voters because of the interest in the election and the sunny Fall weather. Much of the vote was in by 2 P.M., but lines still curled away from many a polling place at the closing hour.
The issues. . . .

Similarly, in a news account of a trial, the *B copy* could begin with the hour at which the judge delivered his charge and gave the case to the jury. An account of a convention fight, leading up to the nomination of a particular candidate, could open with a summary of the remarks of the first speaker and continue chronologically. A baseball game, or other sports account, could fit snugly into the *B copy* pattern by beginning with the action and describing it tersely as it develops, inning by inning or quarter by quarter.

Necessarily, the writer must have a fair idea of which names or titles are to appear in the lead of the story. In order to avoid repeating full names and titles, these would be left out of the *B copy* and only the last names of the principal actors would be used. Such considerations would help to make the *B copy* and lead fit smoothly together.

WRITING BACKWARD

To illustrate the process of writing a story backward, here is a curtailed version of a murder trial verdict as done for a newspaper:

B Copy Getty

The verdict climaxed a long, tense day of courtroom drama. Judge Davis gave the case to the jurors at 11:03 A.M. He charged them to acquit Marilou if they believed her to have been insane at the time of the slaying of her invalid father.

"But," said Judge Davis sternly, "if you find Miss Getty knew the nature and quality of her act, and knew in fact that it was wrong, then you must find her guilty of murder in the first degree."

Marilou was pale but calm as the judge gave his charge. Her mother, a large woman in a crumpled black dress, sobbed audibly.

For much of the afternoon, the courtroom was deserted except for a few clerks and newspaper reporters. Then, toward 4 P.M., word sped about the quiet marble corridors of the court house that the jury was coming in.

Thus, the stage was set for the last act of the drama that has fascinated much of the nation for the past two weeks.

The State had tried to prove that Marilou committed a "mercy murder" when she shot and killed her father with his revolver. District Attorney Lindsey hammered away at the theme that no one has a right to take a human life.

Defense Attorney Streator insisted, throughout, that Marilou was insane at the moment she pulled the trigger. He did not contend, however, that she was out of her mind before or afterward.

Marilou was her own best witness. Testifying in her own defense, a tall, plain-looking girl with short brown hair, she kept a small Bible clutched in her hands. She told jurors quite simply that she could remember nothing of the events on the night her father was fatally shot from the moment she entered his room until she came to in her own room.

The State was never able to shake her story.

End B Copy Getty
A Copy Upcoming

A Copy Getty

Marilou, summoned from the hotel where she had been staying, entered the low-ceilinged, oak-paneled courtoom at 4:16 P.M. to hear the verdict. Her mother and her attorney, Arthur P. Streator, were with her. District Attorney Mead Lindsey followed them.

Marilou still wore the simple black dress, with a small gold pin at the throat, in which she had appeared throughout the trial. A small black hat was pulled down over her straight hair. Her shoes were low, black, and flat-heeled.

Her mother was weeping as Judge Davis entered, short, red-faced, but grave. A few moments later the jury filed in to take its place and the court-room waited tensely for the words that determined Marilou's fate.

End A Copy Getty
Pick Up B Copy

FLASH MARILOU GETTY ACQUITTED GRIMMEL 4:32 PM

Lead Getty

Marilou Getty was acquitted today of the "mercy murder" of her father.

A jury of four men and eight women, most of them in tears, set the tall, 19-year-old choir singer free at 4:31 P.M. They had deliberated five hours and 28 minutes.

Marilou embraced her weeping mother, Mrs. Catherine Getty, and said:

"I was sure they would not find me guilty."

Supreme Court Judge Myron J. Davis dismissed the jurors but did not thank them for their services. To Marilou he said gruffly,

"You are free to go home with your mother. Try to take care of her."

By its verdict the jury showed that it had believed Marilou's story that she was temporarily insane when she fatally shot her father, Morgan R. Getty, a builder who doctors had said would die in a month of cancer. The slaying occurred last October at the Getty home, 365 Baldur Place.

End Lead Getty
Pick Up A Copy Getty, Then B Copy

Dummy Leads In the story of the Getty verdict alternate paragraph leads would have been prepared to cover several possibilities if the paper had been closer to its deadline and unable to wait for a "live" lead from the courtroom. On receipt of the flash the correct *dummy lead* would have been placed atop the A Copy and sent to production with previously prepared headlines to match. Here is how some of the dummy leads would have looked:

Lead Getty — Acquit — Hold for Release

A Supreme Court jury today acquitted Marilou Getty, 19, of the "mercy murder" of her cancer-stricken father, Morgan R. Getty, last October 24.

End Lead Getty — Acquit — Hold for Release

Lead Getty — 1st Degree Murder — Hold for Release

Marilou Getty, 19, was found guilty of first degree murder in Supreme Court today for the "mercy slaying" of her cancer-stricken father, Morgan R. Getty, last October 24.

End Lead Getty — 1st Degree Murder — Hold for Release

Of course other dummy leads would also be prepared to follow the various additional contingencies. The practice, however, is not as wide-spread as it once was because it gives the public nothing it hasn't al-ready received from the broadcast media, and very little of that. In the long run, dummy leads—if overused—are self-defeating because they promise the public more than they actually deliver. It would be far better, many editors argue, for newspapers to wait and deliver a complete account rather than go out with a few lines.

The Competitive Urge Once upon a time newspapers were given to such practices as fudge boxes, a space on Page 1 in which late news could be inserted without stopping the presses, and cold plating, in which alternative plates for Page 1 would be cast in advance based on the outcome of a sports contest or political race in which there was great interest. Very little of that is done nowadays, except in the "Stop Press" boxes on the first page of English language papers abroad. But American newspapers still have the urge to compete with the broadcast media, although not on spot news.

When the press originates its own news, particularly investigative material, broadcasters can't do much about it except to pick it up if they can't deny it. But newspapers also try to be complete on breaking news, especially sports contests. Editors feel foolish when their paper has to carry an incomplete game. They know that anybody who is interested can watch television and find out how it ended. So the dummy lead process still is strong on the sports page. Here, leads are written in such a way that they will stand regardless of the outcome— "State U faced the Aggies today for the Big 7 championship, etc." Then the score is slipped into the second paragraph in one line and the headline is based on it.

The same procedure can be used in almost any type of contest in which there is a winner and loser, but few editors bother with it outside the sports page. In the wonderful world of brawn, time sometimes seems to stand still. There are better and far more valid ways in which the print media can compete with broadcast journalism.

Chapter 14
Human Interest in the News

There is always a place for human interest in the news, but readers sometimes have to search the pages of their newspapers to find it. Actually, more of it is to be seen on television. For while newspaper editors are constantly declaring their fealty to the "human side of the news" or the "human angle," many of them are still so addicted to the daily run of hard news that lighter and more readable pieces take second and third place on their schedules. And hard news is the strength of television, although some broadcasters don't think so.

The editorial dilemma is not particularly new. What makes it of current importance is the emphasis on maintaining newspaper circulation and using news space more efficiently to combat rising costs of newsprint. Almost automatically, that would serve to shove so-called secondary news deeper on the editorial spike if it were not for fear of the "readership crisis," which is annually proclaimed at numerous editorial conferences.

The result, over the years, has been to blur the distinction between hard news and features on many newspapers, with each taking on some of the characteristics of the other. A few have stood firmly for the traditional presentation of news, mostly with disastrous results for the circulation department and eventually the newspaper itself. And a handful of innovators, led by the immensely successful *Wall Street Journal*, have tossed all the rule books out of the city room windows and started afresh.

A DIFFERENT PATTERN

A successful British journalist said recently, "I'll write on anything that appeals to me and readers seem to like it — the pleasures of bicycling in the Highlands or the rotten mess we've made of the Thames."

The Un-Formula If there is any formula at all to the pattern that the *Wall Street Journal* has evolved, that's it. There is a particular flair to this Page 1 *Journal* story on matchbooks:

> Like other U.S. Presidents, Franklin D. Roosevelt kept on hand a supply of presidential matchbooks. But every time he held a press conference, he was cleaned out of matches. In exasperation, he had a batch of matchbooks inscribed: Stolen from Franklin D. Roosevelt.
> Matchbooks certainly get around. Americans burn out roughly 20 billion books of matches a year. Three out of four adults use them, lighting a match an average of once every 45 minutes, day and night. With that kind of ubiquity, the little folders are among the most widely read books in the world. They are useful, of course, for more than just lighting up . . .

The story turned out to be an interesting, thoroughly researched piece that justified the judgment of the *Journal*'s editors in placing it on their first page. But it isn't story values alone that give the *Journal* a vivid touch of originality that pleases 1.5 million purchasers daily at 25 cents a copy. The major hard news stories in the paper seldom read like formula copy liberally sprinkled with "he said, he said," and officialese documentation.

Better Reading The *Journal*'s main story in the same issue was about an investigation of the brewing industry that could have begun with a traditional lead as follows:

> Federal officials said today they were investigating the multi-billion-dollar beer industry for bribery and kickbacks to boost business.

The *Journal* did it differently, beginning with a quote from an anonymous source, something that would have given traditional editors the jitters:

"The name of the game was sales, pure and simple. You did what you had to do to get the business.

"A lot of it was small stuff, like an occasional free keg of beer or a case of glasses for a guy who had a bar, but it got a lot bigger, too. If what you were doing was wrong, well, at least you knew you had a lot of company."

The speaker is a former sales executive for a major U.S. brewery. His comments help illustrate why Federal agencies have marked the multi-billion-dollar beer industry as the first major target in their drive to extend their exposure of foreign bribery and kickbacks by American corporations to the U.S. itself.

The broadest of these inquiries is being conducted by the Securities and Exchange Commission . . .[1]

Laying It on the Line If the *Journal* is given credit for starting a livelier and more readable trend in writing news, and using the "human element" for something more than stories about the zoo, then others may be equally complimented for having the gumption to follow. Here is the way the *Chicago Tribune* began an expose that won the 1976 Pulitzer Prize for General Local Reporting:

It is a hidden disaster, man-made but more destructive to America's cities and towns than any tornado, hurricane or earthquake on record.

In less than seven years it has cut a swath through hundreds of communities the length and breadth of the nation, leaving $4 billion worth of housing destroyed in its wake.

It is a bureaucratic machine set up in Washington to provide housing for the nation's poor that has instead run off course and mangled the homes and lives of thousands of families.

Evidence of the destruction is easy to spot when you know where to look . . .

HUMAN INTEREST – OLD STYLE AND NEW

What appears to be emerging, among the more innovative newspapers in the country, is a pattern of writing that takes advantage of the qualities that were known in the city room for more than a century as "human interest."

The Feature Treatment One of the most perceptive of American journalists, Barry Bingham Sr., of the *Louisville Courier-Journal* and *Times,* has stated the case this way:

"Too many papers still depend on 'hot flashes and late bulletins.' Some otherwise healthy editors suffer from headlineitis, a hangover from past days of hectic street-sale competition.

[1] Both *Journal* stories were published 10 June 1976.

"I'm convinced that readers are showing a failure of appetite, brought on by too much hard, tough, indigestible news. But I want to make the main course—the news—more palatable instead of switching to double portions of cream puffs for dessert.

"More comics? No. More features? No, unless (it) means a feature treatment of solid news. That I go for."

What Bingham and other editors seek to do is to inject the sources of human interest into the news. It is being done now by some more progressive newspapers, large and small, in all parts of the country. What it amounts to is a revival of personal journalism, but with a difference. Instead of the editor and publisher projecting his personality before the public, that enormous privilege is now being given to the men and women of the working press, as it is called.

The Old Style The old editorial division separated stories of special human appeal, but without any particular time element, from the reporting of current events and opinion-molding.

Hard or straight news, as the term implies, was the undiluted record of immediate events written in an impersonal style by all except reporters of special eminence. Features, the generic name for any department, illustration or news account outside the breaking news, could be written almost as fancy dictated. This, it should be remembered, was the age of the sob story.

In that era, hard-boiled editors roughly defined human interest as 'blood, money and broads." The early tabloids proceeded on the general theory that people were interested in reading about pretty girls, babies and animals. As a result, the human interest feature of forty or fifty years ago was likely to be a sensational blood-and-thunder yarn, a Sunday "gee-whiz" story about the electric eel, or some mild little piece of time copy (stories that can be run any old time). Of course, good features were done then, too, but it generally took somebody of the stature of Frank Ward O'Malley of the *New York Sun* to put them over. The sob stories dripped all over Page 1.

And the New Sometimes, change comes to journalism with agonizing slowness. And that was the case with the traditional form of news writing, when a deadpan style was considered standard for all except the few free spirits who wrote as they pleased and got away with it.

The weekly news magazines were the first to make a success out of a less stylized and more personal appeal in writing news. Then came television (radio never did break out of the straight news mold, except by accident). And what has happened with the increasing popularity and influence of television news very largely accounts for the willingness of newspapers to try something different.

It is, however, going to take awhile for the new trend to develop. The hard news habit is very difficult to break.

The Rainbow of Human Interest In today's journalism, the rainbow of human interest arches over the entire field. The news magazines and the remaining magazines of general circulation usually put on the slickest performance as a group. The well-researched, brightly written magazine piece is so far ahead of the old newspaper feature that comparison would be shameful. And in mini-documentaries on the nightly news, the television writers have shown both originality and imagination in projecting events before the public.

The newspapers, therefore, are late converts to the new dispensation and must strive to catch up. Fortunately, the newest generation of journalists has few inhibitions and little feeling for tradition. Demonstrably, the talent for a better kind of news writing is available.

Better Techniques Basically, what is happening is that more and more elements of human interest are being included in news articles that used to be handled in traditional style. The feature patterns, the things that have a special appeal for people, are being included in what was once straight news, deadpanned from beginning to end.

One element of the improved technique is to fit the event into an understandable context. If there is a teen-age gang war on the edge of town, for example, it makes better sense to tell the story in terms of what has happened to individual boys than to wrap up the whole business in a police catch-all about an impersonal mass. And if Americans are being evacuated from a war-torn country in the Mideast, the story of a young mother and child who are forced from their home is of more concern than the flight of hundreds of faceless refugees.

This takes a lot more effort, a great deal of additional reporting, some thought about how to approach a difficult story in the telling, and the willingness of editors to give space to a different approach. It can't be done with the waving of an editorial wand.

Some Precautions This is not to say that hard news must give way to the feature approach in all situations. That would make no sense. For there is no guarantee that all events will be made clearer to the public by writing about them in personal and more colorful terms.

While human interest can add to reader interest, it also entails the inevitable risk of distortion of news values. Little is to be gained, for example, by attempting to report a complicated negotiation with the Russians in terms of a Rotary Club meeting or to attempt to make a new type of missile understandable on the basis of Junior's Fourth of July rocket.

The greatest criticism of journalism is not that it overcomplicates, but that it oversimplifies. One is as great a journalistic fault as the other. Simple things have to be simply told, it is true. But there is no substitute for the explanations that must be made of complicated things to give them depth and meaning.

The human interest touch, therefore, has its uses and its limits.

It can illuminate the news at many levels if it is applied with taste and discrimination in appropriate situations, but nothing is likely to be more embarrassing to a reporter than a mawkish personal story where the news calls for clear writing and a detached position.

Writers must pick the right spot for mingling hard news values with human interest. Sometimes it isn't easy to do. The choice of a journalistic method can only be dictated by knowledge and experience in the field, based on superior judgment.

THE "NEW JOURNALISM"

American journalism is replete with discussions of the "new journalist," going back to Benjamin Franklin, the father of us all. James Gordon Bennett and his son had their era. So did Horace Greeley. And Joseph Pulitzer came on like an angry revolutionary tearing and clawing at the Establishment of his day. Nobody familiar with American journalism needs to be reminded of the contributions of the "Muckrakers," or of the public adulation that came to such idols of newspaper work as Richard Harding Davis.

The News Magazines All of these, their rivals and followers, made distinct contributions to the development of an informed public and to their own craft as well. But very little was done to try to improve the quality of writing in American journalism until the weekly news magazines broke out of the traditional mold in the 1920s. Many of the early experiments with what came to be known as *Timelanguage* were grotesque and aroused scornful critical laughter, but at least the newsbook writers tried to be different. Eventually, they succeeded.

The influence of the news weeklies on journalism as a whole has gone beyond style, however. The old *Time* formula for writing, as popularized by Briton Hadden, was to "start anywhere, go somewhere, then stop." Essentially, this is what newsbook writers still do today. Despite all the complaints about hot-house language, slanting, editorializing in the news columns and dressing up nonessential items to titillate the public, the news magazines thrive on what the journalists of an earlier day called simply "feature writing." And usually, they do it very well indeed—so well that they have numerous imitators in daily newspaper work.

Newest of the New It is scarcely a surprise that the latest crop of "New Journalists" has attracted attention with innovative writing and an inventive choice of the subject matter. This was the lead with which Tom Wolfe, a former *New York Herald Tribune* reporter, caught the attention of a magazine editor with his first article in the mid-1960s:

> There Goes (Varoom! Varoom!) That Kandy-Kolored (Thphhhhhh!) Tangerine-Flake Streamline Baby (Rahghhh!) Around the Bend (Brummmmmmmmmmmmm) . . .

Was this Wolfe some kind of nut—a freak cast up on a fashionable beach by the crazy rip-tide of daily journalism? Indeed not! Thomas Kennerly Wolfe Jr. earned a Ph.D. in American Studies at Yale in 1957 and for more than two decades has been an active and respected journalist in New York. But like other first-rate professionals such as Gay Talese and Jimmy Breslin, he had tired of doing the same old pieces in the same old way. Together they began breaking new ground, mostly in magazines rather than newspapers, where they found a readier reception. And very soon they were joined by the most eminent, and probably the most erratic, of living American novelists, Norman Mailer.

Fact as Fiction What these journalists and their imitators often do is to cast themselves in the guise of writers of highly impressionistic fiction and assume that they have the skill, the judgment and the will power to spin out their narratives as storytellers without actually lying.

The device is interesting and useful at times, but it can be overdone. When Gail Sheehy did a factual article about a prostitute named "Redpants" for *New York* magazine, the *Wall Street Journal* quite accurately reported that there was no "Redpants"—that Miss Sheehy, a "New Journalist," had created a composite character. Her editor eliminated that necessary explanation, however, as he later admitted in an effort to defend her from criticism. As a result, the credibility of the "New Journalists" came under heavy and sometimes unfair attack, but they appear to have survived without much damage.

Tom Wolfe's journalism really belongs in the realm of the magazine and the nonfiction book because it takes so much research to produce anything of consequence. As Wolfe puts the problem:

> You are after not just facts, but scenes—to pull it off you have to stay with the people you are writing about for long stretches. You may have to stay with them days, weeks, even months—long enough so that you are actually there when revealing scenes take place in their lives. You have to be constantly on the alert for chance remarks, odd details, quirks, curios, anything that may serve to bring a scene alive when you're writing—as well as long stretches of dialogue.

The description applies to Woodward and Bernstein's two books about the Nixon Presidency, the more florid works of Norman Mailer when he ventures into journalism (*The Armies of the Night*), Talese's Honor Thy Father, Truman Capote's re-creation of murder, In Cold Blood, and Jimmy Breslin's daily newspaper work.

All may not be right with the newest of the "New Journalists." But all is not wrong with them, either. They have shaken up the more conservative newspaper field.

THE NEWS FEATURE

Almost anything can be turned into an interesting news feature if the writer knows how. It isn't necessary to be catalogued as a "New Journalist" or an "Old Journalist," a freak or a publicist, to produce something that people will want to read. Here is the beginning of a feature about a South Carolinian by William Montalbano of the *Miami Herald* that could have wound up on the financial page in less skillful hands:

> KUWAIT CITY, Kuwait—After World War II, when hardly anybody had heard of Kuwait, Dick Williamson liked to go duck hunting on Kiawah Island off the South Carolina coast. He remembered Kiawah fondly in a long financial career that took him far from his native Columbia, and last year he helped Kuwait buy the island.
>
> Today, Williamson, 47, is a key adviser to the Kuwait Investment Co., a quasi-governmental organization whose job is to find lucrative investment for Kuwait's surplus oil dollars. In recent months Kiawah ($17.4 million) and an Atlanta hotel have seemed small change compared with the nearly half-billion dollars Kuwait has spent for a British real estate company and the controlling interest in the West German manufacturer of Mercedes Benz.
>
> Williamson's Carolina drawl, his business suit and tie, seem wryly misplaced in post offices here where fellow executives speak an English polished at the Harvard Business School and come to work in the traditional Kuwaiti gown (dishdahiya) and head-dress (kufiya). To Williamson, who has been in Kuwait more than five years, such garb is routine for Arab executives . . .

"A Janitor in Surgery" When the *Chicago Tribune* wanted to expose a local hospital after a lengthy investigation, the old-fashioned accusatory lead listing a compendium of alleged crimes was just about the last thing the editors would have ordered. It wasn't that kind of story, although, as matters turned out, there was a great deal wrong with the hospital. But the lead began quietly with the emphasis on a human problem—a little girl in surgery:

> It is a critical period for the 6-year-old girl lying in an anesthetized sleep on the operating table in von Solbrig Memorial Hospital. Only

minutes ago she had undergone two operations, a tonsillectomy and surgical repair of a hernia.

But the only other person in the operating room is a $2-an-hour janitor, in his unsanitary working clothes, who has just put down his mop in the corridor outside and rushed in to watch over the young patient at the request of a nurse.

The surgeon, the nurse, the nurses' aides and the anesthesiologist have all gone. And for several moments, until the nurse returns to relieve him, the janitor is in charge of the patient.

The janitor is Tribune Task Force reporter William Gaines, who found himself summoned into the operating room as many as six times in a single week, often in soiled clothing, to assist patients at Chicago's only for-profit general hospital.

Gaines was a member of the Task Force investigating team that found the 83-bed hospital at 6500 S. Pulaski Rd. poorly maintained, understaffed, and in apparent violation of medical standards and city and state regulations . . .

The rest of the story, the first in a series, developed the shortcomings of the hospital over almost four columns with numerous sidebars. After the series concluded, the hospital was closed.

"Honey! He's Coming Right at Me!" Dial Torgerson of the *Los Angeles Times* was tired of writing about automobile accidents in the same old way. He wanted to do something different and his editors decided to let him try. This was how his emotion-filled Page 1 story opened:

Norman Goodwin's wife, Elizabeth, was talking about their pleasant evening and the stero was playing in Goodwin's Cadillac. They were headed up the Golden State Freeway toward their Van Nuys home.

Suddenly—at 3:30 A.M. Sunday—Goodwin realized that something looked funny about the headlights he saw up ahead. He had been seeing cars pass on the other side of the chain-link center divider since he had swung off north from the Pasadena Freeway.

But these lights were too bright. Goodwin realized why: they were on his side of the fence.

"Honey!" he told his wife. "He's coming right at me! He's on our side!"

For Goodwin, who is 48, it was the most terrifying sight he has ever seen—a freeway driver's nightmare. He was driving north at 60 m.p.h. in the fast lane and another car was heading south in the same lane, right at him.

Within seconds of Goodwin's cry of alarm, three persons were dead, three others injured, one car was torn into hundreds of pieces, three others were demolished, and the northbound Golden State Freeway was closed by wreckage. . . .

There followed a three-column account of how the Goodwins had managed to escape death, and how cars that were behind them had crashed into the wrong-way vehicle. The objective was to explain how it was possible, despite five years' work by accident prevention authorities, for a car to enter the wrong lane on a freeway—and to prevent other such accidents.

SUBJECTS OF HUMAN INTEREST

The field of human interest is broadening constantly. What was once a three-line item about an arrival or departure is now a travel story, based on the increasing yearning of Americans for sights of far places. Advance stories for holidays are mainly given over to reports of cultural and entertainment attractions in and out of town. Anniversaries, especially those of older persons, often include accounts of activities in retirement. Much of the news of education and science, which once would have seemed forbidding, has become of great interest. Anything of substance in the fields of housing, homemaking and gardening commands a large audience. These are some of the results of the steady rise in the standard of living in the United States and the increase in leisure time for millions of Americans.

Expanding News Fronts Issues that would have been ignored by old-time editors are news today and command wide public attention. The energy crisis is big news. The touchy field of consumer news also has been opened up, although newspapers are proceeding with caution on the local front. But for understandable reasons, national consumer news gets a big play, as witness the following:

> WASHINGTON (UPI)—Estrogen drugs used by five million women going through menopause don't keep women feeling young or maintain their soft skin, the Food and Drug Administration said yesterday.
> Nor have the drugs been shown effective in treating simple nervousness during menopause, the agency added. It ordered a crackdown on the way such drugs are labeled, citing scientific reports linking them to cancer of the uterus and birth defects.
> The FDA ordered estrogen manufacturers to print and distribute revised package labeling for physicians within 60 days. It also proposed a special brochure on the risks and benefits of estrogens for distribution to women when they have prescriptions filled.

Travel is another expanding news field. Americans once talked of "the funny little people" they saw abroad. But now they are being obliged to put up with the foreign tourist who stares at them. Tourism in the United States, too, has become respectable and even desirable with the fall in the value of the dollar. But somehow, the features about foreign tourists still display a typically American point of view, as witness the following beginning:

A month ago, Kunio L. Kudos wrote from Nagoya, Japan, seeking permission to visit the Hollyhock House in Hollywood and be allowed to "pollute your good morning by noise, running around in your house, crying with exclamation and photoing."

Monday he showed up with 68 architects and architectural students armed with 68 cameras in a blitz of clicks, whirs and flashes.

Kudos, who had assumed the historic house designed by Frank Lloyd Wright was a private residence, learned it is not only owned by the city but also is being refurbished at a cost of about $500,000.

This is more than we expected," he said of the house and its panoramic view from Barnsdall Park . . .

—Los Angeles Times

The Drama of the Familiar Nobody in journalism is going to escape from the drama of the familiar, however. No matter how many times New York has been described as the "dirtiest city in the world," which it is, the feature goes on and on. And somebody always has to do the St. Patrick's Day Parade, the Easter Parade, the various types of Christmas stories, the features about suffocating traffic on week-days and during rush hours, and all the other time-worn material that is deposited on the nations' doorsteps with the regularity of an incoming tide. Now and then a writer is able to find something just a little different, as the following Santa Claus story shows:

Take it from Nathan Doan: In the Santa Claus business, there are a lot of small things the average person does not think about.

What do you say to a kid who wants a real television station for Christmas? How big is a reindeer? Why the gloves? Do you stand or sit on a parade float?

And then there is the Ho-Ho-Ho bit. Not just anybody with a big stomach and a white beard can master that element of Clausiana.

How does the conscientious Santa learn the tricks of the trade? He goes to school, of course—the Charles W. Howard Santa Claus School in Albion, N.Y., run by Nathan Doan of Bay City, Mich. For a tuition fee (plus room and board) and one week of his time every October, the would-be Santa can learn all sorts of things the average person does not think about.

"We start right out with the basics," Doan said in a telephone interview. "For example, one of the very first things a man must learn is that he has to regulate his kidneys for a day before he rides a float in a parade."

The 15 or so student Santas who matriculate at Albion in October every year learn that a good Santa never stands on a float. He always sits . . .

—Charlotte Observer

And then, there is Father's Day. Is there a journalist who has not faced typewriter or terminal with a hopeless sigh before trying to pump up interest in a feature so familiar? Peter Courtros did a little legwork, which also helps, and came up with something a bit out of the ordinary, which he began as follows:

A high pop is a baseball swatting rain out of low-hanging clouds. A high pop is an ice cream on a stick carried by a tall person.

On the third Sunday of every June, a high pop is Everyman's Father achieving Superman status by federal fiat (Congress made Father's Day a holiday in 1914). Also by virtue of his children's adulation which may take the form of hugs and kisses or a tie that matches nothing in his wardrobe or a phone call from a distant place, which sometimes comes collect.

Down at Washington Square yesterday—under the arch, in the shadow of the statue of the father of our country—a cadre of fathers walked around in a small picket line of sorts, carrying placards and otherwise letting it be known that Father's Day may be just great but who's paying attention to fathers' daze? "Fathers Do More Than Take Out Garbage," complained one sign . . .

—New York Daily News

FAMILY LIFE

The feature based on family interests and family life also takes imaginative reporting and writing to lift an otherwise commonplace situation to the plane of general reader interest. Such a story was produced out of an unpromising scientific survey on the extent of permissible activity for cardiac patients and other cripples. It follows in part:

There's some scientific support for the plaint of the housewife who insists housework is harder than holding a job.

Measurements show that household chores require as much energy expenditure as some heavy male occupations.

Making beds takes more effort than shoe repairing.

Cleaning windows takes 3.7 calories per minute of energy expenditure. Driving a taxi takes 2.8 calories.

Wringing out wash or hanging it is more taxing than plowing with a tractor.

Kneading dough is more work than putting TV parts together.

"Housework is no light occupation," says Dr. Edward E. Gordon of Michael Reese Hospital here, director of the department of physical medicine. "Studies of chores bear out the housewife's opinion that she works harder than her white-collar husband."

Dr. Gordon has been measuring energy expenditures of various tasks as a means of advising cardiacs and other cripples as to the extent of their permissible activities.

—Chicago Daily News

ASSORTED SUBJECTS

Now and then a writer on a regular beat, such as politics or science, will come across an attractive story situation and devote both time and effort to the development of such a feature.

An Off-Beat Story During Jimmy Carter's 1976 Presidential campaign, such things happened frequently. Here is an example of the off-beat political story:

> PLAINS, Ga. — Her father thinks she's spoiled, but her mother disagrees.
>
> "Well, I'd say my Mama was right," she said with a drawl and a little girl's giggle. "Anyway, the men all say that but the women — they think I'm cute."
>
> Amy Carter is that, all right — a freckle-faced, strawberry blonde with a quick smile, a perky nose and silver blue eyes that give away all her secrets.
>
> But she is also the daughter of Jimmy Carter, and like the progeny of most public people, she is both the beneficiary and victim of her father's rapid rise to fame.
>
> Not since 1960 has the Presidential nominee of either major party had a young child — Caroline Kennedy was three years old when her father sought the office — and the contrasts now appearing in Amy's young life seem both familiar and understandable . . .
>
> ©1976 *The New York Times* Co. Reprinted by permission.

Places and Things The fastest airplane, the newest ship, the biggest rocket, the last train — all these have a romantic interest for people the world over. So do the places that are famous and tinged with the golden glow of history — the Statue of Liberty, the United Nations, Broadway and the skyscrapers of New York; the white hills of San Francisco and the Golden Gate; the White House, the Capitol and the massive monuments of Washington, D. C.; the familiar sounds and sights and smells of the cities of foreign lands.

Such stories are written over and over, seen in new ways by different writers. In any town in the nation the places and the things that are dear to people become subjects for features whenever a news peg makes a story appropriate. Here is an example:

> OAKLAND (UPI) — The westbound California Zephyr, serenaded by bands along the route, made its final run into Oakland Sunday night — four hours late for its own funeral.
>
> The historic passenger train, which made its run from Chicago with nearly empty seats in recent years, carried a near capacity load of 300 nostalgic railroad buffs and newsmen on the final run.
>
> "If you write an article," Conductor F. M. Rankin told a newsman. "write a sad story. It's a way of life and it's going."
>
> The gleaming, stainless-steel train with its Vista-Dome passenger lounges was very likely the only great American train left that day. The carnations on the dining car tables were real. So were silverware, crystal, and linen tablecloths and sheets.
>
> "Is any one up there sad about this last trip?" someone called out to the men in the big diesel engine.
>
> "Is there any one up there happy?" Fireman Herbert Briggs called back.

The Zephyr was doomed by order of the Interstate Commerce Commission after the Western Pacific Railroad complained of losing money.

"We lost $2.5 million this year because there wasn't enough passengers," said a Western Pacific official on the last run. "The money is in freight."

The Zephyr carried thousands of persons millions of miles for 21 years, rolling through some of the West's most spectacular scenery. "I was on this train the first day it left," said Porter Willie Owens of Chicago. "I know this train like a book and I love it."

The Travelogue Then there's the familiar story about faraway places, sights and sounds. With the renewed American interest in China, the press was deluged with short pieces of this kind:

PEKING (AP)—Going marketing in Peking is like shopping at a supermarket in the United States—with exceptions.

There are differences in packaging and marketing. The Chinese do not wrap things neatly in cellophane packages; indeed, there's no wrapping at all. Most things are bought fresh. There's no refrigeration now, but in summer some is used.

There are differences in variety. It's difficult to find freshly pressed duck in the United States, but not here. There are stacks on the counter priced at about 4 yuan apiece, which is about $1.70 at the going rate.

Refrigeration is not needed for fish and sea food generally. Most of the fish are live and a young woman had a hard time holding onto a two-foot gray carp. The price varies according to quality; this one fetched about 35 cents a pound.

Dressed chicken, at about 32 cents a pound, and live turkeys were in abundance at this market, a one-floor building with tiled floors and brick walls.

Wang Hsiang, a leading member of the market, not only supervises the 200 workers but also sells. "The supplies," he said, "come directly from the commune. The commune comprises one brigade, with six production teams. They supply the market."

An Animal Tale The animal story is another staple of journalism, ranging from the Sunday feature about the zoo to the halting of construction on a $100 million TVA dam in Tennessee to save a three-inch fish listed among "endangered species." Here is a perennial—the groundhog story that is used every February 2:

PUNXSUTAWNEY, Pa—"Punxsutawney Phil," a dazed and rather frightened groundhog, was snatched today from his warm cage in a local museum, thrust into a freezing earthen burrow outside town, and then coaxed out to pose for television cameras.

He didn't stay very long and 90 members of the local Groundhog Club, standing in seven above zero weather, announced triumphantly that he had seen his shadow. According to legend, this means there will be six more weeks of winter and the club came prepared with signs to proclaim the verdict for the cameras.

Phil didn't seem to mind, once he was pulled out of the burrow and put back in his cage in the museum. Winter won't bother him there.

Chapter 15
Wholesalers
of News

Horse-drawn cabs raced through New York's gas-lit streets in the middle of the nineteenth century to deliver news agency bulletins to newspaper city rooms. In the declining years of the twentieth century, agency services are distributed by computer at speeds of up to 10,000 words per minute. This is the measure of change that has come to the agency business, the wholesalers of news.

DEADLINES EVERY MINUTE

The agencies, also known as wire services and press associations, have to meet deadlines every minute for subscribers all over the world. They supply the news media with news from all sources—local, state, national and foreign. They also provide pictures, features, criticism, cartoons, comics and all the other by-products of the news.

AP and UPI The Associated Press and United Press International, the two American-owned wire services, compete for news on a global basis and serve foreign as well as American press, radio, TV, magazine and other clients. Their familiar initials, AP and UPI, are known wherever newspapers are published. On the air, their electronic services are not credited as often.

The older of the two is the AP, a cooperative nonprofit agency that levies assessments on its members to meet its costs. The AP's rival, UPI, was formed in 1958 when the United Press Associations bought out the Hearst-owned International News Service. UPI sells its service to clients on a contract basis.

Both wire services have thousands of world-wide outlets. In addition to the regular press and broadcast services, subscribers include government agencies, schools and private business concerns with a news service requirement (such as financial and import–export firms). About 400 newspapers use both American services, being members of AP and clients of UPI. Between them, they cover every American daily worthy of the name, many weeklies, television networks and local stations, the news magazines and all but the most insignificant radio stations.[1]

Characteristics Accuracy and speed are the principal characteristics of the American agencies. Quantitatively, both lay down a daily report of several million words from their electronic newsrooms. These, of course, represent the sum total of many different services handled by numerous divisions and subdivisions. Qualitatively, one service may have a few seconds or a minute or two on the other in a major news break but, with rare exceptions, the day of the news beat of hours or days is over. UPI's 30-minute beat on Jimmy Carter's election as President in 1976 is the exception, not the rule.

Their Staffs As far as staffs go, both AP and UPI have many young, capable and well-trained men and a few women who can be trusted to go anywhere and cover anything. They also have a small group of managerial and reportorial veterans who can be used as a kind of modern star reporter.

In writing style UPI is generally under greater pressure to produce colorful accounts of fast-moving events while AP seeks terseness and action. Both are almost fanatical in attempting to observe the first tenet of journalism—accuracy. With some newspaper or other client meeting a deadline every time a breath is drawn, the wire-service reporter has the best of reasons to worry about getting the facts right as well as getting them first.

Each of the wire services maintains several hundred thousand miles

---

[1] The AP had 1,265 newspaper members and 3,500 broadcast members in the United States in 1976, with expenses of $100 million. The UPI had 1,131 newspapers and 3,650 broadcast clients in the United States during the same year, and projected a 1977 budget of $73 million. Each has several thousand foreign clients.

of leased wires in the United States plus leased cable and teleprinter radio circuits overseas. The services also use directional radio beams and communications satellites to get their news and picture services to various points on the globe outside the leased facilities.

The unique part of this flexible communications network is the ease with which main trunk wires on moments' notice can relay the most urgent and dramatic news to the whole country and the rest of the world as well.

THE SWING TO AUTOMATION

The wire services have been in the vanguard of news organizations that have adopted computers and electronic editing devices for their news wires and high speed transmission for stock market tables, tabular sports material and similar data. However, the 66 words per minute teleprinters (effective rate 55 w.p.m.) still putter along in many newsrooms for reasons of economy and editorial convenience. But their day is numbered.

The first move toward automation in the agency business came in 1927 with the invention of teletypesetter tape and its widespread use among smaller newspapers beginning in the 1930s. A teletypesetter wire (TTS, as contrasted with the regular system known as TTY) produced perforated tape that was fed directly into line-casting machines in newspaper composing rooms. Necessarily, this was sent in capital and small letters, or upper and lower case in printers' terminology, and the teletype monitor for the TTS system produced identical copy.

In 1960, the computer and phototypesetter were introduced into newspapers and cold type began replacing hot metal production. Within a few years, realizing that newspapers could now handle copy at a much faster rate in their composing rooms, the wire services developed speedier systems of distribution while retaining TTS. That meant electronic editing, writing and data storage and retrieval.

Using the Computer In 1970, AP and UPI went over to a computerized system. Terminals were used for writing and editing and computers put the product in storage, recalled data as needed for editing and then transmitted the material on the wire services' network as directed. AP began using upper and lower case on most transmissions. UPI retained the all-cap service.

Essentially, the wire services use similar systems but their nomenclature is different. The AP's terminals are called CRTs, for cathode ray tubes, the essential element of most terminals, and the UPI's are VDTs, or video display terminals. Nearly all VDTs are CRTs (the workable exception to date is the Plasma Display which is not in very general use) so the expression, terminal, covers both systems.

Since their introduction, these silent typewriterlike devices with a TV screen above the keyboard have enjoyed unexampled popularity in wire service offices. With staff people writing and editing their own stories for the most part, there has been very little for the old-time "punchers" to do. Like the telegraphers before them, the men who punched and fed tape into the teletype machines have faded steadily in numbers and soon will be out of business altogether.

Once the first stories were filed by terminals late in 1970, it was only a matter of time before they took over the entire operation. It happened two years later, when the AP General Desk in New York went over to terminals completely. So did UPI at about the same time. The result was faster transmission, particularly when the system took hold elsewhere in the country, and much cleaner copy because the computer didn't make "punchers' " mistakes.

High Speed Service Next came the introduction of high speed service. In 1961 the AP DataSpeed Service had broken the old 66 wpm teletype barrier with transmissions at 1,050 wpm but not many editors could handle it. There was more interest in the AP SuperSpeed Sports service in 1970, which delivered sports copy at 1,050 wpm. But it wasn't until 1975, when AP DataStream began operating, that general news copy was sent at 1,200 wpm and newspapers began subscribing in appreciable numbers.

UPI also developed its own high speed services. Its DataNews, the rival of AP's DataStream, is also delivered at 1,200 wpm. UPI has a high speed sports service, too, and is experimenting with additional methods to lay down specialized copy. One of the products is Data-News Limited, for smaller newspapers with computerized operations, which transmits directly to production systems, and DemandNews, which offers selected stories for editors on demand.

AP led the way to still higher speeds with the introduction in 1976 of its DigitalStocks service, which transmits stock market tables computer to computer at 10,000 wpm, the fastest service to date. It completely eliminates the use of tape and tape-handling manpower in newspaper composing rooms. The entire closing stock report of the New York Stock Exchange is thus sent in 3½ minutes. On AP DataSpeed, it took 45 minutes; before that, hours.

UPI has developed its own specialized financial service, Unistox DataBase, by working with market research firms.

WIRE SERVICE CHANNELS

The AP Circuits Both AP and UPI operate a bewildering maze of national, regional and local circuits in the United States and an even more complicated network abroad. These change so frequently in detail, particularly under automation with its exacting requirements, that an editor in the domestic service may have only a very general idea of what overseas practices are, and vice versa. Since the domestic networks are of primary interest here, they will be described in their essentials.

The AP delivers its service over a network of news, sports and financial wires on both the regular (TTY) and the teletypesetter (TTS) circuits. The transcontinental trunk wire that carries the main budget of national and international news is called the *A wire*. It is filed 24 hours a day from New York in two cycles—one for afternoon papers (PMs) starting at 1 A.M., Eastern time, and another for morning papers (AMs) starting at 1 P.M. In addition to the main transmission centers in New York and Washington, AP service is directed through nine "hub" bureaus, each with its own regional computer system, in Atlanta, Chicago, Kansas City, Boston, Columbus, Seattle, Los Angeles, Dallas and Philadelphia. Each "hub" services the satellite bureaus in three to eight states.

It should not be assumed that all AM copy is shut off when the PM cycle begins or vice versa. There is a necessary overlap in which copy is transmitted for both cycles. In addition to breaking news, the PM file consists of copy for an overnight schedule for the first editions of afternoon papers and the regular day-wire schedule for this and later editions. The same cycle carries day leads that often run past 1 P.M., when the night wire opens; similarly, the night wire runs leads past 1 A.M. on continuing stories.

To reduce the piecing together process, AP has a 1,200 wpm DataRecaps service in which up-to-the-minute write-throughs of breaking stories are offered to subscribers in completely assembled form. Mainly, this services copy on the "A" wire.

Paralleling the "A" wire is the "B" wire, carrying the most important regional news coast to coast and from Boston to Florida as well as all-points copy that cannot be accommodated on the "A" wire. Next in importance are numerous regional and state wires, many of which are in effect smaller trunk wires. As the system of hub and satellite bureaus indicates, still further subdivisions exist within specific areas. Very often, too, on subordinate circuits, a system of "splits" is used through which the wire carries general news for part of an hour and state or regional copy for the remainder.

While the "hub" bureaus may take over the "A" wire when they have major news to transmit, most of their copy for the "A" and "B" wires goes first to the general desk in New York City on nine collection wires that are driven by regional computers. It is in New York, therefore, that supervisors, copy editors, and wire filers decide on news priorities and handle the copy for movement on the trunk wires in what is called a *quality control* operation. Washington alone is not "hubbed" and continues to file its copy direct.

The AP teletypesetter operation is separate.

The UPI Circuits The UPI's major news circuits are similar to the AP's in many ways, although the bureau relationships are handled differently. There are four main circuits—the "A" wire, the "B" wire, the teletypesetter version of the "A" wire in caps and lower case and the general TTS wire which carries both national and state or regional news. The PM cycle for afternoon papers begins at midnight, Eastern time, and includes the overnight file, while the AM cycle for morning newspapers begins at noon. All wires are supervised from New York.

The "A" wire is a 24-hour daily circuit, the main transcontinental trunk wire. Although the "B" wire is also a general news wire, a larger portion of its content is regional news and it operates for 20 hours a day except on Sundays when the running time is cut to nine hours. Through the "split" system, the "B" wire is portioned off into regional segments, as are the TTS wires.

The system of picture transmission, which is entirely separate from the news file, is of particular importance to AP and UPI. All bureaus are responsible for both news and pictures, for collecting and for transmitting them. In addition, a bureau manager also may have to serve as chief salesman, promoter and greeter for clients and potential clients. All in all, the wire-service business is the most complicated and demanding in American journalism because it is the basis for the whole system of news collection and dissemination.

Without doubt, in the waning years of this century, the more sophisticated use of communications satellites, laser beams, new generations of computers and other marvels may change the whole concept of wire-service delivery—and perhaps the rest of the news media as well. Certainly, the changes of less than a decade already have added immeasurably to the importance of the news agency system.

Foreign Wire Services Reuters, the British service, is the principal global rival of the two American giants. Although Reuters has fewer major newspaper outlets in the United States, these include some of the leading American papers. It is tailoring its service to meet North American needs. Like the AP-Dow Jones service for commercial clients and UPI's UNICOM, Reuters has a special economic service for business houses, too.

Reuters often runs neck to neck with the Americans on certain types of major foreign stories, and in the Commonwealth it has news sources that normally tend to favor a British rather than an American service. It can scarcely be said, therefore, that the United States is in a dominant position in originating and servicing news outside its borders.

In addition to Reuters, the French wire service, Agence France-

Presse, is a competing factor in the global news business. It is naturally favored in France and French-speaking countries.

It has an English language service, but there are relatively few clients for it. The French service and its predecessor, Havas, have always had a greater attraction in Latin America than in English-speaking countries. Because this is still true, AFP maintains its popularity south of the border. But it is not in a class with the "Big 3" of world wire service journalism — AP, UPI and Reuters.

Tass and Hsinhua Two government-operated news services dominate the dissemination of information in the world areas that are under Communist control. They are Tass, the official service of the Soviet Union, and its rival, Hsinhua (New China News Agency, or NCNA), the official service of the People's Republic of China. With their national newspapers and electronic media, all under the control of their respective governments, the two Communist agencies have a monopoly in their own respective countries.

While the "Big 3" Western agencies are independent of government, deriving their funds for the most part from the media they serve, the Communist agencies devote themselves to the service of their respective states. This means, of course, that both Tass and Hsinhua must be considered propaganda services as well as news agencies, since they frequently bend the news to fit the national purpose and even suppress news when it is convenient to do so. Having no competition, they have nothing to worry about except to keep in favor with the governments they serve.

Yet, despite all these restrictions and the obvious differences with the Western theory of the free press as it has operated for some two centuries, the Communist agencies are the primary sources of news about the Soviet Union and China. No correspondent, either in Peking or Moscow, can afford to ignore them; moreover, no correspondent serving on the periphery of the Communist-dominated land mass in Eurasia can do his job without paying careful attention to what Tass and Hsinhua are saying. Tass, for example, inevitably was first with the notable achievements of the Soviet Union in the race to the moon; Hsinhua, similarly, was the source for much of the news of the turmoil in China during the last days of Mao Tse-tung. And both, scanned on a day-by-day basis, provided the non-Communist world with the details of the power struggle between Moscow and Peking, and Peking's approaches to Washington.

The crude military-type censorship has long since vanished in both the Soviet Union and Communist China, in view of the effectiveness of the governmental control of news in each state. All foreign correspondents are free to send what they wish, in theory; actually, they know that if they persistently offend their hosts in any way, they are subject to immediate expulsion, and, in rare cases, arrest as spies. Thus, the correspondent in effect has to censor himself, an exquisite form of journalistic torture. From the standpoint of the Communist regimes, this is eminently satisfactory. They can contend, with bland innocence, that they do not practice censorship; yet, at the same time, they have assurance of the most effective controls over correspondents.

Despite periods of intense hostility between East and West, and the inner struggles on either side, exchange agreements between the leading news agencies generally have been kept in good faith. Tass, for example, has shared its daily file with the Western agencies on a reciprocal basis for years, regardless of what Washington and Moscow have been saying about each other. And Hsinhua has maintained similar agreements with agencies that were permitted to send correspondents to Peking and, more recently, AP and UPI. But during periods of intense political turmoil, things change in China. It was during one of those periods, at the height of the Cultural Revolution, that a Reuters correspondent, Anthony Grey, was held under house arrest in a single room in Peking for two years. And a Japanese correspondent was jailed for even a longer time.

As for Peking's relationship with the Americans, that began to change from the time that Premier Chou En-lai received an American ping-pong team in Peking in 1971 and turned to John Roderick of the AP, an old China hand, saying, "Mr. Roderick, you have opened the door." From that period on, during negotiations toward mutual recognition following President Nixon's first trip to Peking, the Chinese government has admitted American correspondents for limited periods. But it cannot be doubted that the respective wire services of China and the United States have been granted far greater responsibilities, including exchanges of service.

With the exception of great events such as a Presidential visit to Moscow or Peking, however, it is not often that news furnished by Western or Japanese agencies has been disseminated within the Soviet or Chinese orbits. The same has been true of the newspaper syndicates' material. Usually, news from the non-Communist world has been circulated from Moscow or Peking only when it happens to fit in with the policies of their respective governments. And the Western and Japanese correspondents in these two capitals always have had to be extremely careful of what they do, say and write.

In view of all the obstacles imposed on the wire services and the foreign correspondents for other media, it is almost a miracle that the nations of the world are even partially informed of each others' doings. Because the wire services carry so much of this burden, they in particular are entitled far more to compliments than the brickbats they are accustomed to receive. But that is the way of editors. Few ever can be satisfied with a service they themselves do not direct.

The National Agencies The wire-service communications systems have gradually expanded over the years by hooking a developing chain of national news services into the globe-girdling cables and radio circuits. This is done through various types of agreements. Some of these national agencies are, in effect, extensions of one or more of the global services in particular areas. Thus, Canadian Press is the main agency for wire news in Canada, and Australian Associated Press does the same job for Australia, both being partners of the Associated Press. In Great Britain, the British United Press is an extension of United Press International. In India, the Press Trust of India has agreements with Reuters. And in Japan, Kyodo has exchange arrangements with all the Western "Big 3." Nearly every major country, and a number of smaller ones, have worked out similar exchanges. And where there are no national agencies, governments often buy service directly from the agencies to supply their radios with such material as they select. This is particularly true in Africa.

Understandably, the list of national agencies is very long and their quality varies in accordance with the degree of government supervision, official or unofficial, and the kind of training available to their personnel. Usually, a national agency can be no better than the media it serves — print, electronic or both — because it is often dependent on them for domestic news which it exchanges for a foreign report.

The Local Agencies In the most important news centers of the United States wire services for local news have been in business for as long as there has been a telegraph. Even before 1844, there was cooperative news gathering and distribution by express messenger on horseback, stagecoach and even by ship. Some of the local agencies began independently of the larger wire services. Some were offshoots. Others eventually came under the big agencies' control.

In Washington today both AP and UPI offer a special type of local service for those who want it. In New York the local bureau of the Associated Press covers much of the city on an assignment basis. In Chicago and Los Angeles other city services are offered. As expenses of gathering local news rise, it is likely that still more combinations will be effected where competing news organizations can afford to get their news from the same sources.

SPECIALS AND SYNDICATES

The mounting cost of maintaining correspondents overseas, in Washington, and even in state capitals has brought about a reduction in the number of "specials" — as newspaper correspondents are known — who are permanently assigned outside their offices. This is a loss to the profession. A talented special can do a better job for his own paper on many assignments than an agency that has to service thousands of papers.

News Syndicates The wire services are encountering stiff competition from the newspapers that can afford to maintain large and competent staffs of reporters in the national and international field. The *New York Times*, operating one of the oldest news syndicates in the field, services more than 200 newspapers in the United States and abroad. The *Los Angeles Times*, one of the newest news syndicates, has surged ahead rapidly in a few years, partly because of its loose partnership arrangement with the service offered by the *Washington Post*.

On big news, whether it is in the next county, in Washington, or abroad, the American news media still give saturation coverage and will try, in many cases, to rush specials to the scene, but the firehouse principle of reporting is not really thorough. Specials literally dash from their planes to the scene of an international conference and file their stories. They pick up background and hope for the breaks. Such reporting, on TV or in the press, is not calculated to give wire-service executives sleepless nights.

The habit of depending on the wire services is insidious. Because they are capable and dependable, it is easy for an editor or news director to fall back on them for his national and foreign coverage and salve his conscience by telling himself he does not have a reporter to spare. Almost insensibly the same reasoning can take possession of some editors when it comes time to assign coverage for the state legislature and the governor. The general reporting of important state and national news has, therefore, tended to drift more and more into the domain of the wire service bureaus although newspapers of consequence still do the job that readers expect of them at this level.

The decline of the special has also had its effect on local news reporting and writing. Where there is a good wire service bureau or local wire service in a city, the temptation is great to assign reporters only on the major news of the day and let the agencies handle all the rest. That tendency has led, over the years, to a practice on some newspapers of running locally originated wire-service copy without credit or of rewriting it to make it appear of staff origin. Understandably this has led to a demand for more news writers of ability, originality and—most of all—speed. No matter how flossy the writing, it has not made up for the slackening use of reporters on local, state, national or international news. Good news writing still takes good reporting.

Feature Syndicates Although the wire services also distribute feature material, this function is shared with the big feature syndicates. In their modern form such syndicates are business organizations that contract with assorted experts, artists, writers and photographers for a host of popular features that are sold to hundreds, and often thousands, of newspapers. One of the main characteristics of a feature syndicate is its large sales staff, which is constantly circulating among newspapers both here and abroad with offers of a dazzling variety of circulation-building materials. The wire services and newspaper syndicates sell, too, but very few are able to rival an organization such as the Hearst-owned King Features Syndicate, largest in the field. Feature journalism is the business of such syndicates, and a very big business, too.

Several hundred feature syndicates offer their sales lists to editors. They offer everything that can occur to the brain of an editor and be translated into popular journalistic merchandise. Both fiction and non-fiction best-sellers are offered in serial form by syndicates. They market political columns, cooking columns, children's care columns, bridge columns, fashion news, health columns, editorial cartoons, canned editorials, various kinds of advice not overlooking family counseling, finance and advice to the lovelorn, literary and drama criticism, bedtime stories and other staples.

Newspapers are charged by the feature in accordance with their circulation and their ability to pay. Whereas large newspapers pay a high price for a popular comic, small ones can get a popular columnist for a few dollars a week. Editors often come to New York, headquarters of some of the big syndicates, with long shopping lists.

Contributing to a feature syndicate is scarcely in the same class with the professional work of the journalist who deals primarily in news. If anything, feature syndicate work is a kind of amalgamation of the worlds of art, light literature and journalism. The writers of news seldom know what goes on in it because they have little contact with it until they make a name for themselves.

Despite the promotional aspects of their work, syndicates are not in the same class as advertisers who sponsor television or radio programs. A large advertiser, Xerox, recently sponsored (that is, paid for) a travel series written by a retired *New York Times* reporter, Harrison E. Salisbury, in *Esquire* magazine. Xerox attracted so much protest against the deal that it abandoned further projects.

WIRE SERVICES AT WORK

By the most knowledgeable estimates wire services provide 90 per cent of the foreign news that is published in the American press and 75 per cent or more of the national news. Many newspapers accept at least half their state-wide news from wire services as well. Therefore, except on leading newspapers, it would seem that only local news seems to call for individual exertion. The same is very largely true of the broadcast media.

Standards If the reliance on the wire service for news results in a more or less standardized pattern of foreign, national and state-wide news coverage, it is not primarily the fault of the agencies. In laying heavy demands upon them, the individual newspapers would appear to be somewhat more to blame. Certainly, considering the handicaps of time and diverse other pressures that are put upon them, the agencies perform minor miracles every day to get the news—and occasionally they perform a big miracle.

It would be a grievous error to assume that the agencies, having inherited so much responsibility by default, perform their duties by whim and by chance. Far from it. They are under the most rigorous scrutiny of any organization in the land, for not even a Senate select committee can bore in with more angry vigor than a posse of outraged editors who do not believe that they are getting what they are paying for.

A wire service must meet the standards of thousands of editors of all shades of political and religious beliefs, all nationalities and sympathies. What may be of interest to one news organization may be of no consequence to a wire service, except if an editor requests special coverage, but what may seem interesting to a wire service does not always please its members or clients. Editors being what they are, it is difficult enough to satisfy one of them, let alone hundreds or thousands at a time.

The wire service, therefore, ordinarily takes great care to present all sides of a story that is controversial. It may not be the best way to handle a wire service report, but it is usually the fairest way.

Wire-service people are not paid to take sides. They are the impartial sources of information for all sides. The wire-service reporter or writer, consequently, is closely watched for any shade of editorializing in his copy. For those of experience and proved judgment, permission is given to provide background and interpret the news on stories requiring it. But to tell why something happened, the interpretive process, is quite different from arguing over what should be done about it, the editorial prerogative. This is the first thing that novice wire service reporters must learn, sometimes by being discharged.

Criticisms Every conceivable criticism of wire-service work has been made by editors. They have complained on occasion that wire services send too many bulletins, too many versions of a developing story, too much copy on the average political story, sometimes too little on a good feature. In the rush of putting a report together, hapless agency men are frequently accused of featuring the last thing that happened when it may not be the most important. Or, they may be charged with the particularly heinous crime of glorifying the trivial.

The APME Blue Book records the complaints of editors who called attention to "the vast amount of trivia" in an Associated Press report and asks solemnly, "What are trivia? Suppose we could agree on trivia, what would we substitute?"

Trivia, like the outpouring of new leads on major stories, are a part of wire service work. The wholesalers present a full line of merchandise. The retailers buy. The principle is still *caveat emptor.*

The wire services have their faults and these are many, but they also have virtues. Often, the agencies have been ahead of well-informed diplomats on the great events of world affairs. In the military it is not an earth-shaking secret that many an intelligence officer would be lost in a maze of slow-moving and murky official communications if he did not have a wire service teleprinter in his office.

When a politician has something to say, whether it is of consequence or not, one of the first questions he asks his press secretary is whether the wire services have been informed. Whether the news is big-time or small-town, headline or feature material, sex or science, business or crime, the wire services can be depended on to get it out. They are the basic reporters for the whole top-heavy edifice of modern mass communications.

American journalism could not exist without them. They have made themselves indispensable.

WIRE SERVICE PROCEDURE

The techniques of wire-service handling of developing news differ from newspaper procedure in several respects.

Schedules Preceding the opening of each cycle, a schedule is sent to all editors on a given circuit to let them know what material is available for transmission to them. This schedule, or budget message, tells editors each story that they will get by slug, description and often by word count. It does not, of course, tell the precise time that each specific piece will go on the wire because that is bound to vary. The breaking news, which is handled as it happens, can knock out the most carefully prepared news budget.

There are slight differences between UPI and AP procedure but in the main they follow the same principles because they are always working on some paper's deadline. The various takes of their stories are moved in order, but not necessarily consecutively. They may be put between bulletins of other material that is given precedence.

Wire-Service Slugging For all these reasons it is not practical for a wire-service story to be written in newspaper fashion with the page slugs numbered 1-2-3-4. Instead, wire copy consists of a first take and a series of adds for most stories. Each add is easily identifiable because it bears the slug and dateline of the original and a time sequence of transmission.

Slugs in wire-service work also are devised as a code to indicate urgency of transmission. Those generally used by the American wire services are *Flash, Bulletin* and *Urgent* in descending order of importance.

These are included in the "header" material, made necessary by the computer, that precedes each story. Under arrangements devised by the American Newspaper Publishers Association, both wire services include in their "header" lines such data as the story number, service level designator, pre-header select code, priority and category. All this sounds formidable, but actually it is quite simple to work with and it is necessary for editorial usage.

In this book, for purposes of uniformity and ease of reading, the "header" material will be limited to story numbers, slugs, time designations, signatures and pickup lines. Examples of wire service procedures and copy are presented in upper-and-lower case style for AP and all caps for UPI, as they appear on the printers' copy. In conformity with modern usage, dates are omitted from datelines for all examples except those of historic interest.

Wire-Copy Transmission The two wire-service pieces that follow illustrate what an editor sees when he is an AP member and also subscribes to UPI. The particular examples were selected at random from the file of an ordinary day and are given here in their essentials. Both are about the same announcement. It isn't the kind of story that matters very much as far as time differential is concerned, as long as it is moved promptly on the wire. There also is no particular superiority in presentation between one service and the other. But the editor is given a choice of services, which is the main consideration.

Here is the essential file of both services on the story, with the necessary explanations:

>A110
>PM ROVER 2–28
>BULLETIN
>   WASHINGTON (UPI)—CONGRESS WAS ASKED TODAY FOR $91 MILLION TO BEGIN DEVELOPMENT OF A NUCLEAR-POWERED ENGINE FOR DEEP SPACE PROBES TO BE KNOWN AS THE "ROVER."
>   *MORE*
>   UPI 02–28 11:27 AES

The first number in the bulletin (A110) indicates the dispatch is filed on the "A" wire and that it is the 110th take of the cycle which is, as the PM preceding the slug indicates, the day wire. The slug, "Rover," will be found on all succeeding takes. The final number is unscrambled as follows: UPI signature plus date is followed by the time, 11:27 A.M., Eastern Standard.

In the next take, A111, note that the pickup line is composed of several elements—the number, the cycle, the slug, the number of the add, the number of the previous take, the date, and three Xs to set off the last word of the previous take, which happens to be "Rover." The whole thing is then put together, as follows, with an unintentional garble in the first line of the text:

> A111
> PM —ROVER 1ST ADD A110 2–28
> XXX "ROVER."
> EXPLAINING THAT A NUCLEAR ENGINE, WITH A POTENTIAL OF 200,000 TO 250,000 POUNDS OF THRUST, THE WHITE HOUSE SAID "ROVER" COULD AMOST DOUBLE THE PRESENT SATURN V PAYLOAD.
> IT COULD "BE USED IN FUTURE MANNED LANDINGS AND EXPLORATIONS OF FAR DISTANT PLANETS," A SPOKESMAN SAID.
> CONGRESS WAS ASKED TO ADD THE $91 MILLION TO THE BUDGET FOR THE FISCAL YEAR WHICH BEGINS JULY 1. MONEY FOR "ROVER" WAS PART OF A $149.8 MILLION PROPOSAL WHICH ALSO WOULD PROVIDE TWO SIGNIFICANT NEW NUCLEAR RESEARCH FACILITIES AT A TOTAL COST OF $58.8 MILLION.
> *MORE*
> UPI 02–28 11:30 AES

Two takes of the story are now off the machine in three minutes, but seven minutes elapse until the next take appears. Note that the pickup line specifies that it is the second add and repeats the slug, date, number of the first take and last word of the previous take.

> A112
> PM ROVER 2ND ADD A110 2–28
> XXX MILLION.
> ONE WOULD BE A LABORATORY FOR "BASIC PHYSICAL AND BIOMEDICAL RESEARCH" INVOLVING THE MESON, WHICH THE WHITE HOUSE DESCRIBED AS "ONE OF THE FRAGMENTS OF THE ATOM THAT SCIENTISTS ARE INTERESTED IN STUDYING."
> THE OTHER NEW FACILITY WOULD BE A CENTER FOR ADVANCED RESEARCH INTO "CONTROLLED THERMONUCLEAR FUSION AS A POTENTIAL SOURCE OF ELECTRICITY."
> BOTH RESEARCH PROJECTS WOULD BE BUILT AT THE ATOMIC ENERGY COMMISSION'S LOS ALAMOS SCIENTIFIC LABORATORY IN NEW MEXICO.
> UPI 02–28 11:30 AES

Now, with the end of the story, an observant editor has noted the garble in the first line of the 1st Add and the following correction is filed. Note how instructions are given before and after the correction to show where it fits:

A113
PM ROVER CORRN A110 2ND GRAF: FIXING GARBLE 2–28
THE WHITE HOUSE EXPLAINED THAT ROVER, A NUCLEAR ENGINE WITH A POTENTIAL OF 200,000 TO 250,000 POUNDS OF THRUST, COULD ALMOST DOUBLE THE PRESENT SATURN V PAYLOAD.
PICKUP 3RD GRAF: IT COULD

UPI 02–28 11:38 AES

After 40 minutes elapse, UPI puts out a first lead which is a bit more dramatic and, in its second take, includes somewhat more information. This time, instead of a bulletin, the story is given the next lower order of priority on the wire, urgent, but both takes move with reasonable promptness. Note the wording of the instructions to editors at the beginning and end of the 1st LD to show where it joins with the original story.

A124
PM-ROVER 1ST LD PICKUP 5TH GRAF A110 2–28
URGENT
WASHINGTON (UPI)—THE WHITE HOUSE TODAY ASKED CONGRESS FOR $91 MILLION TO START DEVELOPMENT OF NUCLEAR-POWERED SPACE ROCKETS POWERFUL ENOUGH FOR "FUTURE MANNED LANDINGS AND EXPLORATIONS OF FAR-DISTANT PLANETS."
THE SUPPLEMENTAL FUNDS WOULD GO INTO THE ROVER ENGINE PROGRAM, WHICH IS SHOOTING FOR NUCLEAR PROPULSION OF THE SORT NEEDED IF AMERICANS ARE TO EXPLORE NEIGHBORING PLANETS.
A WHITE HOUSE ANNOUNCEMENT SAID THAT A NUCLEAR ENGINE WITH 200,000 TO 250,000 POUNDS OF THRUST COULD ALMOST DOUBLE THE PAYLOAD OF THE SATURN V ROCKET.

MORE
UPI 02–28 12:18 PES

A125
PM ROVER 1ST ADD 1ST LD A124 XXX 2–28
XXX ROCKET
CHAIRMAN CLINTON P. ANDERSON, D.-N.M., OF THE SENATE SPACE COMMITTEE, PRAISED THE ACTION AS ONE OF "TREMENDOUS IMPACT."
ANDERSON SAID THE DEVELOPMENT OF A STILL MORE POWERFUL ROCKET CALLED NERVA IS EXPECTED TO COST ABOUT $1 BILLION OVER A TEN-YEAR PERIOD. BUT HE SAID HE UNDERSTOOD THIS COULD BE PAID OFF IN ONLY A FEW SPACE MISSIONS "BECAUSE OF THE HIGH PERFORMANCE ACHIEVABLE WITH NUCLEAR RESEARCH PROPULSION."

THE $91 MILLION REQUIRED FOR ROVER WAS PART OF A $149.8 MILLION PROPOSAL WHICH WOULD ALSO PROVIDE TWO IMPORTANT NUCLEAR RESEARCH FACILITIES AT A TOTAL COST OF $58.8 MILLION. *PICKUP 5TH GRAF ONE WOULD*

UPI 02–28 12:31 PES

Here is the way AP ran a bulletin, three succeeding takes and a correction on the Rover story. Note that there is no pickup line between the 1st and 2nd Adds because they follow each other on the wire:

a158
Bulletin
PM Rover
WASHINGTON (AP)—The White House asked Congress today for money to begin the development of a nuclear-powered rocket engine, the "Rover."

0228 1122 AES

a159
PM Rover 1st add a 158 02 28
WASHINGTON: "Rover"
For this and other scientific projects, Congress was asked for a total of $149.8 million for use in the fiscal year beginning July 1.

In addition to the nuclear-powered rocket engine, the White House was asked for funds for a physics laboratory for basic physical and biochemical research and a specialized facility for further exploration into controlled thermonuclear fission as a potential source of electricity.

a160
"The projects will advance America's ability to harness atomic energy for the peaceful exploration of space," a spokesman said. "They will also help us chart new courses in nuclear science."

He said development of a nuclear-powered rocket engine will take time.

0228 1126 AES

a165
URGENT
PM Rover 3rd Add A 158 02 28
WASHINGTON: TIME.
A number of flight and ground tests will precede full use of the engine in space programs, the White House announcement added.

A total of $91 million is sought in the next fiscal year for the rocket development and the remaining $58.8 million to develop the new research facilities.

Both new research facilities will be built by the Atomic Energy Commission at its Los Alamos, N. M., scientific laboratory.

0228 1156 AES

a179
PM Rover Correction
WASHINGTON: Rover A158 Third Graf make read XXX thermonuclear fusion etc. (sted fission)

0228 1247 AES

It will be seen that there is little to choose between the two accounts presented here. Both moved bulletins promptly, the AP a few minutes ahead of UPI. But UPI had more detail in a shorter space of time. Both decided the story should go on the wire at once and therefore marked the first paragraph as a bulletin. The AP used an "urgent" designation on A165 to make certain it was given the next order of priority on the wires. Note the method of identifying the location of corrections because the same procedure is used for placing inserts in moving stories.

Both services use numbered leads in progression. However, after the original story was filed, UPI came up with first lead, second lead, third lead and so on, while AP used lead, second lead, third lead and so on. If a "write-through" is ordered, something newspapers generally call a sub story, wire services often merely use the next numbered lead in the progression and at the end carry the notation "eliminates previous" or "no pickup."

There is another peculiarity in wire service procedure that is not generally in accord with newspaper practice. Because of the confusion in morning papers which carry undated leads with the notation that something happened yesterday, and dated leads of yesterday that something happened today, the wire services use the day of the week and drop all dates for morning papers. However, for afternoon papers, today—and not Monday or Tuesday—is usually used for leads, dated or undated.

Both wire services, whenever possible, carry the total wordage and the number of takes in their "header" material and also include necessary labels and instructions, such as advance stories for a given date or the reason for a particular lead or insert.

But when big news is breaking—news of national and world-wide importance—the wires move the story first and the technicalities take second place.

A PRESIDENTIAL ELECTION

Few Presidential races in this century have been closer than Jimmy Carter's 1976 campaign for the White House against President Gerald R. Ford. After three nationally televised debates and tens of thousands of miles of travel, both candidates surged to what most opinion polls described as a photo finish on election night, November 2. As the returns piled in, Carter seemed within reach of victory for hours but he lacked just a few votes in the electoral college; meanwhile, Ford began catching up by seizing most of the states west of the Mississippi.

It became a question of which of the wire services, networks or major newspapers would make the first call—always a risky business on election night. At 12:59 A.M., EST, November 3, the Albany bureau of United Press International gave New York to Carter, putting him at 250

President-elect Jimmy Carter holding his first news conference at the train depot in Plains, Georgia, the night of November 4, 1976. United Press International photograph. Used by permission.

of the necessary 270 electoral votes by UPI's count. Next came Wisconsin, at 2:34 A.M., with 11 votes, and Hawaii, at 2:45 A.M., with 4 more, giving Carter 265. And at 2:57 A.M., Andy Reese, UPI bureau manager at Jackson, Mississippi, flashed word to Washington that Mississippi's 7 votes had gone to Carter. Immediately, UPI called the election for Carter as follows:

> A 007
> AM-ELECTION 11–3
> *FLASH*
> WASHINGTON—CARTER WINS PRESIDENCY
> UPI 11–03 02:57 AES

> A 008
> AM-ELECTION 300 AM LD—WRITETHRU 11–3
> *BULLETIN*
> AM NIGHT GENL LD ELECTION
> BY STEVE GERSTEL
> WASHINGTON (UPI)—JIMMY CARTER OF GEORGIA WRESTED THE PRESIDENCY AWAY FROM PRESIDENT FORD WEDNESDAY MORNING WHEN MISSISSIPPI GAVE HIM ITS SEVEN ELECTORAL VOTES AND PUSHED HIM OVER THE NECESSARY 270 VOTES.
> *MORE*
UPI 11–03 03:02 AES

> A 009
> AM-ELECTION 300 AM LAD—1ST ADD A-008 11–3
> *URGENT*

XXX VOTES.

CARTER SNATCHED VICTORY FROM A RESURGENT FORD IN ONE OF THE CLOSEST ELECTIONS IN MODERN TIMES BY WINNING THE ELECTORAL VOTES OF WISCONSIN, HAWAII AND FINALLY MISSISSIPPI FOR AN ELECTORAL MAJORITY OF 272 — TWO MORE THAN NEEDED.

CARTER, 52, THE FIRST PRESIDENT ELECTED FROM A DEEP SOUTH STATE SINCE ZACHARY TAYLOR IN 1848, BUILT UP A STRONG LEAD

President-elect Jimmy Carter mingling with reporters after holding his first news conference in Plains, Georgia, on the evening of November 4, 1976. United Press International photograph. Used by permission.

IN HIS NATIVE SOUTH AND BORDER STATES AND THEN SAW IT DWINDLE AS FORD MADE A COMEBACK IN THE WEST AND SOUTH-WEST.

MORE

UPI 11–03 03:06 AES

A 010

AM-ELECTION 300 AM LD – 2ND ADD A 008 11-3

XXX SOUTHWEST.

HIS VICTORY DESTROYED THE HOPES OF GERALD FORD TO WIN ELECTION TO THE WHITE HOUSE IN HIS OWN RIGHT AND ENDED A STUNNING COMEBACK DRIVE BY THE APPOINTED PRESIDENT, WHO PULLED INTO A DEAD HEAT WITH THE FORMER GEORGIA GOVERNOR ON ELECTION EVE AND THEN DENIED HIM VICTORY FOR HOURS BY WINNING KEY STATE AFTER STATE.

BUT FORD'S COMEBACK DRIVE FELL SHORT AND JAMES EARL CARTER, 52, OF PLAINS, GA., CAPPED A 22-MONTH UP-FROM-NO-WHERE PRESIDENTIAL DRIVE ABOUT 3 A.M. EST, BY BECOMING THE 39TH PRESIDENT OF THE UNITED STATES.

THE 3A.M. EST NATIONAL VOTE FOR PRESIDENT, WITH 77 PER CENT (136,716 OUT OF 178, 159) OF THE PRECINCTS REPORTED:

POPULAR VOTE		PERCENTAGE
CARTER	32,091,152	51
FORD	30,109,852	48
McCARTHY	510,090	1
MADDOX	128,586	0

CARTER HAD WON 23 STATES WITH 272 ELECTORAL VOTES AND WAS LEADING IN ONE OTHER STATE. FORD HAD WON 20 STATES WITH 145 ELECTORAL VOTES AND WAS LEADING IN SEVEN OTHERS WITH 76 ELECTORAL VOTES.

MORE

UPI 11–03 03:13 AES

As the night wore on, everybody else made the same call long in advance of a final tabulation of the votes. And although the result was razor-thin in some of the major states of the union, Carter's victory stood up. So UPI's seemingly risky call at 2:57 A.M. paid off. But the AP's Walter Mears won the 1977 Pulitzer Prize for national reporting for his entire Presidential campaign coverage.

A MAJOR INTERNATIONAL EVENT

A wire service must keep up with the news as it happens and has to be prepared for every eventuality. The Associated Press's coverage of the death of the founder and leader of Communist China, Mao Tse-tung, illustrates brilliantly how this is done. In the following extracts of the AP report for September 9, 1976, the essential portions of the bulletin matter and succeeding leads are given with slugging and directions. It was a typical AP performance under pressure, consisting of the death bulletin that moved at 4:11 A.M. EDT, for both cycles of the report (bc), a John Roderick lead and obit for PMs (the obit having been prepared long in advance) and a cleanup first lead.

a 033
bc — Mao, 20
BULLETIN
Tokyo (AP) — Mao Tse-tung died today, the official Chinese news agency Hsinhua announced.

0411 aed 09-09

a 035
bc — Mao, 1st add, a 033, 70
Tokyo: announced.
Hsinhua said the chairman of the Chinese Communist Party died about 16 hours before the announcement, at 12:10 A.M. Peking time (12:10 P.M., EST Wednesday).
He was 82 and had been in failing health for many months.

0418 aed 09–09

a 045
pm — Mao, 490
URGENT
by John Roderick
Associated Press Writer
Tokyo (AP) — Mao Tse-tung, who led the Communist revolution to victory in China in 1949 and dominated the world's most populous nation for the next 27 years, died early today, Peking announced.
He was 82 and had been slowly failing for many months.

MORE
0537 aed 09–09

a 046
pm — Mao, 1st add, a 045
Hsinhua, the official Chinese news agency, said the founding father of the People's Republic of China died at 12:10 A.M. (12:10 P.M. EST Wednesday) "because of the worsening of his illness and despite all treatment, although meticulous medical care was given him in every way after he fell ill."

The announcement of Mao's death was delayed for about 16 hours, the same length of time that intervened before the death of Premier Chou En-lai was announced last Jan. 8.

Mao's death was expected to intensify the power struggle that has shaken Peking intermittently for years and that flared up with renewed intensity after Chou's death.

Presumably Premier Hua Kuo-feng is next in line as chairman of the Chinese Communist Party, a post held by Mao since 1935 . . .

There followed Roderick's 3,200—word biography of Mao, the story being off the wire at 6:28 A.M. Then came a roundup first lead for afternoon papers, summing up world comment and picking up the biography, which was complete at 10:38 A.M. Transmission over the AP's high speed wires naturally expedited handling of the story for member newspapers.

COVERING THE BREAKING NEWS

To Lead or Not to Lead? The tendency of wire services to pile lead on lead is always a puzzle to newcomers to journalism and nonprofessionals in general. And yet, when circumstances change, when erroneous information is given and accepted in good faith, there is nothing a wire service can do except to update the story. The easiest way to do that, and call it to the attention of editors, is to put out a new top. Inserts are generally messy to handle and difficult to place, even with complete instructions.

Natural disasters such as hurricanes and earthquakes and various types of accidents, fires and wrecks cannot be covered in two minutes flat. And yet, wire copy has to start moving once the first bulletin has been sent. The following UPI report of a bus crash, taken from the agency's file, illustrates the manner in which such stories are handled:

A 242
AM BUS 2TAKES 5–21
MARTINEZ, CALIF. (UPI)—A SCHOOL BUS PLUNGED OFF THE APPROACH OF A BRIDGE OVER SAN FRANCISCO BAY FRIDAY, KILLING 27 MEMBERS OF THE YUBA CITY HIGH SCHOOL CHOIR.
THE CALIFORNIA HIGHWAY PATROL SAID AT LEAST 27 OTHERS WERE INJURED WHEN THE BUS CRASHED THROUGH THE GUARDRAIL ON AN OFFRAMP AT THE SOUTH END OF THE MARTINEZ-BENICIA BRIDGE AND PLUNGED 30 FEET TO THE GROUND, LANDING UPSIDE DOWN.
THE ROOF OF THE VEHICLE COLLAPSED, CRUSHING THE HIGH SCHOOLERS AND TRAPPING THEM INSIDE. SOME WERE TRAPPED FOR MORE THAN AN HOUR AS RESCUE WORKERS FOUGHT TO FREE THEM.
THE HIGHWAY PATROL SAID 27 WERE KNOWN DEAD. OFFICIALS AT YUBA CITY HIGH SCHOOL SAID THE BUS WAS CARRYING 51 MEMBERS OF THE SCHOOL CHOIR, TWO ADULT SUPERVISORS AND THE DRIVER . . .

MORE
UPI 05–21 05:05 PED

Once the two takes were off the night wire at 5:11 P.M., that was by no means the end of the story even though it had been developing for the day wire from the time the accident occurred in mid-morning. For the night wire, a write-through began moving shortly before 7 P.M. as follows:

A 263

AM BUS 1ST—2 TAKES A 248 5–21

MARTINEZ, CALIF. (UPI)—TWENTY-EIGHT MEMBERS OF A HIGH SCHOOL CHOIR WERE KILLED FRIDAY AND MORE THAN 20 OTHERS SERIOUSLY INJURED WHEN A SCHOOL BUS CRASHED THROUGH THE GUARD RAIL ON A BRIDGE APPROACH, FLIPPED IN THE AIR AND LANDED 30 FEET BELOW ON ITS TOP.

MORE

UPI 05–21 06:43 PED

A264

AM-Bus 1STADD-1STLD-WRITETHRU 5–21

XXX ITS TOP.

THE TRAGEDY OCCURRED AT MID-MORNING AS THE YOUNG-STERS FROM YUBA CITY HIGH SCHOOL IN THE SACRAMENTO VALLEY WERE EN ROUTE TO ORINDA, CALIF., FOR A PERFORMANCE. THE BIG YELLOW SCHOOL BUS HAD JUST CROSSED THE MARTINEZ-BENICIA BRIDGE OVER SAN FRANCISCO BAY AND WAS LEAVING THE FREEWAY TO MAKE A REST STOP.

ONE OF THE FIRST PERSONS ON THE SCENE WAS HIGHWAY PATROL OFFICER DAN ACKERMAN. "THE TERRIBLE THING ABOUT IT WAS THAT WHEN IT FLIPPED OVER EVERYBODY IN IT WAS THROWN FROM THEIR SEATS TO THE TOP OF THE BUS," HE SAID. "THEN WHEN IT HIT THE GROUND ON ITS TOP THEY WERE ALL SMASHED INTO THE SEATS."

MORE

UPI 05–21 06:45 PED

The two takes of the write-through were off the night wire at 7:03 P.M. and there was no pickup, editors having been informed at the end that the story included material previously sent.

Establishing the Facts It isn't always easy to find out exactly what happened when there is an accident or a natural disaster and a considerable time may elapse before the facts are established. Then, a wire service has to put out leads until the story assumes solid form. Here is an AP report of a bus accident that illustrates the procedure:

a 116

pm—Bus, 25

URGENT

Lafayette, Ore. (AP)—A train slammed into a school bus today in this western Oregon farm town. There were no immediate reports on injuries or fatalities.

03-03-76 12:10 EDT

a 204

pm—Bus crash, 1st LD, a 116, 30

BULLETIN

Lafayette, Ore. (AP)—A train slammed into a school bus today in this western Oregon farm town. State police said there were fatalities but could give no immediate estimate on the number killed.

03-03-76 12:33 EDT

a 205

pm—Bus crash, 1st LD—1st add, a 204

URGENT

Lafayette, Ore., number killed.

It was not immediately known how many youngsters were on the bus. Witnesses said the impact threw the bus a considerable distance. One estimate was that it was more than 300 feet.

03-03-76 12:36 EDT

a 211

pm—Bus, 2nd LD—writethru, a 204

URGENT

Lafayette, Ore. (AP)—A Southern Pacific engine and caboose slammed into a school bus today in this western Oregon farm town. State police said there were fatalities but could give no early estimate on the number killed or injured.

Sheriff W. L. Mekkers of Yamhill County said his officers were at the scene. "I don't think anybody really knows yet what happened out there." he said. "One deputy came back from there and told me he was sick."

03-03-76 13:06 EDT

a 222

pm—Bus, 3rd LD—writethru, a 211

URGENT

Lafayette, Ore. (AP)—A Southern Pacific engine and caboose slammed into a school bus carrying 23 persons today on the second day of school. State police said at least two persons were killed and many were injured.

A witness to the crash, Herb Cline, 35, Lafayette, said the impact threw the bus about 350 feet. He estimated that the engine was going about 40 miles an hour when it hit the right front section of the bus.

Cline said he had just passed the bus and saw the impact in his rear view mirror. He said two children were lying alongside the track crying, but appeared to be not badly hurt."

03-03-76 13:58 EDT

It was 3:18 P.M. before the story was cleaned up for the PM cycle. By that time, a complete story had also moved for the AM cycle, identifying the dead and injured and giving details.

COMPARISON WITH SPECIALS

The specials, who cover for newspapers, news magazines and the broadcast media, have a little more time than wire service reporters to file —but not much. The new technology places pressure on them to get their stuff in and tends to hurry them in the same manner as their wire service competition. It is a trend that specials will have to resist as best they can, for the main reason an editor assigns a special on a story is to get a better rounded, more reflective dispatch.

For "media events," such as a sensational trial or an important national or international meeting, it is sometimes impossible to tell the specials from the tourists—editors who bring wives and kids and pose as correspondents. Also, so many vacationing journalists are attracted by major events that the role of the genuine working press is obscured. Those with long memories can recall when a United Nations meeting drew as many as 3,000 accredited correspondents, of whom perhaps 100 were genuine working press. At the 1976 national political conventions, there were more "reporters" than delegates. Under such circumstances, it is difficult for anybody to produce top-level work.

The special thus has problems of both coverage and identity that complicate most assignments.

How Specials Operate Correspondents seldom do as many leads, inserts and adds as wire service staffers. Their work is for specific editions or news programs. Broadcasters generally dislike interrupting their regular programs, but will do so either with wire service bulletins or a bulletin from their special if the news is big enough.

Newspaper correspondents who file through regular facilities— cable, radio, land wire or leased telephone line—usually handle their stories in the same manner as the wire services with leads, inserts and adds as needed. The principal difference is in the use of B copy, which is impractical for a wire service, but a necessity for most newspaper accounts of a developing story.

Filing through portable terminals also makes a difference in the way a story is handled. For the first time, a scattering of special political correspondents covering the 1976 national political conventions and elections worked their portable terminals under the direct control of their distant offices. For the wire services, of course, filing through terminals was the rule rather than the exception. It was the beginning of a major change in the way political reporters—and a lot of other specials—will be operating in years yet to come.

It is simple enough for even a distant correspondent, using a terminal, to reconstitute a story and top it with late developments. But for those who still use typewriters, or work under a terminal system of which typewriters remain a part, carbon copies of what they write must be retained so that they will know where inserts are to be put and where new leads are to pick up.

SOME HISTORIC STORIES

The wire services cannot wait to polish leads and make sure that every comma is in place when big news is breaking. And yet, despite all the pressures on them, they have conveyed the news with dramatic force on many historic occasions.

When the first American orbited the earth in 1962, before Cape Kennedy was so named, this was the bulletin AP coverage that preceded the final wrap-up:

> *BULLETIN*
>
> CAPE CANAVERAL, FLA., FEB. 20 (AP) ASTRONAUT JOHN H. GLENN JR. PARACHUTED TO A SAFE ATLANTIC OCEAN LANDING TODAY WITHIN SIX MILES OF THE RECOVERY DESTROYER USS NOA. OBSERVERS ON THE NOA WATCHED HIS SPACE SHIP FLOAT DOWNWARD AT 2:43 P.M. THE DESTROYERS SPED TO PICK HIM UP.
>
> THE LANDING WAS FOUR HOURS, 56 MINUTES AFTER BLAST-OFF.
>
> *JN245 PES*

This was the way UPI told the nation of the "eyeball to eyeball" confrontation between the United States and the Soviet Union during the great atomic missile crisis later that year:

> UPI A177 WA
>
> 1ST GENERAL LEAD CRISIS (A156N)
>
> WASHINGTON, TUESDAY, OCT. 23 (UPI) — U. S. PLANES AND SHIPS MOVED INTO POSITION IN THE CARIBBEAN TODAY TO CLAMP AN ARMS BLOCKADE ON CUBA.
>
> PRESIDENT KENNEDY SAID THE ACTION WAS NECESSARY BECAUSE SOVIET MISSILES CAPABLE OF CARRYING NUCLEAR WARHEADS ARE NOW ON CUBAN SOIL.
>
> THE NAVAL FLEET HAD ORDERS TO SHOOT IF NECESSARY TO ENFORCE THE QUARANTINE OF CUBA ORDERED BY KENNEDY AND ANNOUNCED TO THE NATION IN A TELEVISION SPEECH LAST NIGHT.
>
> PICKUP 2ND PGH A 156N: THE ACTION . . .
>
> WO1235AED

Here are the bulletins from Merriman Smith of UPI that gave the first news to the nation of President Kennedy's assassination in Dallas in 1963:

> UPI A7N DA
>
> PRECEDE KENNEDY
>
> DALLAS, NOV. 22 (UPI) — THREE SHOTS WERE FIRED AT PRESIDENT KENNEDY'S MOTORCADE TODAY IN DOWNTOWN DALLAS.
>
> JT1234PCS

> UPI A8N DA
>
> URGENT
>
> 1ST ADD SHOTS DALLAS (A7N) X X X DOWNTOWN DALLAS.
>
> NO CASUALTIES WERE REPORTED.
>
> THE INCIDENT OCCURRED NEAR THE COUNTY SHERIFF'S OFFICE ON MAIN STREET, JUST EAST OF AN UNDERPASS LEADING TOWARD THE TRADE MART WHERE THE PRESIDENT WAS TO MA
>
> *FLASH*

FLASH

KENNEDY SERIOUSLY WOUNDED PERHAPS SERIOUSLY PERHAPS FATALLY BY ASSASSIN'S BULLET

JT1239PCS

UPI 9N
BULLETIN
1ST LEAD SHOOTING
DALLAS, NOV. 22 (UPI) — PRESIDENT KENNEDY AND GOV. JOHN B. CONNALLY OF TEXAS WERE CUT DOWN BY AN ASSASSIN'S BULLETS AS THEY TOURED DOWNTOWN DALLAS IN AN OPEN AUTOMOBILE TODAY.

MORE JT1241PCS

UPI A10N DA
1ST ADD 1ST LEAD SHOOTING DALLAS (9N DALLAS) X X TODAY
THE PRESIDENT, HIS LIMP BODY CRADLED IN THE ARMS OF HIS WIFE, WAS RUSHED TO PARKLAND HOSPITAL. THE GOVERNOR ALSO WAS TAKEN TO PARKLAND.
CLINT HILL, A SECRET SERVICE AGENT ASSIGNED TO MRS. KENNEDY, SAID, "HE'S DEAD," AS THE PRESIDENT WAS LIFTED FROM THE REAR OF A WHITE HOUSE TOURING CAR, THE FAMOUS "BUBBLE-TOP" FROM WASHINGTON. HE WAS RUSHED TO AN EMERGENCY ROOM IN THE HOSPITAL.

*MORE*144PES

The UPI's lead on the Apollo 15 moon landing on July 30, 1971, a perfect operation, followed standard wire-service procedure in this manner:

300 A
URGENT 2ND LD
SPACE CENTER, HOUSTON (UPI) — THE APOLLO 15 LUNAR EXPLORERS SKIMMED OVER A 10,000-FOOT MOUNTAIN RANGE AND MADE A STEEP, DIVING LANDING ON THE MOON FRIDAY NIGHT TO BEGIN MAN'S FOURTH AND MOST AMBITIOUS EXPLORATION OF THE LUNAR SURFACE.
"CONTACT OKAY, HOUSTON, THE FALCON IS ON THE PLAIN AT HADLEY," RADIOED A BREATHLESS DAVID R. SCOTT AS HE AND JAMES B. IRWIN PUT DOWN IN A SMALL VALLEY RINGED ON THREE SIDES BY THE TOWERING LUNAR MOUNTAINS AND CLOSE BY THE MILE-WIDE HADLEY RILLE CANYON.
THEY LANDED ONLY A FEW HUNDRED FEET OFF TARGET AT 6:16.29 P.M. EDT. THEIR 12-MINUTE DESCENT FROM LUNAR ORBIT IN THE LANDING CRAFT FALCON WAS FLAWLESS.

MORE GE645PED

These fragments, the frantic first draft of history, vividly illustrate the basic mission of the wire service — to get the news quickly, report it accurately and remain poised for developments. There is no time here for fine writing — only the short, sharp words and phrases that alert millions of people all over the world to the news.

Chapter 16
Broadcast
Journalism

When Edward Bellamy imagined something akin to modern television in his Utopian romance, *Looking Backward, 2000–1887* A.D., few in the United States believed such things could be. Bellamy was regarded as just another impractical Socialist visionary who had had the good luck to write a best seller that made him wealthy.

Nor were there many more converts on a blustery day in November, 1901, when Guglielmo Marconi proved that long-distance wireless was not a dream. It didn't seem to make much difference to the hard-headed realists of the era that the inventor, flying a kite with copper wire in Newfoundland, had heard the three dots of the letter S in Morse code flashed across the Atlantic with his crude apparatus.

Beginnings Yet, within three years, *The Times* of London was covering naval actions in the Russo-Japanese War with a wireless-equipped vessel. Within eight years, a wireless operator, Jack Binns, was credited with bringing rescue ships to the scene of a maritime disaster in time to save all but six of the 1,600 passengers of the White Star liner *Republic* after a collision.

And in 1912, President William Howard Taft dramatically ordered silence over the air waves so that another wireless operator, David Sarnoff, could direct rescue ships to the sinking *Titanic*. That same Sarnoff, as the founder of the Radio Corporation of America, made possible the first commercial network, the National Broadcasting Company, which on November 11, 1926 began operations with a four-hour program of star-studded entertainment.

The Coming of TV Before long, radio was outstripping the press in the swift presentation of the news. In a little more than two generations after Marconi, beginning in 1947, television was bringing distant scenes into millions of homes with routine daily news programs. Today, with the use of satellites and the introduction of electronic newsgathering that substitutes magnetic tape, miniature cameras and microwave transmission for films, broadcast journalism has come of age. The new system has numerous symbols. Some call it ENG, others EJ, for electronic journalism, and CBS prefers ECC, or electronic camera coverage. But by whatever name it is called, it is remarkable.

Under sensible operation, television has acquired the flexibility of radio and the immediacy of wire service transmission of news. It depicts the set event—from space shots to Presidential news conferences and sports championships—with faithfulness and fidelity. It goes to the spot, often with immediate reports, on demonstrations, riots and wars— sometimes with almost unbearably painful detail. And as a cachet of its reliability, it has gained the right—and the prestige—to share with the older media the responsibility of gathering and presenting all major election returns in the United States.

With broadcast journalism in a continuous state of development and the print media and the wire services breaking out of decades of frozen technology, more surprises are ahead. Any system of communications that can go from a kite to globe-girdling satellites and laser beams in less than man's allotted life span of three-score and ten years has the capacity to create a revolution in the presentation of the news.

There is no doubt that such a revolution is now under way. How far it will go depends almost entirely on the extent to which television news is able to liberate itself from the domination of show personalities and show business. It has the voice, the vision and the genius. It needs the will.

RADIO NEWS OPERATIONS

Outside the United States and other advanced nations, radio is the prime reliance of most of the world's peoples for their daily news.

Where there are no newspapers, or where newspapers are few and under government control, radio is the only source of news for millions in Asia, Africa and parts of Latin America.

Where Radio Rules Inevitably, at the governmental level in these areas, radio has become the principal medium through which a ceaseless struggle is carried on for influence over public opinion. Most of the powerful transmitters owned and operated by governments therefore specialize in news—or what passes for it. In the West, such establishments as the Voice of America and BBC seek credibility by trying on the whole to present news honestly, despite some understandable lapses, over a long period. In the Communist world, and in other forms of closed or partly closed societies, prime sources such as Radio Moscow, Radio Peking and various affiliates seldom put out material that either is critical of their respective governments, or otherwise embarrasses them. The uncommitted nations, in large part, follow variations of these widely conflicting policies, depending on their dominant political philosophies.

Network "Feeds" Although radio does not have the clout of television in the United States, having become a secondary consideration with both advertisers and a large part of the public, it remains a formidable organization for disseminating news quickly. Despite the drawbacks of the all-news radio stations, with their repetitive programming and often bored news listeners, they are making a contribution to public knowledge. When major news breaks, they are always ready to go with it.

It wasn't always so.

Leonard J. Patricelli of WTIC Radio in Hartford, Connecticut, owner of one of the nine original NBC affiliates, recalled at NBC's golden anniversary: "In those days, news departments were nonexistent at local stations. We took our news from the daily papers and did a newscast by reading what was on the front pages. It made a big difference to be able to broadcast news from our own (NBC) source."

NBC and the British Broadcasting Corporation, which was founded two months later, became the models for radio network news. They were soon joined by William S. Paley's Columbia Broadcasting System in 1928. The American Broadcasting Company was formed in 1943 from the NBC Blue Network after government anti-trust action against NBC. And until the coming of television four years later, the three radio networks were supreme in broadcast journalism. Their "feed" system was one of the principal reasons behind the development of radio news.

All-News Radio Despite the dominance of TV from the 1950s onward, radio retained an exclusive market—the motorists and their passengers who drove to and from work in the morning and evening rush hours. Finally, in 1961, the 24-hour all-news radio station began as an experiment to appeal to these captive millions in their automobiles. Today, there are several score of these stations, the larger ones with impressive news staffs. Until the collapse of NBC's News and Information Service (NIS) in 1977, there were more. A number of former NIS clients went on anyway. In the key metropolitan areas of the country, the best all news stations return at least 15 per cent on their investments and the outstanding personalities at their microphones earn anywhere between $100,000 and $225,000 a year.[1]

Broadcast Wire Service News In addition to local news staffs and network feeds, broadcast news is provided by the AP and UPI radio wires and by tape. Those of the 5,000 commercial radio and 700 commercial TV stations that have small or nonexistent news staffs must depend on the wire services. For anybody can handle the material that comes over the radio wire or in tape recordings in their expert, prepackaged formats.

Attitudes Even among broadcast journalists, the radio wire has never acquired the prestige of the regular "A" wire of the agencies although it carries the same news and is written for the ear rather than the eye. The attitude of print journalists toward the radio wire is understandable. To them, it is an illegitimate offspring, not to be acknowledged and generally to be treated with contempt. Broadcasters have aped this attitude.

In the electronic newsrooms, when editors want to be thoroughly insulting, they say, "Why, we always use the 'A' wire and do our own rewrite instead of paying any attention to the radio wire." Historically newspaper specials have always said much the same thing about the supposed unreliability of *their* principal competitor, the "A" wire, only in that case the special insult is, "You know what I told my desk? I told them to spike the 'A' wire copy."

Whether the competition is in the electronic or newspaper field, or both, few specials can ever bring themselves to admit that the news agencies have special virtues of their own. Yet, by glancing over a radio-wire file and then turning the dial to current newscasts at random, it is easily demonstrable that the agencies are the sources for much broadcast news. The radio wires, therefore, are basic to most news programs, even if they are rewritten. This is almost as true of television as it is of radio, although the pictorial requirements of television make it impossible to proceed on the substance of radio wire alone. Despite their lofty attitudes toward agency copy, the networks would no more

[1] Ben H. Bagdikian, "Fires, Sex and Freaks," *New York Times* Sunday Magazine, October 10, 1976, p. 40 *et seq.*

give up the radio wire than the Washington staffs of the *New York Times* and *Washington Post* would give up the "A" wire.

THE RADIO WIRE

In major bureaus such as New York City, the agencies' radio services generally work on a three-cycle basis. These are the "early," from 11 P.M. to 7 A.M., corresponding to the "A" wire overnight file; the "day," from 7 A.M. to 3 P.M., and the "night" from 3 to 11 P.M., both equivalent to the "A" wire day and night cycles. In smaller bureaus and overseas, the early and day files are combined into a single PM cycle and the night file is expanded into a longer AM cycle. But regardless of the system, the agencies' radio wires keep turning out the spot news summaries of headlines, roundups of news and such added broadcast material as sports, financial and weather summaries.

There is a news budget for each cycle of the radio wire, just as there is for the "A" wire. New tops, the radio equivalent of the new lead, are frequently filed to update pending material. Where there is an important new development, the radio wire carries bulletins for immediate use. In general, material is prepared and slugged in much the same basic manner as copy for any other agency wire.

In addition, there are voice recordings made by wire service correspondents who are on the scene at breaking news events.

Brevity Is the Rule Radio writing must be brief. Developing news is usually written in the present tense. The work must be clear and to the point to cut down the risk of misunderstanding, always a radio bugaboo. Consequently, the short sentence and the one and two-syllable words are features of the radio wire.

The following spot summary of five items illustrates the manner in which a radio wire headline roundup is prepared:

Here is the latest news from the Associated Press:

NEW YORK—A Liberian freighter has signaled it is taking on water and is in danger of sinking 470 miles East-Southeast of New York.

NEW YORK—A British freighter has taken aboard three women and two men from the stricken yawl *Petrel*—also at the mercy of the Atlantic storm.

WASHINGTON—The Food and Drug Administration has asked a New York importer to recall all retail stocks of foreign dolls which have been found to be highly inflammable.

BURLINGTON, IOWA—A mysterious but apparently minor illness has affected workers at the Army ammunition plant near here and the Federal government is investigating it.

CHICAGO—A new snowstorm is moving south across the central Rockies.

Expanding the Summary This is expanded into the kind of news summary that is more in evidence on the radio wire than anything else:

A Liberian freighter has signaled it is taking on water and is in danger of sinking in an Atlantic gale. The New York Coast Guard says the ship S. S. *Georgia* gave her position as about 470 miles East-Southeast of New York. A spokesman said the cutter Vigilante out of Provincetown, Massachusetts, has been diverted to help the *Georgia*. The cutter had been en route to the 70-foot yawl *Petrel* — also being pounded by the storm.

A British freighter is standing by the stricken *Petrel* after taking aboard five of its ten passengers 360 miles Southeast of New York. Three women and two men were transferred to the freighter *Cotswold*. The five other passengers — all men — have elected to remain aboard the *Petrel* until a Coast Guard cutter arrives to take it in tow.

The Food and Drug Administration has asked a New York City importer to recall all retail stocks of some imported dolls which have been found to be highly inflammable. The dolls, ranging in size from seven to sixteen inches, have been distributed nationally. Thus far, the administration adds, it has received no reports of any injuries involving the dolls.

A U. S. government report is expected within the next ten days on a mysterious, but apparently minor, illness that has afflicted workers on a project at the Army ammunition plant near Burlington, Iowa. Some 50 to 100 employees have been hit by the ailment in the past six months.

A snowstorm in the Southern Rockies and the intermountain region has prompted heavy snow or hazardous driving warnings for Northern Arizona and Western New Mexico. Several inches of snow fell on Kingman, Arizona, and one to three inches covered the ground today in southern Wyoming, Utah and Nevada.

A New Top With a change in the status of an item in the summary, the new top is sent without fuss and directions are included for the information of station news directors. One way of doing it is as follows:

News Dirs: Following is new top for Ships section above:
(Ships)
The Coast Guard says 29 Greek crewmen aboard a Liberian freighter 470 miles Southeast of New York report they may have to abandon ship. A Coast Guard spokesman says a rescue plane is flying over the stricken vessel — S S *Georgia* — and a rescue ship is only about 20 minutes away. The freighter's position is about 120 miles East of the disabled pleasure yacht *Petrel* which appears to be holding its own. A British freighter has taken aboard five of the *Petrel's* ten passengers and is standing by the 70-foot yawl.
—Dash—
The Food and Drug etc. x x x picking up third graf original item.

In the same manner, the radio wire can and frequently does carry additional material to expand a five-minute summary to ten minutes, if desired. For the 15-minute summaries, which are elaborate for radio, separate treatment is required but the same general methods and rules are observed.

Attribution to Radio Regardless of the time span of a newscast, all copy for radio is intended for the ear and not the eye. It makes a difference in the informality with which radio news is treated. Also, words and phrases that are difficult to pronounce must be dropped. Very often, dependent clauses in a newspaper story are made into a separate sentence for a radio story.

A major difference with newspaper procedure is the use of attribution. In a newspaper, it is considered dull to begin with a routine bit of attribution, such as "Police say . . ." or "The State Department has announced. . . ." But in radio, there is so much concern over misunderstanding that the attribution often comes first. Thus, a proper newspaper lead may be: "A fire at Gamm's Department Store that killed four persons may be the work of a firebug, police reported today." But on radio the dangling attribution is eliminated as follows: "Police say a firebug may have caused the fire at Gamm's Department Store that killed four persons."

Simplifying and Updating The factual precision of newspapers also comes in for relaxed treatment on the radio wire. Middle initials are often dropped and titles curtailed if they are too long. Figures are rounded out wherever practical. Moreover, too many figures in a short newscast are bound to be confusing and some are eliminated. If ages are used, there generally has to be a good reason. And not all precise addresses are considered important in radio wire copy. With these exceptions, the tenets of journalistic accuracy must be observed as rigidly for radio as they are for any other news medium.

In the constant pressure to update the news, so that the listener will hear a "different" newscast on the hour, the radio wire has the same basic weakness as much other agency copy. While the news in essence has not changed, the phrasing is turned and twisted in an effort to infer that something else is about to happen in the brief time between broadcasts. From experience, the listener usually knows he is being conned, sighs, "same old stuff," and turns off his radio. Thus, all the updating—even though the agencies insist on it—actually does very little good. Sometimes, it even does harm, for there is so much updating on a piece of spot news, such as a train wreck, that the listener who has just tuned in cannot tell what has happened, or when.

Nevertheless, the content of the radio wires day in and day out provides solid evidence that a great deal of work is thoroughly if not elegantly done. Improvements are always possible in so detailed a service; from time to time, they are made with good effect. But despite their weak points, the agencies' radio wires remain as essential as network feeds for the news programs of the electronic media.

RADIO NEWS PROGRAMMING

There is an enormous range in radio-news programming. Nothing very elaborate can be expected from a local station of 1,000 watts or less, with a minimal staff, beyond the use of radio wire material. The all-news stations are useful but few have the personnel, the drive and the imagination to vary the dullness of much of their presentation. Therefore, with not many exceptions, the development of significant radio-news programming is left almost by default to the big independents and the networks with their showcase owned and operated stations. These are the places where news staffs of some importance are being developed, and where originality in dealing with the news is being shown.

Organizing the Report In the mystique of broadcast journalism, an inordinate amount of importance is attached to the first item—the lead. It is, in its own way, almost as much of a symbol for radio as a good cover illustration is for a news magazine. For TV, it is even more important because the competition is stiffer.

Once the lead item is decided upon, the business of radio programming proceeds in fits and starts. As the deadline approaches and the news begins to change, rapid switches are made. And very often, while a program is on the air, bulletins come in that make newscasters edit their script as they read it. The only thing certain about radio-news programming is that it is always subject to change.

A good program carries with it a kind of controlled excitement, particularly in the most popular listening periods for news in the morning and early evening. Here is the deadline-and-lead format for one of the oldest network programs of radio news:

> Massive fire in New York . . . German chancellor in Paris . . . New battle in the Middle East . . .
>
> Good morning. This is the CBS World News Roundup . . .
>
> Before dawn today in the City of New York, brilliant flames lit up the sky over the Borough of Queens. Fire had broken out in a large residential area, heavily populated . . . and it raced out of control for several hours . . .

The program quickly switched to a reporter at the fire scene with a vivid taped account of what he heard and saw. This is an example of the flexibility of radio-news programming; in a world-news program, the director did not hesitate to come on strong with a lead of both local and national significance—a fire in the country's largest city.

Sometimes, this kind of material is inserted in a program in an equally dramatic way. NBC's News of the World, for example, once broke into an international summary with this abrupt lead-in: "Now, news by direct report—a big fire in Chicago." On the same program, NBC came through with this vivid bit of writing about a Midwestern storm:

> Blizzard winds on the northern plains . . . They are carrying temperatures as low as 25 below zero. Light snow is flying in the wind. North Dakota, South Dakota, Minnesota, northern Iowa are seriously affected. Gusts up to 100 miles an hour are gouging out old snow cover and piling it up in mountainous drifts. Bus and air travel are halted. Power and communications lines have been ripped out. Hundreds of schools have been closed. Trucks have been blown off the highways in southeastern South Dakota . . .

This illustrates the essentially informal manner of radio news writing. Phrases, partial sentences, vigorous verbs and crisp writing all combine to create a sharp image. That is the essence of the art.

Radio Techniques When news is written for radio, it is often cast in a different context so that listeners can identify their interest with the latest developments. To newspapers, this is the "feature approach," sometimes called "featurizing the news." The news magazines have always done it better than most newspapers, and radio and television, in effect, have tried to rival the news magazines. The trick is effective when it can be done with logic and reason; however, there is an inevitable risk of distortion when the feature angle is overstressed. This is how CBS reported one of the most overworked news stories in Washington—the annual drive for an adjournment of Congress before Christmas:

> Like a horse that quickens its pace when it smells water just ahead, Congress often gets a lot done before a holiday. But in its try for adjournment this week it has come to the crunch, and that crunch is foreign aid . . . Some Senators and Congressmen anxious to head home for Christmas have tried to get around the snarl by passing a resolution that once again would continue foreign aid funding at its present levels until Congress could return next year and settle the matter . . . One other approach suggests a temporary continuation only of foreign-aid salaries and operating expenses, but bars the agency from starting any new aid projects until Congress can debate the whole issue further next year.

A straight news lead on the above, by contrast, would have gone something like this:

> WASHINGTON—A disagreement over foreign aid threatened today to stall Congress's drive for adjournment over the Christmas holiday.

The technique of attracting the attention of the listeners before actually telling them what is happening can be extremely helpful in news of a surprising nature. It comes under the old formula usually stated as follows: "Tell 'em what you're going to tell 'em, then tell 'em what you have to tell 'em, and finally tell 'em that you've told 'em." For example, when the King of Denmark died and was succeeded by his daughter, the NBC teaser at the beginning of the nightly news roundup said that there would be a story telling how "a young woman in Copenhagen, whose father died last night, became Queen of Denmark."

The Roundup While a great deal of radio and television news is told in the present tense, it is by no means an inviolate rule. The roundups, which summarize the day's events, are usually handled very much like summaries in newspapers; moreover, there are newscasters who insist on the use of the word *today* in every past-tensed item just to be sure that the listener understands when the event took place.

At its best, this radio-newswriting technique approximates superior newspaper or news-magazine journalism. But when it is misapplied, the effect is similar to that of reading yesterday's newspaper aloud. Mainly, much depends on who is doing the reading and what sense can be made out of the news.

Comparison with Wire Services The natural development of a story counts for a great deal in broadcast journalism. Here is a compact and colorful account of a skyjacking, as it was used on the CBS World News Roundup, that compressed a number of wire service leads into a good story:

> Another aerial hijacking occurred over the weekend, and it ended in a blaze of gunfire. Three men armed with guns and knives hijacked a Nicaraguan jetliner and directed it to Cuba. But when they landed in San Jose to refuel, the 49 passengers were let off, five crew members escaped, Costa Rican national guardsmen flushed the hijackers out with tear gas and killed one of them. One of the passengers, the son of Nicaragua's agriculture minister, was wounded by a bullet reportedly fired by one of the hijackers. He was hospitalized in satisfactory condition. The plane was on a flight from Miami to Managua, the capital of Nicaragua. The three hijackers boarded at San Salvador. Upon landing at San Jose, the passengers were allowed to leave. President Jose Figueres of Costa Rica told the hijackers from the airport control tower that there would be no reprisals if they released the crew unharmed. The hijackers refused, and the national guardsmen opened up with tear gas, the crew members jumped out the window, and then there was the exchange of gunfire in which one of the hijackers was killed.

Trying to narrate this kind of a fast-moving tale for a listening mass audience, inverted pyramid style, would have been deadly dull. The whole emphasis in writing for radio, therefore, must be on the storytelling values inherent in the news.

MECHANICS

It isn't necessary to be a member in good standing of the Institute of Radio Engineers to be a radio reporter or writer. Nor is a producer or news director required to be expert in the theory and practice of launching communications satellites or constructing efficient micro-wave circuits. It does help to know that radio has progressed beyond the era of the rotary spark gap, that there is a certain amount of differ-ence between a Galena crystal and a transistor, and that the image Or-thicon tube does represent an advance over the DeForest Audiotron and the Western Electric VT-2. While it is undoubtedly possible to do a professional radio-news program without being initiated into the mys-teries of such old and new radio devices, a basic understanding of ra-dio techniques can avert a great deal of woe. For one thing, it enables reporters to communicate with the technicians who operate a station's intricate and expensive equipment. For another, it gives reporters a good idea of what can and cannot be done in gathering, presenting and distributing the news of the day.

Pronunciation When it isn't possible to determine pronunciation of place names through a source book, a telephone call will help. To someone who has never been to New York City, for example, there would be no other way of finding out that Houston Street is pro-nounced *How-ston* and not Hew-ston, as it is in Texas. A book of place names, however, would show that Cairo is pronounced Kay-ro in Illi-nois, whereas Kigh-ro is the city in Egypt.

Some of the simplest mechanical precautions in any radio-news pro-gram are merely the products of good sense. Thus, difficult or unusual names or words are spelled phonetically in scripts to help the news-caster. For example, the Pulitzer Prizes become "*Pull-it-zur* Prizes," Mekong becomes "May-kong," and Zbigniew Brzezinski becomes "Z-big-nee-eF Br-ze-zin-skee."

Timing Aside from such considerations, the dominant mechanical fac-tor in the preparation of any radio or television-news program is time. Most newscasters read from 170 to 180 words a minute and calculate a 16 to 17-line page of typing (with one-inch margins) as requiring about a minute to read. For the average station, only the last few items are timed, with the elapsed time of the script marked in big numerals in the upper right hand side of the page so that the newscaster knows when he must conclude. However, the more important the station, the more rigid are the time controls applied to the radio-news programs. And on the networks, there is usually very little room for maneuvering. A five-minute newscast actually includes only three and one-half minutes of news, allowing for commercial and sign-off, and a 15-minute newscast runs somewhere between 12½ and 13½ minutes, depending on commercials.

Consequently, if there is a 15-minute program beginning at noon, the first thing that must be done after a script is completed is to "back-time" the closing items. The sign-off and station public service announcement take 30 seconds; therefore, the time 12:1430, is marked boldly in the right hand corner of the closing page. The weather, usually inserted before the sign-off, is timed and found to be 20 seconds. At the start of the weather page, therefore, the time is marked: 12:1410 The item directly preceding the weather is a brief sports item of 45 seconds, the time on the page being 12:1325. With these pages laid out on the table beside the newscaster, he or she has a ready check on when to begin the final commercial and be assured of concluding in time. If necessary, filler items may be used or discarded in a prearranged manner. But come what may, the newscast must be concluded on schedule.

To illustrate how little time there really is for very many items in the average five-minute newscast, most stations try to include about eight assorted pieces in the three and one-half minutes actually assigned to the news. This comes down to less than 30 seconds per item, slightly less than eight typewritten lines each. What it means is that all complications will have to be dropped; the best that can be offered, under the circumstances, is bulletin-type coverage. And if there is a taped interview with a news personage or a correspondent, as is usual in most such spots, even fewer items may be included.

In the longer radio-news programs, particularly those of 15 minutes, the script is generally broken into three sections of about five minutes each (including commercials). Thus, tapes may be distributed fairly evenly without crowding out other essential news.

There is nothing in journalism that quite equals the painstaking second-by-second scheduling of the electronic media, the programming jitters, the heightened anticipation as the program goes on the air and the sense of relief when it is over. By contrast, the unscheduled intervention of a reporter with a bulletin is handled with efficiency and smoothness once the basic decision is made to interrupt the usual network or local station routine. Even though the words "News Show" are now regarded with extreme disfavor in broadcast journalism, striving as it does for an image of solidity and prestige, the atmosphere of the theater cannot be exorcised merely by saying it does not exist. It is an intrinsic part of electronic news presentation and accounts in part for the very large audiences it attracts throughout the nation. For radio, news is still a necessity in the United States, particulary in rural areas where so much depends on accurate weather information, and for millions of motorists.

CRITICISMS OF RADIO

Aside from technical criticisms of content, style and pace, radio generally has to face the serious charge that it does little to advance the public interest. In a recent survey of broadcast journalism, Marvin Barrett, director of the duPont-Columbia Awards, wrote that radio was "almost, but not quite, a journalistic desert." Specifically, he found: "Most major markets seemed to have at least one station capable of producing a decent newscast or documentary, whether they did so or not. Some smaller markets frequently did better."[2]

Progress, or Lack of It? There is no built-in reason for radio's current timidity. Listeners of an older generation can remember, in the era immediately before television, when radio was the keeper of the nation's conscience — when broadcasters like Elmer Davis and Edward R. Murrow took the lead in arousing a divided America to the threat of the Axis powers. There was no equivocation at that time, no fumbling over issues that had to be faced, no lack of courage in addressing a confused and even fearful public.

Even after the birth of television, when the McCarthy era had paralyzed much of the press and all save a few strong voices like Murrow's in the broadcast media, it was Davis who counseled the nation over radio:

> The first and great commandment is: Don't let them scare you. For the men who are trying to do that to us are scared themselves. They are afraid that what they think will not stand critical examination; they are afraid that the principles on which this Republic was founded and has been conducted are wrong. They will tell you that there is a hazard in the freedom of the mind, and of course there is, as in any freedom. In trying to think right you run the risk of thinking wrong. But there is no hazard at all, no uncertainty, in letting somebody else tell you what to think: that is sheer damnation.[3]

If radio appears to be producing no new Elmer Davises, Murrows or Eric Sevareids, there still are a few here and there who dare to think for themselves. In Baton Rouge, Louisiana, a small radio station, WJBO, disclosed several local government scandals that led to the prosecution of offenders. And in Richmond, Virginia, WRVA radio did a dramatic documentary on the poisoning of industrial workers at a chemical plant in a nearby Virginia town where an insecticide called Kepone was manufactured.

There were other public service reports that required both digging and courage, but by and large they were too few in number to sustain the crusading image of American radio at its best.

---

[2] Fifth duPont–Columbia Survey of Broadcast Journalism, p. 176.
[3] John Hohenberg, *Free Press/Free People* (New York, 1971), pp. 317–318.

TELEVISION

Television is the most complicated form of journalism, the most dynamic and the most universal in its appeal. Its corporate personality is split between the glitter of show business, the commercial requirements of advertising and the professional demands of good journalism. It is an amalgam of some of the best—and some of the worst—elements of the stage, the movies, the newspapers, wire services and radio. It is the most researched, the most criticized, the most investigated and the recipient of the most free advice of any of the news media. It also is the most rapid in adapting and developing new ideas, spends fantastic amounts of money to cover the top news of the day and patiently tries to invent better ways of informing the public. But it jealously guards its prime time, the main source of its advertising revenue, from intrusion by public service programs of limited appeal.

Pros and Cons Television has many advantages—the immediacy of radio and wire service news, the quick projection of the sights and sounds of daily events into millions of homes, the involvement of people in the news, the flashing brilliance of color film and the dramatic projection of the most personal form of journalism in the shape of eyewitness reporting.

Its limitations are also considerable. Aside from the ever-present threat of government regulation, its most severe handicap is the inability to report the news in depth in its regularly scheduled news programs. It is also a medium that often seems confused by a lack of firm direction and an excessive timidity in the face of controversy.

But when big news breaks—the sudden eruption of war, the assassination of a President, a natural catastrophe such as an earthquake or hurricane, a space shot to the moon or a distant planet—then television is unsurpassed in its coverage of events.

Its Problems In essence, television illustrates in exaggerated form almost every major difficulty the journalist is likely to encounter.

The newspaper reporter, for example, is encumbered at the very worst by such devices as a portable terminal or a tape recorder; generally, all that really is needed is a pad and pencil, a telephone and a stout pair of legs. If still photographers are at the scene, they operate independently. But in television, the newsmen and women must work in cooperation with cameras and other special equipment and those who operate them, which makes quite a difference in the way a story is covered.

Newspaper reporters also have an advantage in both time and space when it comes to transmitting their stories. On a major event, any newspaper of consequence will not blanch at a file of several thousand words from a special; full coverage, in fact, is desirable because it can be cut. But television news people are always conscious of the brevity of their news programs; no matter how much good stuff they have, they know that in the end they will get two or three minutes—400 or 500 words—which will have to be related (probably off camera) against a background of action on videotape or color film that will overshadow anything they can say.

Inside the newsroom, producers do not have the luxury of planning to spread their accounts over two full newspaper pages with illustrations, or perhaps a half-dozen pages of a news magazine or a dozen wire service leads. They must cram their expensive film or tape and narration—obtained at great effort—into the context of a regular news program minus time for commercials and other announcements. And if by chance the event is big enough, they must also worry about how to meet the complaints of the television fanatics who reject all extended or special news programs if they interfere with TV's brand of entertainment.

Finally, television is not its own master in the same manner as printed publications or the independent wire services of the United States, even though newspapers own 65 stations. Let one side of a political issue be covered in the news on television and all the others inevitably clamor for a hearing by invoking the rules of the Federal Communications Commission. Considering all their limitations, it is a tribute to the professionalism of the broadcast journalists that they perform as well as they do in presenting the news on television.

TECHNIQUES OF TV NEWS

It is impossible to work in television journalism without an understanding of the new uses to which video tapes have been put, the development of miniature cameras, the advantages of microwave transmission and the operation of the regular and even more complicated studio equipment. Even if journalists have nothing to do with these technical matters, they must have an appreciation of the problems that are involved and govern themselves accordingly. Otherwise, the best-conceived news assignment can end in utter disaster.

Videotape   Videotape, that most flexible and remarkable process for handling sight and sound, has made possible many of the seeming miracles of television news. It is magnetic and can be played back immediately. It can be reused. It can be stored indefinitely without damage, catalogued, categorized and taken out for a rerun whenever necessary.

In itself, videotape is not new. It has been used for years on large and cumbersome cameras to do commercials and to cover sports events, as anybody knows who has ever watched an instant replay. But it wasn't until after the 1972 political conventions in the United States, when reporters as usual got fouled up in their complicated television equipment, that efforts were made to adapt videotape to news coverage.

With the help of CBS engineers, KMOX-TV in St. Louis, the CBS affiliate there, began experimenting with portable cameras and videotape in 1973 and in the following year abandoned the use of film for news coverage. All kinds of adjustments and improvements had to be made. Different kinds of cameras had to be developed. Cameramen were given backpacks with necessary additional equipment. Correctors had to be invented to make it possible to regenerate the microwave signal of a half- or three-quarter-inch videotape and bring it up to the broadcast quality of a regular two-inch studio tape.

The old Norelco PCP-90, the "Creepie-Peepie" videotape camera that had been standard at sporting events and political conventions, soon had a swarm of competitors. CBS and ABC invested millions of dollars in the Japanese-made Ikegami and NBC spent a comparable amount on the German-made Fernseh KCN cameras. Soon the miniature camera—the now omnipresent minicam—was a fact of life. All three networks used it to cover President Ford's Asian visits.

The Minicam A single operator can handle a 12 pound minicam, with a 20-pound backpack of battery-operated recorders.[4] In essence, therefore, the minicam eliminates the need for the old three-man film camera crews with their mountain of equipment—what Professor Fred W. Friendly used to call television's "thousand-pound pencil." Sometimes, for diplomatic reasons having to do with union relations, two-man tape crews are used on network assignments. But with tape now dominant at the great majority of commercial television stations, the film cameraman in television may soon be as dispensable as the old teletype "puncher" in the wire services and the linotype operators in newspaper composing rooms.

The quality of the color pictures taken by the best minicams is said by network experts to approach, and sometimes exceed, that of 16 mm. newsfilm. It is bound to get better. In any case, the minicams have created more changes in television than anything since the industry-wide adoption of color in 1965.

How Minicams Work Reporters and minicam operators work as a team and closely coordinate with their producers and news directors. It can't be otherwise. They travel in a mobile unit if they are assigned to transmit pictures and narration directly to the newsroom by microwave. In the case of a conference, convention, show or interview, a small electronic relay on a window sill is aimed at the mobile unit outside which transmits a live microwave "feed" back to the studio. Whatever the re-

---

[4] This is for an Ikegami HL-33. Others vary in weight.

porter and minicam operator are doing is thus under the eyes of their news director all the time if he wants to watch them in action.

For outside scenes, the minicam is even more effective. One of the earliest and most striking uses of the new equipment was in CBS's coverage of the crash of an Eastern Airlines Boeing 727 at New York's Kennedy International Airport on June 24, 1975, in which 113 persons were killed. A mobile unit happened to be in the area and began transmitting while eleven survivors were still being pulled out of the wreckage. It was perhaps the fastest and one of the most effective color television news reports in a decade.

But minicams aren't restricted to ground level. KNBC-TV, an NBC affiliate in Los Angeles, has a helicopter equipped with minicam and microwave transmission for the coverage of forest fires, other natural disasters and traffic accidents. The small cameras are so sensitive that they can be used at night with relatively low light levels; they are at their best, of course, by day at brightly colored scenes. Reporters working with them find it easier to do their narration, opening and closing than with film.

At the beginning, there was a considerable amount of concern over the difficult business of learning to edit videotape with its magnetic properties. But that was overcome with patient experimentation. Now, videotape editing proceeds as normally as film editing, and with less trouble.

Difficulties of the New Order The centralized control of news coverage that has always been a strong feature of modern newspaper and wire service work now has come to television with the minicam-videotape, microwave system. Television's control, in fact, is even more sweeping than that of any newspaper editor. For a television news director can see and hear exactly how an interview is going with live coverage and can interrupt with instructions for the crew. Similarly, orders can be given to direct the work of mobile units or large staffs on a convention floor. Everything that comes in may be recorded, as desired, on the TV monitors beside the news director's desk. And both the director and the producer, as a result, have a much better idea of the development of the story.

Like newspaper reporters who groan over their new electronic equipment, television newsmen and women aren't entirely happy over this aspect of their work. As one TV editor put it, "On the positive side, this means that when a camera angle doesn't look right, it can be corrected. And if there is some new information, or an added question to be asked, the reporter can be reached while he still has the interviewee available. Of course, there is also the possibility that the reporter and the editor will disagree on how to conduct the interview.

Some reporters decry this as interference when their editors do not know the details of the story.'' [5]

The Writing When television staffers are working toward a regularly scheduled news program, the pictures and narration accumulated on assignment give editors more time for their work. Cuts can be planned without undue haste, except as the deadline approaches. And there is also more time for writers to work on their scripts, to fit the narration precisely to the pictorial content. It also becomes possible to make more news on deadline and even during the program as it is being shown, always a risky business.

Regardless of how much is written and spoken about these important and complicated procedures, they are actually best learned by doing. Like the intricate problem of putting news and advertising together in a newspaper or magazine and producing a professional product on time, no amount of description or exhortation can be quite as enlightening as meeting the problem head-on. And this is where experience, background and a thorough knowledge of new procedures as well as standard ones count for a great deal.

THE COMPLETED PROGRAM

When a completed, regularly scheduled news program is shown on a national television network, it is generally put together so smoothly that the viewing public is not conscious of the effort that has gone into it.

Making the Scene The cameras move, seemingly in the most natural and agreeable manner, from the principal newscaster in the studio to live, videotaped or filmed segments of other portions of the program. On occasion, there is a pleasant variation of medium and close-up shots of the anchor person. Usually, this key individual is portrayed as calm, decisive, authoritative and—as far as the men are concerned—solemn to the bursting point.

Behind the reader, which is what anchor men and women really are, the device of rear-screen projection may be used to show still pictures, maps, charts, sketches, even headlines on occasion through the use of flipcards on an easel. Or this may be varied by slide devices taking up the whole screen, known as *balops* or *telops*. Almost everything is done to maintain the viewers' interest, from cutting down all unillustrated remarks to working in feature videotape or library film when there aren't enough good new news pictures to give the program a lift.

[5] Phillip O. Kierstead, "ENG, Live News From Almost Anywhere," *The Quill* (May 1976), pp. 25–29.

Except for the few recognized stars, interpreters of the news are not permitted to talk and stare at the home audience for very long; even the best must give their views in two or three minutes as a rule.

The Reaction When the program is over, the public necessarily must judge it by the substance it has just heard and seen. The techniques are applied in such slick fashion that they are seldom detected by the inexperienced eye. Were it not for such technical mastery, editors, writers, reporters and technicians could not even put a program together, for there seems to be no end to television's development as a news medium and to the devices that make it more efficient.

This is at once the strength and the weakness of television, for it is so well managed on the whole that a large section of the public has come to believe that it can get along on a steady diet of television alone. Of course that won't work, as sensible people know. Few of television's professional journalists would dare to give up reading newspapers and magazines and trusting themselves to the vagaries of their own medium. The hard facts of communications today do not justify that kind of exclusivity. For in truth the news media are, to a very large degree, interdependent and other-directed in their motivation.

The Ratings One of the most depressing features of television news is its continued dependence on ratings. The weekly polls of the A. C. Nielsen Company, based on recognized sampling techniques, have been accepted with such finality that they have become the basis for a lot of editorial decision making. And, as any experienced professional journalist knows, that is not the way to build confidence in a news operation.

The Nielsen firm is the largest in marketing research in the country with more than $200 million in annual revenues, of which its controversial TV ratings account for 11 per cent. It is without significant competition nationally although Arbitron, the American Research Bureau, is a rival in local markets and has made attempts to enter the national field.

What Nielsen has been doing in radio since 1942 and TV since 1950 is to record the listening and viewing habits of a small sampling of American homes and project them on a regional or national basis each week. For TV, the sample has consisted of 1,170 homes out of a total of 68.5 million TV-equipped households. The identity of each sample home is carefully guarded and, by means of a device called an audimeter, is connected by special telephone lines to Nielsen computers. These machines sort out the channel selection information and provide the weekly totals on which news and entertainment programs stand or fall.

When it is considered that Nielsen's ratings affect more than $2.5 billion in TV network commercials alone, there is reason to appreciate the influence they exercise over programming. A drop of one percentage point in a network news program rating, for example, is said by some TV executives to be equivalent to a cut of $1.5 million in advertising revenues.

Unlike newspaper sales, the success of TV news is based on its ability to attract millions of viewers—something on the order of 60 million of them for the three network news programs. The critics of the ratings do not say that they are bad or even that they are falsified, except in rare instances. Statistically, social scientists generally agree that they are sound enough. Some argue that participants in the sampling, who get $50 a year and a 50 per cent reimbursement for TV repairs, are by nature viewers in larger volume than the national average and that out-of-home viewing audiences are seldom included. But few have challenged Nielsen's claim to accuracy within 1.3 percentage points of a typical finding that a program has attracted 20 per cent of the viewing audience.

What does seem deplorable is that the merchandising of news is researched on exactly the same basis as Nielson's surveys of everything from chain store food sales, drug store products and wildcat oil wells. It is like surveying the same audience for reactions to a great ballet star and a strip tease dancer, a honky-tonk piano player and Vladimir Horowitz at Carnegie Hall. The judgment of what is worthy and unworthy in the presentation of news ought to be determined by different standards.

Here Come the Clowns Outside consultants, often with little or no journalistic experience, have been hired by local stations in some of the larger market areas of the country in an effort to boost the ratings of news programs. What this has produced makes many a professional wonder whether to laugh or cry; for the nonprofessional consultants, at a stiff fee, have introduced clowns into the news instead of reporters. At first, the notion of attracting larger audiences by making jokes about the news was called "happy talk." It really isn't. Most of it is nonsense; even worse, a lot of the irresponsible banter leads to both misunderstanding and misinformation.

Walter Cronkite had this to say about the plague of consultants:

> Any newsman worth his salt knows that advisers who dictate that no item should run more than 45 seconds, that there must be a film story within the first 30 seconds of the newscast, and that it must have action in it (a barn burning or a jackknifed trailer truck will do); who call a 90-second film piece a mini-documentary; who advise against covering City Hall because it's dull, and who say the anchorman or woman must do all voice-overs for 'identity'—any good newsman knows that is all balderdash. It's cosmetic, pretty packaging—not substance. And I suspect that most station operators know that, too. But I think they've been sold a bill of goods, that

they've been made suckers for a fad: editing by consultantcy. Yes, suckers, because there is no evidence that this formula news broadcasting—the top 20 hit news items—works.[6]

Extending the News Programs Prosperous local stations have been extremely successful with hour-long news programs, not so much on the basis of content as on the agreeable reaction of advertisers. Content tends to be featurelike in tone, sometimes marred by a certain amount of "happy talk," in the absence of enough illustrative news to keep the staff busy.

In consequence, network executives began experimenting with hour-long network news formats in the latter 1970s and CBS was the first to complete a pilot program.

WRITING FOR TELEVISION

If the television correspondent must act as reporter, film director and editor, those who write for television must combine the skills and insights of the playwright, the scriptwriter for motion pictures and the practicing journalist. It is not enough to say that television writers must consider both the eye and the ear. In a real sense, they must unify in word and mood a jumble of sights and sounds and give them meaning. This represents creativeness of the highest degree. Good television reportage, like good drama, is most effective when it appeals to reason rather than emotion, when it strives to make its point through artistry instead of crude histrionics, when it bases itself on the uses of restraint and understatement and lets humankind see at firsthand the stuff of which it is made. To do this with an economy of words and a few carefully selected scenes each day in the span of a television-network news program is no mean feat. It is not recommended for amateurs.

The evening news-roundup programs for the "Big 3" networks— ABC, CBS and NBC—seldom vary in structure on an ordinary day and often duplicate each other in content because of the nature of the day's news. Where they differ is in enterprise material, in which all compete, and in the personalities of their leading figures.

In most roundup news programs for the networks, the writing is so sharply and crisply done that it cannot be viewed as a television script, a radio script, a piece for a wire service or a newspaper. Normally, material for television is put together on a split page, the narration (AUDIO) on one side done in half-lines and the visual effects (VIDEO) on the other side with appropriate directions. A good producer insists on a maximum of information about everything that will be seen on the

[6] *Columbia Journalism Review* (July–August, 1976), p. 24; statistical material on Nielsen ratings from the *Wall Street Journal* (August 2, 1976), p. 1.

Behind the Scenes at CBS Evening News. *A CBS cameraman with a new light-weight miniature camera, the CBS Microcam, gets set for convention coverage while Walter Cronkite checks his script before going on the air. This is a part of CBS's electronic camera coverage (ECC). (Copyright, Columbia Broadcasting System. Used by permission.)*

program and, when necessary, can make split-second decisions to modify his lineup if some segments run shorter or longer than expected.

ASSEMBLING THE NEWS ON TV

Most Americans take their spot news from Walter Cronkite of CBS, John Chancellor and David Brinkley of NBC, and Harry Reasoner and Barbara Walters of ABC. They are the stars of TV news—the most visible, the most publicized and the highest paid. As anchor personnel of the evening news programs, they have also borne the most responsibility.

But despite their importance, they are not the whole show. At CBS, for example, correspondents begin submitting videotaped suggestions early in the day for the evening news programs. Other stories are assigned from New York and Washington. As the news builds up, more material comes in—most of it on videotape, some on film. And once the lead item of the program has been determined and others lined up in order, the writing of the Cronkite script begins.

A Segment Here is how a segment of a CBS Evening News program is written for videotaping and submission to New York. The following is from Richard Roth in Washington, dealing with the findings of the commission on the review of national policy toward gambling:

VIDEO	AUDIO
VTR—	<u>Roth</u>: Not the glittering casinos of Las Vegas—
Las Vegas, begin-	not blackjack, roulette or slot machines—The Com-
ning with exte-	mission found the most exciting gambling game in
riors of strip,	America is horse racing—the thrill biggest for bet-
then interiors of	tors who actually visit the track rather than place
craps, roulette,	their money with bookies or bet at off-track
etc.	offices.
VTR—horse race	Less exciting but far more popular are state lot-
shots	teries, which the Commission said may be the game
VTR—Lottery	best able to compete with the illegal numbers
stuff.	racket.
	Commission officials called gambling—legal or
VTR: Washington	not—an "inevitable" part of the American way of
news conference	life, the criminal justice system largely incapable
	of controlling it, government policies failures.
:20	<u>Ritchie</u>: We promote people's interest—whet
SOF: James	their appetite—We increase their opportunity and
Ritchie, execu-	desire to bet through television—We romanticize
tive director of	former bookmakers_and then we say with a great deal
commission	of pious, sanctimonious, ostrichlike logic: "It's
	against the law to accept a bet."
:10	<u>Roth</u>: The Commission recommends that federal
Roth (OC)	income taxes on gamblers' winnings be abolished as
	the best way to promote legal betting over illegal.

:15	But Commission Chairman Charles Morin admitted the chance of that happening is slim: He wouldn't even lay odds on it. <u>Richard Roth</u>, CBS News, Washington.

The Main Script[7] To illustrate how various segments are fitted into the Cronkite script, here are some of the concluding portions of an evening news program:

VIDEO	AUDIO
Cronkite	The summer—long drought in the upper Midwest is causing new trouble: fire. The hardest hit state is Minnesota. Barry Petersen of WCCO—TV reports:
	TRACK UP
:10	Volunteers are searching the foothills of Wyo-
Petersen VTR	ming's Big Horn mountains tonight for a lost child.
Cronkite	And the search is particularly agonizing. The child is a 4—year—old boy, Ronnie Rea, who has been blind since birth and cannot speak. He wandered away from his ranch home Monday. Temperatures at night in those hills have gone down in the 20s.
:18	The telephone company has computerized itself to
Cronkite	the point that you can't even lament any more that you're all alone by the telephone. Charles Osgood
:09	tells us why:
Osgood VTR	TRACK UP
Cronkite	And thats the way it is . . . This is Walter Cron-
:07	kite, CBS News. Good night.

Ad Libbing a Report The speed and flexibility of videotape has put a great burden on broadcast journalists. Very often, when they are on a breaking story, there is no time to sit at a typewriter and put a script

---

[7] (A note on script terminology: "Track up" means to insert videotape or film track. SOF means sound on film, VOF voice on film or tape. VTR is videotape recording. These and other terms are explained in Appendix I, 3. The detailed material for the video portion—the telops behind the anchor man, etc.—are inserted at the decision of the director of the operation.)

together. They have to ad lib their report as the camera records bits of history, important or not.

For election night, 1976, both videotape and the reporters and cameramen at key vantage points turned in a marvelous on-the-spot record. There was no waiting for film to be developed and studied. Everything was put on live on the three networks and the anchor men and women had to keep the report going all night long, switching back and forth from the various experts in the studio to reporters in the field, until Mississippi put Jimmy Carter over the top. Within a short time, the day shift took over but many reporters who had been on the job all night had to keep going.

At CBS, Hughes Rudd joined Bruce Morton, who had been in the studio working on the returns all night, and both were summing up the results at sunrise when Rudd received word that President-elect Carter had returned to his home in Plains, Georgia, and was greeting the home folks. Here is how the reporters described the scene, under pressure, as the videotape recorded everything in the minicams on the spot for instant transmission: (Speeches by the Carters are not given in full)

VIDEO	AUDIO
Rudd (OC in Studio)	Now I'm told Mr. Carter is back home in Plains, Ga., and Bruce Hall is there. Bruce?
Hall––VTR of Carters entering Plains HQ, with crowd clapping & cheering & band music	Jimmy Carter is returning to his home town in Plains after a short ride back from Atlanta where he spent most of election night. He is being greeted at the railroad depot, which served as a symbolic headquarters for the Carter campaign. There is a crowd of 3–400 with about 75 people running to get near him. The Americus Band has started to play. He is now
More crowd shots––	shaking hands with well-wishers––slowly, very slowly making his way to the podium 100 feet away in his railroad depot where he will be addressing this crowd, which has been here all night in Plains. (Lots of crowd noise in background)
Shots of Carter shaking hands	He is making his way now along a roped off area trying to shake hands with this group. He left about 12–14 hours ago when he said he'd be back and he was coming back a winner. And he did. He put his faith in

the South--it was the South that could help him
through--and it did.

CU, Miss Lillian

Miss Lillian, his mother, is waiting at the top of
the stairs 25 feet from him now. She has been here all
night waiting for his arrival. She said she would not
go home despite the cold weather here until she could
hear her son had been elected President and she kept
waiting through the night to hear the news. When she
heard the news she talked to the crowd here and said
she'd be on hand when he arrived back this morning.

Jimmy Carter is still making his way--he is half
way to the podium--the crowd is swelling--50-75 more
people are coming over--he is continuing to shake

Carter hugging
mother

hands. Now, to the podium where he is being greeted
by his mother, Lillian. Now he is holding up a newspaper saying. "Carter Wins !"

Carter (OC)

Carter: I told you I didn't intend to lose.
(cheering). I came all the way through 22 months and

Carter wipes eyes

didn't get choked up until I. . . . (more cheering) I
believe the sun is rising on a beautiful new day. I
feel good about it and I love every one of you.

Mrs. Carter (OC)
wipes eyes Hall
and crowd shots

I want to thank every one of you . . . I'm glad to
be home.

Hall: Jimmy Carter has returned to Plains after a
night in Atlanta and people waited all night long for
him. Ed Bradley (another reporter) has joined us and
Ed, what was the crowd like in Atlanta as they heard
the returns?

Bradley (OC)

Bradley: It really was a very strange evening.
The Carter people were very confident in Atlanta but
there was some apprehension during the night even
when they decided that there was no way they could
lose. And then, actually, when word came in that Mis-

sissippi would put them over, there was cheering for
awhile but there wasn't the enthusiasm you might

Rudd (OC) in stu-   expect. But there is no doubt they are happy. Hugh?

dio   We'll be back in a couple of minutes.

The Blooper If there are exalted moments in broadcast journalism, as
the reporting of a Presidential election so graphically illustrates, there
also are times when even the best and the brightest commit a blooper.
The legendary radio announcer who solemnly introduced "President
Hoobert Heever" is not alone. This was what viewers saw and heard on
the night of October 4, 1976 when Barbara Walters made her debut
with Harry Reasoner as an anchor person on ABC:

VIDEO   AUDIO

Walters (OC) con-   Harry and I will try to bring you the best darn

cluding 1:45 seg-   news program on the air and we hope that if you've

ment   watched tonight out of curiosity, you'll return

tomorrow to watch us out of conviction. Mr. Rea-

soner?

Reasoner (OC)   Thank you, Barbara. I had a little trouble in

:20   thinking of what to say to welcome you. Not to sound

sexist as in, "You brighten up the place," or

patronizing as in, "That wasn't a bad interview,"

or sycophantic as in, "How in the world do you do

it?" The decision was to welcome you as I would any

respected and prominent colleague of any sex by not-

ing that I kept time on your stories and mine

tonight. You owe me four minutes.

Walters (OC)   (Laughter)

Reasoner (OC)   For Barbara Walters and I, good night.

:05

Next evening, with good grace, Reasoner joked about his grammatical slip. He has had finer moments in his career, some of which are
recorded in this excerpt from a newscast from the Great Wall of China:

VIDEO	AUDIO
VTR--HR via satel-- lite from China :30	HR: It's certainly one of the great sights of the world. The Wall looping over the mountains to the north. The Great Wall is not listed among the seven wonders of the ancient world but that's because the people who made the list never saw it, even though it was there. It was built in 15 years by about 300,000
VTR: Shots of wall. :50	men before the birth of Christ to draw a 1,200-mile line across the top of China to keep out the barbarians.
	Several later dynasties rebuilt it. Now the government is again rebuilding it, this time to draw tourists, not to repel aggressors. Like the Maginot Line, it failed by omission. The invaders came in anyhow through breaks in time of disrepair--around it or through the gates. No one ever successfully stormed it.

It is clear, from the examples provided here, that the best rule to observe in writing or ad libbing for television is the rule of flexibility. Certainly, writing for the electronic media cannot be tossed off; not, at least, for a responsible station and producer. Nor is it possible for the tyro to stand before a microphone and ad lib with professional assurance. That kind of thing requires years of preparation and experience.

Not everything in television news must be of earth-shaking importance. There is time, too, for such mundane matters as the price of eggs which, at the time of programming, were at an all-time low. NBC sent Rebecca Bell to visit the poultry farm of Fred Monroe at Plainfield, Illinois, with the following brief but lively result:

VIDEO	AUDIO
Chancellor (OC) :10	Chancellor: Every time we run a story about farm prices rising, the egg producers complain that we don't say that egg prices are going down. Well, as we see in this report, they are.
VTR: Market scene	Bell (VO) At a time when prices for just about everything are soaring, housewives can find some

:12	relief at the egg counter. Retail prices for eggs are at a 10–year low. Some chain stores are selling eggs as low as 33 ¢ a dozen as compared with 84 ¢ a dozen in 1969.
VTR: Chicago Mer- cantile Exchange :12	The reason is there are too many eggs going to market. People also were buying fewer eggs after a warning by the Heart Association about cholesterol. Traders say the combination has kept market prices consistently below production costs for the past year.
VTR: Bell, Standup :18	Poultry farmers say much of the oversupply results from the introduction last year of a vaccine for a disease that used to kill off as much as 20 per cent of the farmer's hens. Because of the vaccine, chickens are healthier, they're living longer, and they're laying more eggs.
VTR: Chickens on farm, Plainfield, Ill.	A market analyst says another reason is pure greed. It used to be that when egg prices dropped, farmers would sell off some hens for chicken soup. This year, everybody keeps waiting for the other guy to cut his flock. The big companies will be able to hold out, but many small producers are facing bank-ruptcy. (RUNS OF MONROE: 1:20)
VTR: Egg line & farm scenes :18	Bell (VO) Some major producers are backing a bill in Congress that would establish government regu-lation of egg prices. Senate hearings on the pro-posal will begin soon. The bill designed to minimize risks for the poultry farmer, but it also would prob-ably mean that consumers never again would pay so little for eggs. Rebecca Bell, NBC News, Plainfield, Ill.

Writing for television requires study, thought and style just as much as any form of written communication. The style of a writer depends on training, mood, skill, background and above all, the circumstances of the assignment. And in television circumstances change more rapidly than in any other communications medium. Writers, therefore, cannot afford to let themselves be set in any particular mold. What they write is judged by today's standards; tomorrow, the standards may be different. If this means that writing for television is likely to be confusing from time to time, that is the penalty for working in a swiftly developing news medium. The only safeguards are to maintain a sense of balance and a sense of humor. As Harry Reasoner once put it in a New Year's Eve broadcast:

> "Let me offer from all of us my favorite New Year's prayer from the Scots: 'From ghoulies and ghosties and long-legged beasties and things that go bump in the night, the good Lord deliver us.' "

CABLE COMMUNICATIONS

The Federal Communications Act of 1934 limits the spread of communications channels. It is the basis around which the broadcasting industry is organized in its current form. Consequently, it has become the Bible of those who would slow down the development of cable television. Furthermore, it is also the point of attack for others who would limit the growth of the networks and make them more responsive to the wishes of government.

As a result, for all its promise, cable television has been bogged down for years because it is the center of a political struggle. Clay T. Whitehead, the White House television adviser in the Nixon administration, has this to say about the outlook: "The real hope for the future, ... lies in cable TV. With its capacity for infinite expansion of TV channels so that TV programs can be distributed nation-wide or neighborhood-wide or to whatever extent supply and demand allow, cable promises to be to the electronic mass media that the mails are to the print media ...

"Cable's promise is two-fold: more and better TV fare to choose from, and an escape from the First Amendment dilemma in broadcasting that threatens the freedom of all mass media. But cable's threat is equally real: more competition for the broadcasters and political pressure to 'save free TV.' "[8]

However, for as long as the 1934 communications act lasts, cable TV will have to mark time and its fantastic promise will remain unfulfilled. Only a small percentage of the cable systems currently in existence have news programs, even fewer have local reporters and the equipment is skimpy.

---

[8] Fifth duPont–Columbia Survey of Broadcast Journalism, p. 210.

THE FAIRNESS DOCTRINE

One of the weaknesses in the broadcasters' public position is their persistent effort to claim for themselves the same freedom from government regulation that print journalists enjoy under the First Amendment. The difference, of course, is that broadcasters use a limited public facility, the air waves for want of a technical term, and print journalists do not. Therefore, the FCC licenses broadcasters.

Broadcasting advocates are quick to point out, however, that this situation could change if the press, in the forseeable future, resorts to radio facsimile or some process like it for large-scale reproduction of newspapers and magazines. Facsimile has been in use for some years, mainly through leased land lines, but on such a comparatively small scale that no regulatory issue has developed. Nor do newspaper editors believe that this, or similar production processes, would warrant intervention by the Federal Communications Commission. This particular issue, therefore, remains moot.

The Doctrine Struggle The long struggle over the FCC's Fairness Doctrine, however, is another story. Basically, the doctrine obliges broadcasters to devote adequate time to issues of public interest that are important, regardless of how controversial they may be, and to give those with opposing views a fair and reasonable opportunity to state their position.

This represents a lot more than offering political opponents the right of reply. The FCC has removed some station licenses on the ground that the Fairness Doctrine was violated. In addition, even though the networks have not as yet been directly challenged, the threat of government action is always present.

During William S. Paley's long career as CBS board chairman, he argued that the Fairness Doctrine is "a tempting device for use by any administration in power to influence the content of broadcast journalism."[9] And Professor Fred W. Friendly has charged that fear of the doctrine and the FCC has made broadcast news in general "dangerously neutral and bland." [10] Both contend that broadcast journalism should be as free from censorship by the government as the press.

The issue remains difficult, although numerous newspaper editors have come over to the broadcasting position. It will not be easily resolved despite the prospect of temporary relief, in Presidential election years, when the broadcasters are usually given the privilege of refusing to give equal time to everybody who is running—a manifest impossibility in any case.

[9] Fifth duPont–Columbia Survey of Broadcast Journalism, pp. 119–120.
[10] In *The Good Guys, The Bad Guys and the First Amendment* (New York, 1976).

CRITICISMS OF TV NEWS

Despite the built-in handicaps of commercial television in which the news too often has to take second place to a combination of entertainment and advertising, news staffs for the networks and a variety of local stations have developed over a decade into a national asset.

Their performance during elections, particularly Presidential campaigns, is generally first rate. It is flawed only by an understandable anxiety to be first with the results, which sometimes leads even the best broadcasters into error. As for documentaries, that splendid if perennially weak cause, TV has long shown it has the people and the aptitude to do fine work. For example, NBC's "The Sins of the Fathers," which depicts the children the Americans left behind in Vietnam, and CBS's "The Selling of the Pentagon," which is old but still remarkably pertinent. The trouble is that there are so few documentaries that are worth watching.

In the field of public service journalism, television is making considerable progress. It can no longer be said that the electronic journalists leave investigative reporting to their colleagues in print. TV now has its own corps of capable reporters, most of whom had their basic training on newspapers and know how to go after a story. What they need is more opportunity to do so.

The Right of Access Another complaint against network news, which television shares with the newspapers, is that of limited access. Most minority groups campaign for time on the tube, knowing it is the most certain method of attracting national attention, and they generally get it. But not in a form that is satisfactory to them. Too often, minority causes explode before the viewer in the form of riots, demonstrations or other painful scenes; to the minorities, showing this kind of documentation indefinitely amounts to a form of exploitation. What they seek, and what neither television nor the newspapers can give them whenever they demand it, is the right to have a spokesman make a speech about their aims or sign a printed statement to the same effect. That kind of access is, by the very nature of time and news space, confined to the most urgent causes that are linked with the news of the day.

Once, during the 1960s, in the thick of rioting in cities some feared that the mere filming and display of such distressing scenes would serve to spread disorder throughout the land. There was some cause to worry, as well, about the conduct of a few irresponsibles in television who used their cameras to provoke violence. However, in succeeding years, reason has prevailed despite all manner of continuing investigations—a form of intimidation and harassment. The great danger does not lie in exhibiting scenes of disorder in some major news situation, but in suppressing them. Nor can it be truly said that reporters and cameramen deliberately stage unpleasant scenes in order to get some thrilling news footage. The most searching inquiry has failed to uncover anything more than a handful of minor instances of such irresponsible reportage.

Self-Regulation The times require self-restraint of all journalists, regardless of the media they serve. It is no solution to keep newspaper staffers, still cameramen and radio and television personnel out of crisis areas. To do so is to permit irresponsible rumor to sway desperate and frightened people. The turmoil in the cities will not be lessened if somehow reporters will stay away until all danger is past, or delay and censor their own accounts of what little they are able to see. The truth is that wherever there has been partial or total local self-censorship (and it has happened here and there), the news has been circulated promptly outside the affected areas and as promptly played back to them.

In the Soviet Union, where the government controls all media and withholds news at its pleasure, people somehow manage to inform themselves. The intelligentsia circulate their *samizdat,* their underground press. The young people listen to BBC or the "Voice of America." Thus, while great areas of ignorance persist about the non-Communist world, the people of the Soviet Union do have some notion of what is going on outside their own borders. It follows, therefore, that in the United States, with its two-century-old tradition of freedom of information, suppression will not work and falsification of the news even at the highest level will be ultimately found out.

Television's Future The glamor of television's past is exceeded only by its promise for the future. It has become a power in journalism in less than a generation. With the expansion of communications and the perfection of techniques that are now in the experimental stage, television's reach for the news will be limited only by its willingness to increase its capacity for public service. What the medium now requires is not a greater capability for commercial use but a period of industrial and professional statesmanship. For television as entertainment has reached the saturation point, while television as a public service medium is barely on the threshold of its greatest development.

In one sense, it is remarkable that more than 215 million Americans have come to depend so heavily on television's news and public-affairs content in such a short time. But in another sense, it is to be regretted that so little feeling of responsibility permeates an important segment of the electronic media. In the struggle for ratings, even the most prestigious news programs can do silly and even thoughtless things, as witness the work of the ho-ho-ho type of journalist.

The growth of public television, with or without government support, is just about the only competitive means through which all elements in commercial television may be obliged to pay more attention to news and public affairs. For if the proliferation of advertising and the excess of rating-hungry news programs continue to mar commercial television, the public will be ready very soon for almost anything that promises relief.

The success of the Public Broadcasting System in bringing important social and cultural programs to a large public augurs well for the future of the concept of public television. A better and far more vital kind of television-news programming is likely to emerge from a more spirited rivalry between public and commercial television both over the air and on cable, as the Robert MacNeil program has demonstrated. The fine, responsible news programs on commercial television will be strengthened thereby; as for electronic jazz journalism, it will find the going a lot harder than it does now. A greater diversity of views and a broader response to public opinion are bound to make television-news programming more useful to the public interest in the years to come.

Robert MacNeil (left) interviewing Senator Henry Jackson on the Public Broadcasting System's WNET/WETA production of "The MacNeil/Lehrer Report." Photograph: C. Brownie Harris, WNET/Channel 13. Used by permission of WNET.

Part Three
PRINCIPLES OF REPORTING

Chapter 17
The Lives
of a
Reporter

Gene Miller was punched in the mouth. Throughout northwest Florida, he became a marked man. Public officials accused him publicly of lying about them in the *Miami Herald*. He was harassed at every turn, spied upon, frustrated in every attempt he made to prove that he was right—except for the last time.

Then, after eight and a half years, he finally made the gates of Florida State Prison swing open for two indigent black men who had twice been wrongfully convicted of first degree murder and twice sentenced to death. He did it because he had faith in the innocence of the two, Freddie Pitts and Wilbert Lee; because he was able to locate the real culprit and extract a confession, and because the *Miami Herald* backed everything he did.[1]

Once the Governor of Florida freed Pitts and Lee on

---

[1] *Miami Herald,* 19 September 1975. Miller also wrote a book about the case, *Invitation to a Lynching* (Garden City, N.Y., 1975).

the evidence Miller had developed, the reporter's work was done. He said of the case: "It wouldn't go away and it wouldn't go away and it wouldn't go away. There was nothing to do about it but just keep working and writing."

For his efforts, Miller won the Pulitzer Prize for General Local Reporting in 1976, his second Pulitzer. The first was awarded to him for his investigative reporting in 1967, when he produced the evidence that freed a man and a woman in two separate cases after they had been convicted of murders they had not committed.

A HARD ROUTINE

Such feats are rare in the annals of American journalism. Yet, neither Miller nor his editors have ever credited his success to anything more than making accurate basic judgments and following a hard and often unrewarding routine until the work paid off. Much the same thing happened in the Watergate expose conducted by Bob Woodward and Carl Bernstein for the *Washington Post*, except that the paper itself came under as heavy fire as the reporters. Challenges, including some by President Nixon's friends, were filed with the Federal Communications Commission against the *Post*'s ownership of two television stations, causing a drop of almost 50 per cent in *Post* stock on the American Stock Exchange.[2] But the paper never ceased to back its reporters—and the reporters kept on digging.

In all truth, much excellent reporting is based on routine—dull, persistent work such as the checking of records, the location of persons with specialized information, efforts to corroborate material already in hand, long vigils for informants who sometimes never show up. This can go on for months—even years, as in the case of Miller and the Woodward-Bernstein inquiries. And sometimes, despite the best efforts of the most experienced reporters, nothing happens.

The Best Results   But when an investigation works, reporters can achieve remarkable results. Donald Barlett and James B. Steele, the investigative team of the *Philadelphia Inquirer*, pored over records of the Internal Revenue Service for months before they were able to produce their critical series on the IRS. And in Chicago, two other investigative reporters and writers, Arthur M. Petacque and Hugh F. Hough, patiently piled up the evidence that led to a solution of the 1966 murder of Valerie Percy in the *Sun-Times*.

When Oscar Griffin of the *Pecos* (Texas) *Independent* broke the story that led to the downfall of Billie Sol Estes, a Texas tycoon, it was

[2] Bob Woodward and Carl Bernstein, *All The President's Men* (New York 1974), p. 221.

basically an investigation that began with routine. Similarly, when George Thiem of the *Chicago Daily News* traced checks that sent an Illinois State auditor to jail for fraud, it was also routine.

The routine investigation of rumors of a shocking tragedy at My Lai, in South Vietnam, took Seymour M. Hersh all over the country, patiently interviewing exsoldiers, but when he broke the story in his struggling Dispatch News Service his evidence led directly to the trial and conviction of Lieut. William L. Calley Jr. Routine, too, helped Lucinda Franks and Thomas Powers of UPI when they brilliantly researched the life and death of Diana Oughton and wrote their prize-winning series, "The Making of a Terrorist." And when Norman C. Miller of the *Wall Street Journal* broke a salad-oil scandal that cost investors millions of dollars, he was far more the patient examiner of records than a James Bond type.

Morton Mintz of the *Washington Post* once said after breaking an exposé of Thalidomide, the drug blamed for malformed babies: "Many truly important items are actually very dull. Most members of the Washington press corps want the glamor jobs. In doing so, they forgo much that makes significant news."

The point cannot be stressed too much. The basis of nearly all good reporting is hard work. This is why a small paper in Alaska, the *Anchorage Daily News*, was able to expose the operations of the powerful Teamsters Union in the midst of the Alaskan pipeline boom; why another small paper, the *Winston-Salem Journal and Sentinel*, was able to block a strip mining company from destroying a scenic area of North Carolina; why a moderately sized paper, the Riverside (California) *Press-Enterprise*, stood up to powerful and corrupt interests in order to retrieve the stolen property of a hapless Indian tribe.

The reporters whose results are based on either intuition or sheer luck are rare birds. They are found mainly in the paperbacks with lurid covers and in television soap operas. The few broadcast journalists who operate in this field pattern themselves on the way newspaper reporters work. They could do worse.

HOW REPORTERS WORK

It is easy to tell good reporters from poor ones. The good ones know that much of their working time will be spent on routine and are prepared to do it well. The poor ones brush off such mundane details as reading newspapers, checking names and addresses, asking questions about seemingly unimportant details, and taking careful notes when they can.

Another important difference between the two is that the good ones are well aware that they will have to cover all kinds of stories, and most of them will be small, particularly for newspapers, while the poor ones keep hoping for a big news break that may never come their way. Even in the bad old days, reporting was sober, serious business; the glamor of *The Front Page,* if there was any, could be found primarily in the corner saloon.

Beginners usually have to learn such things the hard way. Once a neophyte wire service reporter was sent to a courtroom to pick up an Appeals Court's decision and telephone the results to his desk. When he picked up the papers, he flipped to the last page for the decision and got on the phone with it. Not until he returned to the office did he realize that he had reported a dissenting opinion; the majority's decision was somewhere in the middle of the report but he hadn't bothered to look for it.

The Assignment Sheet In any well-conducted news organization, an assignment sheet is kept to show how the news is being covered and where the reporters and camera people are deployed. This summary shows which staffers are trusted with assignments that require care and judgment and which others receive tasks calling for less-skilled professionals. This is the journalists' "order of battle" in the daily campaign that is waged on all news fronts.

An assignment sheet should be so concisely and neatly kept that even uninformed editors, picking it up without advance briefing, can tell in general what the news of the day is and how it is being covered. Few reporters ever see assignment sheets. On well-conducted newspapers and wire service bureaus, some call in before leaving their homes and get their assignments. Others are summoned to the city desk, given brief instructions and dispatched on their jobs. For broadcast assignments, where so much equipment has to be moved, the work is more complicated but the reporters have to work just as quickly. The news doesn't await the convenience of the media.

Except when reporters are on special assignment, or are sent to work with others on a complicated series, they seldom get detailed guidance from their superiors. It is assumed that they are professionals, that they know what to do, where to go, and what transportation to use. Nobody is going to hold their hand or give them a pep talk.

Going on Assignment Newspaper or wire service reporters, on a spot news assignment, waste no time going directly to the source of the story. It is even more important for the broadcast media to get to the scene, for good pictures can't be taken by remote control and eyewitnesses don't hang around forever to give interviews about accidents, fires, holdups or natural disasters. The saddest reporter in town is always the one who shows up late and has to get a fill-in from a grudging colleague.

Reporters used to rely only on pad and pencil and a good pair of legs if they were working for the print media. Nowadays, particularly on interviews and various types of feature assignments, the better ones lug a tape recorder just to be safe. Unlike British reporters, some of whom are shorthand experts, Americans — with rare exceptions — have never bothered to develop the skill.

Reporters learn from experience when and where to go for certain types of stories. For fires, accidents, and disasters of other kinds the scene of action is often the best source of news. For police news, however, it is not always certain that a visit to the scene of the crime will be the most direct way of picking up the threads of the story unless the principal news sources are there. At political and diplomatic conferences the biggest news is usually made far away from the speakers' platform. In labor negotiations, with both sides sealed up in a conference room, the news can break from any number of places.

The important fact for any reporter to remember is to keep moving. Too often, reporters find that most of their time is spent waiting for people to condescend to see them. When that happens, it is the reporter's business to cut down on the waiting time either by using the telephone, writing a note, or using some other method of reaching a source. In any case, regardless of whether anything or nothing happens while on the assignment, a reporter must call the office at regular intervals of from 30 minutes to an hour. Otherwise the whole news-gathering system is paralyzed through lack of communication.

Every reporter quickly learns that the best approach to a news source largely depends upon circumstances and opportunity. The leisurely business of calling an important person and asking for an appointment is a fine way of doing business — for columnists and editorial writers. A reporter too often has to depend upon a telephone call, a curbstone interview, or a scribbled note submitting a question.

The Basic Approach Professional journalists should not adopt tricks, disguises or other shenanigans without the knowledge and consent of their superiors. It is perfectly true that reporters have made praiseworthy contributions by doing firsthand stories of their work as hospital orderlies, school teachers, policemen, firemen, and even detectives, on occasion, but no news organization wants its reporters doing that kind of thing regularly without some very real and basic need.

It is only when direct methods fail on an assignment that a reporter should even consider a stratagem. Many a news source has been located quickly, not by skulking through supposedly haunted houses at midnight, but by merely looking up a name in a telephone book or city directory. Many a reporter has gained access to a hard-to-see news source by going in the front door.

It is true that Pulitzer Prizes have been won by reporters who posed as relief clients, hospital orderlies, ambulance drivers, Medicaid patients and public welfare caseworkers (see Chapter 24). But these guises were adopted only with the consent of supervisory editors and, in a few instances, the cooperation of responsible public officials. Beginners are not advised to try it on their own.

It is stretching matters to telephone someone and say, as some reporters have, "I'm calling from Police Headquarters." The intimation that a reporter is actually a police official puts him in an indefensible position if he is found out. This kind of thing used to be more common earlier in the century when journalists weren't as carefully scrutinized for errors and bias as they are today. One Chicago veteran used the telephone to pose as anybody from the mayor to the keeper of the morgue if it suited his convenience. Fortunately for journalism, there haven't been many like him since.

Making Your Own Breaks Reporters can make their own breaks by doing their routine work well. Often, by checking both sides of a story, they will find an aggrieved person who will provide good leads for further inquiry. Through firmness and persistence they sometimes can persuade an aloof news source to discuss his position with them. This was the routine adopted by Jack Anderson, the syndicated columnist, when he broke so many major stories in the 1970s, from the disclosure of the background of American opposition to India during the Indo-Pakistan War of 1971 to the lobbying methods in this country and abroad of the International Telephone and Telegraph Company. Like Anderson, many another reporter has found that patience and dogged work have been rewarded with unexpected disclosures, but few have been favored with so many leaks from government sources.

Wherever it is possible, a thorough inquiry should be made into the backgrounds of the principal actors in the news. In a murder trial, during which the defense contended death was due to an accident, a reporter discovered that the judge some years before had shot and killed a hunting companion by accident. During the investigation of a large corporation which was in financial difficulty, it developed that one of its principal officers had been a notorious exconvict who had changed his name. The author of a best-selling book of humor and philosophy was disclosed to have served a prison sentence in connection with a stock fraud, and to have succeeded in rehabilitating himself.

Ask—Ask—Ask! How does a reporter accomplish such feats? Usually this is done by asking questions, often politely but always persistently—not just any question, but one that is so phrased as to produce a newsworthy answer.

The reporter who breezes into the county clerk's office and asks gaily, "What's new?" is likely to be told, "Nothing." But if the reporter goes through court records in a systematic way, the results may be quite different. Donald L. Barlett and James B. Steele went through Philadelphia court records for months on end in an analysis of the administration of justice for the *Philadelphia Inquirer* and came up with a series that showed innocent persons had been sent to jail, judges were inconsistent in sentencing and most of them did less work than others in cities of comparable size.

Aggressiveness All editors want aggressive reporters, but that doesn't mean just a loud voice and tough talk. Loud and brassy reporters are their own worst enemies. The shouted question, the accusing finger, the dramatic manner are not calculated to endear any reporter either to a news source or to professional associates. Mostly, such persons are an embarrassment to their colleagues.

Nor does it ever help reporters to quarrel with their sources, or threaten or anger them. Such histrionics may jar loose one story, but they are likely to cost the reporter the confidence of a good source thereafter. To those who can be persistent, but still maintain an even temper and moderate manner, go most of the rewards of the professional news gatherer.

Sometimes it is the news source who is arrogant, overbearing and even threatening. The most even-tempered reporter may be angered under such pressures. However, as most reporters know, anger is not particularly helpful in gathering news although it is on occasion becoming to an editorial writer. Experienced reporters, regardless of provocation, maintain their poise by staying off the defensive and asking questions.

Young reporters, going on their first assignments, invariably ask themselves before approaching their first awesome news source, "Why should he talk to me?" It is true that few reporters today command a personal following. Young reporters, however, need not feel abashed by lack of experience. They will be received, not because of who they are, but because of what they represent. From such beginnings they will learn quickly enough to make their own way by asking the right questions of the right persons at the right time.

Taking Notes Some good newspaper reporters take a few notes now and then, scribbled on the back of an old envelope or a shred of copy paper. Others have taken notes about the weather even while crossing Times Square on a beautiful spring day. These are the established professionals whose methods vary in accordance with their temperament, their habits and their needs.

Today's reporters, especially the younger ones, are likely to find that considerable note-taking will be more useful to them than the casual attitude of veteran reporters. The reason is that modern reporting must be more careful, more thorough and, if possible, more accurate than the news gathering of thirty-five or forty years ago. There are many methods, both electronic and documentary, of checking the accuracy of newspaper reports today that did not exist in the last generation. It is virtually imperative for a reporter to have a handy record of where he went, what he did, and what was said to him. Not every reporter can cover every assignment with a tape recorder.

Many old-time newspapermen merely grabbed a handful of copy paper, folded it three times sidewise, and scribbled notes whenever it occurred to them. A more regular system of note-taking is advisable in these more complicated days. The pocket-size stenographer's notebook is now standard equipment for the careful reporter. All entries are dated, and nothing is thrown away, even after the notes are used. Customarily, reporters keep copies of their stories with the original notes in some convenient place so that they may be checked if there is ever any question about the story.

When Not to Take Notes Necessarily, there are many occasions on which a reporter cannot take notes. It makes politicians and diplomats nervous to have a notebook thrust under their noses during a casual conversation. That is generally true about others who, for one reason or another, dislike talking for a record. As a rule, whenever reporters find it impossible or inconvenient to take notes during a conversation, they make a record of the event as soon as they can, drawing on their best recollection. Few reporters have anything even approaching total recall, but any well-trained reporter can remember quite accurately the highlights of a conversation or action if notes about it are written immediately after it happens.

Reporters as Participants Whether news organizations like it or not, and usually they do not, reporters are being drawn into the news in these times as never before. This is not merely a matter of doing first-person stories as eyewitnesses to wrecks or natural disasters. Because of the position that some courts have taken in matters affecting judicial hearings, reporters can suddenly find themselves put in very unpleasant and trying positions (see Chapter 23).

No reporter is advised to use individual judgment when ordered to disclose information to a court of law or to agree to withhold facts about a judicial proceeding. Such issues involve the reporter's own organization plus all others represented at the particular proceeding. Unless reporters decide to proceed entirely on their own, hiring their own lawyers and incurring the usually stiff court costs that are involved, it is obvious that the basic decisions for procedure must be made by editors and publishers. And usually, it is not wise for reporters to stake out an individual position in a case involving judicial censorship or contempt proceedings.

There is one other aspect of coverage that may involve a journalist in the news as a participant and that is the presence of a television camera on the scene. In any civil disturbance, demonstrators are likely to put on a special show for television and police sometimes do not appreciate it when they are shown using extreme methods to quell a disturbance. Any reporter or cameraman who ever has been roughed up or clubbed in a riot knows that it is a dangerous matter. For both television correspondents and camera operators, the difficulties can become crucial. Without emergency instructions, the best rule to follow is the rule of good sense.

One Way to Take Notes Unless the reporter wants to be turned into a mere stenographer, there should be some method in prolonged note-taking. Shorthand experts have tried to take down every word of a long and complicated proceeding, only to discover at the end that they are buried under their material and unable to decipher enough quickly to make possible a fast deadline report.

For that reason trained reporters leave a margin at the left of the page on which they take their notes. Beside every block of material, they write a few words in the margin to indicate the subject matter. Even at the end of a day-long court hearing, if this system is adhered to, it is possible to skim quickly over the marginal notes, decide which are the most important, arrange them in the order that will be most fitting for a news story and begin talking to the rewrite bank, dictating or writing.

The Tape Recorder Reporters for the electronic media know from experience how valuable a tape recorder can be either in a prepared sit-down interview or in more informal talks with news sources. But more conservative reporters for the printed media still resist using this essential tool of journalism either because they don't want to be bothered or think it will in some way prejudice their subjects against them. The fact is that most people in public life, both in this country and abroad, now welcome a tape recorder when they have something to say to a reporter and want to make sure that their words are accurately reproduced. James Reston's historic interview with Premier Chou En-lai in Peking, which defined China's policy toward the United States, was conducted by prearrangement with a tape recorder. Other correspondents over the years have successfully used tape recorders in major interviews with such world figures as Indira Gandhi of India when she was Prime Minister. It is not unusual, for that matter, for the source of an important news break to produce a tape recorder for a conversation if the reporter does not do so.

Where an interview or a news conference must be followed at once by a news story, there is nothing to stop qualified reporters from writing or dictating the main part of their material as they remember it, then preparing a more comprehensive account as quickly as possible. No one, least of all an impatient editor, expects that reporters in every situation will have to delay telephoning or filing until they have transcribed every word of their taped material and studied it. For certain types of enterprise assignments, where time is not a factor, the leisurely approach is possible. But even when time is of the essence, the tape recorder remains the best protection against complaints of inaccurate quotations.

One of the principal results of the increasing use of tape recorders is that more news has been put on the record at every level, from the village council to the committees of Congress, from the routine interview with a town police chief to the audience granted by a king. Some old-time reporters, long accustomed to writing politics by referring to mysterious unnamed sources, have found to their dismay that the politicians they once protected so zealously now rush into television talk programs with the most indiscreet remarks. And young reporters with tape recorders think nothing of asking the most exalted figures in the land to say for the record what they once would confide to only the most trusted veteran reporters.

This does not mean that the practice of so-called background reporting is in a decline, as will be seen in the next chapter. It does mean that journalists in general are putting up more of a fight to bring the sources of the news out into the open. The print media, in this respect, owe a debt of gratitude to the electronic journalists who have taken a giant step toward greater honesty in handling the news.

Checking Copy Inexperienced reporters sometimes are placed on the defensive when officials, in public or private industry, demand the right to examine notes or tapes or approve copy before it is submitted to the home office. It is a fixed rule on all news organizations that their editors, alone, have the right to determine what reporters should do with their facts and how a story should be written. Overly aggressive news sources should, of course, be told this in a polite manner. Whenever there is insistence on the right to see a story before it is used reporters can only refer their sources to their superiors and await the outcome. Reporters should never yield copy for examination, except under conditions of acknowledged censorship, or for military clearance when necessary.

In certain types of assignments, such as science writing, a few of the established journalistic experts have voluntarily sent their news stories to the authors of scientific abstracts on which the stories were based. The purpose was to insure accuracy. In no case was the scientist given the right to change or omit facts that were included by the journalist. However, the scientist was asked to point out errors and make any appropriate comments, and editors were consulted on whatever changes were to be made.

Such procedures are almost inevitable on complicated technical stories, but reporters must always be careful to preserve their copy and prevent substantive changes for any reason other than to insure accuracy.

It is, of course, much more difficult for people who seek appearances on live television to make defensive arrangements, such as a series of not-very-difficult questions that are agreed upon beforehand or a pat, memorized speech. True, such things have happened, but they are becoming increasingly rare. Television reporters, no less than their comrades in print, hate to be used by their sources for questionable purposes. As for reviews of tape-recorded conversations by those who participate in them, there really can't be any sound objection to such a request even if it delays the whole editorial process. However, when reporters are able to do so, their editors always ought to be informed of the circumstances under which they have agreed to deletions of tape-recorded material. This is slippery business, and not recommended for amateurs.

REPORTERS AND THEIR OFFICES

The relationship between reporters and their offices is changing in all parts of the news media. Where reporters once were regarded as free-wheeling characters, particularly on fixed newspaper beats like city hall and police headquarters, the rule today is close supervision of all reportorial activity.

There are three main reasons for the change in attitude. The first and foremost is that editors could afford to squander the time of a $35-a-week reporter in the great Depression or let him go off on his own without worrying too much about the ultimate cost. But when wage minimums for average reporters on major news organizations today are in the $350 to $400 range, and up, they are treated quite differently. Their time is important. And if they go into overtime at contractual time and one-half rates, they pose something of an issue. Any editor will ask, "Is this story worth such an expenditure?" And in television, where the cost of technicians and equipment has to be added in, the calculation of news values is anything but philosophical.

As has already been shown, the widespread use of terminals by newspapers and wire services and the swing to electronic coverage by television have in effect linked reporters more closely than ever before to their home offices. Journalists would have to go to the polar ice caps, remote villages in India or China, or the central Sahara before they could properly claim that they were out of touch. In any event, when

editors have the opportunity to supervise, that is what they do and reporters shouldn't be surprised by it. Thus, the concept of "teamwork"
is greatly favored in most city rooms and electronic newsrooms; it gives
a news organization added power and prestige to have special reportorial units available for investigations or other specialized work. Such
units, naturally, are the most closely supervised of all.

Finally, the intricate character of much of the news in the latter part
of the century has obliged editors and reporters to work in closer col-
laboration. When a city trembles on the verge of bankruptcy or a neighborhood is in revolt over the condition of its schools, when small and
distant nations can choke off American oil and gasoline supplies and
poor crops can send food prices soaring, news organizations have to
coordinate all their resources if they are to serve the public properly.
The era of the happy-go-lucky reporter is over.

Pool Reporting Some of the reporting practices of earlier days still survive in this modern era of togetherness, the most important of which is
the "pool."

When there were many more newspapers than there are today, and
competition between newspapers was intense, reporters on beats often
worked together in an unadmitted pool. For example, in the case of a
routine police story, the police headquarters pool would send one reporter to the scene to represent everybody and share the news when he
returned. They would go so far as to hold off telephoning their offices
until the pool leader gave an agreed signal and oblige the wire service
reporter among them to delay filing until everybody else had called in.
A reporter could declare himself out of the pool if he received a special
assignment; otherwise, he cooperated or had to scramble on his own.

Editors tolerated the undeclared pool for many years because it
saved them the trouble and expense of putting on additional reporters,
but there are very few who would countenance it today where it still
exists. In its modern guise, the pool is very official and respectable and
recognized on an international basis as a necessary and legitimate journalistic device. When a President travels by air, for example, it is obvious
that the White House press corps can't go in the same plane. Therefore,
unless he has some special reason for privacy, pool representatives are
appointed by the press corps to go on the Presidential plane and share
whatever they get.

The pool device is resorted to whenever there are large numbers of
reporters and camera operators, both still and television, in a relatively
limited space. Moreover, at major Congressional hearings when public
interest is high, as was the case with the Watergate inquiry, networks
will take turns at providing full daily coverage. Regardless of the complaints of purists, such measures do not deprive the public of any essential information and they are both useful and economical.

Disadvantages of the Pool Nobody contends that the pool is the best way to cover a story. Far from it. For under the informal rules of pool coverage, those in the pool are bound by the agreement of their representatives on material that is to be used for background or put off the record entirely. [See Chapter 18 for gradations of attribution.] Accordingly, those outside the pool, not being bound by the rules, can and do use such material if they hear about it—and that frequently happens.

An even more serious disadvantage occurs when hundreds of reporters are assigned to cover a trial in which there is great public interest, but only a small courtroom is available. Sometimes the judge turns the whole matter over to the reporters themselves, which generally means that smaller papers and radio stations have to organize a pool or be shut out entirely; even if the judge tries to act as arbiter, not everybody receives complete satisfaction.

Almost all pool reporters inevitably face criticism by those who depend on them for not being more observant, for failing to report what the pool subject had for breakfast, or what the subject's demeanor was under certain circumstances. All of which adds to the unpleasantness of pool reporting for everybody concerned.

Call Backs One of the most frustrating experiences for reporters is to call in with a major story and talk with somebody who knows nothing about the assignment. The delays involved in explaining who gave the assignment and why and what has happened since are likely to curdle the spirit of the most enthusiastic reporter. Yet, this kind of faulty liaison is all too common in every news organization.

It is recommended professional practice for call backs by reporters to be handled by the person who originally assigned them or by someone on a later shift who has been briefed on what reporters are doing. Even a casual glance at the assignment sheet often helps. Poor liaison between reporters and editors can quickly lead to demoralization.

Overnight—or Second Day Angle? This matter is a hangover from the era when there were competing afternoon and morning papers in many cities and the hapless staffers assigned to night rewrite on an afternoon paper had to redo morning paper clips with some kind of updated angle. The rule then was for afternoon paper editors to assign reporters on the job to do an overnight story on a continuing assignment—that is, a story that would be fresher than something in the morning papers, warmed over for the first edition.

The practice survives because all news organizations have to face the problem of freshening up a continuing story. A broadcast news program in the morning hours can't keep reporting what a political candidate said last night. Neither can a wire service; news on the PM cycle, even if there is no essential change in the story, has to differ from what has been sent for the AM cycle. And the same is true of afternoon newspapers even if they have no competition.

To illustrate the problem:

In a political campaign, most speeches are made at night to catch the evening news programs and the morning papers. Consequently, the morning broadcast news and the afternoon papers usually have to go with something like this—a fast rewrite with a second-day angle:

> Marvin J. Zugsmith, Republican nominee for U.S. Senator, has accused Democrats in Congress of going on a "spending spree."
>
> In a speech at Central City last night, Mr. Zugsmith warned . . .

This is the way some wire service stories are handled for the overnight wire when there are no new developments. Another possibility, not seen very often nowadays, is the forced second day angle:

> Democrats in Congress were confronted today with a charge by Marvin J. Zugsmith, Republican nominee for U.S. Senator, that they were on a "spending spree."
>
> Mr. Zugsmith's accusation was made last night . . .

What editors prefer, if they have a reporter on the story, is something fresh—an estimate of the candidate's chances, some sidelights on crowd turnouts for the campaign, perhaps an interview with the candidate or his wife, almost anything that will make it unnecessary to rehash an old Form A speech. This is what is meant by a "live" overnight for use in next morning's PM cycle or first edition. Reporters with spark and imagination can do this kind of work and make a story come alive for a newspaper or wire service, just as an inquisitive camera can for television.

DEAD OR ALIVE?

In a static news situation, such as a tugboat strike that has just ended its fourth day, the traditional way to handle the story for an afternoon paper's first edition is to rewrite the clips and the wires. Often, the result will read something like this:

> New York's 3,500 striking tugboatmen entered the fifth day of their strike today without a settlement in sight.
>
> Both union and management negotiators prepared to meet again for talks, with the help of federal and state mediators. The principal issue was the union's demand for more time off for its members . . .

The reader can see at a glance that the "freshened angle" isn't really an angle at all. It is merely a numerical lead which, instead of recounting the events of the fourth day of the strike, triumphantly announces that the fifth day is about to begin. In a word, the story is dead. How can it be brought back to life?

An enterprising reporter produced the following:

By Michael Berlin

Ray Harrison says he's "one of the lucky ones."

"I've been 24 years on tugs, mostly in New York and up and down the coast."

Harrison, a 54-year-old deckhand, has taken his seniority and invested it in one of the better shifts—four days on, two days off—and one of the newer boats, the *Dalzell Eagle*.

"In the old ones," he says, "you sleep in the forepeak below the water line. Tough quarters. Damp small bunks, so a tall man can't fit in 'em."

Most of the city's 3,500 striking tugboatmen work longer shifts, on the boat 24 hours a day, working a full 12.

"You don't sit down, except cruising between jobs, and even then you got the maintenance of the boat—chipping the paint, swabbing the decks. You *want* to keep busy to pass the time."

Harrison, a solid man with thick, calloused fingers from a lifetime of hauling on towlines, says, "That's the big thing we want. More time with our families."

And the strange thing in this strange strike—where there are no pickets, where union and management have the same building, 17 Battery PL.,—is that management wants more time off for the men, too.

"They're beginning to agree that we need more time off," Harrison grudgingly admits.

The issue, as the strike enters its fifth day today, is the cost of the free time. The tug companies have agreed to add a fourth crewman to each tug, which would give the men a day off for each day on.

But to cut the cost, the tug firms want cutbacks in other benefits.

Life on a tug is no bed of roses, but it is cozy.

"Most crews work together pretty much," says Harrison. "On the Eagle, we generally have 11 men on at a time, and the two crews work six hour shifts.

"When there's a ship rush on, we do a lot of ship work, towing ships four—five hours a day. Then we tow barges—oil, cement, trap rock. They keep the boats on the go—there's never a slack time in the 24 hours. You never know where you'll be going from hour to hour. We go up to Albany, over to Jersey, sometimes New Haven . . ."

—The *New York Post*

Thus, the life of a tugboatman emerges in colorful detail from what might have been just a dead rewrite with a conventional second-day angle. A reporter *can* make a difference.

ENTERPRISE REPORTING

This is the generic term given to almost anything off the beaten track of the day's news. It may be nothing more important than overhearing a city official's remark that his wife is house-hunting in the country, which turns out on inquiry to be the clue that he is about to leave office. Or it may be a month-long inquiry by a reportorial team into the county's real estate records, which shows that a city councilman has been involved in questionable dealings. Whatever reporters turn up on their own is credited to their enterprise.

Much of this type of reporting is investigative in character, as might be expected, and is dealt with in detail in Chapter 28. The pertinent matter here is the extent to which enterprise reporting, as a team effort, has subordinated the work of individual reporters. On larger newspapers and in the few broadcast media that go in extensively for original reporting, the juiciest enterprise assignments go to teams primarily because there is a better chance that a team will produce a good series. The odds against an individual reporter in a complicated investigation are naturally much greater than they are against a team.

Still, that has not stopped brilliant reporters like Gene Miller of the *Miami Herald*, Jack Nelson of the *Los Angeles Times*, Peter Arnett of the Associated Press and Seymour Hersh of the *New York Times*, to mention only a few of those who have made major contributions to American journalism through their own efforts.

It follows, therefore, that news organizations of all kinds will have to continue to depend on the enterprise of individuals as well as teams to produce news outside the routine. The imperatives of team reporting do not, by any means, conflict with the individual enterprise of a reporter who follows up a hunch, a tip or even some other news organization's lead. No editor can afford to throttle or ignore this kind of effort, for the individual reporter remains the basis for independent journalism as it is practiced in the United States.

Chapter 18
Ground Rules
for Reporters

While reporters for the *Detroit Free Press* were investigating Michigan's mental hygiene system, they came across information suggesting that a number of mental patients—including four killers—were at large and police weren't searching for them. It was a ticklish matter. Was it really the business of reporters to do police work? And yet, if they didn't find the apparently missing persons, how could they prove the truth of their story?

After a lot of soul-searching, a top-level editorial decision was reached to try to locate ten of the patients involved. The reporters, of necessity, had to adopt various guises to get information. But they determined in advance not to use quotes obtained from innocent persons while posing as someone other than a reporter. And they worried over possible invasion of privacy in the cases of social workers they interviewed and the ethics of obtaining confidential records in such circumstances.

In the end, however, it all worked out well. Seven of the ten persons on the *Free Press* list were located by the reporters, including the four killers. The deficiencies of the State's mental hygiene system were exposed. And widespread reforms were instituted.[1]

A MATTER OF ETHICS

Reporters and editors as a rule are much more concerned about ethical considerations than their critics believe. The old notion that you "get the story, and to hell with everything else" has no responsible defenders in American journalism today.

Even though there are no commonly accepted written rules that reporters carry around with them, they do observe certain basic principles of conduct. Some of these are set down in unenforceable ethical codes that are drawn up from time to time by societies of editors or other professional groups. But mostly, they exist in the minds of responsible journalists. Such practices are handed down from one newsroom generation to another; also, they are discussed in journalism schools and press institutes.

Reportorial ethics, as might be expected, are based in the main on reportorial duties. These are, briefly stated, to cover the news fairly, thoroughly and accurately, to report it as truthfully as possible, to explain what it means, to protect sources whenever necessary and to respect confidences if they are freely offered and willingly accepted.

The practices that reporters have developed to do their work apply in varying degree to every assignment from the smallest school board to the White House, from the playing fields of Berkeley and Cambridge to the desolation of decaying cities and the battlegrounds of foreign wars. If these methods are used with courage and good judgment, they can be effective in penetrating the twin obstacles of public relations and needless official secrecy that have blocked many news sources. Like all procedures, they can be abused or neglected by complacent reporters or sources given to perverting the truth or withholding it entirely.

This does not make them any less necessary. Beginning reporters soon learn that they are judged by their colleagues, their editors, and their sources on how well they know the ground rules, how effectively they use them and how faithfully they observe them.

A STATEMENT OF THE PROBLEM

The problem of sourcing the news in general, and stating the degree of permissible attribution in particular, pervades much of modern journalism. Sources aren't as ready to be identified as they used to be at many levels of government. Some hide behind false fronts. And others

---

[1] Publication of the series in the *Detroit Free Press* began 6 July 1975, and results continued to pile up for more than a year thereafter.

blithely deny having said something that two dozen reporters heard. All of which is viewed by reporters as part of the job.

The Unsourced Story When William F. Woo of the *St. Louis Post-Dispatch* came home from three weeks in China with voluble criticism of American foreign policy by the Peking government, he reported what he had heard in the opening article of his series but used this cautionary paragraph:

> The Chinese insisted that the names of officials interviewed not be mentioned or direct quotes from them used. Paraphrase, attributed to "the Chinese side" or "high Foreign Ministry officials," was permissible.[2]

It did not make Woo's story any less valuable. Nor did it cause the State Department in Washington to disregard the strong indications that China, at that stage, was losing patience with the slow pace of American movement toward recognition of Peking. The point is that the reputation of the journalist and the authority of the newspaper, in such cases, must make up for the lack of attribution of the news. Since Woo was then the editorial page editor of the *Post-Dispatch* and the paper itself was generally on most lists of the best ten papers in the United States, nobody challenged Woo's position even at the highest level of government.

Defending an Unsourced Story Ben H. Bagdikian, another first-rate American journalist, asked in a review of the Woodward-Bernstein book about President Nixon's downfall, *The Final Days*,

> How are we to judge the accuracy of a 476-page book of detailed verbatim conversations, of private emotions and secluded behavior inside a beleaguered and paranoid White House? Where does the lack of attribution and documentation leave the reader?

Pointing out that it was often impossible to give sources on sensitive stories, such as matters involving national security, Bagdikian raised these questions as tests for dropping attribution:

> Is the story important enough to omit the usual obligation to tell the reader where it comes from?
> Is there enough internal evidence in the story to permit reasonable judgment on its plausibility?
> What is the reputation of the journalist whose honesty and judgment we are asked to accept?

He then reviewed the extensive criticism of the authors by the Nixon faithful as well as more disinterested parties, but concluded that the book was "as correct as careful research could make it." In other

[2] *St. Louis Post-Dispatch*, 27 June 1976, p. 1.

words, he took the reporters' work mainly on faith, as was the case with the Woo articles. But the critic added:

> There is a danger that other reporters and less meticulous persons will be encouraged to write unsourced stories without the discipline of Woodward and Bernstein. But that does not cancel the credentials of Woodward and Bernstein or the legitimacy of this kind of work when it is performed with competence and care.[3]

The Dangers Involved This does not mean that a reputable journalist can get away with dropping all attribution if it is inconvenient, or failing to give a source if he has one and can use it. That way lies disaster, as the following incident shows.

> During a fatal uprising at Attica Prison in New York State in 1971, after a final assault by the State Police, an official of the State Department of Corrections announced that hostages held by the prisoners had been found with their throats cut. Almost every reporter on the job was so convinced of the truth of this statement that it was generally used on radio and television and in the press without attribution and without checking. It would have been bad enough to publicize the views of a panicky State official; however, it was compounding a palpable error to drop out all attribution and make most of the nation's news organizations the authorities for the hasty assumption.
>
> It was not until two reporters for the *Rochester* (N.Y.) *Times-Union* obtained autopsy reports next day from a reluctant Monroe County medical examiner that the truth was discovered. The reporters, Richard Cooper and John Machacek, disclosed that the autopsies had shown that the slain hostages died after being shot by police bullets (the rioting convicts had no guns). Thus, the whole focus of the story shifted and the investigation proceeded in a more evenhanded manner. For their work that day, Cooper and Machacek received a Pulitzer Prize in Local Reporting for 1972.

THE USES OF ATTRIBUTION

Few reporters, and even fewer sources, have a precise understanding of the ground rules for giving and receiving information. That is because definitions vary from one person to another and one circumstance to another.

Anybody who has been a reporter for more than a few days knows that everybody can't be quoted on everything at all times. It would be insufferable if a news source couldn't even exchange the time of day with a reporter unless a tape recorder was available. There are many circumstances under which reporters keep their own counsel about what is disclosed to them and maintain the confidentiality of their sources. If they didn't, there would be no investigative reporting wor-

[3] Ben H. Bagdikian, review of *The Final Days*. *The Quill* (June 1976), pp. 21–22.

thy of the name and the whole structure of the practice of journalism would be weakened thereby.

To understand the basics of attribution, therefore, it is well worth analyzing the main gradations as they are generally understood. The following discussion is based on more than 50 years' experience in American journalism and is offered as the view of most professional journalists who are working today:

On the Record Early in this century, reporters were not conscious of their limitations to any great degree. They made it a practice to go to a meeting or interview, take notes on what they heard and write the story with a liberal mixture of direct quotations, whether or not they were exactly what the speaker had said. The same kind of coverage was given lawmaking bodies, the courts, and the various offices of executives either in government or private industry.

Those who made news were named. The things they said were attributed directly to them. If a public official timidly suggested that it might be well to hold up a voluminous document for a few days to give reporters a chance to study and understand it before writing about it, he was accused of betraying the freedom of the press. If he tried to give counsel to reporters on the meaning of the news, but asked not to be quoted as the source, he was hooted down as a propagandist.

In these more complicated and dangerous days the old rule of "everything on the record" has undergone some rather violent changes that old-time reporters and editors would never have accepted. Most public figures have now learned the risks of talking "off the cuff" and often prepare their statements in advance if they intend to speak for publication. The inventions of the tape recorder and video tape have done more than anything else to force reporters to be scrupulously honest about direct quotations.

Today, most American reporters operate on the basic premise that there are certain broad limitations to what is "on the record"—that is, material which can be used by the news media in exactly the form in which it is made available.

One limitation is any specific agreement or understanding made by reporters and their sources to withhold some or all of the news for a valid reason. If there is a matter of principle at stake here, rather than some technical reason, any such limitation should have the approval of the reporter's superiors.

Another limitation, even more important, is the body of law affecting the news media. This includes the law of libel, the law against invasion of privacy, and certain broad statutes forbidding the use of certain kinds of news such as atomic secrets and other matters affecting national defense and, in numerous states, the names of juvenile defendants and relief clients.

Responsible reporters and the news media that employ them are equally insistent on observing the accepted standards of good taste as well.

Finally, reporters like all citizens are bound by the precepts of the Constitution and its interpretation by the courts, as well as the various federal, state and local laws that regulate individual and corporate behavior. These, too, are likely to have an effect on what may or may not be used by the news media, particularly in cases involving such matters as judges' directives concerning publicity, contempt of court or contempt of Congress.

It is good practice for reporters to consider the material that is on the record within the limits here defined. Unless there is a recording of the quoted matter, reporters should take the time to check doubtful quotes for accuracy with the source. News today is far more complicated than it used to be and requires more care and explanation.

In cases involving the public disclosure of official secrets, such as the *New York Times*'s publication of the Pentagon Papers dealing with the Vietnam War, the newspaper's management and ownership make the final decision on the use of such material. It is not done by the reporter although, in the case of the Pentagon Papers, the initiative, knowledge and reputation of the *Times*'s Pentagon correspondent, Neil Sheehan, were decisive factors in what eventually became one of the most celebrated confrontations in American history between the government and the press.

For Attribution, but Not for Direct Quotation The initial variant in the rule of putting as much news as possible on the record is to specify that there may be paraphrase, but no direct quotation. Reporters dislike this kind of limitation because direct quotations give authenticity to the news. Yet, there are times when they must accept it.

Since American reporters as a whole do not take shorthand and they do "fix up" quotes where necessary to make them a fair approximation of what the speaker said, nobody with an important statement of policy is willing to take chances with the system. If an official does not have time to issue the statement in advance, and if no tape recorder is available, then the rule against direct quotation is usually invoked.

Necessarily, the source must be a dominant one in the news to call upon this rule. No mere actress or night club playboy could specify grandly, "You may use what I say, but not in direct quotation." Such a privilege is reserved on occasion for the President of the United States, the Secretary of State, an occasional military briefing of importance, and now and then, major pronouncements on state, local and private industry levels.

However, judges, politicians and diplomats still avail themselves of the "no direct quotations" rule when they can. If reporters are able to overcome the reluctance of sources to be quoted, then the press is doubly responsible to see that the material used is completely accurate and not merely "fixed up." The electronic media here act as good policemen.

Attribution to a Spokesman Before World War II the presence of a spokesman in a news story was not as common as it is today in domestic American journalism. Editors generally insisted that the sources of the news must be identified by name, whether or not they could be quoted directly. The presence of an anonymous figure, who could not be described in any way except in relation to what he represented, was almost an affront to many reporters and editors.

Yet, after World War II spokesmen blossomed in the federal government and at the United Nations. They cropped up in stories from Congress and the legislatures. When it became evident that the editorial bars were down, and the news media were so eager for news that they would accept even anonymous sources, spokesmen appeared as authorities for news about city halls, boards of education, police headquarters and even street cleaning departments.

It is common practice now for spokesmen to make news for even small companies in local papers. They are found on sports pages and in family news. Elizabeth Taylor has a spokesman, so has Catfish Hunter. And the women's rights movement has spokespersons. There even are ecclesiastical press offices in the larger church groups.

Reporters could knock a lot of the nonsense out of the use of anonymous spokesmen by refusing to countenance the practice except where there is good reason for it. They do have a choice. For when government or private sources say, "You may attribute the following to a spokesman for the such-and-such department," reporters may either agree to the conditions or refuse to accept them. If they act in a body, their decision will carry weight.

The trouble is that reporters are competitors, not diplomats, and they have never had much patience for bargaining or negotiation. Consequently, what generally happens is that reporters accept the conditions that are laid down; in rare instances when the proposal is questioned, it is the editors who usually pull the reporters off the job.

Background Anonymous attribution is the most difficult and confusing practice in American journalism, but at the same time it is one of the most important, for it is the key to the use of a lot of news for which nobody will be the authority. The reporter and the news media must take risks, for the only attribution of so-called background news is "well-informed sources," "official sources," "diplomatic sources," "officials" or no source at all but the reporter's name and the name of his organization.

The word "background" is in itself a semantic puzzle. In one sense, when it is used in connection with the writing of a story, background means the historical detail that helps explain some current event. In a reporting sense background means the use of material in a story without any attribution to the source by name or to any nation, state or organization he may represent. The origin of the term in connection with reporting doubtless may be traced to the introduction of such material by a news source:

"Now, I can't be named as the authority for what I'm about to tell you but I'll give it to you for your background."

A variation on this is for a source to remark to a reporter, "This is just background material for your personal use."

It is important for reporters to remember that they need not use background material if they see no real reason to do so. Not all background material, after all, is newsworthy. A lot of it is of trial-balloon character, to be withdrawn if it arouses opposition. Some of it is issued by sources who do not really know what they are talking about. And occasionally, somebody tries to put over background material as out-and-out publicity for some cause, idea or person. It is a human peculiarity that editors who will not print a story when it is put on the record will sometimes fall for the same material when it is put out mysteriously for background by a conniving official (and, in a rare case, maybe a conniving reporter).

Background, as a journalistic practice, is as old as print. European foreign offices have used it as long as there have been favored correspondents and favored newspapers. It was adapted for American use during World War II by Washington reporters who generally credit Ernest K. Lindley, of *Newsweek* magazine, with being the first to employ it. Finding that high officials could not talk to him on the record, and being unwilling to talk to them off the record, Lindley persuaded them to give him needed explanations of current and coming events under a pledge that he would not identify them as his sources. Thus, background came to be a half-way house between on the record and off the record.

Officials and Background The background reporting device has spread from Washington into every state in the union. Few news organizations in the United States today are able to identify all sources of all news because of the growing number of restrictions on use. Therefore, the "informed source" and the "official circle" have moved in as not particularly welcome guests in journalism at all levels. Young or inexperienced reporters should not try background reporting unless they have the firmest kind of instructions from their editors. The reason for this is that there are relatively few news sources experienced enough to be able to handle background material without costly errors in judgment.

For example, when President Carter removed Major General John Singlaub as No. 3 U. S. Army commander in South Korea, the backgrounding practice figured in the incident. The President acted because Singlaub had opposed his program for the withdrawal of U. S. troops from South Korea and for stating it would lead to war with North Korea. Singlaub's defense was that he thought he had talked "for background" with a reporter. At any rate, Singlaub did not deny responsibility.[4]

Reporters and Background Writing in the *New York Times*, James Reston had this to say about background reporting:

> This is a remarkable rule, for it imposes upon the writer what can only be described as a compulsory form of plagiarism. That is to say, the official explains what he has been doing or is about to do or is thinking about doing, on the specific understanding that the writers may publish what he says on their own authority without any attribution to him or his department, or even to "an official source."
>
> The reporters are permitted under these ground rules to say that the government is planning to do these things or thinking about doing them, or if they are inordinately cautious, they can dream up such phrases as "there is one view in the government." But they cannot give any authority for what they are told.
>
> This has many advantages for both the official and the reporters. The official, if he is thinking about introducing a new policy but isn't quite sure how it will be received (officials are almost always in this state), can thus discover the public reaction to his proposal without being identified with it. More important, he can explain some of the intricacies of his problems (including his difficulties with other officials) and thus help win understanding and approval for what he proposes to do.
>
> Similarly the reporters stand to gain, for in such meetings they acquire an understanding of what is going on and are therefore better able to inform their readers. But the trouble is that, if there is a misunderstanding of what is said, or if what is said causes embarrassment to the government, the White House can always repudiate the published stories, and the reporters, who cannot disclose their source, are left without any plausible defense.

Little sympathy should be wasted on the reporter without a "plausible defense" in a background story. Human nature and human conduct being what they are, it is inevitable that the source of a background story of importance eventually will be disclosed if there is controversy about it.

Reporters do try to protect such sources. The difficulty is that those reporters who are left out of a cozy Washington background dinner, which is given by an official to a favored few, invariably disclose what

[4] The Carter decision was announced May 21, 1977 after an interview with the general at the White House. See the *New York Times* and *Washington Post*, May 22, 1977.

happened because they are under no pledge or confidence. On the contary, having been beaten, they are entitled to some slight revenge, and disclosure is one of the best ways they can fight back.

It is the State Department primarily that has developed the backgrounder into a way of journalistic life, although regular backgrounding sessions are part of the routine at the Pentagon, on the Hill during Congressional inquiries, at the White House and elsewhere in government.

During the Eisenhower administration, John Foster Dulles fancied himself as a molder of public opinion who could use the press as a weapon against his enemies. Often, he got away with devious tricks. But once, at Newport, Rhode Island, he gave warning anonymously for background that the United States wouldn't stand for an invasion of Taiwan by the Peking government, then went on the record as secretary of state and was considerably milder for direct quotation. The trouble was that *Time* magazine blew his cover with embarrassment to all concerned.

To get around this kind of disclosure, Secretary of State Dean Rusk in the succeeding Kennedy administration took to talking quietly to a few selected correspondents on what both referred to as "deep background." This meant that the material was primarily for "guidance," a word that can be variously translated, and that the correspondents pledged they would never—well, hardly ever—disclose that the meeting had taken place. In any event, "deep background" soon became a code word in journalism, like the British "D Notice."[5]

When Background Backfires It remained for Secretary of State Henry A. Kissinger, in the Nixon and Ford administrations, to make a travesty of background reporting. He posed so often as a "senior official" in briefing reporters on his plane, while on his many foreign ventures, that both sides took it as a joke.

And yet, after a Federal Court ruled under the Freedom of Information Act that comments made by an "official" at the 1974 Vladivostok arms accord briefing could be attributed directly to Kissinger, the State Department expressed outrage. A State Department lawyer (unnamed) explained that official public statements by the Secretary of State could oblige foreign governments to react, but they could ignore comments made by an "official." The unnamed spokesman had the grace to concede that the position "may sound silly to people who don't know how the game is played."[6]

This resort to secrecy in even the smallest and least consequential

---

[5] The British have a tough Official Secrets Act and, under it, a D (for Defense) Notice, sent to the media, warns that articles on certain subjects may violate the secrets law. Usually, the British press complies and suppresses information. The law carries punitive action.

[6] From the Associated Press night report, 29 May 1976.

matters was what injected Kissinger's methods into the 1976 Presidential campaign despite his recognized ability as a diplomat and his undoubted achievements as secretary of state.

One of the few formal records of his procedures was created when Senator Barry Goldwater, Republican of Arizona, inserted a background briefing for 50 reporters into the Congressional Record during the India-Pakistan War of 1971. This was the way Ron Ziegler, then the White House press secretary, laid down the ground rules:

"What Dr. Kissinger says to you will be background. You can attribute it to White House officials, but no direct quotations. We have, of course, had a number of inquiries and questions about the situation in South Asia. What I am saying to you now is, of course, on background because it relates to this. We thought it might be worth while for Henry to come out this afternoon to discuss our views on a background basis with you to put the matter into further perspective for you."

The reason for Goldwater's action was that he sought to identify Kissinger, then the President's adviser on national security affairs, as the source of unsourced stories defending the American pro-Pakistan policy. However, it didn't seem to bother Kissinger to have his cover blown. Within a short time, on "deep background" for a small group of reporters, he was warning the Soviet Union to restrain the Indians or "the entire U.S.-Soviet relationship might have to be re-examined." This time, the *Washington Post*, not having a reporter at the briefing, blew Kissinger's cover.

There was a flap. There always is over such matters. Various managing editors, including those of the *Washington Post* and the *New York Times*, denounced backgrounders as an insidious device. Some even threatened to pull their reporters out of further background briefings. But nothing happened. As time went on, backgrounding continued to grow although nearly everybody concerned recognized it was a device that concealed more truths than it revealed.

Off the Record The trouble with putting something off the record is that, almost always, it will leak if more than two persons know about it. The leak may take time. Almost a quarter-century elapsed before President Franklin D. Roosevelt's romantic excursions became public knowledge; for President Kennedy, the period of grace was much shorter.

That, however, is not the way reporters look at off the record material in their day-to-day work. To them, off the record means that the information or quotations or documents cannot be used. It is, in effect, a pledge that a confidence will not be violated. And that is how responsible reporters act. This may sound unbelievably holy and high-minded but it is true.

Young reporters and others unfamiliar with the ways of journalism invariably ask why anybody would want to tell the media a secret that should not be revealed. As a matter of public policy, such actions are frequently taken. At the highest level of government, Presidential movements—and sometimes those of other high officials—are not disclosed to the public even though the media receive broad advance notice of travel plans for purposes of coverage. This was particularly true of President Ford immediately after two attempts had been made to assassinate him. The war-time journeys of Presidents Roosevelt and Eisenhower, in World War II and Korea, were similarly handled. In the case of civil disturbances, plans for combating disorders may be disclosed to the media on an off the record basis, again for purposes of eventual coverage. Sometimes, in a kidnapping, authorities ask the media to use nothing until the victim is recovered.

The practice is necessary, but invariably troublesome. For one thing, most sources use "off the record" but really mean "background." And sometimes, sad to say, a sharp-shooting reporter will deliberately misunderstand an "off the record" request. There have been instances in which a reporter was "sealed up" but the confidence was broken by someone else in the same news organization. Moreover, it has happened that a reporter who received a confidence in one city connived with a colleague in another city to break the story.

Nearly always, this sort of thing is sheer, unprincipled opportunism; rarely is a claim made that a confidence must be broken because the public interest demands it. Thus, the general effect of violations of confidence is to reduce the public's belief in the good faith of the news media. About the only defense a reporter has is to refuse to accept anything that is put off the record—but not many try it.

The Leak   Leaking the news is something else again. In Washington and other major capitals of the world, the leak is sometimes used as a weapon against political opponents. Or it may be a strategy to advance the cause of one government department over another, especially at budget time. It has happened that unofficial leaks by officials have put wrongdoers on the spot; and unhappily, in a few cases, leaks have victimized innocent persons and the news media as well. Leaking is a difficult and sometimes a dirty business but it is a part of journalism that cannot be ignored. As James Reston once put the case: "Leaking is the safety valve of democracy."

Who leaks? Wahington's veteran journalists agree that almost everybody does it, given a motive and a story that stands up. Although there is specified punishment for leaking certain kinds of government documents and materials, few are caught at it. One was an Internal Revenue Service employee who was said to have provided the *Providence Journal-Bulletin* with President Nixon's income tax returns. Another was Daniel Ellsberg, who said he made the Pentagon Papers available to the press; although he was tried, he escaped punishment when the case was thrown out of court because the government was shown to have burglarized his psychiatrist's office.

Why do journalists accept leaks? Because, as Clifton Daniel once wrote while chief of the Washington bureau of the *New York Times,* "That is often the only way they can get information they think the public is entitled to have." To which Daniel added philosophically, "They are in a competitive business."[7]

The Battle against Secrecy The attribution of news is a complicated and sometimes confusing business. The public neither cares about it nor understands it. All the fussing over unnamed sources merely makes well-intentioned people wonder.

And yet, reporters are caught in this trap which they have helped to devise. Accordingly, they learn from experience not to make agreements they cannot keep and clear with their offices if they are involved in a difficult ethical situation. The battle against secrecy is never-ending.

In general, where there are gradations of attribution, it is always a sound policy to try to lift the type of attribution by one notch. That is, if material is given for background, a reporter should try to persuade the source that it would receive more attention if it came from a spokesman. The reportorial effort should be unceasing to try to persuade spokesmen and their principals, where it is at all possible, to disclose their identities. Too much secrecy about the sources of the news is likely to undermine public confidence in the gatherers of the news.

Journalists should never forget that their purpose in a free society is not necessarily identical with those of their sources. Dean Acheson, while Secretary of State, put it this way in a letter to a reporter: "If I am about to go abroad to persuade another foreign secretary to agree to something which I wish to discuss with him first in complete confidence, your job would be served by discovering and reporting my plan. But this would frustrate my purpose. So it is fair, and should be understood, that your job requires you to pry; and mine requires me to keep secret."[8]

NEWS BEFORE IT HAPPENS

So much news is issued and processed before it actually happens that the reporter is under a great disadvantage to give life to his copy. It is, after all, impossible to report the colorful details of a political speech or a rocket launching or a parade before they actually occur. Yet, innumerable advance stories have to be written so that the course of events

[7] *New York Times,* 29 June 1974, p. 13.
[8] John Hohenberg, *Between Two Worlds* (New York, 1967), p. 4.

may be followed as they unfold. Nobody likes to do this, particularly for the electronic media where coverage can be immediate as events develop, but there is no choice. The practice of circulating speeches before delivery, and making known other events before they actually occur, gives reporters the responsibility of using or withholding the material.

The Advance For these reasons the "advance" has become an integral part of American journalism. It used to be done solely for the benefit of the press but radio and television have long since dealt themselves in. Now the "advance" is a general technical problem for all concerned.

In essence, the handling of an advance is based on cooperation between the source and the news media, with reporters acting as go-betweens. If the source specifies that the material should be released at a particular time, the news media either comply with the request or do not accept the advance. The practice of holding a story for release is called an *embargo*.

The handling of an important speech, particularly during a political campaign, illustrates this principle in its simplest form. It is axiomatic that candidates running for election seek the widest publicity for their speeches and therefore are willing to have them used even before they are delivered. Assume a speech is to be delivered at 10 P.M.; it is common practice for the embargo to end at 6 P.M. so that the material can appear in all editions of morning newspapers as well as radio and TV newscasts. The embargo directions are always clearly given on the first sheet of the text of advance material.

If the first edition of a morning newspaper hits the street at 7 P.M., it is clear that the text of a speech to be delivered two hours later, or at least a news story about it, will appear under a prominent display. It will also be used by the broadcast media. The manner in which this is justified, both by the source and the editors, is as follows:

The lead will be based on whatever news there is in the speech and it will be written without qualification. But no lower than the second paragraph, it will be noted that the story is based on the release of an advance text with a phrase attributing the news to "a speech prepared for delivery." This qualification usually does not go in the first sentence because the lead then becomes too cumbersome. Here is an example of such an advance lead:

> Governor Williston charged last night that his Republican rival, J. Horton Denfield, intended to increase income taxes in the state if elected.
>
> In a speech prepared for delivery before the Tonawanda Democratic Club's annual dinner at the Hotel Biltmore, the Democratic Governor warned:
>
> "My opponent says our state must match income with outgo. He has pledged a balanced budget, but he refuses to specify what economies he

will make to achieve it. I submit there is only one way in which he can accomplish his aim, and that is to raise the state income tax."

There would, of course, be a lot more of this based on the advance
text. The same material would be used in the radio and TV newscasts
so that it would be thoroughly familiar to any reader or listener by the
time the speech actually was delivered. It would be the duty of the reporter, after writing the advance or giving in the essential facts to rewrite, to check the actual delivery against the advance text. If no substantial changes were made, the reporter would merely call in or
dictate an insert to replace the second paragraph and eliminate all reference to the advance text.

To show that the speech was actually delivered, the sub second
paragraph might read:

The Democratic Governor was interrupted eight times by applause as he
spoke at 10 P.M. before the Tonawanda Democratic Club's annual dinner at
the Hotel Biltmore. He said:

The third paragraph and all the rest of the material culled from the
advance then would be picked up and used as is. There would be no
need for change. Occasionally, if there are interpolations in a speech
that make some difference in the text, an additional insert will be used.
It takes a major shift in emphasis to top an advance that has been used.
Changes have to be kept to a minimum.

The growth of television campaigning in Presidential and major gu-
bernatorial and local elections has greatly reduced the value of advance
texts for newspapers. There is little point in using an advance text
when it differs materially from what actually is said on the air, as has
been the case in recent political campaigns. This and the growth of
what is known as the "basic speech," which candidates use over and
over again in "whistle-stop" campaigning, have led many newspapers
to drop advance texts altogether. Some candidates have been known to
order their staffs to prepare any number of advance texts, merely to
gain newspaper space, with no actual intention of ever delivering them.

Thus, the old reliance on advance texts must be re-examined. In the
future, it is likely that the tape recorder — with machinery for rapid reproduction of the record in type — will be far more useful to newspapers than any canned advance that may or may not be delivered. As for
television, it is safe to say that — given responsible management — its
usefulness as a news medium during political campaigns will be intensified many times over in years to come.

THE EMBARGO

There are numerous types of embargoes. The most familiar one, and the
easiest to work with, is the automatic release which specifies that mate-

rial may be used in all editions that appear on the street after a specified time, and all newscasts as well.

Often, however, an embargo may specify that a release is "expected
at about" a particular hour for all media. In such cases, the story cannot be scheduled definitely but must be held until it is certain that the
speech is about to begin. Customarily, such material is used as soon as
notification has been received that the delivery of the speech has begun. This kind of embargo applies to major advances such as the President's State of the Union message, the various governors' messages to
their state legislatures and similar material.

Use of Embargoes On complicated data, such as federal, state or local
budgets or legislative or private programs to which extraordinary news
significance is attached, several days and sometimes as much as a week
may be given to the preparation of the story. On budgets, it is not unusual for public officials to hold a "budget school" for reporters to give
them special instruction in detail and permit them to question experts.
All material, whether it is printed or given out in the form of interviews or replies to questions, is then embargoed for a particular hour
and issued for use by all media.

Nor are these long embargoes confined to governmental material.
Universities and foundations generally have tried to provide reporters
with sufficient time, in the form of an embargo, to enable them to fa-
miliarize themselves and their editors with complex material. One such
report, dealing with the United States' interest in the United Nations,
was embargoed for several days by the Carnegie Endowment for International Peace so that reporters could interview the leaders of the
study. At the United Nations one of the most famous embargoes was a
four-day period during which reporters frantically tried to inform themselves on the principles of the Baruch Plan for Atomic Control.

Conditional Embargoes The practice of embargoing news in order to
avoid an uninformed deadline scramble among newspapers and even
worse on radio and television has spread to all major sources of information. However, it is not an unmixed blessing to reporters, writers
and commentators for the broadcast media. The news media give far
more than they receive, as a general rule, when they submit to special
conditions for an embargo in order to obtain certain types of news.

For example, after the original failures in the United States missile
program, the Defense Department provided advance information on un-
classified missile or satellite shots for the news media only on condition that no use would be made of it before the actual firing. The object
was to reduce public anticipation, and thereby take the edge off any
continued failures of American space shots in the face of Russia's early
successes. However, as the American space program grew until men

landed on the moon, this kind of precaution was dropped. Classified space shots still take place both in Florida and California without notice to the news media.

Conditional embargoes were used a great deal during the Vietnam War to prevent the news media from giving inadvertent word to the enemy that a particular troop movement was under way. The practice was to permit use of the news when security measures no longer were necessary; however, more than one reporter held guilty of violating such conditional embargoes was denied the right of coverage for limited periods.

When an Embargo Is Broken The universal rule on the breaking of an embargo, either by design or inadvertently, is: "A release that is broken for one is broken for all." The cases of deliberate violations of embargoes on major stories are so rare that each one becomes a *cause celebre.*

When the first color film of the first hydrogen bomb blast was about to be released by the United States Atomic Energy Commission, it was decided to permit advance viewing of the awesome record so that descriptive material could be written. The embargo was to last for one week after the advance showing. However, a syndicated columnist published a review of the H-bomb film almost immediately after he saw it. The Columbia Broadcasting Company then showed the film and the newspapers broke the story.

In addition, there have been instances in which newspapers have deliberately broken releases given to them in advance on the dubious ground that the public interest demanded it. One such case involved a report on the incidence of cancer among habitual cigarette smokers. There have been others, but generally most embargoes have been respected.

At the local and state levels powerful news sources have also succeeded in holding the mass media to an agreed embargo time, but it is somewhat more difficult to contain the aggressively independent Washington press corps. It seems to be a sound rule, however, to notify a news source that an embargo has been broken and that, in consequence, rival reporters no longer feel themselves bound.

False Embargoes The embargo system can be made so complicated that it becomes a burden, rather than a help, to the news media. It can also be put to questionable uses.

When President Ford made his annual trips to Vail, Colorado, for ski practice, the White House staff used to take along bills for him to sign and various messages to approve as press releases in order to give the impression that this was a "working vacation." The Ford administration has not been alone in countenancing such petty chicanery.

Many a governor and mayor have made similar use of the news media.

Of course reporters protest such false embargoes, especially when some material is put out for AM release and others for PM release even though the principal may be anywhere but in the office at the time. But they usually have little choice in the matter. Once reporters accept embargoes, they are bound not to reveal the contents of the embargoed material until the agreed time. They can, and do point out the non-essential nature of the press releases and show, in brief analytical dispatches, that they are mainly cosmetic in nature.

For something of importance that is about to be put out under an embargo, reporters act differently. If they get wind of the story before the embargo is put on it, they are at liberty to use it.

CHANGES IN ADVANCES

Sometimes, even when an embargo is observed in good faith, circumstances beyond anyone's control create such changes in the text that the advance lead is a false statement. There have been instances when speakers dropped dead between the time of the issuance of an advance and the delivery of the text, causing the news media to use an address by a dead man. In other cases, mercurial speakers have discarded an advance text and talked at random.

There have been instances in which public officials have said one thing in their advance and quite another in their actual remarks. Even Presidents of the United States are not immune to such journalistic sinning, as history has amply recorded. Once, when President Eisenhower's television time ran out, he inadvertently omitted the last paragraph of his text, which was the big news point of his advance text, but obligingly covered the reporters by issuing it later as an interview.

Precautions When there are significant changes between the advance and the live statement or speech, reporters should note them in their stories and try to obtain an explanation from the source. If the main point of the story has been nullified, then obviously it may be necessary to shift to some other angle but it is mandatory to report as well what wasn't said and why it wasn't said. It is also accepted practice to let a source change an advance before release time, if there is sufficient reason to do so. But these changes, too, should be reported.

"SEALING UP" REPORTERS

The principal assets of reporters as a group are their ability, their integrity and their freedom from commitments other than those to their news organizations and their immediate families. Very early in their careers, nearly all find out that if one of these qualities is compromised, all are compromised. And that their integrity, basically, is the most precious of all.

For reporters who attain some degree of stature in their profession, it is almost foreordained that attempts will be made to sway their judgment, to persuade them to bend the news just a little in one direction or another. Few are ever affected by such blandishments. Those who are seldom last very long in active, day-to-day journalism.

In rare cases, where reporters are obliged to favor one side or another because of the policies of certain news organizations, they usually find that the very people to whom they are allied begin leaking tips and news to the opposition. Thus, the unfortunates are "sealed up" while the opposition reaps the benefits of being free of any ties. This is the price that extreme partisanship costs a news organization; worse still, where partisan policies continue for any length of time, the organization suffers a complete loss of public respect through lack of confidence in the impartiality of its news presentation.

It was this consideration that caused the American news media to protest disclosures that the Central Intelligence Agency had been using journalists as part-time operatives and demand full identification of those who were so employed. While the CIA declined to identify any of the journalists who were affected, it did announce that it had ended the practice. The rule is without exception: Journalists should stay away from situations in which they may find themselves compromised. The "sealed up" reporter is no reporter at all.

Chapter 19
The News Media and Public Relations

Few Washington correspondents of stature bother with the daily paper blizzard that is created by the public relations machinery of the Department of Agriculture. James Risser, a lawyer turned reporter for the *Des Moines Register*, is an exception. He believes in reading press releases—and sometimes it pays off.

THE STORY OF A HANDOUT

One day when Risser was pursuing his regular routine, he came across a USDA release reporting that bribery indictments had been returned in Houston against five ship inspectors for falsely certifying unacceptable vessels for the loading of grain. These inspectors, although federally licensed, were actually employed by a firm called the Houston Merchants Exchange, which aroused Risser's suspicions. He put the handout in his pocket and went to the headquarters of the USDA

338

grain division in Maryland, where he learned that other grain inspectors had been indicted in New Orleans.

The news media had ignored the story. No other correspondent was bothering with it. But Risser, convinced he was onto something, decided it was worth investigating.

After studying court records in New Orleans and Houston, he began a series of interviews with government investigators, inspection firms and grain companies. Then, he invoked the federal Freedom of Information Act to gain access to USDA files, found evidence that grain shipping figures had been juggled and that foreign grain buyers had lodged more than 100 complaints against short weighting and the shipment of grain that was unfit for use.

Two months after beginning his inquiry, he broke a Page 1 story in the *Des Moines Register* about what he called "widespread corruption in the grading and shipping of U. S. export grains." In addition to his disclosure of the government's investigation, he wrote:

> The Register's own investigation indicates that the government's system of grading export grain and inspecting ships is full of conflicts of interest and the potential for a variety of abuses.
>
> As a result, foreign purchasers and countries that get humanitarian food aid from the United States may have received substandard grain and grain that was contaminated by being transported in dirty or insect-infested ships.

Now the Washington press corps came to life. And leading papers and the electronic media paid attention to the story. Before long, 57 individuals and companies were indicted on charges ranging from bribery to theft in the $12-billion-a-year export grain business. Eventually, more than 50 individuals and companies pleaded guilty to the charges. In the continuing inquiry, Congress approved remedial legislation and different methods of grain inspection were adopted.

And it all began because a reporter read a handout instead of throwing it in the wastebasket. Was he satisfied? Few good reporters ever are. Said Risser: "Many segments of the American press never did focus on the story, dismissing it as a dull farm issue."

THE REPORTERS' PROBLEM

American journalists have good reason to mistrust the powerful public relations apparatus that filters much of today's news flow before it ever reaches the news media. But the problem is not going to be solved by ignoring it, by cold-shouldering all special pleaders and by refusing to listen to them or read what they produce.

Risser's adventure is the best evidence of the error of such judgments. "It is true," he says, "that dirty grain is not as much fun to read about as dirty old men in Congress. But that is not a good enough explanation for the press's failure to cover important issues in depth." [1]

The Credibility Gap It takes a considerable degree of sophistication to deal with public relations pronouncements and attitudes in the higher reaches of government and industry, labor and the professions, and other important segments of public life. And those who direct a large public relations apparatus are most painfully aware of it. The mistrust engendered by the Watergate scandal and the Vietnam War, the undercover machinations of the CIA and the FBI at home and abroad, and the campaigns of bribery undertaken by large American corporations to get business abroad will not soon be forgotten. It is bad enough that one result has been to widen the credibility gap between government and the news media. Worse still, it has contributed to a certain amount of mistrust that has arisen in large segments of public opinion against the press, even though the press contributed to both the Watergate disclosures and the campaign that ended in American withdrawal from Vietnam.

Against so clouded a background, which was scarcely lightened by the carnival atmosphere produced by the American Bicentennial celebration, the best that can be said about the posture of the news media toward public relations is one of extreme doubt. And this extends from the Washington correspondent to the newest and youngest reporter hired by a country weekly. Rarely in this country have so many been willing to believe in so little.

Attitudes toward P. R. Whenever reporters deal with public relations representatives, and it is almost impossible to avoid them except in small towns and modest organizations, their problem is to determine whether the news has been tampered with. Whenever they find distortions, half-truths or no truth at all, it is their job to get the story right before passing it on to the public. Had Risser merely written a two paragraph story based on the USDA handout about inspectors' indictments, he would have served the government's purpose—but not the public's.

Similarly, if reporters had not checked a press release of the Department of Health, Education and Welfare, Secretary Joseph Califano's decision to hire a private cook and disguise him as a "specialist" would not have proved so embarrassing to the Carter administration. The matter of judging between truth and falsehood has been a thankless, well-nigh impossible task since the era of Pontius Pilate. How, then, can a reporter be expected to operate against a position taken by a govern-

---

[1] Risser's opening article in *Des Moines Register*, 4 May 1975; his observations from *The Bulletin* of ASNE (September 1976), p. 17.

ment or major corporation with vast resources, even if there are suspicions of misstatements in public announcements? Granted, few reporters have the freedom of movement and the luxury of weeks of time and a generous expense account, as was the case with Risser's inquiry. A few basic approaches can be taken, however, by any reporter who is willing to put in the effort.

The first and most important step is to seek access to the sources of the news—persons, places, records—within the bounds of law and sound journalistic practice. Such access is one sign of a guarantee of good faith; if it is denied, it may also be one possible sign of danger. In Vietnam, during the early days of the war when the American government continually claimed victory and a light at the end of the tunnel, reporters learned to visit the supposedly victorious units; more often than not, they found the buck privates and the noncoms told the truth, the generals told the lies and the victories were usually defeats. And nobody except the North Vietnamese and the Vietcong ever saw the light at the end of the tunnel.

Translating this experience into terms of local news, reporters who are barred from the meetings of public bodies by closed doors generally learn to be suspicious of such "executive sessions." To be sure, some are necessary. But when a board of supervisors in town or county suddenly decides to hold a closed meeting in a motel at 8 A.M., it doesn't take much imagination to figure out that somebody is trying to conceal something.

The Publicity Specialists This is not to say that anybody who has anything to do with public relations is to be mistrusted from the outset. Many are former journalists who have become government civil servants or corporate officers. Both in ability and reputation they differ widely, probably more so than journalists; moreover, few except at the higher levels appear to derive much satisfaction from the jobs they do. In moments of disillusionment, they apply to themselves every term from press agent to flack, and sometimes worse.

Yet, particularly in government, a well-trained specialist who deals with the news media can be helpful and there are many whose reputations for candor and fairness are well deserved. It is not unknown for such specialists to serve the public interest against the policies of those who employ them, certainly a risky business. But then, "Deep Throat," the key to the earliest Watergate revelations, wasn't exactly a myth. Messrs. Woodward and Bernstein were lucky that he was on their side, rather than the government's.

General Public Relations Because it lacks prestige except perhaps in institutional fields, public relations today goes under many names and an assortment of guises.

The press agent is at the lowest level. There is a stigma attached to the name — a hangover from the days when press agents grabbed news space by doing everything from sitting actresses in milk baths to making a circus out of Rudolph Valentino's funeral. However, today's theatrical press agents go about their job unblushingly and efficiently and most of them are good at it. What they are supposed to do is to get public attention and media time and space for their clients or attractions and they make no bones about it. Often, they work in an engaging and even an informative way.

Corporate and institutional public relations shy away from press agentry. They say they seek goodwill, not mere publicity. Business and industry, foundations and universities, civic, fraternal and charitable groups prefer to be represented by dignified public relations people on a number of levels.

There are the policy consultants, who do not even have mimeograph machines in their offices but make their way by giving sound, shrewd advice on public attitudes. Then there are companies, either separate public relations firms or branches of advertising agencies, that deal with the organization to be publicized. On the working level of the organization itself, if it is large enough, there is an operating staff. They not only serve the external news media but also direct house organs (sometimes called house magazines) for employees. Companies like General Motors, General Electric, Standard Oil of New Jersey, Rockwell International and others are outstanding in their efforts to handle public relations on a professional level.

Government Information The largest of all public relations groupings is in the government at all levels — federal, state and local. Here, because the taxpayers are footing the bill, there is a rather wary reluctance to use even corporate and institutional public-relations terms. The policy consultant is also found in government and used on assignments in which his advice is supposedly likely to cut costs or increase efficiency.

Here, publicity is called by a different name, and it is conscientiously practiced in a different way when directed by responsible officials. Most such efforts in government are termed information work. Those who handle the job are usually called Public Information Officers or Press Officers, the inference being that they deal only in information and do not seek to publicize their respective agencies. If only it were true!

From the working level in government, the progression of titles becomes a dizzy affair. The State Department not only has information personnel, but also Public Affairs Officers. The armed forces have their directors of information, or information services, and briefing officers and information officers as well. So have most of the other major departments of the federal government. In addition, at the policy level, every official of importance has a press secretary who may be called by some such title as special assistant or executive secretary or, to cite only one, Assistant Secretary of State for Public Affairs.

Such personnel are also found at the state and local levels of government wherever there is sufficient pressure for news from the mass media and enough money to pay for the extra service.

The Operation Few in Washington have ever contended that a single reporter could cover the Pentagon, the State Department, the White House or lesser government agencies without a lot of help. That is why government information offices exist. And yet, it is one of the peculiarities of journalism that any move to cut the government's information services is always greeted with cheers from the news media. Undoubtedly, many such staffs are too large and some do too little; however, if they were completely done away with, the news media would be hard put to find out what was happening within so huge — and so secretive — an establishment.

Because of the unpopularity of service in government public relations, not many of the top practitioners stay very long. The list of those who have passed through the government's information network is long and illustrious. James C. Hagerty, President Eisenhower's press secretary, became a vice president of the ABC network. Bill D. Moyers, who served President Johnson in a similar capacity, joined CBS as a producer, writer, commentator. George Reedy, another of President Johnson's press secretaries, became a journalism dean at Marquette for a time. Robert Manning, who handled State Department public relations, was named editor of the *Atlantic* monthly; his associate and successor, James Greenfield, became the foreign editor of the *New York Times*.

By contrast, the role of public relations officials in business and industry, or in institutional work, is fairly stable. They are somewhat removed from the area of public responsibility, in which they are under constant pressure to account for public officials, their departmental responsibility and their expenditures. Except when they are caught up in investigations of wrong-doing, the industrial public relations people usually don't worry too much about Congressional prying. Nor do they often have to rush out the news on a split-second deadline basis. Unless the news is very bad, and therefore likely to leak, they can take their time about making it known.

Their relations with the news media are often of their own making, and the funds at their disposal tend to be more ample than in government. In corporate public relations, the rewards are likely to be greater. But the risks are also larger, as witness the outcome of Congressional investigations of such corporations as Lockheed and International Telephone and Telegraph, to mention only two.

Yet, whether public relations specialists work in government or industry, for corporations such as banks and real estate firms, for labor unions or foundations, their essential worth to the news media is measured by two standards. The first is whether they have access to their principal news source at all times and can influence decisions bearing on the news. The second is whether they have the confidence and good will of the reporters with whom they deal. Public relations people must have both or they cannot operate successfully for very long.

What P. R. Specialists Believe There are some well-intentioned persons in public relations who think of themselves as a part of the staffs of the news media they seek to influence. They believe this so intensely that they fall into the error of thinking of reporters as essentially lazy people, willing to be spoon-fed with information. As the belief of indispensibility takes hold in earnest, they begin arguing that the news media could not function if it were not for public-relations people.

All this, of course, is nonsense. The aim of most of those in public-relations is to represent their clients before the public in the best possible manner. Whatever services they give to the news media in performing their major duty is incidental. They are no more a part of an editorial function than the advertising person who prepares the layouts. It is regretfully true of a minority of poorly trained reporters that they will accept almost anything that is handed to them.

As for newspapers being so dependent on public relations that they could not publish without such material, the truth is that the end product would benefit by printing fewer speeches and official pronouncements and encouraging more competition for news.

This is just as true of television, radio and the news magazines. While they are not as inviting a target for press agents as the newspapers on a day-to-day basis, a public relations coup in a national medium pays enormous dividends. As a result, the electronic media and the magazines are under constant pressure by the persuaders, both hidden and revealed. Some public-relations people contend they are serving the public by putting their "message" over a national, rather than a local setting. That, too, is a dubious proposition.

The "Honest Broker" Realistic public relations operators share no such beliefs. Most of them adhere to the theory of the "honest broker," the go-between who endeavors to do a decent job of representing a client without trying any tricks on the news media. Most public relations professionals are as scornful as journalists are of trying to masquerade propaganda as news and proceed on the basis that truthful reporting is the best policy. But they may not tell all the truth.

Sometimes, that kind of policy turns out to be naive. Then, the public relations professional offends either the reporters or a client, sometimes both. Where the reporter can win praise and prizes, there is no glory for public relations representatives who try to do an honest job.

What Reporters Seek Experienced reporters who deal with public relations agencies expect no favors and ask for none. They expect minimum courtesies — to be told if there is a story, what the subject is and when an announcement may be expected. If a person such as a top official is involved, reporters want a chance for an interview. If claims are to be made, they ask also for substantial proof that the claims are not fictitious. If records are a part of the story, they should be made available.

No public relations agency or person can expect to trifle with the news media and get away with it for very long. A story of public relations origin may wash out once, but the originating agency will find itself ignored if the same thing happens very often.

PRINCIPLES AND METHODS

A reporter working with a responsible and experienced public relations agency or person is guided by a commonly accepted set of standards, principles and methods that have been developed over the years. Since this informal code is not recorded, and only exists because of its usefulness to the participants, it changes from time to time. Therefore, it is always prudent to review the ground rules with the public relations personnel who are directly involved before embarking on any major assignment.

Equal Treatment Reporters have a right to expect equal treatment from public relations sources. This means that no great newspaper or network or news magazine will be given special breaks on a story, always a temptation when a public relations agency has a major news break that will make its client look good. However, other reporters have to demonstrate at least a show of interest to merit consideration — something editors may forget when they are making assignments.

It is generally assumed that a public relations agency or person is obligated to keep the confidence of reporters who check with them on exclusive angles of certain stories. Any attempt to leak the exclusive angle will not gain the gratitude of the press corps for the public relations unit involved; on the contrary, as soon as a violation of confidence is discovered, the unit or person who did the leaking will forfeit the trust of everybody on the story. The pledge of confidence that binds the publicist is no different from the one that seals up the reporter who accepts off-the-record information.

Coverage by Telephone Sometimes reporters have to cover public relations sources by telephone, a usual procedure in government. These routine calls from the news media take much of the office time of busy press officers and even pursue them to their homes at night. Most reporters understand this. Consequently, if they cannot reach the person they want, they ask to have their call returned within a reasonable time.

Reporters as a rule are businesslike on the telephone. They should have a specific query that requires a straight answer. If they get one, they should ask what kind of attribution is requested. However, if they draw a blank or a "no comment," which happens quite often, the best thing they can do is to go on about their business and try other sources.

There is a type of argumentative reporter who likes to draw harassed and usually uninformed public relations officials into long and theoretical discussions about pending news developments. Various theories or possibilities will be presented, under this rather tiresome news-gathering formula, in the hope that one will be singled out as the most reasonable. More often than not, this system produces only confusion and embarrassment. It also costs the reporter some contacts if it happens regularly.

Occasionally reporters encounter new, timid or stupid public relations people who do not know how to handle queries by telephone. Such people invite reporters to try to guess at the news by prompting them to ask all kinds of questions. These incredible guessing games are based on the regulation, current in any civilian or military organization where security is involved, that certain information cannot be disclosed unless an inquiry about it is made. Of course, veteran public relations officials merely tell the inquiring reporter the news and let it go at that.

Handouts When prepared by a trained public relations specialist, the handout may be extremely useful to a reporter. For instance, the text of an important speech is a necessity. An abstract of it, prepared by a knowledgeable writer, can be helpful to the hurried journalist.

Another type of handout generally sought by reporters is the fact sheet, which sums up briefly the essential facts about a news subject, current or anticipated. Such fact sheets are particularly useful in writing about arrivals or departures, new buildings and unfamiliar things such as supersonic airplanes, ballistic missiles and atomic submarines. Chronologies, biographies and brief descriptions of background events are also generally welcome handouts.

No reporter should adopt the attitude that a handout is an insult to his intelligence. If it is important enough to take the time of a public relations agency, a reporter ought at least take the time to read it before discarding it.

JUNKETS, GIFTS AND PARTIES

It may seem incredible to the young and inexperienced, but junkets and cocktail parties have few attractions for serious journalists. Such affairs are part of the job for seasoned political and diplomatic correspondents and must be endured, along with rubber chicken and marble peas on the banquet circuit.

Trick or Treat? News is generally scarce along the commercial party trail and the company is often less than brilliant. As for banquets, the meals are often cold, the drinks watery and the speeches seemingly interminable. After a few years of such public relations largesse, most journalists would be just as happy if they were let alone to stay home.

Nor are gifts much of a problem to experienced journalists who deal in the important news of the day. It is perfectly obvious to them that a substantial gift from any news source, actual or potential, may be prejudicial to their work. Some journalists are so careful that they will even send back boxes of gift cigars or bottles of liquor at Christmastime. Gifts of any kind from public relations sources must be regarded as suspect.

The best rule, and it is insisted upon by all responsible news media, is to permit no staff member to accept any gratuity and to pay for all necessary services including travel costs, hotels and tickets to shows that are being reviewed. At the level of the working press, there is seldom an opportunity for reporters to take two weeks off for an expense-paid airplane junket or something equally glamorous. They are too busy with their daily chores. But in the sports, amusement, family and society departments, both the opportunities and the excuses to attend publicity parties are far greater and it sometimes becomes difficult to tell when some of these specialized journalists are working or playing.

The automobile, airplane and motion picture industries, to name a few of the main problem areas, are adept at mixing their legitimate news announcements with friendly diversions. The same is true of the commercial side of television. But, as sometimes happens, the persuaders may have a full house for a junket and then find that they are drawing more criticism than praise for their clients. It is a touchy business, both for journalists and those who try to win their good opinion. Certainly, on the side of the journalist, there is stricter supervision than ever before of alleged news events that coincide with junketing, gift-giving and partying.

NEWS FROM PUBLIC RELATIONS SOURCES

The news that originates from public relations sources is usually handled in conformity with general journalistic practice. The experienced public relations executive or operative knows this. Only bemused company executives really think that the material put out in their names will be used by the news media in the desired form.

Checking the Facts   A reporter should first check the facts of a public relations source. It is worth a telephone call, for instance, to check the release time of a handout and to be sure that the announcement did in fact originate with the stated source. The day of the journalistic hoax is not over. Beyond that, the business of public relations being what it is, any announcement should be tested for what it does not say as well as for such news as is given.

Writing from P. R. Sources   A public relations announcement generally serves the interests of the issuing agency. There is nothing wrong with this, as long as reporters understand that the interests of their organization and of the public relations agency do not necessarily coincide. For instance, it is a threadbare device to put a propaganda message in quotes, attributed to a prominent person, in the body of a press release. Some of the less imaginative publicity officials also persist in needlessly attributing an announcement to two or three persons or agencies they want to publicize.

Reporters, therefore, should take stock of whatever facts they have from public relations sources, before writing, and ask the simplest of all news questions: "What happened?" The lead and its documentation then may be separated from all the embroidery. The result may not precisely please the issuing agency, but that cannot be helped. The reporter's first responsibility is to the public. It should not be assumed that a public relations announcement must always be discounted. Quite the contrary is true if it is issued from a responsible source and contains news of importance to the community.

Here are some examples of how a sharp-shooting public relations office and a newspaper would handle the same set of facts:

1.   *A Shift in Executive Personnel*

J. Cadwalader Winnefall, president of the J. C. Winnefall Manufacturing Company, announced today that Evans B. Arctander, its general manager, had been designated head of the company's London office.

In accepting the new post, Mr. Arctander wrote in a letter to Mr. Winnefall, "I am most grateful to you and to our executive board for having made the London office my next important post with our company and can assure you that I will do my utmost to serve the company there just as I have in the home office. I have looked forward for some years to a lightening of the heavy load I have been carrying."

The new general manager will be J. Cadwalader Winnefall Jr., who has been promoted from assistant general manager. Mr. Winnefall was graduated from Princeton four years ago . . .

*

The J. C. Winnefall Mfg. Co. today named J. Cadwalader Winnefall Jr. as its new general manager. He replaces Evans B. Arctander, who has been shifted to the London office.

2.   A Fund-Raising Report

Follet Hargreaves, chairman of the trustees of Graditton College, appealed today to its 30,000 living alumni to support its $3,000,000 drive for a new athletic field house.

"Graditton deserves your loyalty and your support," he said at a report luncheon in the Graditton Faculty Club, which was attended by the chairmen of alumni committees. "I am sure that all alumni cherish Graditton traditions and want to see us flourish. To this end, the new athletic field house is a most necessary addition to our plant."

The chairman reported funds in hand and pledges of $62,000, an increase of $24,000 over last month. This brings the total contributions to date to $184,456 for the Graditton Athletic Field House Fund. Checks should be made payable to the fund. All contributions are tax deductible.

*

Graditton College announced today that $62,000 had been contributed to a fund for a new athletic field house, bringing the total to $184,456. The goal of the campaign, which began last year, is $3,000,000.

3.   A Plea for Economy

Mayor Simpson Gravier called upon all department heads in his administration today to "cut to the bone" all budgetary requests for the next fiscal year.

The Mayor acted in line with his campaign pledge, during his successful election drive last year, to introduce new economies in government. "We're going to hold the line," he said. "If my department heads won't cut their requests, then I'll have to do it for them."

The Mayor has received departmental budget requests to date totalling more than $80,000,000 and has referred them to his budget director for examination. The expense budget for the current fiscal year, adopted by the outgoing administration, is $74,340,000.

*

Mayor Gravier's economy drive ran into trouble today.

The Mayor announced that his department heads already had submitted requests for more than $80,000,000 appropriations for the city budget for the next fiscal year. This is $5,700,000 more than the $74,340,000 expense budget of the previous administration, which the Mayor denounced during his campaign as "shocking" and "wasteful."

Furthermore, all requests are not in.

The Mayor, in announcing the record demands, called on his department heads to "cut to the bone" and also pledged to "hold the line." He warned that he would make some cuts if his department heads did not do so, but did not specify where the reductions would be made.

Dealing with Managed News These three examples of managed news are reasonably typical of much of the material that reporters receive from public relations sources. They also demonstrate how the news media try to extract a small amount of truth from the propaganda that descends on them every day. Very often, this is difficult and sometimes impossible. With good reason, the correspondents of American and foreign news media in Saigon labeled the daily American press briefings the "Five O'Clock Follies" during the Vietnam War. From experience, they knew that almost everything they received from American sources would be angled and managed and therefore it was discounted in advance. The result—public disbelief and disenchantment—was foreordained.

Chapter 20
Reporting
on
Public Affairs

Soon after Carol Sutton became managing editor of the *Louisville Courier-Journal*, she was plunged into the midst of a civic crisis. A United States Circuit Court of Appeals had ordered the immediate desegregation of schools in Louisville and surrounding Jefferson County, the twelfth largest school district in the nation. Miss Sutton, like other leading citizens, had thought that the big shift was at least a year away. But the Appeals Court had upset the time table.

BIOGRAPHY OF A BUSING ORDER

Miss Sutton was well aware that it would not be easy to institute busing of school children in Louisville on the large scale that the courts required. She and her top editors had been to Boston and seen the havoc that the anti-busing movement had created there. However, she also had studied the largely successful campaign of the *Boston Globe* to inform the public of what was actually involved in school desegregation in an effort to dispel some of the vicious mythology that was being circulated by opponents.

What Miss Sutton resolved to do was to make a total commitment of the *Louisville Courier-Journal* to the public interest in the crisis over the schools. "We had been developing information we knew people needed and wanted to know," she said. "It was a matter of bringing it together quickly."

There was little time. The court order had been issued on July 17, 1975, just about six weeks before the scheduled opening of the schools for the fall term. Within two weeks, the *Courier-Journal* put out a 32-page tabloid which included 165 separate school zone maps plus detailed information for each. Thus, both parents and children knew well in advance where the changes would come.

To make sure that this vital information was readily available, the *Courier-Journal* donated an extra 25,000 copies of the tabloid to the school board for distribution and then published two additional map supplements. That was just the beginning.

Even though the *Courier-Journal* was probusing (and had to withstand attacks on its staff and property because of it), one of the first moves Miss Sutton made was to provide both coverage and generous space for leaders of the antibusing movement and antibusing rallies. To keep down the possibility of violence, a Page 1 article was run to show how opposition to busing could be carried out legally. Still, more than 7,000 readers canceled subscriptions to the paper and some of its advertisers were harassed

But on the day that desegregation took hold, everything went reasonably well — much quieter than had been expected — and 36 *Courier-Journal* reporters and photographers covered the story in depth. From then on until the end of the year, the paper published almost 1,200 staff-written articles about school desegregation, more than 300 staff photos, 38 editorials, more than 200 maps and enough letters pro and con to fill more than 100 columns of news space. The Society of Professional Journalists–Sigma Delta Chi thereupon gave the Louisville *Courier-Journal* its newspaper public service award for 1976 and the photo staff of the *Courier-Journal* and its sister newspaper, the *Louisville Times*, won a 1976 Pulitzer Prize for Photography.*

The Louisville newspapers were not alone in showing the advantages of a total commitment to the public interest. The *Boston Globe* in 1975 won the Pulitzer Prize for Public Service for its own massive coverage of school desegregation and its problems under even more difficult circumstances. For the future, both the Boston and Louisville papers would serve as models to the nation for a newer, more conscientious and much enlarged concept of public affairs reporting by the American press.

*Miss Sutton was made a member of the publisher's staff in Louisville.

WHAT KIND OF REPORTING?

Critics of the American press have made much of what they call its devotion to event-oriented coverage—what Eric Sevareid has called "the daily needle shower of unrelated facts." However, with the rise of interpretive reporting and the determination of the most powerful newspapers in the nation to go to the heart of some of the problems besetting communities, states, regions and the nation as a whole, there has been much less emphasis on presenting the news in bits and pieces. Like the makers of the path-breaking TV documentaries, most editors do see the relevance of presenting the news of issues in depth and explaining the meaning of events to a concerned public.

Necessarily, all this takes time and money. Even more important, it requires a different type of reporter with a broader education in modern communications methods—one who is familiar with scientific approaches to the measurement of public opinion and the researching of public records (see Chapter 25). Philip Meyer, a national reporter for the Knight-Ridder Newspapers, has popularized and detailed such reportorial concepts and given them a name—"Precision Journalism."[1] It is likely to stick.

The extent of these new approaches to the reporting of public affairs is impressive. Newspapers of all sizes and political orientation, representing every section of the country, have taken up the challenge. The familiar inquiries into political wrong-doing have been matched by equally vigorous examinations of the problems of consumerism, the environment, the energy crisis, the persistent worry over welfare and unemployment and many another subject that would not have attracted much newspaper involvement in former years.

What Smaller Papers Can Do Within recent years, many smaller papers with limited resources have taken on public issues that required both courage and major commitments of their staffs, funds and space. The *Lake Placid News*, a New York weekly, boldly campaigned to protect the natural environment of the Adirondacks by seeking remedial changes in the laws for the development of private lands and land use programs. In Florida, the *Fort Myers News-Press* delved into a mortgage fraud that had victimized local citizens and made a state-wide issue out of the case. On the island of Guam, the *Pacific Daily News* undertook a program to ease the settlement of 50,000 Vietnamese refugees in the United States. In Pennsylvania, the *Sharon Herald* inquired into the effectiveness of a federally funded job program that had been handled by a private firm and came up with some critical answers to a difficult local situation. In Connecticut the *Stamford Advocate* tore into the misdeeds of the city government with resultant dismissals and resigna-

---

[1] Philip Meyer, *Precision Journalism* (Bloomington, Ind., 1973).

tions. And in Texas, the *Lufkin News* won the 1977 Pulitzer Prize gold medal for public service through its inquiry into the suspicious death of a Marine recruit in training, which forced reforms in the recruiting and training practices of the U. S. Marine Corps.

That is just a sampling. The evidence, however, is abundant that even at the smallest level the press is decisively changing its fundamental approach to the news of public affairs.

The Role of Larger Papers It is scarcely a surprise, therefore, to find newspapers in state capitals and medium-sized cities throughout the country making more dramatic presentations of the news of public affairs.

The *Albuquerque Tribune* has campaigned effectively for parole reform in New Mexico. The *Albany Times-Union* has been able to cut down the outrageous amounts of money annually collected by New York legislators "in lieu of expenses," an old local practice known as "lulus." The *Providence Journal* and *Bulletin* are among numerous papers that have attacked local nursing home abuses with heartening results. The *St. Paul Dispatch* and *Pioneer Press* brought about an official inquiry into its charges of abuse in a state prison.

In Tennessee, the *Nashville Tennessean* and the *Banner* have exposed critical mismanagement in the gathering and distribution of funds for various private charities, often an untouchable local subject. In Wisconsin, the *Milwaukee Journal* and the *Sentinel* have given extensive coverage to school desegragation In Iowa, the *Des Moines Register* has done specialized work on consumer problems—something that has caught on in numerous other papers in the Midwest and South. And in Ohio, the *Cleveland Press* has undertaken a long-range campaign for a much-needed regional transit service.

What the Giants Are Doing It has remained for the largest, wealthiest and most powerful papers in the land to tackle some of the most difficult issues. The *Chicago Sun-Times* has undertaken a continuing investigation of the quality of justice in Chicago, an outgrowth of the work of Donald L. Barlett and James B. Steele of the *Philadelphia Inquirer*. The *St. Louis Post-Dispatch* and the *Kansas City Star* both have conducted lengthy inquiries into fraudulent road construction contracts with resultant convictions. The *Washington Post* broke the first of the Congressional sex scandals. The *New York Daily News* uncovered so much mismanagement of the State's lottery that the governor had to suspend the operation for many months to effect safeguards.

The *Philadelphia Inquirer*, a leader in public affairs journalism, has disclosed widespread graft and maladministration in the city's government. The *Detroit News*, after a lengthy inquiry, was able to produce the evidence that freed four men convicted of a murder in New Mexico that they had not committed.

THE POSITION OF THE JOURNALIST

If there ever was any doubt about the position of the journalist as a public figure, the course of events has removed it. The evidence is overwhelming that reporters play an influential and sometimes a decisive part in shaping the news. Bits and pieces of the news, therefore, are no longer good enough. In addition to the day's grist, which must be reported, journalists of consequence invariably try to get beneath the surface of events to probe their meaning. And very often they are able to do it.

Whether reporters like it or not, and some don't, they are unofficial public servants today and their watchdog function in government is of importance to society as a whole. The forces they represent generate influences that are brought to bear in public affairs.

In turn, the pressures on journalists have mounted steadily over the years. Once they were dismissed as ne'er-do-wells, persons of little consequence, know-nothings who preferred the corner bar to the society of upstanding citizens. Now they are pressed to view the manifold operations of government in every detail and make sense out of the process. They must stand up under persuasion by lobbyists and others who apply pressure, fend off private interests representing numerous power centers, put up with the alternate rivalry and camaraderie within journalism itself and contend with the often unspoken but clear desires of publishers. It is thus no easy matter to find what is true and false in the news and present it to their offices and the public in an interesting and timely manner. In this chapter, and in successive ones that deal with journalism, the law and the social sciences, the resources of the journalist in public affairs—both new and old—are analyzed and discussed.

NEWS CONFERENCES

Many serious-minded journalists believe that a news conference is the worst possible way to cover a story because of its undisciplined, helter-skelter character. Nevertheless, it exists and can't be wished out of being. It is something that journalists will have to live with.

When the news conference was a press conference (that is, mainly for newspapers with radio reporters present on sufferance), there is a legend that it was more effective and less bland than it is today under the domination of television. Bland it was not—a Fiorello LaGuardia press conference at New York's City Hall could wind up in a riot—but its effectiveness then, as now, is open to question. In any event, who-ever gives a modern news conference is so conscious of the presence of television cameras and tape recorders that most of the proceedings have the character of a one-month-old baby's mush. As for the reporters, it must be recorded sorrowfully that some try to act or pose as orators when they have no talent for either.

News Conference Rules Whether the news conference is good or bad, or a mixture of both, it is conducted according to a few simple rules that should be well understood by all participants.

On the part of the news source, or a public relations representative, there is a tacit understanding that there is news to impart and explain that will be worth the time of the reporters who are assigned. On the part of the reporters, they agree to listen and report accurately but they make no guarantees of use in any form.

It is the responsibility of the news source to pick a time and place convenient to all, and provide a tape recorder or stenotype record. If TV and still photographers also are expected, the source must make ap-propriate arrangements. Where the news conference is one of a regular series—as at city hall or a state capitol—it is understood that every-thing is on the record and may be quoted. For other conferences, the source's public relations representative announces the ground rules and type of attribution, subject to acceptance by the reporters.

At most news conferences reporters understand that no one is to leave until the last question has been answered and that the door to the conference room will be closed. If there is to be any variation from this practice, it is generally announced before the beginning of the news conference, again subject to agreement.

For the average news conference, reporters expect that about twenty or thirty minutes will be sufficient. If it lasts much more than that, the senior reporter will end the affair abruptly by saying, "Thank you, Gov-ernor or Mayor So-and-So." Without further ado, everybody will leave the room. To avoid such an embarrassing situation, even the most emi-nent news sources have learned to compress their remarks. If they have a great deal to say, they hand out a prepared statement in advance and invite questions on it.

No news source in the world, except for the President of the United States, is supposed to be able to answer without hesitation every ques-tion thrust at him. Therefore, at most news conferences, the principal source will have subordinates answer some of the questions. Only at the White House does a President face the news media of the world and the nation with only a hasty warm-up to guide him.

The White House Influence So great is the influence of the White House on journalistic methods that Presidential news conference procedures have been adopted as standard, not only in government but in institutional and industrial public relations as well. Here and there, a particularly influential news source may be able to insist on having questions written in advance and submitted to him. Various Secretaries General have done this at the United Nations from time to time. For the most part, whether the news source is a captain of industry or a ward heeler, the news conference operates on an ad-lib basis.

Political amateurs sometimes insist on trying to plant questions among supposedly friendly reporters to attempt to create a favorable impression on television. The effort is nearly always discovered and the effect is quite the opposite of what is intended. It takes a lot more guile than the average politician or industrial tycoon has to manage a news conference.

Less guileful but just as unrealistic news sources have tried to make reporters respond to discipline by keeping their questions on a certain point. This tactic involved a simple scheme, used at some of the military academies, to hold up one finger if the question was on the same subject that was being pursued, and two fingers if a new approach was intended. However, the whole thing smacked so much of little boys asking desperately to leave the schoolroom that it didn't last very long.

So, what happens in most places is that reporters gain recognition by standing up, waving a hand or shouting, if there is a large crowd, and then ask their question. At the White House and some state houses and city halls, there is an understanding that a follow-up question may be asked. But usually, the one recognized by the news source or the one with the strongest lungs wins the contest.

Sometimes, reporters arrange in advance to concentrate on one or two main news topics. This may or may not be known to the source, but usually advance briefings take care of all eventualities. It's pretty difficult to surprise or stampede an experienced politician, diplomat or academic.

Even in the presence of TV and tape recorders, the atmosphere at a news conference is relaxed and informal. Reporters do not applaud good answers or groan at bad ones. They do not make jokes, and they refrain from making speeches in the form of questions. The questions, as a rule, are framed so as to produce newsworthy answers, not to satisfy the personal, political or moral prejudices of the reporter or his news organization. That, by reportorial standards, is professional conduct at a news conference.

Finally, after the news conference is over, reporters have learned to check the statements the source has made for accuracy, consistency with past positions and relevance to current issues. This is the one advance that has been made since the McCarthy era, and it is a good one. Not many reporters take anything on trust just because it is said at a news conference, no matter how exalted the source.

THE INTERVIEW

The one-on-one interview, sometimes called the sit-down interview, is potentially an even greater source of misinformation than the news conference. Whenever reporters have to go through a public relations department to see a newsworthy individual, it may be assumed at the outset that the interview will consist of a lot of cosmetic positions. There is a myth that if reporters can only ask exactly the right question in just the right way, and adopt the proper equivalent of the doctor's bedside manner, the interviewee will obligingly respond with the whole truth and nothing but the truth. Alas, but veteran reporters know it doesn't happen that way. The person who has been well coached for an interview, like the one who has been well prepared for a news conference, isn't likely to be caught off guard.

And yet, in the hands of a skillful reporter, the interview still offers the best chance for a highly personal story provided the interviewee does not have firm control. Gerold Frank, a veteran journalist, goes at it with a tape recorder for hours on end and simply wears down the subject—with the subject's permission, of course. Gay Talese, a journalist of equally high repute, once did an excellent and revealing piece about the singer Frank Sinatra, even though Sinatra refused to talk; instead, the reporter got his information from Sinatra's friends and then described exactly how the singer looked, what he did when he was by himself, how he acted.

The point is that interviewing should be conducted in such a way that it gives the journalist more advantages than the subject. And, like standard news conference procedure, any interview should be thoroughly checked for factual accuracy and consistency with past positions before it is written. In the case of television or radio interviews that are spontaneous, particularly involving anything that happens on talk shows, checking is mandatory and subsequent corrections, when necessary, should be made.

Types of Interviews Journalists conduct interviews in many different ways, depending on their own working methods and the person they are interviewing. The types of interviews, briefly described, are as follows:

News Interview When a reporter has important, well-defined questions to submit to newsworthy persons, a meeting may be arranged on generally short notice in an office, a hotel, a restaurant at lunch or dinner, or even the editorial sanctum of a newspaper or a broadcast studio. It all depends on how important the particular news organization is, the general reputation of the reporter involved and the willingness of the source to submit to tough questioning. Presidential candidates, for example, are quite willing to go to a network studio or the editorial board rooms of papers like the *New York Times, Washington Post, Chicago Tribune* or *Los Angeles Times,* to name only a few. But they aren't likely to respond to invitations from lesser news organizations; instead, they can and do sit down with reporters whom they respect. In any event, the news interview is a staple of journalism—the most important of its kind.

Curbstone Interview This is a catch-as-catch-can, risky business both for reporters and sources. As its name implies, the reporter simply has to wait on the curbstone (or some other convenient spot) for the source to come along in order to ask questions. The problem here is to get answers. For as television cameras demonstrate every day, mobs of reporters trailing a news source at a court house and shouting questions don't get very far. The business of herd reporting is a disgrace to journalism and seldom produces any information of consequence, although it is sometimes the only way a reporter has of approaching a source. Still, it is always better to try to work out some individual pattern for a relatively quick exchange of questions and answers away from the herd. That, of course, depends on circumstances, the skill of the journalist and the willingness of the subject to cooperate.

The Informal Survey This is the old journalistic standby, the "man in the street" story, now changed by some to "person in the street," which isn't quite the same thing. Polling organizations with services to sell have been knocking this one for years because it is admittedly unscientific, probably unrepresentative and outrages the sensibilities of social scientists who prefer statistics. Still, editors of all types of news organizations continue to send reporters to talk with almost anybody to pick up opinions and reactions to various current events. Why? It's a fast way of getting colorful and sometimes striking public reactions without having to set up expensive and time-consuming polling arrangements; more often than not, the quotes do reveal some—but not all—public attitudes on given questions. Nobody contends there is anything scientific about such business and all concerned are well aware, at this late date, that reporters can't be expected to come back with firm, statistically sound, representative public positions. So "man in the street" marches on, as do the pursuing reporters.

The Personality Interview This, too, is an old favorite and it has become the basis for many a Sunday TV interview program on the model of "Meet the Press," NBC's pioneering effort. In the earlier part of this century, it was every reporter's dream to have an exclusive interview with the President of the United States but there have been so many now that it isn't the great feat it once was. Still, reporters jump at a chance to interview Presidents, Prime Ministers, oil-rich Arab sheiks, almost any remaining king or queen and as many other renowned foreign figures as possible. The internationally known journalists, naturally, are much better at this than garden variety reporters who must be satisfied with doing Robert Redford or Farrah Fawcett-Majors and other glamorous names in show business.

Telephone Interviews A lot of this is done primarily because it is fast and it is sometimes easier to get a news source by phone than it is to arrange a meeting by appointment. Journalists handle hundreds of such calls in a month and learn from experience to ask the short, sharp questions that will produce a newsworthy answer from a politician as well as the sympathetic manner that will encourage the corner cigar store proprietor to describe the murder that occurred outside his place. Most information for obits and backgrounds of persons involved in the news has to be gathered by telephone, as do details of various kinds of records needed to flesh out the breaking news.

The Prepared Question When all else fails, reporters sometimes make up lists of questions and submit them to news sources with a polite but urgent request for a reply. Sometimes they get answers, but more often they do not. At least, the method is worth trying in a tight spot.

During the Soviet's blockade of Berlin in 1948, J. Kingsbury Smith of International News Service wrote out a list of questions in Paris and wired them to Stalin in Moscow. In his reply Stalin gave the tip that indicated the Russians knew that they had been licked by the American airlift. Negotiations began between East and West, ending with the lifting of the blockade.

METHODS OF INTERVIEWING

The art of interviewing is based on the principle of persuading the other person to do the talking. And that means reporters should know what questions to ask and how to ask them. It sounds easy, but it is not as a reading of the transcript of any Presidential news conference will demonstrate. Sometimes the lords of the Washington press corps, the most prestigious body of reporters in the world, will look like amateurs with long, windy questions, dubious assumptions, rude behavior and sometimes even a failure to ask a question on an important subject. And in New York City, a news conference will wind up in a wild shouting match.

Journalists are familiar with such failings and do not excuse them. It is one thing to discuss the problems of interviewing in a quiet classroom, or elaborate on them in a textbook. It is quite another to go into the public arena, and operate under all the pressures of journalistic competition. At such times, almost anything that can go wrong will go wrong, which is the journalistic equivalent of Murphy's Law.

How to Ask Questions Social scientists have developed a large body of information about the kinds of questions that are most likely to produce responses. They have shown quite convincingly that the wording of a question is of the utmost importance, that a lengthy question is almost always bound to be confusing and that open-ended questions are usually productive of fuzzy responses.

Experienced reporters, like lawyers trained in courtroom techniques, are well aware of both the probable benefits and the probable risks in presenting certain types of questions. They know, for example, that if subjects are shocked, alarmed or frightened, it is extremely difficult to communicate with them and almost useless to ask questions until calmness has been restored, however tentatively, and a certain amount of rapport has been established.

Therefore, if reporters have a chance to prepare for an interview and know the subject, they should go through the clips and records if at all possible to avoid asking silly or unnecessary questions. One bad break at the opening of an interview is likely to destroy it.

In a sit-down interview, the opening gambit — after the reporter briefly states the business at hand — may be a bit of light conversation or some commonplace about a topic of joint interest, almost anything that will establish an easy relationship. Very soon, though, the interviewer must take charge in an unobtrusive way by asking a question that touches on the principal area of the discussion.

The mistake some reporters make, primarily younger ones, is to shoot a lot of short, sharp questions at an interviewee without giving the person any time for reflection. True, questions should be short and pointed. But the Mister District Attorney approach is both offensive and self-defeating. Another major fault, which is found sometimes in reporters of distinction, is an almost complete lack of restraint that produces a reportorial monologue rather than a question. Sometimes, it is argued that this is the way to get a subject to talk freely but the proposition is dubious. It is always sound procedure to ask a question, even a very difficult one, without betraying any sign of urgency or hostility and then wait patiently for a response. Not everybody likes to rattle off quick responses to tough questions.

Listening Somehow, it always seems difficult to train reporters to listen. Certainly, it is the most trying stage of the interviewing process. For a subject may be spouting utter nonsense, perhaps even trying to bait the reporter into nervousness or anger. Or the interview may seem to be reaching a dead end. Still, it is the business of the reporter to try to remain calm and courteous, to keep asking the necessary questions, and — above all — to listen once the subject resumes talking.

Under no circumstances should the reporter be drawn into a lively discussion while the subject, in turn, becomes an openly bored listener.

In the case of hostile subjects, a reporter ought to come directly to the point instead of wasting time. There is no sense in either pleading with or denouncing a person who either doesn't want to talk or is provocative to the level of insult. The necessary questions should be asked, the toughest one last, and the reporter should leave without further ado.

People do not grant interviews to listen to reporters' opinions. For one reason or another they are willing to get themselves into print or on the air and they recognize that submission to an interview is one way of accomplishing their purpose. Yet, it is astonishing to find reporters continually trying to get interviews by declaiming for minutes at a time and giving their subjects no chance to do the talking. The observation may be elementary, but it is important. No talking reporter ever conducted a decent interview.

VERACITY

Dr. Alfred C. Kinsey, who interviewed thousands of men and women in connection with his sex studies, once was asked how he could tell if his subjects were lying.

"Very simple," he said with calm scientific assurance. "I look them right in the eye. I lean forward. I ask questions rapidly, one right after the other. I keep staring them in the eye. Naturally, if they falter, I can tell they are lying."

The reporter who was interviewing Dr. Kinsey nodded sympathetically over this expression of the master's views. A few minutes later, the distinguished scientist was somewhat startled to find the interviewer leaning forward, staring him in the eye, and asking questions rapidly.

The expert protested, "Now look here, that isn't fair. I just don't like what you're doing."

Most experienced reporters have learned that it does not pay to stare their subjects out of countenance. They become just as annoyed as Dr. Kinsey did, when his own methods were turned on him.

The point is that there is no easy way of testing a subject's veracity. If reporters think they are being lied to, their only recourse is to check the statements that have been made in the interview. Subjects who are willing to lie in an interview are usually pretty accomplished, and cannot be upset by stares, grimaces or even outright challenges.

Thirty or forty years ago, when psychology was just a word in the average newsroom, sensation-minded city editors were addicted to notions that liars could not look a reporter in the eye, people with secrets could not keep their fingers from their mouths and criminal types had facial features that betrayed their terrible inner natures. These beliefs die hard, particularly among amateur reporters. Just as the Lombroso theory about criminal types has long ago been disproved, the act of watching subjects' eyes and fingers really proves very little. Nervous people never are easy to interview and should be put at ease, instead of being stared at. Quick, perceptive glances by a reporter, especially when the subject is off guard, are often much more revealing.

Use of the Tape Recorder It is one of the anomalies of human nature that even fairly sophisticated persons will be upset by too much note-taking during an interview, but usually they won't mind a tape recorder. Actually, a tape recorder is the only way to insure the accuracy of a report of an interview or a news conference and wise reporters always use them.

Yes, they are an inconvenience; the notes have to be transcribed, and often this is a chore. Yes, reporters disagree on whether tape recorders inhibit persons who are interviewed or encourage greater frankness. But most younger ones have had excellent experiences with machines in interviews.

I always take a tape recorder with me to interviews and seldom have been refused permission to use it. The more powerful the person to be interviewed, the less objection there usually is to a tape recording. In interviewing a prime minister of Japan, I was once assured that it was necessary to review the tape recording and a transcript would be provided, suitably edited, which was exactly what happened. And one of the few times I was asked not to bring a tape recorder was in an interview with President Ferdinand Marcos of the Philippines at the Malacanang. When I arrived, Marcos had set up his own tape recorder.

The machines should be used whenever possible.

Notes on Interviews When there is no tape recording arrangement, interviewers must trust their memories more often than not. Except for the "puff" interview, when the subject knows something pleasant is going to be written or broadcast, extensive note-taking is seldom possible because it makes the average subject nervous. But after the interview, a reporter should make the most extensive notes as the basis for anything that is to be used later.

CONVENTIONS AND CROWDS

Any assignment to cover a convention or another meeting of a fairly large group usually begins with a visit to the official, agency or public relations firm handling the arrangements. The reporter picks up all available mimeographed material, including the program, schedules, advance copies of speeches, biographies and historical notes. That is the basis for homework on any such session—political, social, academic or scientific. If such advances aren't available, the reporter is in for a dreary time of routine interviewing to get as much background as possible before the meeting opens.

Procedure For most meetings, the story is usually an advance. What reporters try to do is to interview a prominent person involved in the session, perhaps an official or a speaker, to get away from doing a routine story. Sometimes, as in the case of a convention that attracts persons from all over the country, it is possible to do a roundup of national conditions in that particular industry, business or grouping.

Most reporters like to work from advance texts of speeches; or, in the case of a gathering of physicians, scientists or academics, from abstracts of speeches or papers that are to be delivered. If the public relations people in charge of the meeting are efficient, they round up such material in advance. If not, the reporter has to do it—and it is a long, tiresome and often painful job.

In the case of a luncheon, dinner or night meeting, where there is only one featured speaker, the coverage is fairly easy. Following the technique already outlined for the writing of advances, reporters produce their stories based on advanced texts, then check on delivery with whatever changes are necessary. Where there is a filmed or videotaped segment of a speech or meeting, broadcast journalists sometimes arrange for delivery in advance but this is even riskier than going with an advance for a newspaper. In the summer of 1976, while Betty Ford was onstage at a meeting in New York, an elderly rabbi collapsed and died near her; not knowing the man had been fatally stricken, the then First Lady arose and prayed for his recovery and the TV cameras caught it all. Regardless of what newspapers may have to do, there is nothing that matches live TV reporting.

The most dramatic change in coverage has come at the national political conventions where Presidential candidates are nominated. At the 1960 and 1964 conventions of both major parties, the presence of television cameras and TV reporters and commentators led to continual disorder as publicity-conscious candidates and delegates crowded each other for exposure.

That, however, was but a foretaste of what was to come at the disastrous 1968 Democratic National Convention in Chicago when masses of antiwar activists, seeking to punish the Democratic leadership for the escalation of the Vietnam War, disrupted the proceedings with riots and other demonstrations before the television cameras. The Chicago police, surging to attack the demonstrators, helped produce what

Covering a National Convention. *Here is how television reporters worked at the Republican and Democratic National Conventions to cover the nominations of Presidential candidates. The electronic equipment enables them to keep in constant touch with their editors and their anchor people while on the convention floor. (Copyright, Columbia Broadcasting System. Used by permission.)*

turned out to be a political disaster for the Democratic nominee, Senator Hubert H. Humphrey. He was defeated by former Vice President Richard M. Nixon, the Republican candidate, in the November election.

Both parties tried, without much success, to reduce the confusion on the convention floor in 1972 by attempting to restrain television coverage. In 1976, finally, despite the use of hand-held minicams and videotape, TV people were ordered from the floor of the Democratic National Convention several times in order to disperse the crowds around the cameras. The problem of television exposure at conventions can be solved, but it will take a lot more self-restraint by both politicians and reporters than has been in evidence thus far.

Varying the Monotony Conventions are popular in America. Most citizens belong to at least one organization and many are members of several. Committee meetings, luncheons, dinners, discussion groups and fund-raising efforts are part of a way of life. Much of this must be covered by reporters who have no specialized backgrounds, which means that adequate briefings must be arranged whenever the news of a meeting is technical in nature.

The general complaint against most conventions and convention news is that they are dull and repetitious. They need not be. A little drive by reporters, a spark of imagination, a bit of encouragement by an editor rather than the usual air of resignation can do wonders to revive interest in convention news. Not every reporter can cover the quadrennial political conventions, a dramatic space shot or a foreign expedition with the secretary of state. But if they are diligent and watchful of detail, they can help their news organizations and themselves by snapping the deadly routine that blankets so much news of local conventions.

CROWDS AND CROWD FIGURES

At conventions and parades, political meetings and athletic events, street demonstrations and outdoor displays, attendance figures often are bothersome to reporters. It used to be sufficient to get a figure from the police officer in charge, check it with the official or publicist handling arrangements and include it prominently in the story. The public today is a great deal more critical than it used to be, and modern reporters are not as easily satisfied.

The Old Way On a steaming hot Sunday morning in mid-summer years ago, solemn young reporters would follow an elderly official of the Coney Island Chamber of Commerce to the roof of the Half-Moon Hotel in Brooklyn. He would gaze at the crowded beaches for a few minutes and then announce with great deliberation, "Gentlemen, there are 1,000,000 people at Coney Island today." The reporters dutifully noted the figure, used it in their stories, and the headlines on Monday morning recorded the event: "Million Bathe at Coney Island."

The New Way Even with television, it is necessary to arrive at some reasonable crowd figure when the statistic is an important part of the story. Any reporter can make a fairly accurate calculation with little trouble.

In arenas or stadia, such totals are easy to obtain. For instance, for meetings in places like New York's newest Madison Square Garden or the Coliseum, or San Francisco's Cow Palace, the total capacity is known. The number of people in each section also is known, so that each empty section can be subtracted from the capacity figure for a reasonably accurate total attendance. There is no need to rush up to an uninformed police official and take his uninformed guess, merely because he is a policeman. Usually, he knows less than the reporter.

For a parade, the calculation is somewhat more complicated. The number of blocks along the line of march is known, and the average block length can be calculated. By taking samplings of the number of people per 100 feet along the line of march, an average density figure may be obtained. Simple multiplication will then produce a reasonably accurate crowd figure. Similarly, the dimensions of any large and well-known area in a city may be obtained (Times Square in New York, Trafalgar Square in London, Red Square in Moscow) and the crowd density may be observed, thus providing the main figures for a simple calculation. In important cases, a tabulating machine may be used. There is no reason for guesswork in arriving at crowd totals in an age in which so many electronic tabulating devices are available.

Researchers have shown that usual crowd densities may vary from 6.5 to 8.5 square feet per person, with 7 square feet as a reasonable average. Thus, knowing the outer dimensions of a crowd or making a fair approximation of it, anybody can put together very quickly a realistic estimate of the size of measurable gatherings. But if a crowd spreads out for many miles, thin here and dense there, it is foolhardy to put down a supposedly accurate figure and—in these days of omnipresent TV—any viewer knows it.

Still, the urge for headlines or viewer attention dulls good sense. Perhaps it was understandable for an enthusiastic but inaccurate New York police official to announce to the world in 1951, when General Douglas MacArthur paraded through the city after being relieved of his Korean command, that 8 million people had seen him—a figure duly bannered by some big city papers. But surely, in 1976, there was no excuse for banner headlines to proclaim that 6 million people in and around New York City had seen the flotilla of tall ships from many nations that sailed into New York harbor and up the Hudson River to help observe the Bicentennial. How could anybody know? It would have been perfectly honest to say that the crowd was too large to count but must have been in the millions.

At any rate, much of the mythology of crowd reporting has been dispelled. It has been found that Times Square, at best, can hold about 250,000 people. About the same number can line lower Broadway for a ticker-tape parade. As for the millions who supposedly jam the great squares and plazas of foreign cities, that myth also has been shattered, as has the old reliance on police as the all-knowing arbiter of attendance at public events. And a good thing, too.

Chapter 21
The Press
and the Law

A war veteran captured a purse snatcher in a street chase. In writing the story a reporter confused the two and mistakenly identified the war veteran as the thief. The veteran complained he had been libeled, and the newspaper, rather than go to trial, settled the case for $10,000 out of court.

A businessman, accused by a newspaper of "robber baron" tactics, filed suit for libel but later agreed to a settlement out of court. The newspaper contributed $25,000 to his favorite charity.

A writer, after a series of bitter attacks on his personal life by a newspaper columnist, sued for libel and was awarded $75,000 damages by court action.

An auto repairman, accused in a TV program of being part of an illegal car-towing operation, collected $40,000 from the station through a jury verdict after he was exonerated from connection with the racket.

These are illustrations, chosen at random, of the manner in which the law of libel operates. No news organization, in either print or broadcast journalism, can avoid suit if these or other actions make it liable.

368

To be sure, there are numerous defenses that are available to the news media — some complete and some partial — but it is becoming increasingly costly to finance such actions.

It is therefore of basic importance for the professional journalist in all media to know the principles of the law of libel and act in good faith under its tenets.

FREEDOM — AND RESPONSIBILITY

The freedom of the press in the United States is based on the First Amendment to the Constitution:

> Congress shall make no law respecting an establishment of religion, or prohibiting the free exercise thereof; or abridging the freedom of speech, or of the press; or the right of the people peaceably to assemble, and to petition the Government for a redress of grievances.

However, as Justice Oliver Wendell Holmes pointed out, this guarantee of free speech does not permit a citizen to raise a false cry of "Fire!" in a crowded meeting hall and escape punishment. Nor may a political leader incite to riot because there is a constitutional guarantee of free assembly. No newspaper, similarly, may abuse its guarantee of freedom by sending its delivery trucks through street stop lights or refusing to pay its employees.

All news organizations, like citizens, are governed by all the applicable laws of the locality, state and nation.

LIBEL DEFINED

There are so many variations in the libel laws of the various states, and differing court decisions within those states, that it is not easy at all times to define exactly what constitutes libel. Although many definitions exist, no definition is commonly agreed upon in the United States. In addition, circumstances, time and geography all cause changes. As a further complication, so many libel suits are settled out of court and so little is published or broadcast about them that it becomes a chore to compile precedents in this area of the law.

General Definitions The following definition has been used in the Columbia Graduate School of Journalism (and its undergraduate predecessor) for more than 60 years as a statement of general purpose by which a libelous publication may be recognized:[1]

[1] Colonel Henry Woodward Sackett, Harold L. Cross and E. Douglas Hamilton, *What You Should Know about the Law of Libel*, distributed by the Graduate School of Journalism, Columbia University, p. 4.

Libel is defamation expressed in writing, printing or other visible form. . . .

"Any printed or written words are defamatory which impute to the plaintiff that he has been guilty of any crime, fraud, dishonesty, immorality, vice or dishonorable conduct, or has been accused or suspected of any such misconduct; or which suggest that the plaintiff is suffering from any infectious disorder; or which have a tendency to injure him in his office, profession, calling or trade. And so, too, are all words which hold the plaintiff up to contempt, hatred, scorn or ridicule and which, by thus engendering an evil opinion of him in the minds of right-thinking men, tend to deprive him of friendly intercourse and society."—Odgers on Libel and Slander.

Thus, there is a clear distinction between libel—defamation expressed in visible form—and slander—oral defamation—which by its nature is more difficult to prove and to punish. The New York State definition of libel (Section 1340 of the New York Penal Code) is one of the broadest and most useful in the United States:

A malicious publication by writing, printing, picture, effigy, sign or otherwise than by mere speech, which exposes any living person, or the memory of any person deceased, to hatred, contempt, ridicule or obloquy, or which causes, or tends to cause any person to be shunned or avoided, or which has a tendency to injure any person, corporation or association of persons, in his or their business or occupation, is a libel.

Gradations of Libel In general, it should be assumed that defamation in the news media, published or broadcast, constitutes libel *per se* (libel on the face of it), although this does not necessarily mean that successful action may be brought. There are a number of complete and partial defenses against libel and many additional circumstances under which mitigation of damages may be sought.

Most suits for libel are brought as civil actions, since civil libel is an infraction against an individual, and may be punished by the award of substantial damages. Criminal libel, on the other hand, is a crime against the state and it is prosecuted by the state with punishment including both fines and prison terms in the case of individuals. In substance, there is comparatively little difference between the two by definition, except that criminal libel is broad enough to sustain actions that libel entire groups of people. However, these suits, like others that come under the criminal libel statutes, are comparatively rare.

In a civil suit, if a case of libel *per se* has been established and the various defenses struck down, then general or compensatory damages may be granted at the direction of the court and in accordance with the verdict. In such a case, it is not necessary for the plaintiff to prove monetary loss. If he establishes that he has been libeled without justification, that is sufficient; however, in a few celebrated cases, damages have been confined to an insulting sum, six cents. Cases in which monetary loss has been established are subject to an additional award of special damages, but judgments of this kind are not particularly common because financial losses caused by libel are difficult to prove.

Much more common are punitive damages, which must be based on a finding of actual malice in connection with the libel. Actual malice may be predicated on a finding of gross negligence, or ill will, or many other errors of lesser degree. Thus, such a finding constitutes the principal danger in many types of libel suits; it is one reason for the continual insistence by editors and broadcasters on efforts by their reporters to get both sides of a story and use them with a recognizable effort to be fair. Prejudice may be deadly.

The news organization that assumes that it can disregard the laws of libel in dealing with corporations, merely because business concerns do not sue for libel as often as individuals, is also riding for a fall. Obviously, corporations can be damaged by untrue and unprivileged statements that they are violating the law or evading government regulations or cheating their customers. The frequent observation that criminal elements are investing money in legitimate business may be troublesome if a particular corporation is identified without documentation to support the charge, unless the inquiry is part of a public record.

This question of identity is paramount in examining a statement for purported libel. For, if no one is identified, then clearly no libel has been committed. Moreover, the libel must be published (or made known) to a third party in accordance with the general definitions already given before it is actionable. Finally, the publication must have occurred within the statute of limitations in that particular jurisdiction.

Danger Signals It is safe to assume that every derogatory term at one time or another has been made the subject either of a complaint or law suit involving libel. Of all the charges that have been the subject of actions, however, the following are among the least defensible:

An allegation of lack of chastity in a woman.

The publication of an obituary alleging that a person died in disgraceful circumstances, when that person in fact is still alive.

Publishing details of a court action on the supposition that papers would be filed, when in fact the suit was settled before filing.

Use of material such as summonses, affidavits and police blotter entries in the mistaken notion that they are privileged documents, i.e., matters of public record. State laws vary.

Repeating a libel in a report of a proceeding in a libel suit.

Imputing insanity or a deranged mind to a person who has never been confined to an institution of any kind.

Imputing antisocial conduct such as drunkenness and drug addiction to persons of good repute.

Making mistakes in identifying persons of the same name, either by misspellings, wrong addresses or other inaccuracies so that the innocent are confused with the guilty.

Confusing a charge of wrongdoing with a conviction of wrongdoing. Using sarcasm and innuendo to imply wrongdoing.

Libelous Terms Many derogatory terms have been made the subject of libel suits. Among them are such epithets as liar, rascal, villain, swindler, rogue, informer, perjurer and the like. To call a doctor a quack without justification is to invite a libel suit. Similarly, it is libelous to call a clergyman a blasphemer, a teacher an ignoramus or a newspaperman a libelous journalist. While a public official, an actor, a baseball player or other persons in the public eye may be fairly criticized in their public duties or performances, they may not be attacked in their private lives.

Who Is Liable? In all these cases, theoretically, everybody who had anything to do with publication of the item is liable and may be made the subject of an action. As a practical matter, however, the news organization itself is usually the chief target. Often, the more affluent members of its staff from the proprietor or publisher on down may be included in a libel suit as defendants; notably, editors, the more affluent columnists or commentators and other journalists of standing who have greater means of paying damages than ordinary staff members. However, it is also an observable truth that when reporters are involved in libel suits, even if they are wholly or partly to blame, the action serves as a form of job insurance. Such witnesses clearly must be retained on the staff at least until the case is settled.

Regardless of how many staff members may be involved, however, it is the management that bears the principal responsibility in a libel suit. The management is responsible for anything that is published or offered for public viewing or listening attention—news, advertisements, cartoons, pictures, captions, editorials and associated materials. It is never a complete defense to argue that a publication or broadcast was made in good faith and that it was based on something that was said by a public official or issued by a reputable wire service or public relations agency. If it is wrong and if it does not come under the complete defenses against libel, then certainly the management is in trouble.

DEFENSES AGAINST LIBEL

There are a number of complete defenses against libel actions involving the press, which are generally believed to cover the broadcast media as well. Of these, the most familiar are provable truth, the privilege of reporting fairly and truly an official proceeding and the right of fair comment.

The Defense of Truth The provable truth of a story is a complete defense in all but a few states of the Union. While the law in such states specifies that lack of malice must be shown in order to make the defense of truth apply, the qualification is not likely to be of much help to a defendant who relies on it alone. As an entirely practical matter, the defense of truth usually has a decisive effect in any libel suit that is brought to trial, civil or criminal, regardless of what may have motivated the defendant. The exceptions are so rare that they are historical curiosities.

It is, necessarily the duty of the defense to establish the truth of a defamatory charge in a libel suit. Documentary evidence, supported by the testimony of witnesses who can show of their own knowledge that the defamatory story is true, constitutes the best defense against libel. It is, of course, not always possible for a news organization to provide such an airtight defense. In cases that involve persons with a criminal record, for example, efforts may be made by the defendant to show that the plaintiff is of such bad repute that he cannot be libeled. This, however, is at best only a partial defense. In rare instances, the defense of truth may be supported on the evidence of a reporter's notes in order to verify what was said on a particular occasion. A tape recording is much more satisfactory.

In any event, the defense must be centered on proving the substance of the charge, not the manner in which it was made. If it were sufficient only to show that a district attorney had called a defendant a thief outside a courtroom or that one politician had accused another of being a bribetaker, then news organizations would have a comparatively easy time with the libel law.

The general acceptance of truth as a complete defense has disposed of the old English common law plea in criminal libel cases, "The greater the truth, the greater the libel."

The Defense of Privilege A fair and true report of official proceedings is termed privileged. This includes legislative, judicial and other public or official proceedings. However, the exact type of hearing that is covered varies from state to state; consequently, no reporter should automatically assume that everything he believes to be a public proceeding is covered.

The defense of privilege in reporting is based on public policy—the right of the public to receive fair and accurate reports of the acts of its courts, legislatures and other official bodies and governing officials.

Section 337 of the Civil Practice Act in New York contains one of the standard definitions of a privileged document:

> A civil action cannot be maintained against any person, firm or corporation, for the publication of a fair and true report of any judicial proceeding, or for any heading of the report which is a fair and true headnote of the statement published.
>
> This section does not apply to a libel contained in any other matter added by any person concerned in the publication; or in the report of any-

thing said or done at the time and place of such a proceeding which was not a part thereof.

Thus, while New York law makes it clear that a reporter cannot report derogatory matter provided by a legislator or prosecutor except when it is an actual part of the official record, this is not the rule in every state. In Texas and California the protection of privilege is extended to public meetings. In New Jersey, a police chief or a prosecutor or coroner may make official statements that are privileged even though they are not a part of an actual proceeding. In general, however, it is a safe rule for reporters to consider as privileged only material that is part of a trial or legislative record and not random comments of a derogatory nature that are made outside. Even here, there may be exceptions. A legislative reporter once discovered he could not get a record of a speech delivered on the floor of the legislature, so that a libel suit could not be turned aside on that ground. It required an enabling act to make available the record in question.

This points up the primary difficulty of invoking the defense of privilege in all except the clearest cases—the public hearings of Congress, the various legislatures and city and town councils, the records of public trials and the like. In many of the states of the Union and in some areas of the federal government as well, the growth of the cult of secrecy has cast the greatest doubt on what constitutes a public record that is covered by the defense of privilege.

Harold L. Cross, in his book, *The People's Right to Know*, wrote:

> Subject to varying statutory phraseology and common law rules, a newspaper has the privilege (or right), absolute in some states and in others conditioned upon the absence of "actual malice," to publish a fair and true report of certain "proceedings." ... "Legislative proceedings" are almost invariably the subject of such privileged reports. Many states go further and include other "proceedings."
>
> New York, for example, adds "other public and official proceedings." Oklahoma adds "any other proceeding authorized by law." Many other states adopt one or another of these statements or a substantial equivalent thereof.
>
> In ruling upon the availability of the defense of privilege based on reports of "police records," courts in the following states have recognized to varying degrees that "police records" are "public and official," or the substantial equivalent: Colorado, Louisiana, Missouri, New York, Oregon and Washington. Texas seems to have marched off in the opposite direction. Michigan has several decisions, the cumulative impact of which is not clear but appears to squint at the view that written records of police action are "public and official" whereas mere oral statements by peace officers to the press will not support the privilege. ....[2]

---

[2] Harold L. Cross, *The People's Right to Know* (New York, Columbia University Press, 1953), pp. 115–116.

Nor are the police blotter and other police records the only ones open to doubt. Secret proceedings of public bodies, where no records are kept, certainly are dubious supports for the defense of privilege. There is also a very large body of public record that remains secret for reasons of public policy. These include grand jury proceedings, records of juvenile and domestic-relations courts in a number of states, the identities of relief clients in many states, and in Wisconsin the identity of the female in any rape case. The defense of privilege, therefore, is by no means as sweeping as that of truth although it is just as complete when it can be invoked.

The right of a Congressman to speak his mind while on the floor of the Senate or House, regardless of the truth or falsity of his attacks on a person, came to public attention forcibly during the anti-Communist attacks of Senator Joseph R. McCarthy Jr. The defense of privilege in the reporting of all such material is based directly on the Constitution, Section 6, Clause 1:

> The Senators and Representatives shall receive a Compensation for their Services, to be ascertained by Law, and paid out of the Treasury of the United States. They shall in all Cases, except Treason, Felony and Breach of the Peace, be privileged from Arrest during their Attendance at the Session of their respective Houses, and in going to and returning from the same; and for any Speech or Debate in either House, they shall not be questioned in any other Place.

As Professor Edward S. Corwin pointed out in his constitutional analysis: "The protection of this clause is not limited to words spoken in debate but is applicable to written reports, to resolutions offered, to the act of voting and to all things generally done in a session of the House by one of its members in relation to the business before it." [3]

Not even the claim of an unworthy purpose can destroy this defense. Justice Felix Frankfurter ruled in Tenney v. Brandhove in 1951: "Legislators are immune from deterrents to the uninhibited discharge of their legislative duty, not for their private indulgence but for the public good. One must not expect uncommon courage even in legislators."

This, however, does not interfere with the historic right of all citizens in any medium, whether it be a soapbox or television, to criticize their government fairly or unfairly, and regardless of the purity or impurity of their motives. The privilege won by John Peter Zenger at his criminal libel trial in 1735 remains inviolate, as long as the criticism is impersonal. The United States Supreme Court in 1964 reaffirmed that "an otherwise impersonal attack on government operations" is not a libel "of an official responsible for those operations." [4]

---

[3] *The Constitution of the United States, Analysis and Interpretation*, prepared by the Legislative Reference Service, Library of Congress: Edward S. Corwin, ed. (Washington, 1953), pp. 99–100.

[4] *The New York Times v. Sullivan* (376 U.S. 254).

The point at which a public proceeding begins, particularly in a judicial matter, is of crucial importance to the defense of privilege. For instance, the swearing out of an affidavit before a justice of the peace is not usually covered by privilege, nor can a summons be accorded such protective covering except where usage is a matter of practice rather than law, as in minor traffic violations. Papers containing affidavits and complaints must be formally served, or filed, and sometimes both, before they may be quoted under the protection of privilege.

On some newspapers, particularly those of a sensational nature, it is the custom to write in a jocular and pseudo-sophisticated manner about certain types of legal actions such as matrimonials (suits for separation, divorce or annulment). Except in New York and one or two other states, this type of writing is unlikely to be covered by the defense of privilege unless it is proved a "fair and true" report not actuated by malice. The best assurance in all matters affecting the defense of privilege is to give both sides of the story, if it is at all possible.

The Right of Fair Comment Expressions of opinion contained in editorials, critical articles, letters to the editor and news items of an analytical nature are covered chiefly by the defense of the right of fair comment, as applied to a libelous publication. The defense is based on public policy—the right of all persons, and publications, to comment and criticize without malicious intent the work of those who court public attention. Among those who invite such criticism, by the nature of their activities, are holders and seekers of public office, authors and playwrights, public performers—such as actors, actresses and sports participants—and critics as well as others whose careers similarly are based on public attention.

The right of fair comment does not extend to the private life of any person but must be confined to matters of public interest or concern. These include everything from affairs of government to the endeavors of public and semipublic institutions such as colleges and hospitals as well as public entertainment and even advertisements.

While the right of fair comment is confined to expressions of opinion, it is generally true that these opinions must have some basis in fact. It would be manifestly unfair, for instance, to criticize an author for something he had not written or a public official for an ill-considered action he had never taken. Criticism that is founded on fact, therefore, is generally defensible under the right of fair comment even though it may seem poorly based, silly and illogical, provided there is no malicious intent.

THE NEW YORK TIMES RULE

In a landmark decision in 1964, the United States Supreme Court for the first time invoked the First Amendment to provide a defense against libeling a public official. The high court held that if the criticism of the official's public conduct is not a knowing lie or a reckless disregard of the truth, he has no ground for legal complaint.

The case was that of L. B. Sullivan, commissioner of public affairs for Montgomery, Alabama, who sued the *New York Times* after an advertisement by a civil rights group in the newspaper had criticized the police. Because he headed the police force, he contended that he had been libeled even though he had not been named in the advertisement and the Alabama Supreme Court upheld a jury verdict granting him $500,000 in damages.

Although Commissioner Sullivan presented a record in which he argued that the *Times* had been guilty of malice by reason of unretracted falsehoods in the advertisement, the United States Supreme Court reversed the verdict saying:

"The constitutional guarantees require, we think, a Federal rule that prohibits a public official from recovering damages for a defamatory falsehood relating to his official conduct unless he proves that the statement was made with 'actual malice'—that is, with knowledge that it was false or with reckless disregard of whether it was false or not." [5]

Thus, with the high court acting in the liberal tradition exemplified by the Chief Justice, Earl Warren, the journalist was given the right to make errors of fact in his criticism of public officials as long as he did not knowingly lie or recklessly disregard the truth. However, Justice William J. Brennan Jr., in his majority opinion in the *Times* case, did not spell out exactly who may be considered a "public official" and what constituted a "reckless disregard of the truth." Subsequently, in another case, he wrote that the official's position "must be one which would invite public scrutiny and discussion occasioned by the particular charge in the controversy."

The *New York Times* Rule Modified The high court has since modified its position several times, permitting the legal pendulum to swing first toward greater liberalism and then back toward a more conservative position.

In *Rosenbloom v. Metromedia Inc.*, the court voted 5–3 in 1971 to extend the *New York Times* Rule to "public figures," a category that considerably enlarged the press's protection against libel suits involving public officials. In that case, a nudist magazine distributor was held to be a "public figure," defined as a "private individual (involved) in an event of public or general concern" and was required to show "actual malice." The court, with Chief Justice Warren E. Burger presiding, decided the magazine man had not done so and he lost a $750,000 judgment that had been obtained against Metromedia radio station WIP.[6]

---

[5] *The New York Times v. Sullivan* (376 U.S. 254).
[6] *Editor & Publisher* (12 June 1971), p. 9.

There was jubilation among editors and broadcasters. Some actually thought that they no longer had to worry about libel suits because almost any plaintiff could be made out to be a "public figure." The celebration was short-lived.

In *Gertz* v. *Robert Welch Inc.* in 1974, the Supreme Court started the pendulum swinging toward conservatism. Here, a private individual was permitted to collect damages for libel merely by proving a degree of fault, possibly negligence, against a defendant news organization, not the "actual malice" required in the *New York Times* Rule of "public officials"—and extended in *Rosenbloom* to private individuals who became "public figures." Accordingly, Elmer Gertz, a lawyer, was upheld in his defense of a $50,000 award for libel that had been obtained against *American Opinion*, a John Birch Society publication owned by Welch, Inc.

Gertz was a blow to the news media. What it meant was that private individuals under certain circumstances could avoid the difficult task of proving "actual malice" by the high court's definition in the *New York Times* Rule. Instead, they could present evidence of "negligence," which could conceivably be a simple mistake in reporting a complicated proceeding. The state courts have since shown that the area of proving fault against a libel defendant has been greatly confused by *Gertz*.

The American Newspaper Publishers Association accordingly has warned that publishers "no longer have the protection of the *New York Times* Rule when libel is alleged by a private individual, involved in matters of public interest, who seeks to recover actual provable damages." [7] A legal commentator, writing in the *Quill*, added that such a plaintiff could also collect for personal suffering as well as damage to his reputation. But here, it was held that "actual malice" must still be proved by a plaintiff. It was small comfort. [8]

There was worse to come. In 1976, in the libel case of *Mary Alice Firestone* v. *Time Inc.*, the Supreme Court abruptly narrowed the definition of who may be considered a "public figure" and held that all the plaintiff had to do was to show that *Time Inc.* was guilty of "fault" in reporting a lower court's verdict. In other words, it was possible for "negligence" and not "actual malice" to be defined as the standard for judgment.

The case began when socially prominent Mary Alice Firestone sued Time Inc. for libel, charging she had been defamed because the magazine reported in its "Milestones" section that she had been divorced by Russell Firestone "on grounds of extreme cruelty and adultery." A Florida court, holding that Mrs. Firestone had been found guilty only of ex-

---

[7] *Editor & Publisher* (31 August 1974), p. 15. *Columbia Journalism Review*, (May/June, 1975), pp. 38–40.

[8] D. Charles Whitney (August, 1974) p. 22.

treme cruelty, awarded her $100,000 damages by declaring her to be a private individual who did not have to prove "actual malice" by the defendant. The court thus brushed aside contentions by *Time* Inc., that Mrs. Firestone was widely known, had given press conferences during the trial and otherwise had so conducted herself as to be a "public figure."

On appeal, the Supreme Court agreed that Mrs. Firestone was not a "public figure" and did not have to prove "actual malice." The case was sent back to the lower courts for a determination of whether *Time* Inc., was negligent and therefore guilty of "fault." The reason for the high court's action was the ambiguity of the lower court's original decision in the case.

A distinguished legal authority, Alan U. Schwartz, commented:

"Clearly, that (Firestone) decision severely limits the scope of the term 'public figure,' and since mere negligence is all that is required to be proved in a libel case involving someone who is not a public figure, once again the sphere of protection for the press has been reduced. If the Supreme Court cannot agree in any consistent fashion as to who is a public figure, journalists who attempt to make use of this 'qualified privilege' to comment (short of actual malice) on behavior, do so at their peril."[9]

The press was by no means back to Square 1. But it also was very far from the peak attained in *Rosenbloom*.

Other Defenses There are additional defenses against libel, most of them less frequently used. They include the publication or use of defamatory material in self-defense or as a reply, publication resulting from the consent of the person being libeled, the privilege of a participant in an official proceeding including such quasi-judicial agencies as the Federal Communications Commission and other regulatory government bodies, and the shield of the statute of limitations (usually two years or less in the United States).

PARTIAL DEFENSES AGAINST LIBEL

There may on occasion be no complete defense against a defamatory publication. In such cases efforts are made to reduce the amount that may be returned in favor of a plaintiff by submitting partial defenses that tend to mitigate the damages. One of the principal acts available to any defendant, actual or potential, is to publish a retraction, correction

[9]Schwartz's commentary in the *Atlantic*, "Danger: Pendulum Swinging—Using the Courts to Muzzle the Press" (February 1977), p. 29 et seq.; see also Harry W. Stonecipher and Robert Trager, "The Impact of *Gertz* on the Law of Libel," *Journalism Quarterly* (Winter 1976), p. 609 et. seq.

or apology in approximately the same relative position and of the same length as the libelous article. This, plus such expressions as "the alleged crime," "the suspect," "according to police" and others, serve to emphasize that an effort was made to publish a fair and true report, without malicious intent. These expressions will not avert a finding against a defendant but they often help convince a jury that the ends of justice will be served by a finding for general damages, rather than punitive damages.

Recommendations These nine partial defenses are recommended as among the most important:

1. That the general conduct of the plaintiff gave the defendant "probable cause" for believing the charges to be true.
2. That rumors to the same effect as the libelous publication had long been prevalent and generally believed in the community and never contradicted by the accused or his friends.
3. That the libelous article came from a press association or was copied from another newspaper and believed to be true.
4. That the plaintiff's general character is bad.
5. That the publication was made in heat and passion provoked by the acts of the plaintiff.
6. That the charge published had been made orally in the presence of the plaintiff before publication, and he had not denied it.
7. That the publication was made of a political antagonist in the heat of a political campaign.
8. That as soon as the defendant discovered that he was in error he published a retraction, correction or apology.
9. That the defamatory publication had reference not to the plaintiff, but to another person of a similar name, concerning whom the charges were true, and that most readers understood this other individual to be meant.[10]

Practical Defenses Professional journalists can safeguard their news organizations and themselves against libel suits by being accurate, reasonable, fair and impartial in their coverage of the news, and careful to avoid any show of malice as construed by the courts.

It cannot be said too often that nothing must be taken for granted in journalism. It is a safe rule to leave out questionable material until it can be checked and to insist on the letter as well as the spirit of accuracy in everything that is published. The temptation is great, under the pressures of daily journalism, to leap to conclusions, to act as an advocate, to make assumptions based on previous experience, to approach a

[10] Sackett, Cross and Hamilton, *What You Should Know about the Law of Libel*, p. 21.

story with preconceived notions of what is likely to happen. To give way to such tendencies is to invite error, slanted copy and libelous publications for which there is little or no defense. An open mind is the mark of the journalist; the propagandist has made up his mind in advance.

The seeds of libel are sown, broadcast in the news and sprout in the most unexpected places and at the least convenient times. But to anyone who has practiced journalism for many years, it is a familiar observation that successful libel suits are seldom waged over large issues where a news organization has taken a position after long and careful study and full knowledge of the facts. Rather, it is the brief story about a street incident, a switched caption, a wrong address, a misspelled name or any one of a thousand other commonplaces of daily journalism that give rise to the most damaging and least defensible libel suits. Journalists must be on guard constantly to state the facts accurately, to differentiate between a person who has been arrested and one who has been held for questioning, to specify that the placing of a charge against a defendant is not an implication of guilt.

There is something more important then being first with the news. That is to get it right. Nor is safeguarding the office against a libel suit the most compelling reason for emphasizing the care that must be taken with facts. The ultimate stake is public confidence, without which no newspaper can long exist in a democratic country.

THE RIGHT OF PRIVACY

For many years efforts have been made by individuals unable or unwilling to sue for libel to seek relief under the doctrine of the "right of privacy." This right has developed as a common law along with an early New York statute on the subject. While legislative and judicial backing therefore has developed in support of this doctrine, there is as yet no definitive body of law on the right of privacy. Nor is there uniformity of practice in the various states.

The principle of the right of privacy has been invoked for individuals mentioned in textual news, as well as for those whose pictures have been used without their permission in still photographs, movies or TV. However, although the extent of the statute remains to be tested, the use of privacy laws has become a very real threat to the freedom of the press.

The Brandeis-Warren Thesis The first authoritative legal statement on the right of privacy was made by Louis D. Brandeis, later to become an Associate Justice of the United States Supreme Court, and S. D. Warren. Many years ago they wrote as follows:

Instantaneous photographs and newspaper enterprise have invaded the sacred precincts of private and domestic life; and numerous mechanical devices threaten to make good the prediction that "what is whispered in the closet shall be proclaimed from the housetops." For years there has been a feeling that the law must afford some remedy for the unauthorized circulation of portraits of private persons.

The question whether our law will recognize and protect the "right of privacy" in the circulation of portraits and in other respects must soon come before our courts for consideration. . . .

The principle which protects personal writings and other productions of the intellect or of the emotions is the right of privacy, and the law has no new principle to formulate when it extends this protection to personal appearances, sayings, acts and to personal relations, domestic and otherwise. . . .[11]

Brandeis and Warren held, however, that the right of privacy does not extend to privileged communications under the law of libel and slander, nor to publication of matters of public or general interest. They made these sweeping statements:

The right of privacy ceases with the publication of the facts by the individual, or with his consent.

The truth of the matter published does not afford a defense.

The absence of "malice" in the publisher does not afford a defense.

"The Right to Be Let Alone" Since the Brandeis-Warren thesis first defined what has come to be known as "the right to be let alone," most states have recognized the right of privacy in one form or another.

As enunciated by a distinguished legal authority, Wilson W. Wyatt, these are four general situations in which damages have been granted under the law:[12]

1. Appropriation to one's own advantage of the benefit of the name or likeness of another.
2. Unreasonable intrusion upon the privacy or private affairs of another.
3. Unreasonable publicity given to the private life of another, even though the facts are true.
4. Unreasonable publicity which places another in a false light before the public.

The growth of electronic devices that may unreasonably invade the privacy of individuals, and their use by various persons, organizations

[11] S. D. Warren and L. D. Brandeis, "The Right to Privacy," 4 *Harvard Law Review* (1890), p. 193.

[12] Wilson W. Wyatt, "The Right of Privacy Doctrine," *ASNE Bulletin* (November 1967), p. 3.

and public and private agencies, make the law of the right of privacy increasingly important. Just how it may be applied in the future is uncertain, but there is no doubt whatever that it poses major difficulties for all the news media.

Changes in the Privacy Law The legal pendulum has been swinging in the Supreme Court's interpretation of the privacy law, as well as libel.

The most liberal precedent was set in 1967 when the high court made "actual malice" rather than unknowing falsehood the test for violations of the right of privacy, thus extending the *New York Times* Rule. In *Time* Inc. v. Hill, the court decided by 5–4 that a "newsworthy person's" right to privacy did not entitle him to collect damages for reports containing false information unless there was proof that the errors were "knowingly and recklessly" published. Accordingly, a $30,000 judgment against *Life* magazine was set aside in a suit that had been brought by a family allegedly identified as the original of a Broadway drama about the prisoners of three escaped convicts.[13]

But in 1974, the high court decided a privacy law case in favor of a woman because she was the subject of "calculated falsehoods" in a newspaper article about her home and children. Thus, Margaret Mae Cantrell, widow of the victim of a West Virginia bridge disaster, became the victor in a suit against the *Cleveland Plain Dealer* and won a $60,000 judgment in her suit for invasion of privacy. The majority decision held that the newspaper had published "significant misrepresentations" in describing the level at which Mrs. Cantrell and her four children lived, that the reporter had visited her home while she was at work, had talked to her children, but never to her. So, it was shown that private persons could sue under the privacy law and hope to collect if they were depicted in a "false light" by the news media.[14]

However, when a man sued in the following year because an Atlanta TV station had disclosed the name of his daughter after she had been raped and killed by six teen-age boys, the Supreme Court upheld the TV station on appeal. Reversing a judgment for invasion of privacy in favor of the father in the Georgia courts, the high court ruled by 8–1 that "once true information is disclosed in public court documents open to public inspection, the press cannot be sanctioned for publishing it."

As has been its custom in recent years, the Supreme Court then left the door open for later modifications by saying that it was not deciding "the broader question whether truthful publications may ever be subjected to civil or criminal liability." [15]

---

[13] *New York Times* 11 January 1967, pp. 14, 24.
[14] *New York Times* 19 December 1974, p. 39.
[15] *New York Times* 6 March 1975, p. 12.

The Privacy Act There are further complications to the doctrines surrounding the right of privacy in the Family Educational Rights and Privacy Act of 1974, the Privacy Act of 1974 and the Fair Credit Reporting Act, plus later elaborations. In effect, these laws make it difficult for the news media to get certain kinds of information without the permission of those involved. Under the Privacy Act alone, access is restricted to an estimated 8,000 different types of files kept by the federal government. At issue is the question of whether there is a "constitutional right" of privacy and, if so, how it would be construed under the First Amendment. It will take some time for the courts to come around to that matter, but one authority calls privacy "the sexiest issue of today." [16]

Meanwhile so many law suits are being brought under the alleged invasion of the right of privacy that they constitute a serious hazard for the practicing journalist. Just where the public interest ends and invasion of privacy begins is something that is very difficult for the news media to measure, particularly in the absence of a clear verdict from the Supreme Court. Meanwhile, scores of bills affecting the law of privacy go before the Congress each year.

PRIOR RESTRAINTS ON PUBLICATION

Freedom of the press from licensing was recognized under English common law late in the seventeenth century. As summarized in Blackstone's Commentaries, this was stated as follows:

> The liberty of the press is indeed essential to the nature of a free state; but this consists in laying no *previous* restraint upon publications, and not in freedom from censure for criminal matter when published. Every freeman has an undoubted right to lay what sentiments he pleases before the public; to forbid this, is to destroy the freedom of the press; but if he publishes what is improper, mischievous or illegal, he must take the consequences of his own temerity." [17]

Legal authorities are agreed that, with the adoption of the First Amendment in 1791, the United States constitutionally outlawed any system of prior restraint; indeed, no one challenged that basic proposition even though the Supreme Court did not rule on the principle until 1931. Then, in Near v. Minnesota, Chief Justice Charles Evans Hughes in a majority opinion held invalid a Minnesota statute under which an anti-Semitic publication had been prosecuted.

[16] *Editor & Publisher* (1 November 1975), p. 12: Richard M. Schmidt, Jr., counsel for the American Society of Newspaper Editors in the *ASNE Bulletin* (March 1977), p. 9.

[17] Blackstone's *Commentaries on the Laws of England*, vol. 4, pp. 151–152.

The basic Hughes rule was that the principle of "immunity from previous restraint" may be limited "only in exceptional cases" and he wrote in the majority opinion:

> The exceptional nature of its limitations places in a strong light the general conception that liberty of the press, historically considered and taken up in the Federal Constitution, has meant, principally although not exclusively, immunity from previous restraints or censorship.

On the specific case, he stated:

> The fact that the liberty of the press may be abused by miscreant purveyors of scandal does not make any the less necessary the immunity of the press from previous restraint in dealing with official misconduct. Subsequent punishment for such abuses as may exist is the appropriate remedy . . . [18]

The Pentagon Papers Case Despite the breadth of this and other decisions over the years, the right of publication without prior restraint has not been easy to maintain in the United States. Yet, even though strict national security restrictions were laid down in the Atomic Energy Act of 1946, the United States government itself never sought to enjoin publication by court action on the ground of national security until 1971. Then, in the Pentagon Papers case, the issue was posed before the high court.

Through the efforts of its Pentagon correspondent, Neil Sheehan, the *New York Times* had obtained most of the material assembled in a secret and classified 47-volume study ordered by the Defense Department and entitled, *History of U. S. Decision-making Process on Vietnam Policy.* The *Times* published material from this work on June 13, 14 and 15, 1971 before being restrained on the latter date by a court order obtained by the Department of Justice, charging that national security had been imperiled. When the *Washington Post* published articles based on the same study, it also was made the subject of a similar restraining order on June 19.

After both papers had been under government censorship for 15 days, the Supreme Court on June 30 denied by a 6–3 vote the government's right to impose a prior restraint upon publication. The majority opinion held that "any system of prior restraints of expression comes to this court bearing a heavy presumption against its constitutionality." It pointed out that the government "thus carries a heavy burden of showing justification for the enforcement," but it "had not met that burden." [19]

---

[18] *Near v. Minnesota*, 283 U.S. 715–716; 720; see also Thomas I. Emerson, *The System of Freedom of Expression* (New York, 1970), p. 509.

[19] *New York Times*, 1 July 1971, p. 1 et. seq.

However, the battle was far from over. As was pointed out by John S. Knight, a Pulitzer Prize-winning editor, "Actually, a precedent has been set for further or future restraints upon the right to publish." [20]

Judicial Gag Orders Turning away from national security as an issue for the time being, the courts began to take note of what many called a conflict between the First Amendment guarantee of a free press and the Sixth Amendment protection of the right of fair trial. During the 1970s, judges issued at least 50 orders of prior restraints on publication in order to prevent the news media from publishing or broadcasting material held to be a threat to a defendant's fair trial. Coincidentally, numerous cases arose in which reporters were either threatened with jail for contempt or actually put behind the bars by judges when they refused to disclose the sources of their information for investigative and other articles dealing with the administration of justice.

The high court dealt with both issues in decisions on June 30, 1976. In the issue of judicial gag orders, the judges ruled 9–0 in a Nebraska case against prior restraints on publication as a general policy. But on the contempt issue, the court refused to set aside action against reporters that had been ordered by judges on the ground of contempt. [21] Both are discussed in greater detail in Chapter 23.

Freedom of Information Laws When the Freedom of Information Law took effect on July 4, 1967, it contained so many exemptions and restraints that few journalists attempted to invoke it in the battle against undue government secrecy. But in 1975, a series of streamlining amendments passed over President Ford's veto gave the news media— and others—a potent weapon against bureaucratic coverups. True, restrictions still remained,[22] but soon the news media were petitioning various agencies for information under the FoI Law, as it is known, or even going to court to enforce their requests. All requests for data from the FBI increased from 447 to 13,875 a year after the law was streamlined. At the CIA, there was so much activity in the information field that a staff of more than 100 persons was formed to process requests. These agencies, like others, charged 10¢ a page for their copies of records. Some charged much more.

Although some major stories resulted, it was by no means the bonanza that journalists had expected. It also became expensive—some

---

[20] *Miami Herald*, 4 July 1971, p. 6A.

[21] *New York Times*, 1 July 1976, p. 1 *et seq.*

[22] Among them, classified national security papers, personnel and medical files, privileged trade secret information, intergovernment memos, data on internal personnel rules and practices of agencies, and records that could jeopardize the right of fair trial, endanger personal privacy or expose confidential sources.

reports running as high as $10,000. As the situation was described by Frederick Taylor, managing editor of the *Wall Street Journal,* "The act was cumbersome in its old form and it's still cumbersome in its new form."[23]

To help journalists get at the basic material they sought, the Washington-based Reporters Committee for Freedom of the Press issued a paper on search procedures, fees for duplication, relevant procedures, form letters to be addressed to various government agencies and a guide to court action costs, together with an agency address and phone number compilation. If it did nothing else, the reporters' pamphlet kept the government's FoI offices busy.[24]

Even though the news media did make many requests for information, and filed some court suits, the demand for previously secret or otherwise unavailable data was greater among business firms, consumer groups and private citizens who believed that their rights had been jeopardized.

It would seem, based on considerable experience, that the various state laws protecting the public's right to know may sometimes be of more use than federal statutes, including the federal "Sunshine law" of 1976.[25] Many states now have "open meeting" laws requiring government units to operate in public view with specific exceptions, and even more states have "open records" laws that provide broad access to government papers.

An Official Secrets Act? Several measures have been introduced in congress to clamp an Official Secrets Act on the news media of the United States. The basic provisions of such a measure also were incorporated at one time in S-1, a Senate bill of more than 700 pages that sought to revise the federal criminal code, but which was dropped in favor of compromise legislation drafted by Senators John McClellan and Edward Kennedy. The lack of a current majority for an Official Secrets Act should not obscure the danger behind such legislative maneuvering.

The fact is that there is an exaggerated concern, both in the Congress and some areas of the executive branch of government, that the American news media will disclose national defense secrets. This is based, for the most part, on the leaking of classified material during the Vietnam War and other unauthorized disclosures affecting American foreign policy. But in none of these instances did any court find that

[23] *Newsweek* (2 February 1976), p. 50.

[24] The Reporters Committee for Freedom of the Press has headquarters in Room 1112, 1750 Pennsylvania Ave., NW., Washington D. C. 20006. Its steering committee includes Jack C. Landau, Newhouse Newspapers; Fred P. Graham, CBS News; Jack Nelson, *Los Angeles Times,* and Elsie Karper, *Washington Post.*

[25] Associated Press, report for 31 August 1976.

the news media had broken any law; instead, the disclosures served to inform the American public of acts of their government that had been carried out in secret.

What those in favor of press regulation try to do is to assure editors that an Official Secrets Act would do no more than restate, in modern terms, the provisions of the Espionage Act of 1917 which still regulates the publication or broadcasting of material affecting national security. This is sheer nonsense. Both the original provisions of S-1 and the measures proposed in the various contemplated versions of an Official Secrets Act would bind the news media to the government's view of what constitutes national security.

As legal scholars were quick to point out when S-1 was first introduced:

> Because it is impossible to write about national defense matters without including material that ostensibly relates to the 'military capability of the United States,' the only way for a journalist to be safe under S-1 would be to stick to matters made public by the authority of Congress or lawful acts of public servants. Otherwise some legal risks are run.[26]

The revision of S-1 did not remove the threat to the freedom of the press. As Daniel Schorr put it in a discussion of the effect of such maneuvering on his ability to work in Washington as an investigative reporter for the broadcast media, "There could be no investigative reporting under such laws. And it makes no difference whether they are directly applicable to the news media, as in the case of an Official Secrets Act, or whether they serve the same purpose indirectly through an end run in a different piece of legislation."[27]

---

[26] Benno C. Schmidt Jr. and Harold Edgar, "S.1: Would the New Bill Amount to an Official Secrets Law—and Could It Work?" *Columbia Journalism Review* (March/April 1976), pp. 18–21.

[27] In a conversation with me at the University of Tennessee in the fall of 1976.

Chapter 22
Crime
Reporting

The basic policy in the reporting of crime in the American news media should be to safeguard both the rights of free press and fair trial. One cannot exist without the other. Both are vital to the growth of democratic society.

There have been excesses in the coverage of crime in the past; without doubt, such things will occur in the future because of overzealousness and bad judgment on the part of journalists or law enforcement officials, sometimes both. This is a part of the price that must be paid to insure the existence of a free press.

Happily, the leaders of the news media themselves have come to see that self-restraint in the handling of crime news can be a virtue. In many cases, it helps rather than hinders the administration of justice and advances the work of the journalist. A decent sense of balance and a considerable amount of courage are required to deal with crime news in modern journalism.

SOURCES OF CRIME NEWS

The broad coverage of law enforcement is something more than the routine gathering of bits and pieces of crime news. Properly done, it is a public service and perhaps even a deterrent for certain types of criminal acts in an era when the incidence of crime in general is soaring in the cities.

Purpose and Practice The stereotype of crime reporting is based in large part on *The Front Page* era of journalism, when sensational papers fought for hyped up crime news and boosted circulation with boxcar headlines about sensational crimes. With the coming of broadcast journalism's dominance over spot news and the end of newspaper competition in all but a few of the nation's larger cities, that era is over.

It is still true, as it was then, that any editor who wants to fill up his columns with crime news can do so at a very cheap rate per staff working hour. All it takes is a couple of active reporters at police headquarters and the criminal courts plus the local DA's office. But to what end? If the news is consequential, the broadcast media already have taken the edge off it. Moreover, under revised legal procedures made necessary by court rulings, most police and prosecutors are wary about abusing the rights of defendants by releasing all the details of a crime—real and fancied—immediately upon making an arrest. And trial in the news media is more difficult and less popular than it used to be, although an ambitious prosecutor or a clever defense attorney can still get space and time on the air if he takes risks with his case.

The LEAA Intervenes There is little remaining justification for the view held earlier in this century that editors use crime news for the benefit of publishers rather than the public. Today, with crime rates at an all-time high nearly everywhere in the land, what bothers thoughtful journalists a good deal more is the concentrated effort that is being made by government officials and the courts to restrict information about crime and criminal records.

Sometimes these attempts can be overcome by patience, persistence and costly legal appeals. But the net result has been less than satisfactory, both to the news media and those who seek greater protection for the rights of the accused.

The measures taken by the Law Enforcement Assistance Administration (LEAA) of the Department of Justice are a case in point.[1] Created in 1968 under the Omnibus Crime Control and Safe Streets Act, the LEAA in eight years sent $4.5 billion to state and local governments to combat crime. Consequently, when the LEAA in 1975 demanded privacy for most criminal records under a new regulation, many local authorities closed off police blotters and even court records to the press without waiting for the necessary state laws to be passed.

After an uproar of protest, in which civic and business organizations

[1] The *Quill* (July/August 1976), pp. 19–22.

took a more prominent part than the press, LEAA amended its regulations the following year and called upon all states to approve enabling legislation by December 31, 1977, on pain of losing crime-fighting grants. While restrictions were withdrawn from the dissemination of data on convictions and criminal history contained in court records of "public judicial proceedings," access to police blotters remained in doubt under this regulation:

"Police blotters, to be available for access by press people and other interested citizens, must be compiled chronologically and required by law or long standing custom to be made public if such records are organized on a chronological basis (subject to interpretation)."

Critics pointed out at once that this could mean almost anything a public official wanted it to mean. To this, one federal authority replied that the intent was to "stop fishing expeditions." [2] In any event, local practices seemed likely to be the determining factor.

Necessarily, the press must continue to cover the news of crime regardless of difficulties. But it is even more important, as public-spirited editors have shown, to get at the deeper significance of such news. To do it, some papers have formed teams of reporters to do work that used to be done on an individual—and highly competitive—basis at police headquarters, the courts, city hall and prosecutors' offices. It amounts to a pooling of sources and it works.

POLICIES IN CRIME NEWS

The modern movement to curb the news media in the coverage of crime was set in motion by the assassination of President Kennedy in Dallas on November 22, 1963, and the subsequent murder of Lee Harvey Oswald, who was arrested for killing him. The Warren Commission pointed out that it was the clamor of newsmen to see Oswald that made it possible for Jack Ruby to murder him in full view of 50,000,000 television witnesses. Subsequently, the drive of the legal profession to restrict both crime and court coverage was bolstered by two major United States Supreme Court decisions that set sharp limits on what the police could do in interrogating prisoners.

The Escobedo Case In a landmark decision in 1964, the Supreme Court reversed the murder conviction of Danny Escobedo, a 28-year-old Chicago laborer, because he had not been permitted to consult a lawyer before making a murder confession in 1960. The high court held that his rights had been violated because police barred him from legal counsel prior to his admission that he had been implicated in the slaying of his brother-in-law. He had served four years of a 20-year prison term.

[2] The *Quill* (July/August 1970), pp. 19–22; see also the *ASNE Bulletin* (March 1977), pp. 9–12.

Delivering the decision of the court's 5–4 majority, Justice Arthur J. Goldberg wrote: "A system of law enforcement which comes to depend on the confession will, in the long run, be less reliable than a system which depends on extrinsic evidence independently secured through skillful investigation. If the exercise of constitutional rights will thwart the effectiveness of a system of law enforcement, then there is something very wrong with the system.

"We hold only that when the process shifts from investigatory to accusatory — when its focus is on the accused and its purpose is to elicit a confession — our adversary system begins to operate and, under the circumstances here, the accused man must be permitted to consult his lawyer."[3]

The Miranda Case   The Escobedo Rule was extended in 1966 when the United States Supreme Court reversed the conviction of Ernesto A. Miranda, a 25-year-old mentally retarded Arizona truck driver, because he had not been warned of his right to counsel or that his statements might be used against him before he confessed to raping an 18-year-old girl. Miranda had been serving concurrent sentences of 20 to 30 years.

Chief Justice Warren held for the 5–4 majority that police must inform a criminal suspect, when arrested, of his right to remain silent and to obtain counsel. While Miranda remains on the books, it has been weakened by subsequent high court decisions. In 1971, statements made by an accused person before being informed of his rights were admitted under cross examination. Four years later, statements made by an accused person after being informed of his rights were admitted as rebuttal testimony. And in 1976, the Miranda rule was held inapplicable to grand jury testimony.

Copies of the "Miranda card," used by police to inform defendants of their rights upon arrest, were found on Miranda's body after he was stabbed to death in 1976 during a barroom brawl.[4]

The Miranda case laid down guidelines for law enforcement authorities in the States similar to the 1957 Mallory Rule under which the Supreme Court barred prolonged federal interrogation. Under Mallory, a federal defendant upon arrest must be taken "without unnecessary delay" before the nearest U. S. Commissioner who then is charged with reminding him of his rights and providing a lawyer if the prisoner cannot afford one. The Mallory Rule also bars any admissions obtained from a federal defendant during excessive delays in arraignment.

The Consequences   A virtual revolution in police procedures has occurred as a result of these two decisions, along with the Estes and

[3] For Escobedo, *New York Times*, 23 June 1964; for Miranda, *New York Times*, 14 June 1966; *Christian Science Monitor*, 16 August 1974; 8 April 1975; 21 May 1976.

[4] *New York Times*, 2 February 1976, p. 42.

Sheppard cases which are dealt with in a subsequent chapter. The Department of Justice, fortified by the individual actions of various state bar associations, issued a set of press-bar guidelines that counseled police, press and officers of the court to omit references before and during trials to a defendant's prior police record, statements that a case was "open and shut" and "alleged confessions or inculpatory omissions" by an accused person.

Some of the highest State courts, notably in New Jersey, have given such orders on the backing of judicial authority. However, it is clear that while the courts can and will use their contempt power to enforce decisions against recalcitrant prosecutors and defense lawyers, their authority over police and press is on less firm ground. Thus, the thrust of the legal profession has been toward putting its own house in order and, in effect, trying to withhold news and comment from the news media in the interest of protecting the right of fair trial.

THE REARDON RULES

In this spirit, Justice Paul C. Reardon of the Supreme Judicial Court of Massachusetts and a distinguished committee of lawyers placed the authority of the American Bar Association behind a movement to insure punitive action by courts against lawyers or police who issue unauthorized information. For a time, Justice Reardon also sought to impose sanctions against the press on the same ground but was persuaded to drop the notion on constitutional grounds.

The Reardon Rules, as originally formulated, give police the authority to issue only the fact and circumstances of an arrest, the text of the charge, the identity of the arresting officers, the length of the inquiry, and the seizure of evidence, if any. The regulations also call on all parties to withhold the following from the time of the arrest of a suspect until the conclusion of his trial:

1. Any discussion of the strength of the evidence, pro or con, and the possibility of a plea of guilty by the defendant.
2. A defendant's admissions or confession.
3. His previous record, if any.
4. Identities of prospective witnesses.
5. The refusal of a defendant to take various tests, including lie detector tests, or the outcome of tests that he did take.

The next development was the drafting of voluntary press-bar guidelines in many states that included some or all of these provisions and added others with various modifications. Of course there have been disagreements. Few editors, for example, are convinced that the public interest is served by withholding the background of a notorious hoodlum upon his arrest for a serious crime. And judges have resorted to widespread gag orders, punitive action against reporters and even mistrial declarations in cases involving the press in their jurisdictions.

One of the worst shocks to date has been a ruling by Associate Justice Harry A. Blackmun of the U. S. Supreme Court that the voluntary guidelines could be made binding on the press by the courts. This was applied specifically to the Nebraska judicial gag order case, when it was carried to the high court on appeal, but the full court vacated Justice Blackmun's decision. Consequently, the press-bar cooperative movement appears to have survived; editors, in fact, have been attending regional workshops on the issues involved.[5]

A Model Agreement The Washington State agreement on press-bar guidelines is widely regarded as a model. What it does, in effect, is to warn against publication before trial of opinions as to a defendant's guilt or innocence, his character, admissions, alibis or confessions and other information that could be prejudicial.

This represents a concession by the bar in its hitherto inflexible stand against the publication of such data. A request to use reasonable precaution is quite a step down from a legal ban that could lead to punitive sanctions. As for the press, the Washington plan specifies that information may be published on the identity of a defendant and his biographical background with no restraints except to conform to standards of good taste, accuracy and good judgment, on the text of the charge, the identity of the complainant, the investigating agency, the length of the inquiry and the immediate circumstances of the arrest.[6]

The Burger Court The legal pendulum, which swung so far toward the libertarian concept of law enforcement while Earl Warren was the Chief Justice of the United States, has swung back under the more conservative Supreme Court that was created beginning with the appointment of Warren E. Burger as Chief Justice. While the doctrine of freedom from prior restraints on publication has been upheld, notably in the Nebraska "gag order" case, the court has made it increasingly difficult for both reporters and news organizations to safeguard the confidentiality of their sources. As is made evident in the cases cited in Chapter 23, the basic trend is against the news media. The investigative reporter, and particularly the reporter who deals with law enforcement, has many handicaps with which to contend, the courts being among the most serious. Still, on balance, the yield of cooperative action between press and bar has been impressive enough to encourage both

[5] *ASNE Bulletin*, (July/August 1976), p. 24; for Blackmun ruling, see *New York Times*, 22 November 1975, p. 1.
[6] The full text is given in Appendix IV, 4.

professions to continue their voluntary efforts. There is no point whatever to declaring war between the First and Sixth Amendments.

Press Councils The growth of the movement for creating news councils
in the United States, patterned after the successful British model, is
still another sign of the willingness of a substantial part of the American news media to make themselves more accountable to the public,
particularly in cases involving the law.

The British had trouble with their experiment, despite the stimulus
provided by two Royal Commissions that urged a greater share of accountability by the press. After lagging from 1949 to 1964 by failing to
provide the public with sufficient representation, the British Press
Council appointed an impartial chairman, named representatives of
prominent citizens' groups as members and reduced press representation to a minority. It worked—and drew full support from the British
press itself.

The first American groups, which also were concerned mainly with
the press, began at the local level in the 1960s. These were consultative
press councils, in the main, and functioned in Bend, Oregon; Sparta, Illinois; Littleton, Colorado; Honolulu and Seattle. Some public-spirited
newspapers went beyond the Council idea and set up public defenders,
or *ombudsmen* (as they are known in Sweden) to handle the grievances
expressed by their readers.

On September 9, 1971 the first American regional press council was
set up in Minnesota under the chairmanship of C. Donald Peterson, an
associate justice of the Minnesota Supreme Court. Two years later, on
August 1, 1973, the National News Council opened for business at One
Lincoln Plaza, New York, N. Y., 10023. Its declared purpose was "to
advance a free and responsive press," but it soon showed that it intended to monitor complaints affecting broadcast as well as print journalism.

The first chairman was Stanley H. Fuld, former Chief Judge of the
New York State Court of Appeals, who worked with the executive director, William B. Arthur, former editor of *Look* magazine, and 14 others as the News Council's directorate. The initial budget of $271,000
was put up by 10 foundations, but it was soon exhausted and the outlook for the Council's continued existence was grim. Although it handled numerous complaints in its early years without major criticism,
some of the largest and most powerful news organizations in the land,
headed by the *New York Times*, refused to submit their acts to review
by the impartial, nonprofit organization.

The Council had no punitive power. It required plantiffs to waive
court action. All it could do was to publicize the rights and wrongs of
cases that were brought before it. Its procedures were based on a fair

and honest investigation of the facts. First, it decided whether a complaint was worthy of inquiry. If the answer was affirmative, it conducted an investigation. Then, its members returned a ruling based on the information it had been able to gather from both sides. Of course, when a defendant newspaper or broadcast unit refused to cooperate, very little could be done about it.

So the Council dragged along, barely keeping itself alive. One bright spot was an encouraging verdict that came from two inquiring editors, John McMillan, executive editor of the *Huntington* (West Virginia) *Herald-Dispatch and Advertiser*, and Larry Jinks, then the executive editor of the *Miami Herald* and later the executive editor of the *San Jose* (California) *Mercury-News*. In their report, they wrote:

"That they (the Council's members) are meeting together and talking about our business is a reality we shouldn't ignore in the hope that the money crunch facing the foundations will force the Council to die in another year or two." [7]

Still, very little happened until Judge Fuld resigned and the dynamic Norman E. Isaacs, former executive editor of the *Louisville Courier-Journal and Times*, replaced him as chairman. Among the first things Isaacs did was to set the Council on a new track—to defend the freedom of the press as well as to inquire into its shortcomings. In three and a half years, the Council had handled more than 400 complaints. Under Isaacs' direction, and with the continuing assistance of Bill Arthur, the Council became an 18-member group and broadened its nonjournalism membership. More funds were raised to support it. It also intervened, with other journalistic organizations, in cases where the rights of the news media were endangered.

The upshot was a decision by William S. Paley, chairman of the board of the Columbia Broadcasting System, to cooperate with the National News Council. Paley wrote:

> CBS has come to recognize the evidence of the National News Council's ability to strengthen the growth of a free and responsible press in America. Therefore, CBS not only pledges its cooperation with the Council, including reporting by CBS of any Council findings adverse to CBS News, but also affirms its support of the aims and procedures of the Council.[8]

The National Broadcasting Company cooperated, too. Financial support also came from the Gannett Foundation, an enterprise of the Gannett Newspapers; the *Milwaukee Journal & Sentinel*, *Louisville Courier-Journal and Times*, *Denver Post*, Capital Cities Communications, Salt

---

[7] Background on the National News Council in Ronald P. Kriss, "The National News Council at Age One," *Columbia Journalism Review* (November–December 1974), p. 31; McMillan-Jinks report in Larry Jinks, "The News Council Digs In," *ASNE Bulletin* (March 1975), p. 1, and H. L. Stevenson, editor-in-chief, in the UPI *Reporter* (9 December 1976).

[8] William S. Paley's letter to Norman E. Isaacs, 24 January 1977.

Lake Tribune and numerous others. The National News Council still was far from becoming an American institution, but it no longer was facing sudden collapse. With the outbreak of a series of attacks in which small but fanatical propaganda groups held hostages to force publicity for their point of view, the Council in 1977 drew up a set of voluntary guidelines to be followed by the media in such cases. These included self-restraint, cautions against telephoning for interviews with terrorists or hostages, warnings against unedited live TV coverage and appeals for greater cooperation with the authorities. What effect this had was problematical.

CRIME REPORTERS

Crime reporters spend their days—or nights—covering the patient and unspectacular routine of police work. Except on a big break, heroics are not for them. Nor are they often singled out for attention. They do the job to which they are assigned—asking questions, checking facts, refusing to be rebuffed by unsympathetic officials, working in teams with other staff members on occasion. And, when the office is impressed with a tip or a lead they turn in, they get their big chance as investigative reporters.

A Question of Status The old-time police reporter was a king in his little world. Often, he took on the protective coloration of a cop—even talked like a cop. Some became cops.

Today, crime reporters have varied backgrounds and all but the few surviving old-timers are reasonably well educated. In a single office unit at or near police headquarters, one may also find a sociologist turned journalist, a reporter with degrees in both journalism and law, and a specialist in criminology from Harvard. Nor is it any longer strange to find women covering police news or the courts.

Crime reporters, by reason of their achievements, have long outgrown their ranking among the lower orders of journalism. They have achieved prison reforms in several states, the impeachment of a federal judge in Illinois, the imprisonment of a federal judge in New York, the exposure of tax frauds in the Bureau of Internal Revenue, of a veterans' land grant in Texas and of many other instances of wrongdoing. They have, in illustrious cases, freed the innocent and wrongfully convicted from cells in Death Row. And they have precipitated investigations that exposed wholesale corruption in the police departments of some of the nation's larger cities.

For their achievements, they have won the highest prizes that journalism has to offer. But some have paid dearly for their initiative and their bravery by being subjected to savage attacks. In 1926, Don Mellett was murdered in the midst of a campaign, which he was conducting in the *Canton* (Ohio) *Daily News* as its editor, to expose links between police and criminals. In more recent years, Don Bolles, reporter of the Arizona Republic of Phoenix, was fatally injured when his car was destroyed by a bomb in downtown Phoenix. When he died on June 13, 1976, he was involved in a major investigation of the underworld; subsequently, the slaying became a political issue.

HOW CRIME REPORTERS WORK

It isn't always simple for crime reporters to look at police records. As an entirely practical matter, conniving police who have something to hide may make it difficult for an aggressive journalist to examine their work. Laws and practices vary from state to state. Where there are "Sunshine laws" that open records to the public and provide for open meetings of governmental bodies, easy access is provided to certain police files but by no means all of them. Elsewhere, contrary practices exist and the courts are not always cooperative.

The federal government's own "Sunshine law," approved in the fall of 1976 and signed by President Ford, lends Congressional support to the concept of open meetings and open records with certain exceptions. For while the law obliges about 50 federal boards and agencies to conduct much of their business in public, confidentiality is maintained over matters including defense and foreign policy, internal personnel data, private commercial material, criminal and other law enforcement information and data that might invade an individual's privacy.

Reporters, therefore, conduct themselves as their situation requires. Only a few places remain in the nation where a handful of police reporters, ganging together, are permitted to bottle up police news as their exclusive province. The universality of police radio communications broke up that monopoly.

Communications As a result, crime reporters have greater access today to direct reports of law enforcement agencies than they have ever had before. Except in places where listening in on police short wave radio bands is illegal in theory, reporters with a basic knowledge of police and fire alarm codes can keep in touch by using their radio scanners. The interlocking nature of local, state and federal police work also gives reporters more sources.

It is not unknown for an angry local police offical to disclose what the FBI is doing on a case, and vice versa. And the state police, being in the middle, usually have a fair notion of what is happening. In any event, the reporter no longer is dependent on the scrawled police slip. Although few police departments officially welcome the press to their communications rooms, reporters do manage to wangle access to so critical an information source in many places when a major crime story is breaking. But there is still no substitute for actually being where the action is.

Dealing with the Police The first things any reporter must know about the police department are its organization, its regulations, its relationship to other city departments and its point of contact with allied peace-keeping organizations in the state and federal government.

Whether the department is large or small, one official is usually designated to handle the news media. Sometimes it is the chief or commissioner himself, but more often it is a former newspaperman who is known as a secretary, an executive assistant, or some other title covering his public-relations role. Such an official can be helpful, if he is permitted to be, but he also is likely by the nature of his office to withhold more news than he issues.

It is necessary for reporters to protect themselves by maintaining good relationships with other officials who will, for a variety of motives, give them information or check facts. The more reporters know about police organizations, the easier it will be for them to acquire such sources.

Mere procedural knowledge of police routine is never enough. Reporters must also know the substance of criminal law, which varies by terminology and statute in most states, so that they can properly describe police activity. For example, a felony, which is a serious offense, may cover certain types of crime in one state but the same crimes may be called misdemeanors, relatively minor offenses, in another.

Most professional police and court reporters have an excellent practical knowledge of the law, and some even have law degrees. It is virtually impossible to cover police and court news intelligently without acquiring a basic legal background.

THE CRIME STORY

The crime story with universal appeal is likely to attract wide attention, regardless of the status of persons involved and their situation in life. The marital tragedy, the family feud, the kidnaping of children, the search for missing girls and so many other familiar situations therefore receive daily coverage in large or small degree.

Like all other news, there are rough measurements for the importance of crime material. A crime involving persons of prominence, social position, or notoriety is bound to receive attention. Events in better sections of the city are likely to draw reporters to the scene. Spectacular murders, shootings, stabbings, fist fights, or suicides, large monetary losses in robberies or swindles involving property of value all fit into the Page 1 news patterns. So do the tricky crimes and their clever solutions, the eternal build up of mystery and suspense, the drama of unusual arrests, the questioning of prisoners, confrontations and confessions.

The search for the unusual and the unexpected, which is not often rewarded, has in effect created its own type of cliche news situations.

In fact, the very frequency with which the unusual is exploited dulls the attention of the public for the significant case of the well-trained boy who somehow went wrong or the socially prominent girl who is found murdered in a tenement basement. In such matters, reporters must exercise a rare sensitivity and patience if they are to put together the background of the story. It has been done, and it has won prizes, but too often the research has proved to be too troublesome either for news organizations or reporters, often both. In any case, many of the symbol clusters around the crime story deserve to be given painstaking review by the American news media.

The Drama of the Usual The looting of small homes, the snatching of women's pocketbooks, the rumbles between gangs of juvenile delinquents and the small-time offenses of prostitution and gambling and the petty racketeering that flows from them are the commonplaces of crime in American life. Taken individually, they merit but a few lines, if anything at all, in the average paper and no mention at all in the broadcast media. It is the usual run of crime material — routine — uninteresting by old-fashioned editorial standards.

Yet these seemingly small events touch the lives of more people than headline crimes. In many communities, home robberies have outstripped the ability of the police to cope with them and have caused a steep rise in insurance rates. In the nation's largest cities the purse-snatcher and sneak thief are so common that most women and old people fear to walk alone. The rumble that is ignored by today's news media as the outburst of ill-trained and irresponsible street children becomes tomorrow's gang war. As for the streetwalker and the policy-slip salesman, the narcotics addict and the juvenile killer, they make little news by themselves, but in the mass they constitute a major social problem for the nation.

Except for broad public-service campaigns that are methodically conducted by many daily newspapers and the more public spirited broadcast journalists, the issues of inner-city decay, better protection for the home, juvenile delinquency and all the broad problems of crime prevention receive less attention than the stories of commission, detection and punishment of crime. There is not as much alertness over civil rights issues in the bulk of the American news media as there should be; nor, for that matter, is enough encouragement given to such sensitive areas as prison reform. Except when a spectacular crime occurs, a prison is convulsed by rioting or an inner city goes up in flames, crime prevention is treated as a rather dull but necessary aspect of the news.

There is no doubt that it is more difficult to gather such news and that it takes more ingenuity and imagination to develop such stories. But it is not the usual pattern of the crime story as we know it. Hamlet never consulted a psychiatrist. Sherlock Holmes was not a probation officer.

Crime reporting is likely to be broadened considerably in its scope and influence as the public accepts some of the more fundamental developments in modern urban life as a challenge for reform, and not as the kind of existence that must be tolerated indefinitely.

GUIDE TO CRIME REPORTING

Crime reporters often have to go behind the news. The following safeguards are worth following, therefore, in the coverage of the administration of justice:

Arrests It is a serious matter to report that a person has been placed under arrest. When such a report is made, the exact charge against the arrested person should be given and it should be documented by either a record or attribution to a responsible official. If such documentation cannot be obtained, the reporter had better check the facts. The person in question may not have been under arrest at all. There are euphemisms in police work such as holding someone for questioning, asking witnesses to appear voluntarily to cooperate with an investigation and similar statements which indicate the person is being detained, but may or may not be subject to arrest. In many states an arrest is not formally accomplished until a prisoner is booked. The news, in any case, must be handled with care.

Accusations It is commonly written that someone is being sought for robbery, suspected of arson or tried for murder. This is journalistic shorthand, which has gained acceptance through usage, but it is neither precise nor correct.

Persons are sought in connection with a robbery, unless a charge has actually been made, in which case they are charged with robbery. When a person is under suspicion, he is not necessarily going to be charged with a crime, and it is generally not privileged matter to indicate that suspicion is attached to any individual by name. Where the police suspect someone, but lack proof, that person may be held as a material witness — which is far different from being accused of a crime. Therefore, cases of suspicion are not usually given too extensive and detailed news treatment if no privileged material is available for use. The practice of reporting that a defendant is being *tried for murder*, while widely used, is obviously prejudicial and could be more accurately, if less dramatically, stated as "being tried on a charge of murder," or "on a murder indictment."

Confessions The use of the word *confession* to describe statements made by a person to the police or to prosecuting authorities is dangerous when it is not a matter of public record. The fact that a police chief or a prosecutor has claimed to have a confession, except in open court, may be used only at the risk of the news organization. Most press-bar voluntary agreements forbid the use of confessions until they are admitted in open court. The records are full of supposed confessions that backfired later for a variety of reasons and of persons who admitted crimes they could not possibly have committed. Unless and until it is established in fact that a person has confessed, approved procedure for reporters is to use such terms as "statement," "admission," "description," or "explanation." They convey the shade of meaning that is warranted by circumstances and do not subject the news organization to unnecessary risk.

The reporter must always remember that under the law a person is presumed to be innocent until he has been found guilty.

Investigations Certain stages of police investigations require secrecy in the public interest. This also pertains to some of the aspects of prosecutions and trials. The secrecy of the grand jury room and of a trial jury's deliberations are soundly based on public policy. Except under the most extraordinary circumstances, no reporter and no news organization have any right to interfere and few have ever attempted to do so.

Often, during the course of investigations, reporters are confined to listing the identities of witnesses who have entered or left a police station or grand jury room, if the names can be obtained. They have every right to try to interview such witnesses, if the circumstances are favorable, before and after appearances of this kind. But it is the business of the prosecution, defense lawyers and the witnesses themselves to decide whether or not they should talk.

For this reason investigations, in their earliest stages, are likely to produce a crop of speculative reports without much basis in fact unless editors insist on sounder reporting. A clever, publicity-conscious investigator can often hopelessly prejudice the positon of hostile witnesses and others who oppose him if the news media do not hold rigidly to their code of presenting both sides of the story. That is why no claim by any investigator, regardless of his position and personal prestige, should be accepted and published at face value without some effort by a reporter to determine the soundness of the statements that have been issued.

Cases of Violent Death Nowhere is there a greater tendency to jump to conclusions in the field of crime reporting than in the initial reporting of a violent death. The amateur reporter is invariably in a hurry to characterize the event as a suicide or murder when it may be an accidental death. It is advisable, therefore, to report only what is known and avoid speculation in the absence of an official verdict by a coroner, medical examiner or some other competent authority.

An apparent suicide is one of the most difficult crime stories to handle. If the police report that a man was found shot to death with a bullet in his right temple and a revolver in or near his right hand, the story should be written in exactly that way. In the case of a police finding that someone "jumped or fell" to his death, the reporter should not go beyond the facts but use that phrase. If a woman is found dead in bed with an empty bottle labeled sleeping tablets beside her, no conclusions should be drawn.

In all such cases, it is proper to note any other circumstances that have a bearing on the story, particularly as to whether notes were left. It may not always be proper to publish such notes, even if the text is made available by the police, unless the material is privileged. Moreover, unless there is a formal announcement of suicide by a responsible authority, the news account can do no more than to note that an investigation is being made to determine whether the death was a suicide.

When violent deaths occur without any indication as to whether they may be accidents, suicides, murders or combinations of all three, the story should report the indentities of the victims and the manner of their deaths. It is usually fruitless to try to unravel such a mystery in a newsroom. That is the job of the police and the prosecuting authorities. In the absence of any word from them a factual account of the event must suffice.

A murder investigation often tempts reporters to venture into realms for which their profession has not really equipped them. Because a few reporters have achieved fame through phenomenal exploits, all reporters are scarcely justified in trying to play detective when a newsworthy personage has been "done in." Not many even attempt to do so because there is simply not enough time for the routines of both journalism and police work on a fast-breaking story.

There are a few fundamentals of which reporters must take account.

The first is that police and prosecutors rarely will give them information on a silver platter. That means a tremendous amount of interviewing and research must be done in a very short time so that a coherent story may be written.

The second is that there can be no guarantee of police accuracy; in fact, an impressive body of evidence can be amassed to the contrary. That means police versions of names, addresses and other facts must be checked.

The third is that police and journalistic terminology are not necessarily identical. The legal term for a slaying is a homicide, but many news organizations loosely and incorrectly refer to such crimes automatically as murder. In a grand jury indictment the homicide eventually may be defined as first- or second-degree murder, depending on whether there was premeditation; or first- or second-degree manslaughter, depending on whether there was provocation or negligence. Manslaughter is not murder so that care must be used in defining a homicide. Indictments charging murder have been found to be deficient in the past, so that writers should be precise in their statements whenever they refer to the legal basis of any charge.

Assessment of Blame Whenever there is a fist fight, shooting or collision involving police action, it is only human to wonder what happened and who was at fault. Often only a trial can determine this; therefore, most reporters use as many versions of the incident as there are witnesses if such extensive treatment is warranted.

Such accounts begin with a statement that two men had a fist fight in a night club, or that there was a shooting match, or that two automobiles collided. The body of the story then documents the noncommittal lead, giving such versions of the event as are necessary. The attribution of documentation of this type always presents a problem for writers who want to avoid using "he said," or "she said," or "the police said" in every sentence.

There are several ways of doing this. One is to quote the various versions, if they are brief enough. Another is to write, "The police version of the incident follows," and then report it without further attribution. In any case, unless there is some official assessment of blame, it is usually not necessary for the reporter to try to act in such matters.

Identification The identification of persons in crime stories sometimes leads to trouble, no matter how carefully it is checked. Confusion of persons with identical last names, mistakes in middle initials, mixups in addresses, misspellings of names and police errors all conspire against the reporter. There is no real safety in the familiar formula, "The suspect gave his name as . . . ," or, "The prisoner was identified as. . . ." If the identification is incorrect, the reporter and the news organization are in trouble.

It is usually a good rule, in stories that warrant it, to include material showing how the identification was made — by papers in the person's possession, by friends or relatives or by other means. If there is any doubt, the reporter will find it does no harm to add a clause or even a sentence indicating that the identification was partial and remained to be checked. No news organization need regard itself as an oracle, whose word is final, when the public knows that many things are possible between the commission of a crime and the conviction of a defendant.

CIVIL DISORDER

The coverage of civil disorder imposes enormous responsibilities on journalists. On the one hand, they must exercise the greatest care not to spread rumors. On the other, they must expose themselves to danger if necessary to determine the magnitude of any street incident. But whatever they do, they must always be conscious that careless reporting or the provocative appearance of still or television cameras can cause untold harm in a tense situation, particularly in the crowded inner cores of many American cities.

The conduct of the journalist at the scene of action must be circumspect. A hard-hatted, swaggering white reporter in the center of an angry black community can provoke trouble. A television cameraman, training his instrument on a floodlighted crowd, is likely to get more action than he bargains for when fighting has broken out all around him. Nor is there any great sense in sending an armored truck bearing the name of a news organization into a trouble area. These are the things that cause the news media to be blamed for spreading disorder. Complete coverage is desirable at all times, but no one is thereby justified to put on a circuslike performance.

Restraint, such as was maintained in the face of wholesale disorders by street gangs in Detroit in 1976, is a necessity in reporting policy.

In both written and oral reports of any incident, every effort should be made to arrive at accurate evaluations. An isolated act of vandalism, or a street fight between two boys in the midst of a crowd, must not be called a race riot. And if shooting is heard in a crowded neighborhood at night, it is not automatically "sniper fire" until an investigation determines that snipers are at work. Nor are all fires the work of arsonists. Looting, too, should be carefully defined. Great damage can be done if radio, television and published wire service and newspaper reports exaggerate a few small incidents. Consequently, in the early stages of any civil disorder, the basic rule is to work and report with the greatest restraint.

Necessarily, once a news organization's editors have evidence to show that they are dealing with a riot of major proportions, there is no justification for not making a complete report available to the community at large. When reporters see arsonists setting fires and looters carrying merchandise from wrecked stores, these things must be communicated. Yet, the need for restraint and patient inquiry cannot be abandoned even in such circumstances. For when shooting breaks out, the reporter is never justified to leap to conclusions that all the damage is being done by demonstrators or that race is aligned against race. Jittery police and National Guardsmen have been known to fire away at almost anything that moves, sometimes with unfortunate results.

These precautions, which are the product of experience in the coverage of civil disorders, have been incorporated into a number of informal arrangements between the press and the authorities. The oldest is the Chicago plan, which seeks to keep a lid on news of a disorder until it is under control, something that is not always practical. Another procedure, followed in St. Louis, makes a police information center responsible for the clearance of all factual information before it is used by the news media. In Omaha, an attempt has been made to wait at least 30 minutes before broadcasting or publishing news of a disturbance. In addition, a number of individual news organizations have set up their own special instructions of a precautionary nature.

But regardless of how careful journalists may be, it is inevitable that they will be criticized for covering a riot. One of the most pervasive of all prehistoric tribal customs was to kill the messenger who brought bad news, a feeling that still exists in the advanced civilization of today. Journalists, in consequence, must do the best they can. If there is any balm for them in their difficult and even precarious situation, it is the judgment of an Indian journalist who said after the assassination of President Kennedy: "There is one thing of which we can be sure about the United States. Whatever happens there, good or bad, everybody is going to know it and nobody is going to be able to keep it a secret."

WRITING THE NEWS

Variations in the handling of news of violence, rioting and crime in the American news media are illustrated in the following leads, which point up the newer aspects of the problems of reporting in this area.

Tragedy at Kent State One of the most emotional events of recent years occurred on May 4, 1970 at Kent State University, Kent, Ohio, when National Guardsmen fired into an antiwar demonstration on the campus. Under great pressure, the staff of the *Akron Beacon Journal* accurately reported the tragedy as it developed and the story was written with remarkable restraint in the newsroom twelve miles away. Here is the beginning of the account that won a Pulitzer Prize for the *Beacon Journal* staff:

> KENT—Four persons were killed and at least 11 others shot as National Guardsmen fired into a group of rock-throwing protesters at Kent State University today.
>
> Three of the dead were tentatively identified as:
> William Schneider, Jeffrey Miller and Allison Krause.
> The fourth was an unidentified girl.
> Injured were:
> Dean Mahler, Thomas Grace, Joe Lewis, John Cleary, Alan Canford, Rob-

ert Stamp, Dennis Brackenridge, Doug Wrentmore and Bill Hersler. Two of the nine are National Guardsmen.

Six of those taken to Robinson Memorial Hospital suffered gunshot wounds. Three were in critical condition.

Gunshots rang out about 12:30 P.M., half an hour after Guardsmen fired tear gas into a crowd of 500 on the Commons, behind the university administration offices. Demonstrators hurled rocks and tear gas grenades back as they scattered.

A newspaperman, an eyewitness to the shooting, said the gunshots were fired after one student hurled a rock as guardsmen were turning away after clearing the Commons.

"One section of the Guard turned around and fired and then all the Guardsmen turned and fired," he said.

According to the witness, some of the guardsmen were firing in the air while others were firing straight ahead.

Guardsmen and police immediately cordoned off all buildings on the campus, permitting no one to enter or leave.

The shooting broke out after students had rallied on the Commons in defiance of an order not to assemble. An officer in a jeep ordered them over a loudspeaker to disperse. He begged them to break up "for their own good." The protesters laughed and jeered. The troops, wearing gas masks, then began to launch canisters of tear gas.

The troops were en route back to their original positions when about 20 students, both boys and girls, ran toward them from behind Taylor Hall.

Stones and sticks fell on the troops and obscenities filled the air.

Apparently without orders the guardsmen turned and aimed their M–1 rifles at the charging students and began firing . . .

Civil Strife: Busing The opening of school, once a pleasant routine, became a nightmare for some cities in the nation during much of the 1970s. In consequence, the news media were obliged to take undue care not to inflame public sentiment. Often, in cities like Boston, Louisville and Pontiac, Michigan, there were riotous conditions that could have gotten out of hand if the news media had acted in a less responsible manner.

What happened in Little Rock was only a foretaste of what was to occur in the north. But just as the *Arkansas Gazette* pointed the way to sanity and responsibility in Little Rock, so did the *Boston Globe* handle a school problem that was potentially more explosive.

After the Boston and Louisville crises, the latter in 1975, there was a disposition among newspapers to begin preparing a community well in advance to accept court-ordered school busing as long as it remained the law. Looking to the desegregation of Milwaukee's schools, for example, the *Milwaukee Journal* began massive coverage of desegregation plans months in advance. The following was the beginning of one such story in what amounted to an aggressive campaign in 1976 to inform the public of a necessary but unpleasant development:

> Something more than desegregation may come from the efforts of citizens involved in developing plans for racial balance in the Milwaukee public schools.
>
> Across the city, hardly a day goes by without some group gathering to discuss desegregation plans. There are the high school cluster committees, the Committee of 100, the subcommittees.
>
> The cluster committees are at the center of the action. The Committee of 100 members was elected from the clusters and reports back to them. Cecil Brown, cochairman of the Committee of 100, and chairman of the Lincoln Cluster Committee, said he was optimistic about the work being done.
>
> "Parents and children are having, for the first time, an opportunity to have an input into the school system," Brown said . . .

This calm, routine approach to the problem in the news columns, almost mundane in its absence of rhetoric and dramatic appeal, had the desired result. When Milwaukee's desegregated schools opened in the fall of 1976, there was no disorder.

In Louisville, too, massive straight news coverage paid off to a greater extent than desperate editorial appeals to reason in the community. Unlike the clashes of opposing groups over busing in 1975, the opening of school became almost a routine report in 1976 for the *Louisville Courier-Journal* — except that it led the paper:[9]

> Despite boycott calls by antibusing leaders, Jefferson County's 165 public schools opened yesterday with what officials described as "close to normal" enrollment.
>
> They expect 117,000 students to enroll this year, and 94,548 of them — about 81 per cent — showed up as classes opened for the second year of school under a court-ordered desegregation plan.
>
> Superintendent Ernest C. Grayson said at an afternoon press conference, "It is really gratifying to us to know that the community is supporting its schools, that students are in the schools. It reflects a lot of hard work on our part."
>
> Another factor he cited was a statement adopted by both antibusers and probusers pledging to "work to find a peaceful means to achieve the best possible education."
>
> The statement, endorsed by 42 individuals identified with a wide variety of organizations, was read at a press conference by Robert DePrez, chairman of the National Organization to Preserve and Restore Our Freedom (NAPF), and Lyman Johnson, president of the local chapter of the National Association for the Advancement of Colored People (NAACP).
>
> Attendance at almost all of the schools rose dramatically from the first day of school last year when busing for the purpose of desegregation began.

[9] *Milwaukee Journal*, 17 May 1976, p. 1, sec. 2; *Louisville Courier-Journal*, 2 September 1976, p. 1.

On September 4, 1975, only about 55,000 students went to class. That was fewer than half of the 122,000 expected to enroll. Antibusers also had called for a student boycott for the first three days of school last year.

School officials also were generally encouraged by yesterday's transportation effort. The morning movement of students throughout the county was described as "absolutely beautiful" but problems set in during the afternoon . . .

© 1975 The *Courier-Journal*

A Narcotics Inquiry The illicit use of narcotics is so much in the news today that it becomes a routine part of the work of the crime reporter in very short order. The problem is to take it out of routine, to make it the vital and significant issue that it really is. Donald L. Barlett of the *Philadelphia Inquirer*, did exactly that in a thorough investigation of what happened to arrests in narcotics cases. This is the beginning of his series:

Philadelphia police have logged tens of thousands of man-hours the last two years investigating more than 8,000 suspects in narcotics cases as part of a growing crackdown on drug abuse.

Yet, a two and one-half-month *Inquirer* study has found that two of every three persons arrested for violating state drug laws were either acquitted or the charges were dropped.

And one of every two persons indicted at the request of the district attorney's office was either found innocent or the charges were dismissed.

In 8,411 narcotics cases handled by Municipal Court during 1969 and 1970, there were 3,351 acquittals, 224 convictions, and 4,636 defendants were held for grand jury action.

Of 5,280 defendants who were brought to trial on narcotics charges in the last two years in Common Pleas Court, 2,589 were found guilty — a conviction rate of 49 per cent.

The high percentage of acquittals in Philadelphia stems from:

— A large number of bad arrests by police. A bad arrest is one the officer knows, or should know, is improper and will not stand up in court.

— The failure of the district attorney's office to screen out bad cases, including those involving small amounts of marijuana, and dispose of them in Municipal Court rather than press for indictments.

These are a few of the findings to emerge from the *Inquirer's* investigation . . .

SEX CASES AND OBSCENITY

The obscenity issue became a major legal battleground in the latter part of the 1970s because of the ruling of the United States Supreme Court that "community standards" were to be used in assessing obscene materials.

The Miller Decision The "community standards" were set up in the case of *Miller* v. *California* on June 21, 1973. In the same case, the Supreme Court denied the protection of the First Amendment to a work, taken as a whole, if it was found to (1) appeal to prurient interest, (2) exceed the standards of candor in depicting sexual matters, and (3) be "utterly without redeeming social value" or serious literary merit.

Accordingly, Larry Flynt, the publisher of *Hustler* magazine, was convicted in Cincinnati in 1977 and sentenced to 7 to 25 years in jail for "pandering obscenity and engaging in organized crime." The "organized crime" offense was under a state law which specifies that five or more persons who violate the law together are acting as "organized" criminals. Flynt appealed, creating widespread interest in his case.

Flynt's conviction followed two others that also were based on the Miller ruling. In one, Harry Reems, the co-star of the movie "Deep Throat," was found guilty in Memphis, Tennessee, of conspiracy to transport obscene material—the film itself—across state lines, but the conviction was upset on appeal. In the other, Al Goldstein, the publisher of a magazine called *Screw*, was convicted in Wichita, Kansas. The latter appeal, too, was a test of the "community standards" procedure set up by the Supreme Court and of the validity of withholding First Amendment protection from allegedly obscene publications.[10]

Attitudes toward Sex Cases A distinction obviously must be made between the so-called skin magazines such as *Playboy, Penthouse, Hustler, Screw* and the rest of that lot, on one side, and the bulk of the American news media, on the other. Most newspapers and news magazines today have a relatively liberal attitude in the handling of sex cases up to a point. Editors can scarcely forget that their publications go into the home and that the government always has the right, particularly under the "community standards" ruling, to clamp down on borderline material sent through the mails.

Consequently, there is a certain amount of restraint in the use of sex news in the print media. The rules of good taste generally are the guideline—and that, of course, depends on the responsible editor.

What Is the Borderline? There was a lot of editorial soul-searching in both print and broadcast media when the White House romances of Presidents Franklin D. Roosevelt and Kennedy became known, followed by the Congressional sex scandals. The downfall of Representative Wilbur D. Mills, following his involvement with a dancer known as the Argentine firecracker, and the retirement of Representative Wayne L. Hays, as a result of allegations by a secretary—which he de-

[10] Ted Morgan, "The U.S. vs. the Princes of Porn," *New York Times* Magazine, 6 March 1977, p. 15 *et seq.*, and Richard Neville, "Has The First Amendment Met Its Match?" in the same issue, p. 18. See also Thomas L. Emerson, "The System of Freedom of Expression" (New York: Random House, 1970), Chapter 13, Obscenity, p. 467 *et seq.*

nied—that she had been put on the payroll to be his mistress, caused many an editor to wonder how far the news media could really go in delving into an office-holder's private life.

This was the borderline, as described by Benjamin C. Bradlee, executive editor of the *Washington Post*:

"If it does not impinge on their public duties, what they do is their own business."

Alan L. Otten of the *Wall Street Journal* added:

"Many a reporter who feels he can't make a flat-out charge may still strongly suggest what he considers to be the case.

"He won't call the Senator a drunkard but simply tell how the Senator slurs his words or stumbles around the Senate floor. He may not say a prominent political figure has a mistress, but simply report how often the two are seen dining together at posh restaurants.

"Yet the general press rule remains that even politicians are entitled to have their private misdeeds ignored so long as their official activities aren't suffering."

Louis D. Boccardi, as executive editor of the Associated Press, laid down these guidelines in sex cases for all staffers as criteria for using a story or passing it up:

1. Satisfy ourselves that the activity impairs or conflicts with a public official's public responsibility.
2. Satisfy ourselves that there is some documentation beyond an anonymous charge or even a named source of doubtful reliability.
3. Give the item, if we carry it, no more than the prominence it merits and not let that judgment be influenced by the climate surrounding the Hays case.
4. Tell a member (of the AP) who asks for a story, we've decided to pass, that we don't see any news in it. But if the member wants it, give it to him on a one-point basis by whatever means is feasible.
5. Always give the accused a chance for comment on the charge before we move the story.
6. When in doubt about the merits, consult the General Desk (in New York) before moving anything.[11]

Obscenity in the News As for obscenity, the practice varies from the sedate newspaper of record to the alternative press (once called the underground press) and the more juvenile college newspapers. All editors, regardless of what they do or do not print, are agreed that obscenity is

[11] Bradlee quoted on the Merv Griffen Show, Channel 5, New York, July 5, 1976; Otten, quoted in *Wall Street Journal*, June 10, 1976, p. 16, and Boccardi, quoted in AP *Log* (28 June 1976), p. 1.

a part of the permissive spirit of the era. Nor is there any obscene word or expression that is not perfectly well known to the vast majority of the public. In consequence, there is no attention-getting value in obscenity; nor, for that matter, does any shock value exist. The determining factor for the use of obscenity in print journalism, in consequence, becomes a matter of whether it is necessary for an understanding of the news.

When the White House tapes became public during the Congressional Watergate inquiry, most editors decided to use President Nixon's obscenities without resorting to deletions marked by coy dashes. This was, by all odds, a matter of public policy. The reasoning behind it was that the public had a right to know how the President viewed his responsibilities and what kind of language he used in addressing his subordinates.

It usually takes that kind of high drama to persuade most major newspapers to open their columns to obscenities on more than a one-word basis. But even today, one four-letter word may be too much for a newspaper owner to countenance, for one reason or another. The editor and publisher of the *Dayton* (Ohio) *Journal Herald* was obliged to submit his resignation in 1975 because he twice permitted the use of an obscene epithet on Page 1. It was apparently part of the motivation for the fatal shooting of one federal agent by another. However, the Cox Newspapers refused to accept that explanation and engaged a new publisher.[12]

During the 1976 Presidential campaign, rough language in general and obscenity in particular gave numerous editors a difficult time. Some of Jimmy Carter's rough language in his celebrated *Playboy* interview, given while he was campaigning, was widely printed and used on the air. But when President Ford obliged Secretary of Agriculture Earl Butz to resign for telling an obscene story that unjustly reflected on black people, only a few papers of general circulation used the actual quotation. It was considered too offensive.

Aside from these instances, the bulk of the press appears to have overcome much of its traditional reticence. Homosexuality is written about frankly and at length. Prostitution is not disguised by vague terms. Rape is a crime and it is described as such, not as a "statutory offense" or "criminal assault" or similar euphemism of earlier years. In matters of public health, in particular, there is a directness of approach that is welcome and long overdue. It would be a prissy editor, indeed, who would disguise syphilis and gonorrhea today by calling them "social diseases." Moreover, the columns of the press are full of information about the "pill," its advantages and its risks, as well as other contraceptives that are useful in planned parenthood.

---

[12] ASNE *Bulletin* (May/June 1975), p. 23.

True, an old-fashioned newspaper may still be found that calls homosexuals "abnormal persons" and tries to clean up a sordid sex case with fancy writing. But generally, the press no longer is edited for the "Old Lady from Dubuque." Television may have more difficulty getting over its hangups in this area.

Chapter 23
The News Media and the Courts

It has never been easy to reconcile the First Amendment's guarantee of a free press and the Sixth Amendment's equally strong assurance of the right of a fair trial. And yet, it is clear enough that the framers of the Constitution intended both rights to coexist. There have been excesses on both sides—shameful publicity circuses by the news media and unnecessary secrecy by the courts. But the judicial fear of prejudicial publicity and the editorial concern over possible miscarriages of justice cannot be shrugged off despite that. These problems are very real and must be faced case by case and day by day.

THE BACKGROUND

As long ago as the treason trial of Aaron Burr in 1807, Chief Justice John Marshall worried that it would be difficult to select an unbiased jury in view of the widespread publicity against the defendant, led by President Thomas Jefferson. The great Marshall took extraordinary measures in questioning two panels of prospective jurors in Virginia to insure lack of bias. But with Burr's acquittal, the examination of the problem of prejudicial publicity became unnecessary.

Despite the intensely partisan character of the press in the early years of the republic, there were relatively few instances in which the press complicated the work of the courts. Nor did the Supreme Court find the issue worth considering. It was in fact not until 1931 that the high court took a stand against prior restraints on publication in Near v. Minnesota.

There had, however, been numerous cases in which the press contributed to a carnival atmosphere in the courts. During the opening two decades of the twentieth century, there was a great deal of hoopla over such cases as the trial of Harry K. Thaw for the murder of the architect, Stanford White; the Hall-Mills trial and the Snyder-Gray trial. But it was not until the trial of Bruno Richard Hauptmann for the murder of the infant son of Charles and Anne Lindbergh in 1935 in Flemington, New Jersey, that the news media burst all reasonable bounds. The sensational press dominated the proceedings with scant regard for the rights of the defendant. Celebrities surged in and out of the courtroom and photographers plied their trade everywhere. And the elderly trial judge and the opposing attorneys did nothing to maintain order. Nor was any appeal filed on the basis of prejudicial publicity after Hauptmann's conviction.

The only thing that happened as a result of the Hauptmann trial was the adoption of Canon 35 by the American Bar Association, prohibiting picture-taking during trial proceedings. It was amended in 1962 to take account of modern conditions, giving rise to the use of artists in the courtroom and trial sketches on television and in the print media.

Canon 35 now reads:

> Proceedings in court should be conducted with fitting dignity and decorum. The taking of photographs in the courtroom, during sessions of the court or recesses between sessions, and the broadcasting or televising of court proceedings are calculated to detract from the essential dignity of the proceedings, distract the witness in giving his testimony, degrade the court, and create misconceptions with respect thereto in the mind of the public and should not be permitted.

While the canon has not been applied in all 50 states, it has been considered effective in more than half of them. It played a part in the growth of tension over the issues raised by the twin rights of free press and fair trial, as well as reversals of convictions on the ground of prejudicial publicity in the Estes and Sheppard cases. Even more important, however, was the Warren Commission report on the assassination of President Kennedy in 1963 and the subsequent murder of his alleged killer, Lee Harvey Oswald, before national television. The news media as well as the police, the report said, "must share responsibility for the failure of law enforcement which occurred in connection with the death of Oswald." That was the basis for the spreading movement by bench and bar to contain the press in reporting both police proceedings and court actions. These were some of the legal milestones:

THE BASIC DECISIONS

The Estes Case Billie Sol Estes, a Texas financier, won a reversal of his swindling conviction from the Supreme Court in 1965 because his trial in a Texas state court had been televised over his objection. Estes' term in a federal prison based on a federal mail fraud conviction was not affected, and has since been completed.

Justice Tom C. Clark, in a 5–4 decision, wrote that Estes' 1962 trial in Tyler, Texas, had prejudiced his rights because of the presence of live television in the courtroom. Thus, the defendant's eight-year state sentence was nullified and his conviction was set aside in a case that involved the sale of mortgages on nonexistent anhydrous ammonia fertilizer tanks in Texas.

"A defendant on trial for a specific crime is entitled to his day in court, not in a stadium, or a city or a nation-wide arena," Justice Clark wrote. "The heightened public clamor resulting from radio and television coverage will inevitably result in prejudice. Trial by television is therefore foreign to our system . . . The necessity of sponsorship weighs heavily in favor of televising only notorious cases, such as this one." [1]

The Sheppard Case The Sheppard reversal was even more spectacular. After Dr. Samuel Sheppard of Cleveland had served nearly ten years in prison on his 1954 conviction of a charge that he had murdered his wife, the Supreme Court in 1966 reversed the verdict. The high court held that "virulent publicity" and a "carnival atmosphere" had made a fair trial impossible. Again writing for the majority, Justice Clark warned the news media that "trials are not like elections, to be won through the use of meeting halls, radio and the newspaper."

"From the cases coming here," Justice Clark continued, "we note that unfair and prejudicial news comment on pending trials has become increasingly prevalent. Due process requires that the accused receive a trial by an impartial jury free from outside influence . . . Where there is a reasonable likelihood that prejudicial news prior to trial will prevent a fair trial, the judge should continue the case until the threat abates or transfer it to another county not so permeated by publicity." [2]

[1] *New York Times,* 8 June 1965.
[2] *New York Times,* 7 June 1966.

Dr. Sheppard was acquitted at his second trial later in 1966. He died a few years later.

Judicial "Gag Orders" The Sheppard case stimulated judges through-out the land to impose gags on the news media in courtroom proceed-ings. Sometimes, this was a serious and thoughtful effort to insure the impaneling of an impartial jury in a controversial case; at other times, judicial acts appeared to some to be arbitrary and capricious. The Re-porters Committee for Freedom of the Press calculated the movement was slow at first, with 12 such cases from 1967 through 1973. But thereafter, the roof fell in—13 gag orders in 1974, 14 in 1975 and 11 in 1976 for a total of 50 over a period of nine years. The doctrine against prior restraints on publication had been virtually set aside. Some au-thorities argued that the Supreme Court had triggered the movement in the Sheppard case decision by virtually obliging judges and defense counsel to act against the news media as insurance against a possible reversal. And NBC, in an hour-long documentary on the subject, asked, "Is the First Amendment Unconstitutional?"

There were a few judges and appeals courts that stood out against the stampede. At the insistence of the *Chicago Tribune*, the Illinois Su-preme Court relaxed the modification of stringent curbs on coverage by a trial judge in the case of Richard Speck, who was charged with mur-dering eight nurses in Chicago. And in a 1972 case, Stanley H. Fuld, then the Chief Judge of the New York State Court of Appeals, sternly rebuked a trial judge who had acted without sufficient cause to gag the press.

But the tide was running the other way. In addition to deciding what could and could not be published or broadcast in cases before them, numerous judges took to lecturing reporters, warning them and, if they refused to name the sources of information about pending pro-ceedings, sending some of them to jail for contempt of court. In one in-stance, the convicted kidnapper of Reg Murphy, then the editor of the *Atlanta Journal,* won a reversal from an appellate court in Georgia partly because Murphy's own account of his adventure was construed to be "prejudicial publicity." [3]

The Nebraska Gag Case The situation had thus reached a critical stage when a Nebraska man, Erwin Charles Simants, was arrested on October 19, 1975 and accused of murdering a family of six persons in Suther-land, Nebraska, on the previous day. Almost at once a judge put out a "protective order" to limit reporting of the case, which had included sexual assaults. On October 27, Judge Hugh Stuart of the District Court of Lincoln County, Nebraska, issued a substitute order, which was sub-

[3] *New York Times,* 1 July 1976, pp. 1 and 16.

sequently modified by the Nebraska Supreme Court. Judge Stuart was quite open about his reason for restricting the press; he didn't want to be reversed on appeal.

Although Simants was convicted of first degree murder on January 17, 1976, the court-imposed gag order on the pretrial news coverage attained national prominence and was carried to the U. S. Supreme Court by Nebraska news organizations, supported by virtually every major national journalistic body. On June 30, 1976, the high court's 9–0 decision held judicial gag orders unconstitutional except in rare cases and maintained the court's historic position against prior restraints on publication. The Nebraska gag order was struck down. Citing the court's position in the Near and *New York Times* cases, Chief Justice Burger wrote in the majority opinion:

> The thread running through all these cases is that prior restraints on speech and publication are the most serious and the least tolerable infringements on First Amendment rights.
>
> A prior restraint, by contrast and by definition, has an immediate and irreversible sanction. If it can be said that a threat of criminal or civil sanctions after publication 'chills' speech, prior restraint 'freezes' it at least for the time.
>
> The damage can be particularly great when the prior restraint falls upon the communication of news and commentary on current events . . . The authors of the Bill of Rights did not undertake to assign priorities as between First Amendment and Sixth Amendment rights, ranking one as superior to others.

The opinion also pointed out that judges had means other than "gag orders" for maintaining the right of fair trial—changes of venue, sequestration of juries and the disciplining of lawyers and other officers of the court. It was the latter measure that soon began to affect the news media, for instead of trying to gag reporters the lower courts began gagging their sources.

This was not a new development, however. The Reporters Committee for Freedom of the Press tabulated two gag orders in 1967 on prosecution and defense attorneys, but by 1975 there were 18 and the rate for 1976 was even greater.[4]

THE CONTEMPT ISSUE

Although the Supreme Court acted with dispatch to stem the flow of judicial gag orders, it did nothing whatever about the contempt citations that had been imposed on journalists who had refused to disclose their sources upon demand by trial judges. These were two cases that came before the high court in 1976:

[4] *New York Times*, 3 August 1976, p. 35.

The Fresno Four This involved a contempt conviction against four journalists of the *Fresno (California) Bee* for refusing to disclose the source of secret grand jury testimony in a bribery case. When the Supreme Court refused to intervene, Managing Editor George Gruner, ombudsman James H. Bort Jr. and reporters William Patterson and Joe Rosoto served 15 days in jail. Superior Court Judge Hollis Best in Fresno finally freed them on September 17, 1976, saying that "there is an articulated moral principle in the news media" against source disclosure and concluding, as a result, that there was "no substantial likelihood" that the newsmen would give in. He imposed a technical five-day jail term for contempt but suspended the sentences in view of the time served. The case, to quote Gruner, was "more a standoff than a victory."

The Farr Case In the case of William T. Farr, who refused to answer a judge's demand for the source of an article about the Charles Manson murder trial in the *Los Angeles Herald Examiner,* the jury already had been sequestered before the publication of the article. Nevertheless, Farr went to jail for a time because the judge had forbidden court officers to talk for publication and tried to force the reporter to say whether this order had been violated. Here, too, the Supreme Court declined to intervene and the lower courts did not press the issue. Like the Fresno Four case, it was a standoff.[5]

American journalists since John Peter Zenger's time have usually chosen to go to jail rather than give up their right to print what they conceive to be the truth. But where Zenger triumphed when a jury upheld him in his celebrated libel case, the judgment of the contempt issue has generally been fuzzy even under relatively liberal American court procedure.

There have been numerous examples in modern times. One famous case was that of Martin Mooney of the *New York American* who in 1935 refused to reveal his sources to a New York County grand jury during a gambling inquiry conducted by the paper and served 30 days in jail for contempt of court. In 1957, Marie Torre, a *New York Herald Tribune* columnist, served ten days in jail rather than reveal her source in a controversy over the singer Judy Garland. In 1966, a 20-year-old college editor, Annette Buchanan, of the University of Oregon *Daily Emerald,* was fined $300 for refusing to reveal the source of an article about marijuana smoking on the campus.

During the 1970s, it seemed as if both judges and grand juries were bent on trying to break down journalists' sources—something that would have destroyed any serious attempt at investigative reporting.

---

[5] *New York Times,* 1 July 1976, p. 17; UPI file for Saturday, 18 September 1976, on the Fresno Four case outcome.

Demands were made for journalists' notes, radio station tapes, television films and even the so-called out-takes of films — material that had not actually been used. Subpoenas were issued in numerous cases despite the various state "shield laws" that were intended to protect journalists' sources.

Branzburg v. Hayes The Supreme Court, in Branzburg v. Hayes in 1972, ruled on the issue by a 5–4 vote which held in effect that journalists had no right under the First Amendment to refuse to tell grand juries the names of confidential sources and information given to them in confidence.[6] The decision involved Paul M. Branzburg of the *Louisville Courier-Journal*, Earl Caldwell of the *New York Times* and Paul Pappas of Station WTEV, each having been cited for contempt in separate cases for refusing to disclose sources.

In the majority opinion, Justice Byron R. White held that journalists had "no First Amendment privilege to refuse to answer the relevant and material questions asked during a good faith grand jury investigation." However, he did agree that "without some protection for seeking out the news, freedom of the press could be eviscerated." There was a strong dissent by Justice Potter Stewart, who warned that the decision "invites the state and federal authorities to undermine the historic independence of the press by attempting to annex the journalistic profession as an investigative arm of the government."

In retrospect, the lower courts appear to have been governed more often by a suggestion in a concurring majority opinion filed by Justice Lewis Powell than by the sweeping White decision. What Powell held was that a grand jury would have to show a "legitimate need of law enforcement" to challenge the press's refusal to betray a source. What this amounts to, as a practical matter, is that the press is often obliged to rely on its own influence in the community to protect itself instead of seeking the sanction of law. For while more reporters went to jail after Branzburg v. Hayes, notably Peter Bridge of the *Newark* (New Jersey) *Evening News* for refusing to reveal a source to a grand jury, others got off without punishment when the courts followed Powell's dictum.[7]

In an unusual aspect of the controversy, two Louisiana reporters, Larry Dickinson and Gibbs Adams, refused to abide by a federal judge's ruling to refrain from reporting on a case in open court and were held in contempt. Although the Fifth Circuit Court of Appeals held the judge's order unconstitutional, it refused to lift the contempt citation against the reporters. When the Supreme Court in 1974 decided not to review the case, the news media were put on notice that even an unconstitutional court order must be obeyed until it is struck down. The

---

[6] *New York Times*, 30 June 1972, p. 1; *Editor & Publisher* (8 July 1972), p. 11.
[7] Anthony Lewis in the *New York Times*, 19 September 1976, IV: 1; *Columbia Journalism Review* (September/October 1972), p. 18.

high court's failure to act in the Farr and Fresno Four cases in 1976 thus was of a piece with the judicial philosophy about the relationship between the news media and the law.

Medina's Advice The omnibus gag rulings by judges drew this advice for the news media from Harold R. Medina, then in his 88th year and still a senior judge on the United States Court of Appeals for the Second Circuit:

"First, I would stand squarely on the First Amendment itself. I used to think (press–bar) guidelines might be helpful. Now, I believe them to be a snare and a delusion. And the same is true of legislation. . . . Second, I would make no compromise and no concessions of any kind. Third, I say fight like tigers every inch of the way." [8]

The Schorr Case This was precisely the line that was taken by Daniel Schorr, investigative reporter for CBS, when he risked a jail sentence for contempt of Congress on September 15, 1976 by refusing to tell a Congressional committee who had given him a secret report of the House of Representatives on U. S. intelligence activities. Schorr admitted he had given the report to the *Village Voice,* a New York weekly, which published it.

Invoking the First Amendment, Schorr said: "To betray a confidential source would mean to dry up many future sources for many future reporters. The reporters and the news organization would be the immediate losers. The ultimate losers would be the American people and their free institutions. In some 40 years of practicing journalism, I have never yielded to a demand for the disclosing of a source that I had promised to protect. But beyond that, to betray a source would be to betray myself, my career and my life. I cannot do it. To say I refuse to do it is not saying it right. I cannot do it."

A week later, the House Ethics Committee, which had summoned Schorr to testify and spent $150,000 on the investigation without identifying his sources, refused to support a contempt citation against him. Nevertheless, although CBS had stood by him to the extent of paying his legal costs and his salary while he was under suspension during the inquiry, Schorr resigned on September 28, 1976, because of what he called internal staff tensions over the affair.[9]

There was a happier outcome for another obdurate reporter, Lucy Ware Morgan of the *St. Petersburg (Florida) Times,* who for three years

---

[8] Judge Medina's advice in the *New York Times,* 30 November 1975, p. 13; judicial gag order sources include Benno C. Schmidt Jr., "A New Wave of Gag Orders," *Columbia Journalism Review* (November/December 1975), p. 33; E. Barrett Prettyman Jr., "Press Freedom: Legal Threats," *New York Times,* 22 January 1975, p. 39.

[9] Schorr's testimony in AP report for September 15, 1976; House Committee decision, report of September 22; resignation, September 28.

refused under threat of a prison term to disclose the source of her information about a grand jury inquiry into official corruption. On July 30, 1976, Mrs. Morgan was cleared of contempt by the Florida Supreme Court. The majority opinion stated: "The First Amendment is clearly implicated when government moves against a member of the press because of what she has caused to be published."

Nevertheless, it remained a risky business for a reporter to defy either Congress or the courts, or both. But when "Sunshine Laws" and other special legislation proved ineffective, it remained the journalist's only recourse.[10]

The Outlook It is clear that the conflict between the press and the courts will not soon be resolved. Out of the purest of motives, the courts will have further differences with the news media on the degree of coverage of certain cases and the news media will insist on their right to publish whatever they believe to be necessary in the public interest. These continuing tensions provide the public with the best guarantee that both fair trial and free press will be safeguarded.

True, there will be more instances in which journalists overstep the limits of rational conduct, just as there will be more cases in which judges try to halt fair coverage of proceedings in their courts. But because of the voluntary cooperation between press and bar at the working level, these extremes are far less dangerous to our democratic society on the whole today than they were in the twenties, when justice was administered too often in the manner of a three-ringed circus.

THE JUDICIAL PYRAMID

The first thing newly assigned court reporters must do to discharge their responsibilities is to acquire some understanding of the organization of the American court system. At the apex is the United States Supreme Court. To it come appeals from the federal and state appellate court systems. Within each state is a top appellate court that bears various names, such as the Court of Appeals or, again, the Supreme Court (although the name is no indication of the specific powers of the court). Depending on the size of the state's legal network, such a court may have branches.

Under these come the workhorse courts—those of original jurisdiction which may be known as superior, common pleas, circuit or other courts. (Strangely enough, in New York this workhorse court is known as the Supreme Court.) Their functions are generally the same although their jurisdictions may differ. They are the courts of first instance and, in one form or another, are responsible for both civil and criminal matters. Probate courts handle wills.

[10] *Columbia Journalism Review* (November/December 1976), p. 8.

If the case load is very great, separate criminal courts may be formed. They may be called by such names as General Sessions, Oyer and Terminer or simply County Courts. Other specialized courts may hear divorce actions. But regardless of how they are organized, courts of original jurisdiction are courts of record, and cases brought before them are privileged as to publication.

On the lowest rung of the judicial ladder are the inferior courts of limited jurisdiction, which may or may not be courts of record. In a county subdivision a justice of the peace may preside over them. In cities the inferior criminal courts are often Police Courts or Magistrates' Courts. The inferior civil courts, sometimes known as "Poor Men's Courts" because they are supposedly less expensive for litigation, are called City or Municipal Courts and handle cases with judgments limited to a fixed sum, anywhere from $3,000 to $6,000.

There is one new development in the continued proliferation of this court system. Where police judges or magistrates once sat without a jury to handle all minor offenses and bind over prisoners in major cases for possible grand jury action, various cities have created many new types of such inferior courts. Among them are family courts for domestic arguments, adolescents' or children's courts for a variety of cases including juvenile delinquency, and traffic courts where defendants line up by the hundreds to pay fines meekly without any practical chance of saying more than "guilty" or "not guilty."

This crowded judicial ladder of localities and states is roughly paralleled by the less numerous but even more powerful system of federal courts which handle everything from income-tax cases to violations of the Mann Act. From the arraignment proceedings presided over by a United States Commissioner, the judicial authoriy extends upward through the district courts and the various appellate courts to the highest court in the land.

A nation governed by laws, not men and women, has need of many courts, each with a different jurisdiction, each with a line of appeal to a higher court.

What Is Covered The sheer numbers of the courts in the land, their differing functions, and the intricate pattern of local, state and federal jurisdictions provide the best reason for the spot coverage of court news by a large section of the press. In New York City alone, for instance, there are about 300 judges and official referees, who assist them, plus about 3,500 clerks, attendants and other staff workers. By contrast, the entire federal judiciary consists of about 400 judges and some 11,000 other court officers and employees.

The national average for court delays in bringing a case to trial is 30 months, with the worst showing in Chicago where it takes 69 months on the average. Moreover, with new cases coming in at the rate of 8,000 a year in a populous area like New York County, there is little hope that anything will be done to ease the heavy burden of the courts. With two-thirds of all civil cases classified as liability actions, the cause of the tie-up is clear. It can take years in some jurisdictions, to obtain justice.

Such delays in themselves are bound to detract from public interest in all but the most significant and dramatic cases. The pressure of events is very great, and the public memory is lamentably short. It follows that very large areas of civil-court procedures and others of minimal public interest are normally left uncovered, despite their importance. Few newspapers can afford to tie up reporters on long trials that yield little of interest for the news columns.

The emphasis of the news media, therefore, is on criminal courts, matrimonial cases in the civil courts and occasional other ventures such as the coverage of important wills or contests in the probate or surrogates' courts, or the criminal proceedings in the federal courts. Of all the courts in the land, the U. S. Supreme Court is given the broadest and most comprehensive coverage because of its tremendous impact on the states, especially in such matters as integration and other issues affecting civil liberties.

Court Reporting With the decline of the "beat" system of reporting, the numbers of veteran court reporters have been dropping steadily. On many papers there are only one or two reporters at most who spend their days in the courts, and on a growing number of other papers court assignments are given to general-assignment reporters as stories warrant it. The broadcast media cover courts on a firehouse basis.

When a reporter was assigned to the courts and told to develop contacts with lawyers, judges and prosecutors, it was a fruitful area for the gathering of news. Those who still practice it, to the exclusion of all other assignments, are relatively few in number. Over the years most of them have acquired such a wide knowledge of legal backgrounds and precedents that they are sometimes consulted unofficially by the judges whom they cover day by day. Without a continuity of coverage such individuals are bound to be rarities except where they happen to have law degrees.

For those who are assigned on occasion to cover the courts, a basic knowledge of some of the most frequently used legal terms is a must.

TERMINOLOGY

Some of the definitions of legal terms used in court reports follow:

accessory Person who assists in the commission of a crime, either before or after the fact.

action at law   Proceedings instituted to enforce a legal right.

adjournment   Request for more time to find witnesses or important evidence, or other reasons.

administrator   Appointee of a court to administer the estate of a person who has died intestate (without a will.)

affirm   Used by appellate courts to uphold a lower court decision. Failure to affirm is called a reversal.

arraignment   Process through which the prisoner hears the charges against him and pleads to them.

attachment   Authorization by the court in written form to take and hold a person or property.

bail bond   Security, usually furnished by a professional bondsman, to guarantee the appearance of an accused person in court. When a person is ordered held without bail, the seriousness of the charge is such that the court refuses to turn him loose. When a bond of $5,000 is posted, if that is the amount of bail set by the court, the usual phrasing is that the prisoner was liberated in lieu of $5,000 bail, or simply, freed on $5,000 bail.

bench warrant   Court process authorizing an official to apprehend an individual and bring him before the court.

bill of particulars   A statement setting forth the specifications in an indictment, information or complaint.

change of venue   Changing the place of trial.

codicil   Addition to a will.

commutation   Reduction of sentence.

concurrent sentence   Court decision that a convicted defendant serves only the longest of several terms imposed on him. Consecutive sentence means he serves the sum of all terms.

contempt of court   An offense against the court, punishable by a fine, jail term, or both.

consent decree   Court order to which the defendant has consented.

corpus delecti   Essence of the crime.

decree nisi   Final judgment to take effect some time in the future.

defendant   Party against whom an action has begun.

demurrer   Defense plea that the charge does not constitute a crime, or cause of action.

deposition   Taking of testimony from a witness before trial.

directed verdict   Instruction by the court to the jury to bring in a particular verdict.

double jeopardy   Plea that the defendant has already been tried for the same offense.

executor   Person named in a will to administer the estate.

extradition   Process of returning a prisoner from one state to another.

habeas corpus   Writ requiring production of a detained person in court to inquire into the legality of the proceedings.

indeterminate sentence Sentence of "not more than" a certain term, and "not less than" another term of years.

indictment Document brought by the grand jury on evidence submitted to it by the prosecutor. A bill of indictment is also known as a true bill.

information Document filed by the prosecutor under oath instead of by the grand jury.

injunction Court order requiring those named to act or to forbear in certain actions.

interlocutory decree Preliminary mandate of the court.

John Doe inquiry Inquiry by a prosecutor to obtain evidence in connection with an alleged crime.

letters rogatory Document under which a witness in a foreign jurisdiction is examined.

letters testamentary Authority issued to the executor of a will after he has qualified to permit him to perform his functions.

mandamus Court direction requiring someone to perform an act.

mandate A judicial direction.

misdemeanor Minor crime, as distinguished from a *felony*, which is a serious crime such as a homicide.

mistrial End of a trial because of an irregularity.

motion to dismiss Motion attacking the basis of the action.

nolle prosequi Also, simply *nolle pros*; determination not to proceed with a case.

nolo contendere, or *no contest* Plea indicating that defendant will not contest the charge.

obiter dictum A judge's incidental or collateral opinion.

pardon Action by executive relieving criminal from sentence.

parole Release on pledge of reappearance at regular intervals, or on call.

plaintiff Party who initiates litigation.

pleading Document in which the plaintiff's claim or defendant's defense is set forth.

presentment Document brought by a grand jury on its own initiative or upon allegations of private citizens.

quash Motion contending an indictment is defective in form.

quo warranto Writ by which government seeks to recover an office from a public official or a franchise from a corporation.

referee Appointee of court.

replevin Writ requiring production of property.

reprieve Delay in execution of a sentence.

respondent Party against whom an appeal has been taken.

sealed verdict It is rendered in the absence of a judge, but opened by him when court reconvenes.

subpoena Court order requiring witness to appear and testify.

subpoena duces tecum Court order requiring witness to produce certain documents bearing on the case for which he must appear.

suits in equity A proceeding originally brought before a chancellor to compel a defendant to refrain from doing something or to compel him to do something.

summons Process of the court instituting an action.

veniremen Members of a panel (venire) of potential jurors, called to be examined for jury duty.

voir dire Examination of potential jurors.

writ of certiorari Writ from superior to inferior court requiring the record to be sent to the former for review.

writ of supersedas Writ by which proceedings are stayed.

Reporters cannot, of course, use all such terms and others even more complicated in a news story. They would hopelessly confuse the public. Professional practice requires each term to be briefly explained if it is used. For instance: "The defendant pleaded *nolo contendere* (no contest)." Better still, instead of using a term such as *nolle prosequi*, it may be stated as follows: "The prosecution announced it would drop the case." Except in a law journal, there is no reason to clutter up a news story with a lot of legal terminology unless the news cannot be told any other way. This procedure applies particularly to wire service correspondents and specials who cover important legal proceedings in other states for their newspaper. Pleas and other terminology that are familiar to the public in one state are not necessarily known, or even used, in adjacent states.

HOW COURTS ARE COVERED

In the coverage of courts, as in every other aspect of journalism, reporters are only as good as their sources and their knowledge of how to gain access quickly to records. The reporters who are assigned to courts by the story, rather than as a regular beat, quickly discover this to be true. No matter how clever they are and regardless of how hard they work, the veterans on the beat are bound to have many more resources.

Court Sources The key official in any court, as far as reporters are concerned, is the clerk of the court, who keeps all the records and supposedly knows where necessary documents may be found. Under the judge's authority, clerks prepare trial calendars, dockets (abstracts of cases), proceedings, judicial orders and transcripts (the latter for a fee). Clerks also receive applications, motions, fines and transact other necessary court business. They also are the ones who generally make the news media arrangements for coverage at major trials, usually in cooperation with reporters.

Every reporter covering a trial of any consequence should meet the judge, no matter how standoffish that individual may be, even though no judge is willing to act as a day-to-day news source. That function is fulfilled primarily by opposing counsel, their assistants and clerks. The matter of tracking down witnesses is something that is left mainly to reportorial initiative, as is the detailed examination of evidence. As for trial verdicts, particularly if the trial judge orders the courtroom doors closed, there is usually a lot of frantic scrambling and signaling by reporters, notably at major trials.

Prosecution and Grand Juries So much news flows from the offices of prosecutors and their investigators that reporters must be constantly on guard against even an unconscious slant in their copy in the state's favor. Most reporters also make a point of knowing as many minor officials as possible—bailiffs, court stenographers, special police and the like. They learn to check court calendars daily, study the docket for new cases and maintain contact with developing cases. It is their job to keep their editors advised of pending schedules for the organization's "future book."

As for grand jury proceedings, these are secret but reporters often develop a fairly accurate notion of what is going on by talking with witnesses and the prosecuting official who submits the evidence. A grand jury, as distinguished from a trial jury, is charged with the duty of hearing evidence in connection with the commission of a crime and it decides whether to return an indictment or presentment. Often, news of such actions is withheld until those named can be arrested on bench warrants.

It should be remembered that an indictment is an accusation, drafted on the basis of one-sided evidence, and each separate charge or count must be proved in court. Everything in a grand jury action, therefore, must be heavily qualified. If the penalty for the alleged crime is given, reporters should point out that it will apply only upon conviction.

The Defense If Perry Mason never lost a case and the opposing prosecutors never won one, it doesn't really matter very much. The fiction is as harmless as much of television's portrayal of legal talent, and as unrealistic. For most defense attorneys today have a difficult time. On the one hand, if their client is to have any claim on the public sympathy, they must find some way of calling the case to public attention. But on the other, they must be constantly on guard against arousing the ire of the trial judge by disclosing certain kinds of information outside the courtroom. In this unhappy and difficult situation, the burden on the defense is much greater than the prosecution, in most cases. Additionally, when the defense keeps its intentions under wraps, the temptation sometimes arises for reporters to trade information with the prosecution. This kind of journalistic conduct is unethical. Confidences given to reporters are supposed to be inviolate; in the few cases in which reporters have sought to trade tips between defense and prosecution, they have only brought discredit on the news media.

Criminal Procedures In newsworthy cases, reporters generally follow the action from the time the investigation begins. Once an arrest is made, the defendant is arraigned and states his plea. If the lower court has jurisdiction, as in the case of a misdemeanor, the case may be disposed of with a brief hearing; otherwise, it is bound to be postponed. If the court acts to bind over the defendant pending grand jury action, bail is usually set.

When the prosecution has sufficient evidence, grand jury action may be expected quickly. But where the prosecution is having its troubles, or where evidence must be assembled over a long period, months may pass before the grand jury acts. Naturally, if the grand jury fails to act, the defendant is freed. But if the grand jury returns an indictment, the defendant then must be arraigned again to plead to the specific charge and the question of bail is reopened.

Legal strategy begins with the arraignment in the inferior court. So many moves are open to opposing counsel and the courts that there are no set rules of journalistic procedure. Reporters simply have to cover the story, discussing vague points with both sides and attempting to talk with the defendant as well as the lawyers. In some cases it helps to talk with impartial legal sources—lawyers or even judges not connected with the case at hand. It is usually done on a background basis, mainly for the reporter's benefit.

Civil Proceedings Matrimonial suits, actions for damages and occasional petitions in bankruptcy or receiverships are of primary interest to newspapers in civil proceedings. The field of civil law is so great, and complications within states so numerous, that any general plan of procedure would be riddled with exceptions.

A brief outline of the system of law will show why this is so. Civil law, as distinguished from criminal law, may be divided into actions at law and suits in equity. Actions at law deal primarily with property and with personal matters such as damage suits and enforcement of contracts. Suits in equity are brought to compel or bar action. Foreclosures and receiverships are also covered by equity proceedings. Many states have abolished the distinction between actions at law and suits in equity, which is a complicating factor.

Even lawyers of experience, venturing into branches of civil law with which they are not familiar, cheerfully confess that they have to look up considerable material. It is, therefore, mandatory for a reporter not only to have a law dictionary handy, but also to obtain sufficient technical background whenever he is assigned to a particular civil suit.

Sometimes reporters know of civil actions before they are filed through tips from friendly lawyers or court attaches. In any case, by looking over the clerk's docket they can find any complaint, or petition that has been filed in a civil action. They need only its serial number and a helpful official to look up the original petition and get the story from it.

Civil suits begin with the filing of the complaint, but in some states the mere act of filing does not constitute privilege. Once the petition is brought before a judge, however, it becomes a part of a judicial proceeding and is thereby privileged. The issue cannot come to trial, however, until the defendant files his answer and legal skirmishing in the form of pleadings is concluded. As has been pointed out, all this may take many months. The lapse of time and the legal technicalities thereby conspire to limit the news value of many civil actions. They may, in due course, be settled out of court and noted in the record. In major law suits lawyers announce such settlements, but the "run-of-the-mill" civil actions come and go with few except those directly concerned being the wiser.

Covering civil actions involves mainly covering lawyers. And since the pleadings are usually technical and what lawyers say outside court is not privileged, there are probably no more than three news stories in the average civil suit — when it is filed, when it is answered and when a settlement or verdict is made known.

Matrimonials The exception, of course, is the matrimonial action. Newspapers that specialize in them must also be wary of libel suits, since a lawyer may prepare a sizzling complaint for a wife in a divorce suit without knowing that she is, at that moment, about to be reconciled with her husband. Suits for divorce, annulment, separation and alienation of affections are, like crime news, popular with the commercial press. However, they are not particularly popular with reporters who cover them because of the very real difficulty in obtaining material that is privileged and fair to both sides. When the law permits still further complications, such as the sealing of papers in a divorce action, then the use of news of such suits becomes impossible until the trial begins.

It is, therefore, a matter of considerable risk to use an item about a divorce suit or separation involving prominent persons; only in Reno or other jurisdictions that cater to matrimonials can a reporter consider that such work is ever as simple as it seems.

TRIAL STORIES

An outline of the coverage of criminal trials, especially those that attract considerable public attention, may be based at least in part on the various stages of the proceedings. These form the framework for the drama and rising tension of the trial.

Criminal Trial Steps The selection and swearing in of the jury is the first step in a criminal trial.

Then follows the opening address of the prosecutor, in which he details the crime and relates how he intends to prove the defendant guilty. The defense may follow with its opening statement or delay until the end of the prosecution's case, except is such states as New York where the defense must follow the prosecution.

The state puts on its witnesses next, with the prosecutor conducting direct examination and the defense cross-examining. Redirect and recross-examination are permitted, if requested.

When the state's case concludes, the defense always asks for a direct verdict of acquittal on the ground that the charges have not been proved. The court usually denies such requests.

The defense's case follows. Its witnesses go through direct and cross-examination, as have those of the state.

Both sides then may put on rebuttal witnesses.

The summing up follows—invariably a field day for lawyers in a criminal trial. The prosecution generally speaks first, and the defense closes, each seeking to convince the jury with arguments, pleas and rhetoric. Both sides rest their case after that.

The judge then charges the jury. He sums up the law in the case, tells the jury its possible verdicts, and explains the meaning of each verdict. He emphasized that the state must have proved its case beyond a reasonable doubt.

When the jury returns to the courtroom, the foreman or forewoman announces the verdict. If it is a finding of guilt, the judge then may remand the prisoner and set a date for sentencing, or he may pronounce sentence immediately, depending on the law in the state.

Civil Trial Steps Civil trials generally follow this procedure, except that the state is not a party to the case and there may be no jury.

Opening statements are made by the attorneys for the plaintiff and the defendant, in that order. The plaintiff's case then is presented, followed by the defendant's case. Following rebuttal, closing statements are made by the plaintiff and defense. Both sides then rest their case.

A judge, sitting without a jury, generally takes the case under advisement. He may announce his decision in a law journal, or he may permit copies of the decision to be distributed to reporters. He has the option, of course, of announcing his decision as soon as the case is concluded but seldom does so in matters that are at all complicated.

Trial Coverage The basis of efficient trial coverage for the news media is preparation. And this is particularly true for the broadcast media because correspondents can't rely on the camera to tell the story for them. Like newspaper reporters, the television and radio correspondents have to work directly from the testimony as it unfolds before them. It pays, therefore, to have a handy digest of the case beforehand, including all major figures and potential witnesses, plus relevant data on opposing counsel.

Often, reporters need a sixth sense to tell them when to begin taking testimony in Q and A form. Sometimes, through a mistake in judgment, important testimony can be missed; in that event, the only recourse is for the reporter to get a colleague's notes, consult the court stenographer or find somebody who has used a tape recorder.

Sometimes, major testimony comes from persons whose names mean nothing to the public. In such instances, reporters generally say that a state or a defense witness testified to a particular point in the trial, then make the necessary identification in the third or fourth paragraph. An alternative is to describe the charge that was made at the trial, then identify the witness later in the story. Throughout, efficient reporters usually know what to expect next and they make their arrangements with their offices accordingly.

As the time approaches for the judge's charge to the jury, a brief history of the trial should be prepared if it has developed into a major news story. Once the jury retires, the history should be filed for newspaper use as B copy. Further material preceding the verdict, such as a jury's return to the courtroom for instructions, could then be sent as A copy to precede B copy. The jury verdict would, of course, constitute the lead.

Covering the Verdict There isn't much difference in the way trial verdicts are presented by the news media. The broadcast reporters, having the first break, do their reporting in the present tense, the wire services and newspapers in the past tense. But the basic information and the presentation of the story are grounded on historic journalistic practice regardless of the time difference between newspapers and their faster rivals. Here are two verdicts as covered by newspapers, giving the essential portions of the leads for comparative purposes:

The Angela Davis Trial

An all-white jury Sunday found Angela Davis innocent of all charges against her—murder, kidnaping and conspiracy stemming from the Aug. 7,

1970 Marin County escape attempt—and joyous pandemonium erupted in the courtroom.

An ecstatic Miss Davis said later, "This is the happiest day of my life!"

Court Clerk Art Vanek read the verdict of the seven-woman, five-man jury at 12:35 P.M. Moments later, after 16 months in jail cells and court proceedings that carried through more than four months, Miss Davis walked from the jammed, stuffy courtroom into the bright sunshine of freedom.

Jury Foreman Mrs. Mary Timothy handed the verdict to Vanek after the jurors had deliberated for 13 hours over a three-day period. In a quiet, measured manner, Vanek read the verdict on the first charge, kidnaping:

"We, the jury . . . find the defendant not guilty."

The expectant silence in the courtroom was broken by gasps.

Vanek read the verdict on the second charge, murder: "Not guilty."

This time, another gasp and rising murmurs came from the spectators.

Then he read the verdict on the third charge, conspiracy, "Not guilty."

The spectators responded with a roar that can only be likened to that of a baseball crowd when the home team scores the winning run in the seventh game of a World Series. The emotional reaction was so overwhelming that Judge Richard Arnason threatened to clear the courtroom.

Miss Davis, who had been listening intently, half sobbed and half laughed with relief and hugged her close friend, Kendra Alexander, a leading member of the defense committee . . .[11]   —*San Jose Mercury*

The Patty Hearst Trial

SAN FRANCISCO—Patricia Hearst was convicted by a Federal Court jury this afternoon of armed bank robbery and the use of a gun to commit a felony.

Miss Hearst had testified that she had helped a revolutionary group rob the Sunset branch of the Hibernia Bank on April 15, 1974. But she said that she had done so only under threat of death.

After hearing 66 witnesses, viewing almost 1,000 exhibits and measuring that evidence against the instructions of Federal District Judge Oliver J. Carter, the jurors refused to accept Miss Hearst's claim.

Miss Hearst seemed to shrink and her pale face became ashen as the verdict was read. Her parents, Mr. and Mrs. Randolph A. Hearst, sat ten feet away. She did not look at them.

Mrs. Hearst, who left the courtroom in tears yesterday, dropped her gaze to the floor. Mr. Hearst rubbed his forehead and stared into space.

Their daughter, Anne, 20, seated beside them, broke into tears. Two other sisters, Vickie and Mrs. Virginia Bosworth, were in court. A fourth, Catherine, was not present.

After the verdict was announced, Miss Hearst leaned toward her chief lawyer, F. Lee Bailey, and said, "I wonder if I ever had a chance."

The maximum sentence for armed robbery is 25 years in prison. For use of a firearm to commit a felony it is ten years.

The 22-year-old defendant still faces a number of felony counts in state court in Los Angeles . . .[12]

[11] *San Jose* (California) *Mercury,* 5 June 1972.
[12] *New York Times,* 21 March 1976, p. 1.

JUVENILE DELINQUENCY

The rising concern over juvenile crime is weakening the protection that has been given to children who are involved with the law in most states in the union. Instances of 13 and 14-year-old killers preying in gangs on defenseless elderly persons in large cities have outraged law-making bodies in some larger cities. In consequence, there have been moves to lower the age limit for juvenile crime from 16 to 13 or 14. This, combined with the U. S. Supreme Court's restoration of the death penalty for certain types of crimes specifically designated by individual states, raises at least the possibility that children who commit murder may be hanged or put to death in the gas chamber or electric chair.

It may not come to that. And yet, the intensity of the debate about the responsibility of juvenile criminals, habitual or not, indicates that the body of law affecting juvenile delinquents is changing, and not for the better.

Historically, under a U. S. Supreme Court decision in 1967, the nation's 3,000 juvenile courts must give children most of the procedural protections guaranteed to adults in the Bill of Rights. This means that children brought before juvenile judges in delinquency hearings must be given timely notice of the charges against them. They must also have adequate warning of their right to remain silent and not incriminate themselves. Furthermore, they must be accorded the right to have a lawyer, court-appointed if necessary, and to confront and cross-examine their accusers and other witnesses against them.

Until the upsurge of sentiment to tighten provisions for the punishment of child criminals in various states, there was relatively little hard news about juvenile delinquency. Mainly, this was attributed to legal provisions in many states that do not permit the use of names of juvenile defendants and hold juvenile court proceedings without coverage by the news media. By custom as well as law, the news media generally do not use the names of juvenile defendants. What is being done today, to a much greater extent than in the past, is to monitor the sentences that are meted out to convicted child criminals, particularly in capital crimes, and to conduct investigations into the care and treatment of delinquent children.

The time has passed when the news media can ignore the situation of the child before the law. The rise of youth gangs, with children of tender years being used to commit atrocious crimes, creates difficulties for the journalist as well as for the police and the courts. But somehow, the situation must be faced squarely and dealt with wisely if the news media are to retain their privileged status in an open society.

Part Four

INTERPRETIVE JOURNALISM

Chapter 24
Politics,
Government
and the News Media

A utility corporation proposes to build an atomic energy plant on a choice beachfront against the wishes of an outraged village. A town council struggles with the twin problems of what to do about higher taxes and the "For Rent" signs that go up with dismaying regularity in decaying "downtown." An oil terminal imposes on a thriving Long Island rural community and begins gobbling up precious farmland, so necessary to mechanized agriculture, for its ugly tanks. In the dreary hours after midnight, a state legislature worries over how to reduce the bulging welfare rolls without injustice to the helpless and the needy.

These are some of the issues with which the news media must deal in covering the story of politics and government in an expanding United States. There are many more, for the problems of a self-governing nation multiply with the continual growth and shifting of its population as well as the insistence on a good life for everybody. Some of these problems are dealt with after the laggard fashion of the democratic process; others, apparently, are insoluble and must be left to the dubious resort known as the passage of time. But over all, the telling of this complex and ever-changing story gives the news media one of their greatest challenges.

This challenge is being met in many ways. The surviving metropolitan press is pushing into the suburbs, augmenting the thriving newspapers that have sprung up there in little more than a generation. News magazines are trying to expand their services in areas where news coverage of national and international affairs is indifferent to poor. And some leading local television stations have developed a heartening commitment to the cause of good government, adding a potent force to the reporting of local affairs. All these constitute an enlarged resource in bringing the news of government to the public, with local and regional news getting the most attention and national news the least except in Presidential campaign years.

INTERPRETATION AND ANALYSIS

Basic to these changes in journalism as a profession is the development of the twin functions of interpretation and analysis of the news. The outlines of these forms of reporting—*grand reportage*, in the French press—have been apparent since the years before World War II. They are still evolving, amid trials and tests and some misgivings, out of the sound principles and procedures of the past.

There is nothing particularly revolutionary about this. Its roots go as far back into American history as the beginning of the New Deal and the inauguration of new principles in government. The telling of this story revealed the inadequacies of the deadpan news account, but with few exceptions there was no change in professional techniques until the even sterner test of World War II.

A New Concept Since World War II, many American newspapers have adopted a new concept of journalistic responsibility, more universal in its approach to public service. Television, despite its basic fear of controversy and commentary, has contributed programs of brilliance and discernment. As for the news magazines, their fault has been—in the words of a cynical professional—that they "tried to put an angle on everything, including the weather."

Under the leadership of the press, the news media as a whole have progressed. The journalism of analysis and comment has been the principal result. Basically, it seeks to explain as well as to inform. It dares to evaluate, to measure, to teach. By and large, its methods are an adaptation of some of the more practical techniques of mass communication. These are intended to produce a broader interpretation of the news of politics and government at all levels and more accurate ways of evaluating public opinion.

Those who champion this approach to the telling of the news seek to improve newspapers first, hoping the other media will emulate them and thereby help to create a better-informed electorate and better government. There are risks, of course. The public has never really understood the fine professional distinction between the work of editorial writers, columnists and reporters. Interpretive journalism is likely to blur the lines between them still more. Consequently, not all newspapers accept their broadened responsibilities for interpretation and research in public attitudes. As for the electronic media, all save the leaders shy away from it. Only the news magazines, as a group, enthusiastically practice the art in their columns even though the result is not always certain of public approval.

THE POLITICAL STORY

In the past, most news organizations got along fairly well between elections with a city hall reporter and an all-purpose political analyst. The electronic media and the news magazines, of course, left the day-by-day routine very largely to the newspapers and concentrated either on interesting personalities or key issues. The wire services did the rest.

Why Coverage Broadened Today, it is not enough to cover city halls, legislatures, and political clubhouses or headquarters for "official" news. The power of most city political machines has waned. The movement of city people to the suburbs has given rise to many new areas of government responsibility.

In the larger cities, the major newspapers long since have devoted their efforts to covering much more news of government than the political. Some of this has been done by teams, much of it by specialists. The "Metropolitan Section" has become an established part of the newspaper. And in the leading local television stations that pay attention to the needs of their communities, a few good reports in depth and documentaries have helped in the process of informing the public.

The reasons for this change in emphasis are not difficult to find. A suburban campaign for a school bond issue, for instance, can create greater turmoil in the immediate community than an election for a United States senator. An extension of zoning can arouse more passion than the election of a governor. And people who do not know their congressman or assemblyman suddenly find out, when a new bridge or road is to be built near them, that they can appeal only to their elected representatives if all other avenues are closed. The pollution of air and of water has become an expensive and tricky issue. In many cities and towns, where the inner core of business has visibly decayed, bond issues for urban renewal have become major matters for voters to decide. And everybody worries about the energy crisis.

As city voters have shifted to the suburbs, leaving many decaying slum areas to seething minority population groups, problems have multiplied both inside and outside the city boundaries. The agitation for civil rights has been intensified within the ghetto areas. Throughout metropolitan areas, there has also been an enormous increase in voter interest in the provisions for new housing, new streets and highways, new schools, new hospitals, more water and all the other facilities on which the modern urban areas depend. Necessarily, taxes have climbed steeply. The electorate, well aware of the current parlous state of municipal financing, has not been indifferent to the prospect of still more taxes.

It is no wonder that the news media have been hard pressed to tell this story as it should be told. The old theory of telling the news in bits and pieces, just as it happened in a haphazard pattern or no pattern at all, has been shattered.

HOW TO INTERPRET POLITICAL NEWS

Basically, the interpretation of political news adds the factor of judgment to what is called straight news—the unvarnished recital of fact and poll-taking which may or may not represent the truth. For example, a distinguished speaker may make news with a startling statement, but that does not necessarily mean his statement is true; accuracy represents something far greater than putting down the quotes in order and getting middle initials right or reporting on a public-opinion poll. The interpretive writer is given the responsibility of considering the news in this perspective.

The difference between interpretation and editorialization, broadly, is that the interpreter applies the rule of reason to the news but stops short of recommending what should be done about it. The province of the editorial writer is to urge a course of action upon the reader or the viewer. The following are some of the ways in which interpretation may be legitimately used in the news media:

1.   In the print media, interpretation may be written into the main news story or it may be made the subject of an analysis as a separate article. In the electronic media, an interpretive statement may be made during the course of a newscast; or, a separate commentary may follow by an analyst of established reputation.

2.   For all media, the invariable rule is to give the news first and then, at an appropriate point, tell what it means. If there are several possible meanings, with no real indication of which may be correct, the fairest procedure is to give the report in precisely that way. In any event, the public must be given the facts on which an interpretation is based so that each individual may determine the soundness of the analysis in the light of the evidence.

3.   If an interpretive lead is used on a story to give it meaning, the interpretation must be documented immediately. If the explanation is not complete and convincing, a straight news lead is better with a qualified interpretation interjected later.

4.   The interpretive nature of a sidebar should be clearly indicated to the reader at the outset by some such approach as this: "Here is the meaning of the proposed two-cent increase in the state's gasoline tax," or, "This is how the new electric rate will affect your bills." The news, as such, should not be repeated in the sidebar on the assumption that the main story will make the basic facts clear.

5.   The writer's byline goes on an interpretive story and serves as the best guarantee that an impartial explanation of events is being given. While it may be necessary at times to use such phrases as "Authorities said," or "Observers believed" or "Informed sources said," the reporter must in all cases have discussed the story with these unnamed authorities, observers, or informed sources. The opposition often can discover, quickly enough, when a reporter's informed sources are imaginary — sometimes with embarrassing consequences.

6.   When a story explains itself, it should be told without recourse to interpretive techniques. If a story needs perspective in the form of background dates, or a paragraph about a previous action or decision, it should be given but this usually does not constitute interpretation.

7.   While much of the above may be adapted for use by writers for the electronic media, the main problem of presenting interpretation on radio and television is that relatively few journalists are permitted to do it.

8.   In writing for news magazines or Sunday newspaper roundups, the tendency of the journalist often is to overanalyze and overinterpret. Even if readers know the basic facts of a given situation, usually a frail assumption, it is a mistake to ply them with too much opinion when they simply are not interested in it. This is the basic weakness of many an editorial page as well.

EXAMPLES OF INTERPRETATION

These are some of the ways in which interpretation is used to give meaning to the news:

The Interpretive Lead In the following, the routine news lead would have been based on a White House briefing for labor leaders. Instead, the reasonably obvious conclusion was drawn:

> WASHINGTON — A proposal to merge the Labor and Commerce Departments into one super-Cabinet post appeared doomed today.
>
> Leaders of the AFL-CIO emerged from a White House briefing on the Administration's pet project without enthusiasm. Without labor's support,

an Administration source conceded, the plan could not get through Congress.

While the labor leaders reserved comment for the time being, it was learned that they would fight the program if it ever reached the House and Senate. One leader said, "If agriculture is entitled to a separate department, labor is, too." . . .

The Interpretive Paragraph Particularly in reports of legal actions, it is not enough to say that a witness testified or was cross-examined. The purpose of the testimony or the cross-examination must be indicated as quickly as possible. One way in which it can be done follows:

The State hammered away today at a key defense witness in the murder trial of Theron J. Wildener, who is accused of slaying a bank guard during a $100,000 robbery last year.

In an hour-long attack on the testimony of Wildener's girl friend, Emmaline Lindenhurst, District Attorney Millard Carew sought to shake her story that she and the defendant were riding in a car 40 miles from town at the time the robbery occurred.

Repeatedly, he had Miss Lindenhurst tell her story and tried to trap her into inconsistencies. But the witness, a dark-haired, bespectacled, 29-year-old secretary, calmly answered his questions without a trace of nervousness . . .

An Analyst's Conclusions Often, in reporting an election, it is necessary to give conclusions rather than a cumulative total of elected representatives. Thus, the analyst goes beyond the figures at hand in the following lead:

In a stunning upset, the Republicans appeared today to have wrested control of the Legislature from the Democrats for the first time in 20 years.

While the Democrats still held a nominal advantage in the Senate as of 1 A.M., having elected 36 candidates while the Republicans had 33 seats, they were trailing in all nine remaining contests. Thus, it appeared probable that the new Senate would consist of 42 Republicans and 36 Democrats.

In the House, the Republican margin was even greater, with 61 sure seats to 48 for the Democrats, and an even split likely on the remaining ten undecided contests . . .

A Tabular Summary In stories about taxes, budgets, social security, and other matters that vitally affect millions of individuals, a tabular summary is often the simplest and the most effective way of explaining a complicated matter. This is one good method:

WASHINGTON—You'll pay more under the new Social Security Law that goes into effect next month but your retirement benefits will be greater.

The changes were voted at the last session of Congress and signed into law by the President. They affect almost every family in the United States.

Here is a summary, calculated by wage brackets, of what you and your employer will pay under the new law and the net increase: . . .

Fact Sheet Method When a new program of wide public interest is undertaken, one of the easiest ways to present the factual material in a meaningful way is to draw up what amounts to a fact sheet. Thus, if a state undertakes a legalized lottery for the first time, the data could be presented as follows:

> Here is how the state's new lottery will operate when it goes into effect:
> Tickets will be priced at $1 each and will be available at state and city offices. There will be three drawings for prizes during the year, but separate tickets must be purchased for each.
> The winning ticket in each drawing will be worth $100,000, with $75,000 for second place, $50,000 for third place, $20,000 for fourth place and $5,000 each for the holders of the next 11 tickets.
> The lottery will be operated by the State Tax Commission for the benefit of the State Department of Education . . .

Interpretive Sidebar Many newspapers, and nearly all radio and television stations, go out of their way to label separate interpretive pieces as "News Analysis" because they necessarily involve considerable personal judgment by the writer or commentator. The piece is generally all comment because the news is told separately and in detail.

As interpreting the news has become more popular in the news media, this kind of thinking and writing has become one of the imperatives of modern journalism. Certainly, the story of the complications of domestic and international affairs cannot be made comprehensible without recourse to analysis and interpretation. And not all this work can be left by default to syndicated columnists.

Precautions When interpretive writers describe the conclusions of a general body of opinion, such as "critics of the administration," or "independent-minded political leaders," they had better be sure of their ground and check with administrative critics or other representative figures even if such persons sometimes can't be quoted directly. The more conscientious analysts will call 15 or 20 persons and discuss a particular background issue before doing a piece about it. Those inside journalism soon find out who works and who does not.

It is also apparent that the public is becoming increasingly suspicious of those who hack away at a particular candidate, program or objective under the guise of quoting anonymous "observers" or "critics." The reporting of anonymous opinion does have a place in interpretive journalism, sometimes a very important one, but writers should do everything they can to discourage the impression that they are writing about their own prejudices or enthusiasms.

The dividing line between editorialization and interpretation, in this respect, is very clear. Analysts can and should give a balanced presentation of responsible opinion on important questions, but must not overstep the bounds and become an advocate, openly or covertly. Hortatory journalism is the province of the editorialist. During an election year the focus of public and press interest in government is the political contest. Most actions taken by elected executives, councils or legislatures are reported in the light of their effect on the campaign. But in between, when the normal business of government goes on without interruption, a quiet calm descends on the centers of administrative, legislative and judicial action. Without the drama of election, the work-a-day processes of government are handled all too routinely in the news media and become mere adjuncts to the news.

Reporting on Government As in the case of general political coverage, the reporting of government requires primary background knowledge.

Many cities have the mayor-council form of government, but the city manager-commission format is making headway. In counties the traditional method of organization by boards is giving way to a county executive plan. On the state level the governor and the legislature remain the principal sources for the government story. And in metropolitan areas new forms of government that cut across state lines, such as the Port of New York Authority, are developing greater powers.

Reporters must be familiar with these systems and their adjuncts. They must also have a knowledge of the pertinent charters and constitutions, plus the source materials and daily records that are available for inspection, before they can hope to get a maximum of meaning out of public meetings and news conferences with officials.

It is an old reportorial habit to write stories in terms of persons rather than problems, colorful incidents rather than studied analyses of material in which the public should be interested. All journalists know that it is much easier to sell a story if the name of a controversial official is attached to the lead in some way, such as being for or against a particular proposal. The news media like the specific, abhor the abstract.

Sometimes, the government story is abstract. The increasing need for water facilities, the rise in mental hygiene cases that perplexes many states and the public concern over atomic power installations are some of the familiar problems that cannot be made clear in terms of conflict, or whether an alderman points with pride or views with alarm. Such stories have to be told through a reporter's eyes, if they are to be presented in depth. There is no special time element about such accounts, for the problems will be with us for a long time. Magazines for many years have done interesting work in this field, and the other media are following them.

In fact, over and above the day-to-day spot news stories of government, the technique of the "take-out," the delineation of an issue of public importance, is becoming more widely recognized as a useful journalistic tool. As it is regularly practiced by such newspapers as the

Los Angeles Times and the *Wall Street Journal* in special accounts that regularly appear on Page 1, it is contributing to a quickening of interest in the governmental process.

Here is the start of a typical "take-out" that was featured in Column 1, Page 1 of the *Los Angeles Times:*

By Ronald J. Ostrow

WASHINGTON — The truck driver, complaining of persistent chest pains, finally went to the doctor. The physician could find nothing wrong and, unknown to the patient, wrote in his medical record that the man was a "malingerer."

Three years later, the truck driver applied for another job. He listed chest pains as a medical problem. The prospective employer checked with the man's medical insurance carrier and his doctor and learned of the uncomplimentary earlier diagnosis.

The driver did not get the job.

That example, drawn from a hypothetical illustration by Ronald L. Plesser, general counsel of the federal Privacy Protection Study Commission, points up a sensitive area of the privacy issue that soon will draw increased attention.

The commission, created by the Privacy Act of 1974, will conduct its first hearings on medical records June 10 and 11 in Los Angeles.

Because the 1974 legislation covered only federal entities, the commission will pose the same question it has raised in earlier examinations of the credit and insurance industries: Should the principles and requirements of the 1974 act be applied to private entities such as hospitals and doctors?

Particularly touchy are the questions of whether the patient should have access to his medical records (it appears that most doctors and medical institutions oppose the idea) and whether the patient must give an informed consent before medical information about him is given to third parties such as insurers and employers.

"How can you give informed consent if you don't know what's in your records?" Plesser asked . . .[1]

What Is Regularly Covered Most newspapers see to it that the offices of the mayor, the local council and other top local officials are thoroughly covered. But the growing dependence of such authorities on their public relations appointees, usually exjournalists, has tended to remove them from the immediate access they often gave to local reporters assigned to politics. Now, instead of being tossed about in the hurly burly of news conferences, local officials frequently save their news—and their availability—for the much-wanted personal appearances on local television stations.

But the news media have changed, too. Instead of letting a reporter sit and await the pleasure of the mayor, whiling away the hours at penny ante in the press room at city hall, most newspapers insist on

[1] *Los Angeles Times, 17 May 1976.*

enterprise coverage of city affairs. That means reporters get a chance to delve into promising but untouched areas of local government on their own for days at a time in order to produce a special story or series, and most of them welcome it. The growth of the team reporting concept in local affairs has helped open up a lot of different news resources as well.

But if local coverage continues to be emphasized, the same is not true of news at the state level. The tendency now is to send political writers to handle the legislature at its opening and closing stages, unless something of importance develops in between, and to cover the governor with staff writers only when state house actions affect the locality. This means much more state coverage is done today by wire services. It also places a special burden on the press and broadcast reporters who have to hustle to the state capital for a breaking story and frantically try to get a fill-in either from a harassed official or an obliging full-time colleague. The decline in the coverage of news at the state level is one of the depressing aspects of the reporting of politics and government; fortunately, a few major newspapers and broadcast staffs in each state still are willing to spend the money and assign the trained journalists to continue to do the job as it should be done.

ENTERPRISE IN LOCAL COVERAGE

Through detailed investigation of land purchases, tax records and other available official documents, individual reporters and reporting teams have come up with a lot of news that could never have been obtained through the old routine of coverage by the beat.

One of the most brilliant investigations in recent years, which was conducted for six months by the investigative team of the *Indianapolis Star,* exposed widespread corruption in the Indianapolis Police Department and won the Pulitzer Prize for Special Local Reporting in 1975. It resulted in the dismissal of the director of public safety, the removal of the police chief and virtually all ranking police officers, and the defeat at the polls of a prosecuting attorney who was charged with a cover-up of the scandal. Here was the first of more than 400 stories that led to such spectacular results:

> Widespread corruption in the Indianapolis Police Department—including graft and protection for prostitution, narcotics, bootlegging and gambling—has been uncovered in a six-month investigation by the *Indianapolis Star.*
>
> Involvement in corruption by dozens of Indianapolis policemen is not limited to taking money, but has led some members of the department into criminal activities, the probe showed.
>
> Allegations of bribery and wrongdoing over a period of five years are

being investigated by the FBI and other federal agencies. Information obtained by the *Star* has been made available to federal investigators.

The *Star* investigation showed that vice operations in the city over the last decade add up to an estimated $40 million annual "pie" while the illegal narcotics trade is well over that figure.

The majority of illegal money filters up to high-ranking policemen and a few key political figures.

Aided by 28 policemen who—disgusted with what has been occurring—provided statements, tape recordings, records or other assistance, the investigation showed that corruption reaches into many areas of the department and includes high-ranking policemen.

Eight Marion County sheriff's detectives also provided information and other assistance, including statements from persons with direct knowledge of graft.

In all, reporters interviewed more than 400 persons, including a total of 60 policemen plus several former policemen . . .[2]

There followed 15 itemized charges supported by documented evidence, a careful and well-checked case that stood up for the most part under the most searching examination. Even though two of the reporters were indicted in retaliation on trumped-up charges of bribing police, nothing stopped the *Indianapolis Star*. The reporters were cleared, the police were not. The investigation was a model for planning, execution and results.

One of the best individual reportorial inquiries in the area of local government was an investigation of the New York medicaid program—the state complement to federally administered medicare—by William Sherman of the *New York Daily News*. With the secret cooperation of key city officials, the young reporter posed as a medicaid recipient—in effect an undercover agent for the city's Health Department—and uncovered shocking abuses of the system. For example, he found psychiatrists who billed the city for more hours' work than there are in the day, a dentist who billed the city $800,000 in two years, a doctor who claimed to have treated 300 patients in a day, needless medical tests, the use of unapproved drugs and the issuance of unfit eyeglasses. Here is the start of Sherman's series in the *News*:

By William Sherman

Disguised as a welfare client complaining of a cold, a reporter with a medicaid card wandered into a group medical office in Ozone Park, Queens, one day last week and asked to see a doctor.

The patient was first sent to a foot doctor, then twice to an internist with instructions to come back a third time, and then to a psychiatrist who arranged for weekly visits. On his second visit the patient was given an electrocardiogram, three blood tests, two urine tests and an X-ray.

[2] *Indianapolis Star*, 24 February 1974, p. 1.

William Jones, reporter for the Chicago Tribune, sitting in ambulance while at work as an ambulance attendant in a hospital exposé that won him a Pulitzer Prize for Local Reporting. He later became managing editor, news, for the Tribune. (Copyright, Chicago Tribune. Used by permission.)

He was handed six prescriptions in one day and doctors directed him to a pharmacy on the second floor of the center to have them filled. He walked out that day with a mixture of foot powders, a mild foot cream, a vial of sleeping pills, a bottle of powerful tranquilizers, penicillin tablets and a bottle of cough medicine—all in response to his initial complaint of a cold—a feigned cold at that.

The visit to the medical offices in Queens was part of an intensive investigation by the *News* into medicaid and its abuses. The inquiry was conducted with close cooperation of the city's Human Resources Administration and of the Department of Health, which monitored the probe every step of the way . . .[3]

There followed a detailed record, written in a lively and even entertaining style, of how the reporter was fixed up with a temporary medical card, took a number of physical examinations to be certain he was in good health, and then embarked on his adventure. His articles named names, gave addresses and descriptions of persons who were allegedly defrauding the city and state, and resulted among other things

[3] *New York Daily News*, 23 January 1973, p. 7.

William Sherman (right) reporter for the New York Daily News, in the outfit he wore while posing as a Medicaid recipient. He was able to expose millions of dollars in Medicaid frauds and won a Pulitzer Prize in Local Reporting. (Copyright, New York News. Inc. All rights reserved. Reprinted by permission.)

in the forced restitution to the city of more than $1 million in fraudulent billings. Sherman won the 1974 Pulitzer Prize for Special Local Reporting.

It is a touchy business to undertake such roles, but reporters have done it with enormous success from time to time as long as they enjoyed the complete trust and cooperation of their newspapers. Thus, a *Chicago Tribune* Task force exposed substandard conditions in a local hospital when William Gaines, a reporter who worked as a hospital janitor, was called into operating rooms in his janitor's clothes to help patients. In another case, William Jones of the *Chicago Tribune* exposed collusion between police and some of Chicago's largest private ambulance companies to restrict service in low income areas. He knew what he was writing about because he actually worked as an ambulance driver. In still another exploit, Edgar May of the *Buffalo Evening News* worked as an official in the New York State public welfare department and produced a documented series on the shortcomings of the system, "Our Costly Dilemma."

The *Tribune* Task Force, Jones and May won Pulitzer Prizes, the Buffalo reporter being nominated by the commissioner of the department that he investigated.

COVERING BUDGETS AND TAXES

When New York City teetered on the brink of bankruptcy and was lectured for its ills by the President of the United States, it was news of national consequence. Headlines flared across the land and television cameras played on the dismayed faces of the citizens of what had once been considered the wealthiest and most extravagant city in the world. Of its extravagance, there was no doubt. As the federal government pursued its financial inquiries before setting up bailout loans, the extent of the city's budget gimmickry and its wasteful management came out for all to see. The lesson was that budgets and taxes at the local and state level no longer could be pushed into the background. For New York's plight in effect mirrored the desperate situation of many another city in the country. It became an issue in the 1976 Presidential campaign and it will remain an issue for years to come.

The story of budgets and taxes is at the very root of the reporting of public affairs. The excuse that such accounts are dull doesn't wash any more. What happened in New York City turned out to be a cliffhanger that produced a lot of excited comment both in this country and abroad. For in fact, nothing is more important to the cause of democratic self-government than a public presentation of the costs of government and the tax proposals through which officials seek to raise the funds to meet those costs. Without this kind of information, the public is left in the dark and all kinds of tricks can be—and are—played with public funds.

To be sure, reporters with a good background in standard accounting practices and knowledge of computer operations can dig into a government budget presentation at the local level and come up with some unpleasant truths that public officials often seek to conceal. But budget reporting, by and large, isn't all that heroic. It is a part of journalistic routine and it should be done with scrupulous care.

Every budget story must be told with regard for detail—what is to be spent, why it is to be spent, why it is an increased or decreased sum over last year and where economies may be possible. Hand in hand with spending proposals must be an estimate of whether taxes are to be increased and, if so, how much. Necessarily, the tax estimate places an enormous burden on the reporter because public officials, understandably, are usually not very willing to admit that their spending plans are going to cost the public more money. And where there is a tax reduction, writers had best be careful before they break into loud hosannas. Too often, such projections prove on final examination to be less than realistic in an inflationary time.

What is more likely, in most budgets at the local level in this era, is that there will be minimal reductions in jobs and continual tax increases at various levels. What a frustrated public generally does, under such circumstances, is to vote against budget increases whenever it gets the chance, notably on school budgets.

Here is a typical story of a county budget proposal:

A $120.2 million "austerity" budget for Mattox County was recommended yesterday by County Executive Fairfield Winston Jr., who called for the elimination of 200 jobs and a tax increase.

"We will have to balance income with outgo if we want to sell our school bonds and our sewer bonds in a depressed market," he said. "I regret very much having to raise taxes and cut jobs in our county, but I see no alternative. We don't want to be another New York."

Winston, in his budget message to the County Legislature, called for an increase in the property tax rate from $5.15 to $5.26 for each $100 of assessed valuation. The 11-cent increase is the largest in eight years.

As for the proposed dismissals from the county's 4,500-member work force, 60 will come from the police, 50 from the highway department and the rest scattered among other departments.

Winston's Republican opponent, Garfield Sprague, immediately attacked both the proposed dismissals and the tax boost. "Neither one of these moves is necessary," Sprague said. "With just a little economy in the running of our government, we could get by very nicely just as we are but I never heard of a Democrat who wanted to economize. Why, if we eliminate the graft and waste in public welfare alone, we can come through with a balanced budget."

Winston's budget for the next fiscal year is $4 million less than for the current year. Estimated revenues for next year include $60.2 million from property taxes, $51.6 million from state and federal aid programs, and the remainder from miscellaneous sources such as departmental fees, reimbursements and sales of assets.

The biggest expenditure again is for welfare, which takes 40 per cent of the budget. The police are next with 18 per cent. The rest of the spending is for public works, mental health, judicial and miscellaneous services.

Chapter 25

Public Opinion, Polling and Elections

Social science has made possible a thorough-going reform of outworn journalistic methods in measuring
public opinion and keeping pace with electoral campaigns. It has developed powerful statistical tools,
most of which were made possible by the computer, to
enable journalists to do a better job. As Philip Meyer
has put the position:

"Social science has suddenly leaped beyond arm-
chair philosophizing. It is doing what we journalists
like to think of ourselves as best at: finding facts, infer-
ring causes, pointing to ways to correct social problems, and evaluating the efforts of such correction" [1]

JOURNALISM AND SOCIAL SCIENCE

If all editors have not hailed this development with
hosannahs and if all journalists have not hurled them-

[1] Philip Meyer, "Precision Journalism," (Bloomington, Ind., 1973),
p. 4.

453

selves headlong into the breaking statistical waves, that is only characteristic of the innate skepticism of the profession. However, progress
is being made. There are a modest number of reporters in the land
who are capable of conducting a decent scientific study of public
opinion, who are adept at analyzing masses of statistical data and who
are not afraid to work with computers. And there are an increasing
number of editors who are willing to employ them, newspapers that
publish their work, and broadcasting networks and stations that eagerly
use their services.

The Pollsters It is scarcely possible to pick up a paper or turn on a radio or TV set today without getting the results of one poll or another,
listening to a variety of statistical analyses, or becoming aware of the
latest assessment of an ongoing political campaign. Within a brief time,
it has been possible to scan a half-dozen different polls on political issues: an Opinion Research Corporation Poll in which 75 per cent of respondents mistrust big business,[2] a Harris Survey in which 62 per cent
of respondents mistrust big government,[3] a U. S. Census Bureau study
indicating that American women will continue to outnumber men for
the rest of the century,[4] a *New York Daily News* poll in which 77 per
cent of respondents said they had lost trust in politicians and public officials,[5] and a *Los Angeles Times* survey in which most jurors polled
were against judicial press gags.[6] And that constituted only a small
sampling of the American news media.

The Researchers It merely proves, if proof were needed, that the public
opinion survey and social statistical analyses have become the basis for
a major industry.

Within a little more than a generation, the news media, the universities and the commercial polling organizations have established a formidable network for measuring the frequent and sometimes dizzying
shifts in public sentiment. However, it is still as it was almost a century ago when Lord Bryce wrote that "the obvious weakness of government by public opinion is the difficulty of ascertaining it." Wide differences of opinion may be caught very quickly, it is true, but when the
margin of error approaches 3 per cent on either side, most poll-takers
agree, however reluctantly, that the acceptable margin of confidence
usually has been reached.

No one, therefore, can quarrel with Winston Churchill's celebrated
dictum: "Nothing is more dangerous than to live in the temperamental

---

[2] *Bergen Record* (Hackensack, N.J.) 17 May 1976, p. A–8
[3] *Cleveland Plain Dealer*, 17 May 1976, p. B–1
[4] *Albany* (New York) *Times-Union*, 27 April 1976, p. 8
[5] *New York Daily News*, 21 June 1976, p. 5
[6] *Denver Post*, 17 May 1976, p. 6

atmosphere of a Gallup Poll, always taking one's temperature. There is only one duty, only one safe course, and that is to try to be right and not fear to do or say what you believe to be right."

Two of the pioneering polling organizations still remain in the forefront of public opinion research—George Gallup and his American Institute of Public Opinion and Elmo Roper's organization. Among the others, Louis Harris and Daniel Yankelovich are both prominent and widely used. Of the young comers, few have been as publicized as Patrick H. Caddell, who worked for both the George McGovern and Jimmy Carter Democratic Presidential campaigns while still in his twenties.

Of equal importance are the university research centers and the numerous social science researchers in academe, who are so often sought out to help with various types of polls and other statistical studies. Among the oldest are the Michigan Survey Research Center and the National Opinion Research Center.

Finally, some of the stronger and wealthier news organizations are doing much of their own work, as witness the rapid adaptation of social science methods by the Knight-Ridder Newspapers. Others have joined forces and thereby shared costs as well as services, the CBS News–*New York Times* political polls being one example. Then, there are the state-wide polls, some going back for many years, including the *Des Moines Register's* Iowa Poll, the *Minneapolis Tribune's* Minnesota Poll, the *New York Daily News's* New York State Poll, and the Mervin Field organization's California Poll.

MEASURING PUBLIC OPINION

Everybody recognizes the importance of public opinion in an open society but few agree on what it is or how it operates. Nor is it easy to define, even by social scientists.

What Is Public Opinion In a far smaller and less complicated United States nearly a century and a half ago, Alexis de Tocqueville called it the "predominant authority" that acted by "elections and decrees." [7] In a moment of disillusion with the vagaries of the British public, Sir Robert Peel was less admiring; to him, it was "that great compound of folly, weakness, prejudice, wrong feeling, right feeling, obstinacy and newspaper paragraphs which is called public opinion." [8] In the early 1920s, Walter Lippmann argued that it was "primarily a moralized and codified version of the facts," and that "the pattern of stereotypes at the center of our codes largely determines what group of facts we shall see

---

[7] Alexis de Tocqueville. *Democracy in America* (New York, Vintage Press, 1954), vol. 1, p. 129.

[8] Walter Lippmann, *Public Opinion* (New York, 1922), p. 197.

and in what light we shall see them." In our own time, a social scientist, W. Phillips Davison, has concluded that public opinion should be treated as a "consensus that influences the behavior of individuals who contribute to the consensus . . . a form of organization (that) is able to coordinate the thought and action of a large number of people." [9]

Of one thing there is no doubt. Whether it is the "predominant authority," a "great compound of folly," a "pattern of stereotypes," or a "consensus," the measurement of what is called public opinion has become of transcendent importance in modern mass communications. It forms the basis of much advertising and merchandising practice, determines what shall and shall not be seen on television, locates new enterprises as varied in character as food markets and newspapers, provides trends (or the illusion of trends) in political campaigns at all levels of government and dominates the coverage of national elections. The journalist has not been able to escape the implications of this expanding activity. It has placed him squarely in the middle of the computer age.

Since newspapers have taken up "precision journalism," polling assignments have become a part of the regular routine. The *Chicago Tribune*, for example, has found that nine of ten persons surveyed in Chicago favored mandatory hand-gun registration. The *Dayton* (Ohio) *Journal Herald* forecast the outcome of a city tax referendum with less than 2 per cent error. In a survey of "white flight" to the suburbs as a result of school integration, the *Milwaukee Journal* found that the trend was exaggerated. And the Associated Press, in one of a number of surveys, looked for a relationship between cancer death rates and the rate of spending for research.

During political campaigns, obviously, all the news media are heavily involved in polling, with the leaders conducting their own research. For it is the leaders of public opinion, after all, who are more heavily influenced by polling results than the masses. Let a poll show a candidate trailing badly and almost at once his campaign may suffer because funds dry up. Or let a poll show that major opinion is against financial aid by the government to a foreign nation or even a stricken municipality, such as New York City, and all kinds of difficulties ensue for the supplicant.

Social science holds in general that, except in areas where there is a fairly even division of opinion, polls tend to solidify most people in their views instead of changing them. But the elites and the other opinion leaders who generally commission polls *do* base policy decisions on them in numerous instances—sometimes without sufficient evidence.[10]

---

[9] *Ibid*, p. 125; W. Phillips Davison, *International Political Communication* (New York, 1966), p. 66.

[10] Seymour Martin Lipset, "The Wavering Polls," *The Public Interest* (Spring 1976), pp. 70–89.

Before the Polls Were Invented Until George Gallup and Elmo Roper began their surveys of public opinion in 1935, there was a lot of amiable mythology about the course of American public opinion and its values.

Politicians generally took the word of the district captains of the political machines in the big cities, consulted the county chairmen and their henchmen in rural areas, and kept a wary eye on newspaper comment and the size of crowds. Reporters, for better or worse, compared the private views of politicians on the way the campaign was going, talked with voters here and there without attempting a survey on any systematic basis, and usually came up with a consensus by election day.

It follows that a lot of nonsense was circulated about the way people make up their minds. For example, one of the articles of dubious faith was promulgated by James Aloysius Farley, the presiding genius who managed two of President F. D. Roosevelt's successful campaigns. Farley held that people for the most part made up their minds whom they'd vote for directly after the national political conventions and seldom changed. The evidence of last minute switches in voting in 1948, 1956 and 1968 argues powerfully to the contrary, for surveys have shown that President Truman won in 1948 in the last ten days of campaigning, that the Suez crisis of 1956 swung a lot of voters to President Eisenhower and that Senator Hubert H. Humphrey made such headway in the last few days of the 1968 campaign that he almost caught the successful Richard M. Nixon.[11]

The Rise of the Pollsters The practice of poll-taking goes back to 1824 when a Harrisburg *Pennsylvanian* straw poll indicated Andrew Jackson was ahead in the Presidential campaign. Over the course of the next century, such newspapers as the *Boston Globe* and *New York Herald* conducted street corner polls. And at the beginning of the twentieth century, advertisers began experimenting with market surveys, the true forerunner of the modern public opinion poll. The first "social-scientific" poll of public opinion was conducted in 1907–1908 by the Pittsburgh Survey, with the support of the Russell Sage Foundation. Another first was the *Kansas City Star's* quadrennial selection of "sample precincts," from which it would calculate the winner of the Presidential election and banner the result soon after the closing of the election booths in the land.

But none of these was as spectacular a success—and failure—as the *Literary Digest* Poll which began in 1916. For most of the Presidential elections through 1932, the *Digest* sent out postcards to millions of persons and predicted the outcome with reasonable success. By 1935,

[11] George Gallup, *The Sophisticated Poll Watcher's Guide* (Princeton, N.J., 1972), pp. 200–201.

there was so much concern over polling that a bill was introduced in Congress to prohibit the use of the mails for polls and stop this "vicious practice." [12] The bill failed. But in the same year, Elmo Roper began his poll in *Fortune* magazine and the first Gallup Poll was issued by George Gallup's newly founded American Institute of Public Opinion.

In the 1936 Presidential campaign, the *Literary Digest* calculated, on the basis of more than 2 million postcards received mainly from telephone users and automobile owners that President Roosevelt would lose to Alfred M. Landon, his Republican challenger, by 42.9 per cent of the vote to 57.1 per cent. The outcome gave Roosevelt 62.5 per cent of the vote, which enabled him to carry 46 of the 48 states. The *Digest* Poll thereby racked up a polling error of 19.6 per cent, the largest ever known for a Presidential election, and the magazine went out of business. The Gallup Poll, based on a scientific sampling of a few thousand respondents, called the election correctly but itself registered an error of 6.8 per cent, larger than any it has since made. Of course the difference between the two was that the *Digest* sampled only prosperous people in a time of depression, those who had phones and cars, while Gallup reached a better cross-section.[13]

Despite a relatively good record set by Gallup, Roper and other pollsters, the polling industry had to struggle for years to overcome the *Digest* debacle. Just as it was regaining public confidence, however, it came a cropper in the 1948 Presidential election when President Truman upset the favored Thomas E. Dewey. The picture of a grinning Truman holding up the *Chicago Tribune*, with a banner headline proclaiming a Dewey victory, is a favorite in every journalistic album of the era—and one the pollsters will never forget.

In 1948, Gallup was in error by 5.3 per cent, Crossley by 4.7 per cent and Roper by 8.4 per cent and all understated the Democratic vote by these respective amounts. The Social Science Research Council blamed errors of sampling, interviewing and forecasting. Gallup himself argued that he failed because he stopped polling "about 10 to 14 days" before election day and thereafter Democrats who had been "leaning" toward Dewey changed their minds.[14] He changed his sampling methods and began polling up to two days before election day.

The pollsters had some rough times after the Truman disaster, and some bright moments as well. In the close Presidential race between Senator John F. Kennedy and Richard M. Nixon in 1960, both relied heavily on private polling advice, Kennedy on Louis Harris and Nixon on Claude Robinson of the Opinion Research Corp. Kennedy always

---

[12] Daniel J. Boorstin, *The Americans: The Democratic Experience* (New York, 1973), p. 155.

[13] George Gallup, *The Sophisticated Poll Watcher's Guide* (Princeton, N.J., 1972) pp. 65–68.

[14] *Ibid.*, p. 144

gave credit to Harris for the findings on which his successful campaign was based. In the 1968 election, last-minute Gallup and Harris surveys indicated that there was a trend toward Senator Hubert H. Humphrey, the Democratic candidate, that was reflected in Nixon's narrow victory.

Luck as a Factor All poll takers are well aware that they ignore the usual 2.5 to 3 per cent margin of error in any national survey at their own peril. And this was particularly apparent in the exceedingly close 1976 Presidential election, when most major polling organizations came up with predictions of one per cent or less in favor of Jimmy Carter. George Gallup, the dean of pollsters, picked Ford by the same figure. However, Gallup and others covered themselves — pointing to the margin of error — and said the election was "too close to call."

The only one daring enough to make an unqualified forecast was Burns Roper, for the Public Broadcasting System, whose final survey gave Carter 51 per cent, Ford 47 per cent and the minor candidates 2 per cent. He came within one per cent of complete accuracy, the final vote giving Carter 51 per cent, Ford 48 per cent and minor candidates 1 per cent. Said Roper: "Polling is part science and a helluva lot of human judgments. Fortunately, we made the right ones." And Gallup commented drily, "The plain fact of the matter is that you have to be lucky. You have to repeal the laws of probability." [15]

Yet, poll-taking and election forecasting have become so deeply imbedded in the American political system — and in American journalism as well — that they have continued to develop despite all setbacks. Their credibility has suffered from time to time, particularly when hired pollsters of some repute issued findings that tended to support the positions of those who paid them. Yet, on the whole, this has not seemed to affect their public acceptance.

Reasons for Forecasts It may well be asked why the news media go in so heavily for surveys of public opinion in connection with the reporting of politics and government, and elections in particular. One very good reason is that such forecasts, and the basis for them, are a part of the legitimate business of political reporters and their news organizations. An even more compelling reason is that no news organization worthy of the name can act as a mere recording device that plays back speeches and rival claims but does not undertake to evaluate them. When the public asks, "Who's ahead?" the question is worthy of a serious reply by trained reporters and commentators.

POLLING TECHNIQUES

The oldest, least sophisticated and least dependable type of public opinion poll is the reportorial survey in which an editor sends several

[15] AP report (4 November 1976).

staff members out to talk to almost anybody they think will give them a good quote. Before the rise of the aggressive feminine movement, it used to be called the "man-in-the-street" poll and it is still used by editors here and there.

The notion is that any reporter, unschooled in the simplest statistical procedures, can talk to 20 or 30 persons and come up with a valid reflection of the view of the community. Such exercises, no matter how carefully reporters go about their work, come near the truth only by the sheerest accident. The sample has not been picked at random according to the rules of probability and therefore can't be truly representative of the views of all persons in the region under consideration, known in statistical terms as the "universe."

The Random Sample Many journalists still believe that a random sample consists of picking anybody you want to talk to on the street. The folly of that approach is readily apparent in a place like New York City, for example, where people picked at random at the fashionable corner of 50th Street and Park Avenue, in front of the Waldorf Astoria Hotel, will be no more typical of New Yorkers as a whole than those selected at the corner of 125th Street and Lenox Avenue, the crossroads in Harlem.

The definition of a true random sample specifies that everybody living within a given "universe" that is to be surveyed must have an equal chance of being selected for interviewing. If the selection is properly done, the sample need not be large. As statisticians are fond of pointing out, if an experimenter draws 100 balls from two casks of black and white balls, one with 100,000 and the other with 1,000 and each divided into a ratio of three black balls to seven white balls, the likelihood is virtually the same that the drawing will yield 70 white balls and 30 black balls from each cask. Thus, Gallup's usual random sample is about 1,500 and his and other national polling samples during a political campaign run to no more than 3,000 persons.

In any event, reliable research and news organizations always go to considerable trouble and expense to develop a random sample that will represent the "universe," whether it is a village, a county, a state or the nation as a whole. In some instances, a "universe" may consist of groups of people taken by irregular areas depending on the type of survey and the desires of the person in charge.

The Probability Method The most difficult, time-consuming and costly technique is the probability method. It is also the most widely accepted.

In this process, nothing is left to chance that the sample will be truly selected at random. Trained interviewers are given a list of carefully prepared and pretested questions, certain addresses in specified areas, a list of selected apartments in such buildings and a group of persons to be interviewed in order (the oldest male, the oldest woman and so on) at certain times of the day or evening.

The only time they are given a choice is in the event that the address turns out to be an empty lot, or an apartment is vacant, or the type of person to be interviewed isn't available after repeated calls. Then the interviewers are given a list of alternatives to follow, the whole following a statistical pattern developed well in advance.

Various refinements are applied to increase the representative nature of the sample, including stratification. This means simply that where the "universe" includes several identifiable groups of persons, samples will be drawn separately from each group to make certain they are properly represented. This helps maintain the accuracy of the sampling process, whereas clustering—interviewing several designated types of persons in one house or apartment, tends to reduce it.

The Quota Method This is the older type of sampling. It is also the one Gallup and most other poll-takers used through 1948 with disastrous results, causing it to lose favor to the better-rounded probability method. However, quota sampling is still done here and there.

Under this technique, interviewers are given a list of the types of persons to be located and talked to but the choices are pretty much left to their own desires. The trouble here is that, consciously or unconsciously, the personal prejudices of interviewers enter into the selection process.

The principal advantage of the quota method over probability is that it is faster and cheaper; in the end, however, it may not be much more reliable than the "man-in-the-street" poll.

A Question of Confidence Using statistical tables of probability, polling organizations invariably determine the size of their samples on the basis of what is called a "confidence level," in other words a test of accuracy. If a Gallup sample totals 600 persons, for example, he calculates that the chances are 95 in 100 that a poll which divides 60 per cent in favor, 40 per cent opposed (or the reverse) will be within 4 percentage points of the true figure. This means that the number in favor will be somewhere between 56 per cent and 64 per cent. By doubling the sample to 1,200, Gallup holds that the error factor (using the same 95 in 100 criterion) is reduced to 2.8 per cent. Doubled again, there is a further decrease to 2 per cent.

It isn't any great mathematical feat, using statistical tables and relatively basic mathematical procedures, to work out the confidence level for any sample size and confidence level. Most surveys make it their goal to operate within 4 per cent error at the 95 in 100 confidence level, which means a sample of 600 persons is adequate. At 3 per cent, a sample of 1,067 is needed; 2 per cent, 2,401; 1 per cent, 9,605. These figures assume, of course, that there is an absolutely true sample based on probability. As for the size of the "universe" involved, those figures don't make much difference until they get below the 10,000 level.[16]

For many years, it seemed to many that it was sheer madness to try to determine national trends by polling a handful of citizens in a town, a few score in a state, and between 1,200 and 3,000 nationally. And yet, barring technical and human failures that now are usually kept to a minimum, the system works. The Bureau of the Census has been using the probability method of random sampling for years to determine population growth (the house-to-house enumeration process occurs only once a decade). The popularity of TV programs is determined by ratings based on devices attached to sets in fewer than 1,500 homes. Gallup, Roper, Harris and all their competitors sample public opinion on this basis about everything from sex to Presidential elections.

Sampling Techniques The basis of most sampling techniques consists of maps and other data from the Bureau of the Census. If these are reinforced with city directories or comparable tabulations, the raw material for establishing a sample is in hand.

In the probability method, the primary sampling units may be drawn at random (using a table of random numbers) from a list of all the counties and metropolitan areas in the United States. These are then further reduced to urban blocks and rural segments, also selected by the random process as it is known in statistics. Next, within each selected block or segment, every dwelling unit is listed and a fixed number is selected at random. Finally, in the selected dwelling unit, all adults are enumerated; from each, one person is chosen, again at random.

The sample thus selected has a high probability of reflecting all the characteristics of the "universe" from which it is drawn. Factors of age, sex, economic status, ethnic and religious group and other relevant factors are all represented in the sample. It is in this manner that interviewers are provided with their list of persons to be located and asked the precise list of questions drafted by the polling organization.

In telephone polls, which are faster and cheaper, the number of names in a telephone directory in a particular city is divided by the size of the sample (600, 1,067, 2,401 or whatever). The quotient shows the number of names to be skipped, from the beginning to the end of the directory, to produce a true random sample. Then, the designated telephone numbers are called by researchers. To get unlisted numbers, some social scientists advocate adding one digit to each number.

The Uses of Polling It is a familiar argument among pollsters, particularly those with an academic background, that the poll is more sinned against than sinning and that news organizations misuse polls by at-

[16] Gallup, op. cit., pp. 68–69; Meyer, op. cit., pp. 122–123.

tempting to extract more information from them than they are able to give. To a certain extent, this may be true. However, as long as polling organizations offer their wares for sale and as long as they announce certain results within a given range of probabilities, it is only logical to hold them responsible for their output.

No one can claim absolute accuracy for any public opinion study, whether it is done person-to-person, by telephone or questionnaire. The allowance of 3 per cent error on either side is fairly standard in political poll-taking, but the public tends to overlook it in a close political fight when there is perhaps only a 1 per cent difference between the chief rival candidates. Moreover, some polls are put to grotesque uses toward election day when one side or the other will claim victory on the basis of a lead of as little as one-half of 1 per cent.

While political polling is a hurry-up job with a considerable element of risk, and while TV ratings are also under constant criticism for the same reason, the social issues type of poll can be much more leisurely and often just as useful. The *Detroit Free Press*, in a study of black attitudes after the 1967 Detroit riots, took three weeks. A University of California study of the Watts riots took two years to produce. The *Miami Herald* took a considerable period for its inquiry into the militancy of blacks in the Miami area in 1968. And academic studies always take a great deal longer.

Depth Interviews There are some practical-minded social scientists and political experts who have faith in a few depth interviews—solicited from various types of persons at specific locations—as a means of judging the mood of a particular "universe," which may be a small voting unit or even the entire nation. Such depth interviews may be conducted for two or three hours and encompass a variety of subjects. It is hardly fair to say that this kind of work is a projection of the "man-in-the-street" interview, done at a highly sophisticated level. These depth interviews require a rare combination of journalistic skills and social science background, plus shrewd political judgments.

One of the most successful practioners of the art was the political analyst, Samuel Lubell, who did most of his own interviewing and calculated his own results. Lubell might select for a depth interview a man who resides in a low-cost housing development and works in a factory, a housewife who lives in the center of an area torn by controversy over school busing or another emotional issue, a farmer in the center of the mid-West grain belt, a small home owner and other such typical American citizens. Out of the mix of their opinions and his own judgment, he shaped his conclusions.

Is the U. S. Overpolled? Although a recent Gallup survey has indicated that six out of seven Americans over 18 have never been interviewed in a poll, polling organizations agree that there is rising public resistance to their surveys. The work now takes much more time, it is more costly and more people simply don't want to be bothered. The reason is evident: In addition to polls by the government, universities and the news media, more than 1,000 commercial organizations are now in the business—which means the public is being asked to do a lot of the pollsters' work for free. "Perhaps," one pollster suggested, "we are not treating the respondent with respect as a human being." [17]

Checking Trends The use of selected national or state voting units is a favorite indicator of political trends. Every major polling organization has a well-guarded list of such precincts, picked because they have accurately reflected the outcome of elections over a period of years. Of course, in landslides such as 1964 and 1972, it is easy to pick a winner by using the results in the model precincts and projecting them. Sometimes, it can even be done before the polls close by taking a random sample among voters as they emerge from casting their ballot. But in a close election, model precincts are a risky guide.

Among newspapers, it is a time-honored custom for political writers to publish their forecasts on the Sunday or Monday before election. Necessarily, this is nowhere near as informative as it used to be because the publication of weekly surveys before election day has taken the edge off what used to be "the last word." Once again, it is no big deal to call a one-sided election; as for the close ones, predictions continue to be a gamble regardless of when they are made.

Polling Standards Here is a checklist of the information that should accompany any poll:[18]

1. The sponsor of the poll.
2. Exact wording of all questions.
3. Definition of the population sample.
4. Sample size and, where needed, the response rate.
5. Allowance for sampling error.
6. Proportion of "don't knows" and others in sample who may not vote.
7. Method of interviewing and where done.
8. Time period for interviewing.

PREDICTIONS

Any election forecast should have suitable qualifications throughout, even though the result may seem to duplicate many years of similar

---

[17] *New York Times*, 26 October 1975, p. 1

[18] Based on material prepared by National Committee on Published Polls in Philip Meyer, *Precision Journalism*, pp. 185–186.

preelection accounts. This is a sample of the usual type of forecast lead:

> Mayor Hammond Garvell appears likely to win reelection on Tuesday if the vote is as large as expected.
>
> A sampling of typical voter opinion, plus talks with professionals in both parties and the findings of private polls, indicated today that the Mayor was expected to defeat his opponent, Hereford Cates.
>
> But even Mayor Garvell's closest aides emphasized that, as an independent running for reelection, he must count on a heavy turnout at the polls — always a sign in this city that the independent voter is making his influence felt . . .

"Foregrounding" Politics A considerable segment of political writing in newspapers and news magazines and analytical comment on television is based on the summation and interpretation of coming events. The holding of conventions, listing of known candidates and issues and analysis of rival claims is one familiar report of this type. Another is the planning for a campaign during a given period and the conclusions that may be drawn from it in terms of objectives.

Best known of all is the preelection day summation giving the time, places and candidates involved in the voting, the registration figures, probable vote totals, analysis of issues, weather and whatever conclusions the writer or analyst wishes to make. On television, this type of information can only be given in sketchy form. It generally takes two solid pages of newspaper type to give the voter all the material he needs to make a decision on numerous candidates, propositions and referenda. This, certainly, is the place where a good newspaper is priceless and the electronic media are at a complete disadvantage.

COVERING ELECTIONS

The early part of the twentieth century was the golden age for political reporters. They were regarded as seers in their own right, the traveling companions of the great and near-great, the oracles who — in their own time and at their own pleasure — gave the people the Word. Arthur Krock of the *New York Times*, Charles Michelson of the *New York World*, Edward Folliard of the *Washington Post* and their associates were national figures. However, the coming of television changed all that.

The Reporters' Job Today, the exposure of TV plus its astronomical costs limits political campaigning in all except the marathon races of Presidential years. First of all, the wise candidate tries to save his principal pronouncements for TV and gets by the rest of the time with a stock speech. Even more important, except for such millionaire politi-

Walter Mears, winner of the Pulitzer Prize for National Correspondence in 1977 for coverage of the Presidential election. The Associated Press. Used with permission.

cians as the Kennedy brothers, Nelson A. Rockefeller and others, a candidate must be careful that TV costs won't bankrupt the party. And that means a lot less work for political reporters, as well as their news organizations.

Except for Presidential or important state-wide races for a governor or senator, the drive for votes now is concentrated in a matter of a few weeks before election day instead of many months as once was the case. Because TV gets the big news and the major speeches, the newspaper function now is a double one—to analyze the news as well as to present it. Only a few major newspapers can afford to publish the full text of speeches, and even they are now highly selective about what texts they will use. The one all-purpose campaign speech has pretty well destroyed interest in campaign oratory. Furthermore, the old-style political orator has long outlived his usefulness.

Nevertheless, the political reporters for major news organizations outside TV are up against an almost impossible job today. Their work is so concentrated that they have little time to talk to the candidates or their managers, let alone the voters. In a national campaign, if they try to see anybody at an airport or train or motorcade whistle stop, they risk being left behind. Nowadays, candidates will cover several states at a time in a single day. And because most candidates rely on the basic speech, that isn't news after the first few times it is used. Except in the hands of experienced reporters who know how to dig for the unusual in a political campaign, coverage tends to become a humdrum affair. More and more, it is the analysis that counts with many a newspaper.

Team reporting, based on surveys of public opinion, is being used by newspapers that can afford it. And where research is needed, one or two reporters may be assigned to do a lengthy background report on a candidate or an issue. Much of the news, therefore, becomes a matter of reportorial initiative rather than the rewriting of political handouts or the stale coverage of last night's TV appearance. For newspapers and wire services, it is more of a challenge and, on the whole, it leads to better reporting over a period of time.

THE POLITICAL ROUTINE

The electronic revolution that is reshaping the news media has enabled political reporters and commentators to use new and far more effective instruments in their work. At the beginning of the century, the task of obtaining and analyzing registration figures for all but the smallest elections was so time-consuming that only a few great newspapers and the top echelons of wire services made much of an attempt to do it. Now, the computer has made statistical analysis of registration figures almost a routine matter. This, plus social science's new knowledge of the habits of the nation's voters, has given public officials, journalists and office-seekers alike new insights into the operation of the machinery of self-government.

There is no excuse today for any political reporter who does not know the geographical, social and ethnic backgrounds of the various areas of the nation. Nor can any journalist who covers politics ignore the need for a broad academic preparation for his work. It all may seem very glamorous to the beginner, who sees television floor reporters running around national conventions and buttonholing the elect of the country for interviews in front of the ever-present minicams with their instant replay videotapes.

Actually, that is only a small part of the job. Regardless of electronic advances in journalism, a certain amount of routine remains for every political reporter and it has to be done well. For coverage begins with registration and proceeds through the nominating process, the pre-convention maneuvers, the conventions themselves or the primary elections that have replaced them in many states, and then the coverage of the campaigns for all major candidates. What is involved here is a lot of traveling, interviewing, research and writing at all hours of the day and night; the reporter doesn't exist who can cover politics on a regular basis within the neat framework of a seven or eight-hour day.

Election Day The proceedings on election day, once so boisterous in the average American city, are reasonably quiet today. In big cities, with few exceptions, there is almost a holiday air with banks and bars closed and often shcools as well. It is seldom that there is news of such chicanery as stolen ballot boxes, the multiple voting of floaters and other tricks of the bad old days. If an election is being stolen, the few remaining political bosses try not to make a public announcement of it. Trickery at the polls, in consequence, is rather difficult to detect on election day; it comes to light long afterward, if at all.

This does not mean that news staffs have an easy time of it on election day, however. On the contrary, the arduous business of interviewing voters after they have cast their ballots now begins with the opening of the polls. And as the voting progresses, the news no longer is based on an hour-by-hour estimate of how many have voted but on projections at sample precincts of the standings of the various candidates. Of course, not every news organization is equipped to do this because it takes a major outlay of funds and commitments of staff and electronic gear. But those that do can make an election day story much more exciting than it has been in recent years.

Election Night The important thing about election night work is the effort that goes into organizing it. In the press and in the electronic media, the news staff that generally does the best job is the one that prepares for it with the greatest care. Sometimes the preparations for an election night begin as much as six months in advance. During the final weeks, the compilation of background figures, campaign materials, data covering everything from biographies to party platforms and the outlining of actual assignments are almost as important as the day-to-day coverage of the news. No good news organization goes into election night without complete, pretested planning and batteries of the best calculators and computers available, with trained personnel to run them.

Election coverage is the kind of thing the American news media do best. Once the polls close and the first figures start flowing from the newsrooms, partisanship is nearly always forgotten by the working journalists and all effort is concentrated on reporting who won, how victory was achieved and what it means. The union of wire services and the three major television networks for election-night coverage has been of enormous importance in reducing the public's uncertainty over the outcome in all but the very closest of Presidential elections.

Tabulating the Vote The public's attention is riveted on the television screens on election night and the electrifying announcements, as soon as possible, that one candidate or another has won. The electronic performance is risky, but it is in the journalistic tradition. Gradually, the major television news organizations have learned the bitter lesson that newspapers absorbed in the years before the electronic media took primacy in such spot-news reporting. They have become far more careful with the announcement of who won—and why—and have generally adopted a stance of responsibility that befits the journalist far better than a wild-eyed claim of exclusivity. Their cooperation on Presidential elections is in the public interest.

Even though television is first with the results and often first with the announcement of the winners, it cannot—by its very nature—provide the detailed tabulations of the voting down to the smallest districts and the totals amassed by every candidate in the various races. That is something good newspapers have always done superbly and they still continue to do so. Without this kind of service, it would be difficult for a democratic system to operate as well as it does.

HANDLING THE FIGURES

The basis of any voting announcement, whether it is given by the wire services, television or rival media, is the vote total itself, the number of districts it represents and the identities of these districts. No fragmentary vote is worth anything unless the source is identified, so that it can be compared at once with previous records. Thus, any voting result that is important enough to be made known should contain the number of voting districts, the area, and—if possible—the time as follows:

> 442 out of 1,346 election districts in Great Bear County, on the state's northern border, gave these totals at 10:32 P.M.:
>
> | | |
> |---|---|
> | Jones (D) | 60,024 |
> | Smith (R) | 50,555 |

26 election districts in the 64th Ward, in the heart of Central City's south side, gave these totals at 9:30 P.M.:

Brown (D)   2,022
Green (R)   2,366

The names of election units change, of course, from one place to another, but whether they are wards or districts, the practice is the same. On the basis of a sufficient cross-section of the voting, and a knowledge of past performance in the same area, a projection of the figures can be computed and an indicated voting result can be given. Thus, on the basis of a 25 per cent voting return, an experienced political analyst can calculate what will happen and make an announcement that reads something like this:

> On the basis of returns from one-quarter of the city's districts two hours after the polls closed, Smith led by 40,622 to 32,634 for Jones, his Democratic rival. This gave him an actual plurality of 8,028 over Jones and an indicated plurality of more than 30,000 if the same vote ratio continues.

Political analysts know if it is possible for the same ratio to continue. They have all the statistics of past performances and they have tabulating machines and computers, with operators, so that it takes little time to work out a proper projection in all but the closest contests.

Where cities are heavily Democratic and rural districts are overwhelmingly Republican, as is usually true in such states as Illinois, New Jersey and New York, the initial returns from cities, being tabulated faster, often show Democratic candidates far in the lead. But this is where the analysts come in. They point out that the early figures may be misleading. As the returns come in from rural areas, they make projections of the vote to see if the usual Republican majorities are being piled up; if they are, then it is a relatively simple matter to match this projection against those of the cities and arrive at a tentative winner if the swing between the candidates is wide enough. But where the difference between the candidates' vote percentages comes to 3 per cent on either side, the familiar danger point for most statistical compilations, the wise analyst concludes that it is best to await virtually complete results.

It has happened, although rarely, that candidates have conceded defeat on the basis of projected returns and gone to bed, only to find upon arising in the morning that they have won because of a surge of late returns in their favor. And sometimes, when only a handful of votes separates winner and loser, a recount may reverse the result. So caution in close elections is an article of faith in every newsroom on election night.

Doing the Story The writing or telling of the political story, actually, is the simplest part of the election night performance. The coverage of the returns, an unofficial service performed at the national level by a combination of news media working with public officials, is the first business of the journalist. Once the wire services were content to wait until the figures were supplied by slow-moving election board machinery; however, the television networks stepped in and hired hordes of temporary reporters—students, housewives and the like—to go to the precincts and get the returns. It was this kind of competition that finally forced the press to step up its own activity and, eventually, led to the alliance with the electronic media on major elections.

The stories of the election results—written and verbal—are based on the tabulated figures and the majorities and pluralities are calculated accordingly. (A majority is the difference between candidates where only two are running; a plurality between two candidates is the difference where more than two are in the race. A candidate may have a plurality over the second person in a three-way race and a majority over the combined total of the opposition.)

Anchor persons on TV need judgment, stamina and verbal skills to a high degree, but they don't have to worry too much about organizing their remarks. Newspaper work is different.

The key to the successful newspaper story on election night is the organization of the piece. It should be assembled in such a way that it need not be completely rewritten every time a voting total changes. Often, figures are left out of the lead for this reason. The lead is merely based on the fact that one candidate is leading, the actual returns being given immediately afterward in tabular style so that they can be changed quickly by substituting an insert.

Qualifying the Story Until a vote is final, or very close to it, it is difficult to put together a detailed analysis. Consequently, it is well in reporting on election night to use such qualifications as, "On the basis of scattered returns," or, "Partial and unofficial returns showed Smith had a narrow lead 30 minutes after the polls closed." In a newspaper or wire service account, the progress of the vote-reporting, if carried chronologically, can make a detailed and interesting running story. But there is not space for more than one such account in blanket election coverage as a rule. Such things have to be summarized in print, and on the air as well.

The only time a political correspondent can consider the election to be over is after the final figures are in and uncontested, or when all candidates save the winner have conceded defeat. Until then, a careful writer will phrase his lead to read something like this:

> Robert J. Epperson apparently was elected Mayor last night by an indicated plurality of 40,000 votes.
>
> Although no concession of defeat came from his rival, Arthur Ahlgrenson, Epperson claimed victory on the basis of returns from half the city's districts which gave him a commanding lead . . .

Sometimes, in a close election, a candidate may be the victor on the basis of final and unofficial returns and the loser may charge fraud, demand a recount or both. Circumstances dictate how the story should be presented, but it is only logical to report that one candidate has scored a victory which is being contested. The charges of fraud should be used in a lead only when there appears to be some basis for them. But the closeness of an election in itself is not *prima facie* evidence of fraudulent activity. In a famous case in New York State, a judgeship was decided by only one vote. On a recount, the apparent loser was turned into a victor by only one vote. Subsequent court action failed to justify suspicions of fraud in the outcome.

It is also a fallacy for reporters to jump to the conclusion that there is something phony about an election because they find inexplicable contradictions in the figure between votes registered and votes cast. Sometimes, clerical errors in mimeographed handouts prior to election lead to such confused situations. Consequently, while reporters must use the familiar fraud charges invariably made by losers in a close election, they cannot conclude that there is some basis for them until they are able to check the facts with responsible officials and both candidates. It is seldom that such things can be done on election night. Generally, they must await the official count two to three weeks after election day.

Styles vary in the reporting of election results in newspapers. Some carry the actual figures in a box preceding the story, where readers can see them before they look at anything else. Others like to use a lead saying who won, and then immediately summarize the salient figures, even though television has already done the job. Here is a general style in use on many newspapers and wire services, which is also familiar to television audiences who have heard it present-tensed and read by exhausted second-string announcers late at night after the first team has gone home:

> Arthur J. Wingate scored a surprise victory last night over his Democratic opponent, George Berling, who was seeking a third term as governor.
>
> The Republican triumph in the state, which ran counter to a nationwide Democratic trend, was the result primarily of deep inroads that Mr. Wingate made into normally Democratic pluralities in Central City, largest municipality in the state.
>
> Governor Berling conceded defeat at 11:15 last night. The concession followed a conference with Gunnar Dahlquist, chairman of the Democratic State Committee, and Mayor Franklin Quest of Central City.

At 12:32 A.M., with nearly complete state-wide returns in, 10,132 out of 11,110 districts gave:

Wingate (R)   2,834,263
Berling (D)   2,378,767

Nearly complete returns from Central City at that hour indicated that Mr. Wingate, 54-year-old industrialist from Willow Grove, had cut the usual Democratic plurality there to less than 400,000 votes. Four years ago, Governor Berling was able to carry the city by almost 700,000 votes . . .

The unofficial results, reported on election night by the news media, are seldom upset by challenges, charges or recounts, but the final result must await the official canvass. When there is an election upset, it is major news.

Chapter 26
The Big Story: Washington, the UN, the World

In the fall of 1974, a small, soft-voiced Georgian with a toothy smile and a pleasant manner came to the New England hills after the first frosts had set them to sparkling with crimson and gold. On the stone-fenced farmlands and in the quiet villages of New Hampshire, he patiently stopped people, shook hands when he could, and said, "My name is Jimmy Carter and I am running for President." And the response often was, "Jimmy who?"

Jimmy Carter wasn't much of a story then. No Washington reporters bothered to cover him. If local reporters took the time to look him over, it was usually because they thought the Georgian some kind of freak who might make a funny story. But as he finished first in the New Hampshire primary in February, 1976, and proceeded to win a majority of the 30-odd primaries that followed, people began addressing him respectfully as *Governor* Carter, recalling that he had been the chief executive of Georgia. The Washington press corps took to recording his movements, the salient facts of his life, the facets of his character, impressions of his wife, his mother and his small daughter, and even took to repeating the single campaign speech that he used in one form or another wherever he went. And so, Jimmy Carter burst upon the nation as a commanding figure. He won the Democratic Presidential nomination in New York City in the summer of 1976 and defeated President Ford in November, becoming the 39th President of the United States.

THE GREAT PLATFORMS

The ascendancy of President Carter is far from an isolated instance of the growth of a big story from modest beginnings.

Regardless of where the news originates, it becomes magnified to enormous scale as soon as it is picked up in Washington and the other great news centers of the world. This is the basis for global communication of the news of governments and their peoples. It is also, unfortunately, a powerful mechanism that may be seized upon by a single rioter with a fancied grievance, who commits an outrage against public order and thereby has his puny voice amplified a thousandfold. For the news media in effect provide a national and world platform for news makers, good and bad, in every global center of communication. Of these, Washington is by all odds the most powerful.

THE CORRESPONDENTS

Among the 70,000 or so full-time journalists employed by news organizations in the United States, a comparatively small number become Washington, United Nations or foreign correspondents on a permanent basis. For those who have the background, learning, ability and good fortune to survive the rigorous tests of practical journalism, the privilege of covering the outstanding national and international developments of our time is among the finest rewards the profession has to offer.

Whether reporters are at work in the White House, Congress or the United Nations, in the chanceries of Europe, the Great Hall of the People in Peking or in the shadow of the Kremlin, their highest duty is to record and explain the decisions that will lead eventually to world peace or world destruction. Theirs is, in the main, the story of an age of political, social and economic upheaval—an era when man has walked on the moon, sent photographic robots to explore Mars and reached out for more distant planets without being able to solve the essential problems of hunger, shelter and overpopulation on earth.

Characteristics There are always a few daring and courageous youngsters who turn up in the midst of a war or civil disorder overseas and catch on, either as stringers or part-time reporters with the profes-

Helen Thomas, UPI's senior White House correspondent, chatting with President Jimmy Carter aboard the Presidential jet. United Press International. Used with permission.

sionals who represent American news organizations. They work for newspapers or wire services, networks or news magazines, or try to get by on their own as tipsters. Often, the best of them develop into full-fledged correspondents and give a good account of themselves. But they are the exceptions, rather than the rule, in the development of foreign correspondents.

Most of those who represent American news organizations abroad today are mature and reasonably well educated. They may not all have the gift of languages (few Americans do), but they are invariably resourceful, know their own business, and are able to find their way around in difficult situations. Most of them have the ability to soak up the essential history, geography and culture of the areas to which they are assigned. Nearly all of them are aggressive and unlikely to accept much "guidance" from the resident American embassy personnel. For if they have a single dominant characteristic, it is independence.

What the Public Wants If news organizations based their national and international coverage on what they think the public wants, there would be precious little of either except for major news breaks. It is one of the ironies of our time, when the United States remains the most powerful nation on earth and has vast global interests, that the American people are so little interested in the day-by-day coverage of national and world affairs. At peak periods, such as the end of the Vietnam War, the break in the Watergate scandal and national elections, of course there is a demand for news. But otherwise, from Broadway to Main Street, people are more interested in their own affairs at home.

The Foreign News Corps The peaks and valleys of news interest by the public (and by editors) are best illustrated by the assignments of foreign correspondents employed by American news organizations. At the end of World War II, 2,500 correspondents—many of whom had been under fire—were demobilized by their organizations with even greater speed than the American armed forces.

There were temporary buildups of the corps during every crisis, from the Berlin blockade of 1948–1949 to the Vietnam War and the various outbreaks in the Mideast, but it never again achieved its strength of the 1942–1945 period. Even at the height of the Vietnam War, no more than 500 or so correspondents were accredited from American news organizations. Thereafter, when the United States sank into an uncertain peace for the first time in many years, its news media reduced to fewer than 400 the number of full-time, regularly assigned and salaried journalists stationed abroad. And two-thirds of them were in Europe.

It is, therefore, a considerable exaggeration to report, as sometimes happens, that 3,000 or 4,000 American journalists are covering a war in a small country in Asia or Africa. Most of them are stringers, others are hangers-on and on the fringes there are always shadowy characters who are suspected by the bona fide press corps of being intelligence agents.

As an illustration of the falsity of this numbers game, anybody who has visited the United Nations press headquarters on a routine day knows that fewer than 50 full-time, regularly assigned correspondents are there from American news organizations and nowhere near that many from foreign news media. Yet, on a General Assembly opening day, the UN press office usually announces it has accredited anywhere from 1,500 to 2,000 "journalists," who generally vanish as soon as the major personalities return to their regular posts. It invariably serves as a reminder that not everybody who pretends to be a journalist actually is one.

The Washington News Corps Even though some newspapers have pulled their correspondents out of Washington, the nation's capital is still the major news attraction in both domestic and foreign news coverage and the news corps numbers about 2,000 representatives from all countries at peak periods. While many medium and small-size American dailies make no secret of their prejudice against the routine news reports from Washington and abroad, and the local electronic media are even less interested, it takes a petty type of know-nothing editor to cut down on such coverage. At editors' meetings, there is always solemn agreement that this is the kind of news the American public must have but their newspapers don't always show it. Responsible editors, however, take a certain amount of pride in offering solid information from the nation's capital. Those who can't afford to send their own correspondents subscribe to one of the big newspaper syndicates that make national news available at relatively modest cost as a supplement to the wire services.

WASHINGTON NEWS CENTERS

For all the restrictions that are placed upon them, Washington correspondents are broadly representative of newspapers and wire services, news magazines and magazines of commentary, syndicates, radio and TV and news letters. In addition, there are the "one shot" correspondents who are always in and out of Washington on single assignments for their home town papers or stations. And the foreign media frequently do the same thing at times of peak interest.

It is important, therefore, to know how to establish a base in Washington, permanent or temporary, and operate effectively.

Those who are assigned to work in Washington as members of established bureaus are lucky because their associates ease the breaking-in period and provide advice on such problems as housing, commuting, schools for children and so on. But for those who go to the capital for the first time on their own, it is a bewildering and sometimes traumatic experience. Newcomers are well advised to make themselves known to the chiefs of the wire services and syndicates to which their organization subscribes, their Congressional delegation and key information personnel in such strategic spots as the White House, State Department, Pentagon and the House and Senate Press Galleries.

Because of the publicity attached to the National Press Club, and the proximity of news teletype machines, loners in Washington sometimes try to work there on the basis of a temporary membership. However, as a rule, they are likely to be overwhelmed there by press agents of all kinds. It is a much sounder practice to work out of a place like the Senate Press Gallery, when Congress is in session, or to pick a particular story each day and follow it through, whatever the location. One inflexible rule for newcomers in Washington is to get to all assignments well ahead of time to meet the newsmakers and their staff personnel. Another is to insure that there is quick access to a telephone or wire for filing—sometimes far easier said than done in Washington on a major story.

In a book of this nature, which can be only a survey of overall Washington coverage rather than an in-depth study, all that can be attempted is a brief enumeration of the principal points of news and a few suggestions on what to do and what not to do. These are as follows:

The White House The President of the United States, being the single most important news source in the country as well as the most influential, is given intensive daily coverage by every important news organization in the nation and others abroad. So are the members of his family, his friends and close associates.

Yet, the press facilities at the White House are poorer than at many a state house or even a city hall. Only a small number of correspondents regularly assigned to the White House have one of the tiny cubicles plus telephone in the press room; the rest have to scamper for their communications on deadline.

The President's press secretary is generally available once or twice a day for news conferences, announcements or background material. He and his assistants are the gatekeepers who can ease the newcomer's approach to members of the Presidential staff and the various offices directly responsible to the President. The better-known correspondents, of course, make their own appointments and often conduct a substantial part of their business by telephone except on breaking stories. On days when the President is having a news conference, it is usual for 200 or more correspondents to attend if there is advance notice. If the conference is hastily called, only the regulars have time to attend.

The broadcast media are always on call and ready to work at the White House, but are no longer dependent on the unwieldy cameras on tripods that were set up in the reception room to catch important visitors as they left the President's office. With the minicam and videotape, TV people are mobile enough now to vie with other reporters in watching side entrances for visitors who seek to avoid publicity. TV crews can also get into the Rose Garden on short notice if a Presidential news conference is called there on the spur of the moment.

A number of news conferences of subordinate officials, many for background, are held in a medium-sized room called the "Fish Room," after the fish pictures on its walls. And when the President is about to travel, the correspondents accompanying him must make their arrangements through the White House. There may be times on the White House beat when reporters sit around aimlessly and wait for something to happen, but such periods are infrequent. The President, the nation's No. 1 newsmaker, keeps the correspondents occupied with his activities.

Congress If the President of the United States and the principal members of his Cabinet choose to be reticent about a policy or an issue, the Congress of the United States very quickly fills the news vacuum. Next to the White House, the "Hill" is the most important point for news in the capital. Reporters who regularly cover the Senate and the House have a good working relationship with the majority and minority leaders of both Houses, as well as with other legislative officials. They know the committee chairmen and develop efficient methods of keeping in touch with them. Whereas background conferences and other "I'll-tell-you-but-don't-quote-me" expedients are almost the rule in the executive branch of the government, the members of Congress generally put everything on the record. They want their views known. As elected officials, they seek to publicize their actions and their positions on the issues of the day; the voters all too easily forget a senator or a representative from whom nothing is heard for weeks at a time.

For the newcomer, the press galleries in both Houses are about the most convenient places to work in Washington. The superintendents and their small but able staffs in the press galleries know more than most reporters about schedules, speeches, committee hearings and the numerous other facets of the news that may be expected during the course of a Congressional day. Advance copies of major (and a lot of minor) speeches are readily available, either in the press galleries or through the offices of the respective authors. The press gallery officials and other members of Congressional staffs can be exceedingly helpful at times in reaching a Senator or a Representative, either by telephone at his office or by message on the floor of one of the two Houses. Reporters quickly learn that they cannot take the time to make the rounds in the Senate and House office buildings, except where the story makes such a procedure necessary. It is easier to use the telephone.

As the Congressional Directory shows, the sources of news in the Congress are manifold. And as the Congressional Record testifies each day, there are many speeches and other pronouncements that never attract public notice until they are published; moreover, a published speech may be considerably different from the original version because members of Congress have the right of correction and of extending their remarks. A final caution to the newcomer (and to many a veteran as well) is the warning to be familiar with the procedures in both Houses; without such knowledge, much of the intricate maneuvering that takes place during the legislative process cannot be translated into terms understandable to the public. It is a journalistic truism that there is so much news in Washington that it becomes a problem not of what to use, but of what to eliminate.

The State Department In the massive grey building on "Foggy Bottom," about 50 or 60 correspondents regularly cover the affairs of the State Department and several hundred others come rushing in whenever there is a crisis. The inadequate press room, with its tiny cubicles for the reporters, is a chamber of echoes but is used for lack of something better. The wire service staffs, which have slightly larger quarters, do much of their work by dictating to their main offices in Washington.

Primary sources at State are the departmental news divisions, situated near the press room, and the office of the Assistant Secretary of State for Public Affairs on the sixth floor. In addition, the correspondent who is known and respected has access to most of the major officials of the department, up to and sometimes including the Secretary of State himself. Nearly any correspondent can arrange through the small group of press officers to gain access to the desk officials in direct contact with embassies and ministries abroad. This kind of information usually is put out on a background basis. For more direct news reporting, the primary resort is the daily news conference by one of the senior officials in the Public Affairs office. The machinery at State is flexible enough to handle queries or requests for reactions at almost any time of the day, but once the "lid is on" in the evening it takes something akin to a war scare to produce news out of the department.

The Secretary of State and his immediate aides schedule their own news conferences from time to time, but always in consultation with the White House. The printed matter available at State is mountainous in scope, but little of it is new except an occasional White Paper or other policy pronouncement that is issued as a document. Yet, State can be a valuable research facility to those correspondents who know how to operate there and whose offices permit them to spend some time in preparing a story.

With the exception of Secretaries John Foster Dulles in the Eisenhower administration, Dean Acheson in the Truman administration and Henry A. Kissinger in the Nixon and Ford administrations, Secretaries of State since 1933 more often than not have been subordinate to White House political advisers. Such academic figures as Arthur M. Schlesinger Jr. in the Kennedy administration, Walt Whitman Rostow in the Johnson administration and Kissinger in the Nixon administration, while he was national security adviser, received more attention in the news than the entire State Department.

This was particularly true of Kissinger because of his personal diplomacy, his liking for long trips and private negotiations and his penchant for secrecy and press management. Both before and after he became secretary of state, he was a major news figure and took care to see that he never was neglected by the news media. He was in one sense a reporter's delight because of his many personal background briefings; in another sense, because of his secretiveness, he was a reportorial burden. When President Carter pledged a policy of "openness with the American people" in the formulation of foreign policy, he was in effect trying to reverse a trend in American government in general and the handling of international affairs in particular. His Secretary of State, Cyrus Vance, agreed with him. It remained to be seen how far they could really go, for not even President Wilson, who called for "open covenants openly arrived at," actually practiced that ideal.

The Defense Department   Any bona fide correspondent with business in the Defense Department has very little trouble gaining access to the proper officials in the Pentagon. But getting news is something else again. In periods of crisis, restrictions abound. One of the most obnoxious rules, initiated at the time of the Cuban missile crisis, requires all Pentagon officials to report on all contacts with newsmen. While it was enforced, it remained the subject of almost endless controversy.

Regardless of the difficulties of obtaining vital information, the machinery for developing and handling news at the Pentagon is probably the most elaborate ever devised for any department of government in this country. The Defense Department (DOD) has its own information setup under an Assistant Secretary of Defense, which includes representatives of all military services, and a big press room on the second floor of the Pentagon where each service has a desk manned by a number of officers. In addition, the Army, Navy and Air Force each has its own staff of information personnel (Army and Air Force each has a consolidated external and internal information program). Thus, nearly 1,000 officers in the Pentagon are assigned to some facet of public relations activities. In turn, they direct the information and public relations work of small staffs and individuals at each post and base throughout the world; thus, a small army of public relations officers is assigned specifically to work with press and public and within the armed forces themselves.

In the longish and somewhat musty room assigned to Pentagon reporters, opposite the Pentagon press room, there are almost as few places for the working press as there are at the White House. But generally, only a score or so of correspondents turn up daily for the routine chores of coverage. But when the Secretary of Defense holds a news conference, or the Joint Chiefs of Staff figure in the news, the response is very heavy. Otherwise, the Washington press corps does much of its routine business with the various military desks by telephone.

Because of the fierce interservice rivalry within the Pentagon and the equally intense feeling of the military against encroachment on their preserve by the State Department or even the White House, the leaking of secret papers to the news media is a peculiar feature of unauthorized activity there. As long ago as the interservice war over the proposed construction of the B–36 superbomber for the Air Force in the late 1940s, rival military cliques were leaking secret position papers in an effort to discredit the aircraft and block appropriations for it. This situation came to a climax in 1971 and 1972 with the publicly admitted disclosure of the Pentagon Papers by Dr. Daniel Ellsberg, a former Pentagon official, supposedly in the cause of peace, and the leaking of a whole series of papers on secret government policies to the syndicated columnist, Jack Anderson, by other sources that he identified as military in part.

This sort of thing is likely to continue as long as there are huge military appropriations and factions that seek to sway the public's view in one direction or another. The morality of using such material is something that each news organization must decide for itself on the basis of the circumstances and the extent of the public interest that is involved.

The Supreme Court The correspondents assigned to the Supreme Court on a regular basis are few in number and highly specialized in their background and training. Not any reporter can be assigned on a minute's notice to go galloping over to the highest court in the land on a decision day to pick up the text of a ruling in a major case and write an understandable account of the proceedings. Some of the regulars who cover the court are lawyers; others have had some legal training. Even those without special backgrounds in the law have to develop their own knowledge in order to function properly.

Treasury One of the most important innovations developed by the Treasury Department is the "Budget School" which is held for several days prior to the release of the federal budget. Correspondents, many with special training in economic affairs, have a chance to study this formidable document and talk with the nation's leading authorities on it before presenting their accounts to the public.

This kind of preparation is woefully lacking in many other areas of coverage in Washington, where it is needed. The Treasury has shown that it is possible to enter into a workable agreement with the news media on matters of importance to the public, such as government expenditures and the prospect of new taxes, to give correspondents time for study and reflection. In affairs of this nature, the few paragraphs scrambled together for a deadline ten minutes away can sometimes be totally misleading. It is better to wait, in agreement with the source and with the competition, and give the whole story in proper perspective.

In periods of economic tension, the Treasury is also the source of news about monetary policies and the various temporary controls on prices and wages that accompany them from time to time.

Agriculture The correspondents who cover the Department of Agriculture, like those at State, Defense and the Treasury, are generally highly specialized in the field and work for news organizations with a particular interest in the subject. The daily routine of agricultural reports is ably carried by the wire services. But for detailed, in-depth reportage on matters of importance to both farmer and consumer, the news media must turn once more to the specialist.

Other Areas All except the largest and richest news organizations necessarily are unable to staff the many other important government departments daily. Consequently, the Justice Department, the Labor Department, the Departments of Commerce, the Interior and Health, Education and Welfare, to name only a few, are covered by the wire services for the majority of the Washington press corps. Individual correspondents with a special interest in the affairs of Justice or Labor, for example, may spend much more time there than others. Or, the whole group may strain the facilities of a single department, such as Labor, during a national strike emergency. The point is that even the large press corps in the nation's capital has to work on the "firehouse principle" for everything except the top newsmaking sources. And woe betide the unfortunate correspondent who guesses that he can spend a quiet day researching a favorite project at the Department of Health, Education and Welfare only to find out that the President has sent an emergency message to Congress in his absence from contact with his regular news sources.

Among the regulatory agencies, the news media have a natural and abiding interest in almost anything that is done by the Federal Communications Commission. And, with the rising interest in consumerism, more attention is being paid to the Federal Trade Commission. Otherwise, the regulatory agencies and the Postal Service are probably the worst-covered news-making organizations in Washington on a day-to-day basis.

HAZARDS IN RELATIONS WITH NEWS MEDIA

The pressures of public policy and national security sometimes make for difficulties between government and the news media. Disclosures that embarrass the government, mainly in the press, are never accepted with either grace or equanimity. While it may not be general policy to compile a White House "enemies list" and turn it over to the Internal Revenue Service, in line with President Nixon's contribution to the national welfare, no administration is friendly with reporters who are too inquisitive. It also happens, now and then, that when a President or members of his administration try to use the news media as an instrument of public policy, the effort backfires with disastrous consequences.

The Credibility Gap Despite some doubts against the kinds of military information that were put out by the Roosevelt and Truman administrations during World War II, their policies were not widely challenged; in fact, the maintenance of secrecy over the development of the atomic bomb was accounted a national triumph until it became known that spies had leaked essential data to the Soviet Union. However, the credibility gap did not begin until the Eisenhower administration, when the Soviet Union disclosed in 1960 despite White House denials that a U–2 spy plane had been shot down deep inside its territory. It widened in 1961 when President Kennedy tried and failed to cover up the key role of the CIA in organizing the disastrous Bay of Pigs landing in Castro's Cuba. Again in 1963, the Kennedy administration supported the claims of the Diem regime in South Vietnam that "victory" was at hand over the Vietcong.

Thereafter, for the remainder of the Vietnam War, few major statements of the Johnson and Nixon administrations were accepted without challenge and many were proved to be false. The final indignity was, of course, the Watergate scandal cover-up that led to President Nixon's forced resignation.

With such a record, it became a heavy burden for succeeding administrations to try to restore the faith of the American people and of foreign governments in the information provided by the government of the United States on key matters of public policy, particularly those affecting national security. Unhappily, the success of the press in disclosing the shortcomings of government did not endear journalists to the American public. It was their fate to be doubted almost as much as the government — and to be resented by the more zealous partisans of the overthrown President.

FREEDOM AND SECURITY

The government and the news media will always agree to the general proposition that no news should be made public in time of crisis that violates national security. However, no agreement appears to be possible on exactly what constitutes national security in any given set of circumstances. It follows that the responsibility of determining what information should be withheld is exercised primarily by the government. However, when and if the press learns that information is being wrongfully withheld for reasons other than national security, its responsibility is to make prompt disclosures of such material in the public interest. That is the substance of what is known as the adversary relationship with government.

This posture of basic conflict between a democratic government and the free press has been the subject of continuing discussion between journalists and responsible public officials for many years. The relationship is by no means typical only of the United States. As long ago as the Crimean War in the middle of the nineteenth century, William

Howard Russell's disclosures of tragic mismanagement of the British military brought great prestige to *The Times* of London and caused the downfall of the Aberdeen government. Such instances may be documented in every practicing democracy where there is an effective, competent and critical free press.

It is the prevailing theory that the public interest is best served by a continuing rivalry between the two forces. However, if the conflict is pushed to excess, and if all restraint is abandoned by both government and the news media, then the probable result is bound to be anarchy.

In national and international affairs, where so much impinges on national security, correspondents and editors are well aware of all the eloquent philosophy on both sides of the question of whether to reveal or suppress. Despite all the pressures upon them, it will be their decision finally as to what material in their possession will be passed on to the public. This is the highest responsibility of journalists in an open society. To exercise it, they must stand or fall on their own judgment.

THE PRESIDENTIAL NEWS CONFERENCE

It is a peculiarly American custom to have the President of the United States regularly face the questions of newspapermen, wire service, news magazine and radio-TV correspondents. Until the turn of the century, it had occurred to no President to do this, and the newspapers themselves were not particularly interested. Then, President Theodore Roosevelt took to talking with reporters and consigning them to the "Ananias Club" when they published stories he did not like. President Wilson initiated the occasional press conference.

The founding of the Presidential news conference as we know it today was the work of President Franklin Delano Roosevelt. As a past master of the art of handling reporters and editors, and a talented politician who enjoyed jousting with the press, he saw to it that news conferences were held on the average of twice a week during his four terms. President Truman continued F.D.R.'s system. Although he did not hold as many news conferences as his predecessor, they were every bit as expert.

Under President Eisenhower the final shred of protection for a Chief Executive was ripped away. Historically, Presidents had been given the privilege of having their answers to all questions published in indirect discourse. When Presidents permitted direct quotation of a few words or perhaps a sentence, it was a major event. But, once Eisenhower permitted TV cameras to record the Presidential news conference and go on the air with the film, following review, it was impossible to keep the press from using direct quotations. So, after a brief check, Presidential news conferences in the Eisenhower regime were on the record.

The Kennedy Era During President Kennedy's 1,000 days, the televised news conference attained perfection as a dramatic spectacle, whatever may have been said about its usefulness as a device for the public disclosure of news about government. The President generally enjoyed them. He was, in the best sense of the word, a performer. Instead of remaining in the White House and causing the correspondents to line up in an uncomfortable group before his desk, he transferred the whole performance to the capacious auditorium of the State Department. It became a show and he was, in every way, the star. This was the Kennedy style. He did away with the safeguard of reviewing a tape of his televised conference and, with a supreme gesture of self-confidence, let the entire business go out live.

All the Way with LBJ During President Johnson's years in office, the contrast with the Kennedy style was striking. The somber Texan — during much of his tenure in the White House — engaged in a running feud with the press. One casualty was the free-swinging Presidential news conference. Generally, when President Johnson called in reporters, he gave very little advance notice and he also placed the television crews under a considerable handicap. It was his style to crowd people around him and use up a considerable amount of his time with the reading of announcements. He made no secret of his dislike of many of the correspondents. The feeling was mutual. It accounted for a considerable part of the bad press that was characteristic of the Johnson administration.

The Nixon Collapse President Nixon conducted overt warfare against his critics in the news media and news organizations that set reporters to digging into his affairs. Until Vice President Spiro Agnew was forced to resign after pleading "no contest" to tax fraud charges, he was the Nixon Administration's "hatchet" man against the news media. The President himself made no secret of his mistrust of the Washington press corps, holding fewer news conferences than any President since Herbert Hoover. The atmosphere around the White House became poisonous. Following Nixon's resignation, there was little improvement for months.

W.I.N. with Ford Although the nation brimmed over with good will for President Ford when he took over after Nixon's resignation on August 8, 1974, he was in trouble within a month when he issued a Presidential pardon for his predecessor and his press secretary, J. F. ter Horst, resigned in protest. Ford never seemed very happy with his news conferences and held only an average of about three every two months during his somewhat more than two years as the nation's first nonelected President. While he tried to be available to the news media and appointed a professional as his press secretary, Ron Nessen, he had few adherents among the Washington press corps. Like his W.I.N. buttons ("Whip Inflation Now"), his favorable press didn't last long. Too much was made of occasions when he stumbled or bumped his head.

Carter's Promise The Carter administration began with a pledge of open dealing in public office, including a promise, "I will never lie to you." President Carter, however, had his reservations about the press although he promised two news conferences a month. He liked direct communications with the public, restored FDR's "fireside chats" by sitting in a sweater beside a real log fire in his TV talks to the nation, and also invited letters and phone calls from the public. As a result, he was not a great favorite of the Washington press corps, although his efficiency at press conferences won their respect.

THE UNITED NATIONS STORY

In the years when the United States dominated the United Nations, it was a fairly popular assignment among journalists although the American news media seldom paid much attention to the story except at crisis periods. Since the United States has been pushed into a minority position, outvoted or checkmated by a majority of developing countries that have links with the Soviet bloc, China or both, the UN has become unpopular in America. Outbursts of anti-American oratory, crises affecting the Arab states or the black nationalists of Africa, and the pretentious maneuvering of the Soviet bloc have little interest either for the American public or for many correspondents except when it touches a sensitive national nerve.

Yet, for as long as there is a United Nations and for as long as its headquarters remain in New York, it is a story that must be covered. Even if the majority sentiments that are repeated to the point of boredom are repugnant to nearly all Americans, the story continues to be important.

Problems of Coverage The UN is not difficult to cover. The problem, like that of the State Department, is that there is too much paper work, too little action. Most of the large national delegations have press officers, a few of whom are first rate. The UN itself has a small group of capable career press officials who work for Secretary General Kurt Waldheim. At the UN documents counter, relevant materials are easily available; in the UN library, there is a backlog of information on every pending issue and a lot that have been forgotten.

The procedures of the UN, the rules of its main organizations and the interpretations of the Charter are complicated, but not more so than those of any government. Well-qualified correspondents have never had much difficulty in moving around the UN. The main problem of coverage is that there is so little of it.

Methods and Sources These are the four prinicipal sources for the UN story:

1.   The open meetings, speeches and resolutions of the various components of the organization. These are chiefly the General Assembly, Security Council and Economic and Social Council with their subsidiary committees.

2.   The foreign delegations which, however reticent they may be about their own business, generally may be relied on in a highly unofficial way to give background information on what is going on elsewhere behind the scenes. Some, of course, do not; but delegations — like lawyers — are prone to try their cases in the news media at home and abroad if they see some profit in doing so.

3.   The U. S. Mission to the UN. This is an extension of the State Department, but it has its own public affairs and information officers plus an excellent library. The information staff is competent, but it usually does not have too much freedom of action for obvious reasons. Not all negotiations can be carried on with a brass band.

4.   The United Nations' own information staff and the resources of the Secretary General. Over the years the UN has developed a system of chronological reporting of all major meetings, with takes of copy available for correspondents an hour or so after delivery. This small, but qualified, news staff clears through a city desk of its own on the second floor of the UN Secretariat Building and may be consulted by correspondents.

The secretary general, being responsible to all UN members, cannot very well be expected to make earth-shaking pronouncements affecting them, but he manages to make news in his own way at periodic news conferences during the year and in his reports to the organization.

Physically the center of UN press coverage is the third floor of the Secretariat building, where the press liaison, documents center, briefing room and some correspondents' offices are located. Wire, cable, telephone and other communications facilities are available here, too. Accreditation is handled easily, and with a minimum of red tape, the chief requirements being a letter from a managing editor of a newspaper, or other appropriate official, requesting privileges for a correspondent.

FOREIGN CORRESPONDENCE

There is an almost universal feeling in American newsrooms, where such things matter, that the big story overseas is not often told in terms that can be communicated easily to average readers and viewers. The usual surveys, with their findings of minimum use of foreign news in a

Peter Arnett of the Associated Press, winner of a Pulitzer Prize for his war correspondence in Vietnam, going into action with a tank patrol. (Copyright, Associated Press. Used by permission.)

large section of the American press and even less in the broadcast media, are depressing to anybody who has worked in the field and knows how much talent and effort and money go into foreign news coverage.[1] Admittedly, the crisis story, the war story and the personal stories about colorful characters get through in volume. But the straws in the wind, the stories that should put the American public on guard, do not seem to be widely used. It is a fact, too, that fewer than a dozen American correspondents were in Saigon in the crucial years when the United States was slowly enmeshing itself in a war it could not win and was almost certain to lose.

[1] W. Phillips Davison, *International Political Communication* (New York, 1965), p. 51.

The Flow of Foreign News In general, there is much more foreign news that is available on a daily basis than the American news media can possibly use. The AP and UPI distribute around 200,000 words a week each in inbound foreign news. If the average American newspaper uses 10,000 words a week (the electronic media can't absorb anywhere near that amount), wire service editors regard it as something of a triumph. Some of the newspapers that have foreign services and syndicate them probably furnish as much or more to their clients.

The Audience There are hopeful signs that more people in the United States are following foreign news regularly. The millions of Americans who travel abroad each year plus the additional millions of foreigners who visit this country have helped stimulate a less parochial view of the news among editors. The State Department in the decade of the 1970s has reported an increasing volume of communications by letter and telephone from citizens about various problems involving foreign policy. Specialized publications about international issues are slowly expanding; the quarterly *Foreign Affairs*, for example, which had only about 20,000 circulation in 1950, was close to 75,000 in the 1970s. And university courses in international affairs have become increasingly popular.[2] Still, the educational process is inevitably so slow that it is doubtful that more than 10 per cent of the American people have a continuing interest in foreign affairs, and probably the total is closer to 5 per cent in noncrisis periods.

True, surveys have shown continually that the relatively small audience for foreign news contains a disproportionately large number of leading citizens in most communities and decision-makers at all levels of government. But this does not make the job of the foreign editor and the foreign correspondent any easier at a time when the United States has a greater global involvement than at any other era in its history.

The most promising development in the dissemination of foreign news in the United States is the rapid progress of the newspaper syndicates. The *New York Times*, with the largest and most comprehensive foreign service, has more than 300 newspaper clients. The *Los Angeles Times*, within a few years, has more than 200 newspapers and the allied *Washington Post* (in foreign news only) has also expanded considerably. The *Baltimore Sun*, after refusing to syndicate for many years, now offers its foreign news to others and has won a respectable audience. Some of the older foreign services, the *Christian Science Monitor* among them, are being revitalized. And papers like the *Minneapolis Tribune*, *St. Louis Post-Dispatch*, *Miami Herald* and others send out specialists to report on particular issues in the news abroad. But the famous *Chicago Daily News* foreign staff has been disbanded.

[2] W. Phillips Davison. *Mass Communication and Conflict Resolution* (New York, 1974), p. 62.

In areas where there are poor newspapers with minimal national and international coverage, the news magazines sell much of their seven million copies a week with detailed foreign news sections. As for the TV networks, while they still take most of their information from the wire services, they are developing sophisticated staffs of foreign correspondents who work mainly with their cameramen. Business news organizations like the Dow Jones, McGraw-Hill and Fairchild publications have comprehensive staff coverage of major foreign business centers.

Foreign News Space It is difficult to generalize on how much foreign news is used because so much depends on the particular story, the news organization involved and the potential audience. In a time when the United States is at peace all over the world, it is obvious that there is going to be less public interest and less time and space devoted to foreign affairs. In time of war, that situation often changes rapidly; for any prolonged crisis, the space and time devoted to foreign news have a specific co-relation to public anxiety.

Even when things are quiet, the *New York Times* can be expected to publish between 16 and 18 columns a day of foreign dateline news. Under the same circumstances, the *Los Angeles Times* averages ten or 11 columns, the *Washington Post,* nine or ten; the *Baltimore Sun,* eight or nine, with somewhere between four and six columns daily in perhaps 30 other leading papers that have a circulation of about ten million. Added to this, of course, are the foreign news sections in the weekly news magazines and the sometimes important foreign commentaries and presentations on the nightly network news programs.

The *Wall Street Journal* runs a major foreign piece from one of its own excellent correspondents at regular intervals, with a considerable impact on its more than one million national readers. And when the *New Yorker* magazine does a foreign story by one of its small but brilliant group of writers on international affairs, it often has national significance as well. The same is true of the infrequent television documentaries on foreign affairs.

This does not excuse the far from satisfactory performance of the preponderance of American dailies and weeklies in the publication of foreign news, or the paucity of such material on the air when there is no war. But as has been shown, the pattern, on the whole, is mixed. It could be a great deal better. But it also has been a great deal worse.

THE FOREIGN CORRESPONDENT'S JOB

The foreign correspondents who handle the bulk of the news for American news organizations are mature journalists with a superior record of professional performance and a solid education. It is not unusual to

Ovie Carter *(left), photographer, and William Mullen, reporter, both of the* Chicago Tribune, *winners of a Pulitzer Prize in Foreign Correspondence for their coverage of famine in Africa and India. (Copyright,* the Chicago Tribune. *Used with permission.)*

find among them men and women with advanced degrees. Some are Nieman Fellows at Harvard and there are even a few Rhodes Scholars.

They travel a great deal from established bases and usually are given new assignments every three years. If they have to take risks, they do so because it is part of the job and not just for the fun of it. In combat zones, the first thing they learn to do is to keep their heads down. A dead correspondent may be a hero, but news organizations naturally prefer to have their staffers hale of body and sound of wind. And as for rising to the heights and defying dictatorial governments, correspondents find out very soon that being expelled through provocation is not the high road to success.

How to Be One The manner of becoming a foreign correspondent is still as great an uncertainty as ever, despite all the talk about modern personnel methods. Some are chosen for the job and trained rigorously for it with special courses in great universities and hours of practice in a foreign language. Many more happen to be at the right spot at the right time and fall into it. A few adventurers persuade editors to try them, with indifferent results as a rule (although sometimes there are pleasant surprises). The rest of the foreign correspondents work their way up slowly in the news agencies and on newspapers having foreign staffs, and quite often are picked off by the ever-watchful news magazines and electronic media for their own foreign staffs.

While most of the dependable older men and the few women who are established foreign correspondents can count on fairly decent pay, there are youngsters who are willing to work for less than they could earn on a police beat at home. It is only when the action is rough and the risks are very great that the younger people tend to get top preference, particularly in war zones. In television's first war, the Vietnam conflict, the youngsters often dominated the battle coverage.

That, too, was the experience in the trouble-wracked Mideast, especially in the long and brutal Lebanese civil war.

How They Work Most foreign correspondents believe their first duty is to tell the story of the people of the nation to which they are assigned, not merely the official acts of the government and the various press ministry announcements. The job is difficult and demanding, requiring long and sometimes irregular hours of work at periods of the day and night that can break up family life. It is no accident that the divorce rate among foreign correspondents is comparatively high.

Where correspondents are assigned to cover an entire country, such as India, or several countries, such as the northern sector of the South American continent, it is apparent that they have to depend on the local mass communications facilities to keep themselves informed. However, they soon find that they have to do more than read papers, listen to the radio, watch TV, see what the wires are sending and be friendly with American embassy and host country information people. They have to develop their own sources, their own story ideas, their own methods of operation—and that takes time and a lot of money. Without counting transmission tolls, the average news organization excluding wire services can expect to pay at least $75,000 to $100,000 a year to keep a single foreign correspondent in a post—and a good deal more in places like Moscow and Peking.

Correspondents in authoritarian lands, such as the Soviet Union, China and many of the developing countries, can expect to be tied very largely to official sources. In the dwindling number of democratic lands, there is freedom of action if correspondents know what they want to do and how to go about it. It isn't often that editors want to lead correspondents by the hand, or even make the attempt, despite the availability of miracles of modern communication. Foreign correspondence is still a highly individual operation and it is right that it should remain so.

Propaganda It is a great popular delusion that the average American overseas is a ready victim for the wiles of foreign propaganda. The American politician who participates in a foreign conference is usually despaired of in advance. As for foreign correspondents, even their own editors sometimes refuse to believe them if their stories happen to coincide with claims that are being put out by a propaganda agency.

The fundamental difficulty here is to define propaganda and separate it from the journalistic commodity that is called news. Propaganda need not necessarily be based on false or misleading information; the "big lie," in fact, has certainly been less effective in the past than the truth—when the truth happened to serve propaganda ends. Of course, few propagandists are foolish enough to label their more subtle ventures, but no propagandist is likely to deceive an experienced correspondent for very long.

Transmission of Information Under current practice by news organizations with large volumes of news to transmit, circuits are contracted for on a time basis. A global wire service, for example, could keep 24-hour circuits going for two-way transmissions across the Atlantic. Under such circumstances, copy is transmitted in much the same way across or under oceans as it is over land lines or in the newsroom of a major organization. The old coded messages now have only interoffice service functions.

For a foreign service like that of the *New York Times*, transmission of certain kinds of data at 1,000 to 1,500 words a minute is not unusual. The wire services move as fast. Moreover, the system of telephone dictation into recording devices, which are quickly transcribed, is gaining favor at a number of overseas points as a rival to Telex. For television, the satellite system has been a great advantage; with the increase in satellites and the growth of sophisticated cable channels, enormous improvements already are in sight. Transatlantic satellites soon will provide some 42,000 simultaneous voice-data channels or 24 full-time color television channels. And the adaptation of laser technology and transmission by light along glass fibers is bound to broaden current facilities.

Press rates for foreign news are set by the International Telecommunications Union, mainly through the annual meetings of representatives of participating governments at Geneva and elsewhere. It is a general procedure that carriers must charge government-fixed rates and these can vary widely under transmissions paid for by the word rate, instead of a fixed time period.

With rising expenses, it is no wonder that the humble mailer has come back into its own. The jet plane, which joins New York and Europe or Los Angeles and Tokyo in a few hours, makes air mail practical for news that was once sent at deferred cable or radio press rates. It is still necessary to put a dummy dateline on mailers (LONDON, MARCH 00) so that the day of publication may be inserted as needed, but it is questionable how much longer that will be accepted procedure. The supersonic transport (SST) may do more to make foreign news available to small-sized publications than the satellite, the sophisticated cable, and the still popular but less dependable radio teleprinter circuits.

CENSORSHIP

An even greater impediment to the flow of news across national borders than transmission costs is the rise of censorship in new and pernicious forms. In one guise or another, censorship exists over more than three-quarters of the earth's surface and it is gradually gaining even in the home of free expression, Western Europe.

The crude total censorship of the early twentieth century, in which dispatches were held up or mutilated in whole or in part, is no longer as widespread as it once was. Instead, particularly in the Communist world, the system has been changed to place correspondents in the position of censoring themselves for fear of being expelled.

Thus, the Soviet Union formally abolished censorship in 1961 and permitted Western correspondents to inaugurate two-way teletype communication with their home offices if they wished to do so. A certain amount of liberalization followed. Correspondents, cautiously testing the boiling point of the regime, found they could transmit some criticism in low key and even speculate on the course of events behind the Iron Curtain. But they also found out that the Soviet Union was as quick as it ever had been to expel correspondents it deemed unfriendly and to bar from within its territory news organizations it held to be essentially hostile.

In China, too, correspondents found that there was no formal censorship in the accepted sense of the term but they were held on a tight leash in both their movements and what sources they were permitted to contact. An exception was made for correspondents who went to China with either Presidents Nixon or Ford. As a result, Max Frankel of the *New York Times* was able to win the first Pulitzer Prize ever given for China correspondence.

The censor the correspondent never sees and the harsh voice that cuts off a telephone connection in a monitored call are the two figures in a censorship pattern that are the most difficult to bear. These are usually minor officials with set instructions, which they often interpret with unreasonable strictness. All correspondents can do is to file protests and carry their appeals to the authorities of their own embassy as

Max Frankel of the New York Times, winner of a Pulitzer Prize in Foreign Correspondence for his coverage of a Presidential visit to China, standing before the Great Wall of China. (Copyright, the New York Times. Used with permission.)

well as those of the country to which they are accredited. They don't often win a battle of this kind, but they must always stand their ground for as long as possible.

Chapter 27
The
Specialist

When Viking I sent the first color pictures of Mars's red-tinted surface to the space laboratories at Pasadena, California, more than 200 million miles away, no ordinary reporters could have described and explained the achievement for a global audience. It was a well-merited triumph for the specialist in journalism, who has not always received either the attention or the rewards that come to the anchor person, the political columnist or the sports authority.

The lesson of Viking I demonstrates the need for specialized coverage at every level of journalism. The generalists are simply out of their depth in many areas and they know it. Old-fashioned editors may argue that specialists tend to know too much about too little and cost more than they are worth; nevertheless, the younger breed on the whole has a good reputation and its numbers are slowly increasing.

In science, medicine and law, to mention only three fields in which specialists are of demonstrable importance, the news media learned years ago that the generalist couldn't compete with trained experts. In such newer fields as consumerism and the ecology, a certain amount of training, background and experience are also necessary, particularly for investigative reporters. No tyro could have persuaded the leaders of the automotive industry to recall 7.3 million cars to install a safety device; it took a seasoned specialist of the stature of Bob Irvin of the *Detroit News*. Nor could a reporter with no knowledge of computer operations have conducted detailed in-depth studies of race relations in some of the nation's largest and most troubled cities. The director of such an operation had to be both a social scientist and a journalist, as Philip Meyer of the Knight-Ridder Newspapers demonstrated when he did the work.

This kind of know-how is also being recognized, at long last, in numerous other fields from education to housing and from religion to social welfare. Nor do editors of experience and judgment believe it to be a wise policy to assign untrained reporters to consequential areas of service news dealing with home-making, travel, recreation and self-improvement.

Somehow, the leaders among the news media are finding the resources, both human and financial, to satisfy the public's increasing demands for more competent coverage of these and other specialized areas. And more young journalists are being persuaded that it is worth their while to develop an interest in a specialty. The greatest need in an inflationary era is for trained economists who can also write for a mass public.

SCIENCE WRITING

Humankind's giant vault into space, almost at the outset of the atomic age, has done as much as anything else to stimulate the trend toward specialization. It is quite a distance from the first Pulitzer Prize for science writing, granted in 1923 to Alva Johnson of the *New York Times* for his reports on a scientific convention, to William L. Laurence's coverage of the making and dropping of the atomic bomb and the first stories of how men walked on the moon. But when Neil Armstrong in 1969 stepped on the moon's surface and said, "This is one small step for a man, one giant leap for mankind," he also marked a major stage in the development of the reporting of science. True, the public became blasé over the remarkable and repeated moon journeys of American astronauts, but the reporters couldn't afford to be. Through all six moon journeys in which manned landings were made, the journalists told the story behind the marvelous TV pictures from the moon in familiar terms that a mass public could understand. And that, in itself, was a measure of their achievement.

It is the spectacular live coverage of space shots such as the moon journeys, the exploration of Venus in 1975 and the Vikings' 1976 Mars landings that have led the news media to turn to broader methods of communicating science news to mass audiences. Here, the science-trained newscaster and the science reporter for the print media have a great advantage over their less-skilled colleagues because they can explain, in nontechnical language, what the public has seen and heard.

Once, not more than a generation or so ago, just a few hard-bitten science reporters roamed about in the scientific community with little status. Scientists were almost always suspicious of them and seldom cooperated with them. Today, however, a major meeting of pure scientists, physicians or engineers is a national event, covered by most news organizations of standing. And leading scientists have willingly turned themselves into briefing officers, generally with excellent results, for a representative body of journalists who are trained in science reporting.

What Is Covered Out of the enormous amount of material that is published in scientific and scholarly journals, it is obvious that only a small part can be translated into popular terms and used widely by the news media commanding a mass audience. Consequently, a considerable volume of science news of a technical nature appears in specialized publications first. Scientific conventions account for almost as much news of science, being prime sources of new developments and new ideas. Entirely on their own, science writers study almost anything bearing on the development of atomic energy and space exploration for the germ of a significant news account. Sometimes they learn of such developments from their own sources in government and industry; on other occasions, they may be able to deduce clues to future developments from their own background and knowledge.

The increasing emphasis on studies of air and water pollution has deepened public interest in such matters and broadened the scope of the writer of popularized science. This is also true of the emphasis on medical reportage and progress in improving conditions in hospitals. But whole areas of mathematics, physics, and chemistry and other natural sciences are still relatively uncovered in the daily and periodical press because the developments are so far above the level of public understanding. As for television reporting of science, it will never be able to compete with the excellence of press coverage except in such areas as space flights if it waits to develop its own public. The way these things usually are done is for newspapers to educate as they inform.

The Coverage of Controversy With the coming of the energy crisis, the American public needs all the hard information it can get about the future development of alternative resources to augment or replace oil and natural gas. Unfortunately, what the public generally gets in the average newspaper or small radio or TV station is controversy and heated claims by participants.

Nowhere is there greater difficulty and a more critical need for informed and dispassionate reporting than in the field of nuclear fuel development. Through shock treatment, sometimes by well-meaning environmentalists, the public's fear of atomic energy has been exploited to a point where the development of atomic plants for fuel has been endangered in various parts of the nation. California in 1976 rejected a proposal to halt the building of atomic reactors, but it took a major effort at public education to obtain the favorable vote. There is no doubt that there are risks in the broad range of atomic development, and precautions that must be taken. But the old fashioned reporting of controversy—give both sides and let the public judge—is not the best way to handle such an explosive issue. This is one of the areas in which science reporters can help their editors and the public as well to arrive at a solution based on reason rather than panic.

CONSUMERISM

C. A. McKnight, editor of the Charlotte (N. C.) *Observer* and a past president of the American Society of Newspaper Editors, has warned the nation's publishers: "Consumer reporting is one of the big new fields that change has forced upon us. Consumer protection is a fact of life. It is not going away, even if it does set your advertising managers to trembling."

The Challenge To a profession whose support is so dependent on advertising, that indeed is the challenge. It can scarcely be met by a few general assignment reporters, sent out at random, as consumer stories emerge, to cover each one separately. The more responsible news organizations have found it necessary to maintain a group of knowledgeable consumer specialists, who are reinforced from time to time with staff people; even among smaller newspapers with an interest in consumer news, there is usually at least one reporter whose regular assignment is the consumer beat.

More than in any other subject area of journalism, consumer news requires the strict separation of the editorial department from the advertising and business offices if the press is to maintain its credibility with the public. For consumer news cuts across all the traditional departmental lines, from life/style pages to financial, from real estate to sports, and more often than not it dominates Page 1.

Growth of Coverage A few pioneering consumer organizations, with pitifully small resources and skimpy publications, struggled for years to awaken the interest of the public in a crusade against shoddy products, overpricing, misleading advertising and the other signs of an overly commercial age. But for much of this century, few consciences were stirred except among the more progressive editors and managers of the news media. Along Madison Avenue, it was even hinted darkly that people who suspected the good faith of big advertisers were dupes of communism at best and plotters against the security of the republic at worst.

The first to break through the barrier of indifference and neglect was a public-spirited lawyer, Ralph Nader, who managed to marshal the support of a group of talented young adherents in a whole series of campaigns to protect the interests of the consumer. Then, in a period of soaring inflation that sent the cost of living rocketing, the public itself began to face up to a distressing situation. The nation's campuses, ever sensitive to such movements, became staging areas for consumer groups that sought new recruits. And consumerism, at last, became a fact of life for the American press. Even the broadcast media had to take notice when the crusade against cigarettes reached such a pitch that cigarette commercials were eliminated from the air by law.

Range and Methods Editors approach consumer reporting in various ways. The larger news organizations use specialists who do nothing else. Those who want consumer news but can't afford specialists expect their regular reporters to contribute pieces of interest to consumers. Business writers, for example, can do specialized pieces on how consumers can get satisfaction for their complaints. Sports writers can give much more advice than they do on such consumer details as where to park cars outside stadiums, the best methods of travel to various contests, costs, availability of meals and other details. All recipes in the family pages should carry approximate costs. And in travel and entertainment stories, costs should be included as a matter of course.

As the case was put in a report by Jack Foster, editor of the *Palm Beach* (Florida) *Times*, "Consumer reporting is all around us. It is no longer something out of the ordinary, if indeed it ever was." [1]

There is also a greater sensitivity in the handling of news that pertains to health. One of the most controversial health stories of recent years was the national inoculation program proposed by President Ford to ward off a threat of a "swine flu" outbreak in the winter of 1976–1977. Because scientists differed on the necessity for the program, the public was understandably confused. And finally, when too many complications accompanied inoculations, the program was suspended.

On a day-to-day level, science writers have developed an approach that is recommended to those who deal with consumer affairs. Alton Blakeslee, science editor of the Associated Press, points out that scientific breakthroughs "almost never occur in medicine." Instead, as he puts it, "Progress comes in small increments." That may not make for

[1] *AP Log*, 31 May 1976, p. 1.

Page 1 news, but it makes for good sense. These are Blakeslee's precautions:

"An overall guideline is that anything new has a long gauntlet to run to find its real place in the treatment of human ailments. A brand new drug may show promise in the laboratory, but it will likely have unhappy side effects for some people. It may be too expensive.

"We must include such cautions when indicated in order not to add to the burden of the sick and worried people ready to leap at any hint of a miracle." [2]

Results Consumerism has been effective in journalism in several different ways. Leading newspapers are originating their own inquiries in response to complaints, one of the by-products of the various Action Line columns of recent years. And all newspapers, even the most sluggish, are being obliged to reexamine their policies on using material that formerly was considered a harmless bonus for an advertiser. In this respect, television, usually so timid wherever advertisers are concerned, lags behind the printed media.

Campaigns that once were considered taboo are now being undertaken with the helpful resources of a news organization. The *Des Moines Register*, for example, gave full support to Nick Kotz's examination of unsanitary practices in meat packing plants, the result being the passage of the Federal Wholesale Meat Act and a Pulitzer Prize for the reporter. Campaigns against unsanitary restaurants now are considered almost routine in some cities of the nation. And major papers like the *Wall Street Journal* do not hesitate to expose unscrupulous business practices wherever they are found.

The automobile industry, despite its heavy advertising budgets, has been forced on the defensive in numerous instances to justify its safety standards and merchandising practices. The food sections of family pages, so long immune from critical inspection, have undergone an even more searching examination. And the phony plugs to advertisers and the acceptance of favors that have been so disgraceful a part of some financial, real estate and sports sections have come under fire from both within and outside the ranks of professional journalism.

Just how far consumer reporting will develop depends entirely on the skill and devotion of the journalists who undertake this specialty and the amount of support they receive from their news organizations. Several hundred of them are on the job today. But certainly, now that so many barriers have fallen, there can be no return to the comfortable situation where major advertisers felt that the average newspaper would always try to make up in departmental news for whatever injuries they may have received in the headlines on Page 1.

[2] *AP Log*, 15 March 1976, p. 1.

THE ECOLOGY

No less than consumerism, the relationship of people to their environment and the increasing public concern over pollution have generated broadening interest in the news. The great industries that recklessly contaminated the atmosphere, despoiled the earth of its beauty and polluted the water supply are being called to account. Cities that casually dumped their sewage in rivers, lakes and inland seas are finding themselves threatened by their own filth. New York City, a special case, has learned to its cost that it must cease dumping sludge in the ocean because it contaminates beaches for miles around. And even well-meaning citizens have learned that, through their own foolish disposal measures, they are among the worst polluters of all.

A Measure of Progress There has always been a certain amount of interest in the conservation of natural resources in the United States and the development of the resources of the earth for the benefit of all peoples. But for more than a century after the founding of the nation, the constructive measures undertaken by the press were limited to such innovations as those of the editor of the *Pennsylvania Gazette,* Benjamin Franklin, who introduced the yellow willow to America and devised a practical system of lightning rods.

The muckrakers of the early twentieth century were the forerunners of the environmentalists of today. But their influence, in general, was limited to the period of Theodore Roosevelt's presidency, primarily because he had a deep interest in the protection of natural resources and was not afraid to attack "the malefactors of great wealth." However, it was no newspaper but an indignant novelist, Upton Sinclair, who attacked the meat industry in "The Jungle." And it was no national columnist but a little-known chemistry professor and editor, Edwin Fremont Ladd of the *North Dakota Farmer* and *Sanitary Home* magazine, who was among the earliest agitators for pure food and drug legislation. The press, with few exceptions, was preoccupied with the political and economic scandals of the day.

Environmental developments were covered, of course, but there appeared to be no special concern over the state of the earth and the atmosphere even after World War II. Once again, it was a book, *Silent Spring,* by Rachel Carson, that called public attention to a development of consequence—the effect of the pesticide DDT on wild life. Out of the national debate that ensued, a new consciousness was created of the precarious nature of man's estate on earth. It was a time when the public also began paying attention to the historical warnings of overpopulation, diminishing resources for sustaining life and the rising threat of pollution on every side. Ecology, a word that many an editor had to look up before he understood its meaning, became a kind of fad among college people. And eventually, the press seized the issue.

The Press and the Environment It has not taken the nation's newspapers very long to demonstrate their effectiveness as crusaders to protect the environment. Through their accomplishments, they have gone far toward making up for the long years during which they neglected the issue. It has seemed to make no difference whether a paper is large or small; if it has a public-spirited publisher, a determined editor and a talented and devoted staff, it can — and does — obtain results.

A Pulitzer Prize for Public Service has been won by the *Winston-Salem* (N. C.) *Journal* and *Sentinel* for blocking a strip mining operation that would have caused irreparable damage to the beautiful hill country of northwest North Carolina. Other Pulitzer awards have gone to the *Milwaukee Journal* for its successful campaign to stiffen the laws against water pollution in Wisconsin, to the *Louisville Courier-Journal* for its attacks on the Kentucky strip-mining industry and to Robert Cahn of the *Christian Science Monitor* for his critical examination of the future of the American national park system.

For every such prize winner, there have been scores of other papers and individual journalists who have conducted their own campaigns in the public interest. The *Bend* (Oregon) *Bulletin* has defended a great national resource, Rock Mesa, from use by mining interests. The *Casper* (Wyoming) *Star-Tribune* has painstakingly reported the long effort to halt the slaughter of eagles by ranchers. The *Durango* (Colorado) *Herald* has fought against the pollution of the massive Colorado plateau. In the battle against oil pollution and drilling in Santa Barbara Channel in California, the *Santa Barbara News-Press* has been a devoted and painstaking crusader. And on the east coast, such papers as *Newsday,* the *Newark Star-Ledger* and the *Providence Journal-Bulletin* have campaigned against both oil spillage and the dumping of sewage in coastal waters.

New ventures have been undertaken by newspapers of all sizes. The *Chicago Tribune,* with disclosures of the contamination of drinking water, succeeded in forcing the adoption of new standards for drinking water in the Chicago area. The *Manhattan* (Kansas) *Mercury* instituted a "Product Patrol" of reporters who examined products on the shelves of local stores. The *Christian Science Monitor* attacked the illicit traffic in prescription drugs and the *Washington Star* and *Wall Street Journal,* in separate inquiries, disclosed the danger in the use of a pesticide, Kepone, which created a tragic situation at Hopewell, Virginia.

Newspapers and news agencies have demonstrated their effectiveness in the field of consumerism. In good time, once TV realizes it is stronger than any protesting advertiser, broadcast journalists are likely to become the most effective environmentalists of all.

ECONOMIC NEWS

The importance of the economic story, and its impact upon large groups of people, has given it a much higher priority in the declining years of this century than it had at the outset. A rise in the cost of living, a new turn in unemployment statistics, an unexpected swing in interest rates or a dramatic change in other important economic indicators is almost certainly Page 1 news in these times, and worthy of notice on evening news TV programs.

The long-deferred recognition of economic news has been accompanied by equally important changes in the way it is written and told. There is no longer an excuse for making economics dull. In professional hands, such a story can be told in informal, popular and often uninhibited style. Whether the subject is business or labor, the stock market or foreign trade or the innumerable offshoots thereof, the innovators on the *Wall Street Journal* are often the first to show their irreverence for stuffy old forms of writing. This, without doubt, is one of the reasons for the phenomenal growth of the *Journal* into the second largest daily newspaper in the land.

Nor is the *Journal* alone in profiting from changes in the presentation of economic news. All the leading business pages in rival newspapers have been affected by the movement toward improved content and livelier style. The McGraw-Hill magazines, headed by *Business Week,* and the Fairchild group, of which the daily *Women's Wear* is the most prominent, both have found prosperity in their sponsorship of the unorthodox. The financial columnist, Sylvia F. Porter, who began as a writer of advice for housewives at $50 a week, has built a nation-wide audience for her breezy and popular economic column and found wealth and fame for herself as well.

Other popular financial columnists, interpreters of the folkways of business and finance, a constant flow of feature material and a steady emphasis on popular reportage have helped take the dullness out of the business page and given economic journalism its proper place in the news media.

LABOR NEWS

It is a sober and easily observable truth that the coverage of the news of labor has not on the whole kept pace with the surge of new material from the ranks of business and industry. In a nation with so many large and powerful unions, some of which have the power to choke off whole industries and even cities if they choose to do so, the main reliance for labor news is on a mere handful of experienced labor reporters on the major newspapers of the land, the news magazines, and by and large, the weekly labor press. Television and radio are almost not in this specialty, except when there is a labor conflict that attracts picture coverage or results in violent words and actions.

It is perfectly true that the nation's leading newspapers and news magazines have had labor reporters for years and have, on the whole, told the labor story fairly and impartially. It would be unthinkable today for a newspaper of stature in New York, Chicago, Pittsburgh, Detroit or Los Angeles, for example, to fail to maintain regular and detailed coverage of labor affairs. But elsewhere in the country, until very recently, the labor story has usually been told as a series of disconnected episodes. While many smaller newspapers and even a few local stations have tried within their resources to keep a fair balance between labor and management in the news, some have not.

In the columns of a good newspaper, news of labor affairs is by no means confined to strikes and lockouts or violence on the picket lines. A more sophisticated approach to the reporting of conflicts between industry and labor has developed, so that a good newspaper takes care not to label itself a proindustry partisan in every dispute but tries to give both sides to the story.

EDUCATION NEWS

With more than 60 million Americans going to school and about half the nation's population under 25, the coverage of education today is a challenge to all the news media. There is greater room for progress in the reporting of education news than in many another specialty. But it will take well-trained journalists to do the job—men and women who understand the problems of the schools and know how to write about them.

The old journalistic weakness for emphasizing trouble rather than achievement is only a part of the difficulty in achieving a balanced presentation of the news of education. In many cities, the extreme sensitivity of school administrations to criticism handicaps even their defenders when they embark on a purely fact-finding mission. Such sensitivity often is exceeded only by that of the press itself when it is under heavy community criticism. In such situations, there is little possibility for a constructive dialogue and school and press drift into postures of mutual hostility. This is particularly true in some of the struggles over school integration and busing in northern cities.

When the schools are in the forefront of the news, however, cool, careful, impartial reporting must become the order of the day.

This was the pattern to which both the *Boston Globe* and the *Louisville Courier-Journal* and *Times* adhered when integration crises gripped the schools of their respective cities. What they did provided guidance for both hard-pressed parents and teachers as well as much-needed support for the children who went to class daily under difficulty.

It would be well if the noncrisis news of education were covered in the same spirit, but often it is given only minimal attention. Some universities in America are covered by student stringers for major papers and wire services, but not at all by the broadcast media, except when there is a riot or some other disorder. Many an education writer has tried to devise some better method for the daily coverage of higher education, but not many have succeeded.

NEWS OF RELIGION

The news of religion for many years suffered an extremely low priority in the daily press except on week-ends and religious holidays. The changed attitude that is so apparent today in a large section of the press, including television, scarcely means that the editors have suddenly "got" religion.

Rather, the clergy of all the great religions represented in the United States have made a concerted, if uncoordinated, effort to work outside as well as inside the churches and synagogues to a greater extent than ever before. The ecumenical movement, begun with such a flourish by Pope John XXIII and carried on by his earnest successor, Pope Paul VI, did much to focus the attention of both Catholic and non-Catholic on the new life that is pulsing through the Church of Rome. The frequent participation of clergy of all faiths in the various civil rights causes has also stimulated new interest in the work of the churches.

Necessarily, the Monday morning column of sermons (and sometimes on Sundays in communities with large synagogues) is no longer adequate to tell the news of religion. Both the major wire services have editors specializing in religion, as do the weekly news magazines and the better newspapers. And it is not at all unusual to find clergy in the inevitable panel discussions on television, exchanging views with laity and with each other.

THE CULTURAL STORY

The audience for cultural affairs in the United States now is larger than the sports audience in most major metropolitan centers. With few exceptions, however, the news media are not able to turn loose a large and competent staff of critics to assess the cultural activities of their communities.

Certainly, the America of abundant leisure time is entitled to a better display of critical writing on cultural subjects than it presently enjoys except in leading newspapers and magazines. Higher standards among audiences will have to be met in one way or another. If the news media cannot do it by developing critics from younger people on their own staffs with the requisite backgrounds, then they will have to publish more critical material from syndicates or wire services or recruit home-town talent from nearby centers of higher education. But it is nonsense to devote all the energies and wealth of a community to creating a first-rate art center, repertory theatre or symphony orchestra and then permit the local news media to publish hack criticism or no criticism at all.

Among newspapers, there are generally two ways of handling cultural events. The first method, and unhappily the largest in the United States, is the group that runs either a news story on a new book, play, movie, concert or art exhibit or contents itself with a "puff"-type review. The second method, which may be smaller but is by all odds the most influential, endeavors to run both reviews and criticism of cultural events of interest to the community.

There is, of course, a profound difference between a review and a critique. The review is done quickly under pressure, as a rule, while criticism is generally written by someone with expert qualifications after due consideration has been given to a performance, book or exhibit of one kind or another.

The review, far more than the critique or the news story, is the dominant form in serious cultural journalism at the daily level and in the news magazines. The monthlies and specialized publications such as the *New Yorker* go in for critiques because they have the contributors and the time to do them well. Although the style of reviewers varies widely, the exigencies of deadline journalism are bound to influence its structure. In general, therefore, most reviews begin with a general statement of the subject and the writer's reaction to it. If a plot is involved, it is stated briefly—usually in no more than two or three paragraphs. Nothing is worse than a spirited retelling of plot at second hand. The work of the author, composer or players is then summed up, with appropriate comparisons to other attractions or performances. A paragraph or two is given to other detail, if any. And in the concluding paragraph the opening statement is generally amplified and strengthened so that the reader may be in no doubt over the reviewer's position.

In structure, then, the review follows the news story format rather closely, but it is compact and tightly knit. It strives not to say blankly that something is just good or bad, wonderful or terrible, but to define a more precise reaction and give the reasons for it. Moreover, a review should be sportsmanlike. It should not belabor an innocent little high school performance of *Dear Brutus,* pummel a hapless young first novelist or destroy the nice girl soprano who had the bad judgment to try the Bell Song from *Lakme* at a church social. The premise of a professional reviewer is that, in such cases, the less said the better. However, if a novelist of stature writes a trashy book or a renowned playwright gives the public a dull and meaningless drama, then it is obviously the duty of an honest reviewer to say so, and it is the obligation of an honest newspaper to permit him to do it. Sometimes, even good critics make mistakes, but it is better to have mistaken critics than no critics at all.

With the exception of public television, there is very little serious criticism of the arts in the broadcast media outside movie reviews and an occasional 30-second summation of a new play. Books are noticed, if at all, by talk show hosts who brandish a copy of an author's new book, which they usually haven't read, and then proceed to ask what it is about — preferably told in 10 seconds.

Books This is not to say that newspapers pay much attention to books, either. Most of them don't, although the wire services provide a careful and competent flow of compactly written reviews at regular intervals.

Yet, the book boom is one of the cultural phenomena in the United States. Those who moan that reading has gone out of style forget that book sales in this country have increased from $700 million in 1954 to almost $4 billion currently. Book titles have gone from 10,000 to more than 40,000 annually in 20 years. And fortunate authors with hard cover bestsellers have received contracts running into the millions for paperback rights to their work. This is the bonanza that the paperback revolution has provided. And yet, there are still only a handful of daily book reviewers in American journalism — and not very many respectable weekly book sections.

The professional reviewer therefore always has far more business than he can handle. The few full-time critics or reviewers for the book page of less than a score of daily newspapers can cover, at best, only about 300 titles a year. There are, of course, about 300 other papers with Sunday book sections or weekly book pages which are largely filled by contributors. The outstanding papers pay for book critiques or have their own staff people handle literary reviews. The news magazines, for the most part, publish staff reviews while specialized publications have a judicious mixture of staff people and contributors of distinction. Yet, as is the case with the daily paper, only a fraction of the titles that sweep from the presses annually can ever be given critical inspection.

A work by a major writer or an otherwise prominent person is nearly always reviewed, as are the big book-club selections. Books about the famous and infamous, nonfiction books about celebrated events that are written like novels, and novels about thinly disguised celebrities that are written like nonfiction all are given consideration by one reviewer or another. Reviews also are usually given to such books as those topping the lists of the principal publishing houses, an infrequent work of topical interest or local importance and, as for the rest, mainly the luck of the draw.

The Theatre Rival cultural centers for many years have boldly proclaimed the death of Broadway as the home of the American theatre and the demise of New York City as the heart of American culture. It hasn't happened yet and it isn't likely to happen in spite of the city's financial troubles and the moaning over its most fabulous invalid.

Despite the paucity of original works from American playwrights, Broadway came out of a recession in the 1970s with a booming trade in British imports, revivals and musicals mainly carpentered out of old plays. One hit, "Annie," was derived from a comic strip. Even if American creativity was faltering, American audiences were not. And they flocked to Broadway, off-Broadway and off-off Broadway in greater numbers (and at higher prices) than ever before.

However, Broadway doesn't have things its own way completely any more. There are major openings of plays that command respect these days in Los Angeles, Washington and other cities. Chicago, Minneapolis, Boston, Houston and San Francisco can scarcely be thought of any more by the theatrical elite as mere "road show" towns.

All of them have shown that they can and will support a certain amount of serious drama, sometimes more than can be seen on Broadway. Moreover, through the backing of the universities, the little theatre movement no longer is little. It is burgeoning all over the land and is one of the great hopes for the 1980s and beyond, if the American theatre is to continue to flourish without so much dependence on revivals and British imports.

This provides journalism with an opportunity to reestablish criticism of the drama in its rightful place as a necessary feature of newspapers in addition to the all-too-slender cultural resources of television and radio. Outside the news agencies, news magazines and a few monthlies, there is no national theatrical criticism of substance. And in New York, with the number of dailies reduced to three, there are only a handful of critics in the city and suburbia whose opinions matter.

By contrast, major newspapers outside New York have become a good source of critical writing on the drama. While a few combine the theatre with the function of movie reviewing, the better papers see to it that full-time drama critics travel to New York, Washington and other theatrical centers for first-hand reports. And it is not unheard of now for New York critics to go to Los Angeles, Washington and other centers for openings. Although the time limit is still rigidly adhered to, some of the capsule drama criticism on TV is both competent and entertaining. Maybe, some day, a daring station will give a drama reviewer all of four minutes.

Motion Pictures Many newspapers merely relate the story of motion pictures but seldom attempt to evaluate them. Only the leaders generally publish film reviews that mean something and are intended to guide the public with the same fundamental honesty as those of the other lively arts. The magazines, on the whole, have fewer inhibitions because they are far less nervous about movie advertising. As for television, the presence of a first rate reviewer is an event. There is, indeed, no reason why television should not review as diligently and as sharply as a great newspaper. Because of its vastly larger audience, it has more reason to do so.

Perceptive critics have not increased in number, scope or authority despite the need for more of them. It is an area in which most newspapers could make sharp and immediate improvements with benefit to themselves, their readers and — ultimately — the movies as well. It is also a subdivision of critical journalism that television could practice with much greater vigor if it chose to do so.

The Media Criticism, as a function of journalism, is regarded by many hardheaded editors as more of a nuisance than an attraction — a troublemaker that does not attract readers or viewers and pleases none but a few intellectuals. The one famous radio program that criticized newspapers, "CBS Views the Press," had a comparatively small but fanatical following. The few attempts to revive the program or match it have failed. As for the newspapers, the consistently effective critics of television and radio are confined for the most part to the leaders in large metropolitan areas. But even the best have not yet managed to approach in vigor or in eloquence Edward R. Murrow's famous warning: "During the daily peak viewing periods, television in the main insulates us from the realities of the world in which we live. If this state of affairs continues, we may alter an advertising slogan to read: 'Look now, pay later.' For surely we shall pay for using this most powerful instrument of communication to insulate the citizenry from the hard and demanding realities which must be faced if we are to survive."

Just as Murrow headed the critics of TV, the most effective criticism of newspapers has come from outspoken newspapermen and women. The various journalism reviews, the ombudsmen at papers like the *Washington Post* and *Louisville Courier-Journal* and the in-house critiques that are so much a feature of newspaper editors' meetings all have contributed to a balanced view of the press. However, it is still true, as it was when Robert M. Hutchins issued the report of his Commission on the Freedom of the Press, that newspaper people fiercely resent criticism by outsiders and resist it almost as much as they ever did. It is a professional weakness that seems to be without remedy.

SERVICE NEWS

Changes in American society have helped turn the long-neglected women's pages of newspapers into sections that deal with information and comment on home and family, fashions, domestic attitudes, social problems, arts and crafts. On a majority of newspapers, they are called almost anything except women's pages now, with variants including life/style pages, family pages, design-for-living pages and home-making pages. Like the service magazines, they specialize in service news.

One of the results of the change has been to sweep out a lot of the stale publicity and product plugs that cluttered women's pages for years. Also, sensible editors have put a limit on junketing by food companies and others, realizing full well that most junkets imply the existence of eventual publicity payoffs.

It is difficult to eliminate the evil of "puffery" in a part of the press that is a prime target for hordes of press agents. But where controls have been applied, improvement has been noted.

Service pages, in consequence, now run a lot of more or less interesting material on social problems, family interests, public health and the manifold uses of leisure time as well as the old standbys—food and drink, fashions, home decorating and the like. A more sophisticated use of graphics has helped. Instead of the eternal "mugg" shots of engaged girls and brides and local society leaders, most of them homely, original and unusual pictures, sketches and caricatures enliven the service departments.

The ultimate has been the declared objective of a few women activists in journalism to eliminate the former women's pages altogether and distribute their content in the general news section of the newspaper. Admittedly, this radical solution has not caught on; nor is it likely to do so. But subjects that have been forbidden for years on service pages, from abortion to narcotics addiction and prostitution, are now acceptable on numerous newspapers. Contrasted with the traditional product, almost any change in the press is likely to be for the better. As for television, this is an area in which the tube has a built-in superiority over anything that can be done in print.

SPORTS WRITING

The sports pages have produced some of the best writing in American journalism; also, some of the worst. The superior sports reporters have always been on good terms with the English language, as well as sports, and have handled both with loving care. They have taken advantage of the freedom of expression that is the birthright of every sports writer and used it to communicate with a mass public in more or less original terms.

Television's superior attraction—the presentation of the game itself in all its fascinating detail—has not solved the problem of bad sports writing, as some had hoped. There are few sports commentators who let the viewer watch the game, giving him only the most necessary information and explanation. For the most part, between the nonstop talk of the commentators, much of it graceless, and the deluge of advertising, the viewer must cope with mangled and sometimes incomprehensible English.

What it comes down to is this:

The amateur sports reporters have never quite grasped either the disciplines of sports or the English language. They have written and spoken in overexpert terms of simple games and loaded their reportage with faded cliches, a frequent source of annoyance. Instead of using their freedom of expression with grace and meaning, they have cluttered it with nonessentials. They have fawned on the great names of sports, whether the great names deserved it or not, and trafficked with the gristle, the shabby hangers-on. They have sought to ignore the rising interest in women's sports, and written of women athletes as if they were subhuman creatures, to be degraded and made the subject of bad jokes.

They have, on occasion, shrilly rebuked the boy who dropped a fly ball in the last of the ninth inning and lost the game. And that is the heart of the matter. The amateurs have never learned to play the game—the most important facet of a sports reporter's work. And this is the difference between them and the relatively small group of professionals who dominate sports on and off the field.

Patterns of Sports Writing Because most of the sports public knows the final score of a game from radio or television before the paper comes out, what becomes important in the written story is to relate how and why the result was achieved. It means that the techniques of the feature writer have now become all-important on the sports pages, although some editors still insist on the fast summary straight-away lead (just as if television didn't exist). It is almost pathetic to pick up even a great newspaper and note that a sports writer has described the first-quarter of a night football game, which ended long before the paper was purchased. The newspapers have taken many years to adjust to the electronic realities and some have not quite made it yet. But the sensible ones have adapted the methods that make general news writing more effective and readable and applied them to the sports page.

Neither the radio and television talkers nor the writers, of course, can take on a sports assignment without an intimate knowledge of the events they are describing. In both fields of reporting, the two greatest necessities are accuracy and restraint. Sports followers invariably pride themselves on being experts. They like to hear and read about "inside" strategy, just as the literati gossip endlessly about the famous people on whom characters in a sensational new novel are supposedly patterned. However, some games are more easy to describe than others—and that depends on the patterns of the sport.

An essentially simple game like baseball is easily reported. The game's play-by-play, the result and the reasons for it can be quickly summarized, then documented with a description of the key plays. A few other details, and the account is complete enough for a post-game electronic roundup or a sports story. Not every baseball game, after all, is handled as if it were a World Series drama.

Boxing and horse-racing, too, have essentially simple patterns and need not be told in too complicated a fashion. What matters here, particularly in television, is the detail that makes the tiny images on the small screen come alive—the blow by blow in a fight and the enormously intricate "call" in a horse race. By comparison, accounts of competitions in crew, swimming, tennis, polo and golf are handled with relative ease.

In football, however, the pattern of the game becomes increasingly complicated and difficult to follow. The effort of a play-by-play commentator here must be to simplify, wherever possible, and to explain to the viewer what happened and why it happened instead of prattling excitedly about the confusing technicalities. In a summary, oral as well as written, it becomes necessary to analyze the result, to select the principal plays and to give the public a sense of participation in the reporting.

The many events in track and field, each with special complications, also require a good deal of guidance from professionals who are intimately acquainted with the sport. This is particularly true during the great spectacle of the Olympic Games every four years; in inexpert hands, such reportage may be the worst, rather than the best, of the year because some American commentators and reporters know only their own competitors as a rule and habitually tend to give the results of each race as a triumph of American righteousness or a blow to the Stars and Stripes. Actually, in any track meet, the reporting can be done very nicely—and interestingly—if the expert-for-the-day will bother to acquaint himself with the teams in advance, look up the necessary background and records, and come to the field an hour before the meet begins to do a final checkup. To wait until the first event begins is to bog down completely in detail. But if it is known in advance that the pole vault, the mile run and the hurdles are likely to develop the most interesting contests, then the meet becomes a relatively easy matter to cover. What can never be anticipated is the unexpected event, such as the murders of Israeli athletes by Arab guerrillas that made so tragic a spectacle out of the 1972 Olympic Games in Munich and the wholesale withdrawal of black African nations from the 1976 Games in Montreal. The American Broadcasting Company, nevertheless, did a first-rate job in bringing the 1976 games to the U. S.

As for basketball, with its seven-footers and its statistical labyrinths, this is less a job for a sports reporter than for a certified public accountant. It is hard to follow on television and even worse to describe in print, but it has such a large and devoted following that it receives major coverage.

It is clear, therefore, that the patterns of sport have much to do with the pattern of sports journalism. The big money sports such as horse racing, boxing, baseball and football are the ones with the most public appeal; in general, professional sports have the widest following. The amateur sports frequently are interesting only to alumni of schools and friends of participants except for the football and basketball colleges that compete for national championships annually and reap profit and fame from their TV contracts.

However, two new developments have broadened the audiences for both the sports page and the sports events on the tube. The most important is the rise in participation for women's sports and the broader attention and funding that universities have been forced to give to them. In some parts of the nation, even at the high school level, the excitement over women's sports has become a matter of such consequence that women sports writers have been hired for formerly all-male staffs. Nor are the new sports writers mere tokens; like their male counterparts, they cover all kinds of games, not merely women's events, and some of them carry 25-pound terminals to get their stories to the office quickly.

When women sports writers first began attending professional contests for some of the larger papers, there was a lot of superior male grousing over their presence in the press boxes and, even worse, in the dressing rooms of the teams. But the initial notion of embarrassment — imagine someone like Joe Namath being embarrassed! — quickly passed and the women evidently got over the shock of glimpsing an occasionally nude athlete striding from the showers. After all, nudism has been a part of the theatre ever since the production of "Hair." The sports arenas have not fallen apart. The teams have not been stricken with paralysis. And women sports writers and women athletes have become a part of the national scene in the United States, just as they have elsewhere in the world. The development was long overdue.

The second new break in the traditional sports pages has been the interest in such audience participation events as stock car racing, motor boating and sailing, hunting and fishing, skating and skiing and the like. Such events are not easy for TV to cover, and therefore offer something to newspapers that can interest their readers. The boom in soccer, so long considered a "foreign" sport, benefits all the news media.

Handling the Sports Story The incomparable Red Smith, viewing an Army-Navy football game at Philadelphia, began his account as follows:

> As some churlish historian of America's great undergraduate pastime wrote years ago, "It was an ideal day for football—too cold for the spectators and too cold for the players." For 100,000 citizens of assorted nations, including Russia and Monaco, whose chattering teeth rattled like castanets upon the necks of bottles in Municipal Stadium yesterday, that just about sums up the match of Army and Navy.

Eventually, Smith got around to mentioning the size of the Army's victory, 22–6, which wasn't particularly important to him because everybody who read him knew it anyway. What was more important to his readers was his point of view:

> The entertainment seemed flat by comparison with Army—Navy contests of the past. It was just too perishing cold. Reluctant to quit a slugging match which they had traveled many miles to watch, the customers nevertheless started making their numbed way toward the exits when the first half ended, longing for a warm hotel room with the guy across the courtyard beating his wife . . .

Unlike Red Smith, the average sports writer and commentator immerse themselves in technicalities to such an extent that they often forget entirely about the game itself and the people who contest it and who watch it. The electronic reporters become slaves to their equipment. The newspaper reporters worry about writing three separate accounts of a single event in order to cover all editions of a newspaper—a time-consuming and expensive procedure that provides no advantage in these times of instant communication.

Because the technique of doing multiple stories of one sports event is still practiced in a large section of the daily press, the essentials are recorded here without assurance that they will survive many more years:

1. *The Advance Story.* The advance begins with a situation lead, relating that two teams are facing each other or that a field of seven horses is ready for the big race of the day. The remainder of the story merely discusses the background of the event, gives whatever detail there is on the participants and the crowd, and winds up in such a way that the running account of the early part of the game can be added on. If the contest is under way before the edition closes, a brief high insert can give the early scoring. Necessarily, even in an early edition, the advance is bound to look foolish. It assumes that the public is entirely dependent on the newspaper to find out what happened and will buy a

later edition to get the full details. This used to happen, but it hasn't been true for many years.

2. *The Running Story.* Depending on the style of the paper, the chronological story of the game is told as B copy or B matter or merely slugged "Running" or "Play by Play." As an edition approaches, a two-paragraph lead is written by the reporter at the scene or an editor in the office and put on top of the opening of the chronological account. Once the event is over, a final wrap-up lead is written and the details of the end of the game are put at the bottom of the piece.

3. If the running story is well done within reasonable space, it should stand. But frequently, sports writers have the urge to do the whole exercise over again on the dubious theory that they will produce magnificent prose the second time around. Unfortunately, it rarely turns out that way.

Nobody can do his best under these wretched circumstances. If the objective is to keep pace with radio and television, it is impossible to attain. If it is to "save space" for the final story, the theory is lacking in practicality. Such "saved space" is always wasted space. The news magazines manage to do pretty well with their weekly summaries of sports and do not arouse great feeling among the sports-minded public that it is being cheated. Sooner or later, the newspapers will come around to the obvious — that the best way to do a sports story is to wait until the event is over and then give it the well-considered treatment it deserves. Few sports events are big enough to call for edition-by-edition coverage against electronic competition.

A generation that was thrilled by the "Ah, wonderful!" sports writing of an expert Heywood Broun has been succeeded by a generation that prefers the inexpert sports commentaries of his son Heywood Hale Broun on television. And that is the measure of the generation gap in sports.

Chapter 28
Public Service Journalism

Under a revised federal pension law, nearly 2,000,000 federal pensioners were given an extra one per cent permanent pension increase beginning in 1969 whenever their checks were adjusted to meet changes in the cost of living.

For years, nobody in the White House or Congress thought anything more about it. But one day, Dick Barnes of the Associated Press did a projection that showed the unintended bonus would cost taxpayers $100 billion or more by 1990. The figures also showed that a typical federal employee's retirement check could go up by 57 per cent even though the cost of living rose by 46 per cent. Stated another way, such an employee could draw more than $27,500 in pension funds beyond what he would have received if his pension had just kept even with the cost of living index.

When the AP story was published under Barnes's name, it developed that Congress had made no such simple cost projection and that not even the watchdog agency, the General Accounting Office, had costed out the revised pension law. The result: still more revisions and this time there was some basic cost accounting before passage.

THE NEWS MEDIA AND THE PUBLIC

The tale of the "one per cent kicker" is one example of the manner in which public service journalism works in the United States. Another is *Newsday's* expenditure of $300,000 to uncover the French and Turkish connections in the heroin traffic across the Atlantic to the United States. There are many more. If newspapers are the acknowledged leaders in this kind of journalism, it is primarily because the press has a tradition of public service going back to Benjamin Franklin's crusade in his *Pennsylvania Gazette* to beef up police protection in Philadelphia. It took awhile for the electronic media to realize it was part of their responsibility to the public, too.

Newspaper Campaigns There have been public spirited campaigns, sometimes called crusades, by newspapers of all sizes in every part of the land. One of the most unusual was that of the *Miami Herald*, which obtained an 8–0 ruling from the U. S. Supreme Court, striking down a challenge to the First Amendment. Nor did the press neglect itself. The *Minneapolis Star* published a series that considered the shortcomings of the news media, including itself and its sister paper, the *Minneapolis Tribune*, in the Twin Cities area. The *National Observer*, the Dow Jones weekly, did some editorial soul-searching and dropped the secret coding of its public opinion surveys, which it called "The Invisible Ink Caper." It has, unhappily, gone out of business since.

The *St. Louis Post-Dispatch* investigated the U.S. Civil Service Commission, resulting in several resignations, and the *Washington Star*, among others, took a close look at the Social Security system and its failings. A score of newspapers delved into widespread charges of profiteering and price gouging by major oil companies. In addition to breaking Watergate and the Congressional sex scandals, the *Washington Post* demonstrated that some senators were using committee personnel for their own benefit. The *New York Times*, in a searching examination of the nursing home industry, uncovered abuses that resulted in indictments and jail sentences for offenders. And the *Philadelphia Bulletin* exposed spying on taxpayers by officials of the Internal Revenue Service.

The record is replete, as well, with instances in which newspapers and their editors took unpopular positions based on principle.

A woman reporter and a small Texas daily—Caro Brown and the Alice *Echo*—combined to lead a campaign that interrupted the rule of a political gang in neighboring Duval County. In Oregon, Editor Robert

W. Ruhl and the *Medford Mail Tribune* performed a similar service in a political situation that was no less dangerous. In California, the *Watsonville Register-Pajaronian* exposed corruption in local office and forced the resignation of a district attorney, no mean feat for a small newspaper. The *Boston Globe* showed what a large newspaper could do in a similar situation by helping to obtain more than 100 indictments following an investigation of local government in Somerville, Mass. And *Newsday* attacked the land deals of a Long Island political machine, forcing numerous resignations from local public and political offices.

Campaigning by Broadcasters If the broadcast journalists have not generally received the same opportunities for public service as their colleagues of the press, those who did conduct campaigns have demonstrated both the value and the power of the medium. One of the most memorable was Fred Freed's three-hour documentary on "The Energy Crisis" for NBC News. Others were "The Food Crisis—Feast and Famine" for CBS Reports and a three-hour NBC documentary on violence. Local broadcasters, too, distinguished themselves. In Miami, WPLG-TV attracted attention with its crime reporting, particularly its "Crime Watch" series. And in Los Angeles, KNBC-TV contributed a documentary shocker, "Prison Gangs."

The expose of wrongdoing by public servants has been impressively handled, too. WPVI-TV, Philadelphia, did it well in "Public Bridges and Private Riches," dealing with a scandal in the Delaware River Valley. WCKT-TV, Miami, established a good record with its investigations of local government corruption. In Hartford, Connecticut, WFSB-TV attacked questionable emergency ambulance operations in "Scandal Rides the Ambulance." WCVB-TV, Boston, examined the safety of one of the world's largest air terminals, Boston's own Logan Airport. And KERA-TV, Dallas, delved into environmental reporting in "Big Thicket."

There have been times, as well, when TV has gone into areas that create difficulties among viewers and management. One such was the sensitive matter of race relations, which was handled by WKY-TV, Oklahoma City, in "Through the Looking Glass Darkly." Miami's WTVJ-TV tackled the problem of sex criminals in "The Sex Offenders." And through sheer persistence, WMC-TV, Memphis, managed to find the money to keep open for an additional year a small local hospital in a Mississippi town that served poor people, white and black.

Juvenile crime, drug addiction, alcoholism, rape, off-shore oil spillage and the problems of minorities are among other topics that have attracted broadcasters with a purpose. The pity of it is that their numbers have been so few. But as Marvin Barrett of Columbia University observed: "As long as the networks and courageous individual commercial stations continued to support and take pride in their news and public affairs departments . . . the situation, though depressing, was not desperate." [1]

News Areas of Public Service While the role of the news media as watchdogs in the governmental processes is the most familiar and the most celebrated, public service journalism today also includes such growing areas as civil rights, consumerism, inflation, health protection and the war on poverty in all its phases. Numerous newspapers and broadcasters have done exhaustive studies of the black, Puerto Rican and Mexican American communities and what can be done to improve their lot. The same is true of other modern issues. One of the most interesting experiments in recent years was the Gannett Newspapers' effort to find and print stories of civil rights successes in order to counteract the massive impression of conflict and failure.

The cause of prison reform was taken up by a large group of newspapers and broadcasters, usually with printed reports and filmed documentaries about conditions inside penal institutions. But Harold Eugene Martin of the *Montgomery Advertiser* and *Alabama Journal* broke the pattern with an expose of a commercial scheme for using Alabama prisoners for drug experimentation and obtaining blood plasma from them. And KLZ Denver broadcast interviews with five convicts awaiting execution, two of whom later were shot and killed while attempting to escape.

In the struggle for legislative reapportionment following the United States Supreme Court's ruling that districts should be of approximately equal size—the "one man, one vote" decision—several newspapers took decisive action to bring about vote reforms in their states. One of the great successes was in Kansas, where the *Hutchinson News* went to court in order to help achieve true legislative reapportionment. In New York, WMCA Radio played a key role in another reapportionment battle.

There have been other major efforts in news areas of public interest. The *St. Louis Post-Dispatch* led a drive to obtain a bond issue to renew the decaying center of the city and succeeded, but only after an initial failure. In two score or more communities, newspapers also were the main reliance of civic improvement groups for similar crusades for urban renewal. The *Chicago Daily News* originated one of the most unusual campaigns—a drive to popularize birth control among underprivileged families in Illinois and provide them with information at State expense. And the *Detroit Free Press* did much to spread both

[1] Fifth duPont-Columbia Survey of Broadcast Journalism, p. 136.

news and understanding of the ecumenical movement originated by the Vatican Council.

Much more can and will be done by the news media in these and other new areas of public service.

What Public Service Is Not There are, of course, many ways to counterfeit journalistic public service. But it is to the credit of American journalism that only a few newspapers, magazines and radio-television stations are cynical enough to attempt to gain public favor through such questionable tactics.

Here and there, a news organization may be found that makes feeble gestures for traffic safety, control of drug addicts, harsh treatment for sex deviates and the like while prudently keeping at a safe distance from a fight with an unscrupulous political machine. Sometimes, a newspaper maintains a facade of righteous opposition to gambling in any form while publishing lottery numbers results for the policy racketeers. Now and then, a station, magazine or newspaper will whip up a ten-minute crusade against sin and, having exposed the fact that sin exists, drop the matter to go on to something else to capture public curiosity.

Such phony crusades fool nobody, least of all the public. Whatever circulation or listener or viewer interest is aroused during the brief spurt of activity drops off sharply when it ends. And very real damage is done to the news staff, which recognizes at once that its leadership has an integrity quotient of zero. Good people will not stay with such a shabby organization for very long.

A Tradition of Conscience Contrast such parodies of public-service journalism with the concern voiced by Harry Ashmore at the twentieth anniversary of the Nieman Fellowships at Harvard over whether serious newspapers were really informing the American people.

> Perhaps what we need most of all is simply the courage of our own convictions—to recognize that news is not merely a record of ascertainable facts and attributable opinions, but a chronicle of the world we live in cast in terms of moral values. We will err, certainly, and we will be abused—but we will at least be in position in the watchtowers, trying to tell the story in all its dimensions.

This is the kind of editorial conviction that has brought Pulitzer Prizes for public service in journalism to editors and newspapers that have served the public interest. For every prize winner there have been many in the ranks of journalism who have labored without awards and with precious little recognition on the smaller but no less important aspects of the news of the day.

That is the highest tradition of journalism—the tradition of conscience, as Joseph Pulitzer, Jr. has aptly phrased it. Without it an editor becomes a rubber stamp for the prejudices of the mob, and a newspaper is nothing more than a wad of paper for shelving or a wrapping for fish instead of a respected chronicler of life itself.

EDITORIALS

The editorial page is undergoing a much-needed revival and the editorial voice of radio and television is a little stronger. Even some news magazines are coming around to the need for a separate section for editorial comment. The new stress on editorial opinion is due in large part to the expansion of public-service journalism; for, without the strongest kind of editorial support and the total mobilization of the resources of the entire news organization, many a crusade would wither and die in a few days.

There are many definitions of what editorial opinion should be, and how a properly conducted editorial page or editorial program should operate. Certainly, it must be something more than the voice of the proprietor, the vehicle for promoting his own interests and prejudices and those of his leading editors. Properly conducted, an editorial section should represent a community or region of the country; many, of course, contend that they speak for the nation but not very many could prove it if challenged. Moreover, such a section should be a marketplace of ideas, and not a grab-bag of columns and reprints intended to please all segments of the audience.

What Editors Believe It is customary, in any discussion of the editorial function, to note that editorial pages rank comparatively low in any survey of readership of newspapers and programs devoted to editorial opinion are close to the bottom in radio and television audience measurements. What these surveys do not show, however, is the quality of those who read the editorial page and listen to editorial programs. In most communities and regions, it is primarily the leaders who pay the closest attention to editorial content and who are the most likely to be influenced by it. Thus, despite low total diffusion, the editorial section can have an impact on the decision-making process and community leaders are well aware of it.

Much has been made of the tendency of some radio and television stations to editorialize, but actually the function as yet does not have the importance of press comment and is not likely to equal the press in impact in the forseeable future. There are too many limitations on the electronic media, for one thing. For another, electronic editorialists are still in the process of trying to establish a place for themselves in a section of the mass media that is heavily devoted to entertainment. And finally, there just aren't very many talented editorial writers who are willing to devote their services entirely to television.

This is not to say that television and radio both have not made a good beginning on the use of the editorial function. In some instances, the electronic editorializing has been both courageous and brilliant; without doubt, there will be more to come. But it is a fact that of the television stations owned completely or in large part by some 130 newspapers in the nation, few have editorialized on the air with the same abandon as their brothers do in print. Stimson Bullitt, owner of three West Coast television stations, said of some broadcast editorials: "They endorse Christmas seals." Inevitably, as the electronic media gain in stature and experience, more stations are going to emulate the independent policies of the newspapers and news magazines. But it may take some time for the movement to gain momentum.

The effect of the written word, consequently, remains the standard by which editorial influence is judged in American journalism. It can be profound. Because editors in the American colonies believed in freedom, they laid the basis for the Declaration of Independence in the minds of their readers. Because Mohandas K. Gandhi read Henry David Thoreau's essay on "Civil Disobedience," he molded a powerful weapon of public opinion that helped free the whole Indian subcontinent from British rule.

On newspaper editorial pages the evidence is more than sufficient to indicate that editorial writers can be an effective force in their communities if they have the material with which to work and the freedom to use it for the public good.

On Editorial Writing A good editorial page has so few restrictions that effective editorials vary widely in both style and organization. It would, therefore, be a waste of time and effort to draw up a blueprint for a good editorial, or an outline for a bad one. By their very nature editorials generally reflect the taste and character of the writer as well as the flavor of the newspaper. On editorial pages of large newspapers, where conferences are held daily to determine policy, select agreeable topics and discuss assignments, the style variations of individual editorial writers may in addition be affected by the personality of the editor. On small papers, where editors write their own editorials when and if they get around to it, the style is likely to be more vigorous.

Yet, allowing for all these variables, most editorials have certain things in common. They are generally short, varying from a sentence or two to 1,000 words or more. They usually have a news peg, an introductory statement announcing the subject of the editorial and tying it to a news development.

In the development of a point of view on the subject, the most forceful and persuasive arguments are marshaled in a logical pattern to convince the reader. In addition, the editorial writer is bound to consider what arguments are likely to be used in rebuttal and to raise them for the purpose of answering them in advance. Finally, the editorial must end in a firm conclusion, clearly and reasonably stated, if it is to have any effect at all.

The most convincing editorials are cool, informal and well-reasoned, devoid of cliches. Even the least sophisticated reader has learned to laugh at the traditional piece that "views with alarm," "points with pride," indulges in a judicious weighing of alternatives without coming to a conclusion or ends with a stentorian warning to the reader: "It's UP to YOU!" (Capitalization of individual words, by the way, went out with Arthur Brisbane, a Hearst editorial columnist of the old school.) Equally annoying to readers is the lofty attitude of some editorialists who do not bother to explain the issues and wind up with vague talk.

Here is one of the most famous editorials in American journalism:

TO AN ANXIOUS FRIEND

You tell me that law is above freedom of utterance. And I reply that you can have no wise laws nor free enforcement of wise laws unless there is free expression of the wisdom of the people—and, alas, their folly with it. But if there is freedom, folly will die of its own poison, and the wisdom will survive. That is the history of the race. It is the proof of man's kinship with God. You say that freedom of utterance is not for time of stress, and I reply with the sad truth that only in time of stress is freedom of utterance in danger. No one questions it in calm days because it is not needed. And the reverse is true also; only when free utterance is suppressed is it needed, and when it is needed, it is most vital to justice. Peace is good. But if you are interested in peace through force and with free discussion, that is to say, free utterance decently and in order—your interest in justice is slight. And peace without justice is tyranny, no matter how you may sugarcoat it with expediency. This state today is in more danger from suppression than from violence, because in the end, suppression leads to violence. Violence, indeed, is the child of suppression. Whoever pleads for justice helps to keep the peace; and whoever tramples upon the plea for justice, temperately made in the name of peace, only outrages peace and kills something fine in the heart of man which God put there when we got our manhood. When that is killed, brute meets brute on each side of the line.

So, dear friend, put fear out of your heart. This nation will survive, this state will prosper, the orderly business of life will go forward if only men can speak in whatever way given to them to utter what their hearts hold— by voice, by posted card, by letter or by press. Reason never has failed men. Only force and repression have made the wrecks in the world.

—*William Allen White in the Emporia (Kan.) Gazette,*
July 27, 1922; Pulitzer Prize, 1923

COLUMNISTS AND COMMENTATORS

A different kind of personal journalism is developing in the United States. This has nothing to do with the old personal rule of the press typefied by Greeley and Dana, Pulitzer and Hearst, Victor Fremont Lawson, Adolph S. Ochs and their associates. Rather, it marks the development of the individual who has no proprietory interest in the press and sometimes even opposes the interests of most of the proprietors.

In their most important manifestation, these writers are editorial columnists with signed articles that appear at regular intervals in newspapers or commentators who give their opinions with equal regularity on major network news programs. Both are national forces and have national followings.

There are as many columnists as there are existing editorial positions on political, social and economic interests, and then some. Commentators are fewer in number because the breed is in comparatively rare supply on the broadcast media. The most controversial columnist and investigator is Jack Anderson, the combative successor to his friend and mentor, Drew Pearson. On the liberal side, the leaders for some years have been James Reston of the *New York Times*, David Broder of the *Washington Post*, Mary McGrory of the *Washington Star* and Joseph Kraft of the *Chicago Sun-Times*. Among the conservatives, William F. Buckley, George Will and James J. Kilpatrick have been widely syndicated. Carl Rowan, the leading black commentator, also has been one of the few who have worked successfully in both print and television. The vendor of gossip, who came to prominence in the 1930s, has made a comeback in the checkout counter tabloids and the more sensational daily papers. As for humorists, typefied by Art Buchwald, Russell Baker and a few others, they have always been in short supply in journalism.

In radio and television, Walter Cronkite of CBS remains the leading commentator and newscaster but he is facing continual challenges from the stars of the other networks. However, except for the regulars on the evening news, few are measuring up as potential national figures.

The "Op Ed" Page The urge to put something in the paper that will please almost everybody has resulted in the reincarnation of what Herbert Bayard Swope used to call his "Op Ed" page in the *New York World* of treasured memory. But whereas Swope's page opposite editorial sparkled with some of the great names of American journalism—critics, essayists, artists, even humorists—the revived version runs heavily to political cómment. With the exception of established columnists, the contributed material—solicited or not—is generally serious in nature and heavy in tone. It has the substance of good, cold, well water, but no sparkle.

Letters to the Editor A glance at the morning mail on an editor's desk will usually determine very quickly a newspaper's credibility with its particular public. The published letters, judged by their sources and content, are an equally good measurement. For if the letters column is not given serious treatment, or if it is filled with the efforts of the semi-pros who like to see their names in the paper, then it may very well be a reflection on the degree of acceptance the paper has in the community. No paper with any interest in the public-service field is going to neglect one of its chief points of contact with its readers—the daily letters column. It should be as carefully edited as anything else.

THE ALTERNATIVE PRESS

During the Nazi occupation of much of Western Europe in World War II, newspapers were published clandestinely in France, Italy and the low countries to keep hope alive among oppressed peoples and maintain resistance to the conquerors. This marked the birth of the underground press in its modern guise. With the overthrow of Hitler and his Axis allies, the best of the underground papers surfaced and took their rightful place in their communities. The rest died.

The American Underground In the United States, at the height of resistance to the Vietnam War, a fledgling antiestablishment press took form because many young people, particularly those on the nation's campuses, had serious doubts that the so-called straight press could ever represent them properly. This move toward an alternative press, which for some years called itself the underground, had nothing in common with its European predecessors except the will to resist. Originally, it was written by the alienated for the alienated.

The alternative newspapers that took the trouble to build a professional staff survived when the antiwar movement collapsed with the end of the Vietnam conflict. The rest went out of business, leaving little behind except debts. Of the press that began as an alternative, the leaders are facing the same challenges as their commercial counterparts. For example, the *Village Voice*, a fat and sassy New York weekly, was snatched up by Rupert Murdoch, the Australian press baron, in a deal through which he also acquired *New York* magazine. It's going to be a different *Voice* from now on. And *Rolling Stone*, the tough newcomer from California, is now settled comfortably in a New York setting where its image is not exactly one of youthful defiance. The rest of the alternative survivors also retain little of their rebelliousness and few are distinguishable from the established press.

INVESTIGATIVE REPORTING

So much of this volume has been given over to investigative reporting that this relatively brief section of the final chapter serves mainly as a summation. In most of the public service journalism conducted by the

Gene Miller, reporter for the Miami Herald and winner of two Pulitzer Prizes in Local Reporting for helping free four persons in three separate and unrelated cases by proving that they had not been guilty of the murders for which they had been convicted. He is shown with two of those he saved from cells in Death Row, Freddy Lee Pitts (left) and Wilbert Lee, as a result of an eight-and-a-half-year effort. (Copyright, Miami Herald, Used by Permission.)

news media, the investigators are all-important. Without these "diggers," it is seldom possible to document the rights and wrongs of governmental processes or the shortcomings of the private sector. In consequence, the practice of investigative reporting has become a specialty in its own right. Among leaders of the news media, the practitioners of the art have status, work singly or in teams and even have their own national organization for the discussion of common problems.

An experienced investigative reporter who is on a continuing inquiry works all hours. The men and the few women who are engaged in such inquiries very often keep their own counsel until they have something worth reporting to their superiors. It is tiring work, sometimes dangerous work.

The Bolles Case The case of Don Bolles of the Arizona Republic should serve as a constant reminder to all journalists both of the dedication and the courage that are required of investigative reporters who venture into dangerous situations. The reaction to his murder in downtown Phoenix, while he was on the track of gangland connections with official Arizona, should also serve as an inspiration.

After Bolles was killed, 36 reporters and editors from different news organizations came to Arizona and many of them spent up to six months in the state, under the leadership of Bob Greene of *Newsday*, to try to finish the work that the Arizonan had begun. It was a unique cooperative effort, financed in part by most of the 20 news organizations that were represented, to show that no investigative reporter could be harassed or slain without inviting the most serious consequences.

The series of articles produced by the Investigative Reporters and Editors Inc., as the group called itself, was published and broadcast in whole or in part by a number of the participating organizations. The charges of links between business and politics and organized crime in Arizona, in a number of instances, bore out allegations that had been made first by Bolles.[2]

The Scope of the Work   By its very nature, investigative reporting has come to be considered gumshoe work in the field of crime. But reporters in other areas have had just as difficult a time as the crime specialists in getting at sources, piercing official and unofficial secrecy and achieving results. It isn't a simple matter to uncover trickery in governmental accounting practices, to conduct inquiries in institutions for juvenile offenders, hospitals or facilities for criminals or the mentally ill; to check on the bill that is slipped through Congress or a state legislature to give a favored concern a tax break. Of course there are supposed to be governmental agencies that protect the citizens of the land; but more often than not, it takes the press, the outsider, to do the job.

Methods   Bob Greene of *Newsday*, the successful leader of several major investigations by the Long Island newspaper, has always advised members of his team to study public records—land sales, tax payments, mortgages and the like—to see if they could detect a pattern of curious events involving office-holders or others that might indicate wrongdoing. This kind of work, colorless and uninspiring, is the very backbone of investigative reporting. It is both time-consuming and expensive in terms of the length of reportorial assignments.

Another familiar tactic, particularly when an inquiry deals with government sources, leads a reporter to work directly with a public official or a committee that has the right of subpoena. While public office-holders are not supposed to work exclusively with one reporter or a single team of reporters, it frequently happens that a cooperative invest-

[2] Associated Press file, 14 March 1977.

igative reporter who knows his way around can get help from official sources.

Wallace Turner, whose investigative work helped expose labor racketeering while he was a member of the *Portland Oregonian* staff, gives this advice on method:

> The most important official to the investigative reporter is the prosecutor. You have to rely on him. A newspaper which tolerates an ineffective prosecutor is short-sighted in both its own and in the public's interest. Get him out of the box! The vast powers of a Congressional committee can help or hurt your exposé efforts, depending on what the staff and the committee want to do. Your decision whether to cooperate must be made on the basis of the facts that present themselves at the time.

Then, too, experienced reporters sometimes do undercover work, infiltrating the agency or organization they are investigating and working at various jobs. On occasion, reporters deliberately go to prison or have themselves committed to mental institutions—a far cry from the play-acting assignment of putting on a Santa Claus suit to get a feature at Christmas time. But such roles, in difficult investigations, are not for untrained beginners; in fact, most news organizations are quite wary of assigning anybody to undercover work unless the stakes are very high and the story is a matter of the utmost urgency.

Katharine Graham, publisher of the Washington Post, *with her star investigative reporters, Carl Bernstein (left) and Bob Woodward, who broke the Watergate scandal. (Copyright, the Washington Post. Used by permission.)*

Lucinda Franks and Thomas Powers who shared a Pulitzer Prize for their investigation written for UPI of the life and death of a twenty-eight-year old revolutionary, Diana Oughton, "The Making of a Terrorist." United Press International. Used with permission.

But whatever the campaign may be and wherever the investigation may lead reporters, they are often helpless unless somebody talks. For in most inquiries, it is not enough for an editor or a reporter to satisfy the requirements of the paper or the station. They can never forget that they must pile up proof in so convincing a manner that it will stand up in court. And that is the most difficult part of any investigation.

Some Leaders Jack Anderson, the syndicated columnist, says that he became an investigative reporter because he was "brought up with a sense of duty and a sense of outrage." He calls himself a "watchdog on government" in Washington and few would deny either his capacity or his effectiveness. Like his fellows in the field, Anderson and his staff are always on the lookout for the angry man or angry woman in government, the disgruntled official who is so opposed to a particular practice or policy that he is willing to risk both livelihood and career to help with an expose. These are among the sources that account for the leaking of secret papers and proceedings. But that isn't all there is to Anderson's work. He meets his sources in out-of-the-way places, checks their credentials and their credibility, and tries to avoid the charge of being careless about his facts. Yet, in the case of Senator Thomas Eagleton of Missouri, who resigned under pressure in 1972 as the Democratic Vice Presidential candidate, Anderson had to apologize for wrongfully accusing him in a broadcast of convictions for drunken driving. Still, as one government official said of Anderson, "He keeps a lot of people honest."

Clark Mollenhoff, once a leading investigator for the *Des Moines Register-Tribune,* tried for a while to be a government investigator but came back to journalism considerably chastened. Out of his earlier experiences, when he played a leading part in exposing such Presidential favorites as Sherman Adams in the Eisenhower administration and Robert G. (Bobby) Baker in the Johnson administration, he put the position this way:

> It is doubtful if we will ever eliminate corruption in the federal government but it must be kept under closer control or it can spread with devastating impact. Nothing speeds the growth of corruption more than policies that foster arbitrary secrecy. Secrecy allows little scandals to become major scandals, costly to the taxpayers, devastating to our foreign-aid programs, to our position of defense readiness and to our national morale.

Neil Sheehan, who obtained the Pentagon Papers for the *New York Times,* never doubted that there was a moral right to publish such material in the public interest. He put the case in this manner:

> We are told that in writing the First Amendment, that "Congress shall make no law abridging the freedom of speech, or of the press," the Founding Fathers meant to give us a mere privilege to report and publish, a license that can be revoked or restricted when those who govern us see fit to revoke or restrict it for what they believe to be the greater good of the nation. Those who hold this view will learn that journalists who take their work seriously reject it, regardless of the personal consequences. The Founding Fathers did not give us a privilege, a license that is held at the convenience of government. Rather, in writing the First Amendment, they imposed upon us a duty, a responsibility to assert the right of the American people to know the truth and to hold those who govern them to account.

There are numerous smaller newspapers such as the *St. Petersburg* (Florida) *Times* that proceed with investigations as a matter of public policy and sometimes achieve results out of proportion to their size. In one instance, a staff of *Times* reporters demonstrated that the Florida highway system was being extended through costly and questionable administrative practices. As a result, the highway administration was revised from top to bottom; in the reforms that followed, Florida taxpayers were assured savings of millions of dollars and better roads as well.

The investigative art is by no means confined to men, although they are usually given the fattest assignments and the most prominent roles. Lois Wille of the *Chicago Daily News* and the late Miriam Ottenberg of the *Washington Star* both won Pulitzer Prizes for their investigative reporting and Ann deSantis of the *Boston Globe*, Lucinda Franks of UPI and Myrta J. Pulliam of the *Indianapolis Star* were members of prizewinning teams. The evidence is abundant that women investigators do their jobs with as much skill and spirit as the men.

William Gaines, a member of the Chicago Tribune's Investigative Task Force, which won a Pulitzer Prize for Local Reporting because of its hospital and housing exposes. Gaines, shown at work in a janitor's uniform at a Chicago hospital, also had to assist nurses and doctors in surgery without changing his clothes. (Copyright, Chicago Tribune. Used with permission.)

The Action Line There are numerous offshoots of the spreading interest in investigative reporting. One of the most popular and useful is the Action Line column in newspapers and the similar services offered by some broadcast organizations. This specialty was originated by the *Houston Chronicle* and quickly picked up by hundreds of other news organizations. The purpose is to help readers, listeners or viewers who have complaints and apparently are unable to proceed by themselves.

Someone may write in or telephone to an "Action Line" reporter about a tax matter, a piece of condemned property, a case of official neglect or even a missing pet such as a talking crow. The "Action Line" (it has many different names) then is supposed to get action on the complaint. Surprisingly many are handled, the results being publicized in the column or on the air.

The Secret Witness Another aspect of investigative reporting is the "Secret Witness" program originated by the *Detroit News* with striking results. This is a variation of the well-established newspaper practice of offering a reward for information leading to the arrest and conviction of persons sought for a particular crime. What the *Detroit News* did was to go into the whole field of unsolved crimes in its area, and sometimes beyond, with a blanket offer of both rewards and protection for persons who would come forward with legitimate evidence. Those who gave information were assured that their identities would never be revealed, a prerequisite in any successful investigation. And a remarkable part of the program was that people *did* trust the *Detroit News*. They did come forward. And a lot of unsolved crimes were cleared up. Although the program proved to be both expensive and time-consuming, other papers picked it up and some still use it.

WRITING

Investigative stories may be done in a variety of ways. When the subject matter is familiar and little explanation is needed, straight news style usually applies. But when the investigation deals with a complicated matter, particularly in the field of government, it is essential to weave interpretive material into the account wherever necessary. However, an investigative story should not resemble an editorial or a signed column unless a considered decision is made by top management to present the case in this manner. Generally, an investigative piece gains in effect if it is written in a calm, restrained and detached style which depends on reason rather than a heavy-handed emotional appeal. If there is a crime in investigative writing, it is compounded of inaccuracy and dullness.

Here is the way Carl Bernstein and Bob Woodward began one of their earliest pieces about the Watergate scandals for the *Washington*

Post, soon after five men were arrested for the break-in at Democratic National Committee headquarters in the Watergate complex, Washington, D. C., on June 17, 1972:

> FBI agents have established that the Watergate bugging incident stemmed from a massive campaign of political spying and sabotage conducted on behalf of President Nixon's reelection and directed by officials of the White House and the Committee for the Reelection of the President.
>
> The activities, according to information in FBI and Department of Justice files, were aimed at all the major Democratic Presidential contenders and — since 1971 — represented a basic strategy of the Nixon reelection effort.
>
> During their Watergate investigation, federal agents established that hundreds of thousands of dollars in Nixon campaign contributions had been set aside to pay for an extensive undercover campaign aimed at discrediting individual Democratic Presidential candidates and disrupting their campaigns.
>
> "Intelligence work" is normal during a campaign and is said to be carried out by both political parties. But federal investigators said that what they uncovered being done by the Nixon forces is unprecedented in scope and intensity.
>
> They said it included:
>
> Following members of Democratic candidates' families and assembling dossiers on their personal lives; forging letters and distributing them under the candidates' letterheads; leaking false and manufactured items to the press; throwing campaign schedules into disarray; seizing confidential campaign files, and investigating the lives of dozens of Democratic campaign workers.
>
> In addition, investigators said the activities included planting provocateurs in the ranks of organizations expected to demonstrate at the Republican and Democratic conventions, and investigating potential donors to the Nixon campaign before their contributions were solicited.
>
> Informed of the general contents of this article, the White House referred all comment to the Committee for the Reelection of the President. A spokesman there said, "The *Post* story is not only fiction but a collection of absurdities." . . .

This was, of course, the first disclosure of the "dirty tricks" department of the Republican campaign, which victimized Senator Edmund S. Muskie of Maine, a contender for the Democratic Presidential nomination, and brought about the conviction of a loyal Nixon supporter, Donald H. Segretti, and others. It was quite a way from these early stories in the *Washington Post's* Watergate campaign — when the *Post* alone was doing the investigating — until President Nixon finally was obliged to resign the Presidency after the White House tapes disclosed he had indeed directed the Watergate cover-up despite his long record of denials. But when he stepped down after a majority of the House Judiciary Committee voted for articles of impeachment, there was no hint of triumph in Carroll Kilpatrick's cool, highly professional story for the *Washington Post* on August 9, 1974. Here is the beginning of that historic account:

Richard Milhous Nixon announced last night that he will resign as the 37th President of the United States at noon today.

Vice President Gerald R. Ford of Michigan will take the oath as the new President at noon to complete the remaining 2½ years of Mr. Nixon's term.

After two years of bitter public debate over the Watergate scandals, President Nixon bowed to pressures from the public and leaders of his party to become the first President in American history to resign.

"By taking this action," he said in a subdued yet dramatic television address from the Oval Office, "I hope that I will have hastened the start of the process of healing that is so desperately needed in America."

Vice President Ford, who spoke a short time later in front of his Alexandria home, announced that Secretary of State Henry A. Kissinger will remain in his Cabinet.

The President-to-be praised Mr. Nixon's sacrifice for the country and called it "one of the very saddest incidents I have ever witnessed."

Mr. Nixon said he decided he must resign when he concluded that he no longer had "a strong enough political base in Congress" to make it possible for him to complete his term of office.

Declaring that he has never been a quitter, Mr. Nixon said that to leave office before the end of his term "is abhorrent to every instinct in my body."

But "as President, I must put the interests of America first," he said.

While the President acknowledged that some of his judgments "were wrong," he made no confession of the "high crimes and misdemeanors" with which the House Judiciary Committee charged him in its bill of impeachment.

Specifically, he did not refer to the Judiciary Committee charges that in the cover-up of Watergate crimes he misused government agencies such as the FBI, Central Intelligence Agency and the Internal Revenue Service.

After the President's address, Special Prosecutor Leon Jaworski issued a statement declaring that "there has been no agreement or understanding of any sort between the President or his representatives and the special prosecutor relating in any way to the President's resignation." . . .

This is the way such things are handled by professional news organizations. And it is the same for small ones as for the giants, for the struggling, little-known reporters as for Woodward and Bernstein. Here, for example, is the beginning of the Teamsters Union series, copyrighted by the *Anchorage Daily News,* as it appeared under the bylines of Howard Weaver and Bob Porterfield, staff writers. Like the *Washington Post's* Watergate expose, winner of the Pulitzer Prize gold medal for Public Service in 1973, the *Anchorage Daily News's* Teamster series was awarded the gold medal for 1976.

Teamsters Union Local 959 is fashioning an empire in Alaska, stretching across an ever-widening slice of life from the infant oil frontier to the heart of the state's major city.

Secure under the unquestioned leadership of Secretary-Treasurer Jesse L. Carr, the empire has evolved in just 18 years into a complex maze of political, economic and social power which towers above the rest of Alaska's labor movement—and challenges at times both industry and government itself.

In recent weeks the union has come under increasing observation in Alaska and outside, but basic, key questions have been left unanswered. How has the union amassed its power? Where does its structure reach? Who are its primary architects? What lies ahead?

To answer these and other questions, the *Daily News* made a lengthy study of the empire. These are the basic facts:

Local 959 has amassed its power in a number of ways:

—With 23,000 registered members, the union is by far the most influential and successful special interest group in the state.

—No other group—including the Republican party which elected the governor—even approaches the concentration of power which Teamsters have vested in Carr, the secretary-treasurer and moving force of the union.

—By means of a pension fund rapidly approaching the $100 million level and an investment policy, which gives it considerable influence over the state's major financial institutions, 959 represents the most potent financial force of any Alaska-directed organization. Measured in terms of Alaska interest, this appears true even in comparison with the oil giants and emerging native corporations now operating in the state.

—Despite an occasional upset, no other group has displayed such consistent political power here as the Alaska Teamsters. Spanning as it does both party and ideological boundaries, the union outstrips either political party in this respect.

The web of Teamster power stretches across the face and beneath the surface of Alaska society, manifesting itself in a wide variety of forms . . .

When a reporter has done undercover work, the approach is different. Often, if a personal angle is involved, the writing may take on an intensely personal tone. This was the style adopted by William Jones of the *Chicago Tribune* when he described his first day as a private ambulance driver in Chicago as follows:

The ambulance siren gave a final growl as we arrived in front of the blighted south-side building.

I leaped from the vehicle, my heart pounding. It was my first day on the job as an ambulance attendant and my first emergency call.

I had good reason to be nervous. Reporting for work less than an hour before, I was immediately assigned to an ambulance. Now, with no training in the handling of a stretcher or the use of oxygen, I was to be confronted with a reported heart-attack victim who could be fighting for her life. The city code requires only first-aid training to be licensed as an attendant.

It was the first in what would quickly become a long list of horror stories involving the misery merchants who operate some of Chicago's private ambulance companies. The two-month investigation, conducted in cooperation with the Better Government Association, revealed widespread mismanagement, welfare fraud, sadism and payoffs to police in the multimillion-dollar-a-year private ambulance business.

Before this 24-hour shift was over, I would witness some of this mistreatment of the ill and injured. I would also be threatened with a beating when one of my employers suspected I was a private investigator . . .

THE ANATOMY OF A CAMPAIGN

Newspaper people are not very demonstrative as a rule. Although the public and a few more emotional editorialists pin the crusading label on a variety of public service material, reporters prefer almost any other term—campaigns, investigations, series, reports or (depending on who is doing the work) a "hatchet job." Most of them feel uncomfortable if they are called crusaders, although it was a term that perfectly suited the first Joseph Pulitzer, one of its most eminent practitioners.

How Campaigns Begin A campaign may begin by design, by degree or entirely by accident, depending on circumstances.

A woman wrote a letter of protest to the *Detroit News*, touching off its campaign to free four men who had been wrongfully convicted of murder in New Mexico. A Congressional secretary confided her woes to a sympathetic stranger seated next to her on a bus, who happened to be a *Washington Post* reporter, and who proceeded to break the Congressional sex scandals. Somebody at the *New York Daily News* noticed that a lot of unsold lottery tickets were being drawn as winners in the New York State lottery, leading to an investigation that caused suspension of the drawings and subsequent reforms.

A photographer in Buffalo happened to take a picture of a city truck unloading supplies at a private contracting job, thus revealing a major municipal scandal that rocked the City Hall. A penciled notation on a card, found by a reporter for the *Seattle Times*, resulted in clearing a University of Washington professor of charges of Communist activity. A wrinkled newspaper clipping about an Air Force lieutenant who was losing his commission because some of his relatives were left-wing sympathizers led to a great television expose by Edward R. Murrow.

It sometimes happens, but not as often as romantics believe, that an angry reporter will start an investigation on his own and thereby commit his newspaper to a campaign that it would not otherwise have undertaken. But it never happens that a managing editor, or a publisher, comes into the office on a Monday morning, jumps on a desk and announces to a palpitating staff: "This morning, ladies and gentlemen, we undertake a great crusade." That is the stuff of politics, not journalism.

Development of Campaigns Sometimes a campaign turns entirely on the results of the work of one reporter, although in this era of data banks and computerized procedures this is becoming increasingly rare. Usually, anywhere from two to a dozen reporters will work together under the direction of an editor who is taken off regular duties. It all depends on the size of the news organization and the type of assignment.

Whatever the size of the reportorial staff, most successful campaigns depend for their success on the whole symphony of journalism—the investigators, the editorialist, the columnist, the photographer and cartoonist, the editor and publisher, working together as a team. For without a firm commitment by top management to persevere, no editor and no reporter can conduct a campaign for very long. Nor can the staff work very effectively if it has the slightest doubt that top management will support a reporter who becomes too deeply involved in one way or another. When campaigns have failed, despite the production of sufficient information, lack of top management support rather than a lack of effort has been the primary reason.

This is as true of the news magazines and television as it is of newspapers and wire services. A single reporter or a team of reporters can accomplish little, no matter how worthy the objective, unless all the resources of the news organization are mobilized to give them the firmest kind of support. A copout by top management—and it has happened—spells disaster.

Objectives It used to be said that the primary objective of most campaigns was to put wrongdoers in jail and get innocent persons out of jail. These, naturally, are the most spectacular results of campaigning. But there are many others, as this discussion has made abundantly clear. It sometimes happens that, without any declared intent, a major public service is performed because a news organization and its staff do their work of informing the public under extreme difficulties and in superlative fashion. This often occurs in the coverage of natural disasters or civil disorders. It results occasionally when a reporter, out of sheer conviction, risks life and limb to get a story that can be obtained in no other way.

Such was the first account of the upheaval in Cambodia following the Communist takeover, which was sent by Sydney H. Schanberg to the *New York Times* when he reached Thailand on May 8, 1975, after despairing weeks in Phnom Penh: He began his story as follows:

> BANGKOK, THAILAND, May 8—The victorious Cambodian Communists, who marched into Phnom Penh on April 17 and ended five years of war in Cambodia, are carrying out a peasant revolution that has thrown the entire country into upheaval.
>
> Perhaps as many as three or four million people, most of them on foot, have been forced out of the cities and sent on a mammoth and grueling exodus into areas deep in the countryside where, the Communists say, they will have to become peasants and till the soil.
>
> No one has been excluded—even the very old, the very young, the sick and the wounded have been forced out onto the roads—and some will clearly not be strong enough to survive.
>
> The old economy of the cities has been abandoned, and for the moment money means nothing and cannot be spent. Barter has replaced it.
>
> All shops have either been looted by Communist soldiers for such things as watches and transistor radios, or their goods have been taken away in an organized manner to be stored as communal property.

Even the roads that radiate out of the capital and that carried the nation's commerce have been virtually abandoned, and the population living along the roads, as well as that in all cities and towns that remained under control of the American-backed government, has been pushed into the interior. Apparently the areas into which the evacuees are being herded are at least 65 miles from Phnom Penh.

In sum the new rulers—before their overwhelming victory they were known as the Khmer Rouge—appear to be remaking Cambodian society in the peasant image, casting aside everything that belonged to the old system, which was generally dominated by the cities and towns and by the elite and merchants who lived there . . .

For his work, which was made possible only because he refused to obey orders from his superiors to leave Cambodia before it fell, Schanberg won the Pulitzer Prize for International Reporting for 1976. It is a prime example of the type of public service journalism that is conducted for the sake of providing information alone. In a sense, that is the continual campaign of any worthy news organization.

The campaign that attempts to sound an alarm also has a long and honorable history. It goes back almost to the beginning of the republic when editors were imprisoned for protesting the Alien and Sedition Acts and includes many of the heroes of American journalism, from Isaiah Thomas to William Lloyd Garrison and Elijah Lovejoy. In modern times, these journalistic sentinels have included those who warned against the rise of Hitler, who foretold disaster for the United States in the earliest days of the Vietnam commitment, who fought against the destruction of the nation's natural resources. In substance, their deeds have ranged from the bravery of Mel Ruder, editor of the weekly *Hungry Horse News* in Montana, who risked his life to warn his community of rising flood waters, to the persuasive editorial warnings of Philip F. Kerby of the *Los Angeles Times* against judicial censorship of the press.

Numerous newspapers have tackled the problem of oil spillage. The situation has created an editorial mood that has spread across the country and involved even the smallest papers. Here, for example, is the way a California weekly, the *Pacifica Tribune*, presented the issue:

Oil! Oil! Oil!
Untold gallons of it fouled Pacifica's beaches yesterday, killing unknown numbers of marine birds, maiming others, and bringing an estimated 1,000 people swooping down on Pacifica to engage in the great oil battle.
The oil seeped ashore Monday night, the early morning high tides leaving great gobs of the stuff high up on the beach, the surf covered with oil streaks, and two more huge oil slicks lingering off shore . . .

In attacking a housing crisis brought on by the deliberate burning of slum buildings for whatever insurance could be collected, the *St. Louis Globe-Democrat* began its piece this way:

Last April City Fire Marshal Arthur C. Newman called arson a grave threat to the future of the city. Since then, a fire captain and others have died in arson fires, and untold thousands of dollars worth of slum property has been deliberately destroyed.

And the fires continue to burn, in many cases, fire officials say, so someone can make a buck . . .

In some campaigns, the news stories are quite factual and restrained in tone but the alarm is sounded on the editorial page with thunderous emphasis. This was the case in the successful effort of the *Winston-Salem* (North Carolina) *Journal* and *Sentinel* to prevent strip miners from tearing apart the beautiful hill country of northwest North Carolina. One of the major editorials took this approach:

The rolling hills and valleys in northwest North Carolina are among the most beautiful anywhere. But the land in Ashe, Alleghany, Wilkes and Surry counties won't be beautiful much longer if strip-mining gets a foothold in the area.

Strip-mining might get that foothold if landowners and concerned citizens in the northwest aren't careful. The Gibbsite Corporation of America, which has obtained options on thousands of acres in the northwest and in southwest Virginia, is conducting studies to see if gibbsite—a mineral found in the area—can be extracted easily and cheaply from the soil for use in producing aluminum. If the studies prove that strip mining would be profitable, Gibbsite apparently will exercise its options . . .

One weapon against an unwelcome intruder is a public outcry. Such a protest helped Orange County keep Texas Gulf Sulphur from spoiling its beauty, and perhaps widespread resistance would make Gibbsite think twice.

If the people of the northwest should allow strip-mining to get a substantial foothold and if large parts of that scenic countryside become a virtual wasteland in a decade or so, they will have nobody to blame but themselves.

The point cannot be overemphasized. If a campaign is to mean anything, it must be undertaken with vigor and supported by the resources of the entire newspaper—from Page 1 to editorial, from pictures to cartoons.

This is something that few broadcasters have learned to date in their laudable efforts to emulate the crusading press; it is one thing to do an effective documentary, it is quite another to arouse the public without the editorial intervention of the management itself.

Does Campaigning Pay? There have been few campaigns of consequence that have added substantially to the circulation of a newspaper or the audience of a radio or TV station. Nor have very many reporters become as wealthy almost overnight as Woodward and Bernstein.

The record shows depressing instances in which campaigners for worthy causes in the press and broadcast media have lost circulation and advertising, become the targets for boycotts and even lost their jobs. The exposé is not the royal road to success, by any means.

The *Arkansas Gazette* paid for its championship of school integration in Little Rock with heavy monetary losses and the eventual resignation of its editor, Harry Ashmore. Several newspapers that ran campaigns against unscrupulous used car dealers lost automobile advertising. And in a classic case, the *Wall Street Journal* lost its General Motors advertising because it published information about new models before the auto giant was ready; however, GM soon came back into the paper.

One discouraged small-city editor, who tried and failed with a perfectly good campaign, even thought of giving up crusading altogether because it was so little appreciated. And J. Montgomery Curtis, while director of the American Press Institute, once came across an old Maine editor who refused point-blank to have anything to do with a campaign to improve his community, saying, "Son, the durn town ain't worth it."

True, crusading isn't easy. Nor can anything of consequence in a community be accomplished quickly or cheaply merely by viewing with alarm. Most campaigns are won simply by hard, consistent work, backed by a determined editor and publisher. Such was the case in the *Louisville Courier-Journal's* drive to tighten Kentucky's laws against strip-mining, which took four years before the Kentucky Legislature finally passed what was then called "the toughest strip-mining legislature in America." More often than not, even a modest crusade takes a good deal longer than either editors or reporters anticipate at the outset.

The issue is not whether crusading journalism pays but whether it is necessary. The answer must be overwhelmingly yes.

TOWARD THE FUTURE

If anything at all is certain about the concluding years of the twentieth century and the opening of the twenty-first, it is that American society will undergo drastic changes and journalism will have to reflect them. In no sense can it be said that social and economic pressures on this nation are likely to decrease; the outlook is quite the opposite. Even such necessary and long-delayed political reforms as government consolidation, an equitable taxing system and the elimination of towering injustices in the treatment of the sick and the needy, helpless children and the elderly may have a chance of success.

The nation will have need of a more efficient and broadened system for the dissemination of news, ideas and opinions. What we are seeing today in the adaptation of newspapers and wire services to the computer age and the development of the electronic media is only the beginning of the changes that are ahead for journalism. It is useless to speculate on whether there will be giant screens for TV across our living room walls, instant production of newspapers in the basement whenever we want them or production of voluminous statistics from distant data banks at the touch of a finger. The genius of science, interacting with the laws of supply and demand, will determine how much instant journalism we can have, what form it will take and how much we can actually absorb.

There are several things that are more important to the journalist than research and development, much as they are needed in a profession that has been backward for too long in such matters. The first and greatest of these is the continued protection of the freedoms guaranteed in the First Amendment, which are under increasing challenge in times of social change and world-wide political upheaval. For without a free press, the journalist becomes a mouthpiece for government, a lackey of the powerful, a robot who performs mindless duties in a graceless style.

While it is a temporary relief to have the U.S. Supreme Court strike down judicial gag orders and other prior restraints on publication, no journalist can feel secure if reporters sit in jail in violation of judicial orders to disclose their sources to the authorities and act, in fact, as servants of the government. It is a disturbing, even a threatening, trend.

Second only to the perpetuation of the rights of a free press is a reconsideration of the substance of journalism. And that bears upon the preparation and the beliefs of those who are intimately concerned with the identification, gathering, distribution and presentation of the news. Because, whatever definition may be offered, news actually tends to be what the journalist says it is. And the current definition of what the journalist treats as news is simply not good enough. Television and radio will have to be something more than glorified bulletin boards; newspapers, wire services and news magazines will be obliged to shape their reports to a greater extent toward areas that more deeply affect the public interest.

Finally, journalism must stand for something if it is to continue to be respected in a democratic society and given constitutional protection. It is not enough to be the harbinger of bad tidings; in primitive societies, such messengers were killed and journalists, in modern times, have frequently felt the sting of public animus merely because they did their duty. No less than the holding of public office, the difficult task of informing the public is a public trust. It is therefore inevitable that the concept of journalism as a public service is bound to increase in strength. Today, it is a trend. Tomorrow, it will be a necessity.

APPENDIXES

I A GLOSSARY FOR JOURNALISTS

1. For Newspapers and Wire Services
2. For Computer Technology
3. For the Broadcast Media

II A MODEL STYLE BOOK

III COPY EDITING TERMS AND SYMBOLS

IV STANDARDS FOR JOURNALISTS

Appendix I
A Glossary for Journalists

This glossary is divided into three parts. The first consists of terminology commonly used in newspapers and wire services. The second includes the principal terms used in computer technology for newspapers and wire services, and has some limited application to the electronic media where computers are used. The third applies solely to broadcast journalism.

1. FOR NEWSPAPERS AND WIRE SERVICES

A copy Also known as *A matter*. Part of a news story, based mainly on advance material, that is later completed by placing a lead on top of it. Used by newspapers mainly.

ad An advertisement.

add Additions of any kind to a news story.

advance News story based on factual material about a forthcoming event, such as the advance text of a speech, parade line of march, etc.

agate 5½ point type; as a unit of advertising, 14 agate lines equal one column inch.

AMs Morning newspapers.

angle   An approach to a story; also, various parts of a story.

ANPA   American Newspaper Publishers Association.

AP   Associated Press.

APME   Associated Press Managing Editors.

assignment   Duty given to a journalist.

bank   Also called a *deck;* the part of a headline that usually follows the top or the cross line, often both.

banner   A headline across Page 1, of four columns or more; sometimes known as a *streamer.* It is often confused with a *binder,* a headline across the top of an inside page.

B copy   Also known as *B matter.* Part of a news story, based mainly on advance material, which may be completed by topping it first with A copy and then with a lead. Many newspapers omit the A copy and top B copy with a lead directly.

beat   An exclusive story; also, a series of places regularly visited by a reporter to gather news.

Ben Day   Process named for Editor Ben Day of the *New York Sun.* It is a shading pattern of dots or lines used in photoengraving as background for photos, type or line drawings.

BF   Bold-face type. It is heavier and darker than regular type.

body   Part of a story that follows the lead. Also, the name of type in which regular newspaper reading matter is set.

box   Brief story enclosed by a border; many modern boxes have only top and bottom borders. Those put in the middle of a related story are called **drop-ins.**

bulldog   Early newspaper edition.

bulletin   Brief dispatch containing major news. Usually no more than 40-50 words.

byline   Signature on a story.

caps   Capital letters. Also called *upper case.*

c & lc   Caps and lower case (small letters).

caption   Descriptive material accompanying illustrations, cartoons, etc.

center spread   Also called a *double truck* on tabloids. The two pages in the center fold of a newspaper.

city editor   Boss of the local news staff in the United States. Now called Metropolitan Editor by some papers.

city room   Properly, the news room. Seat of the editorial operation of a newspaper.

clip   A newspaper clipping. Called a *cutting* by the British.

copy   Universally known as the name of material written by a journalist.

copy desk   Where copy is edited, cut and headlined.

copy editors   Also called *copyreaders.* They edit and headline the copy. Not to be confused with *proofreaders,* a function of the pre-computer mechanical staff, whose duty was to catch errors in proof.

correspondent When a reporter goes out of town, he sometimes calls himself a correspondent. In broadcast media, a correspondent is a job classification of more importance than the basic *newsman.*

cover To obtain news.

credit line To credit a picture, cartoon, etc., to the source.

crop Reducing the size of an illustration before it is put into printed form.

crusade Also known as a *campaign,* a *series,* a *long reporting job.* It is an effort by all parts of an editorial staff to persuade the public to act, or to refuse to act, in some matter involving the public interest.

cub An untrained newspaper person, usually a reporter. A term used more by the public than by newspaper people, who generally call a beginner a first-year reporter.

cut An engraving, but also applied to all kinds of newspaper illustrations.

cutlines The part of a caption that describes an illustration.

dateline The place from which a news story is sent. Many newspapers now omit the date from the dateline.

deadline Closing time for all copy for an edition. There are different deadlines for the city desk, news desk, copy desk, closing of pages in the composing room, etc.

deskman or woman An editor in the newsroom.

dingbat Decorations in type.

dope story Also called a *think piece;* soft news, supposedly based on reliable opinion, which seeks to develop trends.

dummy A drawing, usually freehand, outlining the position of news stories and cuts on a page by designating slugs and kinds of headlines.

dupe Also called a *blacksheet.* Carbon copy of a story. Virtually extinct in computerized newsrooms.

ears Boxes on either side of the nameplate on Page 1 of a newspaper—one usually encloses the weather, the other the name of the edition.

edition Remake, or revision of some of the pages of a newspaper, including Page 1.

editorial Comment on the news in the name of the news organization itself.

em Through usage this term has become interchangeable with a pica, the name applied to a lineal measurement of 12 points (one-sixth of an inch) or to a square of 12-point type. Originally an em was the square of any size of type.

en Half an em. Also called a *nut* to avoid phonetic confusion.

file The act of dispatching copy to or from a news center, except when it is sent by a messenger.

filler Small items used to fill out columns where needed.

flag   Newspaper nameplate on Page 1.

flash   In general news, a rarely used message of a few words describing a momentous event.

folio   Page number and name of the paper.

folo   Also called *follow, follow-up, follow story.* Sequence of news events after a news break.

future book   Date book of future events.

handout   Generic term for written publicity.

head   Name for all headlines.

hellbox   Repository for dead or discarded type in a precomputer composing room.

hold for release   Instruction placed on news that must not be used until receipt of a release, either automatic or by message.

HTK   Abbreviation of *Head to Kum* (printers' spelling). Placed on copy when the headline is to be written after the copy is cleared.

human interest   News or features with emotional appeal.

insert   Addition to a story written in such a way that it can be placed anywhere between the end of the first paragraph and the beginning of the last paragraph.

italics   Type face with characters slanted to the right, as contrasted with roman, or upright, characters.

Jim-dash   A 3-em dash.

jump   Continuation of a story to another page.

jump line   A continuation line.

justify   To fill out a line of type, a column of type or a page of type.

kill   Elimination of news material at any stage in the processing.

layout   Arrangement of illustrations.

lead   Beginning of a story, which may be a sentence, a paragraph or several paragraphs, depending on the complications involved.

libel   Any defamatory statement expressed in writing, printing or other visible form.

ligature   Two or more united characters of type, such as æ, fi.

lobster   The working shift that usually begins with midnight and runs through to about 10 or 11 A.M.

logotype   Also called a *logo.* A single matrix containing two or more letters used together, such as AP or UPI. It is also another name for the flag, or nameplate.

lower case   Small letters.

makeover   Redoing a page.

makeup   Assembling the newspaper or magazine.

markup   A proof or clipping, pasted on paper and marked to show where changes are to be made and what new material is to be used.

masthead   Statement, usually on the editorial page, of the newspaper's ownership, place of publication and other offices. Sometimes confused with the flag or nameplate.

morgue   News library.

must   When this word is put on copy, it means the story must be used.

new lead   Also called a *New top, Nulead or NL.* It is a fresh beginning on a story already sent or in the paper and is so written that it joins with the old story smoothly at a paragraph that can be designated at the end of the new lead. A *lead all* is a short top that fits on a new lead.

offset   A system of printing. Also known as "cold type."

obit   An obituary.

overnight   Also called *overnite* or *overniter.* It is a story for the first edition of an afternoon newspaper of the following day; also, for the overnight cycle of a wire service. In morning newspaper terminology an overnight refers to an assignment to be covered the next day.

overset   Type left over from an edition. Usually wasted.

photo composition   Typesetting by photography, replacing metal.

pi   To upset or otherwise mix up type.

pica   12-point type, and also a lineal measurement of 12 points.

pick up   Also written *pikup* in printers' shorthand. This is the name for that portion of a story in type that should be placed at the end of a new lead, or other news material.

pickup line   Line at top of wire service copy that includes the word "add," the point of origin of the story and the last few words of the preceding page. It is used to assemble the whole story in order.

play   The display given to a story or picture. Most editors talk of playing a story, rather than playing it up or down; these latter expressions are more frequently used by the public.

point   Basic printing measurement, roughly equivalent to one-seventy-second of an inch.

PMs   Afternoon newspapers.

pool   Selection of one journalist or a small group of them to cover for a large group.

precede   Brief dispatch, such as a bulletin or editorial note, that introduces a story but is separated from it by a dash.

printer   Also called a *Teletype* or *TWX.* It produces copy by electrical impulses actuated by a perforated tape, or some other means.

proof   Inked impressions of type for the purpose of making corrections.

rewrite   A writer for a newspaper or wire service, whose work consists in part of redoing stories and in part of writing original copy for the reporters who turn in notes by telephone or wire.

rim   Outer edge of copy desk. Extinct where terminals are used to read copy.

running story   Another name for the B Copy—A copy—lead process. Usually it means a chronological story of an event topped by successive leads as the news changes.

runover   Another name for a *jump.*

scoop   An exclusive story.

shirttail   Additional material, related to a longer story, and separated from it by a dash.

short   A brief story.

sidebar   A separate piece, related to a main story on the same subject.

situationer   An interpretive story describing a particular news situation.

slot   Seat of the head of an old-fashioned horseshoe copy desk.

slug   Each story has a name, which is called a slug.

split page   First page second section in a paper of two sections.

spread   Any story that takes a headline big enough to be used at the top of an inside page.

stereotype   Plate cast from a mold or image of a page of hot type.

stet   Copy editors' and printers' instruction, "Let it stand."

stick   About two inches of type.

stringer   Occasional correspondent paid by the amount of space per story. The length of the clippings is called the "string."

swing shift   A shift operated by workers who swing from one shift to another on different days.

take   A page of copy.

thirty   Telegraphers' Morse code symbol for "The End."

turn rule   Sometimes written as *T.R.* "T.R. for 2d ADD STORM" means a second addition to a story about a storm is expected.

UPI   United Press International.

wire service   A press association, a wholesaler of news.

wrapup   Also called a roundup. Summary of events in a broadly developed news situation.

2.   For Computer Technology

autofunctions   Commands placed on copy to instruct computer on types sizes, column widths, etc.

automatic purge   Function on some computer models that automatically kills copy stored more than 24 hours without change.

baud   Transmission speed. In computer language, a typical rate would be 1,200 bits (or 150 characters) per second.

code   Assignment of functions or routines.

coding form   Prepared programming instructions.

commands   Use of various symbols on a terminal to tell computer how a story is to be processed.

computer   Electronic machine for storing and processing news and other data.

core   Principal storage place of a computer, its main memory.

CPU Central Processing Unit of a computer for input, output and storage.

CRT Cathode Ray Tube. The AP calls its terminals CRTs. Most CRTs are Video Display Terminals.

cursor Indicator for editing changes on a terminal which is the size of a single character and takes the form of a mobile block of light.

data Information processed by a computer.

database All the text stored in a computer system.

database manager A computer that oversees all database operations, handling incoming stories for editing and sending outgoing to composing room.

directories Schedules that may be called up on terminals to see what stories are available.

DM A control function of terminals, enabling key users to obtain a master directory of stories.

drum full Signal from computer on terminal that storage drum has reached its capacity.

dump Changing stored material from one computer unit to another.

edit Programs for handling textual material.

edit mode Position of terminal after a story has been called to the screen for handling.

font Face and size of a type face.

hardware The entire production system, as distinguished from software, the news and other data it processes.

head This still means headlines in terminal-computer usage and they are written on terminals and handled by computers.

header Basic information placed at head of story including writer's name, date, slug of story and department for which it is intended.

index In some computer programs, it means directory or schedule showing the first three to five lines of a story.

insert Placing additional material in a story already on a terminal or stored in a computer.

interface An electrical command between parts of hardware—the machines "speaking" to each other.

invalid command When one is made, the terminal screen reports it.

keyboarding Keystrokes through which data is put into the system.

kill One of the basic commands on a terminal.

modem Device that uses an interface between two other parts of the hardware of a production system.

more Instruction typed at end of a take of copy when it is to be continued.

multiplexor Device through which computer handles material at the same time from several interconnected machines.

OCR Optical Character Reader, also known as a scanner, which converts specialized typewritten material into electrical impulses which then are recorded either on punched tape or stored in a computer for later editing on a VDT.

on line   Units interfaced into the computer system, as contrasted with units that operate independently.

output   Data from a computer system, either in the form of tape or a printout.

paper tape reader   Device used to put OCR output in computer when OCR is not part of system.

purge   Elimination of data from system.

queue   Order of priority in various schedules, each schedule being known as a queue.

reperf   A tape perforator.

roll up, roll down   Commands moving text on a terminal screen.

slug   In a terminal, this may be the name of the story, registered in six to eight characters after the writer's name, or it may designate all the header material placed at the top of the story.

sort   Arranging material in desired sequence.

system   Combination of computer programs.

terminal   Generic name for electronic typewriterlike devices with TV-type screens on which news and other editorial material is written and processed.

UF, CF   Instructions for typesetting on certain types of terminals.

VDT   Video Display Terminals, the most widely used form of CRTs, sometimes called a "super typewriter" because it has a type-writerlike extension from what looks like a small TV screen. Used to write, correct, change and edit stories, write headlines and process the material through the computer system to the composing room. Also stores material in memory banks.

wrap   Command used in editing on some types of VDTs.

3.   For the Broadcast Media

ABC   American Broadcasting Company.

academy leader   Film marked off in seconds, spliced to newsfilm, as a lead-in.

anchor man or woman   Chief newscaster.

Arbitron   Audience measuring device used by American Research Bureau.

atmospherics   Electrical disturbances in atmosphere.

audio   Sound transmission, or reception.

audio frequency   Vibrations normally audible to human ear.

audiometer   Audience measuring device used by A. C. Nielsen Co.

BBC   British Broadcasting Corporation.

back timing   Exact length of closing segment of newscast, timed in advance, to determine moment when segment should begin for program to end on schedule.

balop   Card, picture or similar object flashed electronically on a viewing screen. (The term is derived from Balopticon, an opaque projector trademarked by Bausch and Lomb, used for such work.)

blooper   Embarrassing error.

blow up   Enlargement of portion of picture, chart or map.

bridge   Written segment joining film clips of a differing nature.

bring it up   Order for increase in volume.

CATV   See cable television.

CBC   Canadian Broadcasting Company.

CBS   Columbia Broadcasting System.

CU   Close up.

cable television, or CATV   A system of wired television in which programs are received by a central source and redistributed to subscribers for a monthly fee plus original installation fee. Central reception is based on efficient high antenna that intercepts signals, which then are channeled by wire to subscribers.

cathode ray tube   Tube that produces picture on its large fluorescent end surface by means of electron beam emanating from its cathode, or negative, electrode.

call letters   Station's signature.

communications satellite   Space vehicle placed in orbit about earth to facilitate global transmission of data by radio, TV and radio-telephone signals. Echo I, launched in 1960, was the first. Other early examples Telstar, Relay, Syncom.

coaxial cable   Long copper tubing containing large number of wire conductors held in place by insulating discs, making possible transmission of television signals, telephone and telegraph messages simultaneously.

compatibility   System in which color broadcasts may be received in black and white on sets not specially equipped to receive color.

cue   Signal in script or by hand or word to start or stop speech, movement, film, tape, sound effects, music or other parts of program.

cut   To eliminate, to halt.

cutaway   Subsidiary scenes that can be fitted by film editor into main action.

dead area   Also called "blind spot." It refers to areas where reception is difficult.

diode   Two-element electron tube or semiconductor that changes (rectifies) alternating current into pulsating direct current.

double projection   A system in which two projectors are used, one for sound and the other for visual material, in producing a segment of integrated newsfilm and sound.

ECU   Extreme close up.

ENG   Electronic newsgathering, a combination of the use of the mini-cams (which see) and videotape which makes possible immediate transmission and replaces film. Also called EJ (electronic journalism) and ECC (electronic camera coverage).

easel shot   Also called limbo; an object such as a still photo or a chart or map that can be picked up by a studio camera.

electron   Particle of matter, a constituent of the atom, that carries an elementary charge of negative electricity.

ether   Upper region of space, or the rarified element that is supposed to fill it.

FCC   Federal Communications Commission.

FM   Frequency modulation, a virtually static-free system of broadcasting by radio. It adjusts the frequency of the transmitting wave in accordance with sound being sent, as contrasted with AM, or amplitude modulation, which adjusts the wave in accordance with its maximum departure from normal.

fading   Fluctuation of sound or image in broadcasting.

feedback   Sharp noise or hum, such as may be caused by a microphone placed too close to a speaker.

fidelity   Degree of accuracy with which sound or visual material is reproduced in radio or television.

flip card   Card containing material (charts, pictures, credits, etc.) that may be flipped before camera in studio.

fluff   An error in speaking or reading from a script.

frame   One of a series of pictures on film; there may be 24 to 28 frames of film shown in a second.

from the top   Begin all over.

facsimile   System of electronic transmission of written, printed or photographed material. It is done regularly over 800 miles in Japan in reproducing the newspaper Asahi in editions in Tokyo, Sapporo on the northern island of Hokkaido and elsewhere. The process is put to numerous uses in Britain and the U.S., as well.

Geiger counter   Device for detecting radioactivity.

generator   A machine that converts mechanical into electrical power.

ground   Connection from broadcast receiver to the earth.

Heaviside Layer   Also called Kennelly-Heaviside Layer. It is the ionosphere region of electrically charged air that begins about 25 miles above the earth's surface and makes possible the transmission of radio waves over great distances.

high frequency   A frequency is the number of complete cycles of alternating current that occur in one second; high frequencies are between 6,000 and 30,000 kilocycles.

Iconoscope   A trademarked electron pickup or camera tube that uses an electron scanning beam to convert photo-emissions into television signals.

Image Orthicon Tube   A trademarked electron pickup or camera tube, a refinement of the Iconoscope.

interlock   Separate projection of sound and film, locked together in synchronization. Expression describes a type of film, for example, as "16 mm color interlock."

interference   The effect of two electrical waves on each other.

intro   Introduction of a filmed or taped portion of a program in script or spoken form.

jamming   Interference from an undesired source, effectively blocking the reception of signals.

jump cut   Undesirable element of television, in which there is an irregular or unnatural continuation of movement.

Kenotron   An electron rectifying tube.

Kinescope   Trademarked picture receiving tube, either by direct view or projection. It also refers to the film, sometimes called a "kinnie," that is made from the monitor kinescope as the program is in progress.

kilowatt   A unit of electric power. A watt is the work done by one ampere electric current under a pressure of one volt. A kilowatt is one thousand watts.

LS   Long shot.

laser   Concentrated light beam. Acronym for "light amplification by stimulated emission of radiation."

level   Volume of transmitted sound.

live   On the spot broadcast or telecast.

live mike   An open microphone.

light wave technology   Use of glass fibers 90 microns in diameter (a micron is one millionth of a meter) to carry light in the form of a laser beam which, when activated into electrical impulses, substitutes for copper coaxial cables for cable TV, computers, aircraft systems and telephones.

limbo   Objects such as charts, pictures, etc,, that can be picked up by studio cameras. Also called easel shots.

long wave   Radio waves with a length of 600 meters or more and frequencies under 500 kilocycles.

low frequency   A frequency below radio frequencies, usually between 10 and 100 kilocycles, one that can be heard by the human ear; an audio frequency.

LTP   Living telop (which see).

MCU   Medium close up.

minicam   Hand-held miniature TV cameras using videotape that can transmit pictures direct to studios for instant use, eliminating costly and time-consuming film processing.

MS   Medium shot.

microwave   Very short electromagnetic waves, usually between one and 100 centimeters in length; basis for microelectronic circuits in line of sight transmissions and in space technology.

monochrome image   Black and white.

monitor   To view or hear a program.

NAB   National Association of Broadcasters.

NBC   National Broadcasting Company.

newsfilm   Film of current events designed for use on television, usually developed in the negative, after which a positive print is made for use on the air.

night effect   Attenuation of transmitted or received signals, usually after sunset, often attributed to changes in the ionized upper atmosphere.

on camera   Script notation of what is to be shown.

out cue   Last few words of a strip of sound on film or sound on tape, indicating that next section of newscast must be started.

out takes   Material that is filmed or videotaped but not used.

PBS   Public Broadcasting System.

pan   Moving the camera horizontally to include several objects or scenes in its sweep.

photoelectric cell   Cell containing a substance sensitive to light that controls emissions of electrons, either from a Cathode Ray tube or similar source.

prop   Various devices—so-called stage properties—used in a televised news program or documentary.

RP   Rear screen projection, requiring the use of a positive transparency that projects a picture in back of the television newscaster on a full screen.

RPM   Refers to revolutions per minute of a recording—commonly 33, 45 and 78 RPMs.

radiation   Transmission of radio waves through space in every direction; in its widest sense, the term refers to all forms of ionized radiation, including electromagnetic, particle and acoustic.

radio channel   The band or bands of frequencies within which a transmitter is permitted to operate by law.

radio frequency   It is incapable of being heard by the human ear, as contrasted with audio frequency which refers to radio waves that can be heard.

radio wire   The wire service teletypes that are hooked up specifically to a central source that provides news written for radio and television use at periodic intervals.

roll cue   Three to four seconds' signal before newsfilm segment must be shown on a news program.

SL   Silent film.

SOF   Sound on film.

SOT   Sound on tape.

scan Causing a beam of electrons to sweep rapidly across a surface in a succession of narrow lines, varying in brightness, so that a transmitted image is faithfully reproduced. In the U.S., the standard is 525 lines every one-thirtieth of a second.

segue Overlapping of dialogue, sound effects or music, one fading in as the other fades out. Pronounced "seg-way."

signal Electric energy that conveys coherent messages.

split page Method by which television news script is written, with audio directions in one column on one side of the page, and video directions on the other side of the page in a second and separate column.

static Disturbing electrical effects, caused by atmospheric electrical phenomena that disrupt sound in electronic receivers.

still Single photograph used in television, usually an 8 × 10 inch glossy. Less satisfactory copy, of course, is also used at times.

standby Written account of an event, held for use in case filmed version fails for any reason. Standby copy is then read.

slug Title for each piece of film considered for use in a news program; also used as a title for each piece of radio copy.

straight up When the second hand reaches 12, "straight up."

switch Shifting from one locale to another, introducing the change in scene with a call in throw cue and signaling the switch back to headquarters with a return cue. A hot switch is a switch without warning.

switcher One who does the actual switching of the program at an order from the news director.

TCU Tight close up.

telop Like a balop, this is a card or picture flashed electronically on a viewing screen from an opaque projector. TP is abbreviation.

Telenews Newsfilm syndicate, formally titled News of the Day.

track up Insert videotape or film track.

transistor Arrangement of semiconductor materials, usually germanium and silicon, separated by a vacuum, that takes the place of a vacuum tube; used as a voltage and current amplifier and for other functions of a vacuum tube.

UHF Ultra high frequency band, consisting of Channels 14 through 83, as contrasted with VHF, very high frequency, the commercial broadcast band consisting of Channels two through 13.

UPI Newsfilm Newsfilm, formerly Movietone News, distributed by United Press International.

VCU Very extreme close up.

VHF Very high frequency, Channels two through 13, the commercial broadcasting band.

VO Voice over, meaning dialogue or live narration over silent film or studio action.

VOF   Voice on film or tape.

VTR   Videotape recording.

video   Pertaining to or used in the reception or transmission of an image on television, as contrasted with audio, which refers to sound only.

videotape   A band of magnetic tape that records image and sound simultaneously and can be played back and rewound in seconds. It can be stored indefinitely, erased, used many times over a period of years.

vidicon   Type of television camera often used for closed circuit, industrial and military work.

Vizmo   A 5 × 7 transparency used in rear screen projection.

Viznews   British Commonwealth newsfilm group, titled Brzina Viznews, to indicate the countries involved—Britain, Australia, New Zealand, India and some others.

Vizs   Plural of Vizmo.

Voice of America   U.S. government broadcasting service overseas, a part of the U.S. Information Agency.

wave   Moving electronic disturbance in a medium, such as space, having a regularly recurring time period.

wavelength   Distance between any point in a wave and the corresponding point in the wave immediately preceding and following it.

wave trap   A circuit that can be tuned to cut out any undesired signal.

wired radio   Form of radio transmission in which current carrying the signals is sent over established wire systems, such as telephone or telegraph lines. The equivalent for television is the system known as CATV, which generally provides its own wire system hooked to telephone poles already in place.

wrapup   Rounded narration and/or filmed news program that summarizes a single major event or the day's news.

Appendix II
A Model
Stylebook

(Note: With the exception of the news writing instructions, the following is mainly adapted from the AP–UPI Stylebook. It should be remembered that wire service copy is prepared on terminals, rather than typewriters and copy paper, and that much newspaper copy is also terminal-prepared. Therefore, in the copy preparation instructions, an effort has been made to satisfy both the new and the old styles.)

NEWS WRITING INSTRUCTIONS

1. The purpose of all news writing is to communicate information, opinions and ideas in an interesting and timely manner. It must be accurate, terse, clear and easily understood.
2. Writers should use relatively short, simple sentences and paragraph liberally. A sentence, or two or three to a paragraph should be sufficient. Unity and coherence should be maintained.
3. Wherever possible, one idea to a sentence should be used. To attain this end separate sentences may be made out of qualifying or descriptive phrases or clauses when desirable.

4. Short, familiar words should be used in preference to long, strange words. Unfamiliar words should be defined for the reader. Geographical points should be located.

5. Try to use vigorous verbs. Wherever possible, use the active rather than the passive voice. Use adjectives sparsely and make each one count.

6. Writers must be specific. Instead of reporting that a woman is tall, she should be described as being six feet. Instead of writing that a speaker is disturbed, say he shouted and banged on the table.

7. Writers should try to relate an event to the particular community or public. The death of five in a fire in Atlanta is of relatively little interest to people in Chicago, unless there is something about the victims that particularly interests Chicago.

8. Try to relate statistics to something the public can quickly grasp. Instead of writing that India is a needy nation, say that the average Indian earns less than $100 a year. Instead of describing Lebanon as a tiny country, write that its coastline is 120 miles long, or about the same size as Long Island's South shore.

9. The simplest form of news story is divided into two parts—the lead and body. The lead tells what happened, simply, briefly and effectively. Do not crowd in everything that happened—just the main news. The body of the story documents the lead with facts in a diminishing order of importance.

10. In a hard, or spot, news story everything should be attributed to an identifiable source. If that cannot be done, the public should be told why.

11. In a speech or interview or public statement, all statements made by a speaker must be attributed directly to him. In reporting an arrest it must be specified that the police version of the alleged crime is being given.

12. News must be explained. To that end, experienced writers are given the privilege of interpretation. In this process the news should be told first. Then the public should be told what it means, if the writer is in a position to know. But no reporter has any right to urge a course of action on the basis of the news. That is editorialization.

13. Use meaningful quotations whenever possible but use partial quotations sparingly. They are misleading, at times. Whenever a quotation is used, it should begin a new paragraph.

14. *Don'ts:*
Do not write tortured, unnatural or excitable prose.
Do not write topsy-turvy sentences.

Do not overwrite, either in length or in meaning. The uses of restraint are of great importance in journalism.

Do not inject a personal point of view in a news story, unless you are given permission to do so. Do not use the pronouns "I" or "we" except when you are writing a first-person story. News is generally told in the third person. Do not switch tenses continually in writing news. Most news is best told in the past tense for newspapers, and in the present tense for the electronic media. The rule for sequence of tenses should be observed.

Do not neglect to feature the time element in a news lead. Today is the key word for the electronic media and in most afternoon newspaper leads, while yesterday is used in most local stories written for a morning newspaper. If in doubt use the day of the week.

15. When in doubt about anything in a story, leave it out until it can be checked. Never take anything for granted in journalism.

16. Always meet deadlines. Go with what you've got.

COPY PREPARATION

(Note: Copy preparation for radio, television and wire services is summed up in chapters that refer to the particular requirements of these media. The following applies to newspapers.)

A. Terminals

1. Scanners

These optical character recognition machines are capable of turning copy into type at speeds of up to 1,800 words a minute. They are also used for deletions and insertions.

It is necessary in the first instance to use a particular kind of electric typewriter with a special type face—the IBM Selectric is the usual machine.

All typing procedures are specified in a manual and must be carefully followed. These deal with the setting of correct margins, proper alignment and insertion of copy paper, slugging of a story, proper marking for instructions and basic coding procedures.

Copy is generally triple spaced.

Corrections must be made with a special pen using special ink and are provided by the newspaper.

2. VDTs and CRTs

These immensely versatile machines substitute for typewriters and copy paper and scanners, as well.

The keyboard duplicates the usual typewriter keyboard, but has numerous additional keys for instructions. At the lower right is a cluster that moves the cursor—the rectangle of light that marks the spot on the TV-like screen above the keyboard where the work is being done.

Complete instructional manuals are issued for the use of terminals by each news organization that installs them. That of the *Milwaukee Journal*, for example, runs to 44 single-spaced pages. Nothing is left to chance.

While it is impossible in a brief space to detail such instructions, the basic steps are these:

Signing on   Procedures vary, but generally writers use the first four letters of their names or their initials, plus the call letter of the queue or story to be placed on the screen if there is editing to be done. Otherwise, initials and a code word will produce a "sign on" response when the SIGN ON button is pushed.

Execute mode   A light on the right side of the keyboard will show under the label EXEC. That means the terminal is in the execute mode. Touch the SLUG key and a one or two-line slug form will appear at the top of the screen—and the cursor light rectangle will be positioned in the first blank space behind the word SLUG. The writer fills in the destination of the copy (city desk, sports desk, etc., name, date, slug of the story, etc.) and is now ready to proceed.

Cursor   There is no guesswork about where to start the story. The cursor positions itself where the writing should begin when the home key is pressed. Copy may be corrected, edited, shifted, inserted and otherwise changed by using the cursor and following simple instructions.

Continuation   If the story is to be continued, write "more," after ending the last sentence and paragraph on the take and route the story to the editing desk by touching the proper button. The SLUG key will produce a form to be filled in for the top of the second take and the writing proceeds until the story is ended.

End/send   Whenever the story ends, on the first take or the tenth, press the END/SEND button and the terminal will return to the Execute Mode.

Again, it must be emphasized that terminal systems and newspaper instructions vary considerably. What has been set down here constitutes the barest basic general instructions for preparing copy on a particular type of machine.

3.   For Typewriters Using Copy Paper

a   Copy is typewritten on one side of a sheet of 8½ × 11 copy paper.

b   The name goes in the upper left-hand corner, the source of the story on the same line. If the reporter has covered the story, the source is "assigned."

c The story begins one-third of the way down the paper, with paragraphs generously indented and large margins on all sides. Double or triple space, the latter preferably. On the second take the story resumes an inch from the top. All sentences and paragraphs end on a page. No runovers.

d If the story continues, write "More" at the bottom of the take. If it ends, write "End" or use a mark such as XXX, ### or 30, give the writer's initials and the time.

e The slug is the name of the story. Use a one-word slug that describes the story—*snow* for snowstorm, *heat* for heat wave, *crash* for an accident, etc. Where there are many stories in one category, such as obits, use two words—*Smith-obit*.

f There are two principal ways of numbering news stories.
1. Most newspapers use the consecutive method. Thus, the slug is written on the first page, about two inches under your name. If the story is continued, the slug goes at the top left of the second page and the figure two is written after it. The third page would be identified similarly.
2. Wire service copy generally is written with a slug on the first page, just as newspaper copy is prepared. But the second page begins with a pickup line—the slug, the word "ADD," the point of the story, and the last words of the previous page. Thus, the second page of a UPI story about a rocket shot would carry the top line: "1st ADD ROCKET HOUSTON . . . SUCCESSFULLY FIRED."

g Check the spelling of any unfamiliar word and all proper nouns and put a light check mark above each one. Read copy carefully before handing it in. Nothing is more annoying to an editor than bad spelling and grammatical errors. Make certain that copy is clean in all respects.

CAPITALIZATION

1. Titles preceding a name are capitalized, but are used in lower case when they stand alone or follow a name.
2. Titles of foreign religious leaders are capitalized when they precede a name, but are used in lower case when they stand or follow a name. The Pope is an exception, but pontiff, when referring to the Pope, is lower cased.
3. Titles of authority are capitalized when they precede a name, but are used in lower case when they stand alone or follow a name.
4. When titles are long and cumbersome, they should follow a name. They are then lower cased.
5. As a general rule, false titles should not be used. However,

when it becomes necessary to use a false title such as defense attorney before a name, it is lower cased.

6. When such terms as Republic, Union or Colonies refer to the United States, they are capitalized. Similarly, capitalize the French Fifth Republic or the Republic of Korea.

7. Capitalize the Capitol, meaning the building. Lower case capital, meaning the city. The U.S. Congress, Senate, House and Cabinet are capitalized. So is Legislature, when preceded by the name of the state; City Council and Security Council.

8. Committees such as House Ways and Means Committee are capitalized, but not the word committee when used by itself. Similarly, such titles as International Atomic Energy Authority and Interstate Commerce Commission are capitalized, but not authority and commission when used alone.

9. Courts are capitalized — Supreme Court, Court of Appeals and the like.

10. When referring to the U. S. system, Social Security is capitalized but it is lower cased when used in a general sense.

11. Titles of U. S. armed forces are capitalized, but foreign armed forces are lower cased with the exception of Royal Air Force, Royal Canadian Air Force and French Foreign Legion.

12. The title, Joint Chiefs of Staff, is capitalized but not chiefs of staff.

13. Historic events, holidays, ecclesiastical feasts, special events, fast days and names of hurricanes and typhoons are capitalized.

14. Arctic Circle and Antarctica are capitalized but not arctic or antarctic.

15. Specific regions are capitalized — New York's West Side, the Far East and Michigan's Upper Peninsula, for example.

16. Political or ideological areas are capitalized (East-West) but not just a direction.

17. Names of fraternal organizations are capitalized.

18. The Deity, He, His and Him — when denoting God — are capitalized but not who, whose and whom. Satan and Hades are capitalized but not hell or devil.

19. Names of wars are capitalized.

20. Indian, Negro, Chinese, Caucasian and other names of races are capitalized but red, black, yellow and white are not. While it is correct to use "colored" in African usage, it is not used in the United States except in the title of an organization: National Association for the Advancement of Colored People.

21. Capitalize common nouns when they are part of a formal name (Columbia River, Aswan Dam) but not river and dam standing alone.

22. Species of animals, flowers and so on, are capitalized (Afghan, hound; Peace, rose;) but not the common nouns standing alone.

23. Trade names and trademark names are capitalized. Coke and Thermos, for example, are registered trademarks, the former for a soft drink and the latter for a vacuum jug. Instead of trademark names, it is preferable to use a broad term.

24. Books, plays, musical compositions in general, and formal dance titles are capitalized and used in quotation marks. This is standard newspaper usage. Titles of books, plays and dance are italicized in book usage.

25. Names of formal organizations are capitalized (World's Fair, Boy Scouts) but not common nouns (fair, scouts).

26. Capitalize nicknames of states or of well-known organizations (Evergreen State, Leathernecks).

27. Capitalize awards and decorations.

28. Where proper names have acquired a common meaning, they are lower cased (dutch oven, brussels sprouts).

29. Capitalization of names in all cases should follow the preference of the individual.

ABBREVIATIONS

1. Spell out names of organizations, firms, agencies, groups and committees when they are first mentioned, then abbreviate when they are referred to again in the same story. AFL–CIO is an exception.

2. Military terms, time zones, airplane designations, ships and distress calls are abbreviated. Periods are dropped in such abbreviations as EST, MP, USS New Jersey, SS France, SOS and B747.

3. Names of business firms are abbreviated. (Lehman Bros., Jones & Co.)

4. In addresses, abbreviate Ave., St., Blvd., Ter. but not Lane, Road, Oval, Drive, Place, Plaza, Circle or Port. Ordinal numbers are used in addresses, such as 22 W. 38th St. In a Washington address, such as 2525 16th Ave. NW, there are no periods in NW. When no addresses are given, it is Fifth Avenue, Sunset Boulevard, Main Street.

5. Use periods with most lower case abbreviations. At the first mention of speed, it should be miles per hour, thereafter m.p.h. Exceptions to the period rule are film sizes (16 mm) or armament (155 mm rifle).

6. For versus use vs. (with period).

7. Names of states are abbreviated when they follow cities, towns, air bases, Indian agencies, national parks and so on, but not

when they are used alone. Alaska, Hawaii, Idaho, Iowa, Ohio, Maine and Utah are never abbreviated. Reasonably well known areas, such as Canadian provinces or Caribbean islands, are also abbreviated if they are preceded by a city or town but obscure places must be spelled out.

8. To avoid confusion, B. C. the era must be preceded by a date and B. C., the Canadian province, must be preceded by a city or town.

9. United States and United Nations may be abbreviated in titles, but periods must be used with both: U. N. Educational, Scientific and Cultural Organization; U. S. Civil Service Commission. Standing by themselves, U. S. A. and U. N. may be used in direct quotations or in texts. But United States and United Nations must be spelled out when used as nouns.

10. Religious, academic, fraternal or honorary degrees may be abbreviated, capitalized and used with periods (M.A.) but lower cased when spelled out (master of arts).

11. Titles may be abbreviated and capitalized: Mr., Mrs., Ms., M., Mlle., Dr., Prof., Sen., Rep., Asst., Lt. Gov., Gov. Gen., Dist. Atty. If used after a name, these are lower cased and spelled out.

12. The title Mr. is never used with the full name of a man except on the society page. Once the full name is used, Mr. may be put before the last name the next time it is mentioned (John Johnson the first time, then Mr. Johnson).

13. Do not abbreviate Christmas. Do not abbreviate San Francisco (Frisco). Do not abbreviate guaranteed annual wage (GAW).

14. Do not abbreviate such nouns as association, port, point, detective, department, commandant, commodore, field marshal, general manager, secretary-general, secretary, treasurer, fleet admiral or general of the armies. (Use Gen. Smith and Adm. Jones, both correct).

15. Months are abbreviated when used with dates, except for March, April, May, June or July. Days of the week are abbreviated only in tabular matter or financial routine.

16. St. and Ste. are abbreviated (as in St. Louis or Sault Ste. Marie) but not Saint John, N. B. The mountain is abbreviated (Mt. Rainier) but not the city, Mount Vernon. An army post is abbreviated (Ft. Monmouth) but not the city, Fort Lauderdale.

17. Unless the individual himself does it, do not abbreviate names such as Alexander, Benjamin, Frederick, William.

PUNCTUATION

Punctuation is used to clarify meaning. When it does not do so, it should be omitted. These are some common rules:

The Period

1. Use a period after a declarative sentence.
2. Use a period after an imperative sentence that is not exclamatory.
3. Use a period after a letter or number in a group, series or list of items.
4. Omit periods after most headings, captions, subheads, figures, roman numerals and chemical symbols.
5. Omit periods after nicknames, after per cent and after tabulated matter.
6. Use a series of periods to indicate that quoted matter has been omitted. Usually it is a series of three.
7. Use a period with abbreviations and as a decimal point.
8. Use a period before the closing parenthesis mark when an entire sentence is enclosed. If the final words of the sentence are parenthetical, the period goes outside the closing parenthesis.
9. Use a period after Mr. and Mrs.

The Comma

1. Use a comma to clarify meaning by separating words and figures when necessary: Whatever is, is right. Jan. 12, 1984.
2. Use commas to separate a series of qualifying words, except before "and" and "or" as follows: He was stocky, bald, short and talkative. It is either red, white or brown.
3. Use commas to separate parenthetical matter.
4. Use commas between name, title and organization, in scores of games, to set off appositives.
5. Omit the comma between the name and abbreviation of persons, before the dash or ampersand, in telephone numbers, street addresses, years and serial numbers. Omit comma before "of": Jones of Columbia.

The Semicolon

1. The semicolon is used principally to separate phrases containing commas in order to avoid confusion, to separate statements of contrast and statements too closely related.
2. The semicolon is used in sports scores and balloting: Giants, 6; Dodgers, 5. Yeas, 52; Nays, 52.
3. Use a semicolon in a series of names and addresses; John Jones, Massapequa; Doris Smith, Amityville; David Johnson, Riverhead.

The Colon

1. The colon's principal use is to introduce listings. It also introduces statements and marks discontinuity.

2. It is used in reporting time. He ran the mile in 3:59.
3. It is used in introducing a resolution. Resolved:
4. It separates chapter and verse in scriptual references.

Quotation Marks

1. Quotation marks enclose direct quotations, complete or partial.
2. They are put about words or phrases in political argument, ironical use, accepted phrases or nicknames, coined words or words of unusual meaning. Use sparingly in such cases.
3. When there are several paragraphs of continuous quotations, each paragraph should be started with a quotation mark, but it should be omitted from the end of all paragraphs except the final one.
4. Commas and final periods go inside quotations marks. Other punctuation marks go inside quotation marks only when they are part of the quoted matter.
5. Semicolons and colons always follow quotation marks.
6. Interior quotes take single quotation marks.
7. Titles of books, plays, movies, operas, statuary, paintings, TV and radio programs and songs all take quotation marks. Again, this is standard newspaper usage. Titles of books, plays, movies, operas, statuary, paintings, ships and aircraft are italicized in book usage.
8. Fire engines, ships, aircraft, horses, cattle, sleeping cars, homes, characters in fiction or on the stage and common nicknames do not take quotation marks.
9. Do not quote the names of newspapers or magazines.
10. Do not quote trial testimony. Simply list it as Q. and A.

The Apostrophe

1. The apostrophe is used for possessives and in some abbreviations.
2. In possessives, the apostrophe generally is used between a singular noun and the added "s" (except when the noun ends in "s"). For plural nouns ending with "s" or "ce" the apostrophe only is added.
3. Use the apostrophe to mark the omission of such word contractions as it's, I've, etc. (Do not use with pronoun its.)
4. Omit the apostrophe where it is not a part of a proper name (as Governors Island.)
5. One apostrophe only is used to indicate common possession, as The Army, Navy and Air Force's ideals. Use in Court of St. James's.

Parenthesis

1. Parentheses set off material that is not a part of the main statement.

2. They also set off an identification or grammatical element of a sentence that is closely related to the main statement.
3. They set off figures or letters in a tabular series in a sentence.
4. Unless the parenthetical matter is a complete sentence, it is placed before the period. Do not use around such designations as Sen. Long, D Louisiana.
5. Parentheses, like quotes, are used only at the beginning of a series of parenthetical paragraphs except for the final paragraph, where a closing parenthesis is placed after the final period.

The Dash

1. The dash marks an abrupt change of thought.
2. The dash is used to separate.
3. It is used after the logotype in a dateline and before the first word of the story.

The Hyphen

1. Just as the dash separates, the hyphen joins. It is used to form compound words. It is also used in abbreviations and in scores. As a rule, "like" characters take the hyphen, "unlike" characters do not.
2. Two or more words that form a compound adjective are hyphenated unless one of them is an adverb ending in "ly." The combined adjective elements that follow a noun do not take a hyphen, however.
3. Do not hyphenate commander in chief, vice president, today.
4. Use a hyphen for like characters in abbreviations (A-bomb, U-boat) but not for unlike characters (B52, W7ERD, MIG15, IC4A).
5. Do not use a hyphen for upstate, downstate, homecoming, cheerleader, textbook, makeup, cannot, bookcase.
6. Use the hyphen in prefixes to proper names, in writing figures, in various types of measures if used as adjectives.

Exclamation Point

It is used to indicate surprise, appeal, incredulity or other strong emotions. Use sparingly.

Question Mark

It follows a direct question, marks a gap or uncertainty. In the use of question and answer material, paragraph both Q. and A. when they run to some length.

Ampersand

It is used in abbreviations and firm names: AT&T, Smith, Barney & Co.

NUMERALS

1. The general rule is spell below 10, use numerals for 10 and above.
2. Use numerals excusively in all tabular and statistical records, latitude and longitude, election returns, times, speeds, temperatures, highways, distances, dimensions, heights, ages, ratios, proportions, military units, political divisions, orchestra instruments, court divisions or districts, handicaps, dates and betting odds.
3. Use July Fourth or Fourth of July.
4. Figures should be used for all human or animal ages. For inanimates, spell out under 10. Spell out casual numbers such as Gay Nineties.
5. Use Roman numerals for personal sequence — World War II, Pope Pius VI, Act I, Shamrock X.
6. Designate highways U.S. 17, Interstate 40, New York 58.
7. In amounts of more than a million, round numbers take the dollar sign and million, billion and so on, are spelled. Carry decimals to two places: $4.75 million. For exact amounts: $4,756,342.
8. For less than a million, use $500, $1,000, $440,000.
9. Use same decimal style for figures other than money, such as population, automobile registration, etc.
10. In amounts of less than a dollar spell out "cents."
11. Use figures in stories dealing with percentages and time sequences.
12. Use bracketed letter (M) after a figure in the millions, bracketed letter (B) after figure in the billions.
13. Confine fractions to 8ths — ⅛, ¼, ⅜, ½. Others require a hyphen — 3-16, 7-20, 9-10. Used alone, fractions are spelled out: three-eights of a mile.

Appendix III
Copy Editing
Terms and Symbols

(Note: Wherever copy editing is done on terminals, complete instructions are provided by news organizations for the use of editing marks and symbols. The procedure is standardized for each organization. The following, therefore, applies only to those organizations where copy is still edited with an old-fashioned soft lead pencil on copy paper.)

SYMBOL	MEANING
. . . worry. ⌐She said . . .	Begin a new paragraph. Use right angle symbol.
NO ₱ There was . . .	No paragraph. Use indicated symbol.
	Story is continued. Circle word "more" or use arrow.
(30) xxx # # #	End of story. Use one of the three symbols.
John Smith	Set in capitals. Use double line under letter or word.
Is it really true?	Set in italics. Use single line under word.

BF	Set in bold face. Use symbol as indicated.
⊙－ ⊗	Period. Circle a period or a cross.
⸴/	Comma. Use comma and diagonal mark for emphasis.
⸜Hamlet⸝	Quotes. Use carets as indicated.
(meaning/) The was unclear. ∧	Insert a letter or word. Use caret and write it in.
/–/ Dingdong ∧	Insert a hyphen. Use caret and hyphen above.
⑥ (Gov.)	Spell out figure or word. Use circles.
(Mister) (twelve)	Abbreviate word or use numeral. Use circles.
w̲ou̲ld	Underscore U's and W's. Draw lines under them.
n̄evermōre	Overscore N's and M's. Draw lines over them.
STET Then he said,	Restore text, eliminated by mistake. Use word STET.
thunderous	Transpose letter or word. Draw indicated symbol.
⌐	Indent from left. Use indicated symbol.
⌐	Indent from right. Use indicated symbol.
⌐ ⌐	Center: indent on both sides. Use indicated symbol.
gentle⌣man	Close up. Draw marks as indicated.
Boy/Scout	Separate. Use slash as indicated.
Here is the Model.	Make it a small letter. Use diagonal mark.
The beautiful girl . . .	Eliminate. Cross it out and close it up.
(set 2 col 10 pt)	Printer: Do not set this in type. Circle it.

Appendix IV Standards for Journalists

American journalists have always been wary of codes of conduct. While they may generally agree with the principles of such codes, they have invariably raised the possibility that government in some fashion will try to enforce them. That, of course, would lead directly to the licensing of journalists and the end of the free press.

Thus, in the following presentation of documents in part or as a whole that bear on the standards of journalists, it should be borne in mind that no enforcement is provided for any code or declaration.

1. A STATEMENT OF PRINCIPLES

The following Statement of Principles was adopted in 1975 by the American Society of Newspaper Editors to replace its 52-year-old Code of Ethics or Canons of Journalism:[1]

PREAMBLE

The First Amendment, protecting freedom of expression from abridgment by any law, guarantees to the people through their press a

[1] *Editor & Publisher* (13 December 1975).

constitutional right, and thereby places on newspaper people a particular responsibility.

Thus journalism demands of its practitioners not only industry and knowledge but also the pursuit of a standard of integrity proportionate to the journalist's singular obligation.

To this end the American Society of Newspaper Editors sets forth this Statement of Principles as a standard encouraging the highest ethical and professional performance.

ARTICLE I - Responsibility

The primary purpose of gathering and distributing news and opinion is to serve the general welfare by informing the people and enabling them to make judgments on the issues of the time. Newspapermen and women who abuse the power of their professional role for selfish motives or unworthy purposes are faithless to that public trust.

The American press was made free not just to inform or just to serve as a forum for debate but also to bring an independent scrutiny to bear on the forces of power in the society, including the conduct of official power at all levels of government.

ARTICLE II - Freedom of the Press

Freedom of the press belongs to the people. It must be defended against encroachment or assault from any quarter, public or private.

Journalists must be constantly alert to see that the public's business is conducted in public. They must be vigilant against all who would exploit the press for selfish purposes.

ARTICLE III - Independence

Journalists must avoid impropriety and the appearance of impropriety as well as any conflict of interest or the appearance of conflict. They should neither accept anything nor pursue any activity that might compromise or seem to compromise their integrity.

ARTICLE IV - Truth and Accuracy

Good faith with the reader is the foundation of good journalism. Every effort must be made to assure that the news content is accurate, free from bias and in context and that all sides are presented fairly. Editorials, analytical articles and commentary should be held to the same standards of accuracy with respect to facts as news reports.

Significant errors of fact, as well as errors of omission, should be corrected promptly and prominently.

ARTICLE V - Impartiality

To be impartial does not require the press to be unquestioning or to refrain from editorial expression. Sound practice, however, demands a clear distinction for the reader between news reports and opinion. Articles that contain opinion or personal interpretation should be clearly identified.

ARTICLE VI - Fair Play

Journalists should respect the rights of people involved in the news, observe the common standards of decency and stand accountable to the public for the fairness and accuracy of their news reports.

Persons publicly accused should be given the earliest opportunity to respond.

Pledges of confidentiality to news sources must be honored at all costs, and therefore should not be given lightly. Unless there is clear and pressing need to maintain confidences, sources of information should be identified.

These principles are intended to preserve, protect and strengthen the bond of trust and respect between American journalists and the American people, a bond that is essential to sustain the grant of freedom entrusted to both by the nation's founders.

2. THE TELEVISION CODE OF THE NATIONAL ASSOCIATION OF BROADCASTERS (EXCERPT)

V. Treatment of News and Public Events
NEWS

1. A television station's news schedule should be adequate and well-balanced.

2. News reporting should be factual, fair and without bias.

3. A television broadcaster should exercise particular discrimination in the acceptance, placement and presentation of advertising in news programs so that such advertising should be clearly distinguishable from the news content.

4. At all times, pictorial and verbal material for both news and comment should conform to other sections of these standards, wherever such sections are reasonably applicable.

5. Good taste should prevail in the selection and handling of news:

Morbid, sensational or alarming details not essential to the factual report, especially in connection with stories of crime or sex, should be avoided. News should be telecast in such a manner as to avoid panic and unnecessary alarm.

6. Commentary and analysis should be clearly identified as such.

7. Pictorial material should be chosen with care and not presented in a misleading manner.

8. All news interview programs should be governed by accepted standards of ethical journalism, under which the interviewer selects the questions to be asked. Where there is advance agreement materially re-

stricting an important or newsworthy area of questioning, the interviewer will state on the program that such limitation has been agreed upon. Such disclosure should be made if the person being interviewed requires that questions be submitted in advance or if he participates in editing a recording of the interview prior to its use on the air.

9. A television broadcaster should exercise due care in his supervision of content, format and presentation of newscasts originated by his station, and in his selection of newscasters, commentators and analysts.

PUBLIC EVENTS

1. A television broadcaster has an affirmative responsibility at all times to be informed of public events, and to provide coverage consonant with the ends of an informed and enlightened citizenry.

2. The treatment of such events by a television broadcaster should provide adequate and informd coverage.

VI. Controversial Public Issues

1. Television provides a valuable forum for the expression of responsible views on public issues of a controversial nature. The television broadcaster should seek out and develop with accountable individuals, groups and organizations, programs relating to controversial public issues of import to his fellow citizens; and to give fair representation to opposing sides of issues which materially affect the life or welfare of a substantial segment of the public.

2. Requests by individuals, groups or organizations for time to discuss their views on controversial public issues should be considered on the basis of their individual merits, and in the light of the contribution which the use requested would make to the public interest and to a well-balanced program structure.

3. Programs devoted to the discussion of controversial public issues should be identified as such. They should not be presented in a manner which would mislead listeners or viewers to believe that the program is purely of an entertainment, news or other character.

4. Broadcasts in which stations express their own opinions about issues of general public interest should be clearly identified as editorials. They should be unmistakably identified as statements of station opinion and should be appropriately distinguished from news and other program material.

VII. Political Telecasts

1. Political telecasts should be clearly identified as such. They should not be presented by a television broadcaster in a manner which would mislead listeners or viewers to believe that the program is of any other character.

(Ref. Communications Act of 1934, as amended, Secs. 315 and 317, and FCC Rules and Regulations, Secs. 3, 654, 3, 657, 3, 663, as discussed in NAB's "A Political Catechism.")

3. NAB RADIO CODE OF GOOD PRACTICES (EXCERPT)

I. Program Standards

A. NEWS

Radio is unique in its capacity to reach the largest number of people first with reports on current events. This competitive advantage bespeaks caution—being first is not always as important as being right. The following standards are predicated upon that viewpoint.

1. News Sources Those responsible for news on radio should exercise constant professional care in the selection of sources—for the integrity of the news and the consequent good reputation of radio as a dominant news medium depend largely upon the reliability of such sources.

2. News Reporting News reporting shall be factual and objective. Good taste shall prevail in the selection and handling of news. Morbid, sensational or alarming details not essential to factual reporting should be avoided. News should be broadcast in such a manner as to avoid creation of panic and unnecessary alarm. Broadcasters shall be diligent in their supervision of content, format and presentation of news broadcasts. Equal diligence should be exercised in selection of editors and reporters who direct news gathering and dissemination, since the station's performance in this vital information field depends largely upon them.

3. Commentaries and Analyses Special obligations devolve upon those who analyze and/or comment upon news developments, and management should be satisfied completely that the task is to be performed in the best interest of the listening public. Programs of news analysis and commentary shall be clearly identified as such, distinguishing them from straight news reporting.

4. Editorializing Broadcasts in which stations express their own opinions about issues of general public interest should be clearly distinguished from news and other program material.

5. Coverage of News and Public Events In the coverage of news and public events the broadcaster has the right to exercise his judgment consonant with the accepted standards of ethical journalism and especially the requirements for decency and decorum in the broadcast of public and court proceedings.

6. Placement of Advertising A broadcaster should exercise particular discrimination in the acceptance, placement and presentation of advertising in news programs so that such advertising should be clearly distinguishable from the news content.

B.   CONTROVERSIAL PUBLIC ISSUES

1.   Radio provides a valuable forum for the expression of responsible views on public issues of a controversial nature. The broadcaster should develop programs relating to controversial public issues of importance to his fellow citizens, and give fair representation to opposing sides of issues which materially affect the life or welfare of a substantial segment of the public.

2.   Requests by individuals, groups or organizations for time to discuss their views on controversial public issues should be considered on the basis of their individual merits, and in the light of the contributions which the use requested would make to the public interest.

3.   Programs devoted to the discussion of controversial public issues should be identified as such. They should not be presented in a manner which would create the impression that the program is other than one dealing with a public issue.

C.   COMMUNITY RESPONSIBILITY

1.   A broadcaster and his staff occupy a position of responsibility in the community and should conscientiously endeavor to be acquainted with its needs and characteristcs in order to serve the welfare of its citizens.

2.   Requests for time for the placement of public service announcements or programs should be carefully reviewed with respect to the character and reputation of the group, campaign or organization involved, the public interest content of the message and the manner of its presentation.

4.   FREE PRESS AND FAIR TRIAL

The following is excerpted from the Press-Bar Guidelines of the State of Washington, an example of the kind of cooperative relationship that exists in many states to protect the right of free press and the right of fair trial:

GUIDELINES FOR THE REPORTING OF CRIMINAL PROCEEDINGS

The proper administration of justice is the responsibility of the judiciary, bar, the prosecution, law enforcement personnel, news media and the public. None should relinquish its share in that responsibility or attempt to override or regulate the judgment of the other. None should condone injustices on the ground that they are infrequent.

The greatest news interest is usually engendered during the pretrial stage of a criminal case. It is then that the maximum attention is received and the greatest impact is made upon the public mind. It is then that the greater danger to a fair trial occurs. The bench, the bar and the news media must exercise good judgment to balance the possible release of prejudicial information with the real public interest. However, these considerations are not necessarily applicable once a jury has been empaneled in a case. It is inherent in the concept of freedom of the press that the news media be free to report what occurs in public proceedings, such as criminal trials. In the course of the trial it is the responsibility of the bench to take appropriate measures to insure that the deliberations of the jury are based upon what is presented to them in court.

These guidelines are proposed as a means of balancing the public's right to be informed with the accused's right to a fair trial before an impartial jury.

1. It is appropriate to make public the following information concerning the defendant:

(a) The defendant's name, age, residence, employment, marital status and similar background information. There should be no restraint on biographical facts other than accuracy, good taste and judgment.

(b) The substance or text of the charge, such as complaint, indictment, information or, where appropriate, the identity of the complaining party.

(c) The identity of the investigating and arresting agency and the length of the investigation.

(d) The circumstances immediately surrounding an arrest, including the time and place of arrest, resistance, pursuit, possession and use of weapons and a description of items seized at the time of arrest.

2. The release of certain types of information by law enforcement personnel, the bench and bar, and the publication thereof by news media generally tends to create dangers of prejudice without serving a significant law enforcement or public interest function. Therefore, all concerned should be aware of the dangers of prejudice in making pretrial public disclosures of the following:

(a) Opinions about a defendant's character, his guilt or his innocence.

(b) Admissions, confessions or the contents of a statement or alibis attributable to a defendant.

(c) References to the results of investigative procedures, such as fingerprints, polygraph examinations, ballistic tests or laboratory tests.

(d) Statements concerning the credibility or anticipated testimony of prospective witnesses.

(e) Opinions concerning evidence or argument in the case, whether or not it is anticipated that such evidence or argument will be used at trial.

Exceptions may be in order if information to the public is essential to the apprehension of a suspect, or where other public interests will be served.

3. Prior criminal charges and convictions are matters of public

record and are available to the news media through police agencies or court clerks. Law enforcement agencies should make such information available to the news media after a legitimate inquiry. The public disclosure of this information by the news media may be highly prejudicial without any significant addition to the public's need to be informed. The publication of such information should be carefully reviewed.

4. Law enforcement and court personnel should not prevent the photographing of defendants when they are in public places outside the courtroom. They should not encourage pictures or televising nor should they pose the defendant.

5. Photographs of a suspect may be released by law enforcement personnel provided a valid law enforcement function is served thereby. It is proper to disclose such information as may be necessary to enlist public assistance in apprehending fugitives from justice. Such disclosure may include photographs as well as records of prior arrests and convictions.

6. The news media are free to report what occurs in the course of the judicial proceeding itself. The bench should utilize available measures, such as cautionary instructions, sequestration of the jury and the holding of hearings on evidence after the empaneling of the jury, to insure that the jury's deliberations are based upon evidence presented to them in court.

7. It is improper for members of the bench-bar-news media or law enforcement agencies to make available to the public any statement or information for the purpose of influencing the outcome of a criminal trial.

8. Sensationalism should be avoided by all persons and agencies connected with the trial or reporting of a criminal case.

Index